INFORMATION TECHNOLOGY
PROJECT MANAGEMENT

INFORMATION TECHNOLOGY PROJECT MANAGEMENT

Eighth Edition

Kathy Schwalbe, Ph.D., PMP
Professor Emeritus, Augsburg College

CENGAGE
Learning·

Australia • Brazil • Mexico • Singapore • United Kingdom • United States

CENGAGE
Learning®

Information Technology Project Management, Eighth Edition

Kathy Schwalbe

Product Director: Mike Schenk

Senior Product Manager/Team Lead: Joe Sabatino

Content Development Manager: Jennifer King

Content Developer: Anne Merrill

Product Assistant: Adele Scholtz

Intellectual Property Analyst: Christina Ciaramella

Senior Intellectual Property Manager: Kathryn Kucharek

Marketing Manager: Eric La Scola

Manufacturing Planner: Ron Montgomery

Art and Cover Direction, Production Management, and Composition: Lumina Datamatics, Inc.

Cover Images:

©everything possible/shutterstock.com (man looking at a network structure)

©Stuart Jenner/shutterstock.com (back view of group of people)

> For product information and technology assistance, contact
> **Cengage Learning Customer & Sales Support, 1-800-354-9706.**
>
> For permission to use material from this text or product, submit all requests online at **cengage.com/permissions**
>
> Further permissions questions can be e-mailed to **permissionrequest@cengage.com**

Library of Congress Control Number: 2015950371

Student Edition:

ISBN-13: 978-1-285-45234-0

Cengage Learning

20 Channel Center Street

Boston, MA 02210

USA

Printed in the United States of America

Print Number: 01 Print Year: 2015

For Dan, Anne, Bobby, and Scott

BRIEF CONTENTS

TABLE OF CONTENTS

The future of many organizations depends on their ability to harness the power of information technology, and good project managers continue to be in high demand. Colleges have responded to this need by establishing courses in project management and making them part of the information technology, management, engineering, and other curricula. Corporations are investing in continuing education to help develop and deepen the effectiveness of project managers and project teams. This text provides a much-needed framework for teaching courses in project management, especially those that emphasize managing information technology projects. The first seven editions of this text were extremely well received by people in academia and the workplace. The Eighth Edition builds on the strengths of the previous editions and adds new, important information and features.

It's impossible to read a newspaper, magazine, or web page without hearing about the impact of information technology on our society. Information is traveling faster and being shared by more people than ever before. You can buy just about anything online, surf the web on a mobile phone, or use a wireless Internet connection just about anywhere. Companies have linked their systems together to help them fill orders on time and better serve their customers. Software companies are continually developing new products to help streamline our work and get better results. When technology works well, it is almost invisible. But did it ever occur to you to ask, "Who makes these complex technologies and systems happen?"

Because you're reading this text, you must have an interest in the "behind-the-scenes" aspects of technology. If I've done my job well, you'll begin to see the many innovations society is currently enjoying as the result of thousands of successful information technology projects. In this text, you'll read about IT projects in organizations around the world that went well, including the National University Hospital in Singapore, which used critical chain scheduling to decrease patient admission times by more than 50 percent; retailer Zulily, one of a growing number of organizations developing software in-house to meet their need for speed and innovation; Dell's green computing project that saves energy and millions of dollars; Google's driverless car project, striving to reduce traffic accidents and save lives; and many more.

Of course, not all projects are successful. Factors such as time, money, and unrealistic expectations, among many others, can sabotage a promising effort if it is not properly managed. In this text, you'll also learn from the mistakes made on many projects that were not successful.

I have written this book in an effort to educate you, tomorrow's project managers, about what will help make a project succeed—and what can make it fail. You'll also see how projects are used in everyday media, such as television and film, and how companies use best practices in project management. Many readers tell me how much they enjoy reading these real-world examples in the What Went Right?, What

Went Wrong?, Media Snapshot, and Best Practice features. As practitioners know, there is no "one size fits all" solution to managing projects. By seeing how different organizations in different industries successfully implement project management, you can help your organization do the same.

Although project management has been an established field for many years, managing information technology projects requires ideas and information that go beyond standard practices. For example, many information technology projects fail because of a lack of executive support, poor user involvement, and unclear business objectives. This book includes many suggestions for dealing with these issues. New technologies can also aid in managing information technology projects, and examples of using software to assist in project management are included throughout the book.

Information Technology Project Management, Eighth Edition, is the only textbook to apply all 10 project management knowledge areas and all five process groups to information technology projects. As you will learn, the project management knowledge areas are project integration, scope, time, cost, quality, human resource, communications, risk, procurement, and stakeholder management. The five process groups are initiating, planning, executing, monitoring and controlling, and closing.

This text builds on the *PMBOK® Guide, Fifth Edition,* an American National Standard, to provide a solid framework and context for managing information technology projects. It also includes an appendix, Guide to Using Microsoft Project 2013, that many readers find invaluable.

In addition to the physical text, several resources are available online. Additional case studies, including the one from the Seventh Edition, Manage Your Health, are available, as well as over fifty template files that students can use to create their own project management documents. The author's personal website (*www.kathyschwalbe.com* or *www.pmtexts.com*) also provides additional, up-to-date resources and links related to the field of project management, including topics like Agile, PMP and CAPM certification, simulation software, leadership, mind mapping, sample student projects, and more.

Information Technology Project Management, Eighth Edition, provides practical lessons in project management for students and practitioners alike. By weaving together theory and practice, this text presents an understandable, integrated view of the many concepts, skills, tools, and techniques of information technology project management. The comprehensive design of the text provides a strong foundation for students and practitioners in project management.

NEW TO THE EIGHTH EDITION

Building on the success of the previous editions, *Information Technology Project Management, Eighth Edition,* introduces a uniquely effective combination of features. The main changes in the Eighth Edition include the following:

- A new running case at the end of Chapters 4–13, the ten knowledge area chapters. Instructors often like to assign running cases to reinforce application of key concepts. The "Manage Your Health" running case from the Seventh Edition is provided online along with several additional running cases.

- Updated and additional exercises to enhance student learning and give instructors more options for in-class or out-of-class work.
- Additional content on important topics like leadership and agile.
- New examples that highlight IT project management at work in real, newsworthy companies. These timely, relevant examples help illustrate the real-world applications and impact of key project management concepts. They also serve as mini-case stories, suitable for class discussion.
- Many recent studies of IT project management and related topics. Summaries of classic, updated, and the most current research throughout the text build a rich context for essential IT project management concepts.
- User feedback is incorporated. Based on feedback from reviewers, students, instructors, practitioners, and translators, you'll see a variety of changes that help clarify information. (This book has been translated into Chinese, Japanese, Russian, and Czech.)

Many people have been practicing some form of project management with little or no formal study in this area. New books and articles are written each year as we discover more about the field and as project management software continues to advance. Because the project management field and the technology industry change rapidly, you cannot assume that what worked even a few years ago is still the best approach today. This text provides up-to-date information on how good project management and effective use of software can help you manage projects, especially information technology projects. Distinct features of this text include its relationship to the Project Management Body of Knowledge, its value in preparing for certification, its detailed guide for using Microsoft Project 2013, its inclusion of running case studies and online templates, its emphasis on IT projects, its coverage of several software tools that assist with project management, and its companion website.

Based on *PMBOK® Guide, Fifth Edition* and Preparing for Certification

The Project Management Institute (PMI) created the Guide to the Project Management Body of Knowledge (the *PMBOK® Guide*) as a framework and starting point for understanding project management. It includes an introduction to project management, brief descriptions of all 10 project management knowledge areas, and a glossary of terms. The *PMBOK® Guide* is, however, just that—a guide. This text uses the *PMBOK® Guide, Fifth Edition* (2013) as a foundation, but goes beyond it by providing more details, discussing the how and why of the knowledge areas, highlighting additional topics, and providing a real-world context for IT project management. This text is an excellent resource for preparing for PMI certifications, such as the Project Management Professional (PMP) and Certified Associate in Project Management (CAPM).

Detailed Guide to Microsoft Project 2013

Software has become a critical tool for helping project managers and their teams effectively manage information technology projects. *Information Technology Project Management, Eighth Edition,* includes a detailed guide in Appendix A for using the leading project management software on the market—Microsoft Project 2013. Examples that use Project 2013 and other software tools are integrated throughout the text. Appendix A, Guide to Using Microsoft Project 2013, teaches you in a systematic way to use this powerful software to help in project scope, time, cost, human resource, and communications management.

Emphasis on IT Projects and Use of Software Tools

Most of the examples of projects in this text are based on IT projects. Research studies and advice are specific to managing IT projects, and include expanded information on agile. Each of the knowledge area chapters includes examples as well as a separate section describing how software can be used to assist in managing that knowledge area. For example, Chapter 5, Project Scope Management, includes examples of using mind maps created with MindView Business software to create a work breakdown structure. Chapter 11, Project Risk Management, shows an example of using Monte Carlo simulation software to help quantify project risk.

Exercises, Running Cases, Templates, and Sample Documents

Based on feedback from readers, the Eighth Edition continues to provide challenging exercises and running cases to help students apply concepts in each chapter. The text includes more than 50 templates and examples of real project documents that students can use to help them apply their skills to their own projects.

Students can access all of these materials for free through the companion CourseMate product, and for an additional fee, students who purchase the CourseMate product will gain access to a complete, interactive e-book, crossword puzzles, and additional study tools.

ACCESSING THE COURSEMATE SITE

To access the CourseMate site, open a web browser and go to *www.cengagebrain .com*. Search by ISBN, author name, or title, and click Create My Account to begin the registration process.

ORGANIZATION AND CONTENT

Information Technology Project Management, Eighth Edition, is organized into three main sections, which provide a framework for project management, a detailed description of each project management knowledge area, and an appendix of practical information for applying project management. The first three chapters form the first section, which introduces the project management framework and sets the stage for the remaining chapters.

Chapters 4 through 13 form the second section, which describes each of the project management knowledge areas—project integration, scope, time, cost, quality, human resource, communications, risk, procurement, and stakeholder management—in the context of information technology projects. An entire chapter is dedicated to each knowledge area. Each of these chapters includes sections that map to their major processes as described in the *PMBOK® Guide, Fifth Edition.* For example, the chapter on project quality management includes sections on planning quality management, performing quality assurance, and controlling quality. Additional sections highlight other important concepts related to each knowledge area, such as Six Sigma, testing, maturity models, and using software to assist in project quality management. Each chapter also includes detailed examples of key project management tools and techniques as applied to information technology projects. For example, the chapter on project integration management includes samples of various project-selection techniques, such as net present value analyses, ROI calculations, payback analyses, and weighted scoring models. The project scope management chapter includes a sample project charter, a project scope statement, and several work breakdown structures for information technology projects.

Appendix A forms the third section of the text, which provides practical information to help you learn how to use the most popular project management software available today. By following the detailed, step-by-step guide in Appendix A, which includes more than 60 screen illustrations, you will learn how to use Project 2013. You can download a free trial from the Microsoft website, use your school or company license, or purchase this powerful software.

PEDAGOGICAL FEATURES

Several pedagogical features are included in this text to enhance presentation of the materials so that you can more easily understand the concepts and apply them. Throughout the text, emphasis is placed on applying concepts to current, real-world information technology project management.

Opening Case and Case Wrap-Up

To set the stage, each chapter begins with an opening case related to the material presented in that chapter. These real-life case scenarios, most of which are based on the author's experiences, spark student interest and introduce important concepts in a real-world context. As project management concepts and techniques are discussed, they are applied to the opening case and other similar scenarios. Each chapter then closes with a case wrap-up—with some ending successfully and some failing—to further illustrate the real world of project management.

What Went Right? and What Went Wrong?

Failures, as much as successes, can be valuable learning experiences. Each chapter of the text includes one or more examples of real information technology projects that went right, as well as examples of projects that went wrong. These examples further illustrate the importance of mastering key concepts in each chapter.

Media Snapshot

The world is full of projects. Television shows, movies, newspapers, websites, and other media highlight project results that are good and bad. Relating project management concepts to the types of projects highlighted in the media helps you understand the importance of this growing field. Why not get excited about studying project management by seeing its concepts at work in popular television shows, movies, or other media?

Best Practice

Every chapter includes an example of a best practice related to topics in that chapter. For example, Chapter 1 describes best practices written by Robert Butrick, author of *The Project Workout,* from the *Ultimate Business Library's Best Practice* book. He instructs organizations to ensure that their projects are driven by their strategy and to engage project stakeholders.

Global Issues

Every chapter includes an example of global issues of importance today. For example, Chapter 2 describes some of the problems with outsourcing, such as rioting in Beijing when customers could not buy the latest iPhones. Chapter 12 describes the recent development of urban onshoring, one response to problems with offshoring.

Key Terms

The fields of information technology and project management include many unique terms that are vital to creating a workable language when the two fields are combined. Key terms are displayed in boldface and are defined the first time they appear. Definitions of key terms are provided in alphabetical order at the end of each chapter and in a glossary at the end of the text. You can also find them by chapter on the companion website.

Application Software

Learning becomes much more dynamic with hands-on practice using the top project management software tool in the industry, Microsoft Project 2013, as well as other tools, such as spreadsheet software and the Internet. Each chapter offers many opportunities to get hands-on experience and build new software skills. This text is written from the point of view that reading about something only gets you so far—to really understand project management, you have to do it for yourself. In addition to the exercises and running cases at the end of each chapter, several challenging exercises are provided at the end of Appendix A, Guide to Using Microsoft Project 2013.

STUDENT AND INSTRUCTOR RESOURCES

Student and Instructor Companion Websites

The free Student Companion Website accessed through www.cengagebrain.com provides the template files mentioned in the text, Project 2013 files, a case study describing initiating through closing the ResNet project for Northwest Airlines (now part of Delta), and additional running cases that instructors can assign to students to practice their skills. There is also a link to the author's website, which provides up-to-date resources on important topics like agile, certifications, and more.

The Instructor Companion Website, also accessed with a single sign-on (SSO) account through www.cengagebrain.com, contains even more resources only for instructors:

- **Instructor's Manual** The Instructor's Manual that accompanies this textbook includes additional instructional material to assist in class preparation, such as suggestions for lecture topics and additional discussion questions.
- **Solution Files** Solutions to end-of-chapter questions are available on the Instructor Companion Website.
- **PowerPoint Presentations** This text comes with Microsoft PowerPoint slides for each chapter. These slides are included as a teaching aid for classroom presentation, to make available to students on the network for chapter review, or to print for classroom distribution. Instructors can add their own slides for additional topics they introduce to the class.

- **Test Banks** In addition to the Test Bank available online through Cognero (see below), the Test Bank is also available in a number of file formats on the Instructor Companion Website. Each chapter's bank of questions includes dozens of True/False, Multiple Choice, and Essay questions. Instructors can retrieve the appropriate file formats to administer tests through their schools' learning management systems (Blackboard, Canvas, Moodle, Desire2Learn, etc.), or they can opt for Word documents.

NEW! Test Banks in Cognero

The Test Bank for *Information Technology Project Management, Eighth Edition,* is now available online in the new Cognero system. Cengage Learning Testing Powered by Cognero is a flexible, online system that allows instructors to:

- Author, edit, and manage test bank content.
- Use searchable metadata to ensure tests are complete and compliant.
- Create multiple test versions in an instant.
- Deliver tests from your learning management system (LMS), classroom, or wherever you want.

Cengage Learning Testing Powered by Cognero works on any operating system or browser with no special installs or downloads needed. With its intuitive tools and familiar desktop drop-down menus, Cognero enables instructors to easily create and edit tests from school or home—anywhere with Internet access.

IT Project Management CourseMate

Engaging, trackable, and affordable, the IT Project Management CourseMate website offers a dynamic way to bring course concepts to life with interactive learning, study, and exam preparation tools that support the printed edition of the text. Watch student comprehension soar with all-new flashcards and engaging crossword puzzles, test-prep quizzes, and more. A complete e-book provides students and instructors alike with the choice of an entire online learning experience. IT Project Management CourseMate goes beyond the book to deliver what students need.

The complete CourseMate companion product is available for an additional fee, but students can also use the CourseMate website to access the text's supplemental materials, including project documents, templates, and cases, at no additional charge.

ACKNOWLEDGMENTS

I never would have taken on the project of writing this book, including all the prior editions, without the help of many people. I thank the staff at Cengage Learning, including Joe Sabatino, Jason Guyler, Anne Merrill, Jennifer King, Eric LaScola, Christina Ciaramella, and Kathy Kucharek, for their dedication and hard work in helping me produce this book and in doing such an excellent job of marketing it. I'd also like to thank Marilyn Freedman for her excellent assistance in researching and preparing the manuscript, and many more people who did a great job in planning and executing this book and its supplemental materials.

I thank my many colleagues and experts in the field who contributed information to this book. Joseph W. Kestel, PMP, provided outstanding feedback on the agile information in this text based on his personal experience in leading agile projects. David Jones, Rachel Hollstadt, Cliff Sprague, Michael Branch, Barb Most, Jodi Curtis, Rita Mulcahy, Karen Boucher, Bill Munroe, Tess Galati, Joan Knutson, Neal Whitten, Brenda Taylor, Quentin Fleming, Jesse Freese, Nick Matteucci, Nick Erndt, Dragan Milosevic, Bob Borlink, Arvid Lee, Kathy Christenson, Peeter Kivestu, and many other people provided excellent materials included in this book. I enjoy the network of project managers, authors, and consultants in this field who are passionate about improving the theory and practice of project management.

I also thank my students and colleagues at Augsburg College and the University of Minnesota for providing feedback on the earlier editions of this book. I received many valuable comments from them on ways to improve the text and structure of my courses. I learn something new about project management and teaching all the time by interacting with students, faculty, and staff.

I also thank the faculty reviewers for providing excellent feedback for me in writing this book over the years. I thank the many instructors and readers who have contacted me directly with praise as well as suggestions for improving this text. I appreciate the feedback and do my best to incorporate as much as I can. In particular, I'd like to thank the following:

Jody Allen, Mid-America Christian University
William Baker, Southern New Hampshire University
Tonya Barrier, Missouri State University
Kevin Daimi, University of Detroit Mercy
Antonio Drommi, University of Detroit Mercy
Roger Engle, Franklin University
Lisa Foster, Walsh College of Business & Accountancy
Esther Frankel, Santa Barbara City College
Guy Garrett, Gulf Coast State College
James Gibbs, Mount St Joseph University
Thomas Haigh, University of Wisconsin, Milwaukee
Kay Hammond, Lindenwood University
Sam Hijazi, Saint Leo University
Henry Jackson, Schreiner University
Karen Johnson, Indiana University Northwest
Donna Karch, The College of St. Scholastica
Carol Kaszynski, Inver Hills Community College
Cyril Keiffer, Owens Community College
Thomas King, Pennsylvania State University
Sang Joon Lee, Mississippi State University
Sunita Lodwig, University of South Florida
Barbara Miller, Zane State College
Kimberly Mitchell, Illinois State University
Tim Moriarty, Waubonsee Community College
Brandon Olson, The College of St. Scholastica
Olga Petkova, Central Connecticut State University
April Reed, East Carolina University

Jason Riley, Sam Houston State University
Carl Scott, University of Houston
Ferris Sticksel, Webster University
David Syverson, Embry-Riddle Aeronautical University
Barbara Warner, Wake Technical Community College
Steven White, Anne Arundel Community College

Most of all, I am grateful to my family. Without their support, I never could have written this book. My wonderful husband, Dan, has always supported me in my career, and he helps me keep up-to-date with software development because he is a lead architect for Milner Technologies, Inc. (formerly ComSquared Systems, Inc.). Our three children, Anne, Bobby, and Scott, think it's cool that their mom writes books and speaks at conferences. They also see me managing projects all the time. Anne, now 31, a research analyst for The New Teacher Project, teases me for being the only quilter she knows who treats each quilt as a project. (Maybe that's why I get so many done!) After her colleagues at The Minnesota Evaluation Studies Institute at the University of Minnesota heard about my work and books, they hired me to teach a workshop on project management to evaluators, which was sold out. Our two sons are working as software developers in Texas and Oregon and may become IT project managers soon. Our children understand the main reason I write—I have a passion for educating future leaders of the world, including them.

As always, I am eager to receive your feedback on this book. Please send comments to me at *schwalbe@augsburg.edu*.

Kathy Schwalbe, Ph.D., PMP
Professor Emeritus, Department of Business Administration
Augsburg College

ABOUT THE AUTHOR

Kathy Schwalbe, Professor Emeritus in the Department of Business Administration at Augsburg College in Minneapolis, taught courses in project management, problem solving for business, systems analysis and design, information systems projects, and electronic commerce until her retirement in May 2015. She retired from teaching to focus on writing, traveling, and enjoying life. Kathy was also an adjunct faculty member at the University of Minnesota, where she taught a graduate-level course in project management in the engineering department. She also provides training and consulting services to several organizations and speaks at numerous conferences. Kathy's first job out of college was as a project manager in the Air Force. She worked for 10 years in industry before entering academia in 1991. She was an Air Force officer, project manager, systems analyst, senior engineer, and information technology consultant. Kathy is an active member of PMI, having served as the Student Chapter

Liaison for the Minnesota chapter, VP of Education for the Minnesota chapter, Editor of the ISSIG Review, Director of Communications for PMI's Information Systems Specific Interest Group, member of PMI's test-writing team, and writer for the community posts. Kathy earned her Ph.D. in Higher Education at the University of Minnesota, her MBA at Northeastern University's High Technology MBA program, and her B.S. in mathematics at the University of Notre Dame. She was named Educator of the Year in 2011 by the Association of Information Technology Professionals (AITP) Education Special Interest Group (EDSIG). Kathy lives in Minnesota with her husband. Visit her personal website at www.kathyschwalbe.com or www.pmtexts.com.

Other books by Kathy Schwalbe:

An Introduction to Project Management, Fifth Edition (Minneapolis: Schwalbe Publishing, 2015).

Healthcare Project Management, co-authored with Dan Furlong (Minneapolis: Schwalbe Publishing, 2013).

CHAPTER **1**

INTRODUCTION TO PROJECT MANAGEMENT

LEARNING OBJECTIVES

After reading this chapter, you will be able to:

- Understand the growing need for better project management, especially for information technology (IT) projects

- Explain what a project is, provide examples of IT projects, list various attributes of projects, and describe the triple constraint of project management

- Describe project management and discuss key elements of the project management framework, including project stakeholders, the project management knowledge areas, common tools and techniques, and project success

- Discuss the relationship between project, program, and portfolio management and the contributions each makes to enterprise success

- Understand the role of project managers by describing what they do, what skills they need, and career opportunities for IT project managers

- Describe the project management profession, including its history, the role of professional organizations like the Project Management Institute (PMI), the importance of certification and ethics, and the advancement of project management software

OPENING CASE

Anne Roberts, the director of the Project Management Office for a large retail chain, stood in front of 500 people in the large corporate auditorium to explain the company's new strategies during a monthly all-hands meeting. She was also streaming live video to thousands of other employees at other locations, suppliers, and stockholders throughout the world. The company had come a long way in implementing new information systems to improve inventory control, sell products online, streamline the sales and distribution processes, and improve customer service. However, a recent security breach had alarmed investors and the stock price plummeted. People were anxious to hear about the company's new strategies.

Anne began to address the audience, "Good morning. As many of you know, we have completed many projects successfully, including the advanced data networks project. That project enabled us to provide persistent broadband between headquarters and our retail stores throughout the world, allowing us to make timely decisions and continue our growth strategy. Our customers love that they can return items to any store, and any sales clerk can look up past sales information. Local store managers can make timely decisions using up-to-date information. Of course, we've had some failures, and we need to continually assess our portfolio of projects to meet business needs.

Two big IT initiatives this coming year include providing the best computer security possible and providing enhanced online collaboration tools for our employees, suppliers, and customers. Our challenge is to work even smarter to decide what projects will most benefit the company, how we can continue to leverage the power of information technology to support our business, and how we can exploit our human capital to successfully plan and execute those projects. If we succeed, we'll continue to be a world-class corporation."

"And if we fail?" someone asked from the audience.

"Let's just say that failure is not an option," Anne replied.

1.1 INTRODUCTION

Many people and organizations today have a new—or renewed—interest in project management. Until the 1980s, project management primarily focused on providing schedule and resource data to top management in the military, computer, and construction industries. Today's project management involves much more, and people in every industry and every country manage projects. Project management is a distinct profession with degree programs, certifications, and excellent career opportunities.

New technologies have become a significant factor in many businesses. Computer hardware, software, networks, and the use of interdisciplinary and global work teams have radically changed the work environment. The following statistics demonstrate the significance of project management in today's society, especially for projects involving information technology (IT):

- Worldwide IT spending was $3.8 trillion in 2014, a 3.2 percent increase from 2013 spending. Telecom services accounted for 45 percent of the spending.[1]
- The Project Management Institute estimates demand for 15.7 million project management jobs from 2010 to 2020, with 6.2 million of those jobs in the United States.[2]

- The unemployment rate for IT professionals is generally half the rate of the overall labor market in the United States. Between 2011 and 2014, and during the recession, the average unemployment rate for workers not in science, technology, engineering, and mathematics (STEM) was 7.4 percent, as opposed to just above 3 percent for STEM workers.[3]
- In 2013 (the most recent year of PMI's salary survey), the average salary in U.S. dollars for someone in the project management profession was $108,000 per year in the United States; $134,658 in Australia, (the highest-paid country); and $24,201 in Egypt (the lowest-paid country). Of the 11,150 people from the United States who responded to PMI's salary survey, 80 percent had the Project Management Professional (PMP) credential, and their salary was over 20 percent higher than professionals without it.[4]
- The top skills employers look for in new college graduates are all related to project management: team-work, decision-making, problem-solving, and verbal communications. The three degrees most in demand are business, engineering, and computer and information sciences.[5]
- Organizations waste $109 million for every $1 billion spent on projects, according to PMI's Pulse of the Profession® report. Excelling at project management definitely affects the bottom line.[6]

The complexity and importance of IT projects, which involve using hardware, software, and networks to create a product, service, or result, have evolved dramatically. Today's companies, governments, and nonprofit organizations are recognizing that to be successful, they need to use modern project management techniques, especially for IT projects. Individuals are realizing that to remain competitive in the workplace, they must develop skills to become good project team members and project managers. They also realize that many of the concepts of project management will help them in their everyday lives as they work with people and technology on a day-to-day basis.

(X) WHAT WENT WRONG?

In 1995, the Standish Group published an often-quoted study titled "The CHAOS Report." This consulting firm surveyed 365 IT executive managers in the United States who managed more than 8,380 IT application projects. As the title of the study suggests, the projects were in a state of chaos. U.S. companies spent more than $250 billion each year in the early 1990s on approximately 175,000 IT application development projects. Examples of these projects included creating a new database for a state department of motor vehicles, developing a new system for car rental and hotel reservations, and implementing a client-server architecture for the banking industry. The study reported that the overall success rate of IT projects was *only* 16.2 percent. The surveyors defined success as meeting project goals on time and on budget. The study also found that more than 31 percent of IT projects were canceled before completion, costing U.S. companies and government agencies more than $81 billion. The study authors were adamant about the need for better project management in the IT industry. They explained, "Software development projects are in chaos, and we can no longer imitate the three

continued

monkeys—hear no failures, see no failures, speak no failures."[7] Although this study was done 20 years ago, it was significant in making senior executives pay attention to the importance of IT project management.

In another large study, PricewaterhouseCoopers surveyed 200 companies from 30 different countries about their project management maturity and found that *over half of all projects fail*. The study also found that only 2.5 percent of corporations consistently meet their targets for scope, time, and cost goals for all types of projects.[8]

Although several researchers question the methodology of such studies, the results have prompted managers throughout the world to examine ways to improve their practices in managing projects. Many organizations assert that using project management techniques provides advantages, such as:

- Better control of financial, physical, and human resources
- Improved customer relations
- Shorter development times
- Lower costs and improved productivity
- Higher quality and increased reliability
- Higher profit margins
- Better internal coordination
- Positive impact on meeting strategic goals
- Higher worker morale

This chapter introduces projects and project management, explains how projects fit into programs and portfolio management, discusses the role of the project manager, and provides important background information on this growing profession. Although project management applies to many different industries and types of projects, this text focuses on applying project management to IT projects.

1.2 WHAT IS A PROJECT?

To discuss project management, it is important to understand the concept of a project. A **project** is "a temporary endeavor undertaken to create a unique product, service, or result."[9] Operations, on the other hand, is work done in organizations to sustain the business. Projects are different from operations in that they end when their objectives have been reached or the project has been terminated.

1.2a Examples of IT Projects

Projects can be large or small and involve one person or thousands of people. They can be done in one day or take years to complete. As described earlier, IT projects involve using hardware, software, and networks to create a product, service, or result. Examples of IT projects include the following:

- A large network of healthcare providers updates its information systems and procedures to reduce hospital acquired diseases.
- A team of students creates a smartphone application and sells it online.
- A company develops a driverless car.
- A college upgrades its technology infrastructure to provide wireless Internet access across the whole campus as well as online access to all academic and student service information.
- A company develops a new system to increase sales force productivity and customer relationship management that will work on various laptops, smartphones, and tablets.
- A television network implements a system to allow viewers to vote for contestants and provide other feedback on programs via social media sites.
- A government group develops a system to track child immunizations.
- A large group of volunteers from organizations throughout the world develops standards for environmentally friendly or green IT.
- A global bank acquires other financial institutions and needs to consolidate systems and procedures.
- Government regulations require monitoring of pollutants in the air and water.
- A multinational firm decides to consolidate its information systems into an integrated enterprise resource management approach.

Gartner, Inc., a prestigious consulting firm, identified the top 10 strategic technologies for 2015. A few of these technologies include the following:

- *Computing everywhere*: The needs of mobile users in diverse contexts and environments will continue to drive companies to develop new products and services.
- *The Internet of things*: Expanding digitization and connectivity will continue to enable companies to combine information from people, places, and things to extend services, improve how assets or machines operate, or create new sources of revenue. One example, according to Gartner, is that "the pay-per-use model can be applied to assets (such as . . . equipment), services (such as pay-as-you-drive insurance), people (such as movers), places (such as parking spots), and systems (such as cloud services)."
- *3D printing*: Worldwide shipments of 3D printers are expected to nearly double in 2015 compared to 2014 and double again in 2016. New applications continue to be found for producing items at lower costs through improved designs, streamlined prototyping, and short-run manufacturing.
- *Advanced, pervasive, and invisible analytics*: Analytics continues to grow in importance as the volume of data generated by embedded systems increases. The challenge is analyzing data to provide "the right information to the right person at the right time."[10]

As you can see, a wide variety of projects use information technologies, and organizations rely on them for success.

One of Gartner's top 10 strategic technologies for 2012 included application stores and marketplaces for smartphones and tablets. Gartner predicted that by 2014 there would be more than 70 billion mobile application downloads every year, but the actual number was almost double![11] Facebook is by far the most downloaded app, and the most popular category of all apps continues to be games.

There are over 1.3 million apps in Apple's App store and another 1.3 million in Google's Play Store. Of course, business professionals use phone applications for productive purposes. The challenge is to develop useful apps and get workers to focus on them instead of the many distracting options available. *Business Insider*, *Forbes*, *PC Magazine*, and website Lifehacker.com provide lists of top productivity apps "to keep you focused and get things done."[12]

1.2b Project Attributes

Projects come in all shapes and sizes. The following attributes help define a project further:

- *A project has a unique purpose.* Every project should have a well-defined objective. For example, Anne Roberts, the director of the Project Management Office in the chapter's opening case, might sponsor an IT collaboration project to develop a list and initial analysis of potential IT projects that might improve operations for the company. The unique purpose of this project would be to create a collaborative report with ideas from people throughout the company. The results would provide the basis for further discussions and selecting projects to implement. As you can see from this example, projects result in a unique product, service, or result.

- *A project is temporary.* A project has a definite beginning and end. In the IT collaboration project, Anne might form a team of people to work immediately on the project, and then expect a report and an executive presentation of the results in one month.

- *A project is developed using progressive elaboration.* Projects are often defined broadly when they begin, and as time passes, the specific details of the project become clearer. Therefore, projects should be developed in increments. A project team should develop initial plans and then update them with more detail based on new information. For example, suppose that a few people submitted ideas for the IT collaboration project, but they did not clearly address how the ideas would support the business strategy of improving operations. The project team might decide to prepare a questionnaire for people to fill in as they submit their ideas to improve the quality of the inputs.

- *A project requires resources, often from various areas.* Resources include people, hardware, software, and other assets. Many projects cross departmental or other boundaries to achieve their unique purposes. For the IT collaboration project, people from IT, marketing, sales, distribution, and other areas of the company would need to work together to develop ideas. The company might also hire outside consultants to provide input. Once the collaboration project team has selected key projects for implementation, each of those will probably require additional resources. To meet objectives of these new projects, people from other companies—product suppliers and consulting companies—may be added to the team. Resources, however, are limited and must be used effectively to meet project and other corporate goals.

- *A project should have a primary customer or sponsor.* Most projects have many interested parties or stakeholders, but for a project to succeed someone must take the primary role of sponsorship. The **project sponsor** usually provides the direction and funding for the project. Executive support is crucial to project success, as described in later chapters. Anne Roberts would be the sponsor for the IT collaboration project. Once further IT projects are selected, however, the sponsors for those projects would be senior managers in charge of the main parts of the company affected by the projects. For example, the sponsor of a project to improve online product sales would be the vice president of sales. In this situation, Anne might become part of a project steering committee, helping other managers understand different project objectives, resolve priorities, research issues, or alter constraints within a given project or across multiple projects.

- *A project involves uncertainty.* Because every project is unique, it is sometimes difficult to define its objectives clearly, estimate how long it will take to complete, or determine how much it will cost. External factors also cause uncertainty, such as a supplier going out of business or a project team member needing unplanned time off. This uncertainty is one of the main reasons project management is so challenging, especially on projects involving new technologies.

An effective **project manager** is crucial to a project's success. Project managers work with the project sponsors, team, and the other people involved to achieve project goals.

1.2c Project Constraints

Every project is constrained in different ways, often by its scope, time, and cost goals. These limitations are sometimes referred to in project management as the **triple constraint**. To create a successful project, a project manager must consider scope, time, and cost and balance these three often-competing goals:

- *Scope*: What work will be done as part of the project? What unique product, service, or result does the customer or sponsor expect from the project? How will the scope be verified?
- *Time*: How long should it take to complete the project? What is the project's schedule? How will the team track actual schedule performance? Who can approve changes to the schedule?
- *Cost*: What should it cost to complete the project? What is the project's budget? How will costs be tracked? Who can authorize changes to the budget?

Figure 1-1 illustrates the three dimensions of the triple constraint. Each area—scope, time, and cost—has a target at the beginning of the project. For example, the IT collaboration project might have an initial scope of producing a 40- to 50-page report and a one-hour presentation on about 30 potential IT projects. The project manager might further define project scope to include providing a description of each potential project, an investigation of what other companies have implemented for similar projects, a rough time and cost estimate, and assessments of the risk and potential payoff as high, medium, or low. The initial time estimate for this project might be one month, and the cost estimate might be $45,000–$50,000. These expectations provide targets for the scope, time, and cost dimensions of the project.

Note that the scope and cost goals in this example include ranges—the report can be 40 to 50 pages long and the project can cost between $45,000 and $50,000. Because projects involve uncertainty and limited resources, projects rarely finish according to their original scope, time, and cost goals. Instead of discrete target goals, it is often more realistic to set a range for goals, such as spending between $45,000 and $50,000 and having a 40- to 50-page report. These goals might require hitting the target, but not the bull's eye.

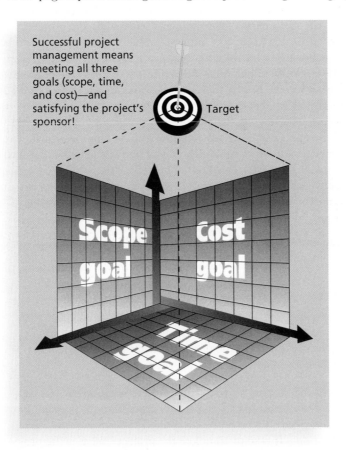

© Cengage Learning 2016

FIGURE 1-1   Project constraints

Managing the triple constraint involves making trade-offs between scope, time, and cost goals for a project. For example, you might need to increase the budget for a project to meet scope and time goals. Alternatively, you might have to reduce the scope of a project to meet time and cost goals. Experienced project managers know that you must decide which aspect of the triple constraint is most important. If time is most important, you must often change the initial scope and cost goals to meet the schedule. If scope goals are most important, you may need to adjust time and cost goals.

To generate project ideas for the IT collaboration project, suppose that the project manager sent an e-mail survey to all employees, as planned. The initial time and cost estimate may have been one week and $5,000 to collect ideas using this e-mail survey. Now, suppose that the e-mail survey generated only a few good project ideas, but the scope goal was to collect at least 30 good ideas. Should the project team use a different method like focus groups or interviews to collect ideas? Even though it was not in the initial scope, time, or cost estimates, it would really help the project. Because good ideas are crucial to project success, it would make sense to inform the project sponsor that adjustments are needed.

Although the triple constraint describes how the basic elements of a project inter-relate, other elements can also play significant roles. Quality is often a key factor in projects, as is customer or sponsor satisfaction. Some people, in fact, refer to the *quadruple constraint* of project management, which includes quality as well as scope, time, and cost. A project team may meet scope, time, and cost goals but might fail to meet quality standards and satisfy the sponsor. For example, Anne Roberts may receive a 50-page report describing 30 potential IT projects and hear a presentation that summarizes the report. The project team may have completed the work on time and within the cost constraint, but the quality may have been unacceptable.

Other factors might also be crucial to a particular project. On some projects, resources are the main concern. For example, the entertainment industry often needs particular actors for movies or television shows. Project goals must be adjusted based on when particular people are available. Risk can also affect major project decisions. A company might wait to start a project until the risks are at an acceptable level. The project manager should be communicating with the sponsor throughout the project to make sure it is meeting expectations. Chapter 10, Project Communications Management, and Chapter 13, Project Stakeholder Management, address communicating with stakeholders and understanding their expectations in greater detail.

How can you avoid the problems that occur when you meet scope, time, and cost goals, but lose sight of customer satisfaction? The answer is *good project management, which includes more than managing project constraints.*

1.3 WHAT IS PROJECT MANAGEMENT?

Project management is "the application of knowledge, skills, tools, and techniques to project activities to meet project requirements."[13] Project managers must strive not only to meet specific scope, time, cost, and quality goals of projects, they must also facilitate the entire process to meet the needs and expectations of people involved in project activities or affected by them.

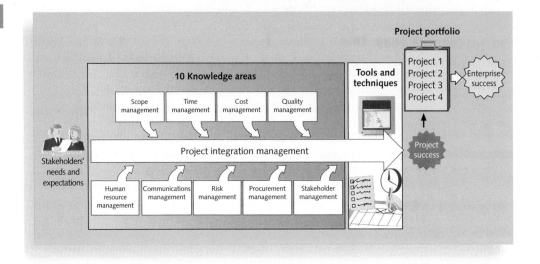

© Cengage Learning 2016

FIGURE 1-2 Project Management Framework

Figure 1-2 illustrates a framework to help you understand project management. Key elements of this framework include the project stakeholders, project management knowledge areas, project management tools and techniques, and the contribution of successful projects to the enterprise.

1.3a Project Stakeholders

Stakeholders are the people involved in or affected by project activities, and include the project sponsor, project team, support staff, customers, users, suppliers, and even opponents of the project. These stakeholders often have very different needs and expectations. A familiar example of a project is building a new house. There are several stakeholders in a home construction project.

- The project sponsors would be the potential new homeowners who would be paying for the house. They could be on a very tight budget, so would expect the contractor to provide a realistic idea of what type of home they could afford given their budget constraints. They would also need a realistic idea of when they could move in. Regardless of budget, they would expect the contractor to provide accurate estimates for the building costs. The new homeowners would have to make important decisions to keep the costs of the house within their budget. Can they afford to finish the basement right away? If they can afford to finish the basement, will it affect the projected move-in date? In this example, the project sponsors are also the customers and users of the product, which is the house.
- The house may require financing by a bank or other financial institution like a credit union, which will secure a legal interest (lien) in the property and

the finished home. This institution is an example of a legal stakeholder who must be informed of any changes to the plans or schedule because the project is part of a legal contract.

- The project manager in this example would normally be the general contractor responsible for building the house. The project manager needs to work with all the project stakeholders to meet their needs and expectations.
- The project team for building the house would include several construction workers, electricians, and carpenters. These stakeholders would need to know exactly what work they must do and when they need to do it. They would need to know if the required materials and equipment will be at the construction site or if they are expected to provide the materials and equipment. Their work would need to be coordinated because many interrelated factors are involved. For example, the carpenter cannot put in kitchen cabinets until the walls are completed.
- Support staff might include the buyers' employers, the general contractor's administrative assistant, and people who support other stakeholders. The buyers' employers might expect their employees to complete their work but allow some flexibility so they can visit the building site or take phone calls related to building the house. The contractor's administrative assistant would support the project by coordinating meetings between the buyers, the contractor, suppliers, and other parties.
- Building a house requires many suppliers. The suppliers would provide the wood, windows, flooring, appliances, and other materials. Suppliers would expect exact details on the items they need to provide, and where and when to deliver those items.
- A project might have opponents. In this example, a neighbor might oppose the project because the workers make so much noise that she cannot concentrate on her work at home, or the noise might wake her sleeping children. She might interrupt the workers to voice her complaints or even file a formal complaint. Or, the neighborhood might have association rules concerning new home design and construction. If the homeowners do not follow these rules, they might have to halt construction due to legal issues. Even without such complaints, the home must comply with certain building codes and other restrictions; these considerations may also result in changes to the project's requirements, making the local government a stakeholder in the project.

As you can see from this example, projects have many different stakeholders, and they often have different interests. Stakeholders' needs and expectations are important in the beginning and throughout the life of a project. Successful project managers develop good relationships with project stakeholders to understand and meet their needs and expectations.

1.3b Project Management Knowledge Areas

Project management knowledge areas describe the key competencies that project managers must develop. The center of Figure 1-2 shows the 10 knowledge areas of project management.

1. Project scope management involves defining and managing all the work required to complete the project successfully.
2. Project time management includes estimating how long it will take to complete the work, developing an acceptable project schedule, and ensuring timely completion of the project.
3. Project cost management consists of preparing and managing the budget for the project.
4. Project quality management ensures that the project will satisfy the stated or implied needs for which it was undertaken.
5. Project human resource management is concerned with making effective use of the people involved with the project.
6. Project communications management involves generating, collecting, disseminating, and storing project information.
7. Project risk management includes identifying, analyzing, and responding to risks related to the project.
8. Project procurement management involves acquiring or procuring goods and services for a project from outside the performing organization.
9. Project stakeholder management includes identifying and analyzing stakeholder needs while managing and controlling their engagement throughout the life of the project.
10. Project integration management is an overarching function that affects and is affected by all of the other knowledge areas.

Project managers must have knowledge and skills in all 10 of these areas. This text includes an entire chapter on each of these knowledge areas because all of them are crucial to project success.

1.3c Project Management Tools and Techniques

Thomas Carlyle, a famous historian and author, stated, "Man is a tool-using animal. Without tools he is nothing, with tools he is all." As the world continues to become more complex, it is even more important for people to develop and use tools, especially for managing important projects. **Project management tools and techniques** assist project managers and their teams in carrying out work in all 10 knowledge areas. For example, some popular time-management tools and techniques include Gantt charts, project network diagrams, and critical path analysis. Table 1-1 lists some commonly used tools and techniques by knowledge area. You will learn more about these and other tools and techniques throughout this text.

A survey of 753 project and program managers was conducted to rate several project management tools. Respondents rated tools on a scale of 1–5 (low to high) based on the extent of their use and the potential of the tools to help improve project success. "Super tools" were defined as those that had high use and high potential for improving project success. These super tools included software for task scheduling (such as project management software), scope statements, requirement analyses, and lessons-learned reports. Tools that are already used extensively and have been found to improve project performance include progress reports, kick-off meetings, Gantt charts, and change requests.

These super tools appear in column 3 of Table 1-1.[14] Note that project stakeholder management was not a separate knowledge area at the time of this survey. Of course, different tools can be more effective in different situations. It is crucial for project managers and their team members to determine which tools will be most useful for their particular projects.

TABLE 1-1   Common project management tools and techniques by knowledge area

Knowledge Area/Category	Tools and Techniques	Super Tools
Integration management	Project selection methods Project management methodologies Stakeholder analyses Work requests Project charters Project management plans Change control boards Project review meetings	Project management software Change requests Lessons-learned reports
Scope management	Statements of work Scope management plans Scope verification techniques Scope change controls	Scope statements Work breakdown structures Requirements analyses
Time management	Project network diagrams Critical path analysis Crashing Fast tracking Schedule performance measurements	Gantt charts
Cost management	Project budgets Net present value Return on investment Payback analysis Earned value management Project portfolio management Cost estimates Cost management plans Cost baselines	
Quality management	Quality metrics Checklists Quality control charts Pareto diagrams Fishbone diagrams Maturity models Statistical methods Test plans	
Human resource management	Motivation techniques Empathic listening Responsibility assignment matrices Project organizational charts Resource histograms Team building exercises	

(continued)

TABLE 1-1 Common project management tools and techniques by knowledge area (*continued*)

Knowledge Area/Category	Tools and Techniques	Super Tools
Communications management	Communications management plans Conflict management Communications media selection Status reports Virtual communications Templates Project websites	Kick-off meetings Progress reports
Risk management	Risk management plans Risk registers Probability/impact matrices Risk rankings	
Procurement management	Make-or-buy analyses Contracts Requests for proposals or quotes Source selections Supplier evaluation matrices	

© Cengage Learning 2016

 WHAT WENT RIGHT?

Follow-up studies by the Standish Group (publisher of the annual CHAOS study; see "What Went Wrong?") have shown some improvement in the success rates of IT projects:

- The number of successful IT projects more than doubled, from 16 percent in 1994 to 39 percent in 2012.
- The number of failed projects decreased from 31 percent in 1994 to 18 percent in 2012.

"This year's results represent a high watermark for success rates in the history of CHAOS research. The increase in success is a result of several factors, including looking at the entire project environment of processes, methods, skills, costs, tools, decisions, optimization, internal and external influences, and team chemistry. Advances in the understanding of the skills needed to be a good executive sponsor have proved to be very valuable for increasing success rates. Increases in project management as a profession and trained project management professionals can be tied directly to increases in success rates."[15]

The 2013 CHAOS study also compared small projects (under $1 million) with large projects (over $10 million). Not surprisingly, the success rate for small projects was much higher than for large projects—76 percent versus 10 percent. It is easier to manage smaller projects, and researchers suggest that organizations strive to break large projects into a sequence of smaller ones in a process they call optimization.[16]

Despite its advantages, project management is not a silver bullet that guarantees success on all projects. Project management is a very broad, often complex discipline. What works on one project may not work on another, so it is essential for project managers to continue to develop their knowledge and skills in managing projects. It is also important to learn from the mistakes and successes of others.

1.3d Project Success

How do you define the success or failure of a project? The list that follows outlines a few common criteria for measuring the success of a project, illustrating each with an example of upgrading 500 desktop computers within three months for $300,000:

1. *The project met scope, time, and cost goals.* If all 500 computers were upgraded and met other scope requirements, the work was completed in three months or less, and the cost was $300,000 or less, you could consider the project successful. The Standish Group studies used this definition of success, but several people question this simple definition of project success and the methods used for collecting the data. (Search for articles by Robert L. Glass to read more about this debate.)

2. *The project satisfied the customer/sponsor.* Even if the project met initial scope, time, and cost goals, the users of the computers or their managers might not be satisfied. Perhaps the project manager or team members never returned calls or were rude. Perhaps users had their daily work disrupted during the upgrades or had to work extra hours due to the upgrades. If the customers were not happy with important aspects of the project, it would be deemed a failure. Conversely, a project might not meet initial scope, time, and cost goals, but the customer could still be very satisfied. Perhaps the project team took longer and spent more money than planned, but they were very polite and helped the users and managers solve several work-related problems. Many organizations implement a customer satisfaction rating system to measure project success instead of tracking only scope, time, and cost performance.

3. *The results of the project met its main objective, such as making or saving a certain amount of money, providing a good return on investment, or simply making the sponsors happy.* Even if the project cost more than estimated, it took longer to complete, and the project team was hard to work with, the project would be successful if users were happy with the upgraded computers, based on this criterion. As another example, suppose that the sponsor approved the upgrade project to provide a good return on investment by speeding up work and therefore generating more profits. If those goals were met, the sponsor would deem the project a success, regardless of other factors involved.

Why do some IT projects succeed and others fail? Table 1-2 summarizes the results of the 2013 CHAOS study. The factors that contribute most to the success of IT projects are listed in order of importance. Executive support is the most important factor, followed by user involvement. A few of the top success factors relate to good scope management, such as having clear business objectives and optimizing scope. Project management expertise continues to be a key success factor. In fact, experienced project managers, who can often help influence all of these factors to improve the probability of project success, led 97 percent of successful projects, based on an earlier CHAOS study in 2001.

16

TABLE 1-2   What helps projects succeed?

1. Executive support
2. User involvement
3. Clear business objectives
4. Emotional maturity
5. Optimizing scope
6. Agile process
7. Project management expertise
8. Skilled resources
9. Execution
10. Tools and infrastructure

Source: The Standish Group, "CHAOS Manifesto 2013: Think Big, Act Small" (2013).

A 2011 U.S. government report listed the top three reasons why federal technology projects succeed:

1. Adequate funding
2. Staff expertise
3. Engagement from all stakeholders

Notice that the CHAOS study list does not include adequate funding. Most nongovernment companies must either find adequate funds for important projects or cancel projects if they cannot be funded or get an adequate return. Government projects often require that funds be allocated a year or more before they even start, and estimates often fall short. "The government has struggled when acquiring technology thanks to the convoluted nature of the federal contracting process and the shortage of qualified contracting officers and technical personnel. Critics argue that federal agencies get little return for the $80 billion the government spends annually on IT. . . . 'History has shown that government IT projects frequently face challenges of meeting cost, schedule or performance goals,' said Sen. Susan Collins (R-Maine) in a statement."[17]

It is interesting to compare success factors for IT projects in the United States with those in other countries. A 2004 study summarizes the results of a survey of 247 information systems project practitioners in mainland China. One of the study's key findings was that relationship management is viewed as a top success factor for information systems in China, while it is not mentioned in U.S. studies. The study also suggested that having competent team members is less important in China than in the United States. The Chinese, like the Americans, included top management support, user involvement, and a competent project manager as vital to project success.[18]

It is also important to look beyond individual project success rates and focus on how organizations as a whole can improve project performance. Research comparing companies that excel in project delivery—the "winners"—from those that do not found four significant best practices:

1. *Use an integrated toolbox.* Companies that consistently succeed in managing projects clearly define what needs to be done in a project, by whom, when,

and how. They use an integrated toolbox, including project management tools, methods, and techniques. They carefully select tools, align them with project and business goals, link them to metrics, and provide them to project managers to deliver positive results.

2. *Grow project leaders.* The winners know that strong project managers—referred to as project leaders—are crucial to project success. They also know that a good project leader needs to be a business leader as well, with strong interpersonal and intrapersonal skills. Companies that excel in project management often grow or develop their project leaders internally, providing them with career opportunities, training, and mentoring.

3. *Develop a streamlined project delivery process.* Winning companies have examined every step in the project delivery process, analyzed fluctuations in workloads, searched for ways to reduce variation, and eliminated bottlenecks to create a repeatable delivery process. All projects go through clear stages and clearly define key milestones. All project leaders use a shared road map, focusing on key business aspects of their projects while integrating goals across all parts of the organization.

4. *Measure project health using metrics.* Companies that excel in project delivery use performance metrics to quantify progress. They focus on a handful of important measurements and apply them to all projects. Metrics often include customer satisfaction, return on investment, and percentage of schedule buffer consumed.[19]

Project managers play an important role in making projects, and therefore organizations, successful. Project managers work with the project sponsors, the project team, and other stakeholders to meet project goals. They also work with sponsors to define success for particular projects. Good project managers do not assume that their definition of success is the same as the sponsors'. They take the time to understand their sponsors' expectations and then track project performance based on important success criteria.

1.4 PROGRAM AND PROJECT PORTFOLIO MANAGEMENT

As mentioned earlier, about one-quarter of the world's gross domestic product is spent on projects. Projects make up a significant portion of work in most business organizations or enterprises, and managing those projects successfully is crucial to enterprise success. Two important concepts that help projects meet enterprise goals are the use of programs and project portfolio management.

1.4a Programs

A **program** is "a group of related projects, subprograms, and program activities managed in a coordinated way to obtain benefits and control not available from managing them individually."[20] As you can imagine, it is often more economical to group projects together to help streamline management, staffing, purchasing, and other work. The following are examples of common programs in the IT field.

- *Infrastructure*: An IT department often has a program for IT infrastructure projects. This program could encompass several projects, such as providing more wireless Internet access, upgrading hardware and software, enhancing computer security, and developing and maintaining corporate standards for IT.
- *Applications development*: This program could include several projects, such as updating an enterprise resource planning (ERP) system, purchasing a new off-the-shelf billing system, or developing a new capability for a customer relationship management system.
- *User support*: In addition to the many operational tasks related to user support, many IT departments have several projects to support users. For example, a project might provide a better e-mail system or develop technical training for users.

A **program manager** provides leadership and direction for the project managers heading the projects within a program. Program managers also coordinate the efforts of project teams, functional groups, suppliers, and operations staff supporting the projects to ensure that products and processes are implemented to maximize benefits. Program managers are responsible for more than the delivery of project results; they are change agents responsible for the success of products and processes developed by those projects. For example, the NASA International Space Station Program is led by a program manager who oversees all U.S. projects involved with the station and is accountable for achieving their objectives, funding, and contribution to scientific knowledge.

Program managers often have review meetings with all their project managers to share important information and coordinate important aspects of each project. Many program managers worked as project managers earlier in their careers, and they enjoy sharing their wisdom and expertise with their project managers. Effective program managers recognize that managing a program is much more complex than managing a single project. They recognize that technical and project management skills are not enough—program managers must also possess strong business knowledge, leadership capabilities, and communication skills.

1.4b Project Portfolio Management

In many organizations, project managers also support an emerging business strategy of **project portfolio management** or **portfolio management**, as called in this text, in which organizations group and manage projects and programs as a portfolio of investments that contribute to the entire enterprise's success. Portfolio managers help their organizations make wise investment decisions by helping to select and analyze projects from a strategic perspective. Portfolio managers may or may not have previous experience as project or program managers. It is most important that they have strong financial and analytical skills and understand how projects and programs can contribute to meeting strategic goals.

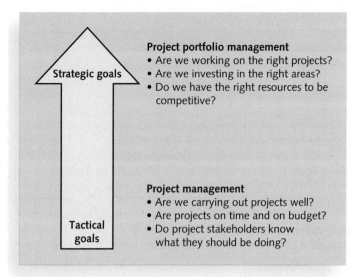

Strategic goals

Project portfolio management
- Are we working on the right projects?
- Are we investing in the right areas?
- Do we have the right resources to be competitive?

Project management
- Are we carrying out projects well?
- Are projects on time and on budget?
- Do project stakeholders know what they should be doing?

Tactical goals

© Cengage Learning 2016

FIGURE 1-3   Project management compared to project portfolio management

Figure 1-3 illustrates the differences between project management and project portfolio management. Notice that the main distinction is a focus on meeting tactical or strategic goals. Tactical goals are generally more specific and short-term than strategic goals, which emphasize long-term goals for an organization. Individual projects often address tactical goals, whereas portfolio management addresses strategic goals. Project management addresses questions like "Are we carrying out projects well?", "Are projects on time and on budget?", and "Do project stakeholders know what they should be doing?"

Portfolio management addresses questions like "Are we working on the right projects?", "Are we investing in the right areas?", and "Do we have the right resources to be competitive?" Pacific Edge Software's product manager, Eric Burke, defines project portfolio management as "the continuous process of selecting and managing the optimum set of project initiatives that deliver maximum business value."[21]

Many organizations use a more disciplined approach to portfolio management by developing guidelines and software tools to assist in it. The Project Management Institute (described later in this chapter) first published the *Organizational Project Management Maturity Model (OPM3) Knowledge Foundation* in 2003.[22] OPM3 describes the importance not only of managing individual projects or programs well but the importance of following organizational project management to align projects, programs, and portfolios with strategic goals. OPM3 is a standard that organizations can use to measure their organizational project management maturity against a comprehensive set of best practices.

🎗 BEST PRACTICE

A **best practice** is "an optimal way recognized by industry to achieve a stated goal or objective."[23] Rosabeth Moss Kanter, a professor at Harvard Business School and well-known author and consultant, says that visionary leaders know "the best practice secret: Stretching to learn from the best of the best in any sector can make a big vision more likely to succeed."[24] Kanter also emphasizes the need to have measurable standards for best practices. An organization can measure performance against its own past, against peers, and, even better, against potential. Kanter suggests that organizations need to continue to reach for higher standards. She suggests the following exercise regimen for business leaders who want to adapt best practices in an intelligent way to help their own organizations:

- Reach high. Stretch. Raise standards and aspirations. Find the best of the best and then use it as inspiration for reaching full potential.
- Help everyone in your organization become a professional. Empower people to manage themselves through benchmarks and standards based on best practice exchange.
- Look everywhere. Go far afield. Think of the whole world as your laboratory for learning.

Robert Butrick, author of *The Project Workout*, wrote an article on best practices in project management for the *Ultimate Business Library's Best Practice* book. He suggests that organizations need to follow basic principles of project management, including these two mentioned earlier in this chapter:

- Make sure your projects are driven by your strategy. Be able to demonstrate how each project you undertake fits your business strategy, and screen out unwanted projects as soon as possible.
- Engage your stakeholders. Ignoring stakeholders often leads to project failure. Be sure to engage stakeholders at all stages of a project, and encourage teamwork and commitment at all times.[25]

As you can imagine, project portfolio management is not an easy task. Figure 1-4 illustrates one approach for project portfolio management in which one large portfolio exists for the entire organization. This allows top management to view and manage all projects at an enterprise level. Sections of the portfolio are then broken down to improve the management of projects in each sector. For example, a company might have the main portfolio categories shown in the left part of Figure 1-4—marketing, materials, IT, and human resources (HR)—and divide each of those categories further to address its unique concerns. The right part of this figure shows how the IT projects could be categorized in more detail to assist in their management. In this example, there are three basic IT project portfolio categories:

- *Venture*: Projects in this category help transform the business. For example, the large retail chain described in the opening case might have an IT project to provide kiosks in stores and similar functionality on the Internet where customers and suppliers could quickly provide feedback on products or services. This project could help transform the business by developing closer partnerships with customers and suppliers.

- *Growth*: Projects in this category would help the company increase its revenues. For example, a company might have an IT project to provide information on its corporate website in a new language, such as Chinese or Japanese. This capability could help the company grow its business in those countries.
- *Core*: Projects in this category must be accomplished to run the business. For example, an IT project to provide computers for new employees would fall under this category.

In Figure 1-4, the costs of Core IT projects are nondiscretionary, which means that the company has no choice in whether to fund them. Core IT Projects must be funded for the company to stay in business. Projects in the Venture or Growth category are discretionary costs because the company can use its own discretion or judgment in deciding whether to fund them; these projects are not critical to the company fulfilling its mission. The arrow in the center of Figure 1-4 indicates that the risks and value of projects normally increase as you move from Core to Growth to Venture projects. In addition, timeliness becomes increasingly important; growth and venture projects, more than core projects, must be done within a certain time frame to be effective. However, some core projects can also be high risk, have high value, and require good timing. As you can see, many factors are involved in portfolio management.

Many organizations use specialized software to organize and analyze all types of project data into project portfolios. **Enterprise project management software** or **project and portfolio management software** integrates information from multiple projects to show the

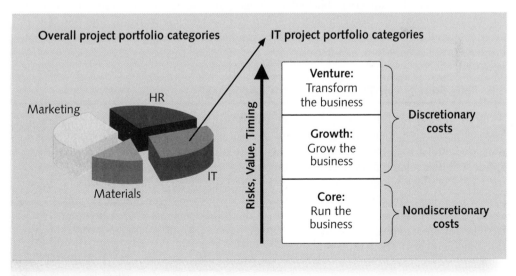

© Cengage Learning 2016

FIGURE 1-4   Sample project portfolio approach

Source: Microsoft, "PPM Solution Guide" (October 2013).

FIGURE 1-5   Microsoft project portfolio management capabilities

status of active, approved, and future projects across an entire organization. It also helps organizations prioritize project portfolio investment to deliver results with the best business value. In 2014, Capterra published an infographic listing the top 20 project management software tools. Microsoft Project continues to lead the market with over 880,000 customers and 22 million users.[26] Figure 1-5 summarizes the capabilities of the Microsoft Project Portfolio Management solution.

1.5 THE ROLE OF THE PROJECT MANAGER

You have already read that project managers must work closely with the other stakeholders on a project, especially the sponsor and project team. They are also more effective if they are familiar with the 10 project management knowledge areas and the various tools and techniques related to project management. Experienced project managers help projects succeed. But what do project managers do, exactly? What skills do they really need to do a good job? The next section provides brief answers to these questions, and the rest of this book gives more insight into the role of the project manager. Even if you never become a project manager, you will probably be part of a project team, and it is important for team members to help their project managers.

1.5a Project Manager Job Description

A project manager can have many different job descriptions, which can vary tremendously based on the organization and the project. In fact, PMI includes a page on their website to answer the question, "Who are project managers?" In addition to saying that project managers are organized, passionate, and goal-oriented individuals who drive business results by leading projects, PMI emphasizes that they are also change agents who work well under pressure and enjoy challenging work environments.

Project management jobs can be found in every country and every industry. Sites like indeed.com listed hundreds of thousands of job openings in 2015. Monster.com has a job category for project management, and their site says that project managers "smoothly link management, clients and staff to keep projects rolling. To be successful in a project management job, you'll need people skills, business acumen and technical competence."[27] Here are a few edited postings:

- *Project manager for a consulting firm*: Plans, schedules, and controls activities to fulfill identified objectives applying technical, theoretical, and managerial skills to satisfy project requirements. Coordinates and integrates team and individual efforts and builds positive professional relationships with clients and associates.
- *Project manager for a computer systems firm*: Works independently within established practices to assist in the development and implementation process of projects involving departmental, vendor relationships, and/or cross-functional teams. Coordinates with internal/external clients to gather business requirements and coordinate project plans. Monitor projects from initiation through delivery ensuring completion of the project on schedule.
- *IT project manager for a nonprofit consulting firm*: Responsibilities include business analysis, requirements gathering, project planning, budget estimating, development, testing, and implementation. Responsible for working with various resource providers to ensure development is completed in a timely, high-quality, and cost-effective manner.

The job description for a project manager can vary by industry and by organization, but most project managers perform similar tasks regardless of these differences. In fact, project management is a skill needed in every major IT field, from database administrator to network specialist to technical writer. Because demand for project managers is high, some organizations have hired new college graduates to fill positions normally held by experienced professionals. For example, Boom Lab, a consulting company, is growing quickly by finding, training, and placing talented people as project coordinators. As new project coordinators gain experience and credentials, they often continue their careers by managing larger projects, becoming program managers, or transitioning into other management positions.

1.5b Suggested Skills for Project Managers

Project managers need to have a wide variety of skills and be able to decide which skills are more important in different situations. *A Guide to the Project Management Body of Knowledge*—the *PMBOK® Guide*—recommends that the project management team understand and use expertise in the following areas:

- The Project Management Body of Knowledge
- Application area knowledge, standards, and regulations

- Project environment knowledge
- General management knowledge and skills
- Soft skills or human relations skills

This chapter introduced the 10 project management knowledge areas, as well as some general tools and techniques project managers use. The following section focuses on the IT application area, including skills required in the project environment, general management, and soft skills. Note that the *PMBOK® Guide, Fifth Edition* describes three dimensions of project management competency: project management knowledge (knowing about project management), performance competency (being able to apply project management knowledge), and personal competency (attitudes and personality characteristics). Consult PMI's website at *www.pmi.org* for further information on skills for project managers and PMI's Career Framework for Practitioners.

The project environment differs from organization to organization and project to project, but some skills will help in almost all project environments. These skills include understanding change and understanding how organizations work within their social, political, and physical environments. Project managers must be comfortable leading and handling change, because most projects introduce changes in organizations and involve changes within the projects themselves. Project managers need to understand the organization in which they work and how that organization develops products and provides services. The skills and behavior needed to manage a project for a Fortune 100 company in the United States may differ greatly from those needed to manage a government project in Poland. Chapter 2, The Project Management and Information Technology Context, provides detailed information on these topics.

Project managers should also possess general management knowledge and skills. They should understand important topics related to financial management, accounting, procurement, sales, marketing, contracts, manufacturing, distribution, logistics, the supply chain, strategic planning, tactical planning, operations management, organizational structures and behavior, personnel administration, compensation, benefits, career paths, and health and safety practices. On some projects, it will be critical for the project manager to have a lot of experience in one or several of these general management areas. On other projects, the project manager can delegate detailed responsibility for some of these areas to a team member, support staff, or even a supplier. Even so, the project manager must be intelligent and experienced enough to know which of these areas are most important and who is qualified to do the work. The project manager must make all key project decisions and take responsibility for them.

Achieving high performance on projects requires soft skills, otherwise called human relations skills. Some of these soft skills include effective communication, influencing the organization to get things done, leadership, motivation, negotiation, conflict management, and problem solving. Why do project managers need good soft skills? One reason is that to understand, navigate, and meet stakeholders' needs and expectations, project managers need to lead, communicate, negotiate, solve problems, and influence the organization at large. They need to be able to listen actively to what others are saying, help develop new approaches for solving problems, and then persuade others to work toward achieving project goals. Project managers must lead their project teams by providing vision, delegating work, creating an energetic and positive environment, and setting an example of appropriate and effective behavior. Project managers must focus on teamwork skills to employ people effectively. They need to be able to motivate different types of people and develop *esprit de corps* within the project team and with other project stakeholders. Because most projects involve changes and trade-offs between competing goals, it is important for project managers to have strong coping skills as well. Project managers need to be able to cope with criticism and constant change. Project managers must be flexible, creative, and sometimes patient in working toward project goals; they must also be persistent in making project needs known.

Finally, project managers, especially those managing IT projects, must be able to make effective use of technology as it relates to the specific project. Making effective use of technology often includes special product knowledge or experience with a particular industry.

Project managers must make many decisions and deal with people in a wide variety of disciplines, so it helps tremendously to have a project manager who is confident in using the special tools or technologies that are the most effective in particular settings. Project managers do not normally have to be experts on any specific technology, but they have to know enough to build a strong team and ask the right questions to keep things on track. For example, project managers for large IT projects do not have to be experts in the field of IT, but they must have working knowledge of various technologies and understand how the project would enhance the business. Many companies have found good business managers can be very good IT project managers because they focus on meeting business needs and rely on key project members to handle the technical details.

A 2013 survey by CIO.com listed seven skills project managers need in order to be effective and successful in leading IT projects:

1. Be highly organized.
2. Take charge and know how to lead.
3. Be an effective communicator.
4. Know how and when to negotiate.
5. Be detail-oriented.
6. Recognize and solve problems quickly.
7. Possess the necessary technical skills.[28]

All project managers should continue to develop their knowledge and experience in project management, general management, soft skills, and the industries they support. IT project managers must be willing to develop more than their technical skills to be productive team members and successful project managers. Everyone, no matter how technical they are, should develop business and soft skills.

1.5c Importance of People Skills and Leadership Skills

Project management experts from various industries were asked to identify the 10 most important skills and competencies for effective project managers. Table 1-3 shows the results.

TABLE 1-3 Ten most important skills and competencies for project managers

1. People skills
2. Leadership
3. Listening
4. Integrity, ethical behavior, consistency
5. Strength at building trust
6. Verbal communication
7. Strength at building teams
8. Conflict resolution, conflict management
9. Critical thinking, problem solving
10. Understanding and balancing of priorities

Source: Jennifer Krahn, "Effective Project Leadership: A Combination of Project Manager Skills and Competencies in Context," *PMI Research Conference Proceedings* (July 2006).

Respondents were also asked what skills and competencies were most important in various project situations:

- *Large projects*: Leadership, relevant experience, planning, people skills, verbal communication, and team-building skills were most important.
- *High-uncertainty projects*: Risk management, expectation management, leadership, people skills, and planning skills were most important.
- *Innovative projects*: Leadership, people skills, vision- and goal-setting, self-confidence, expectations management, and listening skills were most important.[29]

Notice that a few skills and competencies not cited in the top 10 list were mentioned when people thought about the context of a project. To be most effective, project managers require a changing mix of skills and competencies depending on the project being delivered.

Also notice the general emphasis on people and leadership skills. As mentioned earlier, all project managers, especially those working on technical projects, need to demonstrate leadership and management skills. *Leadership* and *management* are terms often used interchangeably, although there are differences. Generally, a **leader** focuses on long-term goals and big-picture objectives while inspiring people to reach those goals. A **manager** often deals with the day-to-day details of meeting specific goals. Some people say: "Managers do things right, and leaders do the right things." "Leaders determine the vision, and managers achieve the vision." "You lead people and manage things."

However, project managers often take on the role of both leader and manager. Good project managers know that people make or break projects, so they must set a good example to lead their team to success. They are aware of the greater needs of their stakeholders and organizations, so they are visionary in guiding their current projects and in suggesting future ones. As mentioned earlier, companies that excel in project management grow project "leaders," emphasizing development of business and communication skills. Yet, good project managers must also focus on getting the job done by paying attention to the details and daily operations of each task. Instead of thinking of leaders and managers as specific people, it is better to think of people as having leadership skills, such as being visionary and inspiring, and management skills, such as being organized and effective. Therefore, the best project managers have leadership and management characteristics; they are visionary yet focused on the bottom line. Above all else, good project managers focus on achieving positive results!

1.5d Careers for IT Project Managers

As shown earlier, the IT industry continues to grow, and the need for people to lead IT projects has remained solid. In fact, every IT worker needs some skills in project management.

Computerworld's 2014 annual forecast survey supports this career projection. Forty-three percent of the 194 respondents said that they expect their IT budgets to increase, and overall IT budgets are expected to increase by 4.3 percent. The top five priorities include spending on:

1. security technologies,
2. cloud computing,
3. business analytics,
4. application development,
5. wireless/mobile.[30]

IT executives listed the "ten hottest skills" they planned to hire for in 2015. Programming and application development remained in first place, mainly due to the increased need for programmers with mobile development expertise and experience building secure applications. Project management skills continue to make the list, as these skills are crucial to prioritizing business needs and implementing effective solutions. Table 1-4 shows the results of the latest survey, as well as the percentage of respondents who listed the skill as being in demand. Even if you choose to stay in a technical role, you still need project management knowledge and skills to help your team and your organization succeed.

TABLE 1-4 Ten hottest IT skills

Skill	Percentage of Respondents
Programming and application development	48
Project management	35
Help desk/technical support	30
Security/compliance governance	28
Web development	28
Database administration	26
Business intelligence/analytics	24
Mobile application and device management	24
Networking	22
Big data	20

Source: Mary K. Pratt, "10 Hottest IT Skills for 2015," *Computerworld*, November 18, 2014.

1.6 THE PROJECT MANAGEMENT PROFESSION

The project management profession is growing at a very rapid pace. To understand this line of work, it is helpful to briefly review the history of project management, learn about the Project Management Institute (PMI) and some of its services (such as certification), and examine the growth in project management software.

1.6a History of Project Management

Most people think that project management is a 20th century invention. But Mark Kozak-Holland, certified PMP and author of books that mine history for insight about project management, says that's wrong. He notes that major historical projects closely resemble today's project management best practices. About his 2011 book *The History of Project Management*, he said, "The general perception of most people is that project management started in the mid-20th century, or started earlier with Henry Gantt and his charts. . . . Yet, how were all the great projects of the past delivered? Think about the Giza Pyramid, the Parthenon, the Coliseum, the Gothic Cathedrals of Medieval Europe, the great voyages of exploration, the Taj Mahal, and the mega projects of the industrial revolutions. Was project management used on these projects? Were the concepts of project management even understood? Can we connect modern and ancient project management?" Kozak-Holland's answer to these questions is "yes." You can see the PMBOK process groups and techniques from the knowledge areas in all of these historical projects. Project management has been around since 2550 B.C.E.[31]

Although people have worked on projects for centuries, most agree that the modern concept of project management began with the Manhattan Project, which the U.S. military led to develop the atomic bomb in World War II. The Manhattan Project involved many people with different skills at several different locations. It also clearly separated the overall management of the project's mission, schedule, and budget under General Leslie R. Groves and the technical management of the project under the lead scientist, Dr. Robert Oppenheimer. The Manhattan Project lasted about three years and cost almost $2 billion in 1946.

In developing the project, the military realized that scientists and other technical specialists often did not have the desire or the necessary skills to manage large projects. For example, after being asked several times for each team member's responsibilities at the new Los Alamos laboratory in 1943, Dr. Oppenheimer tossed the project organization chart at his director and said, "Here's your damn organization chart."[32] Project management was recognized as a distinct discipline requiring people with special skills and, more importantly, the desire to lead project teams.

In 1917, long before the Manhattan project, Henry Gantt developed the famous Gantt chart for scheduling work in factories. A **Gantt chart** is a standard format for displaying project schedule information by listing project activities and their corresponding start and finish dates in calendar form. Initially, managers drew Gantt charts by hand to show project tasks and schedule information. This tool provided a standard format for planning and reviewing all the work on early military projects.

Today's project managers still use the Gantt chart as the primary tool to communicate project schedule information, but with the aid of computers, it is no longer necessary to draw the charts by hand, and they are easier to share and disseminate to project stakeholders. Figure 1-6 displays a Gantt chart created with Project 2013, the most widely used project management software today. You will learn more about using Project 2013 in Appendix A.

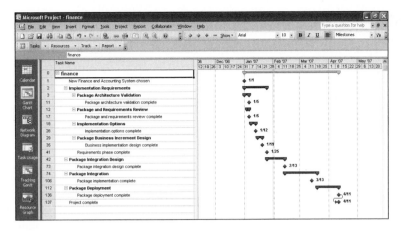

FIGURE 1-6   Sample Gantt chart created with project 2013

During the Cold War years of the 1950s and '60s, the military continued to play an important role in refining several project management techniques. Members of the U.S. Navy Polaris missile/submarine project first used network diagrams in 1958. These diagrams helped managers model the relationships among project tasks, which allowed them to create schedules that were more realistic. Figure 1-7 displays a network diagram created using Project 2013. Note that the diagram includes arrows that show which tasks are related and the sequence in which team members must perform the tasks. The concept of determining relationships among tasks is essential in helping to improve project scheduling. This concept allows you to find and monitor the **critical path**—the longest path through a network diagram that determines the earliest completion of a project. It shows you which tasks affect the target completion date of a project, and it can change as work proceeds and more information becomes available. You will learn more about Gantt charts, network diagrams, critical path analysis, and other time management concepts in Chapter 6, Project Time Management.

By the 1970s, the U.S. military and its civilian suppliers had developed software to assist in managing large projects. Early project management software was very expensive to purchase, and it ran exclusively on mainframe computers. For example, Artemis was an early project management software product that helped managers analyze complex schedules for designing aircraft. A full-time employee was often required to run the complicated software, and expensive pen plotters were used to draw network diagrams and Gantt charts.

As computer hardware became smaller and more affordable and software companies developed graphical, easy-to-use interfaces, project management software became less expensive and more widely used. This made it possible—and affordable—for many industries worldwide to use project management software on all types and sizes of projects. New software makes basic tools such as Gantt charts and network diagrams inexpensive, easy to create, and available for anyone to update. See the section later in this chapter on project management software for more information.

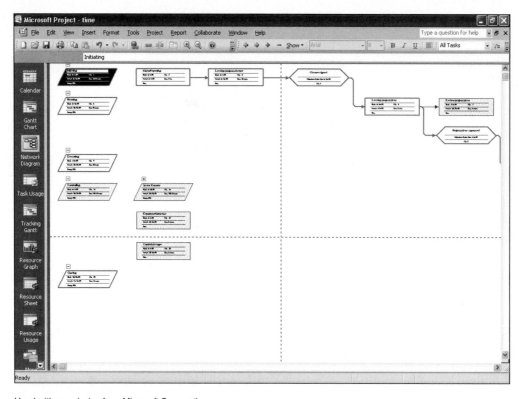

Used with permission from Microsoft Corporation

FIGURE 1-7   Sample network diagram created with project 2013

In the 1990s, many companies began creating Project Management Offices to help them handle the increasing number and complexity of projects. A **Project Management Office (PMO)** is an organizational group responsible for coordinating the project management function throughout an organization. A 2014 study found that 80 percent of U.S. companies reported having PMOs. Figure 1-8 shows the percentage of companies with PMOs based on past surveys.[33] For large organizations, 90 percent reported having PMOs in 2014, while 61 percent of small organizations did. The percentage of large organizations with PMOs was about the same in 2010, but only 48 percent of small organizations had PMOs in 2010. This increase shows the growing importance of using standard project management processes in organizations of all sizes.

There are different ways to structure a PMO, and they can have various roles and responsibilities. Organizations continue to modify their PMOs to ensure they add value to their unique situations. For some organizations with very mature project management processes and experienced managers, a small PMO focusing on organizing all project data might be all that is needed. For an organization new to project management, a larger PMO might be needed focusing on training and standards. PM Solutions identified three key factors that are playing major roles in the growth of PMOs:

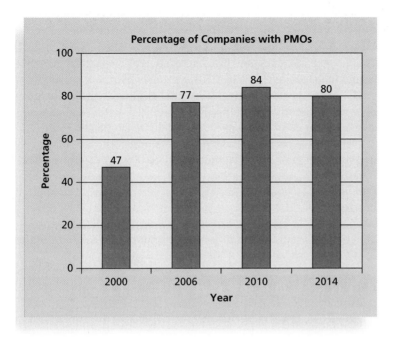

Source: PM Solutions, "The State of the PMO 2010" (2010).

FIGURE 1-8   Growth in the Number of Project Management Offices

1. The growing strategic value of the PMO
2. The increased role of the PMO in training
3. The ever-present challenge of resource management

Below are possible goals of a PMO:

- Collect, organize, and integrate project data for the entire organization.
- Ensure that the organization's approaches for project management include accepted and validated best practices.
- Audit project documentation and offer feedback on project managers' approaches and compliance with standards.
- Develop and maintain templates, tools, and standards for project documents and project methodologies to be used.
- Develop or coordinate training in various project management topics.
- Provide a formal career path for project managers.
- Provide project management consulting services.
- Provide a structure or department that project managers belong to while they are assigned to a project or are between projects.

By the end of the 20th century, people in virtually every industry around the globe began to investigate and apply different aspects of project management to their projects. The sophistication and effectiveness with which project management tools are being applied and used today is enabling companies to do business, use resources, and respond to market requirements with greater speed and accuracy.

Many colleges, universities, and companies around the world now offer courses related to different aspects of project management. You can even earn bachelor's, master's, and doctoral degrees in project management. In late 2014, a *gradschools.com* search for "project management" found 370 campus and online accredited graduate, certificate, and doctoral programs from all types of institutions. PMI reported in 2015 that formal education programs in project management continue to grow, especially in China and India, where many infrastructure projects are needed. "In China, for example, the 104 institutions offering project management programs receive more than 20,000 applications each year." As projects become more global and teams are no longer stationed in the same city or even country, students are learning a common project management language no matter where they seek their education.[34]

The problems organizations have in managing projects, increasing education in project management, and the belief that it can make a difference continue to contribute to the growth of this field.

1.6b The Project Management Institute

Although many professional societies suffer from declining membership, the **Project Management Institute (PMI)**, an international professional society for project managers founded in 1969, has continued to attract and retain members, reporting more than 449,000 members worldwide by late 2014. Because so many people work on projects in different industries across the globe (51 million total according to PMI), PMI has created communities of practice that enable members to share ideas about project management in their particular application areas, such as information systems. PMI also has communities

 GLOBAL ISSUES

Based on a survey of more than 1,000 project management leaders across a variety of experience levels and industries, several global dynamics are forcing organizations to rethink their practices:

- Talent development for project and program managers is a top concern. Seventy percent of organizations have a career path for project and program management, but most are still informal and not documented.
- Basic project management techniques are core competencies. Seventy percent of organizations said that they always or often use basic practices like change management and risk management on their projects.
- Organizations want to use more agile approaches to project management. One-quarter of survey respondents said they now use agile techniques, and agile project management was the most requested article topic.
- Benefits realization of projects is a key metric. Organizations know that they need to align projects and programs with the organization's business strategy.[35]

PMI STUDENT MEMBERSHIP

As a student, you can join PMI for a reduced fee ($32 versus $139 in 2015). Consult PMI's website (*www.pmi.org*) for more information. With student membership, you can network with other project management students by joining a local PMI chapter. Many welcome students to attend free events, including talks and job networking. You can volunteer your services to help develop your skills and serve your community. You can also qualify for the Certified Associate in Project Management (CAPM) certification with just a bachelor's degree and a course in project management.

for aerospace/defense, financial services, government, healthcare, and agile techniques, to name a few. Note that there are other project management professional societies, such as the International Project Management Association (IPMA) and the Association for Project Management (APM).

1.6c Project Management Certification

Professional certification is an important factor in recognizing and ensuring quality in a profession. PMI provides certification as a **Project Management Professional (PMP)** —someone who has documented sufficient project experience and education, agreed to follow the PMI code of professional conduct, and demonstrated knowledge of project management by passing a comprehensive examination. Note that you do not need work experience to qualify for CompTIA's Project+ certification or PMI's CAPM certification, so college graduates just entering the workforce can earn these certifications and become more marketable.

The number of people earning PMP certification continues to increase. In 1993, there were about 1,000 certified project management professionals. At the end of April 2015, there were 658,523 active PMPs.[36] Figure 1-9 shows the rapid growth in the number of people earning project management professional certification from 1993 to 2014.

Several studies show that organizations supporting technical certification programs tend to operate in more complex IT environments and are more efficient than organizations that do not support certification. Likewise, organizations that support PMP certification see the value of investing in programs to improve their employees' knowledge in project management. Many employers today require specific certifications to ensure that their workers have current skills, and job seekers find that they often have an advantage when they earn and maintain marketable certifications. Global Knowledge listed PMP certification as number 5 in their list of top-paying certifications for 2014.[37]

As IT projects become more complex and global in nature, the need for people with demonstrated knowledge and skills in project management will continue. Just as passing the CPA exam is a standard for accountants, passing the PMP exam is becoming a standard for project managers. Some companies require that all project managers be PMP certified. Project management certification is also enabling professionals in the field to share a common base of knowledge. For example, any person with PMP certification can list, describe, and use the 10 project management knowledge areas. Sharing a common base of knowledge is important because it helps advance the theory and practice of project management. PMI also offers additional certifications, including agile techniques, scheduling, risk, and program management.

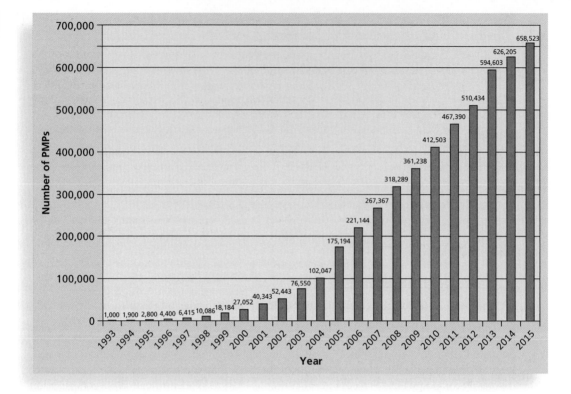

© Cengage Learning 2016

FIGURE 1-9   Growth in PMP Certification, 1993–2014

1.6d Ethics in Project Management

Ethics, loosely defined, is a set of principles that guides decision making based on personal values of what is considered right and wrong. Making ethical decisions is an important part of project managers' personal and professional lives because it generates trust and respect with other people. Project managers often face ethical dilemmas. If project managers can make more money by taking bribes, should they? No! Should project managers accept subpar work to meet a deadline? No! Ethics guide us in making these types of decisions.

PMI approved a Code of Ethics and Professional Conduct that took effect in January 2007. This code applies not only to PMPs but to all PMI members who hold a PMI certification, apply for a PMI certification, or serve PMI in a volunteer capacity.

It is vital for project management practitioners to conduct their work in an ethical manner. Even if you are not affiliated with PMI, these guidelines can help you conduct your work in an ethical manner, which helps the profession earn the confidence of the public, employers, employees, and all project stakeholders. The PMI Code of Ethics and Professional Conduct includes short chapters addressing vision and applicability, responsibility, respect, fairness, and honesty. A few excerpts from this document include the following:

"As practitioners in the global project management community:

2.2.1   We make decisions and take actions based on the best interests of society, public safety, and the environment.

2.2.2   We accept only those assignments that are consistent with our background, experience, skills, and qualifications.

2.2.3   We fulfill the commitments that we undertake—we do what we say we will do.

3.2.1   We inform ourselves about the norms and customs of others and avoid engaging in behaviors they might consider disrespectful.

3.2.2   We listen to others' points of view, seeking to understand them.

3.2.3   We approach directly those persons with whom we have a conflict or disagreement.

4.2.1   We demonstrate transparency in our decision-making process.

4.2.2   We constantly reexamine our impartiality and objectivity, taking corrective action as appropriate.

4.3.1   We proactively and fully disclose any real or potential conflicts of interest to appropriate stakeholders.

5.2.1   We earnestly seek to understand the truth.

5.2.2   We are truthful in our communications and in our conduct."[38]

In addition, PMI added a new series of questions to the PMP certification exam in March 2002 and continues to include this topic to emphasize the importance of ethics and professional responsibility.

1.6e Project Management Software

Unlike the tale of the cobbler who neglected to make shoes for his own children, the project management and software development communities have definitely responded to the need to provide more software to help manage projects. As mentioned earlier, Microsoft Project continues to lead the market with over 880,000 customers and 22 million users. See Appendix A for details on the various configurations available for Microsoft Project and detailed instructions for using Project Professional 2013, the product available for a free trial. TopTenReviews.com has a category for online project management software and listed Clarizen, GeniusProject, and AtTask as the top three products in 2014. There are also several smartphone and tablet apps for project management. There are enough options that deciding which project management software to use has become a project in itself. This section summarizes the basic types of project management software available and provides references for finding more information.

Many people still use basic productivity software such as Microsoft Word and Excel to perform many project management functions, including determining project scope, time, and cost, assigning resources, and preparing project documentation. People often use productivity software instead of specialized project management software because they

MICROSOFT PROJECT 2013

Appendix A includes a *Guide to Using Microsoft Project 2013*, which will help you develop hands-on skills for using this popular project management software.

already have it and know how to use it. However, hundreds of project management software tools provide specific functionality for managing projects and performing portfolio management. These software tools can be divided into three general categories based on functionality and price:

- *Low-end tools*: These tools provide basic project management features and generally cost less than $200 per user. Smartphone and tablet apps are available for much less, but they often have limited functionality. Low-end tools are often recommended for small projects and single users. Most of these tools allow users to create Gantt charts, which cannot be done easily using current productivity software.
- *Midrange tools*: A step up from low-end tools, midrange tools are designed to handle larger projects, multiple users, and multiple projects. All of these tools can produce Gantt charts and network diagrams, and can assist in critical path analysis, resource allocation, project tracking, and status reporting. Prices range from about $200 to $1,000 per user, or less per month for online tools. Several tools require additional server software for using workgroup features.
- *High-end tools*: These tools are sometimes referred to as enterprise project management software. They provide robust capabilities to handle very large projects and dispersed workgroups, and they have enterprise and portfolio management functions that summarize and combine individual project information to provide an enterprise view of all projects. These products are generally licensed on a per-user basis, can be integrated with enterprise database management software, and are accessible via the Internet.

Several free or open-source tools are also available. For example, Basecamp, Trello, and Asana offer free online tools that may work for some projects and offer paid products to meet more complex needs. Most companies, including Microsoft, offer free trials of their project management software. ProjectLibre, LibrePlan, and OpenProject are all free open-source project management tools. Remember, however, that open-source tools are developed, managed, and maintained by volunteers and may not be well supported.

There are many reasons to study project management, particularly as it relates to IT projects. The number of IT projects continues to grow in almost every industry the complexity of these projects continues to increase, and the profession of project management continues to expand and mature. As more people study and work in this important field, the success rate of IT projects should continue to improve.

CASE WRAP-UP

Anne Roberts worked with the VPs and the CEO to form teams to help identify potential IT projects that would support their business strategies. They formed a project team to implement a portfolio project management software tool across the organization. They formed another team to develop project-based reward systems for all employees. They also authorized funds for a project to educate all employees in project management, to help people earn PMP and related certifications, and to develop a mentoring program. Anne had successfully convinced everyone that effectively managing projects was crucial to their company's future.

Chapter Summary

Many people and organizations have a new or renewed interest in project management as the number of projects continues to grow and their complexity continues to increase. The success rate of IT projects has more than doubled since 1995, but still only about one-third are successful in meeting scope, time, and cost goals. Using a more disciplined approach to managing projects can help projects and organizations succeed.

A project is a temporary endeavor undertaken to create a unique product, service, or result. An IT project involves the use of hardware, software, and networks. Projects are unique, temporary, and developed incrementally; they require resources, have a sponsor, and involve uncertainty. The triple constraint of project management refers to managing the scope, time, and cost dimensions of a project. It is important to address these dimensions as well as other constraints (such as quality, resources, and risks) and to satisfy the project sponsor.

Project management is the application of knowledge, skills, tools, and techniques to project activities to meet project requirements. Stakeholders are the people involved in or affected by project activities. A framework for project management includes the project stakeholders, project management knowledge areas, and project management tools and techniques. The 10 knowledge areas are project integration management, scope, time, cost, quality, human resource, communications, risk, procurement, and stakeholder management. There are many tools and techniques in each knowledge area. There are different ways to define project success, and project managers must understand the criteria that define success for their unique projects.

A program is a group of related projects, subprograms, and program activities managed in a coordinated way to obtain benefits and control that are not available from managing the projects individually. Project portfolio management involves organizing and managing projects and programs as a portfolio of investments that contribute to the entire enterprise's success. Portfolio management emphasizes meeting strategic goals, while project management focuses on tactical goals. Studies show that user involvement is crucial to project success, as are other factors like executive support and clear business objectives.

Project managers play a key role in helping projects and organizations succeed. They must perform various job duties, possess many skills, and continue to develop skills in project management, general management, and their application area, such as IT. Soft skills, especially leadership, are particularly important for project managers.

The profession of project management continues to grow and mature. In the United States, the military took the lead in project management and developed many tools such as Gantt charts and network diagrams, but today people use project management in virtually every industry around the globe. The Project Management Institute (PMI) is an international professional society that provides certification as a Project Management Professional (PMP) and upholds a code of ethics. Today, hundreds of project management software products are available to assist people in managing projects.

Quick Quiz

1. The _____ field includes the top skills employers look for in new college graduates.

    a. communications

    b. project management

    c. financial management

    d. customer service

2. Which of the following is not a potential advantage of using good project management?

   a. shorter development times

   b. higher worker morale

   c. lower cost of capital

   d. higher profit margins

3. A _____ is a temporary endeavor undertaken to create a unique product, service, or result.

   a. program

   b. process

   c. project

   d. portfolio

4. Which of the following is not an attribute of a project?

   a. Projects are unique.

   b. Projects are developed using progressive elaboration.

   c. Projects have a primary customer or sponsor.

   d. Projects involve little uncertainty.

5. Which of the following is not part of the triple constraint of project management?

   a. meeting scope goals

   b. meeting time goals

   c. meeting communications goals

   d. meeting cost goals

6. _____ is the application of knowledge, skills, tools, and techniques to project activities to meet project requirements.

   a. Project management

   b. Program management

   c. Project portfolio management

   d. Requirements management

7. Project portfolio management addresses _____ goals of an organization, while project management addresses _____ goals.

   a. strategic, tactical

   b. tactical, strategic

   c. internal, external

   d. external, internal

8. Several application development projects done for the same functional group might best be managed as part of a _____.

   a. portfolio

   b. program

   c. investment

   d. collaborative

9. Which of the following is not true?

    a. Most American companies have a project management office.

    b. You can earn an advanced degree in project management from hundreds of colleges and universities.

    c. Employers are looking for project management skills in new graduates.

    d. Project management certification does not affect pay.

10. What is the name of one of the popular certifications provided by the Project Management Institute?

    a. Certified Project Manager (CPM)

    b. Project Management Professional (PMP)

    c. Project Management Expert (PME)

    d. Project Management Mentor (PMM)

Quick Quiz Answers

1. b; 2. c; 3. c; 4. d; 5. c; 6. a; 7. a; 8. b; 9. d; 10. b

Discussion Questions

1. Why is there a new or renewed interest in the field of project management?

2. What is a project, and what are its main attributes? How is a project different from what most people do in their day-to-day jobs? What is the triple constraint? What other factors affect a project?

3. What is project management? Briefly describe the project management framework, providing examples of stakeholders, knowledge areas, tools and techniques, and project success factors.

4. What is a program? What is a project portfolio? Discuss the relationship between projects, programs, and portfolio management and the contributions that each makes to enterprise success.

5. What is the role of the project manager? What are suggested skills for all project managers and for IT project managers? Why is leadership so important for project managers? How is the job market for IT project managers?

6. Briefly describe some key events in the history of project management. What role do the Project Management Institute and other professional societies play in helping the profession?

7. What functions can you perform with project management software? What are the main differences between low-end, midrange, and high-end project management tools?

8. Discuss ethical decisions that project managers often face. Do you think a professional code of ethics makes it easier to work in an ethical manner?

Exercises

1. Read at least two of the first five references cited in this chapter with statistics about the importance of IT and project management. Write a summary of the reports, key conclusions, and your opinion of them.

2. Find someone who works as a project manager or someone who works on projects involving IT, such as a worker in your school's IT department or a project manager active in a professional group, like PMI. Prepare several interview questions to learn more about projects and project management, and then ask your questions in person, through e-mail, over the phone, or using other technology. Write a summary of your findings.

3. Write a paper summarizing key information available on the Project Management Institute's website (*www.pmi.org*). Also read and summarize two recent reports from PMI, including "Pulse of the Profession®: The High Cost of Low Performance" (2014). Note: Instructors can break this into two exercises by specifying the second report.

4. Find any example of a real project with a real project manager. Feel free to use projects in the media (such as the Olympics, television shows, or movies) or a project from your work, if applicable. Write a paper describing the project in terms of its scope, time, and cost goals. Also describe other impacts on a project, such as quality, resources, and risks. Discuss what went right and wrong on the project and the role of the project manager and sponsor. Also describe whether the project was a success, and why. Include at least one reference and cite it on the last page.

5. Watch a free online video on the history of project management created by Mark Kozak-Holland. Summarize how the project management knowledge areas can be applied to building the Giza Pyramid Project.

6. Research articles and tools on project portfolio management. Summarize the advantages of performing project portfolio management as well as challenges.

7. Skim through Appendix A on Microsoft Project 2013. Review information about Project 2013 from the Microsoft website (*www.microsoft.com*). Research three other project management software tools, including at least one smartphone or tablet app. Write a paper answering the following questions:

   a. What functions does project management software provide that you cannot do easily using other tools such as a spreadsheet or database?

   b. How do the different tools you reviewed compare with Project 2013, based on cost of the tool, key features, and other relevant criteria?

   c. How can organizations justify investing in enterprise or portfolio project management software?

8. Research information about PMP and CAPM certifications. Find at least two articles on this topic. What are benefits of certification in general? Do you think it is worthwhile for most project managers to get certified? Is it something you would consider? Write a paper summarizing your findings and opinions.

9. Review PMI's Code of Ethics and Professional Conduct. Find and summarize two articles related to ethics in project management.

Key Terms

End Notes

1   Gartner, Inc., "Gartner Says Worldwide IT Spending on Pace to Grow 3.2 Percent in 2014" (April 2, 2014).

2   Project Management Institute, "Project Management Talent Gap" (March 2013).

3   Change the Equation, "Vital Signs," *vitalsigns.changetheequation.org/#us-United%20States-Demand (2014).*

4   Project Management Institute, *Project Management Salary Survey*, Eighth Edition (2013).

5   Adams, Susan, "The 10 Skills Employers Most Want in 2015 Graduates," *Forbes* (November 12, 2014).

6   Project Management Institute, "Pulse of the Profession®: The High Cost of Low Performance" (2014).

7   Standish Group, "The CHAOS Report," *www.standishgroup.com* (1995). Another reference is Jim Johnson, "CHAOS: The Dollar Drain of IT Project Failures," *Application Development Trends* (January 1995).

8   PricewaterhouseCoopers, "Boosting Business Performance Through Programme and Project Management" (June 2004).

9   Project Management Institute, *A Guide to the Project Management Body of Knowledge (PMBOK® Guide)*, Fifth Edition (2013).

10   Gartner, Inc. "Gartner Identifies the Top 10 Strategic Technologies for 2015," Gartner Press Release (October 8, 2014).

11   Niall McCarthy, "Mobile App Usage by the Numbers," *Forbes* (October 29, 2014).

12   Steven Tweedie, "The App 100: The World's Greatest Apps," *Business Insider* (October 1, 2014).

13   Project Management Institute, *A Guide to the Project Management Body of Knowledge (PMBOK® Guide)*, Fifth Edition (2013).

14 Claude Besner and Brian Hobbs, "The Perceived Value and Potential Contribution of Project Management Practices to Project Success," *PMI Research Conference Proceedings* (July 2006).

15 Standish Group, "CHAOS Manifesto 2013: Think Big, Act Small" (2013).

16 Ibid.

17 Gautham Nagesh, "GAO Tells Congress Why Federal IT Projects Succeed," *The Hill* (November 22, 2011).

18 Chao Dong, K.B. Chuah, and Li Zhai, "A Study of Critical Success Factors of Information System Projects in China," *Proceedings of PMI Research Conference, London* (2004).

19 Dragan Milosevic and And Ozbay, "Delivering Projects: What the Winners Do," *Proceedings of the Project Management Institute Annual Seminars & Symposium* (November 2001).

20 Project Management Institute, *A Guide to the Project Management Body of Knowledge (PMBOK® Guide)*, Fifth Edition (2013).

21 Eric Burke, "Project Portfolio Management," *PMI Houston Chapter Meeting* (July 10, 2002).

22 Project Management Institute, *Organizational Project Management Maturity Model (OPM3) Knowledge Foundation* (2003).

23 Ibid., p. 13.

24 Ultimate Business Library, *Best Practice: Ideas and Insights from the World's Foremost Business Thinkers* (New York: Perseus, 2003), p. 1.

25 Ibid., p. 8.

26 Capterra, "Top Project Management Software Products" (October 2014).

27 Monster, "Project Management Industry Overview," *jobs.monster.com/v-project-management.aspx* (accessed January 31, 2015).

28 Jennifer Lonoff Schiff, "7 Must-Have Project Management Skills for IT Pros," *CIO.com* (January 15, 2013).

29 Jennifer Krahn, "Effective Project Leadership: A Combination of Project Manager Skills and Competencies in Context," *PMI Research Conference Proceedings* (July 2006).

30 Stacy Collett, "Forecast 2015: IT Spending on an Upswing," *Computerworld*, (November 3, 2014).

31 "The History of Project Management—Author's Perspective," YouTube video, Narration from "An Introduction to the History of Project Management," Posted by Projectlessons, December 19, 2010, *youtube/dYgMT57I7UI*.

32 Regents of the University of California, Manhattan Project History, "Here's Your Damned Organization Chart" (1998–2001).

33 PM Solutions, "The State of the PMO 2014" (2014).

34 Project Management Institute, "Project Management Education Articles," www.pmiteach.org (January 2015).

35 Project Management Institute, *PMI's Pulse of the Profession: Driving Success in Challenging Times* (March 2012).

36 Project Management Institute, *PMI Today* (June 2015).

37 John Hales, "15 Top-Paying Certifications for 2014," Global Knowledge (2014).

38 Project Management Institute, *PMP Credential Handbook* (August 31, 2011), pp. 48–51.

THE PROJECT MANAGEMENT AND INFORMATION TECHNOLOGY CONTEXT

LEARNING OBJECTIVES

After reading this chapter, you will be able to:

- Describe the systems view of project management and how it applies to information technology (IT) projects

- Understand organizations, including the four frames, organizational structures, and organizational culture

- Explain why stakeholder management and top management commitment are critical for a project's success

- Understand the concept of a project phase and the project life cycle, and distinguish between project development and product development

- Discuss the unique attributes and diverse nature of IT projects

- Describe recent trends affecting IT project management, including globalization, outsourcing, virtual teams, and agile project management

OPENING CASE

Tom Walters recently accepted a new position at his college as the Director of Information Technology. Tom had been a respected faculty member at the college for the past 15 years. The college—a small, private institution in the Southwest—offers a variety of programs in the liberal arts and professional areas. Enrollment includes 1,500 full-time traditional students and about 1,000 working adults who attend evening programs. Many instructors supplement their courses with information on the Internet and course websites, but the college does not offer distance-learning programs. The college's niche is serving students in the region who like the setting of a small liberal arts college and want to make connections with each other and their community.

Like other institutions of higher learning, the use of IT at the college has grown tremendously in the past 10 years. Wi-Fi is available everywhere on campus. But only a few classrooms on campus have computers for the instructors and students, and most other classrooms have only instructor stations and projection systems. Tom knew that several colleges throughout the country require that all students lease or own laptops or tablets and that these colleges incorporate technology into most courses. This idea fascinated him. He and two other members of the IT department visited a local college that had required all students to lease laptops for the past three years, and they were very impressed with what they saw and heard. Because tablets were becoming more popular, they thought it would make more sense to require tablets instead of laptops. Tom had heard how easy it was for faculty members to create interactive course materials that would run on tablets; these materials also could help reduce the cost of textbooks, a concern expressed by many students. Tom and his staff developed plans to start requiring students either to lease or purchase tablets at their college starting the next academic year.

Tom sent an e-mail to all faculty and staff in September, and briefly described his plans. He did not get much response, however, until the February faculty meeting. As he described some of the details of his plan, the chairs of the History, English, Philosophy, and Economics departments all voiced opposition to the idea. They eloquently stated that the college was not a technical training school and that they did not have time to write their own course materials to run on tablets. They liked the books they used, and students could already buy books in an electronic format, but most preferred the print versions. Members of the Computer Science department voiced their concern that almost all of their students already had state-of-the art laptops and would not want to pay a mandatory fee to lease less-powerful tablets. The director of the adult education program expressed her concern that many adult-education students would balk at an increase in fees or required technology. Tom was in shock to hear his colleagues' responses, especially after he and his staff had spent a lot of time planning how to implement tablets at their campus. Now what should he do?

Many of the theories and concepts of project management are not difficult to understand. What *is* difficult is implementing them in various environments. Project managers must consider many different issues when managing projects. Just as each project is unique, so is its environment. This chapter discusses some of the concepts involved in understanding the project environment, such as using a systems approach, understanding organizations, managing stakeholders, matching product life cycles to the project environment, understanding the context of IT projects, and reviewing recent trends that affect IT project management.

2.1 A SYSTEMS VIEW OF PROJECT MANAGEMENT

Even though projects are temporary and intended to provide a unique product or service, you cannot run projects in isolation. If project managers lead projects in isolation, it is unlikely that they will ever truly serve the needs of the organization. Therefore, projects must operate in a broad organizational environment, and project managers need to consider projects within the greater organizational context. To handle complex situations effectively, project managers need to take a holistic view of a project and understand how it relates to the larger organization. **Systems thinking** describes this holistic view of carrying out projects within the context of the organization.

2.1a What Is a Systems Approach?

The term **systems approach** emerged in the 1950s to describe a holistic and analytical approach to solving complex problems that includes using a systems philosophy, systems analysis, and systems management. Systems are sets of interacting components that work within an environment to fulfill some purpose. For example, the human body is a system composed of many subsystems, including the nervous system, the skeletal system, the circulatory system, and the digestive system. Organizations are also systems, with people in various roles working together to design, develop, deliver, and sell various products and services. A **systems philosophy** is an overall model for thinking about things as systems.

Systems analysis is a problem-solving approach that requires defining the scope of the system, dividing it into components, and then identifying and evaluating its problems, opportunities, constraints, and needs. Once this is completed, the systems analyst then examines alternative solutions for improving the current situation; identifies an optimum, or at least satisfactory, solution or action plan; and examines that plan against the entire system. **Systems management** addresses the business, technological, and organizational issues associated with creating, maintaining, and modifying a system.

Using a systems approach is critical to successful project management. If top management and project managers are to understand how projects relate to the whole organization, they must follow a systems philosophy. They must use systems analysis to address needs with a problem-solving approach. They must use systems management to identify key issues in business, technological, and organizational spheres related to each project in order to identify and satisfy key stakeholders and do what is best for the entire organization.

In the chapter's opening case, Tom Walters planned the tablet project without using a systems approach. Members of his IT department did all of the planning. Even though Tom sent an e-mail describing the tablet project to all faculty and staff, he did not address many of the organizational issues involved in such a complex project. Most faculty and staff are very busy at the beginning of the fall term, and many may not have read the entire message. Others may have been too busy to communicate their concerns to the IT department. Tom was unaware of the effects the tablet project would have on other parts of the college. He did not clearly define the business, technological, and organizational issues associated with the project. Tom and the IT department began work on the tablet project in isolation. If they had taken a systems approach, considering other dimensions of the project and involving key stakeholders, they could have identified and addressed many of the issues raised at the February faculty meeting *before* the meeting.

2.1b The Three-Sphere Model for Systems Management

Many business and IT students understand the concepts of systems and performing a systems analysis. At the same time, they often overlook systems management. However, addressing the three spheres of systems management—business, organization, and technology—can have a huge impact on selecting and managing projects successfully.

Figure 2-1 provides a sample of business, organizational, and technological issues that could be factors in the tablet project. In this case, technological issues, though not simple by any means, are probably the least difficult to identify and resolve. However, projects must address issues in all three spheres of the systems management model. Although it is easier to focus on the immediate and sometimes narrow concerns of a particular project, project managers and other staff must recognize the effects of any project on the interests and needs of the entire system or organization. The college president and senior administrators, in particular, will focus on whether the tablet project adds value to the college as a whole.

Many IT professionals become captivated with the technology and day-to-day problem solving involved in working with information systems. They tend to become frustrated with many of the "people problems" or politics involved in most organizations. In addition, many IT professionals ignore important business questions, such as "Does it make financial sense to pursue this new technology?" or "Should the company develop this software in-house or purchase it off the shelf?" Using a more holistic approach helps project

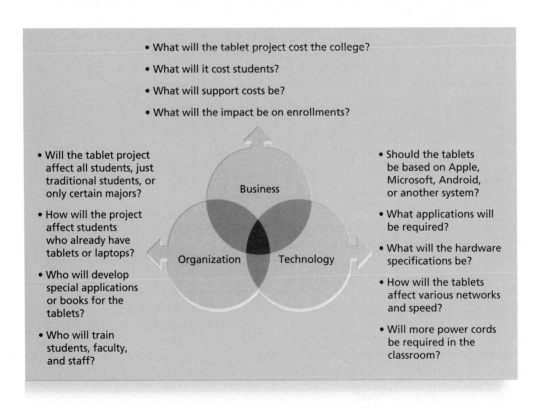

© Cengage Learning 2016

FIGURE 2-1   Three-sphere model for systems management

managers integrate business and organizational issues into their planning. It also helps them look at projects as a series of interrelated phases. When you integrate business and organizational issues into project management planning and look at projects as a series of interrelated phases, you do a better job of ensuring project success.

2.2 UNDERSTANDING ORGANIZATIONS

The systems approach requires that project managers always view their projects in the context of the larger organization. Organizational issues are often the most difficult part of working on and managing projects. In fact, many people believe that most projects fail because of organizational issues like company politics. Project managers often do not spend enough time identifying all the stakeholders involved in projects, especially the people opposed to the projects. Also, project managers often do not spend enough time considering the political context of a project or the culture of the organization. To improve the success rate of IT projects, it is important for project managers to develop a better understanding of people as well as organizations.

2.2a The Four Frames of Organizations

As shown in Figure 2-2, you can try to understand organizations better by focusing on different perspectives. Organizations can be viewed as having four different frames: structural, human resources, political, and symbolic.[1]

- The **structural frame** deals with how the organization is structured (usually depicted in an organizational chart) and focuses on different groups' roles and responsibilities to meet the goals and policies set by top management. This frame is very rational and focuses on coordination and control. For example, within the structural frame, a key IT issue is whether a company should centralize the IT personnel in one department or decentralize across several departments. You will learn more about organizational structures in the next section.
- The **human resources (HR) frame** focuses on producing harmony between the needs of the organization and the needs of people. It recognizes that mismatches can occur between the needs of the organization and those of individuals and groups, and works to resolve any potential problems. For example, many projects might be more efficient for the organization if employees worked 80 or more hours a week for several months. However, this work schedule would conflict with the personal lives and health of many

Structural frame: Roles and responsibilities, coordination, and control. Organizational charts help describe this frame.	**Human resources frame:** Providing harmony between needs of the organization and needs of people.
Political frame: Coalitions composed of varied individuals and interest groups. Conflict and power are key issues.	**Symbolic frame:** Symbols and meanings related to events. Culture, language, traditions, and image are all parts of this frame.

Source: Bolman and Deal

FIGURE 2-2   Perspectives on organizations[2]

employees. Important IT issues related to the human resources frame are the shortage of skilled IT workers within the organization and unrealistic schedules imposed on many projects.

- The **political frame** addresses organizational and personal politics. **Politics** in organizations take the form of competition among groups or individuals for power, resources, and leadership. The political frame emphasizes that organizations are coalitions composed of varied individuals and interest groups. Often, important decisions need to be made about the allocation of scarce resources. Competition for resources makes conflict a central issue in organizations, and power improves the ability to obtain those resources. Project managers must pay attention to politics and power if they are to be effective. It is important to know who opposes your projects as well as who supports them. Important IT issues related to the political frame are the differences in power between central functions and operating units or between functional managers and project managers.

- The **symbolic frame** focuses on symbols and meanings. In this frame, the most important aspect of any event in an organization is not what actually happened, but what it means. Was it a good sign that the CEO came to a kick-off meeting for a project, or was it a threat? The symbolic frame also relates to the company's culture. How do people dress? How many hours do they work? How do they run meetings? Many IT projects are international and include stakeholders from various cultures. Understanding those cultures is also a crucial part of the symbolic frame.

Project managers must learn to work within all four frames to function well in organizations. Organizational issues are discussed further in Chapter 9, Project Human Resource Management, Chapter 10, Project Communications Management, and Chapter 13, Project Stakeholder Management. The following sections on organizational structures, organizational culture, stakeholder management, and the need for top management commitment provide additional information related to the structural and political frames.

 WHAT WENT WRONG?

In a paper titled "A Study in Project Failure," two researchers examined the success and failure of 214 IT projects over an eight-year period in several European countries. The researchers found that only one in eight (12.5 percent) were considered successful in terms of meeting scope, time, and cost goals. The authors made the following conclusions about factors that contribute to a project's failure:

"Our evidence suggests that the *culture* within many organisations is often such that leadership, stakeholder and risk management issues are not factored into projects early on and in many instances cannot formally be written down for *political* reasons and are rarely discussed openly at project board or steering group meetings although they may be discussed at length behind closed doors. … Despite attempts to make software development and project delivery more rigorous, a considerable proportion of delivery effort results in systems that do not meet user expectations and are subsequently cancelled. In our view this is attributed to the fact that very few organisations have the infrastructure, education, training, or management discipline to bring projects to successful completion."[3]

2.2b Organizational Structures

Many discussions of organizations focus on their structure. Three general classifications of organizational structures are functional, project, and matrix. Many companies today use all three structures somewhere in the organization, but using one is most common. Figure 2-3 portrays the three organizational structures. A **functional organizational structure** is the hierarchy most people think of when picturing an organizational chart. Functional managers or vice presidents in specialties such as engineering, manufacturing, IT, and human resources report to the chief executive officer (CEO). Their staffs have specialized skills in their respective disciplines. For example, most colleges and universities have very strong functional organizations. Only faculty members in the business department teach business courses; faculty in the history department teach history; faculty in the art department teach art, and so on.

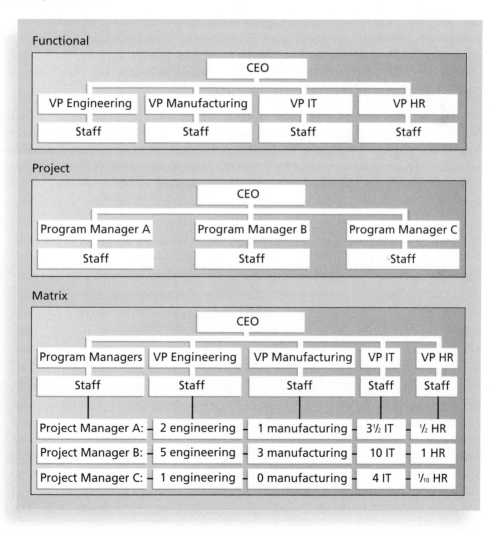

© Cengage Learning 2016

FIGURE 2-3 Functional, project, and matrix organizational structures

A **project organizational structure** also is hierarchical, but instead of functional managers or vice presidents reporting to the CEO, program managers report to the CEO. Their staffs have a variety of skills needed to complete the projects within their programs. An organization that uses this structure earns its revenue primarily from performing projects for other groups under contract. For example, many defense, architectural, engineering, and consulting companies use a project organizational structure. These companies often hire people specifically to work on particular projects.

A **matrix organizational structure** represents the middle ground between functional and project structures. Personnel often report both to a functional manager and one or more project managers. For example, IT personnel at many companies often split their time between two or more projects, but they report to their manager in the IT department. Project managers in matrix organizations have staff from various functional areas working on their projects, as shown in Figure 2-3. Matrix organizational structures can be strong, weak, or balanced, based on the amount of control exerted by the project managers. Problems can occur if project team members are assigned to several projects in a matrix structure and the project manager does not have adequate control of their time.

Table 2-1 summarizes how organizational structures influence projects and project managers, based on information from several versions of the *PMBOK® Guide*. Project managers have the most authority in a pure project organizational structure and the least amount of authority in a pure functional organizational structure. It is important that project managers understand their current organizational structure. For example, if someone in a functional organization is asked to lead a project that requires strong support from several different functional areas, he or she should ask for top management sponsorship. This sponsor should solicit support from all relevant functional managers to ensure that they cooperate on the project and that qualified people are available to work as needed. The project manager might also ask for a separate budget to pay for project-related trips, meetings, and training or to provide financial incentives to the people supporting the project.

TABLE 2-1 Organizational structure and its influences on projects

Project Characteristics	Organizational Structure Type				
	Functional	Matrix			Project
		Weak Matrix	Balanced Matrix	Strong Matrix	
Project manager's authority	Little or none	Limited	Low to moderate	Moderate to high	High to almost total
Percent of organization's personnel assigned full-time to project work	Virtually none	0–25%	15–60%	50–95%	85–100%
Who controls the project budget	Functional manager	Functional manager	Mixed	Project manager	Project manager
Project manager's role	Part-time	Part-time	Full-time	Full-time	Full-time
Common title for project manager's role	Project coordinator/ project leader	Project coordinator/ project leader	Project manager/ project officer	Project manager/ program manager	Project manager/ program manager
Project management administrative staff	Part-time	Part-time	Part-time	Full-time	Full-time

© Cengage Learning 2016

Even though project managers have the most authority in the project organizational structure, this type of organization is often inefficient for the company as a whole. Assigning staff full-time to the project often creates underutilization and misallocation of staff resources. For example, if a technical writer is assigned full-time to a project, but has no project work on a particular day, the organization is wasting money by paying that person a full-time wage. Project organizations may also miss economies of scale that are available through pooling requests for materials with other projects.

Disadvantages such as these illustrate the benefit of using a systems approach to managing projects. For example, the project manager might suggest hiring an independent contractor to do the technical writing work instead of using a full-time employee. This approach would save the organization money while still meeting the needs of the project. When project managers use a systems approach, they are better able to make decisions that address the needs of the entire organization.

2.2c Organizational Culture

Just as an organization's structure affects its ability to manage projects, so does its culture. **Organizational culture** is a set of shared assumptions, values, and behaviors that characterize the functioning of an organization. It often includes elements of all four frames described previously. Organizational culture is very powerful, and many people believe the underlying causes of many companies' problems are not in the organizational structure or staff; they are in the culture. It is also important to note that the same organization can have different subcultures. The IT department may have a different organizational culture than the finance department, for example. Some organizational cultures make it easier to manage projects.

According to Stephen P. Robbins and Timothy Judge, authors of a popular textbook on organizational behavior, there are 10 characteristics of organizational culture:

1. *Member identity*: The degree to which employees identify with the organization as a whole rather than with their type of job or profession. For example, project managers or team members might feel more dedicated to their company or project team than to their job or profession, or they might not have any loyalty to a particular company or team. As you can guess, an organizational culture in which employees identify more with the whole organization are more conducive to a good project culture.
2. *Group emphasis*: The degree to which work activities are organized around groups or teams, rather than individuals. An organizational culture that emphasizes group work is best for managing projects.
3. *People focus*: The degree to which management's decisions take into account the effect of outcomes on people within the organization. A project manager might assign tasks to certain people without considering their individual needs, or the project manager might know each person very well and focus on individual needs when assigning work or making other decisions. Good project managers often balance the needs of individuals and the organization.
4. *Unit integration*: The degree to which units or departments within an organization are encouraged to coordinate with each other. Most project managers strive for strong unit integration to deliver a successful product, service, or result. An organizational culture with strong unit integration makes the project manager's job easier.

5. *Control*: The degree to which rules, policies, and direct supervision are used to oversee and control employee behavior. Experienced project managers know it is often best to balance the degree of control to get good project results.

6. *Risk tolerance*: The degree to which employees are encouraged to be aggressive, innovative, and risk seeking. An organizational culture with a higher risk tolerance is often best for project management because projects often involve new technologies, ideas, and processes.

7. *Reward criteria*: The degree to which rewards, such as promotions and salary increases, are allocated according to employee performance rather than seniority, favoritism, or other nonperformance factors. Project managers and their teams often perform best when rewards are based mostly on performance.

8. *Conflict tolerance*: The degree to which employees are encouraged to air conflicts and criticism openly. It is very important for all project stakeholders to have good communications, so it is best to work in an organization where people feel comfortable discussing differences openly.

9. *Means-ends orientation*: The degree to which management focuses on outcomes rather than on techniques and processes used to achieve results. An organization with a balanced approach in this area is often best for project work.

10. *Open-systems focus*: The degree to which the organization monitors and responds to changes in the external environment. As you learned earlier in this chapter, projects are part of a larger organizational environment, so it is best to have a strong open-systems focus.[4]

As you can see, there is a definite relationship between organizational culture and successful project management. Project work is most successful in an organizational culture where employees identify more with the organization, where work activities emphasize groups, and where there is strong unit integration, high risk tolerance, performance-based rewards, high conflict tolerance, an open-systems focus, and a balanced focus on people, control, and means orientation.

2.3 FOCUSING ON STAKEHOLDER NEEDS

Recall from Chapter 1 that project stakeholders are the people involved in or affected by project activities. Stakeholders can be internal or external to the organization, directly involved in the project, or simply affected by the project. Internal project stakeholders include the project sponsor, project team, support staff, and internal customers of the project. Other internal stakeholders include top management, other functional managers, and other project managers. Projects affect these additional internal stakeholders because they use the organization's limited resources. Thus, while additional internal stakeholders may not be directly involved in the project, they are still stakeholders because the project affects them in some way. External project stakeholders include the project's customers (if they are external to the organization), competitors, suppliers, and other external groups potentially involved in the project or affected by it, such as government officials or concerned citizens.

Because the purpose of project management is to meet project requirements and satisfy stakeholders, it is critical that project managers take adequate time to identify, understand, and manage relationships with all project stakeholders. Using the four frames of organizations to think about project stakeholders can help you meet their expectations. See Chapter 13, Project Stakeholder Management, for more information.

Consider again the tablet project from the opening case. Tom Walters seemed to focus on just a few internal project stakeholders. He viewed only part of the structural frame of the college. Because his department would do most of the work in administering the tablet project, he concentrated on those stakeholders. He did not even involve the main customers for this project—the students at the college. Even though Tom sent an e-mail to faculty and staff, he did not hold meetings with senior administrators or faculty at the college. Tom's view of the project stakeholders was very limited.

During the faculty meeting, it became evident that the tablet project had many stakeholders in addition to the IT department and students. If Tom had expanded his view of the structural frame of his organization by reviewing an organizational chart for the entire college, he could have identified other key stakeholders. He would have been able to see that the project would affect academic department heads and members of different administrative areas, especially if he wanted faculty members to develop customized course materials themselves. If Tom had focused on the human resources frame, he would have been able to tap into his knowledge of the school and identify people who would most support or oppose requiring tablets. By using the political frame, Tom could have considered the main interest groups that would be most affected by the project's outcome. Had he used the symbolic frame, Tom could have tried to address what moving to a tablet environment would really mean for the college. He then could have anticipated some of the opposition from people who were not in favor of increasing the use of technology on campus. He also could have solicited a strong endorsement from the college president or dean before talking at the faculty meeting.

Tom Walters, like many new project managers, learned the hard way that technical and analytical skills were not enough to guarantee success in project management. To be more effective, he had to identify and address the needs of different stakeholders and understand how his project related to the entire organization.

MEDIA SNAPSHOT

The media have often reported on mismanaged IT projects. One that really stands out was the high profile website created for U.S. citizens to sign up for healthcare under the Obama administration. When the new site opened on October 1, 2013, only about 3 in 10 people could successfully log in and even after they logged in, many were kicked off due to numerous bugs. An article in *Forbes* put its finger on the source of the problems: "HealthCare.gov Diagnosis: The Government Broke Every Rule of Project Management."

The Centers for Medicare & Medicaid Services (CMS) was in charge of overseeing the project, which suffered from several classic mistakes: unrealistic requirements, technical complexity, poor integration, fragmented authority, loose metrics, an aggressive schedule, and not reporting problems to senior management. The author of the *Forbes* article suggests that CMS should have let more competent people run the project from the start.[5]

What happened soon after the disastrous launch? President Obama asked White House chief of staff Denis McDonough to determine if the site could be fixed or if it should be totally scrapped. McDonough asked Jeff Zients, a highly regarded businessman slated to be director of the National Economic Council, and Todd Park, the White

continued

House chief technology officer, to work full-time to fix HealthCare.gov. They assembled a team of elite technologists from several firms, dubbed the "Obama Trauma Team," including Gabriel Burt, CTO of Civis Analytics; Mikey Dickerson, site-reliability engineer at Google; Paul Smith, deputy director of the Democratic National Committee's tech operation; Marty Abbott, former CTO of eBay; Jini Kim, former Google employee turned CEO of her own healthcare data-analytics service; and key engineers from QSSI and CGI (the companies that developed the site). The team realized there was no dashboard to measure what was really going on with the site, and in only five hours they coded one.

Burt soon recruited Mike Abbot, a partner at Kleiner Perkins Caufield & Byers venture capital firm, to lead the team of technologists. Abbot had successfully led projects at Twitter, Microsoft, and Palm, and people loved his low-key, results-driven leadership style. Abbot successfully led the new team in fixing the site. They quickly implemented solutions, like caching key data to speed up the site, and in about two months, the website was remarkably stable and much faster than before. "In about a tenth of the time that a crew of usual-suspect, Washington contractors had spent over $300 million building a site that didn't work, this ad hoc team rescued it and, arguably, Obama's chance at a health-reform legacy."[6]

2.3a The Importance of Top Management Commitment

A very important factor in helping project managers successfully lead projects is the level of commitment and support they receive from top management. Without this commitment, many projects will fail. Some projects have a senior manager called a **champion** who acts as a key advocate for a project. The sponsor can serve as the champion, but often another manager can more successfully take on this role. As described earlier, projects are part of the larger organizational environment, and many factors that might affect a project are out of the project manager's control. Several studies cite executive support as one of the key factors associated with virtually all project success.

Top management commitment is crucial to project managers for the following reasons:

- Project managers need adequate resources. The best way to kill a project is to withhold the required money, human resources, and visibility. If project managers have top management commitment, they will also have adequate resources and not be distracted by events that do not affect their specific projects.
- Project managers often require approval for unique project needs in a timely manner. For example, on large IT projects, top management must understand that unexpected problems may result from the nature of the products being developed and the specific skills of people on the project team. The team might need additional hardware and software halfway through the project for proper testing, or the project manager might need to offer special pay and benefits to attract and retain key project personnel. With top management commitment, project managers can meet these needs.
- Project managers must have cooperation from people in other parts of the organization. Because most IT projects cut across functional areas, top management must help project managers deal with the political issues that often

arise. If certain functional managers are not responding to project managers' requests for necessary information, top management must step in to encourage the functional managers to cooperate.

- Project managers often need someone to mentor and coach them on leadership issues. Many IT project managers come from technical positions and are inexperienced as managers. Senior managers should take the time to give advice on how to be good leaders. They should encourage new project managers to take classes to develop leadership skills and allocate the time and funds for managers to do so.

IT project managers work best in an environment in which top management values IT. Working in an organization that values good project management and sets standards for its use also helps project managers succeed.

2.3b The Need for Organizational Commitment to Information Technology

Another factor that affects the success of IT projects is the organization's commitment to IT in general. It is very difficult for an IT project to be successful if the organization itself does not value IT. Many companies have realized that IT is integral to their business and have created a vice president or equivalent position for the head of IT, often called

 BEST PRACTICE

A major element of good practice concerns **IT governance**, which addresses the authority for and control of key IT activities in organizations, including IT infrastructure, IT use, and project management. (The term *project governance* can also be used to describe a uniform method of controlling all types of projects.) The IT Governance Institute (ITGI) was established in 1998 to advance international thinking and standards in directing and controlling an organization's use of technology. Effective IT governance helps ensure that IT supports business goals, maximizes investment in IT, and addresses IT-related risks and opportunities. A 2004 book by Peter Weill and Jeanne Ross titled *IT Governance: How Top Performers Manage IT Decision Rights for Superior Results*[7] includes research indicating that firms with superior IT governance systems have 20 percent higher profits than firms with poor governance.

A lack of IT governance can be dangerous, as evidenced by three well-publicized IT project failures in Australia: Sydney Water's customer relationship management system, the Royal Melbourne Institute of Technology's academic management system, and One. Tel's billing system. Researchers explained how these projects were catastrophic for their organizations, primarily due to a severe lack of IT governance, which the researchers dubbed *managerial IT unconsciousness* in a subsequent article:

"All three projects suffered from poor IT governance. Senior management in all three organizations had not ensured that prudent checks and balances were in place to enable them to monitor either the progress of the projects or the alignment and impact of the new systems on their business. Proper governance, particularly with respect to financial matters, auditing, and contract management, was not evident. Also, project-level planning and control were notably absent or inadequate—with the result that project status reports to management were unrealistic, inaccurate, and misleading."[8]

the Chief Information Officer (CIO). Some companies assign people from non-IT areas to work full-time on large projects and increase involvement from end users of the systems. Some CEOs even take a strong leadership role in promoting the use of IT in their organizations and empower employees to use IT effectively.

The leadership style of the CIO plays a crucial role in gaining organizational commitment to IT as well as motivation and support for IT workers. A 2014 survey found that 76 percent of CIOs in companies in Europe, the Middle East, and Africa (EMEA) need to adapt their leadership style to fully embrace digital business. "Command-and-control leadership doesn't suit this digital world," said Dave Aron, vice president and Gartner Fellow. "In fact, it can be an obstacle. Vision and inspiration are typically the most powerful attributes of digital leaders. CIOs must accept to flip from 'control first' to vision first. In EMEA, 65 percent of CIOs said that they need to decrease their time on commanding IT, while 45 percent of them said they need to increase their visionary leadership."[9]

Empowering employees at all levels to effectively use IT is also crucial. For example, Hilton Worldwide won a prestigious Customer Relationship Management (CRM) award by enabling its employees to create their own solution for improving customer service and loyalty. In addition to using the company's Satisfaction and Loyalty Tracking (SALT) customer analytics software to deliver key information in a timely manner, team members created a more personal process to focus on using data to improve the guest experience called HEART: Hear the Guest; Empathize with the Guest; Apologize to the Guest; Resolve the Issue; and Thank the Guest. By following this process along with timely data, Hilton Worldwide dramatically increased their customer loyalty score, which leads to higher profits.[10]

2.3c The Need for Organizational Standards

Another problem in most organizations is a lack of standards or guidelines to follow when performing project management. These standards or guidelines might be as simple as providing standard forms or templates for common project documents, examples of good project management plans, or guidelines for how project managers should provide status information to top management. The content of a project management plan and instructions for providing status information might seem like common sense to senior managers, but many new IT project managers have never created plans or created a nontechnical status report. Top management must support the development of these standards and guidelines, and encourage or even enforce their use. For example, an organization might require all potential project information to be reported in a standard format to make project portfolio management decisions. If a project manager does not submit a potential project in the proper format, it could be rejected.

As you saw in Chapter 1, some organizations invest heavily in project management by creating a project management office or center of excellence, which assists project managers in achieving project goals and maintaining project governance. Rachel Hollstadt, founder and retired CEO of a project management consulting firm, suggests that organizations consider adding a new position, a Chief Project Officer (CPO). Some organizations develop career paths for project managers; some require that all project managers have Project Management Professional (PMP) certification and that all employees have some type of project management training. The implementation of such standards demonstrates an organization's commitment to project management.

2.4 PROJECT PHASES AND THE PROJECT LIFE CYCLE

Because projects operate as part of a system and involve uncertainty, it is good practice to divide projects into several phases. General phases in traditional project management are often called the concept, development, implementation, and close-out phases. The *PMBOK® Guide, Fifth Edition* calls these phases starting the project, organizing and preparing, carrying out the project work, and finishing the project. (These phases should not be confused with the project management process groups of initiating, planning, executing, monitoring and controlling, and closing, which are described in Chapter 3.) Project phases vary by project or industry.

A **project life cycle** is a collection of phases. Phases break projects down into smaller, more manageable pieces, which will reduce uncertainty. Some organizations specify a set of life cycles for use in all of their projects, while others follow common industry practices based on the types of projects involved. Project life cycles define what work will be performed in each phase, what deliverables will be produced and when, who is involved in each phase, and how management will control and approve work produced in each phase. A **deliverable** is a product or service, such as a technical report, a training session, a piece of hardware, or a segment of software code, produced or provided as part of a project. (See Chapter 5, Project Scope Management, for detailed information on deliverables.)

In early phases of a project life cycle, resource needs are usually lowest and the level of uncertainty is highest. Project stakeholders have the greatest opportunity to influence the final characteristics of the project's products, services, or results during the early phases of a project life cycle. It is much more expensive to make major changes to a project during later phases. During the middle phases of a project life cycle, the certainty of completing the project improves as it continues and as more information is known about the project requirements and objectives. Also, more resources are usually needed than during the initial or final phase. The final phase of a project focuses on ensuring that project requirements were met and that the project sponsor approves completion of the project.

The first two traditional project phases (concept and development) focus on planning, and are often referred to as **project feasibility**. The last two phases (implementation and close-out) focus on delivering the actual work, and are often referred to as **project acquisition**. Each phase of a project should be successfully completed before the team moves on to the next phase. This project life cycle approach provides better management control and appropriate links to the ongoing operations of the organization.

Figure 2-4 provides a summary of the general phases of the traditional project life cycle. In the concept phase, managers usually develop a business case, which describes the need for the project and basic underlying concepts. A preliminary or rough cost estimate is developed in this first phase, and an overview of the required work is created.

One tool for creating an overview of the required work is a work breakdown structure (WBS). A WBS outlines project work by decomposing the work activities into different levels of tasks. The WBS is a deliverable-oriented document that defines the total scope of the project. In the concept phase, a WBS usually has only two levels. (You will learn more about the WBS in Chapter 5, Project Scope Management.)

In the opening case, Tom Walters could have followed the project life cycle instead of moving full steam ahead with the tablet project. He could have initiated a concept phase and created a committee of faculty and staff to study the concept of increasing the use of technology on campus. This committee might have developed a business case and plan that included an initial, smaller project to investigate alternative ways of increasing the

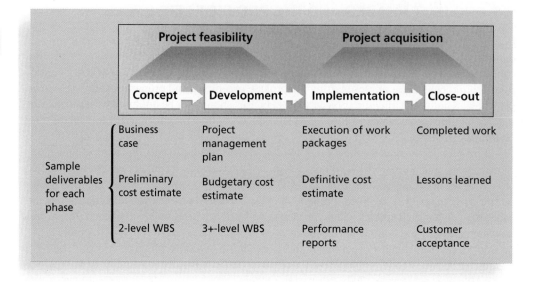

© Cengage Learning 2016

FIGURE 2-4   Phases of the traditional project life cycle

use of technology. The committee might have estimated that it would take six months and $20,000 to conduct a detailed technology study. The WBS at this phase of the study might have three levels and partition the work to include a competitive analysis of what five similar campuses were doing; a survey of local students, staff, and faculty; and a rough assessment of how using more technology would affect costs and enrollments. At the end of the concept phase, the committee would be able to deliver a report and presentation on its findings. The report and presentation would be examples of deliverables.

After the concept phase is completed, the next project phase—development—begins. In the development phase, the project team creates more detailed project management plans, a more accurate cost estimate, and a more thorough WBS. In the example under discussion, suppose the concept phase report suggested that requiring students to have tablets was one means of increasing the use of technology on campus. The project team could then further expand this idea in the development phase. The team would have to decide if students would purchase or lease the tablets, what type of hardware and software the tablets would require, how much to charge students, how to handle training and maintenance, and how to integrate the use of the new technology with current courses. However, if the concept phase report showed that tablets were not a good idea for the college, then the project team would no longer consider increasing the use of technology by requiring tablets and would cancel the project before development. This phased approach minimizes the time and money spent developing inappropriate projects. A project idea must pass the concept phase before evolving into the development phase.

The third phase of the traditional project life cycle is implementation. In this phase, the project team creates a definitive or very accurate cost estimate, delivers the required work, and provides performance reports to stakeholders. Suppose Tom Walters' college took the idea of requiring students to have tablets through the development phase. During the implementation phase, the project team would need to obtain the required hardware and software, install the necessary network equipment, deliver the tablets to the students, create a process for collecting fees, and provide training to students, faculty, and staff. Other people on campus would also be involved in the implementation phase. Faculty would need to consider how best to take advantage of the new technology. The recruiting staff would have to update their materials to reflect this new feature of the college. Security would need to address new problems that might result from students carrying around expensive equipment. The project team usually spends the bulk of its efforts and money during the implementation phase of projects.

The last phase of the traditional project life cycle is the close-out phase. In it, all of the work is completed, and customers should accept the entire project. The project team should document its experiences on the project in a lessons-learned report. If the tablet idea made it all the way through the implementation phase and all students received tablets, the project team would then complete the project by closing out any related activities. Team members might administer a survey to students, faculty, and staff to gather opinions on how the project fared. They would ensure that any contracts with suppliers were completed and that appropriate payments were made. They would transition future work related to the tablet project to other parts of the organization. The project team could also share its lessons-learned report with other colleges that are considering a similar program.

Many projects, however, do not follow this traditional project life cycle. They still have general phases with some similar characteristics, but they are much more flexible. For example, a project might have just three phases—the initial, intermediate, and final phases. Or, there may be multiple intermediate phases. A separate project might be needed just to complete a feasibility study. Regardless of the project life cycle's specific phases, it is good practice to think of projects as having phases that connect the beginning and end of the process. This way, people can measure progress toward achieving project goals during each phase and the project is more likely to be successful.

2.4a Product Life Cycles

Creating a product like a new automobile or a new operating system is a complicated endeavor. For example, developing just the engine for a new electric or hybrid car is a full-fledged project. Companies often use a program—a coordinated group of projects—to develop products and bring them to market. And just like a project has a life cycle, so does a product.

All products—cars, buildings, even amusement parks—follow some type of life cycle. The Walt Disney Company, for example, follows a rigorous process to design, build, and test new products. Project managers oversee the development of all new products, such as rides, parks, and cruise lines.

IT projects are used to develop products and services such as new software, hardware, networks, research reports, and training on new systems. Most IT professionals are familiar with the concept of a product life cycle, especially for developing software.

Software development projects are one subset of IT projects. Many IT projects involve researching, analyzing, and then purchasing and installing new hardware and software with little or no actual software development required. Other projects involve minor modifications to enhance existing software or to integrate one application with another. Still other projects involve a major amount of software development. Many argue that developing software requires project managers to modify traditional project management methods, depending on a particular product's life cycle.

A **systems development life cycle (SDLC)** is a framework for describing the phases of developing information systems. Some popular models of an SDLC include the waterfall model, the spiral model, the incremental build model, the prototyping model, and the Rapid application development (RAD) model. These life cycle models are examples of a **predictive life cycle**, meaning that the scope of the project can be articulated clearly and the schedule and cost can be predicted accurately. The project team spends a large portion of the project attempting to clarify the requirements of the entire system and then producing a design. Users are often unable to see any tangible results in terms of working software for an extended period. Below are brief descriptions of several predictive SDLC models:[11]

- The waterfall life cycle model has well-defined, linear stages of systems analysis, design, construction, testing, and support. This life cycle model assumes that requirements will remain stable after they are defined. The waterfall life cycle model is used when risk must be tightly controlled and when changes must be restricted after the requirements are defined. The waterfall approach is used in many large-scale systems projects where complexity and cost are so high that the more rigid steps of the approach help to ensure careful completion of all deliverables.
- The spiral life cycle model was developed based on refinements of the waterfall model as applied to large government software projects. It recognizes the fact that most software is developed using an iterative or spiral approach rather than a linear approach. The project team is open to changes and revisions later in the project life cycle, and returns to the requirements phase to more carefully clarify and design the revisions. This approach is suitable for projects in which changes can be incorporated with reasonable cost increases or with acceptable time delays. Figure 2-5 illustrates the differences between the waterfall and spiral life cycle models.

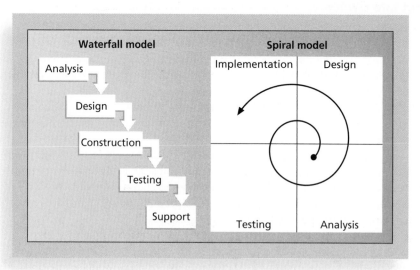

© Cengage Learning 2016

FIGURE 2-5 Waterfall and spiral life cycle models

- The incremental build life cycle model provides for progressive development of operational software, with each release providing added capabilities. This type of approach is often used by organizations like Microsoft, which issues a specific release of a software package while working on future revisions that will be distributed later in another release with a higher "build" or version number. This approach helps to stage the priorities of the features and functions with user priorities or the costs, time, and scope of the revisions.

- The prototyping life cycle model is used for developing software prototypes to clarify user requirements for operational software. It requires heavy user involvement, and developers use a model to generate functional requirements and physical design specifications simultaneously. Developers can throw away or keep prototypes, depending on the project. This approach is often used in systems that involve a great deal of user interface design, such as website projects, in systems that automate previously manual functions, or in systems that change the nature of how something is done, such as mobile applications.

- The RAD life cycle model uses an approach in which developers work with an evolving prototype. This life cycle model also requires heavy user involvement and helps produce systems quickly without sacrificing quality. Developers use RAD tools such as computer-aided software engineering (CASE), joint requirements planning (JRP), and joint application design (JAD) to facilitate rapid prototyping and code generation. These tools are often used in reporting systems in which programmers enter parameters into software to generate reports for user approval. When approved, the same parameters will generate the final production system without further modification by the programmer.

In contrast to the predictive models, the **adaptive software development (ASD)** life cycle model assumes that software requirements cannot be clearly expressed early in the life cycle, so software is developed using a less structured, flexible approach. Software developers focus on the rapid creation of working code and an evolution of the entire software system. Instead of planning in detail what the software should do, developers have a basic idea of user needs and work to create code that will meet those needs. If some of the code needs to change, a developer changes it. The software is never really finished; there are stable periods between new releases. ASD grew out of RAD, but RAD allows for a time period when the software is finished, while ASD does not.

ASD was first described in a 1974 paper written by Dr. Ernest A. Edmonds, where he stated,

> The aim of the paper is to describe the process of software development as it often occurs unintentionally, in a way that might make it easier to recognize what is happening. An approach to the problem of controlling the process is indicated, as are the areas where detailed investigation would be necessary in any particular case. The nontechnical users that concern us are people who do not write their own programs and do not wish to use the computer for a technical, well defined process. The development of software for such users is often made difficult because one cannot predict just which facilities are the best ones to provide. There may not be an existing system to analyse, and the analyst may not be able to invent one. It is suggested that the solution proposed may also allow users to adapt their methods at the same rate as the development of the software, giving a smooth and well understood change in the system.[12]

Examples of ASD include extreme programming, feature driven development, dynamic systems development model, and scrum. Today ASD approaches are collectively referred to as **agile software development**, named after the Agile Manifesto published in 2001. The last section of this chapter provides more information on agile as it applies to project management, and Chapter 3 includes a brief case study of an agile project.

Whether predictive or agile, all of these models are examples of SDLCs. The type of software and complexity of the information system in development determines which life cycle models to use. Most important, to meet the needs of the project environment, the project manager needs to understand the product life cycle. (For more information, you can find detailed descriptions of each model on many websites and in management information systems textbooks.)

Most large IT products are developed as a series of projects or as part of a program. For example, the systems planning phase for a new information system can include a project to hire an outside consulting firm to help identify and evaluate potential strategies for developing a particular business application, such as a new order processing system or general ledger system. The planning phase can also include a project to develop, administer, and evaluate a survey of users to get their opinions on the current information systems used in the organization. The systems analysis phase might include a project to create process models for certain business functions in the organization. This phase can also include a project to create data models of existing company databases related to the business function and application. The implementation phase might include a project to hire contract programmers to code a part of the system. The close-out phase might include a project to develop and run several training sessions for users of the new application. It is often good practice to view large projects as a series of smaller, more manageable ones, especially when extensive uncertainty is involved. Successfully completing one small project at a time will help the project team succeed in completing the larger project.

Some aspects of project management need to occur during each phase of the product life cycle. Therefore, it is critical for IT professionals to understand and practice good project management throughout the product life cycle.

2.4b The Importance of Project Phases and Management Reviews

Due to the complexity and importance of many IT projects and their resulting products, it is important to take time to review the status of a project at each phase. A project should successfully pass through each of the main project phases before continuing to the next. Because the organization usually commits more money as a project continues, a management review should occur after each phase to evaluate progress, potential success, and continued compatibility with organizational goals.

Management reviews, called **phase exits** or **kill points**, are very important for keeping projects on track and determining if they should be continued, redirected, or terminated. Recall that projects are just one part of the entire system of an organization. Changes in other parts of the organization might affect a project's status, and a project's status might likewise affect events in other parts of the organization. By breaking projects into phases, top management can make sure that the projects are still compatible with other needs of the organization.

Take another look at the opening case. Suppose Tom Walters' college conducted a study sponsored by the college president on increasing the use of technology. At the end of the concept phase, the project team could have presented information to the president, faculty, and other staff members that described different options for increasing the use of technology, an analysis of what competing colleges were doing, and results of a survey of local stakeholders' opinions on the subject. This presentation at the end of the concept phase represents one form of a management review. Suppose the study reported that 90 percent of surveyed students, faculty, and staff strongly opposed the idea of requiring all students to have tablets, and that many adult students said they would attend other colleges if they were required to pay for the additional technology. The college would probably decide not to pursue the idea any further. Had Tom taken a phased approach, he and his staff would not have wasted time and money developing detailed plans.

In addition to formal management reviews, it is important to have top management involvement throughout the life cycle of most projects. It is unwise to wait until the end of project or product phases to have management inputs. Many projects are reviewed by management on a regular basis, such as weekly or even daily, to make sure they are progressing well. Everyone wants to be successful in accomplishing goals at work, and having management involvement ensures that a company can accomplish its project and organizational goals.

✓ WHAT WENT RIGHT?

Having specific deliverables and kill points at the end of project or product phases helps managers make better decisions about whether to proceed, redefine, or kill a project. Improvement in IT project success rates reported by the Standish Group has been due in part to an increased ability to know when to cancel failing projects. Standish Group Chairman Jim Johnson made the following observation: "The real improvement that I saw was in our ability to—in the words of Thomas Edison—know when to stop beating a dead horse. ... Edison's key to success was that he failed fairly often; but as he said, he could recognize a dead horse before it started to smell. ... In information technology we ride dead horses—failing projects—a long time before we give up. But what we are seeing now is that we are able to get off them; able to reduce cost overrun and time overrun. That's where the major impact came on the success rate"[13]

Another example of the power of management oversight comes from Huntington Bancshares, Inc. This company, like many others, has an **executive steering committee**, a group of senior executives from various parts of the organization who regularly review important corporate projects and issues. The Ohio-based, $26 billion bank holding company completed a year-long website redesign using XML technology to give its online customers access to real-time account information as well as other banking services. The CIO, Joe Gottron, said there were "four or five very intense moments" when the whole project was almost stopped due to its complexity. The executive steering committee met weekly to review the project's progress and discuss work planned for the following week. Gottron said the meetings ensured that "if we were missing a beat on the project, no matter which company [was responsible], we were on top of it and adding additional resources to make up for it."[14]

Some projects still go on for a long time before being killed. Blizzard, producer of the popular massive multiplayer online (MMO) game World of Warcraft, decided to cancel their Titan game project after spending over seven years in development. According to Blizzard co-founder and CEO Mike Morhaime, "We set out to make the most ambitious thing that you could possibly imagine. And it didn't come together. We didn't find the fun. We didn't find the passion. ... We'd rather cut out a game we put a lot of time and resources into than put out something that might ...." Chris Metzen, Blizzard's senior vice president of story and franchise development, finished Morhaime's sentence: "Damage the relationship. Smash the trust."[15]

2.5 THE CONTEXT OF INFORMATION TECHNOLOGY PROJECTS

The project context has a critical impact on which product development life cycle will be most effective for a particular software development project. Likewise, several issues unique to the IT industry have a critical impact on managing IT projects. These include the nature of projects, the characteristics of project team members, and the diverse nature of technologies involved.

2.5a The Nature of IT Projects

Unlike projects in many other industries, IT projects are diverse. Some involve a small number of people installing off-the-shelf hardware and associated software. Others involve hundreds of people analyzing several organizations' business processes and then developing new software in a collaborative effort with users to meet business needs. Even for small hardware-oriented projects, a wide diversity of hardware types can be involved—personal computers, mainframe computers, network equipment, kiosks, laptops, tablets, or smartphones. The network equipment might be wireless, cellular based, or cable-based, or might require a satellite connection. The nature of software development projects is even more diverse than hardware-oriented projects. A software development project might include creating a simple, stand-alone Microsoft Excel or Access application or a sophisticated, global e-commerce system that uses state-of-the-art programming languages and runs on multiple platforms.

IT projects also support every possible industry and business function. Managing an IT project for a film company's animation department requires different knowledge and skills than a project to improve a federal tax collection system or to install a communication infrastructure in a third-world country. Because of the diversity of IT projects and the newness of the field, it is important to develop and follow best practices in managing these varied projects. Developing best practices gives IT project managers a common starting point and method to follow with every project.

2.5b Characteristics of IT Project Team Members

Because IT projects are diverse, the people involved come from diverse backgrounds and possess different skills. The resulting diverse project teams provide a significant advantage because they can analyze project requirements from a more robust systems view. Many companies purposely hire graduates with degrees in other fields such as business, mathematics, or the liberal arts to provide different perspectives on IT projects. Even with these different educational backgrounds, however, there are common job titles for people working on most IT projects, such as business analyst, programmer, network specialist, database analyst, quality assurance expert, technical writer, security specialist, hardware engineer, software engineer, and system architect. Within the category of programmer, several other job titles describe the specific technologies used, such as Java programmer, PHP programmer, and C/C++/C# programmer.

Some IT projects require the skills of people in just a few job functions, but some require inputs from many or all of them. Occasionally, IT professionals move between these job functions, but more often people become technical experts in one area or they decide to move into a management position. It is also rare for technical specialists or project managers to remain with the same company for a long time. In fact, many IT projects include a large number of contract workers. Working with this "army of free agents," as author Rob Thomsett calls them, creates special challenges.

2.5c Diverse Technologies

Many of the job titles for IT professionals reflect the different technologies required to hold those positions. Differences in technical knowledge can make communication between professionals challenging. Hardware specialists might not understand the language of database analysts, and vice versa. Security specialists may have a hard time communicating with business analysts. People within the same IT job function often do not understand each other because they use different technology. For example, someone with the title of programmer can often use several different programming languages. However, if programmers are limited in their ability to work in multiple languages, project managers might find it more difficult to form and lead more versatile project teams.

Another problem with diverse technologies is that many of them change rapidly. A project team might be close to finishing a project when it discovers a new technology that can greatly enhance the project and better meet long-term business needs. New technologies have also shortened the time frame many businesses have to develop, produce, and distribute new products and services. This fast-paced environment requires equally fast-paced processes to manage and produce IT projects and products.

2.6 RECENT TRENDS AFFECTING INFORMATION TECHNOLOGY PROJECT MANAGEMENT

Recent trends such as increased globalization, outsourcing, virtual teams, and agile project management are creating additional challenges and opportunities for IT project managers and their teams. Each of these trends and suggestions for addressing them are discussed in this section.

2.6a Globalization

In his popular book *The World Is Flat*, Thomas L. Friedman describes the effects of globalization, which has created a "flat" world where everyone is connected and the "playing field" is level for many more participants.[16] Lower trade and political barriers and the digital revolution have made it possible to interact almost instantaneously with billions of other people across the planet, and for individuals and small companies to compete with large corporations. Friedman also discusses the increase in "uploading," in which people share information through blogging, podcasts, and open-source software.

IT is a key enabler of globalization. In 2014, more than 1.3 billion people were using Facebook, spending an average of 21 minutes a day.[17] Other social networks, such as Twitter and LinkedIn, also continue to grow. In 2014, there were over 284 million Twitter users and 332 million LinkedIn users. According to LinkedIn's website, in the third quarter of 2014, 75 percent of new members came from outside the United States. Globalization has significantly affected the field of IT. Even though major IT companies such as Apple, IBM, and Microsoft started in the United States, much of their business is global—indeed, companies and individuals throughout the world contribute to the growth of information technologies, and work and collaborate on various IT projects.

It is important for project managers to address several key issues when working on global projects:

- *Communications*: Because people work in different time zones, speak different languages, have different cultural backgrounds, and celebrate different holidays, it is important to address how people will communicate in an efficient and timely manner. A communications management plan is vital. For details, see the plan described in Chapter 10, Project Communications Management.
- *Trust*: Trust is an important issue for all teams, especially when they are global teams. It is important to start building trust immediately by recognizing and respecting others' differences and the value they add to the project.
- *Common work practices*: It is important to align work processes and develop a modus operandi with which everyone agrees and is comfortable. Project managers must allow time for the team to develop these common work practices. Using special tools, as described next, can facilitate this process.
- *Tools*: IT plays a vital role in globalization, especially in enhancing communications and work practices. Many people use free tools such as Skype, Google Docs, or social media to communicate. Many project management software tools include their own communications and collaboration features in an integrated package. IBM continues to be the leader in providing collaboration tools to businesses in over 175 companies, followed by Oracle in 145 countries, SAP in 130 countries, and Microsoft in 113 countries.[18] Work groups must investigate options and decide which tools will work best for their projects. Security is often a key factor in deciding which tools to use.

After researching over 600 global organizations, KPMG International summarized several suggestions for managing global project teams:

- Employ greater project discipline for global projects; otherwise, weaknesses within the traditional project disciplines may be amplified by geographical differences.
- Think globally but act locally to align and integrate stakeholders at all project levels.
- Consider collaboration over standardization to help balance the goals and project approach.
- Keep momentum going for projects, which will typically have a long duration.
- Consider the use of newer, perhaps more innovative, tools and technology.[19]

2.6b Outsourcing

As described in detail in Chapter 12, Project Procurement Management, **outsourcing** is an organization's acquisition of goods and services from an outside source. The term **offshoring** is sometimes used to describe outsourcing from another country. Offshoring is a natural outgrowth of globalization. IT projects continue to rely more and more on outsourcing, both within and outside their country boundaries.

Some organizations remain competitive by using outsourcing to their advantage. Many organizations have found ways to reduce costs by outsourcing, even though the practice can be unpopular in their home countries. For example, outsourcing was an important topic in the 2012 U.S. Republican presidential debates, as candidates discussed why Apple hires half a million low-paid workers in the Far East to assemble its products. A *New York Times* article explained that outsourcing is not just about low costs. "One former executive described how [Apple] relied upon a Chinese factory to revamp iPhone manufacturing just weeks before the device was due on shelves. Apple had redesigned the iPhone's screen at the last minute, forcing an assembly line overhaul. New screens began arriving at the plant near midnight. A foreman immediately roused 8,000 workers inside the company's dormitories, according to the executive. Each employee was given a biscuit and a cup of tea, guided to a workstation and within half an hour started a 12-hour shift fitting glass screens into beveled frames. Within 96 hours, the plant was producing over 10,000 iPhones a day. 'The speed and flexibility is breathtaking,' the executive said. 'There's no American plant that can match that.' "[20]

Because of the increased use of outsourcing for IT projects, project managers need to become more familiar with many global and procurement issues, including working on and managing virtual teams.

2.6c Virtual Teams

Several factors, such as the cost and time required for travel or employee relocation, the ability to communicate and work across vast distances, the advantages of hiring people in locations that have a lower cost of living, and worker preferences for flexible work hours, have contributed to a significant increase in virtual project teams. A **virtual team** is a group of people who work together despite time and space boundaries using communication technologies. Team members might all work for the same company in the same country, or they might include employees as well as independent consultants, suppliers, or even volunteers providing their expertise from around the globe.

The main advantages of virtual teams include:

- Lowering costs because many virtual workers do not require office space or support beyond their home offices.
- Providing more expertise and flexibility or increasing competitiveness and responsiveness by having team members across the globe working any time of day or night.

 GLOBAL ISSUES

Outsourcing also has disadvantages. For example, Apple benefits from manufacturing products in China, but it had big problems there after its iPhone 4S launch in January 2012 caused fighting between migrant workers who were hired by scalpers to stand in line to buy the phones. When Apple said it would not open its store in Beijing, riots resulted and people attacked security guards. The Beijing Apple Store has had problems before. In May 2011, four people were injured when a crowd waiting to buy the iPad 2 turned ugly. Market analysts blamed Apple for not marketing or distributing its products well in China.[21]

- Improving the balance between work and life for team members by eliminating fixed office hours and the need to travel to work.

Disadvantages of virtual teams include:

- Isolating team members who may not adjust well to working in a virtual environment.
- Increasing the potential for communications problems because team members cannot use body language or other nonverbal communications to understand each other and build relationships and trust.
- Reducing the ability for team members to network and transfer information informally.
- Increasing the dependence on technology to accomplish work.

Like any team, a virtual team should focus on achieving a common goal. Research on virtual teams reveals a growing list of factors that influence their success:

- *Team processes*: It is important to define how the virtual team will operate. For example, teams must agree on how and when work will be done, what technologies will be used, how decisions will be made, and other important process issues.
- *Leadership style*: The project manager's leadership style affects all teams, especially virtual ones.
- *Trust and relationships*: Many virtual teams fail because of a lack of trust. It is difficult to build relationships and trust from a distance. Some project managers like to have a face-to-face meeting so team members can get to know each other and build trust. If such a meeting is not possible, phone or video conferences can help.
- *Team member selection and role preferences*: Dr. Meredith Belbin defined a team role as "a tendency to behave, contribute and interrelate with others in a particular way."[22] It is important to select team members carefully and to form a team in which all roles are covered. All virtual team members must also understand their roles on the team. (Visit *www.belbin.com* for more information on this topic.)
- *Task-technology fit*: IT is more likely to have a positive impact on individual performance if the capabilities of the technologies match the tasks that the user must perform.
- *Cultural differences*: It is important to address cultural differences, including how people with authority are viewed, how decisions are made, how requests or questions are communicated, and how workers prefer to operate (in collaboration or individually). These cultural differences vary from location to location and affect many aspects of the team.
- *Computer-mediated communication*: It is crucial to provide reliable and appropriate computer-mediated communication to virtual team members, including e-mail, instant messaging, text messaging, and chat rooms. If you rely on these technologies to bring the virtual team together, you need to ensure that they actually work, or you risk increasing the distance that can exist across virtual boundaries.

- *Team life cycles*: Just as projects and products have life cycles, so do teams. Project managers must address the team life cycle, especially when assigning team members and determining deliverable schedules.
- *Incentives*: Virtual teams may require different types of incentives to accomplish high-quality work on time. They do not have the benefit of physical contact with their project managers or other team members, so it is important to provide frequent positive incentives, such as a thank-you via e-mail or phone, or even a bonus on occasion. Negative incentives, such as fines or withholding payment, can also be effective if virtual team members are not being productive.
- *Conflict management*: Even though they might never physically meet, virtual teams still have conflicts. It is important to address conflict management, as described in more detail in Chapter 9, Project Human Resource Management.

Several studies have tried to determine factors that are correlated positively to the effectiveness of virtual teams. Research suggests that team processes, trusting relationships, leadership style, and team member selection provide the strongest correlations to team performance and team member satisfaction.[23]

2.6d Agile Project Management

Earlier the agile approach to product development was discussed. **Agile** means being able to move quickly and easily, but some people feel that project management, *as they have seen it used*, does not allow people to work quickly or easily. Early software development projects often used a waterfall approach, but as technology and businesses became more complex, the approach often became difficult to use because requirements were unknown or continuously changing. Agile today means using a method based on iterative and incremental development, in which requirements and solutions evolve through collaboration. Agile can be used for software development or in any environment in which the requirements are unknown or change quickly. In terms of the triple constraint, an agile approach sets time and cost goals but leaves scope goals flexible so the project sponsors or product owners can prioritize and reprioritize the work they want done. An agile approach makes sense for some projects, but not all of them.

Many seasoned experts in project management warn people not to fall for the hype associated with agile. For example, J. Leroy Ward, Executive Vice President at ESI International, said that "Agile will be seen for what it is ... and isn't." According to Ward, "Project management organizations embracing Agile software and product development approaches will continue to grow while being faced with the challenge of demonstrating ROI through Agile adoption. In addition, they will need to disabuse their stakeholders and executives of the expectations set by IT consultants, the media and the vendor community that Agile is the next 'silver bullet.' Organizations that do it right—including selecting the right projects for Agile—will reap significant rewards."[24]

2.6e The Manifesto for Agile Software Development

In the business world, the term *agile* was first applied to software development projects. In February 2001, a group of 17 people that called itself the Agile Alliance developed and agreed on the Manifesto for Agile Software Development, as follows:

We are uncovering better ways of developing software by doing it and helping others do it. Through this work we have come to value:

- Individuals and interactions over processes and tools
- Working software over comprehensive documentation
- Customer collaboration over contract negotiation
- Responding to change over following a plan[25]

The person or organization that implements Agile is responsible for interpreting and applying the preceding values.

Some people associate Agile with specific techniques such as Scrum.

2.6f Scrum

According to the Scrum Alliance, **Scrum** is the leading agile development method for completing projects with a complex, innovative scope of work. The term was coined in 1986 in a Harvard Business Review study that compared high-performing, cross-functional teams to the scrum formation used by rugby teams. The basic Scrum framework is summarized in the following list and illustrated in Figure 2-6:

- A *product owner* creates a prioritized wish list called a *product backlog*.
- During *sprint planning*, the team pulls a small chunk from the top of that wish list, a *sprint backlog*, and decides how to implement those pieces.
- The team has a certain amount of time, a *sprint*, to complete its work— usually two to four weeks—but meets each day to assess its progress (*daily Scrum*).
- Along the way, the *ScrumMaster* keeps the team focused on its goal.

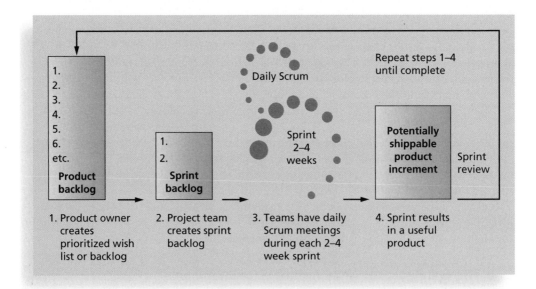

© Cengage Learning 2016

FIGURE 2-6 Scrum framework

- At the end of the sprint, the work should be *potentially shippable*, as in ready to hand to a customer, put on a store shelf, or show to a stakeholder.
- The sprint ends with a *sprint review* and *retrospective*.
- As the next sprint begins, the team chooses another chunk of the product backlog and begins working again.

The cycle repeats until enough items in the product backlog have been completed, the budget is depleted, or a deadline arrives. Which of these milestones marks the end of the work is entirely specific to the project. No matter which of these reasons stops work, Scrum ensures that the most valuable work has been completed when the project ends.[26]

In the Axosoft video "Scrum in 10 Minutes," Hamid Shojaee, an experienced software developer who has worked with several major corporations, briefly explains key concepts like product backlogs, team roles, sprints, and burndown charts.[27] Techniques from the just-in-time inventory control method **Kanban** can be used in conjunction with Scrum. Kanban was developed in Japan by Toyota Motor Corporation. It uses visual cues to guide workflow. For example, teams can place cards on boards to show the status of work in the backlog, such as new, in progress, and complete. Cards on the board are moved to the right to show progress in completing work. Kanban also helps limit work in progress by making a bottleneck visible so people can collaborate to solve problems that created the bottleneck. Kanban helps improve day-to-day workflow, while Scrum provides the structure for improving the organization of projects.[28] Scrum was initially applied to software development projects, but today other types of projects use this technique to help focus on teamwork, complete the most important work first, and add business value. Chapter 3 includes a case study that illustrates an agile approach to project management.

2.6g Agile, the *PMBOK® Guide*, and a New Certification

The *PMBOK® Guide* describes best practices for *what* should be done to manage projects. Agile is a methodology that describes *how* to manage projects. One could view Agile and the Scrum framework as methods that break down a big project into several smaller projects, defining the scope for each one. Project teams can have brief meetings each day to decide how to get the most important work done first without calling the meetings "scrums."

As stated earlier in the chapter, several different methods are related to developing information systems and other products. Because projects are unique, someone must decide what processes are needed and how they should be performed. Project teams can follow one specific process, a hybrid of several, or their own customized approach.

The Project Management Institute (PMI) recognized the increased interest in Agile, and introduced a new certification in 2011 called Agile Certified Practitioner (ACP). As stated on the PMI website, "The use of agile as an approach to managing projects has been increasing dramatically over the last several years. Gartner predicts that by the end of 2012, agile development methods will be used on 80 percent of all software development projects. PMI's research has shown that the use of agile has tripled from December 2008 to May 2011. Furthermore, research demonstrates the value that agile can have in decreasing product defects, improving team productivity, and increasing delivery of business value. The PMI-ACP is positioned to recognize and validate knowledge of this important approach."[29]. At the end of April 2015, there were 8,255 people who earned the Agile Certified Practitioner Certification.[30]

CASE WRAP-UP

After several people voiced concerns about the tablet idea at the faculty meeting, the president of the college directed that a committee be created to formally review the concept of requiring students to have tablets. Because the college was dealing with several important enrollment-related issues, the president named the vice president of enrollment to head the committee. Other people soon volunteered or were assigned to the committee, including Tom Walters as head of Information Technology, the director of the adult education program, the chair of the Computer Science department, and the chair of the History department. The president also insisted that the committee include at least two members of the student body. The president knew everyone was busy, and he questioned whether the tablet idea was a high-priority issue for the college. He directed the committee to present a proposal at next month's faculty meeting, either to recommend creating a formal project team to fully investigate requiring tablets or to recommend terminating the concept. At the next faculty meeting, few people were surprised to hear the recommendation to terminate the concept. Tom Walters learned that he had to pay much more attention to the needs of the entire college before proceeding with detailed IT plans.

One reason for increased interest in Agile is the hope that it will somehow make project management easier. Many books, courses, and consultants are capitalizing on this "new" approach. However, seasoned project managers understand that they have always had the option of customizing how they run projects. They also know that project management is not easy, even when using Agile.

As you can see, working as an IT project manager or team member is an exciting and challenging job. The excitement and challenge come from the focus on successfully completing projects that will have a positive impact on the organization as a whole.

Chapter Summary

Projects operate in an environment broader than the project itself. Project managers need to take a systems approach in order to successfully manage projects; they need to consider projects within the greater organizational context. To ensure project success, IT project managers need to integrate business and organizational issues as well as technology into project planning.

Organizations have four different frames: structural, human resources, political, and symbolic. Project managers need to understand all of these aspects of organizations to be successful. The structural frame focuses on different groups' roles and responsibilities to meet the goals and policies set by top management. The human resources frame focuses on producing harmony between the needs of the organization and the needs of people. The political frame addresses organizational and personal politics. The symbolic frame focuses on symbols and meanings.

The structure of an organization has strong implications for project managers, especially regarding the amount of authority they have. The three basic organizational structures are functional, matrix, and project. Project managers have the most authority in a pure project organization, an intermediate amount of authority in a matrix organization, and the least amount of authority in a pure functional organization.

Organizational culture also affects project management. Projects are more likely to succeed in a culture where employees have a strong identity with the organization, where work activities emphasize groups, and where there is strong unit integration, high risk tolerance, performance-based rewards, high conflict tolerance, an open-systems focus, and a balance among the dimensions of people focus, control, and means orientation.

Project stakeholders are individuals and organizations who are actively involved in the project or whose interests may be positively or negatively affected by the project's execution or successful completion. Project managers must identify and understand the different needs of all stakeholders involved with their projects.

Top management commitment is crucial for project success. Because projects often affect many areas in an organization, top management must assist project managers if they are to do a good job of project integration. Organizational commitment to IT is also important to the success of IT projects. Development standards and guidelines assist most organizations in managing projects.

A project life cycle is a collection of phases. Traditional project phases include concept, development, implementation, and close-out. Projects often develop products, which follow product life cycles. Examples of product life cycles for software development include the waterfall, spiral, incremental build, prototyping, RAD, and adaptive software development models. Project managers must understand the specific life cycles of their products as well as the general project life cycle model.

A project should successfully pass through each project phase in order to continue to the next phase. A management review should occur at the end of each project phase, and more frequent management inputs are often needed. These management reviews and inputs are important for keeping projects on track and determining if projects should be continued, redirected, or terminated.

Project managers need to consider several factors affected by the unique context of IT projects. The diverse nature of these projects and the wide range of business areas and technologies involved make IT projects especially challenging to manage. Leading project team members with a variety of specialized skills and understanding rapidly changing technologies are also important considerations.

Several recent trends have affected IT project management. Increased globalization, outsourcing, virtual teams, and agile project management have changed the way many IT projects are staffed and managed. Project managers must stay abreast of these and other trends and discover ways to use them effectively.

Quick Quiz

1. Which of the following is not part of the three-sphere model for systems management?
   a. business
   b. information
   c. technology
   d. organization

2. Which of the four frames of organizations addresses how meetings are run, employee dress codes, and expected work hours?
   a. structural
   b. human resources
   c. political
   d. symbolic

3. Personnel in a _____ organizational structure often report to two or more bosses.
   a. functional
   b. project
   c. matrix
   d. hybrid

4. Project work is most successful in an organizational culture where all of the following characteristics are important except _____.
   a. member identity
   b. group emphasis
   c. risk tolerance
   d. control

5. A _____ is a product or service, such as a technical report, a training session, or hardware, produced or provided as part of a project.
   a. deliverable
   b. product
   c. work package
   d. tangible goal

6. Which of the following statements is false?
   a. An analysis project life cycle is a collection of project phases.
   b. A product life cycle is the same as a project life cycle.
   c. The waterfall approach is an example of a predictive life cycle model.
   d. Agile is an example of an adaptive life cycle model.

7. Which of the following terms describes a framework of the phases involved in developing information systems?

   a. systems development life cycle

   b. rapid application development

   c. predictive life cycle

   d. extreme programming

8. The nature of IT projects is different from the nature of projects in many other industries because they are very _____.

   a. expensive

   b. technical

   c. diverse

   d. challenging

9. What term describes an organization's acquisition of goods and services from an outside source in another country?

   a. globalization

   b. offshoring

   c. exporting

   d. global sourcing

10. _____ is the leading agile development method.

   a. Extreme programming

   b. Sprint

   c. Kanban

   d. Scrum

Quick Quiz Answers

1. b; 2. d; 3. c; 4. d; 5. a; 6. b; 7. a; 8. c; 9. b; 10. d

Discussion Questions

1. What does it mean to take a systems view of a project? How does taking this view apply to project management?

2. Explain the four frames of organizations. How can they help project managers understand the organizational context for their projects?

3. Briefly explain the differences between functional, matrix, and project organizations. Describe how each structure affects the management of a project.

4. Describe how organizational culture is related to project management. What type of culture promotes a strong project environment?

5. Discuss the importance of top management commitment and the development of standards for successful project management. Provide examples to illustrate the importance of these items based on your experience on any type of project.

6. What are the phases in a traditional project life cycle? How does a project life cycle differ from a product life cycle? Why does a project manager need to understand both?

7. What makes IT projects different from other types of projects? How should project managers adjust to these differences?

8. Define globalization, outsourcing, virtual teams, and agile project management, and describe how these trends are changing IT project management.

Exercises

1. Summarize the three-sphere model for systems management in your own words. Then use your own project experience or interview someone who recently completed an IT project, and list several business, technology, and organizational issues addressed during the project. Which issues were most important to the project, and why? Summarize your answers in a short paper or presentation.

2. Apply the four frames of organizations to a possible project that involves the development of a new technology like mobile banking, online retail, or social media. Work with two other class members in a virtual environment on this exercise. Write a short paper or presentation that summarizes your analysis and opinions of how working virtually helped or hindered your results.

3. Search the Internet for two interesting articles about software development life cycles, including agile development. Review the website *www.agilealliance.org*. What do these sources say about project management? Write a summary of your findings and opinions on this topic, and cite your references.

4. Search the Internet and scan IT industry magazines or websites to find an example of an IT project that had problems due to organizational issues. Write a short paper summarizing the key stakeholders for the project and how they influenced the outcome.

5. Write a short summary of an article that discusses the importance of top management support for successful IT projects. Your summary should include your opinion on this topic.

6. Research the trend of using virtual teams. Review the information on team role theory from *www.belbin.com* and other related sources. Write a summary of your findings, and cite at least three references. Also include any personal experience and your opinion on the topic. For example, what role(s) would you prefer to play on a team? Do you like working on virtual teams? If you have not yet worked on one, how do you think it would be different from working on a face-to-face team?

7. Research the agile movement as it applies to software development and other types of projects. See how many books and websites are available on the topic. Is there evidence to show that agile projects are more successful than others? What agile principles can be applied to all types of projects? Write a short paper that summarizes your findings, and cite at least three references. Also include any personal experience and your opinion on the topic.

8. Watch videos about Scrum and Kanban by Axosoft or other organizations. Summarize what you learned and any questions you have in a short paper. Try to find answers to your questions and cite your sources.

Key Terms

adaptive software development (ASD)   p. 61

agile   p. 69

agile software development   p. 62

champion   p. 54

deliverable   p. 57

executive steering committee   p. 63

functional organizational structure   p. 49

human resources (HR) frame   p. 47

IT governance   p. 55

kanban   p. 71

kill point   p. 62

matrix organizational structure   p. 50

offshoring   p. 66

organizational culture   p. 51

outsourcing   p. 66

phase exit   p. 62

political frame   p. 48

politics   p. 48

predictive life cycle   p. 60

project acquisition   p. 57

project feasibility   p. 57

project life cycle   p. 57

project organizational structure   p. 50

scrum   p. 70

structural frame   p. 47

symbolic frame   p. 48

systems analysis   p. 45

systems approach   p. 45

systems development life cycle (SDLC)   p. 60

systems management   p. 45

systems philosophy   p. 45

systems thinking   p. 45

virtual team   p. 67

End Notes

[1] Lee G. Bolman and Terrence E. Deal, *Reframing Organizations* (San Francisco: Jossey-Bass, 1991).

[2] Ibid.

[3] John McManus and Trevor Wood-Harper, "A Study in Project Failure," *BCS* (June 2008).

[4] Stephen P. Robbins and Timothy A. Judge, *Organizational Behavior*, 16th edition (Upper Saddle River: Pearson/Prentice Hall, 2015).

[5] Loren Thompson, "HealthCare.gov Diagnosis: The Government Broke Every Rule of Project Management," *Forbes*, *www.forbes.com/sites/lorenthompson/2013/12/03/healthcare-gov -diagnosis-the-government-broke-every-rule-of-project-management/* (December 3, 2013).

[6] Steven Brill, "Obama's Trauma Team," *Time*, *time.com/10228/obamas-trauma-team/* (March 10, 2014).

[7] Peter Weill and Jeanne Ross, *IT Governance: How Top Performers Manage IT Decision Rights for Superior Results* (Boston, MA: Harvard Business School Press, 2004).

[8] David Avison, Shirley Gregor, and David Wilson, "Managerial IT Unconsciousness," *Communications of the ACM* 49, no. 7 (July 2006), p. 92.

[9] Gartner, "Gartner Survey Reveals That 76 Percent of EMEA CIOs Must Change Their Leadership Style to Succeed as a Digital Leaders," press release (November 12, 2014).

10 Cynthia Clark, Elizabeth Glagowski, Thomas Hoffman, and Anna Papachristos, "Meet the Winners," Gartner (2014).

11 Douglas H. Desaulniers and Robert J. Anderson, "Matching Software Development Life Cycles to the Project Environment," *Proceedings of the Project Management Institute Annual Seminars & Symposium* (November 1–10, 2001).

12 Ernest A. Edmonds, "A Process for the Development of Software for Non-Technical Users as an Adaptive System," *General Systems* 19 (1974), pp. 215–218.

13 Jeannette Cabanis, "A Major Import: The Standish Group's Jim Johnson on Project Management and IT Project Success," *PM Network* (PMI) (September 1998), p. 7.

14 Lucas Mearian, "Bank Hones Project Management Skills with Redesign," *Computerworld* (April 29, 2002).

15 Philip Kollar, "Blizzard Cancels Its Next-Gen MMO Titan After Seven Years," *Polygon* (September 23, 2014).

16 Thomas L. Friedman, *The World Is Flat: A Brief History of the Twenty-First Century* (Farrar, Straus, and Giroux, 2005).

17 Craig Smith, "By the Numbers: 170 Amazing Facebook User and Demographic Statistics," *DMR Digital Marketing Ramblings* (October 30, 2014).

18 IBM, "IBM Leads in Collaboration and Building Exceptional Digital Experiences," www.ibm.com (2014).

19 KPMG International, "Managing Global Projects: Observations from the Front-Line," www.kpmg.com (2007).

20 Charles Duhigg and Keith Bradsher, "How the U.S. Lost Out on iPhone Work," *The New York Times*, www.nytimes.com/2012/01/22/business/apple-america-and-a-squeezed-middle-class.html?_r=0 (January 21, 2012).

21 Sharon LaFraniere, "All iPhone Sales Suspended at Apple Stores in China," *The New York Times*, www.nytimes.com/2012/01/14/technology/apple-suspends-iphone-4s-sales-in-mainland-china-stores.html (January 13, 2012).

22 Belbin® Team Role Theory, www.belbin.com (accessed July 1, 2008).

23 Jeremy S. Lurey and Mahesh S. Raisinghani, "An Empirical Study of Best Practices in Virtual Teams," *Information & Management* 38, no. 8 (2001), pp. 523–544.

24 J. Leroy Ward, "The Top Ten Project Management Trends for 2011," *projecttimes.com* (January 24, 2011).

25 Agile Manifesto, www.agilemanifesto.org.

26 Scrum Alliance, "The Scrum Framework in 30 Seconds," www.scrumalliance.org/pages/what_is_scrum.

27 Hamid Shojaee, "Scrum in 10 Minutes," *Axosoft* (blog), www.axosoft.com (February 23, 2012).

28 Axosoft, "Intro to KanBan in Under 5 Minutes," *YouTube* (vlog), May 13, 2013, *www.youtube.com/watch?v=R8dYLbJiTUE*.

29 The Project Management Institute, PMI Agile Certified Practitioner (PMI-ACP)® (accessed January 23, 2012).

30 Project Management Institute, *PMI Today* (June 2015).

THE PROJECT MANAGEMENT PROCESS GROUPS: A CASE STUDY

LEARNING OBJECTIVES

After reading this chapter, you will be able to:

- Describe the five project management process groups, the typical level of activity for each, and the interactions among them

- Understand how the project management process groups relate to the project management knowledge areas

- Discuss how organizations develop information technology (IT) project management methodologies to meet their needs

- Review a case study of an organization applying the project management process groups to manage an IT project, describe outputs of each process group, and understand the contribution that effective initiating, planning, executing, monitoring and controlling, and closing make to project success

- Review a case study of the same project managed with an agile focus and compare the key differences between an agile approach and a predictive approach

- Describe several templates for creating documents for each process group

OPENING CASE

Erica Bell is in charge of the Project Management Office (PMO) for her consulting firm, JWD Consulting, which has grown to include more than 200 full-time consultants and even more part-time consultants. JWD Consulting provides a variety of consulting services to assist organizations in selecting and managing IT projects. The firm focuses on finding and managing high-payoff projects and developing strong metrics to measure project performance and benefits to the organization after the project is implemented. The firm's emphasis on metrics and working collaboratively with its customers gives it an edge over many competitors.

Joe Fleming, the CEO, wanted his company to continue to grow and become a world-class consulting organization. Because the core of the business is helping other organizations with project management, he felt it was crucial for JWD Consulting to have an exemplary process for managing its own projects. He asked Erica to work with her team and other consultants in the firm to develop several intranet site applications that would allow them to share their project management knowledge. He also thought that the firm should make some of the information available to the firm's clients. For example, the firm could provide project management templates, tools, articles, links to other sites, and an Ask the Expert feature to help build relationships with current and future clients. Because JWD Consulting emphasizes the importance of high-payoff projects, Joe also wanted to see a business case for this project before proceeding.

Recall from Chapter 1 that project management consists of 10 knowledge areas: integration, scope, time, cost, quality, human resources, communications, risk, procurement, and stakeholder management. Another important concept to understand is that projects involve five project management process groups: initiating, planning, executing, monitoring and controlling, and closing. Tailoring these process groups to meet individual project needs increases the chance of success in managing projects. This chapter describes each project management process group in detail through a simulated case study based on JWD Consulting. It also includes samples of typical project documents applied to this case. You can download templates for these and other project documents from the companion website for this text. Although you will learn more about each knowledge area in Chapters 4 through 13, it is important first to learn how they fit into the big picture of managing a project. Understanding how the knowledge areas and project management process groups function together will lend context to the remaining chapters.

3.1 PROJECT MANAGEMENT PROCESS GROUPS

Project management is an integrative endeavor. Decisions and actions taken in one knowledge area at a certain time usually affect other knowledge areas. Managing these interactions often requires making trade-offs among the project's scope, time, and cost—the triple constraint of project management described in Chapter 1. A project manager may also need to make trade-offs between knowledge areas, such as between managing risk and human resources. Consequently, you can view project management as a number of related processes.

A **process** is a series of actions directed toward a particular result. **Project management process groups** progress from initiating activities to planning activities, executing activities, monitoring and controlling activities, and closing activities. Recall that a project can have different combinations of phases. One project might have concept, development, implementation, and close-out phases, and another might have initial, intermediate, and final phases. But all projects and all project phases need to include all five process groups. You cannot equate process groups with project phases. For example, project managers and teams need to reexamine the business need for the project, part of monitoring and controlling activities, during every phase of the project life cycle to determine if the project is worth continuing.

- **Initiating processes** include defining and authorizing a project or project phase. Initiating processes take place during *each* phase of a project. For example, in the close-out phase, initiating processes are used to ensure that the project team completes all the work, that someone documents lessons learned, and that the customer accepts the work.
- **Planning processes** include devising and maintaining a workable scheme to ensure that the project addresses the organization's needs. Projects include several plans, such as the scope management plan, schedule management plan, cost management plan, and procurement management plan. These plans define each knowledge area as it relates to the project at a particular point in time. For example, a project team must develop a plan to define the work needed for the project, to schedule activities related to that work, to estimate costs for performing the work, and to decide what resources to procure to accomplish the work. To account for changing conditions on the project and in the organization, project teams often revise plans during each phase of the project life cycle. The project management plan, which is described in Chapter 4, coordinates and encompasses information from all other plans.
- **Executing processes** include coordinating people and other resources to carry out the various plans and create the products, services, or results of the project or phase. Examples of executing processes include acquiring and developing the project team, performing quality assurance, distributing information, managing stakeholder expectations, and conducting procurements.
- **Monitoring and controlling processes** include regularly measuring and monitoring progress to ensure that the project team meets the project objectives. The project manager and staff monitor and measure progress against the plans and take corrective action when necessary. A common monitoring and controlling process is reporting performance, where project stakeholders can identify any necessary changes that may be required to keep the project on track.
- **Closing processes** include formalizing acceptance of the project or project phase and ending it efficiently. Administrative activities are often involved in this process group, such as archiving project files, closing out contracts, documenting lessons learned, and receiving formal acceptance of the delivered work as part of the phase or project.

The process groups are not mutually exclusive. For example, project managers must perform monitoring and controlling processes throughout the project's life span.

That is, monitoring and controlling processes occur concurrently throughout a project with initiating, planning, executing, and closing processes. Initiating and planning processes can occur concurrently with executing processes, and so on for each process group.

The level of activity and length of each process group varies for every project. Normally, executing tasks require the most resources and time, followed by planning tasks. Initiating and closing tasks are usually the shortest (at the beginning and end of a project or phase, respectively), and they require the least resources and time. However, every project is unique, so exceptions are possible.

You can apply the process groups for each major phase or iteration of a project, or you can apply the process groups to an entire project. The first example of the JWD Consulting case study applies the process groups to the entire project. The second example shows how you can use a more agile approach to manage the same project; several process groups are repeated for each iteration of the project.

Many people ask for guidelines on how much time to spend in each process group. In his book *Alpha Project Managers: What the Top 2% Know That Everyone Else Does Not*, Andy Crowe collected data from 860 project managers in various companies and industries in the United States. He found that the best—the alpha—project managers spent more time on every process group, except executing, than their counterparts as shown in Figure 3-1. Notice that the alpha project managers spent almost *twice* as much time on planning (21 percent versus 11 percent) as other project managers. Spending more time on planning should lead to less time spent on execution, which should reduce the time and money spent on projects. The best project managers know and practice this important concept—do a good job of planning.[1]

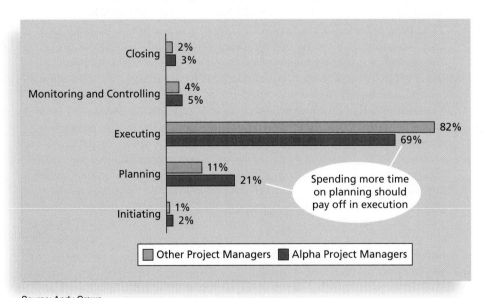

Source: Andy Crowe

FIGURE 3-1   Percentage of time spent on each process group

⊗ WHAT WENT WRONG?

Many readers of *CIO magazine* commented on its cover story about problems with information systems at the U.S. Internal Revenue Service (IRS). The article described serious problems the IRS has had in managing IT projects. Philip A. Pell, PMP, believes that having a good project manager and following a good project management process would help the IRS and many organizations tremendously. Pell provided the following feedback to the article:

> *Pure and simple, good, methodology-centric, predictable, and repeatable project management is the SINGLE greatest factor in the success (or in this case failure) of any project. When a key stakeholder says, 'I didn't know how bad things were,' it is a direct indictment of the project manager's communications management plan. When a critical deliverable like the middleware infrastructure that makes the whole thing work is left without assigned resources and progress tracking, the project manager has failed in his duty to the stakeholders. When key stakeholders (people and organizations that will be affected by the project, not just people who are directly working on the project) are not informed and their feedback incorporated into the project plan, disaster is sure to ensue. The project manager is ultimately responsible for the success or failure of the project.*[2]

The IRS continues to have problems managing IT projects. A 2014 U.S. Government Accountability Office (GAO) report stated that the IRS had significant cost and schedule variances in over 68 percent (13 of 19) of its major IT projects that auditors evaluated between June 2013 and April 2014. "The IRS is in the midst of several high-profile, long-term, high-dollar IT projects to improve electronic tax filing, prepare the systems to manage subsidy calculations and penalties under the 2010 health care law, and modernize its central taxpayer database and processing system. The success or failure of those projects will affect the government's ability to collect taxes and distribute refunds efficiently and accurately."[3]

Each of the five project management process groups is characterized by the completion of certain tasks. While initiating processes for a new project, the organization recognizes that a new project exists and completes a project charter as part of this recognition. (See Chapter 4 for more information on project charters.) Tables are provided later in this chapter with detailed lists of possible outputs for each process group by knowledge area. For example, Tables 3-3 through 3-7 list potential outputs for the initiating and planning process groups. Samples of some outputs are provided for each process group in a case study of JWD Consulting's project management intranet site project. Project managers and their teams must decide which outputs are required for their particular projects.

Outputs of the planning process group include completing the project scope statement, the work breakdown structure, the project schedule, and many other items. Planning processes are especially important for IT projects. Anyone who has ever worked on a large IT project that involves new technology knows the saying, "A dollar spent up front in planning is worth one hundred dollars spent after the system is implemented." Planning is crucial in IT projects because once a project team implements a new system, considerable effort is needed to change it. Research suggests that companies working to implement best practices should spend at least 20 percent of project time in initiating and planning.[4] This percentage is backed up by evidence from Alpha project managers, as described earlier.

The executing process group takes the actions necessary to complete the work described in the planning activities. The main outcome of this process group is delivering the actual work of the project. For example, if an IT project involves providing new hardware, software, and training, the executing processes would include leading the project team and other stakeholders to purchase the hardware, develop and test the software, and deliver and participate in the training. The executing process group should overlap the other process groups, and generally requires the most resources.

Monitoring and controlling processes measure progress toward the project objectives, monitor deviation from the plan, and take corrective action to match progress with the plan. Performance reports are common outputs of monitoring and controlling. The project manager should be monitoring progress closely to ensure that deliverables are being completed and objectives are being met. The project manager must work closely with the project team and other stakeholders and take appropriate actions to keep the project running smoothly. The ideal outcome of the monitoring and controlling process group is to complete a project successfully by delivering the agreed-upon project scope within time, cost, and quality constraints. If changes to project objectives or plans are required, monitoring and controlling processes ensure that these changes are made efficiently and effectively to meet stakeholder needs and expectations. Monitoring and controlling processes overlap all of the other project management process groups because changes can occur at any time.

During the closing processes, the project team works to gain acceptance of the end products, services, or results and bring the phase or project to an orderly end. Key outcomes of this process group are formal acceptance of the work and creation of closing documents, such as a final project report and lessons-learned report.

MEDIA SNAPSHOT

Just as IT projects need to follow the project management process groups, so do other projects, such as the production of a movie. Processes involved in making movies might include screenwriting (initiating), producing (planning), acting and directing (executing), editing (monitoring and controlling), and releasing the movie to theaters (closing). Many people enjoy watching the extra features on a DVD that describe how these processes lead to the creation of a movie. For example, the DVD for *Lord of the Rings: The Two Towers Extended Edition* includes detailed descriptions of how the script was created, how huge structures were built, how special effects were made, and how talented professionals overcame numerous obstacles to complete the project. This material acted "not as promotional filler but as a serious and meticulously detailed examination of the entire filmmaking process."[5] New Line Cinema made history by shooting all three *Lord of the Rings* films consecutively during one massive production. It took three years of preparation to build the sets, find the locations, write the scripts, and cast the actors. Director Peter Jackson said that the amount of early planning they did made it easier than he imagined to produce the films. Project managers in any field know how important it is to have good plans and to follow a good process. Jackson continued his movie making success by directing *The Hobbit*, produced as a film trilogy, with movies released in 2012, 2013, and 2014.

3.2 MAPPING THE PROCESS GROUPS TO THE KNOWLEDGE AREAS

You can map the main activities of each project management process group into the 10 project management knowledge areas. Table 3-1 provides a big-picture view of the relationships among the 47 project management activities, the process groups in which they are typically completed, and the knowledge areas into which they fit. The activities listed in the table are the main processes for each knowledge area listed in the *PMBOK® Guide, Fifth Edition*. This text includes additional activities not listed in the *PMBOK® Guide*, such as creating a business case and team contract, which can also assist in managing projects. Note that the *PMBOK® Guide* can serve as a guide for all types of projects that use all types of methods, including Agile. It is up to each project team to decide what processes and outputs are required based on their specific needs.

Several organizations use PMI's *PMBOK® Guide* information as a foundation for developing their own project management methodologies, as described in the next section. Notice in Table 3-1 that many of the project management activities occur as part of the planning process group. Because each project is unique, project teams are always trying to do something that has not been done before. To succeed at unique and new activities, project teams must do a fair amount of planning. Recall, however, that the most time and money is normally spent on executing. It is good practice for organizations to determine how project management will work best in their own organizations.

TABLE 3-1 Mapping project management process groups to knowledge areas

	Project Management Process Groups				
Knowledge Area	**Initiating**	**Planning**	**Executing**	**Monitoring and Controlling**	**Closing**
Project Integration Management	Develop project charter	Develop project management plan	Direct and manage project work	Monitor and control project work, perform integrated change control	Close project or phase
Project Scope Management		Plan scope management, collect requirements, define scope, create WBS		Validate scope, control scope	
Project Time Management		Plan schedule management, define activities, sequence activities, estimate activities resources, estimate activity durations, develop schedule		Control schedule	

(continued)

TABLE 3-1   Mapping project management process groups to knowledge areas (*continued*)

Knowledge Area	Project Management Process Groups				
	Initiating	Planning	Executing	Monitoring and Controlling	Closing
Project Cost Management		Plan cost management, estimate costs, determine budget		Control costs	
Project Quality Management		Plan quality management	Perform quality assurance	Control quality	
Project Human Resource Management		Plan human resource management	Acquire project team, develop project team, manage project team		
Project Communications Management		Plan communications management	Manage communications	Control communications	
Project Risk Management		Plan risk management, identify risks, perform qualitative risk analysis, perform quantitative risk analysis, plan risk responses		Control risks	
Project Procurement Management		Plan procurement management	Conduct procurements	Control procurements	Close procurements
Project Stakeholder Management	Identify stakeholders	Plan stakeholder management	Manage stakeholder engagement	Control stakeholder engagement	

Source: Project Management Institute *A Guide to the Project Management Body of Knowledge (PMBOK® Guide)*—Fifth Edition, Project Management Institute, Inc., (2013). Copyright and all rights reserved. Material from this publication has been reproduced with the permission of PMI.

3.3 DEVELOPING AN IT PROJECT MANAGEMENT METHODOLOGY

Some organizations spend a great deal of time and money on training efforts for general project management skills, but after the training, project managers may still not know how to tailor their project management skills to the organization's particular needs. Because of this problem, some organizations develop their own internal IT project management methodologies. The *PMBOK® Guide* is a **standard** that describes best practices for *what* should be done to manage a project. A **methodology** describes *how* things should be done, and different organizations often have different ways of doing things.

In addition to using the *PMBOK® Guide* as a basis for project management methodology, many organizations use other guides or methods, such as the following:

- **PRojects IN Controlled Environments (PRINCE2)**: Originally developed for IT projects, PRINCE2 was released in 1996 as a generic project management methodology by the U.K. Office of Government Commerce (OCG). It is the de facto standard in the United Kingdom and is used in over 50 countries. (See *www.prince2.com* for more information.) PRINCE2 defines 45 separate subprocesses and organizes them into eight process groups as follows:

  1. Starting up a project
  2. Planning
  3. Initiating a project
  4. Directing a project
  5. Controlling a stage
  6. Managing product delivery
  7. Managing stage boundaries
  8. Closing a project

- **Agile methods**: As described in Chapter 2, agile software development is a form of adaptive software development. All agile methods include an iterative workflow and incremental delivery of software in short iterations. Popular agile methods include extreme programming, Scrum, feature-driven development, lean software development, Agile Unified Process (AUP), Crystal, and Dynamic Systems Development Method (DSDM). See websites like *www.agilealliance.org* for more information. The second case in this chapter provides an example of using Scrum.

 GLOBAL ISSUES

The first study on the state of agile methods in India was published in 2011. The survey included feedback from 770 respondents from 330 organizations across India that are already using Agile, piloting Agile, or planning for Agile. The study was undertaken to understand the progress, challenges, and opportunities that firms face in evaluating and implementing Agile. Only 14 percent of respondents reported having expert experience in Agile methods, 39 percent considered themselves intermediate users, 35 percent were beginners, and 12 percent had no experience. A summary of findings included the following:

- Two-thirds of organizations in some stage of Agile adoption are realizing key software and business benefits in terms of faster delivery of products to the customer, an improved ability to manage changing requirements, and higher quality and productivity in IT.
- Organizations struggle with the magnitude of the cultural shift required for Agile, opposition to change, a lack of coaching and help in the Agile adoption process, and a lack of qualified people.
- The daily stand-up, iteration planning, and release planning are the most commonly used practices, while paired programming and open workspaces are not popular.

continued

Sudhir Tiwari, managing director of ThoughtWorks India, which sponsored the study, noted that some organizations "are approaching the holy grail of Continuous Delivery." He said, "We live in an age where Flickr releases 40 patches a week into production. The overall Agile suite is built to cater to teams which are looking at agility and going into production very rapidly."[6] A 2014 survey conducted by VersionOne found that 88 percent of survey respondents were knowledgeable about agile software development techniques. Executive sponsorship was the main success factor when scaling agile beyond a single team. The main barriers to further adoption of agile were an inability to change organizational culture and resistance to change.[7]

- **Rational Unified Process (RUP) framework**: RUP is an iterative software development process that focuses on team productivity and enables all team members to deliver software best practices to the organization. According to RUP expert Bill Cottrell, "RUP embodies industry-standard management and technical methods and techniques to provide a software engineering process particularly suited to creating and maintaining component-based software system solutions."[8] Cottrell explained that you can tailor RUP to include the PMBOK process groups because several customers asked for that capability. Several other project management methodologies are used specifically for software development projects, such as Joint Application Development (JAD) and Rapid Application Development (RAD). See websites such as *www.ibm.com/software/awdtools/rup* for more information.
- **Six Sigma methodologies**: Many organizations have projects that use Six Sigma methodologies. The work of many project quality experts contributed to the development of today's Six Sigma principles. Two main methodologies are used on Six Sigma projects: Define, Measure, Analyze, Improve, and Control (DMAIC) is used to improve an existing business process, and Define, Measure, Analyze, Design, and Verify (DMADV) is used to create new product or process designs to achieve predictable, defect-free performance. (See Chapter 8, Project Quality Management, for more information on Six Sigma.)

Many organizations tailor a standard or methodology to meet their unique needs. Even if organizations use the *PMBOK® Guide* as the basis for their project management methodology, they still have to do a fair amount of work to adapt it to their unique work environment.

 WHAT WENT RIGHT?

Organizations that excel in project management complete 89 percent of their projects successfully compared to only 36 percent of organizations that do not have good project management processes. PMI estimates that poor project performance costs over $109 million for every $1 billion invested in projects and programs.[9]

continued

Very large, complex projects often benefit the most from using proven project management methodologies. Several well-respected companies are teaming up to bid on an $11 billion military health-record contract in 2015. IBM and Epic announced that they were preparing to work on the project by running an instance of the Epic health-record system (the most popular system on the market) on a secure, IBM-operated data center. PriceWaterhouseCoopers (PWC) plans to work with Google to provide a solution based on an open-source version of the Vista health-record system used by the Department of Veterans Affairs.[10] If this huge contract is managed well, it will save taxpayers over $1.2 billion in potential wasted dollars.

The following sections present two examples of applying the project management process groups to a project at JWD Consulting. Both examples use some of the ideas from the *PMBOK® Guide, Fifth Edition*, some ideas from other methodologies, and some new ideas to meet unique project needs. The first case study follows a more predictive or waterfall approach, while the second case study follows a more adaptive approach using Scrum. Even though they are tailored for JWD Consulting's organizational needs, they both still use the project management process groups and several outputs or deliverables described in the *PMBOK® Guide*.

3.4 CASE STUDY 1: JWD CONSULTING'S PROJECT MANAGEMENT INTRANET SITE PROJECT (PREDICTIVE APPROACH)

The following fictitious case provides an example of the elements involved in managing a project from start to finish. This example also uses Microsoft Project to demonstrate how project management software can assist in several aspects of managing a project. Several templates illustrate how project teams prepare various project management documents. Files for these and other templates are available on the companion website for this text. Details on creating many of the documents shown are provided in later chapters, so do not worry if you do not understand everything right now. These two cases are provided to give you a sense of the big picture of IT project management. You might want to read this section again later to enhance your learning.

3.4a Project Pre-Initiation and Initiation

In project management, initiating includes recognizing and starting a new project. An organization should put considerable thought into project selection to ensure that it initiates the right kinds of projects for the right reasons. *It is better to have a moderate or even small amount of success on an important project than huge success on a project that is unimportant.* The selection of projects for initiation is therefore crucial, as is the selection of project managers. Ideally, the project manager would be involved in initiating a project, but often the project manager is selected after many initiation decisions have already been made. You will learn more about project selection in Chapter 4, Project Integration Management.

It is important to remember that strategic planning should serve as the foundation for deciding which projects to pursue. The organization's strategic plan expresses the vision, mission, goals, objectives, and strategies of the organization. It also provides the basis for

IT project planning. IT is usually a support function in an organization, so the people who initiate IT projects must understand how those projects relate to current and future needs of the organization. For example, JWD Consulting's main business is providing consulting services to other organizations, not developing its own intranet site applications. Information systems, therefore, must support the firm's business goals, such as providing consulting services more effectively and efficiently.

An organization may initiate IT projects for several reasons, but the most important reason is to support business objectives. As mentioned in the chapter's opening case, JWD Consulting wants to follow an exemplary process for managing its projects because its core business is helping other organizations manage projects. Developing an intranet to share its project management knowledge could help JWD Consulting reduce internal costs by working more effectively, and by allowing existing and potential customers to access some of the firm's information. JWD Consulting could also increase revenues by bringing in more business. Therefore, the firm will use these metrics—reducing internal costs and increasing revenues—to measure its performance on this project.

3.4b Pre-Initiation Tasks

It is good practice to lay the groundwork for a project *before* it officially starts. Senior managers often perform several tasks to lay the groundwork, sometimes called pre-initiation tasks, including the following:

- Determine the scope, time, and cost constraints for the project.
- Identify the project sponsor.
- Select the project manager.
- Develop a business case for a project.
- Meet with the project manager to review the process and expectations for managing the project.
- Determine if the project should be divided into two or more smaller projects.

As described in the opening case, the CEO of JWD Consulting, Joe Fleming, defined the high-level scope of the project. He wanted to sponsor the project himself because it was his idea and it was strategically important to the business. He wanted Erica Bell, the PMO Director, to manage the project after proving there was a strong business case for it. If there was a strong business case for pursuing the project, then Joe and Erica would meet to review the process and expectations for managing the project. If there was not a strong business case, the project would not continue.

As for the necessity of the last pre-initiation task, many people know from experience that it is easier to successfully complete a small project than a large one, especially for IT projects. It often makes sense to break large projects down into two or more smaller ones to help increase the odds of success. In this case, however, Joe and Erica decided that the work could be done in one project that would last about six months.

To justify investing in this project, Erica drafted a business case for it, getting input and feedback from Joe, from one of her senior staff members in the PMO, and from a member of the Finance department. She also used a corporate template and sample business cases from past projects as a guide. Table 3-2 provides the business case. (Note that this example and others are abbreviated.) Notice that the following information is included in this business case:

- Introduction/background
- Business objective
- Current situation and problem/opportunity statement
- Critical assumptions and constraints
- Analysis of options and recommendation
- Preliminary project requirements
- Budget estimate and financial analysis
- Schedule estimate
- Potential risks
- Exhibits

Because this project is relatively small and is for an internal sponsor, the business case is not as long as many other business cases. Erica reviewed the business case with Joe, and he agreed that the project was definitely worth pursuing. He was quite pleased to see that payback was estimated within a year and that the return on investment was projected to be 112 percent. He told Erica to proceed with the formal initiation tasks for this project, which are described in the next section.

TABLE 3-2   JWD Consulting's business case

1.0 Introduction/Background

JWD Consulting's core business goal is to provide world-class project management consulting services to various organizations. The firm can streamline operations and increase business by providing information related to project management on its intranet site, making some information and services accessible to current and potential clients.

2.0 Business Objective

JWD Consulting's strategic goals include continuing growth and profitability. The project management intranet site project will support these goals by increasing visibility of the firm's expertise to current and potential clients by allowing client and public access to some sections of the intranet. The project will also improve profitability by reducing internal costs by providing standard tools, techniques, templates, and project management knowledge to all internal consultants.

3.0 Current Situation and Problem/Opportunity Statement

JWD Consulting has a corporate website as well as an intranet. The firm currently uses the website for marketing information. The primary use of the intranet is for consultant human resource information, such as entering hours on projects, changing and viewing benefits information, and accessing an online directory and Web-based e-mail system. The firm also uses an enterprise-wide project management system to track all project information, focusing on the status of deliverables and meeting scope, time, and cost goals. There is an opportunity to provide a new section on the intranet dedicated to sharing consultants' project management knowledge across the organization. JWD Consulting only hires experienced consultants and gives them freedom to manage projects as they see fit. However, as the business grows and projects become more complex, even experienced project managers are looking for suggestions on how to work more effectively.

4.0 Critical Assumptions and Constraints

The proposed intranet site must be a valuable asset for JWD Consulting. Current consultants and clients must actively support the project, and it must pay for itself within one year by reducing internal operating costs and generating new business. The Project Management Office manager must lead the effort, and the project team must include participants from several parts of the company, as well as from current client organizations. The new system must run on existing hardware and software, and it should require minimal technical support. It must be easily accessible by consultants and clients and be secure from unauthorized users.

(continued)

TABLE 3-2   JWD Consulting's business case (*continued*)

5.0 Analysis of Options and Recommendation

There are three options for addressing this opportunity:

1. Do nothing. The business is doing well, and we can continue to operate without this new project.
2. Purchase access to specialized software to support this new capability with little in-house development.
3. Design and implement the new intranet capabilities in-house, using mostly existing hardware and software.

Based on discussions with stakeholders, we believe that option 3 is the best option.

6.0 Preliminary Project Requirements

The main features of the project management intranet site include the following:

1. Access to several project management templates and tools. Users must be able to search for templates and tools, read instructions for using these templates and tools, and see examples of how to apply them to real projects. Users must also be able to submit new templates and tools, which should first be screened or edited by the Project Management Office.
2. Access to relevant project management articles. Many consultants sense an information overload when they research project management information. They often waste time they should be spending with their clients. The new intranet should include access to important articles on project management topics, which are searchable by topic, and should allow users to ask the Project Management Office staff to find additional articles to meet their needs.
3. Links to other, up-to-date websites, with brief descriptions of the main features of the external sites.
4. An Ask the Expert feature to help build relationships with current and future clients and share knowledge with internal consultants.
5. Appropriate security to make the entire intranet site accessible to internal consultants and certain sections accessible to others.
6. The ability to charge money for access to some information. Some of the information and features of the intranet site should prompt external users to pay for the information or service. Payment options should include credit card or similar online payment transactions. After the system verifies payment, the user should be able to access or download the desired information.
7. Other features suggested by users, if they add value to the business.

7.0 Budget Estimate and Financial Analysis

A preliminary estimate of costs for the entire project is $140,000. This estimate is based on the project manager working about 20 hours per week for six months and other internal staff working a total of about 60 hours per week for six months. The customer representatives would not be paid for their assistance. A staff project manager would earn $50 per hour. The hourly rate for the other project team members would be $70 per hour, because some hours normally billed to clients may be needed for this project. The initial cost estimate also includes $10,000 for purchasing software and services from suppliers. After the project is completed, maintenance costs of $40,000 are included for each year, primarily to update the information and coordinate the Ask the Expert feature and online articles.

Projected benefits are based on a reduction in hours that consultants spend researching project management information, appropriate tools, and templates. Projected benefits are also based on a small increase in profits due to new business generated by this project. If each of 400 consultants saved just 40 hours each year (less than one hour per week) and could bill that time to projects that generate a conservative estimate of $10 per hour in *profits*, then the projected benefit would be $160,000 per year. If the new intranet increased business by just 1 percent, using past profit information, increased profits due to new business would be at least $40,000 each year. Total projected benefits, therefore, are about $200,000 per year. Exhibit A summarizes the projected costs and benefits and shows the estimated net present value (NPV), return on investment (ROI), and year in which payback occurs. It also lists assumptions made in performing this preliminary financial analysis. All of the financial estimates are very encouraging. The estimated payback is within one year, as requested by the sponsor. The NPV is $272,800, and the discounted ROI based on a three-year system life is excellent at 112 percent.

(continued)

TABLE 3-2 JWD Consulting's business case (*continued*)

8.0 Schedule Estimate

The sponsor would like to see the project completed within six months, but there is some flexibility in the schedule. We also assume that the new system will have a useful life of at least three years.

9.0 Potential Risks

This project carries several risks. The foremost risk is a lack of interest in the new system by our internal consultants and external clients. User inputs are crucial for populating information into this system and realizing the potential benefits from using the system. There are some technical risks in choosing the type of software used to search the system, implement security, process payments, and so on, but the features of this system all use proven technologies. The main business risk is investing the time and money into this project and not realizing the projected benefits.

10.0 Exhibits

Exhibit A: Financial Analysis for Project Management Intranet Site Project

Discount rate	8%				
Assume the project is done in about 6 months		Year			
	0	1	2	3	Total
Costs	140,000	40,000	40,000	40,000	
Discount factor	1	0.93	0.86	0.79	
Discounted costs	140,000	37,037	34,294	31,753	243,084
Benefits	0	200,000	200,000	200,000	
Discount factor	1	0.93	0.86	0.79	
Discounted benefits	0	186,185	171,468	158,766	515,419
Discounted benefits - costs	(140,000)	148,148	137,174	127,013	
Cumulative benefits - costs	(140,000)	8,148	145,322	272,336 ← NPV	
		Payback in Year 1			
Discounted life cycle ROI----------->	112%				
Assumptions					
Costs	# hours				
PM (500 hours, $50/hour)	25,000				
Staff (1500 hours, $70/hour)	105,000				
Outsourced software and services	10,000				
Total project costs (all applied in year 0)	140,000				
Benefits					
# consultants	400				
Hours saved	40				
$/hour profit	10				
Benefits from saving time	160,000				
Benefits from 1% increase in profits	40,000				
Total annual projected benefits	200,000				

© Cengage Learning 2016

3.4c Initiating

To officially initiate the project management intranet site project, Erica knew that the main tasks were to identify all of the project stakeholders and to develop the project charter. Table 3-3 shows these processes and their outputs, based on the *PMBOK® Guide, Fifth Edition*. The main outputs are a project charter and a stakeholder register. Additional outputs that Erica found very useful for initiating projects were a stakeholder management strategy and a formal project kick-off meeting. Descriptions of how these outputs were created and sample documents related to each of them are provided for this project. Recall that every project and every organization is unique, so not all project charters, stakeholder registers, and other outputs will look the same. You will see examples of several of these documents in later chapters.

TABLE 3-3 Project initiation knowledge areas, processes, and outputs

Knowledge Area	Initiating Process	Outputs
Project Integration Management	Develop project charter	Project charter
Project Stakeholder Management	Identify stakeholders	Stakeholder register

Source: *PMBOK® Guide, Fifth Edition*, 2013.

Identifying Project Stakeholders Erica met with Joe Fleming, the project's sponsor, to help identify key stakeholders. Recall from Chapter 1 that stakeholders are people involved in project activities or affected by them, and include the project sponsor, project team, support staff, customers, users, suppliers, and even opponents to the project. Joe, the project sponsor, knew it would be important to assemble a strong project team, and he was confident in Erica's ability to lead that team. They decided that key team members should include one of their full-time consultants with an outstanding record, Michael Chen; one part-time consultant, Jessie Faue, who was new to the company and supported the Project Management Office; and two members of the IT department who supported the current intranet, Kevin Dodge and Cindy Dawson. They also knew that client inputs would be important, so Joe agreed to ask the CEOs of two of the firm's largest clients if they would be willing to provide representatives to work on this project at their own expense. All of the internal staff Joe and Erica recommended agreed to work on the project, and the two client representatives were Kim Phuong and Page Miller. Because many other people would be affected by this project as future users of the new intranet, Joe and Erica also identified other key stakeholders, including their directors of IT, Human Resources (HR), and Public Relations (PR), as well as Erica's administrative assistant.

After Joe and Erica made the preliminary contacts, Erica documented the stakeholders' roles, names, organizations, and contact information in a **stakeholder register**, a document that includes details related to the identified project stakeholders. Table 3-4 provides an example of part of the initial stakeholder register. Because this document would be public, Erica was careful not to include information that might be sensitive, such as how strongly the stakeholders supported the project and their potential influence on the project. She would keep these issues in mind discreetly and use them in developing the stakeholder management strategy.

TABLE 3-4 Stakeholder register

Name	Position	Internal/External	Project Role	Contact Information
Joe Fleming	CEO	Internal	Sponsor	joe_fleming@jwdconsulting.com
Erica Bell	PMO Director	Internal	Project manager	erica_bell@jwdconsulting.com
Michael Chen	Senior Consultant	Internal	Team member	michael_chen@jwdconsulting.com
Kim Phuong	Business Analyst	External	Advisor	kim_phuong@client1.com
Louise Mills	PR Director	Internal	Advisor	louise_mills@jwdconsulting.com

© Cengage Learning 2016

TABLE 3-5 Stakeholder management strategy

Name	Level of Interest	Level of Influence	Potential Management Strategies
Joe Fleming	High	High	Joe likes to stay on top of key projects and make money. Have a lot of short, face-to-face meetings and focus on achieving the financial benefits of the project.
Louise Mills	Low	High	Louise has a lot of things on her plate, and she does not seem excited about this project. She may be looking at other job opportunities. Show her how this project will help the company and her resume.

A stakeholder analysis is a technique that project managers can use to help understand and increase the support of stakeholders throughout the project. Results of the stakeholder analysis can be documented in a stakeholder register or in a separate stakeholder management strategy. This strategy includes basic information such as stakeholder names, level of interest in the project, level of influence on the project, and potential management strategies for gaining support or reducing obstacles from each stakeholder. Because much of this information can be sensitive, it should be considered confidential. Some project managers do not even write down this information, but they do consider it because stakeholder management is a crucial part of their jobs. Table 3-5 provides an example of part of Erica's stakeholder management strategy for the project management intranet site project. You will see other examples of documenting stakeholder information in later chapters.

Drafting the Project Charter Erica drafted a project charter and had the project team members review it before showing it to Joe. Joe made a few minor changes, which Erica incorporated. Table 3-6 shows the final project charter. (Charters can include more details than are shown in this example. See Chapter 4 for more information on project charters.) Note the items included in the project charter and its short length. JWD Consulting believes that project charters should be one or two pages long, and they may refer to other documents, such as a business case, as needed. Erica felt the most important parts of the project charter were the signatures of key stakeholders (not included for brevity) and their individual comments. It is hard to get stakeholders to agree on even a one-page project charter, so everyone has a chance to make their concerns known in the comments section. Note that Michael Chen, the senior consultant asked to work on the project, was concerned about participating when he felt that his other assignments with external clients might have a higher priority. He offered to have an assistant help as needed. The IT staff members mentioned their concerns about testing and security issues. Erica knew that she would have to address these concerns when managing the project.

TABLE 3-6 Project charter

Project Title: Project Management Intranet Site Project	
Project Start Date: May 2	**Projected Finish Date:** November 4

Budget Information: The firm has allocated $140,000 for this project. The majority of costs for this project will be internal labor. An initial estimate provides a total of 80 hours per week.

Project Manager: Erica Bell, (310) 555-5896, erica_bell@jwdconsulting.com

Project Objectives: Develop a new capability accessible on JWD Consulting's intranet site to help internal consultants and external customers manage projects more effectively. The intranet site will include several templates and tools that users can download, examples of completed templates and related project management documents used on real projects, important articles related to recent project management topics, an article retrieval service, links to other sites with useful information, and an Ask the Expert feature, where users can post questions about their projects and receive advice from experts in the field. Some parts of the intranet site will be accessible free to the public, other parts will only be accessible to current customers and internal consultants, and other parts will be accessible for a fee.

Main Project Success Criterion: The project should pay for itself within one year of completion.

Approach:

- Develop a survey to determine critical features of the new intranet site and solicit input from consultants and customers.
- Review internal and external templates and examples of project management documents.
- Research software to provide security, manage user inputs, and facilitate the article retrieval and Ask the Expert features.
- Develop the intranet site using an iterative approach, soliciting a great deal of user feedback.
- Develop a way to measure the value of the intranet site in terms of reduced costs and new revenues, both during the project and one year after project completion.

ROLES AND RESPONSIBILITIES (PARTIAL LIST)

Name	Role	Position	Contact Information
Joe Fleming	Sponsor	JWD Consulting, CEO	joe_fleming@jwdconsulting.com
Erica Bell	Project Manager	JWD Consulting, manager	erica_bell@jwdconsulting.com
Michael Chen	Team Member	JWD Consulting, senior consultant	michael_chen@jwdconsulting.com
Jessie Faue	Team Member	JWD Consulting, consultant	jessie_faue@jwdconsulting.com
Kevin Dodge	Team Member	JWD Consulting, IT department	kevin_dodge@jwdconsulting.com
Cindy Dawson	Team Member	JWD Consulting, IT department	cindy_dawson@jwdconsulting.com
Kim Phuong	Advisor	Client representative	kim_phuong@client1.com
Page Miller	Advisor	Client representative	page_miller@client2.com

Sign-Off: (Signatures of all the above stakeholders)

Comments: (Handwritten or typed comments from above stakeholders, if applicable)

"I will support this project as time allows, but I believe my client projects take priority. I will have one of my assistants support the project as needed."—Michael Chen

"We need to be extremely careful testing this new system, especially the security in giving access to parts of the intranet site to the public and clients."—Kevin Dodge and Cindy Dawson

Holding a Project Kick-Off Meeting Experienced project managers like Erica know that it is crucial to get projects off to a great start. Holding a good kick-off meeting is an excellent way to do this. A **kick-off meeting** is a meeting held at the beginning of a project so that stakeholders can meet each other, review the goals of the project, and discuss future plans. The kick-off meeting is often held after the business case and project charter are completed, but it could be held sooner, as needed. Even if some or all project stakeholders must meet virtually, it is still important to have a kick-off meeting.

Erica also knows that all project meetings with major stakeholders should include an agenda. Figure 3-2 shows the agenda that Erica provided for the project management intranet site project kick-off meeting. Notice the main topics in an agenda:

- Meeting objective
- Agenda (lists in order the topics to be discussed)
- A section for documenting action items, who they are assigned to, and when each person will complete the action
- A section to document the date and time of the next meeting

---

Kick-Off Meeting
[Date of Meeting]

Project Name: Project Management Intranet Site Project

Meeting Objective: Get the project off to an effective start by introducing key stakeholders, reviewing project goals, and discussing future plans

Agenda:
- Introductions of attendees
- Review of the project background
- Review of project-related documents (business case and project charter)
- Discussion of project organizational structure
- Discussion of project scope, time, and cost goals
- Discussion of other important topics
- List of action items from meeting

Action Item	Assigned To	Due Date

Date and time of next meeting:

© Cengage Learning 2016

FIGURE 3-2 Kick-off meeting agenda

It is good practice to focus on results of meetings, which is why a good agenda has sections for documenting action items and deciding on the next meeting date and time. It is also good practice to document meeting minutes, focusing on key decisions and action items. Erica planned to send the meeting minutes to all meeting participants and other appropriate stakeholders within a day or two after the meeting.

3.4d Project Planning

Planning is often the most difficult and unappreciated process in project management. Because planning is not always used to facilitate action, many people view planning negatively. The main purpose of project plans, however, is *to guide project execution*. To guide execution, plans must be realistic and useful, so a fair amount of time and effort must go into the planning process. People who are knowledgeable about the work need to plan the work. Chapter 4, Project Integration Management, provides detailed information on preparing a project management plan, and Chapters 5 through 13 describe planning processes for each of the other knowledge areas.

Table 3-7 lists the project management knowledge areas, processes, and outputs of project planning according to the *PMBOK® Guide, Fifth Edition*. If you plan to earn PMP or CAPM certification, it will be helpful to study this table and similar ones found in this chapter to understand the potential outputs of each process group. There are many potential outputs from the planning process group, and every knowledge area is included. Just a few planning documents from JWD Consulting's project management intranet site project are provided in this chapter as examples, and later chapters include many more examples.

Recall that the *PMBOK® Guide* is only a guide, so many organizations may have different planning outputs based on their particular needs, as is the case in this example. You can also use many templates for planning; several are listed in the last section of this chapter.

TABLE 3-7 Planning processes and outputs

Knowledge Area	Planning Process	Outputs
Project Integration Management	Develop project management plan	Project management plan
Project Scope Management	Plan scope management	Scope management plan Requirements management plan
	Collect requirements	Requirements documentation Requirements traceability matrix
	Define scope	Project scope statement Project documents updates
	Create WBS	Scope baseline Project documents updates
Project Time Management	Plan schedule management	Schedule management plan
	Define activities	Activity list Activity attributes Milestone list Project management plan updates

(continued)

TABLE 3-7 Planning processes and outputs (*continued*)

Knowledge Area	Planning Process	Outputs
	Sequence activities	Project schedule network diagrams Project documents updates
	Estimate activity resources	Activity resource requirements Resource breakdown structure Project documents updates
	Estimate activity durations	Activity duration estimates Project documents updates
	Develop schedule	Schedule baseline Project schedule Schedule data Project calendars Project management plan updates Project documents updates
Project Cost Management	Plan cost management	Cost management plan
	Estimate costs	Activity cost estimates Basis of estimates Project documents updates
	Determine budget	Cost baseline Project funding requirements Project documents updates
Project Quality Management	Plan quality management	Quality management plan Process improvement plan Quality metrics Quality checklists Project documents updates
Project Human Resource Management	Plan human resource management	Human resource plan
Project Communications Management	Plan communications management	Communications management plan Project documents updates
Project Risk Management	Plan risk management	Risk management plan
	Identify risks	Risk register
	Perform qualitative risk analysis	Project documents updates
	Perform quantitative risk analysis	Project documents updates
	Plan risk responses	Project management plan updates Project documents updates
Project Procurement Management	Plan procurement management	Procurement management plan Procurement statement of work Procurement documents Source selection criteria Make-or-buy decisions Change requests
Project Stakeholder Management	Plan stakeholder management	Stakeholder management plan Project documents updates

Source: *PMBOK® Guide, Fifth Edition*, 2013.

Because the project management intranet site project is relatively small, Erica believes some of the most important planning documents to focus on are the following:

- A team contract (not listed in Table 3-7, which is based only on the *PMBOK®️ Guide*)
- A project scope statement
- A work breakdown structure (WBS), a key part of the scope baseline
- A project schedule, in the form of a Gantt chart with all dependencies and resources entered
- A list of prioritized risks (part of a risk register)

All of these documents, as well as other project-related information, will be available to all team members on a project website. JWD Consulting has used project websites for several years, and has found that they help facilitate communications and document project information. For larger projects, JWD Consulting also creates many of the other outputs listed in Table 3-7. (You will learn more about these documents by knowledge area in the following chapters.)

Soon after the project team signed the project charter, Erica organized a team-building meeting. An important goal of the meeting was helping the project team members get to know each other. Erica had met and talked to each member separately, but this was the first time the project team would spend much time together. Jessie Faue worked in the Project Management Office with Erica, so they knew each other well, but Jessie was new to the company and did not know any of the other team members. Michael Chen was a senior consultant and often worked on the highest-priority projects for external clients. He attended the meeting with his assistant, Jill Anderson, who would support the project when Michael was too busy. Everyone valued Michael's expertise, and he was extremely straightforward in dealing with people. He also knew both of the client representatives from past projects. Kevin Dodge was JWD Consulting's intranet guru, who tended to focus on technical details. Cindy Dawson was also from the IT department and had experience working as a business consultant and negotiating with outside suppliers. Kim Phuong and Page Miller, the two client representatives, were excited about the project, but they were wary of sharing sensitive information about their companies.

Erica knew that it was important to build a strong team and have everyone work well together. She had all participants introduce themselves, and then she led an icebreaking activity so everyone would be more relaxed. She asked all participants to describe their dream vacations, assuming that cost was no issue. This activity helped everyone get to know each other and show different aspects of their personalities.

Erica then explained the importance of the project, again reviewing the signed project charter. She explained that an important tool to help a project team work together was to have members develop a team contract that everyone felt comfortable signing. JWD Consulting believed in using team contracts for all projects to help promote teamwork and clarify team communications. She explained the main topics covered in a team contract and showed them a team contract template. She then had the team members form two smaller groups, with one consultant, one IT department member, and one client representative in each group. These smaller groups made it easier for everyone to contribute ideas. Each group shared its ideas for what should go into the contract, and then everyone worked together to form one project team contract.

TABLE 3-8   Team Contract

Code of Conduct: As a project team, we will:

- Work proactively, anticipating potential problems and working to prevent them.
- Keep other team members informed of information related to the project.
- Focus on what is best for the entire project team.

Participation: We will:

- Be honest and open during all project activities.
- Encourage diversity in team work.
- Provide the opportunity for equal participation.
- Be open to new approaches and consider new ideas.
- Have one discussion at a time.
- Let the project manager know well in advance if a team member has to miss a meeting or may have trouble meeting a deadline for a given task.

Communication: We will:

- Decide as a team on the best way to communicate. Because a few team members cannot often meet face to face, we will use e-mail, a project website, and other technology to assist in communicating.
- Have the project manager facilitate all meetings and arrange for phone and video conferences, as needed.
- Work together to create the project schedule and enter actuals into the enterprise-wide project management system by 4 p.m. every Friday.
- Present ideas clearly and concisely.
- Keep discussions on track.

Problem Solving: We will:

- Encourage everyone to participate in solving problems.
- Only use constructive criticism and focus on solving problems, not blaming people.
- Strive to build on each other's ideas.

Meeting Guidelines: We will:

- Have a face-to-face meeting the first and third Tuesday morning of every month.
- Meet more frequently the first month.
- Hold other meetings as needed.
- Record meeting minutes and send them via e-mail within 24 hours of all project meetings, focusing on decisions made and action items from each meeting.

© Cengage Learning 2016

Table 3-8 shows the resulting team contract, which took about 90 minutes to create. Erica could see that there were different personalities on this team, but she felt they all could work together well.

Erica wanted to keep the team-building meeting to its two-hour time limit. The next task would be to clarify the scope of the project by developing a project scope statement and WBS. She knew it would take time and several future meetings to develop these documents, but she wanted to get a feel for what everyone thought were the main deliverables for this project, their roles in producing those deliverables, and what areas of the project scope needed clarification. She reminded everyone what their budget and schedule goals were so they would keep the goals in mind as they discussed the scope of the project.

She also asked each person to provide the number of hours he or she would be available to work on this project each month for the next six months. She then had each person write answers to the following questions:

1. List one item that is most unclear to you about the scope of this project.
2. What other questions do you have or issues do you foresee about the scope of the project?
3. List what you believe to be the main deliverables for this project.
4. Which deliverables do you think you will help create or review?

Erica collected everyone's inputs. She explained that she would take this information and work with Jessie to develop the first draft of the scope statement that she would e-mail to everyone by the end of the week. She also suggested that they all meet again in one week to develop the scope statement further and to start creating the WBS for the project.

Erica and Jessie reviewed all the information and created the first draft of the scope statement. At their next team meeting, they discussed the scope statement and got a good start on the WBS. Table 3-9 shows a portion of the scope statement that Erica created after a few more e-mails and another team meeting. Note that the scope statement lists the product characteristics and requirements, summarizes the deliverables, and describes project success criteria in detail.

TABLE 3-9 Scope statement draft

Project Title: Project Management Intranet Site Project
Date: May 18   **Prepared by:** Erica Bell, Project Manager, erica_bell@jwdconsulting.com
Project Summary and Justification: Joe Fleming, CEO of JWD Consulting, requested this project to assist the company in meeting its strategic goals. The new intranet site will increase visibility of the company's expertise to current and potential clients. It will also help reduce internal costs and improve profitability by providing standard tools, techniques, templates, and project management knowledge to all internal consultants. The budget for the project is $140,000. An additional $40,000 per year will be required for operational expenses after the project is completed. Estimated benefits are $200,000 each year. It is important to focus on the system paying for itself within one year of its completion.
Product Characteristics and Requirements:

1. Templates and tools: The intranet site will allow authorized users to download files they can use to create project management documents and to help them use project management tools. These files will be in Microsoft Word, Excel, Access, Project, or in HTML or PDF format, as appropriate.
2. User submissions: Users will be encouraged to e-mail files with sample templates and tools to the Webmaster. The Webmaster will forward the files to the appropriate person for review and then post the files to the intranet site, if desired.
3. Articles: Articles posted on the intranet site will have appropriate copyright permission. The preferred format for articles will be PDF. The project manager may approve other formats.
4. Requests for articles: The intranet site will include a section for users to ask someone from the Project Management Office (PMO) at JWD Consulting to research appropriate articles for them. The PMO manager must first approve the request and negotiate payments, if appropriate.
5. Links: All links to external sites will be tested on a weekly basis. Broken links will be fixed or removed within five working days of discovery.
6. The Ask the Expert feature must be user-friendly and capable of soliciting questions and immediately acknowledging that the question has been received in the proper format. The feature must also be capable of forwarding the question to the appropriate expert (as maintained in the system's expert database) and capable of providing the status of questions that are answered. The system must also allow for payment for advice, if appropriate.

(continued)

TABLE 3-9 Scope statement draft (*continued*)

7. Security: The intranet site must provide several levels of security. All internal employees will have access to the entire intranet site when they enter their security information to access the main, corporate intranet. Part of the intranet will be available to the public from the corporate website. Other portions of the intranet will be available to current clients based on verification with the current client database. Other portions of the intranet will be available after negotiating a fee or entering a fixed payment using pre-authorized payment methods.

8. Search feature: The intranet site must include a search feature for users to search by topic and key words.

9. The intranet site must be accessible using a company-approved Internet browser. Users must have appropriate application software to open several of the templates and tools.

10. The intranet site must be available 24 hours a day, 7 days a week, with one hour per week for system maintenance and other periodic maintenance, as appropriate.

Summary of Project Deliverables

Project management-related deliverables: Business case, charter, team contract, scope statement, WBS, schedule, cost baseline, progress reports, final project presentation, final project report, lessons-learned report, and any other documents required to manage the project.

Product-related deliverables:

1. Survey: Survey current consultants and clients to help determine desired content and features for the intranet site.

2. Files for templates: The intranet site will include templates for at least 20 documents when the system is first implemented, and it will have the capacity to store up to 100 documents. The project team will decide on the initial 20 templates based on survey results.

3. Examples of completed templates: The intranet site will include examples of projects that have used the templates available on the site. For example, if there is a template for a business case, there will also be an example of a real business case that uses the template.

4. Instructions for using project management tools: The intranet site will include information on how to use several project management tools, including the following as a minimum: work breakdown structures, Gantt charts, network diagrams, cost estimates, and earned value management. Where appropriate, sample files will be provided in the application software appropriate for the tool. For example, Microsoft Project files will be available to show sample work breakdown structures, Gantt charts, network diagrams, cost estimates, and applications of earned value management. Excel files will be available for sample cost estimates and earned value management charts.

5. Example applications of tools: The intranet site will include examples of real projects that have applied the tools listed in number 4.

6. Articles: The intranet site will include at least 10 useful articles about relevant topics in project management. The intranet site will have the capacity to store at least 1,000 articles in PDF format with an average length of 10 pages each.

7. Links: The intranet site will include links with brief descriptions for at least 20 useful sites. The links will be categorized into meaningful groups.

8. Expert database: In order to deliver an Ask the Expert feature, the system must include and access a database of approved experts and their contact information. Users will be able to search for experts by predefined topics.

9. User Requests feature: The intranet site will include an application to solicit and process requests from users.

10. Intranet site design: An initial design of the new intranet site will include a site map, suggested formats, and appropriate graphics. The final design will incorporate comments from users on the initial design.

11. Intranet site content: The intranet site will include content for the templates and tools sections, articles section, article retrieval section, links section, Ask the Expert section, User Requests feature, security, and payment features.

12. Test plan: The test plan will document how the intranet site will be tested, who will do the testing, and how bugs will be reported.

(continued)

TABLE 3-9 Scope statement draft (*continued*)

13. Promotion: A plan for promoting the intranet site internally and externally will describe various approaches for soliciting inputs during design. The promotion plan will also announce the availability of the new intranet site.

14. Project benefit measurement plan: A project benefit plan will measure the financial value of the intranet site.

Project Success Criteria: Our goal is to complete this project within six months for no more than $140,000. The project sponsor, Joe Fleming, has emphasized the importance of the project paying for itself within one year after the site is complete. To meet this financial goal, the intranet site must have strong user inputs. We must also develop a method for capturing the benefits while the intranet site is being developed and tested, and after it is rolled out. If the project takes a little longer to complete or costs a little more than planned, the firm will still view it as a success if it has a good payback and helps promote the firm's image as an excellent consulting organization.

© Cengage Learning 2016

As the project team worked on the scope statement, it also developed the work breakdown structure (WBS) for the project. The WBS is a very important tool in project management because it provides the basis for deciding how to do the work. The WBS also provides a basis for creating the project schedule and for measuring and forecasting project performance. Erica and her team decided to use the project management process groups as the main categories for the WBS, as shown in Figure 3-3. They included completed work from the initiating process to provide a complete picture of the project's scope. The team members also wanted to list several milestones on their schedule, such as the completion of key deliverables, so they prepared a separate list of milestones that they would include on the Gantt chart. You will learn more about creating a WBS in Chapter 5, Project Scope Management.

After preparing the WBS, the project team held another face-to-face meeting to develop the project schedule, following the steps outlined in Section 2.5 of the WBS. Several of the project schedule tasks are dependent on one another. For example, the intranet site testing was dependent on the construction and completion of the content tasks. Everyone participated in the development of the schedule, especially the tasks on which each member would be working. Some of the tasks were broken down further so the team members had a better understanding of what they had to do and when. They also kept their workloads and cost constraints in mind when developing the duration estimates. For example, Erica was scheduled to work 20 hours per week on this project, and the other project team members combined should not spend more than 60 hours per week on average for the project. As team members provided duration estimates, they also estimated how many work hours they would spend on each task.

After the meeting, Erica worked with Jessie to enter all of the information into Microsoft Project. Erica was using the intranet site project to train Jessie in applying several project management tools and templates. They entered all of the tasks, duration estimates, and dependencies to develop the Gantt chart. Their initial inputs resulted in a completion date that was a few weeks later than planned. Erica and Jessie reviewed the critical path for the project, and Erica had to shorten the duration estimates for a few critical tasks to meet their schedule goal of completing the project within six months. She talked to the team members working on those tasks, and they agreed that they could plan

1.0 Initiating
    1.1 Identify key stakeholders
    1.2 Prepare project charter
    1.3 Hold project kick-off meeting
2.0 Planning
    2.1 Hold team planning meeting
    2.2 Prepare team contract
    2.3 Prepare scope statement
    2.4 Prepare WBS
    2.5 Prepare schedule and cost baseline
        2.5.1 Determine task resources
        2.5.2 Determine task durations
        2.5.3 Determine task dependencies
        2.5.4 Create draft Gantt chart
        2.5.5 Review and finalize Gantt chart
    2.6 Identify, discuss, and prioritize risks
3.0 Executing
    3.1 Survey
    3.2 User inputs
    3.3 Intranet site content
        3.3.1 Templates and tools
        3.3.2 Articles
        3.3.3 Links
        3.3.4 Ask the Expert
        3.3.5 User requests feature
    3.4 Intranet site design
    3.5 Intranet site construction
    3.6 Intranet site testing
    3.7 Intranet site promotion
    3.8 Intranet site roll-out
    3.9 Project benefits measurement
4.0 Monitoring and Controlling
    4.1 Progress reports
    4.2 Change requests
5.0 Closing
    5.1 Prepare final project report
    5.2 Prepare final project presentation
    5.3 Lessons learned

FIGURE 3-3   JWD Consulting intranet project work breakdown structure (WBS)

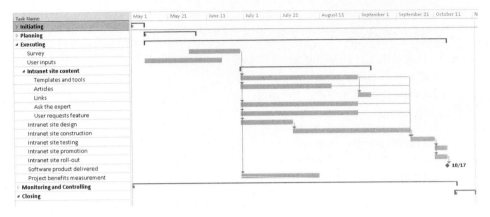

© Cengage Learning 2016

FIGURE 3-4   JWD Consulting intranet site project baseline Gantt chart

to work more hours each week on those tasks, if required, to complete them on time. Figure 3-4 shows the resulting Gantt chart created in Microsoft Project. Only the executing tasks are expanded to show the subtasks under that category. (You will learn how to use Project 2013 in Appendix A. Chapter 6, Project Time Management, explains Gantt charts and other time management tools.)

The baseline schedule projects a completion date of November 1. Also notice that there is only one delivery of the software, shown as a milestone near the end of the project, on October 17. The project charter had a planned completion date of November 4. Erica wanted to complete the project on time, and although three extra days was not much of a buffer, she felt the baseline schedule was realistic. She would do her best to help everyone meet their deadlines.

Erica decided to enter the resource and cost information after reviewing the schedule because the majority of the costs for this project were internal labor. Aware of the connection between time spent and cost on the project, the team kept its labor hour constraints in mind when developing task duration estimates. Erica and Jessie entered each project team member's name and labor rate in the resource sheet for their Microsoft Project file. The client representatives were not being paid for their time, so she left their labor rates at the default value of zero. Erica had also included $10,000 for procurement in the financial analysis she prepared for the business case. She showed Jessie how to enter that amount as a fixed cost split equally between the Ask the Expert and User Requests features, because she thought they would have to purchase external software and services for those. Erica then helped Jessie assign resources to tasks, which involved entering the projected number of hours everyone planned to work each week on each task. They then ran several cost reports and made a few minor adjustments to resource assignments to make their planned total cost meet their budget constraints. Their cost baseline was very close to their planned budget of $140,000.

TABLE 3-10 List of prioritized risks

Ranking	Potential Risk
1	Lack of inputs from internal consultants
2	Lack of inputs from client representatives
3	Security of new system
4	Outsourcing/purchasing for the article retrieval and Ask the Expert features
5	Outsourcing/purchasing for processing online payment transactions
6	Organizing the templates and examples in a useful fashion
7	Providing an efficient search feature
8	Getting good feedback from Michael Chen and other senior consultants
9	Effectively promoting the new system
10	Realizing the benefits of the new system within one year

© Cengage Learning 2016

The last deliverable her team needed to create within the planning process group was a list of prioritized risks. As the project progresses, this information will be updated and expanded in a risk register, which also includes information on root causes of the risks, warning signs that potential risks might occur, and response strategies for the risks. (See Chapter 11, Project Risk Management, for more information on risk registers.) Erica reviewed the risks she had mentioned in the business case as well as the comments team members made on the project charter and in their team meetings. She held a special meeting for everyone to brainstorm and discuss potential risks. They listed all of the risks they identified and then categorized them to analyze how likely (high, medium, or low probability) each was and how big an impact (high, medium, or low) each could have. Only one risk was in the high probability and high impact category, and several had medium impact. They chose not to list the low-probability and low-impact risks. After some discussion, the team developed the list of prioritized risks shown in Table 3-10.

3.4e Project Execution

Executing the project involves taking the necessary actions to complete the activities in the project plan. The products of the project are created during project execution, and it usually takes the most resources to accomplish this process. Table 3-11 lists the knowledge areas, executing processes, and outputs of project execution from the *PMBOK® Guide, Fifth Edition.*

Many project sponsors and customers focus on deliverables related to providing the products, services, or results desired from the project. However, it is equally important to document change requests and update planning documents as part of execution. Templates related to this process group are listed later in this chapter.

TABLE 3-11 Executing processes and outputs

Knowledge Area	Executing Process	Outputs
Project Integration Management	Direct and manage project work	Deliverables Work performance data Change requests Project management plan updates Project documents updates
Project Quality Management	Perform quality assurance	Change requests Project management plan updates Project documents updates Organizational process assets updates
Project Human Resource Management	Acquire project team	Project staff assignments Resource calendars Project management plan updates
	Develop project team	Team performance assessments Enterprise environmental factor updates
	Manage project team	Change requests Project management plan updates Project documents updates Enterprise environmental factors updates Organizational process assets updates
Project Communications Management	Manage communications	Project communications Project documents updates Project management plan updates Organizational process assets updates
Project Procurement Management	Conduct procurements	Selected sellers Agreements Resource calendars Change requests Project management plan updates Project documents updates
Project Stakeholder Management	Manage stakeholder engagement	Issue log Change requests Project management plan updates Project documents updates Organizational process assets updates

Source: *PMBOK® Guide, Fifth Edition, 2013.*

Erica knew that providing strong leadership and using good communication skills were crucial to good project execution. For this relatively small project, she was able to work closely with all the team members to make sure they were producing the desired work results. She also used her networking skills to get input from other people in the firm and from external sources at no additional cost to the project. She made sure that everyone who would use the resulting intranet application understood what the team was producing as part of the project and how the intranet application would help them in the future.

Erica also knew that working efficiently was critical for successful execution, regardless of the size of the project. Therefore, she used resources throughout the company when they were available. For example, she used the firm's formal change request form, even though it had primarily been used for external projects. The firm also had contract specialists and templates for several procurement documents that the project team members would use for the portions of the project it planned to outsource.

Erica kept in mind that Joe, the CEO and project sponsor, liked to see progress on projects through milestone reports. He also wanted Erica to alert him to any potential issues or problems. Erica met with most of her project team members often, and she talked to Joe about once a week to review progress on completing milestones and to discuss any other project issues. Although Erica could have used project management software to create milestone reports, she used word-processing software instead because this project was small and she could more easily manipulate the report format. Table 3-12 shows a sample of a milestone report for the project management intranet site project that Erica reviewed with Joe in mid-June.

TABLE 3-12   Milestone report as of June 17

Milestone	Date	Status	Responsible	Issues/Comments
Initiating				
Stakeholders identified	May 2	Completed	Erica and Joe	
Project charter signed	May 10	Completed	Erica	
Project kick-off meeting held	May 13	Completed	Erica	Went very well
Planning				
Team contract signed	May 13	Completed	Erica	
Scope statement completed	May 27	Completed	Erica	
WBS completed	May 31	Completed	Erica	
List of prioritized risks completed	June 3	Completed	Erica	Reviewed with sponsor and team
Schedule and cost baseline completed	June 13	Completed	Erica	
Executing				Poor response so far!
Survey and analysis completed	June 28		Erica	
Intranet site design completed	July 26		Kevin	
Project benefits measurement completed	August 9		Erica	
User inputs collected	August 9		Jessie	
Articles completed	August 23		Jessie	
Templates and tools completed	September 6		Erica	
Ask the Expert completed	September 6		Michael	
User Requests feature completed	September 6		Cindy	
Links completed	September 13		Kevin	
Intranet site construction completed	October 4		Kevin	
Intranet site testing completed	October 18		Cindy	

(continued)

TABLE 3-12 Milestone report as of June 17 (*continued*)

Milestone	Date	Status	Responsible	Issues/Comments
Intranet site promotion completed	October 25		Erica	
Intranet site roll-out completed	October 25		Kevin	
Monitoring and Controlling				
Progress reports	Every Friday		All	
Closing				
Final project presentation completed	October 27		Erica	
Sponsor sign-off on project completed	October 27		Joe	
Final project report completed	October 28		Erica	
Lessons-learned reports submitted	November 1		All	

© Cengage Learning 2016

Human resource issues often occur during project execution, especially conflicts. At several of the team meetings, Erica could see that Michael seemed to be bored and often left the room to make phone calls to clients. She talked to Michael about the situation, and she discovered that Michael was supportive of the project, but he knew he could only spend a minimal amount of time on it. He was much more productive outside of meetings, so Erica agreed to have Michael attend a minimal number of project team meetings. She could see that Michael was contributing to the team by the feedback he provided and his leadership on the Ask the Expert feature for the intranet site. Erica adjusted her communication style to meet his specific needs.

Another problem occurred when Cindy was contacting potential suppliers for software to help with the Ask the Expert and User Requests features. Kevin wanted to write all of the software for the project himself, but Cindy knew it made better business sense to purchase these new software capabilities from a reliable source. Cindy had to convince Kevin that it was worth buying some software from other sources.

Cindy also discovered that their estimate of $10,000 was only about half the amount they needed for software services. She discussed the problem with Erica, explaining the need for some custom development no matter which supplier they chose. Erica agreed that they should go with an outside source, and she asked their sponsor to approve the additional funds. Joe agreed, but he stressed the importance of still having the system pay for itself within a year.

Even near the beginning of the project, Erica had tapped Joe for help when the team received a low response rate to their survey and requests for user inputs. Joe sent an e-mail to all of JWD Consulting's consultants describing the importance of the project. He also offered five extra vacation days to the person who provided the best examples of how they used tools and templates to manage their projects. Erica then received informative input from the consultants. Having effective communication skills and strong top management support are essential to good project execution.

BEST PRACTICE

One way to learn about best practices in project management is by studying recipients of PMI's Project of the Year award. The Quartier International de Montréal (QIM), Montreal's international district, was a 66-acre urban revitalization project in the heart of downtown Montreal. This $90 million, five-year project turned a once un-popular area into a thriving section of the city with a booming real estate market, and has generated $770 million in related construction. Clement Demers, PMP, was the director general for the QIM project. He said the team "took a unique project execution approach by dividing work into packages that allowed for smaller-scale testing of management techniques and contract awards. Benefiting from experience gained in each stage, managers could then adjust future work segments and management styles accordingly."[11]

Other strategies that helped the team succeed included the following:

- The team identified champions in each stakeholder group to help inspire others to achieve project goals.
- The team's communications plan included a website dedicated to public concerns.
- There were two-day reviews at the beginning of each project phase to discuss problems and develop solutions to prevent conflict.
- Financial investors were asked for input to increase their stake in the project.
- The team recognized the value of hiring high-quality experts, such as architects, engineers, lawyers, and urban planners. They paid all professionals a fixed price for their services and paid their fees quickly.
- Another Canadian firm won the Project of the Year award in 2014. The CA $1.3 billion AP60 Phase 1 Project produced an upgraded aluminum smelting facility in Jonquiere, Quebec. In 2013, the Adelaide desalination project in Adelaide, Australia, won the award. This project, which supplies water during times of drought, was completed early and within 1 percent of its AU$1.4 billion budget.[12] The 2012 award went to a high-risk chemical agent disposal project in Hermiston, Oregon, which was completed ahead of schedule, under budget, and with a low injury rate that was striking given the deadly nature of the chemicals involved.[13] See PMI's website for more information on award criteria and winners.

3.4f Project Monitoring and Controlling

Monitoring and controlling is the process of measuring progress toward project objectives, monitoring deviation from the current plan, and taking corrective action to match progress with the current plan. Monitoring and controlling is done throughout the life of a project and involves 9 of the 10 project management knowledge areas. Table 3-13 lists the knowledge areas, monitoring and controlling processes, and outputs, according to the *PMBOK® Guide, Fifth Edition*. Templates related to this process group are listed later in this chapter.

TABLE 3-13 Monitoring and controlling processes and outputs

Knowledge Area	Monitoring and Controlling Process	Outputs
Project Integration Management	Monitor and control project work	Change requests Work performance reports Project management plan updates Project documents updates
	Perform integrated change control	Approved change requests Change log Project management plan updates Project documents updates
Project Scope Management	Validate scope	Accepted deliverables Change requests Work performance information Project documents updates
	Control scope	Work performance information Change requests Project management plan updates Project documents updates Organizational process assets updates
Project Time Management	Control schedule	Work performance information Schedule forecasts Change requests Project management plan updates Project documents updates Organizational process assets updates
Project Cost Management	Control cost	Work performance information Cost forecasts Change requests Project management plan updates Project documents updates Organizational process assets updates
Project Quality Management	Control quality	Quality control measurements Validated changes Validated deliverables Work performance information Change requests Project management plan updates Project documents updates Organizational process assets updates
Project Communications Management	Control communications	Work performance information Change requests Project documents updates Organizational process assets updates
Project Risk Management	Control risks	Work performance information Change requests Project management plan updates Project documents updates Organizational process assets updates

(continued)

TABLE 3-13   Monitoring and controlling processes and outputs (*continued*)

Knowledge Area	Monitoring and Controlling Process	Outputs
Project Procurement Management	Control procurements	Work performance information Change requests Project management plan updates Project documents updates Organizational process assets updates
Project Stakeholder Management	Control stakeholder engagement	Work performance information Change requests Project documents updates Organizational process assets updates

Source: *PMBOK® Guide, Fifth Edition*, 2013.

On the project management intranet site project, several updates to the project management plan were made to reflect changes made to the project scope, schedule, and budget. Erica and other project team members took corrective action when necessary. For example, when they were not getting many responses to their survey, Erica asked Joe for help. When Cindy had trouble negotiating with a supplier, she got help from another senior consultant who had worked with that supplier in the past. Erica also had to request more funds for that part of the project.

Project team members submitted a brief progress report every Friday to show work performance information. They were originally using a company template for progress reports, but Erica found that by modifying the old template, she received better information, which then helped her team work more effectively. She wanted team members not only to report what they did but also to focus on what was going well or not going well, and why. This extra information helped team members reflect on the project's progress and identify areas in need of improvement. Table 3-14 is an example of one of Cindy's progress reports.

TABLE 3-14   Sample weekly progress report

Project Name: Project Management Intranet Project

Team Member Name: Cindy Dawson, cindy_dawson@jwdconsulting.com

Date: August 5

Work completed this week:

–Worked with Kevin to start the intranet site construction
–Organized all the content files
–Started developing a file naming scheme for content files
–Continued work on Ask the Expert and User Requests features
–Met with preferred supplier
–Verified that their software would meet our needs
–Discovered the need for some customization

Work to complete next week:

–Continue work on intranet site construction
–Prepare draft contract for preferred supplier
–Develop new cost estimate for outsourced work

(continued)

TABLE 3-14 Sample weekly progress report *(continued)*

What's going well and why:
The intranet site construction started well. The design was very clear and easy to follow. Kevin really knows what he's doing.
What's not going well and why:
It is difficult to decide how to organize the templates and examples. Need more input from senior consultants and clients.
Suggestions/Issues:
–Hold a special meeting to decide how to organize the templates and examples on the intranet site.   –Get some sample contracts and help in negotiating with the preferred supplier.
Project changes:
I think we can stay on schedule, but it looks like we'll need about $10,000 more for outsourcing. That's doubling our budget in that area.

© Cengage Learning 2016

In addition to progress reports, an important tool for monitoring and controlling the project was using project management software. All team members submitted their actual hours worked on tasks each Friday afternoon by 4 p.m. via the firm's enterprise-wide project management software. They were using the enterprise version of Microsoft Project 2013, so they could easily update their task information via the Web. Erica worked with Jessie to analyze the information, paying special attention to the critical path and earned value data. (See Chapter 6, Project Time Management, for more information on critical path analysis; Chapter 7, Project Cost Management, for a description of earned value management; and Appendix A for more information on using Project 2013 to help control projects.) Erica wanted to finish the project on time, even if it meant spending more money. Joe agreed with that approach, and approved the additional funding Erica projected they would need based on the earned value projections and the need to make up a little time on critical tasks.

Joe again emphasized the importance of the new system paying for itself within a year. Erica was confident that they could exceed the projected financial benefits, and she decided to begin capturing benefits as soon as the project team began testing the system. When she was not working on this project, Erica was managing JWD Consulting's Project Management Office (PMO), and she could already see how the intranet site would help her staff save time and make their consultants more productive. One of her staff members wanted to move into the consulting group, and she believed the PMO could continue to provide its current services with one less person due to this new system—a benefit Erica had not considered before. Several of the firm's client contracts were based on performance and not hours billed, so she was excited to start measuring the value of the new intranet site to their consultants as well.

3.4g Project Closing

The closing process involves gaining stakeholder and customer acceptance of the final products and services and then bringing the project or project phase to an orderly end. It includes verifying that all of the deliverables are complete, and it often includes a

TABLE 3-15   Closing processes and output

Knowledge Area	Closing Process	Outputs
Project Integration Management	Close project or phase	Final product, service, or result transition Organizational process assets updates
Project Procurement Management	Close procurements	Closed procurements Organizational process assets updates

Source: *PMBOK® Guide, Fifth Edition*, 2013.

final project report and presentation. Even though many IT projects are canceled before completion, it is still important to formally close any project and reflect on what can be learned to improve future projects. As philosopher George Santayana said, "Those who cannot remember the past are condemned to repeat it."[14]

It is also important to plan for and execute a smooth transition of the project into the normal operations of the company. Most projects produce results that are integrated into the existing organizational structure. For example, JWD Consulting's project management intranet site project will require staff to support the intranet site after it is operational. Erica included support costs of $40,000 per year for the projected three-year life of the new system. She also created a transition plan as part of the final report to provide for a smooth transition of the system into the firm's operations. The plan included a list of issues that had to be resolved before the firm could put the new intranet site into production. For example, Michael Chen would not be available to work on the intranet site after the six-month project was complete, so the team had to know who would support the Ask the Expert feature and plan some time for Michael to work with that person.

Table 3-15 lists the knowledge areas, processes, and outputs of project closing based on the *PMBOK® Guide, Fifth Edition*. During the closing processes of any project, project team members must deliver the final product, service, or result of the project and update organizational process assets, such as project files and a lessons-learned report. If project team members procured items during the project, they must formally complete or close out all contracts. Templates related to project closing are listed later in this chapter.

Erica and her team prepared a final report, final presentation, contract files, and lessons-learned report in closing the project. Erica reviewed the confidential, individual lessons-learned reports from each team member and wrote one summary lessons-learned report to include in the final documentation, part of which is provided in Table 3-16. Notice the bulleted items in the fourth question, such as the importance of having a good kick-off meeting, working together to develop a team contract, using project management software, and communicating well with the project team and sponsor.

Erica also had Joe sign a client acceptance form, one of the sample templates on the new intranet site that the project team suggested all consultants use when closing their projects. (You can find this and other templates on the companion website for this text.)

TABLE 3-16 Lessons-learned report (abbreviated)

Project Name:	JWD Consulting Project Management Intranet Site Project
Project Sponsor:	Joe Fleming
Project Manager:	Erica Bell
Project Dates:	May 2 – November 4
Final Budget:	$150,000

1. Did the project meet scope, time, and cost goals?

   We did meet scope and time goals, but we had to request an additional $10,000, which the sponsor approved.

2. What were the success criteria listed in the project scope statement?

   Below is what we put in our project scope statement under project success criteria:

   "Our goal is to complete this project within six months for no more than $140,000. The project sponsor, Joe Fleming, has emphasized the importance of the project paying for itself within one year after the intranet site is complete. To meet this financial goal, the intranet site must have strong user input. We must also develop a method for capturing the benefits while the intranet site is being developed and tested, and after it is rolled out. If the project takes a little longer to complete or costs a little more than planned, the firm will still view it as a success if it has a good payback and helps promote the firm's image as an excellent consulting organization."

3. Reflect on whether you met the project success criteria.

   As stated above, the sponsor was not too concerned about going over budget as long as the system would have a good payback period and help promote our firm's image. We have already documented some financial and image benefits of the new intranet site. For example, we have decided that we can staff the PMO with one less person, resulting in substantial cost savings. We have also received excellent feedback from several of our clients about the new intranet site.

4. What were the main lessons your team learned from managing this project?

   The main lessons we learned include the following:

   - *Having a good project sponsor was instrumental to project success. We ran into a couple of difficult situations, and Joe was very creative in helping us solve problems.*
   - *Teamwork was essential. It really helped to take time for everyone to get to know each other at the kick-off meeting. It was also helpful to develop and follow a team contract.*
   - *Good planning paid off in execution. We spent a fair amount of time developing a good project charter, scope statement, WBS, schedules, and so on. Everyone worked together to develop these planning documents, and there was strong buy-in.*
   - *Project management software was very helpful throughout the project.*

5. Describe one example of what went right on this project.

6. Describe one example of what went wrong on this project.

7. What will you do differently on the next project based on your experience working on this project?

© Cengage Learning 2016

Table 3-17 provides the table of contents for the final project report. The cover page included the project title, date, and team member names. Notice the inclusion of a transition plan and a plan to analyze the benefits of the system each year in the final report. Also, notice that the final report includes attachments for all the project management and product-related documents. Erica knew how important it was to provide good final documentation on projects. The project team produced a hard copy of the final

TABLE 3-17   Final project report table of contents

1. Project Objectives
2. Summary of Project Results
3. Original and Actual Start and End Dates
4. Original and Actual Budget
5. Project Assessment (Why did you do this project? What did you produce? Was the project a success? What went right and wrong on the project?)
6. Transition Plan
7. Annual Project Benefits Measurement Approach

Attachments:

A Project Management Documentation

- Business case
- Project charter
- Team contract
- Scope statement
- WBS and WBS dictionary
- Baseline and actual Gantt chart
- List of prioritized risks
- Milestone reports
- Progress reports
- Contract files
- Lessons-learned reports
- Final presentation
- Client acceptance form

B Product-Related Documentation

- Survey and results
- Summary of user inputs
- Intranet site content
- Intranet site design documents
- Test plans and reports
- Intranet site promotion information
- Intranet site roll-out information
- Project benefits measurement information

© Cengage Learning 2016

documentation and an electronic copy to store on the new intranet site for other consultants to use as desired.

Erica also organized a project closure luncheon for the project team right after the final project presentation. She used the luncheon to share lessons learned and celebrate a job well done.

3.5 CASE STUDY 2: JWD CONSULTING'S PROJECT MANAGEMENT INTRANET SITE PROJECT (AGILE APPROACH)

This section demonstrates an agile approach to managing JWD Consulting's project management intranet site project. Instead of repeating the sample documents shown in the first, predictive case study, this section emphasizes the differences of using an agile approach in each process group. Recall that an agile approach is often used for projects in which the business team cannot clearly express the scope early in the product life cycle, but the team wants to provide a potentially shippable product earlier rather than later. An agile project team typically uses several iterations or deliveries of software instead of waiting until the end of the project to provide one product.

Note that teams do not normally make a snap decision about whether to manage a project using an agile approach or not. Likewise, you don't just decide whether to take a plane or a car on a long trip without specific logic. If you need to get somewhere quickly, have little concern for sightseeing along the way, and have no problems with flying, you will probably take a plane. If you want to take your time getting somewhere, see sights along the way, and enjoy driving, you will take a car. Likewise, organizations should use logic to decide when to use a predictive approach or an agile approach to managing specific projects. Projects with heavy constraints, inexperienced and dispersed teams, large risks, generally clear up-front requirements, and a fairly rigid completion date are best done using a predictive approach. In contrast, projects with less rigid constraints, experienced and preferably co-located teams, smaller risks, unclear requirements, and more flexible scheduling would be more compatible with an agile approach. The same project is used in this section to highlight the main differences between the processes and outputs of these two approaches.

When using agile techniques and its most popular method, Scrum, a team uses specific roles, artifacts, and ceremonies.

3.5a Scrum Roles, Artifacts, and Ceremonies

Recall from Chapter 2 that Scrum includes three main roles for project participants:

- **Product owner**: The person responsible for the business value of the project and for deciding what work to do and in what order, as documented in the product backlog. In this case, Joe Fleming is the product owner. He is the CEO of JWD Consulting and the person who suggested the project.
- **ScrumMaster**: The person who ensures that the team is productive, facilitates the daily Scrum, enables close cooperation across all roles and functions, and removes barriers that prevent the team from being effective. ScrumMasters have authority over the process but not the people on the team. They must be comfortable surrendering control to the product owner and team. Some experts suggest that traditional project managers do not make great Scrum-Masters. In this case, Erica Bell will take on the challenge and serve as the ScrumMaster.
- **Scrum team or development team**: A cross-functional team of five to nine people who organize themselves and the work to produce the desired results for each sprint. A **sprint** normally lasts two to four weeks, during which specific work must be completed and made ready for review. Large projects might require teams of teams. In this case, Michael Chen, Jessie Faue, Kevin Dodge, Cindy Dawson, Kim Phuong, and Page Miller are development team members. Their positions are listed in the project charter shown earlier in Table 3-6. Kim and Page are client representatives who do not work for JWD Consulting, but they are key team members, especially for developing the parts of the intranet that external clients would use.

In Scrum, an **artifact** is a useful object created by people. An artifact can be called a deliverable in other project management approaches. The following three artifacts are created with Scrum:

- **Product backlog**: A list of features prioritized by business value. The highest-priority items should be broken down in enough detail for the team to estimate the effort involved in developing them. Some experts suggest scheduling about 10 workdays for each item. Size and complexity of the work dictates the estimate.
- **Sprint backlog**: The highest-priority items from the product backlog to be completed within a sprint. The Scrum team breaks down the highest-priority items into smaller tasks that take about 12 to 16 hours to complete. Examples of a sprint backlog and product backlog are provided later in this section under Planning.
- **Burndown chart**: Shows the cumulative work remaining in a sprint on a day-by-day basis. An example burndown chart is provided later in this section under Monitoring and Controlling.

The ScrumMaster facilitates four ceremonies or meetings when using Scrum methods:

- Sprint planning session: A meeting with the team to select a set of work from the product backlog to deliver during a sprint. This meeting takes about four hours to a full day.
- **Daily Scrum**: A short meeting for the development team to share progress and challenges and plan work for the day. Ideally the team members are in the same place, the meeting usually lasts no more than 15 minutes, and it is held at the same time and place each day. If that is not possible, teams can use videoconferencing to have short virtual meetings. The ScrumMaster asks what work has been done since yesterday, what work is planned for today, and what impediments or stumbling blocks might hamper the team's efforts. The ScrumMaster documents these stumbling blocks and works with key stakeholders to resolve them after the daily Scrum. Many teams use the term *issues* for items that do not have to be solved in the next 24 hours and *blockers* for items that need to be addressed immediately. This allows a ScrumMaster to maintain focus on highest-priority items (blockers) first and then manage the resolution of other issues over the next day or so.
- Sprint reviews: A meeting in which the team demonstrates to the product owner what it has completed during the sprint.
- Sprint retrospectives: A meeting in which the team looks for ways to improve the product and the process based on a review of the actual performance of the development team.

Figure 3-5 displays how you can view the Scrum framework shown in Chapter 2 in terms of the project management process groups. Creating the product backlog, developing the sprint backlog, and discussing plans during the daily Scrum would fall under planning. Performing the daily work and sprint, and creating the potentially shippable product increment would fit under executing. Holding the sprint review and discussing challenges as part of the daily Scrum can be viewed as monitoring and controlling. Reflecting during the sprint retrospective would fit under closing. Initiating the entire project is a phase that falls outside the Scrum framework in this example.

Table 3-18 summarizes some of the unique Scrum activities by each process group. The following sections provide more detail on these activities.

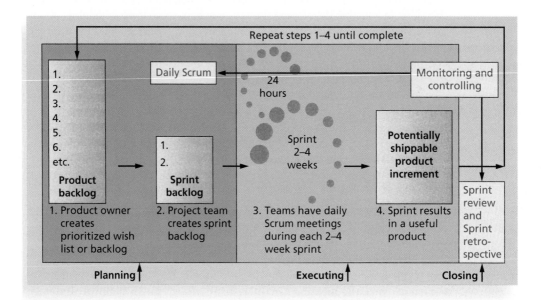

© Cengage Learning 2016

FIGURE 3-5 Scrum framework and the process groups

TABLE 3-18 Unique scrum activities by process group

Initiating:

- Determine roles
- Decide how many sprints will compose each release and the scope of software to deliver

Planning:

- Create product backlog
- Create sprint backlog
- Create release backlog
- Plan work each day in the daily Scrum
- Document stumbling blocks in a list

Executing:

- Complete tasks each day during sprints
- Produce a shippable product at the end of each sprint

(continued)

TABLE 3-18 Unique scrum activities by process group (*continued*)

Monitoring and Controlling:

- Resolve issues and blockers
- Create and update burndown chart
- Demonstrate the completed product during the sprint review meeting

Closing:

- Reflect on how to improve the product and process during the sprint retrospective meeting

© Cengage Learning 2016

3.5b Project Pre-Initiation and Initiation

The main differences between pre-initiation in this case and the first case would be determining roles and deciding what functionality would be delivered as part of each release, how many sprints will be required to complete a release, and how many releases of software to deliver. This is similar to dividing the project into several smaller projects. A project charter, stakeholder register, stakeholder management strategy, and kick-off meeting would still be created as part of initiation, just as they were in the predictive version of this case. Using the Scrum roles, however, Joe Fleming would be the product owner, Erica Bell the ScrumMaster, and the other people listed in the project charter would be team members.

Joe met with Erica to discuss what functionality would be delivered in each release, how many sprints would be needed for each release, how many software releases would be required, and the approach required to complete the project. They realized that before they could pin down functionality, releases, and sprints, they needed to survey potential users to collect requirements for the new software and determine a way to measure the value of the intranet site after it was implemented. They estimated that collecting and analyzing information from potential users would take about two months.

Working together, Joe and Erica would create a survey that specifically asks potential users which features would provide the most value. For example, instead of listing general ideas, they would list specific features and have respondents rank them in order of importance. They would also ask survey respondents to submit sample templates, tools, and other useful information to Cindy Dawson, a project team member in the IT department. Collecting this information up front would streamline the software development process.

Joe and Erica decided that three software releases would be realistic, given the time and cost constraints. Each sprint would be targeted to last four weeks, and reviews and creation of the product and sprint backlogs would be an ongoing activity within each sprint.

Joe and Erica met with Cindy and other team members several times. Cindy had the most experience working on agile projects. She discussed the importance of submitting several graphical user interface designs to prospective users to gain their feedback. This approach was extremely useful in the past, based on Cindy's experience, and it would save a lot of rework during development. For example, a team member would create one to four designs of a particular interface for prospective users to review in sessions hosted by a marketing team. Cindy explained that the feedback would help lead to a better, more intuitive user interface. Also, asking prospective users to rate the "look and feel" would be very beneficial. Users may be distracted by a selected color scheme, for example, so team members should craft the same interface in various color schemes to gauge which one has the greatest appeal and generates the most positive usability score. Cindy explained that user interface designers are not normally development team members, but organizations might use them to provide detailed design specifications that provide a consistent user interface. Erica and Joe learned a lot from Cindy and would incorporate her recommendations into future plans.

3.5c Planning

Instead of creating a team contract, WBS, Gantt chart, and list of prioritized risks for the whole project, the team follows the Scrum method. A preliminary scope statement for the entire project can still be a useful tool for planning, even though the team knows that more details will be added and changes will be made. Because Scrum implies that team members work as a self-directed group, coached by the ScrumMaster, a team contract should not be necessary.

In place of a WBS, high-level descriptions of the work to be completed would be identified in the product and sprint backlogs. The team would develop a more detailed list of technical stories and associated tasks to complete during each sprint. The team must also establish a velocity (or capacity) estimate for each sprint based on team member availability each day of the sprint. Estimates can be provided as hours of work, assuming that all developers are contractors who can code eight hours per day. Estimates can also be provided as points, assuming that developers are employees who code less than eight hours per day. For example, six hours per day would equal a point, so 36 hours of effort would equal 6 points.

A Gantt chart for the entire project could still be created, as shown in Figure 3-6. Notice that the process groups do not follow a simple linear pattern. Several process groups are repeated for each sprint, resulting in several releases of a usable software product, as shown by the milestones. Recall that in the predictive version of this case, there was only one release or delivery of software near the end of the project, on October 17. In this case, two additional deliveries of software are scheduled, one on August 3 and one on September 11. Some teams create a release road map, as described later in this section, for each software release. The entire project is still scheduled for completion on November 1.

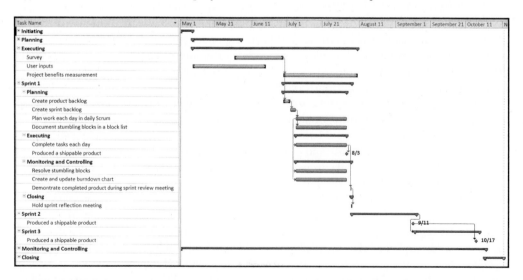

FIGURE 3-6   Intranet site project baseline Gantt chart using Scrum approach

In addition to listing all of the preliminary project requirements in a scope statement, as shown in section 6.0 of the business case (see Table 3-2), Joe, the product owner, created a product backlog to prioritize the most important functions of the new intranet software in terms of adding value to the business. Joe created the product backlog after analyzing the survey results and discussing options with several people. He included separate items for the most important templates and tools, instead of grouping them in one item, and requested a point person from their firm's pool of consultants to contact for questions about each template or tool as well. Notice that this approach combined a few items in the scope statement shown in the first case to focus on what would add the most value. Having a point person would be useful before the team developed the more complex Ask the Expert feature. After reviewing the product backlog, the Scrum team would do its planning and update the sprint backlog based on the items the team could complete in the first sprint. Table 3-19 provides an example of the product backlog and a sprint backlog for the first sprint. The team would then have its first daily Scrum meeting to plan the day.

The Scrum team breaks down the items in the sprint backlog into more specific work items, often in the form of user stories, technical stories, and related tasks. **User stories** are short descriptions written by customers of what they need a system to do for them. These descriptions should be about three sentences long. They provide the basis for time estimates for the sprint planning meeting. User stories should be testable and small enough that programmers can complete and unit test their code in a timely manner.

Developers break down user stories into technical stories. Then they use technical stories to translate user requirements into the technical specifications necessary to create the defined user functionality. The technical stories can contain one or more technical tasks that developers use to chart progress on a sprint board as work is conducted throughout a sprint. A task should fit within a day. One item in the sprint backlog may or may not be documented

TABLE 3-19 Product and sprint backlogs

Product Backlog	Sprint Backlog
1. User story templates, samples, and point person	1. User story templates, samples, and point person
2. WBS templates, samples, and point person	2. WBS templates, samples, and point person
3. Project schedule templates, samples, and point person	3. Project schedule templates, samples, and point person
4. Ability to charge customers for some intranet products and services	4. Ability to charge customers for some intranet products and services
5. Ability to collect user suggestions	5. Ability to collect user suggestions
6. Business case templates, samples, and point person	
7. Ask the Expert feature	
8. Stakeholder management strategy templates, samples, and point person	
9. Risk register templates, samples, and point person	
10. Etc.	

© Cengage Learning 2016

in one user story, one technical story, and one task, based on its complexity. There could be a one-to-one relationship or a many-to-one relationship if the item is highly complex.

For example, someone in the finance area of the company could write a user story called "Ability to charge customers for some intranet products and services." It might read as follows: "As a financial manager, I want our site to use Company B to process payments so that we save money on transaction and customer service costs." User stories are broken down into a detailed technical story and then into tasks, similar to tasks in a work breakdown structure.

Some organizations use a release road map to lay out all the work for an entire release, which can include more than one sprint. This road map is usually represented as a chart consisting of several columns. The release road map provides a clear picture of what stories (scope) will be contained in each sprint. This tool enables the Scrum team to easily review and update velocity estimates versus actuals. A release road map should be derived from data in the Project Management Information System (PMIS) or a related agile management system, such as Microsoft's Team Foundation Server, Rally, VersionOne, or JIRA.

3.5d Executing

As discussed earlier in this chapter, the most time and money should be spent on executing, when plans are implemented to create the desired product. The team would complete tasks each day, as it would in the predictive version of this case. But by using an agile approach, the team would produce several iterations of a potentially shippable product. For example, at the end of the first sprint, JWD Consulting would have some functionality available on its new project management intranet site. Users would be able to access templates, samples, and a point person for user stories, WBSs, and project schedules, as listed in the first sprint backlog. Users would also be able to make suggestions for functionality they would like to see in the intranet site as it was being developed. The first iteration of the software would also provide the ability to charge customers for some products and services. By using Scrum methods, the business could benefit from these new features a few months earlier than they could using the predictive approach described in the first case.

Because Erica and some of the project team would be inexperienced in using Scrum, they would have to work out several challenges. For example, communications are very different because the project team meets every morning, physically or virtually. There would also be communications issues with users of the new intranet site, who might be confused by getting three iterations of the product instead of just one. See Chapters 10 and 13, Project Communications Management and Project Stakeholder Management, for additional information.

3.5e Monitoring and Controlling

The two main tools for monitoring and controlling in the Scrum framework are the daily Scrum and the sprint review. Daily Scrums are held each morning to plan and communicate work for the day and discuss any risks, issues, or blockers. The daily Scrum includes a brief discussion of any issues and blockers the team is facing. The ScrumMaster would work with the appropriate stakeholders to address these problems as part of monitoring and controlling. Removing obstacles so the team can perform well is one of the main job duties of the ScrumMaster. The ScrumMaster documents issues and blockers, similar to a list of prioritized risks.

The work progress within a sprint can be represented on a sprint board maintained by the ScrumMaster. The sprint board contains a card to represent each task to be worked on during the sprint. Each task card contains the control number, task name, estimated time to complete, rank or priority number, and team member assigned. As tasks are opened, worked on, and closed, their cards are moved physically to the appropriate section on the board. These sections include Not Started, In Progress, Ready to Test, Tested, and Closed. Developers update the status of tasks in the Not Started, In Progress, and Ready to Test sections. Testers update the status for tasks in the Tested section. The product owner is responsible for reviewing functionality, confirming that it is working as expected, and changing a task's status to Closed.

A burndown chart is an important artifact used to graphically display progress on each sprint. The burndown chart in Figure 3-7 shows progress during the first sprint for the JWD Consulting intranet project, which was scheduled to last four weeks and produce five items or user stories listed in the sprint backlog. Remember that during planning, each user story was broken down into specific tasks, and the team estimated how long it would take to complete each task for each user story. During the daily Scrum meeting, the work a team member claims should fit within a day. Each day, the team should again estimate the number of hours or points remaining for each task. Some tasks might be added and some might be dropped as the scope becomes clearer. It does not matter how many hours have been spent; what matters is how many hours of work remain to complete the user stories for that sprint.

The burndown chart plots each day's sum of estimated hours or points remaining. It also shows an idealized burndown line, as if the team were completing an equal amount of work each day, or 10 tasks each day in this example. The chart then clearly shows

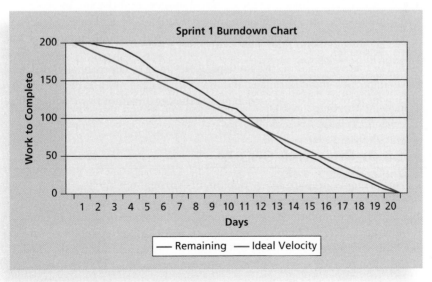

© Cengage Learning 2016

FIGURE 3-7 Burndown chart

whether the team is doing well in that sprint or if there is potential for trouble. Burndown charts help the team understand whether user stories might not be completed within that sprint. The chart provides an indicator that stories are at risk and should be removed. If progress is better than anticipated, the burndown chart can indicate that stories should be added to the sprint.

At the end of each sprint, the ScrumMaster—Erica in this example—leads the sprint demonstration review meeting. The team demonstrates to the product owner what it has completed during the sprint. In this case, Joe would review the five features created during the first sprint. After the sprint demonstration review, he would update the product backlog based on the latest information and business needs, and the next sprint cycle would begin.

3.5f Closing

After the sprint review, the ScrumMaster leads a sprint retrospective. During this short meeting (about half an hour), the team reflects on what happened during the sprint. The ScrumMaster normally solicits team member feedback via e-mail first and collates these results before the meeting. This saves time and focuses the discussion on items that are most important. The retrospective is similar to a lessons-learned report, but it focuses on a shorter period of time. The sprint retrospective is intended to answer two fundamental questions:

- What went well during the last sprint that we should continue doing?
- What could we do differently to improve the product or process?

The sprint retrospective meeting is usually led by the ScrumMaster, who documents a list of action items for implementation. Those items may be added to the product backlog if the product owner agrees with them. For example, after the first sprint for the JWD project management intranet site project, the team might suggest that the site be mobile enabled. This new requirement could be added to the product backlog and selected as an item for the next sprint. Recall that an agile approach welcomes new requirements as long as they focus on business value.

As demonstrated in the two cases on the same project, the agile approach and predictive approach have similarities and differences. If done well, an agile method can produce several releases of useful software. This approach allows the organization to work together quickly to address changing business needs.

3.6 TEMPLATES BY PROCESS GROUP

As you can see, project teams prepare many documents throughout the life of a project. Many people use templates to apply a standard format for preparing those documents. Table 3-20 lists templates used to prepare the documents shown in this chapter and later chapters. The table lists the template name, chapter number, process group(s) in which you normally use the template, the application software used to create it, and the file name for the template. You can download all of these templates in one compressed file from the companion website for this text or from the author's website at *www.kathyschwalbe.com*. Feel free to modify the templates to meet your needs.

TABLE 3-20 Templates by process group

Template Name	Process Group	Chapter(s) Where Used	Application Software	File Name
Business Case	Pre-initiating	3	Word	business_case.doc
Business Case Financial Analysis	Pre-initiating	3, 4	Excel	business_case_ financials.xls
Stakeholder Register	Initiating	3, 13	Word	stakeholder_register.doc
Stakeholder Management Strategy	Initiating	3, 13	Word	stakeholder_strategy.doc
Kick-off Meeting	Initiating	3	Word	kick-off_meeting.doc
Payback Chart	Initiating	4	Excel	payback.xls
Weighted Decision Matrix	Initiating	4, 12	Excel	wtd_decision_matrix.xls
Project Charter	Initiating	3, 4, 5	Word	charter.doc
Team Contract	Planning	3	Word	team_contract.doc
Requirements Traceability Matrix	Planning	5	Word	reqs_matrix.doc
Scope Statement	Planning	3, 4, 5	Word	scope_ statement.doc
Statement of Work	Planning	12	Word	statement_of_work.doc
Request for Proposal	Planning	12	Word	rfp_outline.doc
Software Project Management Plan	Planning	4	Word	sw_project_mgt_plan.doc
Work Breakdown Structure	Planning	3, 5, 6	Word	wbs.doc
Gantt Chart	Planning, Executing	3, 5, 6	Project	Gantt_chart.mpp
Network Diagram	Planning, Executing	3, 6	Project	network_ diagram.mpp
Project Cost Estimate	Planning	7	Excel	cost_estimate.xls
Earned Value Data and Chart	Monitoring and Controlling	7	Excel	earned_value.xls
Burndown Chart	Monitoring and Controlling	3, 7	Excel	burndownchart.xls
Quality Assurance Plan	Executing	8	Word	quality_assurance_ plan.doc
Pareto Chart	Monitoring and Controlling	8	Excel	pareto_chart.xls
Project Organizational Chart	Planning, Executing	9	Power-Point	project_org_chart.ppt
Responsibility Assignment Matrix	Planning, Executing	9	Excel	ram.xls
Resource Histogram	Planning, Executing	9	Excel	resource_histogram.xls
Communications Management Plan	Planning	10	Word	comm_plan.doc
Project Description (text)	Planning	10	Word	project_desc_text.doc

(continued)

TABLE 3-20 Templates by process group (*continued*)

Template Name	Process Group	Chapter(s) Where Used	Application Software	File Name
Project Description (Gantt chart)	Planning	10	Project	project_desc_Gantt.mpp
Milestone Report	Executing	3, 6	Word	milestone_report.doc
Change Request Form	Planning, Monitoring and Controlling	4	Word	change_request.doc
Progress Report	Monitoring and Controlling	3, 10	Word	progress_report.doc
Probability/Impact Matrix	Planning, Executing, Monitoring and Controlling	11	Power-Point	prob_impact_matrix.ppt
List of Prioritized Risks	Planning, Executing, Monitoring and Controlling	3, 11	Word	list_of_risks.doc
Risk Register	Planning, Monitoring and Controlling	11	Excel	risk_register.xls
Top 10 Risk Item Tracking	Planning, Monitoring and Controlling	11	Excel	top_10.xls
Breakeven/Sensitivity Analysis	Planning	11	Excel	breakeven.xls
Expectations Management Matrix	Monitoring and Controlling	13	Word	expectations.doc
Issue Log	Monitoring and Controlling	13	Word	issue_log.doc
Client Acceptance Form	Closing	10	Word	client_acceptance.doc
Lessons-Learned Report	Closing	3, 10	Word	lessons_learned_ report.doc
Final Project Documentation	Closing	3, 10	Word	final_documentation.doc

© Cengage Learning 2016

The project management process groups—initiating, planning, executing, monitoring and controlling, and closing—provide a useful framework for understanding project management. They apply to most projects, both IT and non-IT, and along with the project management knowledge areas, help project managers see the big picture of managing a project in their organization.

CASE WRAP-UP

Erica Bell and her team finished the project management intranet site project on November 4, as planned in their project charter. They went over budget, but Joe had approved Erica's request for additional funds, primarily for purchasing external software and customization. Like any project, they had a few challenges, but they worked together as a team and used good project management to meet their sponsor's and users' needs. They received positive initial feedback from internal consultants and some of their clients on the new intranet site. People were asking for templates, examples, and expert advice even before the system was ready. (If they had used an agile approach, these features could have been delivered earlier.) About a year after the project was completed, Erica worked with a member of the Finance department to review the benefits of the new system. Although the Project Management Office lost one of its staff members, it did not request a replacement because the new system helped reduce its workload. This saved the firm about $70,000 a year for the salary and benefits of that staff position. The team also had data to show that the firm saved more than $180,000 on contracts with clients because of the new system, compared with their projection of $160,000. The firm was breaking even with the Ask the Expert feature during the first year, and Erica estimated that the system provided $30,000 in additional profits the first year by generating new business, instead of the $40,000 the team had projected. However, savings from the PMO staff position salary and the extra savings on contracts more than made up for the $10,000 difference. Joe was proud of the project team and the system they produced to help make JWD Consulting a world-class organization.

Chapter Summary

Project management involves a number of interlinked processes. The five project management process groups are initiating, planning, executing, monitoring and controlling, and closing. These processes occur at varying levels of intensity throughout each phase of a project, and specific outcomes are produced as a result of each process. Normally the executing processes require the most resources and time, followed by the planning processes.

Mapping the main activities of each project management process group into the 10 project management knowledge areas provides a big picture of what activities are involved in project management.

It is important to tailor project management methodologies to meet an organization's particular needs. Some organizations develop their own IT project management methodologies, often using the standards in the *PMBOK® Guide* as a foundation. Popular methods like PRINCE2, Agile, RUP, and Six Sigma include project management processes.

The JWD Consulting case study demonstrates how one organization managed an IT project from start to finish. The case study provides samples of outputs produced for initiating, planning, executing, monitoring and controlling, and closing:

- Business case
- Stakeholder register
- Stakeholder management strategy
- Project charter
- Kick-off meeting agenda
- Team contract
- Work breakdown structure
- Gantt chart
- List of prioritized risks
- Milestone report
- Progress report
- Lessons-learned report
- Final project report

The second version of the same case study illustrates how to use Scrum, the leading agile method, to manage the project. Instead of releasing the new intranet software just once near the end of the project, the team could release three iterations of the software. This version of the case study introduced some new tools, including a product backlog, sprint backlog, and burndown chart. Later chapters provide detailed information for creating these and other project management documents and using several of the tools and techniques described in both versions of this case study.

Quick Quiz

1. A _____ is a series of actions directed toward a particular result.

   a. goal

   b. process

   c. plan

   d. project

2. _____ processes include coordinating people and other resources to carry out project plans and create the products, services, or results of the project or phase.

   a. Initiating

   b. Planning

   c. Executing

   d. Monitoring and controlling

   e. Closing

3. Which process group normally requires the most resources and time?

   a. Initiating

   b. Planning

   c. Executing

   d. Monitoring and controlling

   e. Closing

4. What methodology was developed in the United Kingdom, defines 45 separate subprocesses, and organizes them into eight process groups?

   a. Six Sigma

   b. RUP

   c. *PMBOK® Guide*

   d. PRINCE2

5. Which of the following outputs is often completed before initiating a project?

   a. stakeholder register

   b. business case

   c. project charter

   d. kick-off meeting

6. A work breakdown structure, project schedule, and cost estimates are outputs of the _____ process.

   a. initiating

   b. planning

   c. executing

   d. monitoring and controlling

   e. closing

7. Initiating involves developing a project charter, which is part of the project _____ management knowledge area.

   a. integration

   b. scope

   c. communications

   d. risk

8. _____ involves measuring progress toward project objectives and taking corrective actions.

   a. Initiating

   b. Planning

   c. Executing

   d. Monitoring and controlling

   e. Closing

9. Which of the following is not a typical reason that project teams would use a predictive approach versus an agile approach to managing a project?

   a. The project has unclear up-front requirements.

   b. The project team is inexperienced and dispersed.

   c. Large risks are involved.

   d. The completion date is fairly rigid.

10. Many people use _____ to have a standard format for preparing various project management documents.

   a. methodologies

   b. templates

   c. project management software

   d. standards

Quick Quiz Answers

1. b; 2. c; 3. c; 4. d; 5. b; 6. b; 7. a; 8. d; 9. a; 10. b

Discussion Questions

1. Briefly describe what happens in each of the five project management process groups (initiating, planning, executing, monitoring and controlling, and closing). What types of activities occur before initiating a project?

2. Approximately how much time do good project managers spend on each process group, and why?

3. Why do organizations need to tailor project management concepts, such as those found in the *PMBOK® Guide*, to create their own methodologies?

4. What are some of the key outputs of each process group?

5. What are some of the typical challenges project teams face during each of the five process groups? You can frame your discussion based on a project described in one of the feature boxes in this chapter (for example, the What Went Right? or What Went Wrong? feature). You can also frame your discussion on one of PMI's Project of the Year Award winners or on a well-known project failure like the Denver International Airport baggage handling system.

6. What are the main differences between the two versions of the JWD Consulting case study? When should you use a more prescriptive or agile approach? Do you think users of the JWD Consulting Intranet site would prefer one release of the software or several incremental ones? What are some pros and cons of each approach?

Exercises

1. Study the WBS and Gantt charts provided in Figures 3-3 and 3-4. Enter the WBS into Project 2013, indenting tasks as shown to create the WBS hierarchy. Do not enter durations or dependencies. Print the resulting Gantt chart. See the scope management section of Appendix A for help using Project 2013.

2. Research a project management method, such as PRINCE2, Agile, RUP, or Six Sigma, and how organizations use it, citing at least two references. Why do you think organizations spend time and money tailoring a methodology to their environment? Write a summary of your findings and your opinion on the topic.

3. Read the "ResNet Case Study," which is available from the companion website for this text under Chapter 3. This real case study about Northwest Airlines' reservation system illustrates another application of the project management process groups. Write a paper summarizing the main outputs produced during each project process group in this case. Also, include your opinion of whether Peeter Kivestu was an effective project manager. If you prefer, find another well-documented project and summarize it instead.

4. JWD Consulting wrote a business case before officially initiating the project management intranet site project. Review the contents of this document in Table 3-2 and find two articles that describe the need to justify investing in IT projects. In addition, describe whether you think most projects should include a business case before the project sponsors officially approve the project. Write a short paper summarizing your findings and opinions.

5. Read an article or watch a video about a recipient of PMI's Project of the Year award. Search online for information from PMI's website. Write a one-page paper summarizing a winning project, focusing on how the project manager and team used good project management practices.

6. Review the product backlog, sprint backlog, and burndown chart provided in this chapter. Read articles or watch a video about using a Scrum method that mentions these artifacts. Write a short paper that describes more details about how to create these artifacts; cite at least two references.

7. You are a project consultant for the ACME Company and are helping to develop an agile method using Scrum. The company has always used predictive project management methods for software development, but company managers have heard that Agile can have significant advantages if implemented properly. Prepare a proposal that suggests what training, documentation, executive support, and team management approaches are needed to start a pilot for Agile. Provide justification for your recommendations.

8. Review at least two surveys about the use of agile methodologies, such as the annual survey on the state of agile by VersionOne. Also find a critical analysis of these surveys as they are sponsored by companies that sell agile products or surveys. Summarize your findings in a short paper.

9. Download the template files used in this text from the companion website or from *www .kathyschwalbe.com*. Review several of the files, and look at examples of how they are used in this text. Also search the Internet for other template files. Write a short paper to summarize what you think about using templates and how you think they can help project managers and their teams. Also discuss potential problems with using templates.

Key Terms

agile methods p.87

artifact p.119

burndown chart p.199

closing processes p.81

daily Scrum p.119

executing processes p.81

initiating processes p.81

kick-off meeting p.97

methodology p.86

monitoring and controlling processes p.81

planning processes p.81

process p.81

product backlog p.119

product owner p.118

project management process groups p.81

PRojects IN Controlled Environments (PRINCE2) p.87

Rational Unified Process (RUP) framework p.88

ScrumMaster p.118

Scrum team or development team p.118

Six Sigma methodologies p.88

sprint p.118

sprint backlog p.119

stakeholder register p.94

standard p.86

user stories p.123

End Notes

[1] Andy Crowe, *Alpha Project Managers: What the Top 2% Know That Everyone Else Does Not* (Atlanta, GA: Velociteach Press, 2006).

[2] Phillip A. Pell, Comments posted at Elaine Varron, "No Easy IT Fix for IRS" [formerly "For the IRS, There's No EZ Fix"], *CIO.com* (April 1, 2004).

[3] Adam Mazmanian, "GAO: IRS Should Improve IT Investment Reporting," *FCW: The Business of Federal Technology* (April 3, 2014).

[4] PCI Group, "PM Best Practices Report" (October 2001).

[5] Brian Jacks, "Lord of the Rings: The Two Towers Extended Edition (New Line)," *Underground Online*, *UGO.com* (accessed August 4, 2004).

[6] ThoughtWorks, "Agile Adoption in India Survey Report—2011" (2011).

[7] Version One Inc., "8th Annual State of Agile™ Survey," *VersionOne.com* (2014).

[8] Bill Cottrell, "Standards, Compliance, and Rational Unified Process, Part I: Integrating RUP and the PMBOK," *IBM Developer works* (May 10, 2004).

[9] Project Management Institute, "Pulse of the Professions®: The High Cost of Low Performance" (2014).

[10] Adam Mazmanian, "Google Joins PwC's Vista-Based Bid for Military Health Records," *FWC: The Business of Federal Technology* (January 14, 2015).

[11] Libby Ellis, "Urban Inspiration," *PM Network* (January 2006), p. 30.

[12] PMI, "2013 PMI Project of the Year Award Winner: Adelaide Desalination Project," October 31, 2013, *www.youtube.com/watch?v=SIPleb0y0jg*.

[13] PMI, "2012 PMI Project of the Year Winner: Umatilla Chemical Agent Disposal Facility," October 20, 2012, *www.youtube.com/watch?v=d0hSS_e7ABo&feature=share&list =UUMA-ZzWeWAipboxxBRjzedg*.

[14] George Santayana, *The Life of Reason: Reason in Common Sense* (New York: Scribner's, 1905), p. 284.

CHAPTER **4**

PROJECT INTEGRATION MANAGEMENT

LEARNING OBJECTIVES

After reading this chapter, you will be able to:

- Describe an overall framework for project integration management as it relates to the other project management knowledge areas and the project life cycle

- Discuss the strategic planning process and apply different project selection methods

- Explain the importance of creating a project charter to formally initiate projects

- Describe project management plan development, understand the content of these plans, and describe approaches for creating them

- Explain project execution, its relationship to project planning, the factors related to successful results, and tools and techniques to assist in directing and managing project work

- Describe the process of monitoring and controlling a project

- Understand the integrated change control process, planning for and managing changes on information technology (IT) projects, and developing and using a change control system

- Explain the importance of developing and following good procedures for closing projects

- Describe how software can assist in project integration management

OPENING CASE

Nick Carson recently became project manager of a critical biotech enterprise at his Silicon Valley company. This project involved creating the hardware and software for a next generation (next-gen) DNA-sequencing instrument used in assembling and analyzing the human genome. Several companies were competing to build smaller, faster sequencing instruments that would reduce the costs and improve the quality of data analysis in this rapidly changing field. The biotech project was the company's largest endeavor, and it had tremendous potential for future growth and revenue.

Unfortunately, there were problems managing this large project. It had been under way for three years and had already gone through three different project managers. Nick had been the lead software developer on the project before top management made him the project manager. The CEO told him to do whatever it took to deliver the first version of the product in four months and a production version in nine months. Negotiations for a potential corporate buyout with a larger company influenced top management's sense of urgency to complete the project.

Highly energetic and intelligent, Nick had the technical background to make the project a success. He delved into the technical problems and found some critical flaws that kept the next-gen DNA-sequencing instrument from working. Nevertheless, he was having difficulty in his new role as project manager. Although Nick and his team got the product out on time, top management was upset because Nick did not focus on managing all aspects of the project. He never provided them with accurate schedules or detailed plans of what was happening on the project. Instead of performing the work of project manager, Nick had taken on the role of software integrator and troubleshooter. Nick, however, did not understand top management's complaints—he delivered the product, didn't he? Didn't they realize how valuable he was?

4.1 WHAT IS PROJECT INTEGRATION MANAGEMENT?

Project integration management involves coordinating all of the other project management knowledge areas throughout a project's life cycle. This integration ensures that all the elements of a project come together at the right times to complete a project successfully. According to the *PMBOK® Guide, Fifth Edition*, six main processes are involved in project integration management:

1. *Developing the project charter* involves working with stakeholders to create the document that formally authorizes a project—the charter.
2. *Developing the project management plan* involves coordinating all planning efforts to create a consistent, coherent document—the project management plan.
3. *Directing and managing project work* involves carrying out the project management plan by performing the activities included in it. The outputs of this process are deliverables, work performance information, change requests, project management plan updates, and project documents updates.
4. *Monitoring and controlling project work* involves overseeing activities to meet the performance objectives of the project. The outputs of this process are change requests, project management plan updates, and project documents updates.

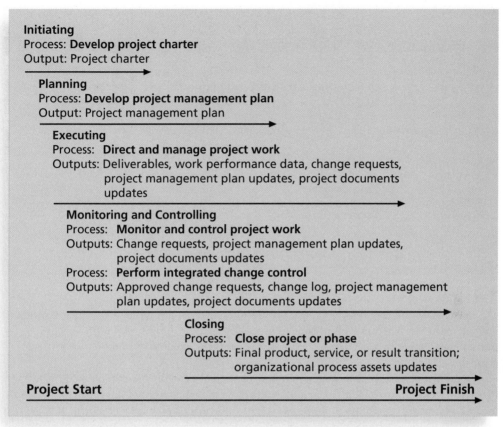

Initiating
Process: **Develop project charter**
Output: Project charter

Planning
Process: **Develop project management plan**
Output: Project management plan

Executing
Process: **Direct and manage project work**
Outputs: Deliverables, work performance data, change requests, project management plan updates, project documents updates

Monitoring and Controlling
Process: **Monitor and control project work**
Outputs: Change requests, project management plan updates, project documents updates
Process: **Perform integrated change control**
Outputs: Approved change requests, change log, project management plan updates, project documents updates

Closing
Process: **Close project or phase**
Outputs: Final product, service, or result transition; organizational process assets updates

Project Start   **Project Finish**

© Cengage Learning 2016

FIGURE 4-1   Project integration management summary

5. *Performing integrated change control* involves identifying, evaluating, and managing changes throughout the project life cycle. The outputs of this process include change request status updates, project management plan updates, and project documents updates.
6. *Closing the project or phase* involves finalizing all activities to formally close the project or phase. Outputs of this process include final product, service, or result transition and organizational process assets updates. Figure 4-1 summarizes these processes and outputs, and shows when they occur in a typical project.

Many people consider project integration management the key to overall project success. Someone must take responsibility for coordinating all of the people, plans, and work required to complete a project. Someone must focus on the big picture of the project and steer the project team toward successful completion. Someone must make the final decisions when conflicts occur among project goals or people. Someone must communicate key project information to top management. These responsibilities belong to the project manager, whose chief means for accomplishing all these tasks is project integration management.

⊗ WHAT WENT WRONG?

Understanding an organization's needs and making the right staffing decisions for a project is much easier said than done, as senior British police officer Mark Rowley discovered after failure of the Surrey Integrated Reporting Enterprise Network (Siren) project.

The Surrey police force began looking into replacing its criminal intelligence system in 2005, and they awarded a contract to develop a new one in 2009. The police force spent £14.8 million (over $22 million) on the project until it was canceled in 2013. It was finally replaced with a much less expensive system used by thirteen other forces.

Surrey Police and Crime Commissioner Kevin Hurley said that Mark Rowley, chief constable at the time and the person in charge of Siren, should take responsibility for the project failure. Rowley was reassigned to the Metropolitan Police Service, and he insisted that no misconduct occurred. An audit report by Grant Thornton said Siren was an "ambitious project that was beyond the in-house capabilities and experience of the police force and police authority."[1]

Particularly on large projects, the project manager's main job is project integration management. To perform well in that role, it is important to understand the organization's needs and staff your project with skilled workers capable of making the project a success.

Good project integration management is critical to providing stakeholder satisfaction. Project integration management includes **interface management**, which involves identifying and managing the points of interaction between various elements of a project. The primary tools for interface management are communication and relationships. The number of interfaces can increase exponentially as the number of people involved in a project increases. Thus, one of the most important jobs of a project manager is to establish and maintain good communication and relationships across organizational interfaces. The project manager must communicate well with all project stakeholders, including customers, the project team, top management, other project managers, and opponents of the project.

What happens when a project manager does not communicate well with all stakeholders? In the chapter's opening case, Nick Carson seemed to ignore a key stakeholder for the next-gen DNA-sequencing instrument project—his top management. Nick was comfortable working with other members of the project team, but he was not familiar with his new job as project manager or the needs of the company's top management. Nick continued to do his old job of software developer and took on the added role of software integrator. He mistakenly thought project integration management meant software integration management and focused on the project's technical problems. He totally ignored what project integration management is really about—integrating the work of all of the people involved in the project by focusing on good communication and relationship management. Recall that project management is applying knowledge, skills, tools, and techniques to meet project requirements, while also meeting or exceeding stakeholder needs and expectations. Nick did not take the time to find out what top management expected from him as the project manager; he assumed that completing the project on time and within budget was sufficient to make them happy. Yes, top management should have made its expectations more clear, but Nick should have taken the initiative to get the guidance he needed.

In addition to not understanding project integration management, Nick did not use holistic or systems thinking (see Chapter 2). He burrowed into the technical details of his particular project. He did not stop to think about what it meant to be the project manager, how this project related to other projects in the organization, or top management's expectations of him and his team.

Project integration management must occur within the context of the entire organization, not just within a particular project. The project manager must integrate the work of the project with the ongoing operations of the organization. In the opening case, Nick's company was negotiating a potential buyout with a larger company. Consequently, top management needed to know when the next-gen DNA-sequencing instrument would be ready, how big the market was for the product, and if the company had enough in-house staff to continue to manage projects like this one in the future. Top management wanted to see a project management plan and a schedule to help monitor the project's progress and show the potential buyer what was happening. When top managers tried to talk to Nick about these issues, he soon returned to discussing the technical details of the project. Even though Nick was very bright, he had no experience or real interest in many of the company's business aspects. Project managers must always view their projects in the context of the changing needs of their organizations and respond to requests from top management. Likewise, top management must keep project managers informed of major issues that could affect their projects and strive to make processes consistent throughout their organization.

Following a standard process for managing projects can help prevent some of the typical problems new and experienced project managers face, including communicating with and managing stakeholders. Before organizations begin projects, however, they should go through a formal process to decide what projects to pursue.

4.2 STRATEGIC PLANNING AND PROJECT SELECTION

Successful leaders look at the big picture or strategic plan of the organization to determine what types of projects will provide the most value. Some may argue that project managers should not be involved in strategic planning and project selection because top management is usually responsible for these types of business decisions. But successful organizations know that project managers can provide valuable insight into the project selection process.

4.2a Strategic Planning

Strategic planning involves determining long-term objectives by analyzing the strengths and weaknesses of an organization, studying opportunities and threats in the business environment, predicting future trends, and projecting the need for new products and services. Strategic planning provides important information to help organizations identify and then select potential projects.

Many people are familiar with **SWOT analysis**—analyzing Strengths, Weaknesses, Opportunities, and Threats—which is one tool used in strategic planning. For example, a group of four people who want to start a new business in the film industry could perform a SWOT analysis to help identify potential projects. They might determine the following based on a SWOT analysis:

Strengths:

- As experienced professionals, we have numerous contacts in the film industry.
- Two of us have strong sales and interpersonal skills.
- Two of us have strong technical skills and are familiar with several filmmaking software tools.
- We all have impressive samples of completed projects.

Weaknesses:

- None of us have accounting or financial experience.
- We have no clear marketing strategy for products and services.
- We have little money to invest in new projects.
- We have no company Web site and limited use of technology to run the business.

Opportunities:

- A potential client has mentioned a large project she would like us to bid on.
- The film industry continues to grow.
- There are two major conferences this year where we could promote our company.

Threats:

- Other individuals or companies can provide the services we can.
- Customers might prefer working with more established individuals and organizations.
- There is high risk in the film business.

Based on their SWOT analysis, the four entrepreneurs outline potential projects as follows:

- Find an external accountant or firm to help run the business.
- Hire someone to develop a company website, focusing on our experience and past projects.
- Develop a marketing plan.
- Develop a strong proposal to get the large project the potential client mentioned.
- Plan to promote the company at two major conferences this year.

Some people like to perform a SWOT analysis by using **mind mapping**, a technique that uses branches radiating from a core idea to structure thoughts and ideas. The human brain does not work in a linear fashion. People come up with many unrelated ideas. By capturing those ideas in a visual mind map format, you can often generate more ideas than by creating lists. You can create mind maps by hand, using sticky notes, using presentation software such as Microsoft PowerPoint, or by using mind mapping software.

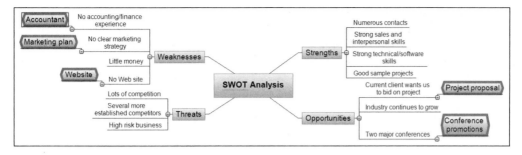

© Cengage Learning 2016

FIGURE 4-2 Mind map of a SWOT analysis to help identify potential projects

Figure 4-2 shows a sample mind map for the new film industry business SWOT analysis. This diagram was created using MindView Business Edition software by MatchWare. Notice that this map has four main branches representing strengths, weaknesses, opportunities, and threats. Ideas in each category are added to the appropriate branch, and sub-branches are shown for some ideas under those categories. Notice that several branches end with a project idea, such as Project proposal, Conference promotions, Accountant, Marketing plan, and Website. You can easily format the project ideas to make them stand out, as shown in Figure 4-2. From this example, you can see that no project ideas are identified to address strengths or threats, so these areas should be discussed further.

4.2b Identifying Potential Projects

The first step in project management is deciding what projects to do in the first place. Therefore, project initiation starts with identifying potential projects, using realistic methods to select which projects to work on, and then formalizing their initiation by issuing some sort of project charter.

In addition to using a SWOT analysis, organizations often follow a detailed process for project selection. Figure 4-3 shows a four-stage process for selecting IT projects. Note the hierarchical structure of this model and the results produced from each stage.

In the first stage of the selection process, starting at the top of the hierarchy, a steering committee develops an IT strategic plan that is tied to the organization's overall strategic plan. In many organizations, this steering committee consists of managers from departments throughout the company to ensure that all projects are selected in the best interests of the entire organization. The head of the Project Management Office (PMO) would be part of this committee because the PMO acts as the central location for keeping track of all project activities. It is very important to have managers from outside the IT department assist in developing the IT strategic plan, as they can help IT personnel understand organizational strategies and identify the business areas that support them. At the end of this stage, the organization should have a well-defined list of IT strategic goals.

After identifying strategic goals, the next stage in the process for selecting IT projects is to perform a business area analysis. This analysis outlines business processes that are central to achieving strategic goals and helps determine which processes could most benefit from IT. In the next stage, the organization starts defining the scope, benefits, and constraints of potential IT projects. The last stage in the process for selecting IT projects is choosing which projects to do and assigning resources for working on them.

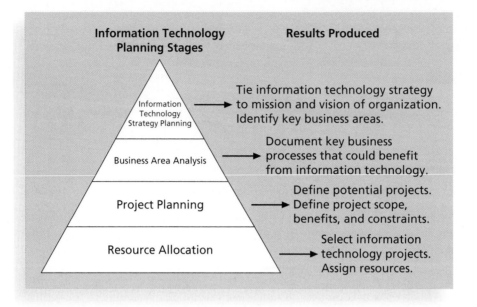

© Cengage Learning 2016

FIGURE 4-3   Planning process for selecting IT projects

4.2c Aligning IT with Business Strategy

Notice that aligning IT projects with business strategy is at the heart of selecting IT projects. This is consistently a top concern for CIOs. It is often difficult to educate line managers on technology's possibilities and limitations and keep IT professionals in tune with changing business needs. Most organizations face thousands of problems and opportunities for improvement. To get the most value from technology, an organization's strategic plan should guide the IT project selection process. Recall from Chapter 2's Best Practice feature that IT governance is an important part of ensuring that IT supports business goals. IT governance helps organizations maximize their investments in IT and address IT-related risks and opportunities.

An organization must develop a strategy for using IT to define how it will support the organization's objectives. This IT strategy must align with the organization's strategic plans. In fact, research shows that supporting explicit business objectives is the top reason cited for why organizations invest in IT projects. Other top criteria for investing in IT projects include supporting implicit business objectives and providing financial incentives, such as a good internal rate of return (IRR) or net present value (NPV).[2] In a 2014 survey, responses from 178 CIOs suggested that the majority of organizations (87 percent) are planning to maintain or increase IT budgets with an average budget increase of 4.9 percent. Investments in core technologies, such as infrastructure, networks, and storage, received the largest budget allocation. Annual spending increased by 5 percent to 32 percent on edge technologies, such as mobile, social, customer relationship management (CRM), and marketing automation. The focus of new IT projects continues to be revenue growth, a strategic objective of many organizations.[3]

Information systems often are central to business strategy. Author Michael Porter, who developed the concept of the strategic value of competitive advantage, and many other experts have emphasized the importance of using IT to support strategic plans and provide a competitive advantage. Many information systems are classified as strategic because they directly support key business strategies. For example, information systems can support an organizational strategy of being a low-cost producer. As one of the largest retailers in the United States, Walmart's inventory control system is a classic example of such a strategic system. Information systems can support a strategy of providing specialized products or services that set a company apart from others in the industry. Consider the classic example of Federal Express's introduction of online package tracking systems. FedEx was the first company to provide this type of service, which gave it a competitive advantage until others developed similar systems. Information systems can also support a strategy of selling to a particular market or occupying a specific product niche. Owens Corning developed a strategic information system that boosted the sales of its home-insulation products by providing its customers with a system for evaluating the energy efficiency of building designs. In 2012, the editor in chief of *CIO* magazine stated, "The smart use of technology is always a key component in driving innovation and creating a competitive edge. We see IT value proving itself across the board in many organizations."[4]

 BEST PRACTICE

In a 2013 survey, CEOs and senior executives identified the companies they most admired for their ability to apply IT-related business capabilities for competitive advantage. The executives identified the best practices of 21 companies, as follows:

- Customer-driven IT is essential. The best organizations excel at managing complex e-commerce systems and platforms, supporting multichannel management, and innovating quickly to meet customer needs.
- IT can enable branding and customer recruitment. Many of the top companies use customer success stories to show how IT helped them create new markets and solve customer problems. These testimonials drive recruitment efforts for analytics, cloud computing, and systems integration work.
- Keep improving. Successful organizations did not get complacent with their use of IT. For example, many leveraged the disruptive power of cloud computing and mobility to improve their enterprise systems.[5]

The top companies admired for using IT as a competitive advantage, in alphabetical order, include:

Accenture	Hospital Corporation of America	Nestle
Amazon	IBM	Procter & Gamble
Apple	Intermountain Healthcare	Progressive Insurance
Cleveland Clinic	JP Morgan Chase	Schlumberger
General Electric	Kaiser Permanente	Target
Goldman Sachs	Mayo Clinic	Toyota
Google	Microsoft	Wells Fargo

4.3 METHODS FOR SELECTING PROJECTS

Organizations identify many potential projects as part of their strategic planning processes, and they need to narrow down the list of potential projects to the ones that will be of most benefit. They often rely on experienced project managers to help them make project selection decisions. Selecting projects is not an exact science, and many methods exist for selecting projects. Five common techniques are:

- Focusing on broad organizational needs
- Categorizing IT projects
- Performing net present value or other financial analyses
- Using a weighted scoring model
- Implementing a balanced scorecard

In practice, many organizations use a combination of these approaches to select projects. Each approach has advantages and disadvantages, and it is up to management to determine the best approach for selecting projects based on their particular organization.

4.3a Focusing on Broad Organizational Needs

Top managers must focus on meeting their organizations' many needs when deciding what projects to undertake, when to undertake them, and to what level. Projects that address broad organizational needs are much more likely to be successful because they will be important to the organization. For example, a broad organizational need might be to improve safety, increase morale, provide better communications, or improve customer service. However, it is often difficult to provide a strong justification for many IT projects related to these broad organizational needs. For example, estimating the financial value of such projects is often impossible, even though everyone agrees that they have a high value. As the old proverb says, "It is better to measure gold roughly than to count pennies precisely."

One method for selecting projects based on broad organizational needs is to determine whether they first meet three important criteria: *need*, *funding*, and *will*. Do people in the organization agree that the project needs to be done? Does the organization have the desire and capacity to provide adequate funds to perform the project? Is there a strong will to make the project succeed? For example, many visionary CEOs can describe a broad need to improve certain aspects of their organizations, such as communications. Although they cannot specifically describe how to improve communications, they might allocate funds to projects that address this need. As projects progress, the organization must reevaluate the need, funding, and will for each project to determine if it should be continued, redefined, or terminated.

4.3b Categorizing IT Projects

Another method for selecting projects is based on various categorizations, such as the project's impetus, time window, and general priority. The impetus for a project is often to respond to a problem, an opportunity, or a directive.

- **Problems** are undesirable situations that prevent an organization from achieving its goals. These problems can be current or anticipated. For example, users of an information system may be having trouble logging on to the system or getting information in a timely manner because the system has reached its capacity. In response, the company could initiate a project to enhance the current system by adding more access lines or upgrading the hardware with a faster processor, more memory, or more storage space.

- **Opportunities** are chances to improve the organization. For example, the project described in the chapter's opening case involves creating a new product that can make or break the entire company.
- **Directives** are new requirements imposed by management, government, or some external influence. For example, many projects that involve medical technologies must meet rigorous government requirements.

Organizations select projects for any of these reasons. It is often easier to get approval and funding for projects that address problems or directives because the organization must respond to these categories to avoid hurting their business. Many problems and directives must be resolved quickly, but managers must also apply systems thinking and seek opportunities for improving the organization through IT projects.

Another categorization for IT projects is based on timing: How long will it take to complete a project and what is the deadline for completing it? For example, some potential projects must be finished within a specific time window; otherwise, they are no longer valid projects. Some projects can be completed very quickly—within a few weeks, days, or even minutes. Many organizations have an end-user support function to handle very small projects that can be completed quickly. However, even though many IT projects can be completed quickly, it is still important to prioritize them.

Organizations can also categorize IT projects as having high, medium, or low priority based on the current business environment. For example, if it is crucial to cut operating costs quickly, projects that have the most potential to do so would be given a high priority. An organization should always complete high-priority projects first, even if a low- or medium-priority project could be finished in less time. Usually an organization has many more potential IT projects than it can undertake at one time, so it is crucial to work on the most important projects first.

4.3c Performing Financial Analyses

Financial considerations are an important aspect of the project selection process, whether economic times are tough or the economy is growing. As authors Dennis Cohen and Robert Graham put it, "Projects are never ends in themselves. Financially they are always a means to an end, cash."[6] Many organizations require an approved business case before pursuing projects, and financial projections are a critical component of the business case. (See Chapter 3 for a sample business case.) Three primary methods for projecting the financial value of projects include net present value analysis, return on investment, and payback analysis. Because project managers often deal with business executives, they must understand how to speak business language, which often boils down to the following important financial concepts.

Net Present Value Analysis

Most people know that a dollar earned today is worth more than a dollar earned five years from now—a principle called the time value of money. Many projects have financial implications that extend into the future. In order to evaluate potential projects equally, you need to consider their net present value.

Net present value (NPV) analysis is a method of calculating the expected net monetary gain or loss from a project by calculating the value of all expected future cash inflows and outflows at the present time. An organization should consider only projects with a positive NPV if financial value is a key criterion for project selection. A positive NPV means that the return from a project exceeds the **cost of capital**—the return available from investing the capital elsewhere. In other words, the cost of capital is the rate of return that could have been earned by putting the same money into a different investment with equal risk. Projects with higher NPVs are preferred to projects with lower NPVs, if all other factors are equal.

To calculate NPV, you must assume a certain discount rate. The **discount rate** is the interest rate used to discount cash flows. It takes into account not just the time value of money but also the risk or uncertainty of future cash flows. The greater the uncertainty of future cash flows, the higher the discount rate. It is also called the **capitalization rate** or the **opportunity cost of capital**.

Figure 4-4 illustrates this concept in Microsoft Excel for two different projects. Note that this example starts discounting immediately in Year 1 and uses a 10 percent discount rate. You can use the NPV function in Excel to calculate the NPV quickly. Detailed steps for performing this calculation manually are presented later.

Figure 4-4 lists the projected benefits first, followed by the costs, and then the calculated cash flow amount. Note that the sum of the **cash flow**—benefits minus costs or income minus expenses—is the same for both projects at $5,000. The net present values are different, however, because they account for the time value of money. Project 1 has

	A	B	C	D	E	F	G
1	Discount rate	10%					
2							
3	**PROJECT 1**	YEAR 1	YEAR 2	YEAR 3	YEAR 4	YEAR 5	TOTAL
4	Benefits	$0	$2,000	$3,000	$4,000	$5,000	$14,000
5	Costs	$5,000	$1,000	$1,000	$1,000	$1,000	$9,000
6	Cash flow	($5,000)	$1,000	$2,000	$3,000	$4,000	$5,000
7	NPV⟶	$2,316					
8		Formula =npv(b1,b6:f6)					
9							
10	**PROJECT 2**	YEAR 1	YEAR 2	YEAR 3	YEAR 4	YEAR 5	TOTAL
11	Benefits	$1,000	$2,000	$4,000	$4,000	$4,000	$15,000
12	Costs	$2,000	$2,000	$2,000	$2,000	$2,000	$10,000
13	Cash flow	($1,000)	$0	$2,000	$2,000	$2,000	$5,000
14	NPV⟶	$3,201					
15		Formula =npv(b1,b13:f13)					
16							
17							

Note that totals are equal, but NPVs are not because of the time value of money

© Cengage Learning 2016

FIGURE 4-4 Net present value example

a negative cash flow of $5,000 in the first year, while Project 2 has a negative cash flow of only $1,000 in the first year. Although both projects have the same total cash flows without discounting, they are not of comparable financial value. Project 2's NPV of $3,201 is better than Project 1's NPV of $2,316. NPV analysis, therefore, is a method for making equal comparisons between cash flows for multiyear projects.

To determine NPV, follow these steps:

1. Determine the estimated costs and benefits for the life of the project and the products it creates. For example, JWD Consulting assumed its project would produce a system in about six months that would be used for three years, so costs are included in Year 0, when the system is developed. Ongoing system costs and projected benefits are included for Years 1, 2, and 3.
2. Determine the discount rate. In Figure 4-4, the discount rate is 10 percent per year.
3. Calculate the net present value. Most spreadsheet software has a built-in function to calculate NPV. For example, Figure 4-4 shows the formula that Microsoft Excel uses: =npv(discount rate, range of cash flows), where the discount rate is in cell B1 and the range of cash flows for Project 1 are in cells B6 through F6. (See Chapter 7, Project Cost Management, for more information on cash flow and other cost-related terms.) To use the NPV function, you must have a row or column in the spreadsheet for the cash flow each year, which is the benefit amount for that year minus the cost amount.

The result of the formula yields an NPV of $2,316 for Project 1 and $3,201 for Project 2. Because both projects have positive NPVs, they are good candidates for selection. However, because Project 2 has an NPV that is 38 percent higher than Project 1, it would be the better choice. If the two numbers are close, then other methods should be used to help decide which project to select.

The mathematical formula for calculating NPV is:

$$\text{NPV} = \sum_{t=0 \ldots n} A_t / (1 + r)^t$$

where t equals the year of the cash flow, n is the last year of the cash flow, A is the amount of cash flow each year, and r is the discount rate.

If you cannot enter the data into spreadsheet software, you can perform the calculations by hand or with a calculator. First, determine the annual **discount factor**—a multiplier for each year based on the discount rate and year—and then apply it to the costs and benefits for each year. The formula for the discount factor is $1/(1 + r)^t$, where r is the discount rate, such as 8 percent, and t is the year. For example, the discount factors used in Figure 4-5 are calculated as follows:

Year 0 : discount factor $= 1/(1 + 0.08)^0 = 1$

Year 1 : discount factor $= 1/(1 + 0.08)^1 = 0.93$

Year 2 : discount factor $= 1/(1 + 0.08)^2 = 0.86$

Year 3 : discount factor $= 1/(1 + 0.08)^3 = 0.79$

After determining the discount factor for each year, multiply the costs and benefits each year by the appropriate discount factor. (Note discount factor in this case is rounded

Discount rate	8%					
Assume the project is completed in Year 0			Year			
	0	1	2	3	Total	
Costs	140,000	40,000	40,000	40,000		
Discount factor	1	0.93	0.86	0.79		
Discounted costs	**140,000**	**37,200**	**34,400**	**31,600**	**243,200**	
Benefits	0	200,000	200,000	200,000		
Discount factor	1	0.93	0.86	0.79		
Discounted benefits	**0**	**186,000**	**172,000**	**158,000**	**516,000**	
Discounted benefits - costs	(140,000)	148,800	137,600	126,400	**272,800**	←NPV
Cumulative benefits - costs	(140,000)	8,800	146,400	272,800		
ROI ──────────────→	112%					
	Payback In Year 1					

© Cengage Learning 2016

FIGURE 4-5   JWD Consulting net present value and return on investment example

to two decimal places). For example, in Figure 4-5, the discounted cost for Year 1 is $40,000 × 0.93 = $37,200. Next, sum all of the discounted costs and benefits each year to get a total. The total discounted costs in Figure 4-5 are $243,200. To calculate the NPV, subtract the total discounted costs from the total discounted benefits. In this example, the NPV is $516,000 − $243,200 = $272,800.

When calculating NPV, some organizations refer to the investment year or years for project costs as Year 0 and do not discount costs in Year 0. Other organizations start discounting immediately based on their financial procedures; it's simply a matter of preference for the organization.

The discount rate can also vary, often based on the prime rate and other economic considerations. Some people consider it to be the rate at which the organization could borrow money for the project. Financial experts in your organization can tell you what discount rate to use.

When calculating NPV, you can enter costs as negative numbers instead of positive numbers, and you can list costs first and then benefits. For example, Figure 4-5 shows the financial calculations used in the JWD Consulting business case for the project management intranet site project described in Chapter 3. Note that the discount rate is 8 percent, costs are not discounted in Year 0, the discount factors are rounded to two decimal places, costs are listed first, and costs are entered as positive numbers. Also note that costs and benefits are discounted before they are summed. The NPV and other calculations are the same; only the format is different. A project manager needs to check with the organization to learn its guidelines for when discounting starts, what discount rate to use, and what format the organization prefers.

Return on Investment

Another important financial consideration is return on investment. **Return on investment (ROI)** is the result of subtracting the project costs from the benefits and then dividing by the costs. For example, if you invest $100 today and next year it is worth $110, your ROI is ($110 – 100)/100 or 0.10 (10 percent). Note that the ROI is always a percentage. It can be positive or negative. For multiyear projects, it is best to use discounted costs and benefits when calculating ROI. Figure 4-5 shows an ROI of 112 percent, which you calculate as follows:

ROI = (total discounted benefits – total discounted costs)/discounted costs

ROI = (516,000 – 243,200)/243,200 = 112%

The higher the ROI is, the better. An ROI of 112 percent is outstanding.

Many organizations have a required rate of return for projects. The **required rate of return** is the minimum acceptable rate of return on an investment. For example, an organization might have a required rate of return of at least 10 percent for projects. The organization bases the required rate of return on what it could expect to receive elsewhere for an investment of comparable risk. You can also determine a project's **internal rate of return (IRR)** by finding what discount rate results in an NPV of zero for the project. You can use the Goal Seek function in Excel to set the cell that contains the formula for NPV to the value 0 by changing the cell that contains the discount rate. The resulting discount rate is the IRR. For example, in Figure 4-4, you could set cell b7 to zero while changing cell b1 to find that the IRR for Project 1 is 27 percent.

Payback Analysis

Payback analysis is another important financial tool when selecting projects. **Payback period** is the amount of time it will take to recoup the total dollars invested in a project, in terms of net cash inflows. In other words, payback analysis determines how much time will elapse before accrued benefits overtake accrued and continuing costs. Payback occurs when the net cumulative benefits equal the net cumulative costs or when the net cumulative benefits minus costs equal zero. Figure 4-5 shows how to find the payback period. The cumulative benefits minus costs for Year 0 are ($140,000). Adding that number to the discounted benefits minus costs for Year 1 results in $8,800. Because that number is positive, the payback occurs in Year 1.

Creating a chart helps illustrate more precisely when the payback period occurs. Figure 4-6 charts the cumulative discounted costs and cumulative discounted benefits each year using the numbers from Figure 4-5. Note that the lines cross around Year 1. This is the point where the cumulative discounted benefits equal the cumulative discounted costs, so that the cumulative discounted benefits minus costs are zero. Beyond this point, discounted benefits exceed discounted costs and the project shows a profit. Because this project started in Year 0, a payback in Year 1 actually means the project reached payback in its second year. An early payback period, such as in the first or second year, is considered very good.

Many organizations have requirements for the length of the payback period of an investment. They might require all IT projects to have a payback period of less than two years or even one year, regardless of the estimated NPV or ROI. Dan Hoover, vice president and area director of Ciber Inc., an international systems integration consultancy, suggests that organizations, especially small firms, should focus on payback period when making IT investment decisions. "If your costs are recovered in the first year," Hoover said, "the project is worthy of serious consideration, especially if the benefits are high. If the payback

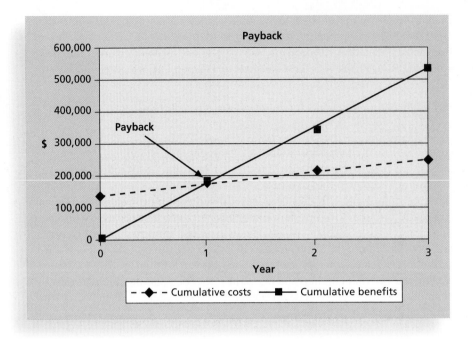

© Cengage Learning 2016

FIGURE 4-6   Charting the payback period for the JWD Consulting project

period is more than a year, it may be best to look elsewhere."[7] However, organizations must also consider long-range goals when making technology investments. Many crucial projects cannot achieve a payback so quickly or be completed in such a short time period.

To aid in project selection, project managers must understand the organization's financial expectations for projects. Top management must also understand the limitations of financial estimates, particularly for IT projects. For example, it is very difficult to develop good estimates of projected costs and benefits for IT projects. You will learn more about estimating costs and benefits in Chapter 7, Project Cost Management.

4.3d Using a Weighted Scoring Model

A **weighted scoring model** is a tool that provides a systematic process for selecting projects based on many criteria. These criteria can include factors such as meeting broad organizational needs; addressing problems, opportunities, or directives; the amount of time needed to complete the project; the overall priority of the project; and projected financial performance of the project.

The first step in creating a weighted scoring model is to identify criteria that are important to the project selection process. It often takes time to develop and reach agreement on these criteria. Holding facilitated brainstorming sessions or using groupware to exchange ideas can aid in developing these criteria. Possible criteria for IT projects include:

- Supports key business objectives or strategies
- Has strong internal sponsor

- Has strong customer support
- Uses realistic level of technology
- Can be implemented in one year or less
- Provides positive NPV
- Has low risk in meeting scope, time, and cost goals

Next, you assign a weight to each criterion based on its importance. Once again, determining weights requires consultation and final agreement. You can assign weights based on percentages; the weights of the criteria must total 100 percent. You then assign numerical scores to each criterion (for example, 0 to 100) for each project. The scores indicate how much each project meets each criterion. At this point, you can use a spreadsheet application to create a matrix of projects, criteria, weights, and scores. Figure 4-7 provides an example of a weighted scoring model to evaluate four different projects. After assigning weights for the criteria and scores for each project, you calculate a weighted score for each project by multiplying the weight for each criterion by its score and adding the resulting values.

	A	B	C	D	E	F
1	**Criteria**	**Weight**	**Project 1**	**Project 2**	**Project 3**	**Project 4**
2	Supports key business objectives	25%	90	90	50	20
3	Has strong internal sponsor	15%	70	90	50	20
4	Has strong customer support	15%	50	90	50	20
5	Uses realistic level of technology	10%	25	90	50	70
6	Can be implemented in one year or less	5%	20	20	50	90
7	Provides positive NPV	20%	50	70	50	50
8	Has low risk in meeting scope, time, and cost goals	10%	20	50	50	90
9	**Weighted Project Scores**	**100%**	**56**	**78.5**	**50**	**41.5**
10						
11						
12						
13						
14						
15						
16						
17						
18						
19						
20						
21						
22						
23						
24						
25						
26						

Weighted Score by Project

FIGURE 4-7 Sample weighted scoring model for project selection

For example, you calculate the weighted score for Project 1 in Figure 4-7 as:

$$25\% * 90 + 15\% * 70 + 15\% * 50 + 10\% * 25 + 5\% * 20 + 20\% * 50 + 10\% * 20 = 56$$

Note that in this example, Project 2 would be the obvious choice for selection because it has the highest weighted score. Creating a bar chart to graph the weighted scores for each project allows you to see the results at a glance.

If you create the weighted scoring model in a spreadsheet, you can enter the data, create and copy formulas, and perform a "what-if" analysis. For example, suppose that you want to change the weights for the criteria. By having the weighted scoring model in a spreadsheet, you can easily change the weights and update the weighted scores and charts automatically. This capability allows you to investigate various options for different stake-holders quickly. Ideally, the result should reflect the group's consensus, and any major disagreements should be documented.

You can also establish how well projects meet criteria by assigning points. For ex-ample, a project might receive 10 points if it definitely supports key business objectives, 5 points if it somewhat supports them, and 0 points if it is totally unrelated to key busi-ness objectives. With a point model, you can simply add all the points to determine the best projects for selection, without having to multiply weights and scores and sum the results.

You can also determine minimum scores or thresholds for specific criteria in a weighted scoring model. For example, suppose that an organization should not consider a project if it does not score at least 50 out of 100 on every criterion. You can build this type of threshold into the weighted scoring model to reject projects that do not meet these minimum standards. As you can see, weighted scoring models can aid in project selection decisions.

4.3e Implementing a Balanced Scorecard

Drs. Robert Kaplan and David Norton developed another approach to help select and manage projects that align with business strategy. A **balanced scorecard** is a strategic planning and management system that helps organizations align business activities to strategy, improve communications, and monitor performance against strategic goals. The Gartner Group estimates that over half of large U.S. organizations use this approach. The balanced scorecard has evolved over time. "The 'new' balanced scorecard trans-forms an organization's strategic plan from an attractive but passive document into the 'marching orders' for the organization on a daily basis. It provides a framework that not only provides performance measurements but helps planners identify what should be done and measured."[8] You can find several examples of balanced scorecards from manu-facturing companies like Shat-R-Shield to non-profits like the Kenya Red Cross at *www.balancedscorecard.org*.

As you can see, organizations can use many approaches to select projects. Many project managers have some say in which projects their organizations select for imple-mentation. Even if they do not, they need to understand the motives and overall business strategies for the projects they are managing. Project managers and team members are often called upon to explain the importance of their projects, and understanding project selection methods can help them represent the project effectively.

4.4 DEVELOPING A PROJECT CHARTER

After top management decides which projects to pursue, it is important to let the rest of the organization know about these projects. Management needs to create and distribute documentation to authorize project initiation. This documentation can take many different forms, but one common form is a project charter. A **project charter** is a document that formally recognizes the existence of a project and provides direction on the project's objectives and management. It authorizes the project manager to use organizational resources to complete the project. Ideally, the project manager plays a major role in developing the project charter.

155

Instead of project charters, some organizations initiate projects using a simple letter of agreement, while others use much longer documents or formal contracts. Key project stakeholders should sign a project charter to acknowledge agreement on the need for and intent of the project. A project charter is a key output of the initiation process, as described in Chapter 3.

The *PMBOK® Guide, Fifth Edition* lists inputs, tools, techniques, and outputs of the six project integration management processes. The following inputs are helpful in developing a project charter:

- *A project statement of work*: A statement of work is a document that describes the products or services to be created by the project team. It usually includes a description of the business need for the project, a summary of the requirements and characteristics of the products or services, and organizational information, such as appropriate parts of the strategic plan, showing the alignment of the project with strategic goals.
- *A business case*: As explained in Chapter 3, many projects require a business case to justify their investment. Information in the business case, such as the project objective, high-level requirements, and time and cost goals, is included in the project charter.
- *Agreements*: If you are working on a project under contract for an external customer, the contract or agreement should include much of the information needed for creating a good project charter. Some people might use a contract or agreement in place of a charter. However, many contracts are difficult to read and can often change, so it is still a good idea to create a project charter.
- *Enterprise environmental factors*: These factors include relevant government or industry standards, the organization's infrastructure, and marketplace conditions. Managers should review these factors when developing a project charter.
- *Organizational process assets*: **Organizational process assets** include formal and informal plans, policies, procedures, guidelines, information systems, financial systems, management systems, lessons learned, and historical information that can influence a project's success.

The main tools and techniques for developing a project charter are expert judgment and facilitation techniques, such as brainstorming and meeting management. Experts from inside and outside the organization should be consulted when creating a project charter to make sure it is useful and realistic. Facilitators often make it easier for experts to collaborate and provide useful information.

The only output of the process to develop a project charter is the charter itself. Although the format of project charters can vary tremendously, they should include at least the following basic information:

- The project's title and date of authorization
- The project manager's name and contact information
- A summary schedule, including the planned start and finish dates; if a summary milestone schedule is available, it should also be included or referenced
- A summary of the project's budget or reference to budgetary documents
- A brief description of the project objectives, including the business need or other justification for authorizing the project
- Project success criteria, including project approval requirements and who signs off on the project
- A summary of the planned approach for managing the project, which should describe stakeholder needs and expectations, important assumptions, and constraints, and should refer to related documents, such as a communications management plan, as available
- A roles and responsibilities matrix
- A sign-off section for signatures of key project stakeholders
- A comments section in which stakeholders can provide important comments related to the project

Unfortunately, many internal projects, like the one described in the opening case of this chapter, do not have project charters. They often have a budget and general guidelines, but no formal, signed documentation. If Nick had a project charter to refer to—especially if it included information for managing the project—top management would have received the business information it needed, and managing the project might have been easier. Project charters are usually not difficult to write. The difficult part is getting people with the proper knowledge and authority to write and sign the project charter. Top management should have reviewed the charter with Nick because he was the project manager. In their initial meeting, they should have discussed roles and responsibilities, as well as their expectations of how Nick should work with them. If there is no project charter, the project manager should work with key stakeholders, including top management, to create one. Table 4-1 shows a possible charter that Nick could have created for completing the next-gen DNA-sequencing instrument project.

Many projects fail because of unclear requirements and expectations, so starting with a project charter makes a lot of sense. If project managers are having difficulty obtaining support from project stakeholders, for example, they can refer to the agreements listed in the project charter. Note that the sample project charter in Table 4-1 includes several items under the Approach section to help Nick in managing the project and the sponsor in overseeing it. To help Nick make the transition to project manager, the charter said that the company would hire a technical replacement and part-time assistant for Nick as soon as possible. To help Ahmed, the project sponsor, feel more comfortable with how the project was being managed, items were included to ensure proper planning and communications. Recall from Chapter 2 that executive support contributes the most to successful IT projects. Because Nick was the fourth project manager on this project, top management at his company obviously had problems choosing and working with project managers.

TABLE 4-1 Project charter for the next-gen DNA-sequencing instrument completion project

Project Title: Next-gen DNA-Sequencing Instrument Completion Project

Date of Authorization: February 1

Project Start Date: February 1   **Projected Finish Date:** November 1

Key Schedule Milestones:

- Complete first version of the software by June 1
- Complete production version of the software by November 1

Budget Information: The firm has allocated $1.5 million for this project, and more funds are available if needed. The majority of costs for this project will be internal labor. All hardware will be outsourced.

Project Manager: Nick Carson, (650) 949-0707, ncarson@dnaconsulting.com

Project Objectives: The Next-gen DNA-sequencing instrument project has been under way for three years. It is a crucial project for our company. This is the first charter for the project; the objective is to complete the first version of the instrument software in four months and a production version in nine months.

Main Project Success Criteria: The software must meet all written specifications, be thoroughly tested, and be completed on time. The CEO will formally approve the project with advice from other key stakeholders.

Approach:

- Hire a technical replacement for Nick Carson and a part-time assistant as soon as possible.
- Within one month, develop a clear work breakdown structure, scope statement, and Gantt chart detailing the work required to complete the Next-gen DNA-sequencing instrument.
- Purchase all required hardware upgrades within two months.
- Hold weekly progress review meetings with the core project team and the sponsor.
- Conduct thorough software testing per the approved test plans.

ROLES AND RESPONSIBILITIES

Name	Role	Position	Contact Information
Ahmed Abrams	Sponsor	CEO	aabrams@dnaconsulting.com
Nick Carson	Project Manager	Manager	ncarson@dnaconsulting.com
Susan Johnson	Team Member	DNA expert	sjohnson@dnaconsulting.com
Renyong Chi	Team Member	Testing expert	rchi@dnaconsulting.com
Erik Haus	Team Member	Programmer	ehaus@dnaconsulting.com
Bill Strom	Team Member	Programmer	bstrom@dnaconsulting.com
Maggie Elliot	Team Member	Programmer	melliot@dnaconsulting.com

Sign-off: (Signatures of all the above stakeholders)

Ahmed Abrams   *Nick Carson*

Susan Johnson   *Renyong Chi*

Erik Haus   *Bill Strom*

Maggie Elliot

Comments: (Handwritten or typed comments from above stakeholders, if applicable)

"I want to be heavily involved in this project. It is crucial to our company's success, and I expect everyone to help make it succeed."—ahmed abrams

"The software test plans are complete and well documented. If anyone has questions, do not hesitate to contact me."—Renyong Chi

Taking the time to discuss, develop, and sign off on a simple project charter could have prevented several problems in this case.

After creating a project charter, the next step in project integration management is preparing a project management plan.

4.5 DEVELOPING A PROJECT MANAGEMENT PLAN

To coordinate and integrate information across project management knowledge areas and across the organization, there must be a good project management plan. A **project management plan** is a document used to coordinate all project planning documents and help guide a project's execution and control. Plans created in the other knowledge areas are considered subsidiary parts of the overall project management plan. Project management plans also document project planning assumptions and decisions regarding choices, facilitate communication among stakeholders, define the content, extent, and timing of key management reviews, and provide a baseline for progress measurement and project control. Project management plans should be dynamic, flexible, and subject to change when the environment or project changes. These plans should greatly assist the project manager in leading the project team and assessing project status.

To create and assemble a good project management plan, the project manager must practice the art of project integration management, because information is required from all of the project management knowledge areas. Working with the project team and other stakeholders to create a project management plan will help the project manager guide the project's execution and understand the overall project.

The main inputs for developing a project management plan include the project charter, outputs from planning processes, enterprise environment factors, and organizational process assets. The main tool and technique is expert judgment, and the output is a project management plan.

4.5a Project Management Plan Contents

Just as projects are unique, so are project management plans. A small project that involves a few people working over a couple of months might have a project management plan consisting of only a project charter, scope statement, and Gantt chart. A large project that involves 100 people working over three years would have a much more detailed project management plan. It is important to tailor project management plans to fit the needs of specific projects. The project management plans should guide the work, so they should be only as detailed as needed for each project.

Most project management plans have common elements. A project management plan includes an introduction or overview of the project, a description of how the project is organized, the management and technical processes used on the project, and sections describing the work to be performed, the schedule, and the budget.

The introduction or overview of the project should include the following information at a minimum:

- *The project name*: Every project should have a unique name, which helps distinguish each project and avoids confusion among related projects.
- *A brief description of the project and the need it addresses*: This description should clearly outline the goals of the project and strategic reason for it. The

description should be written in layperson's terms, avoid technical jargon, and include a rough time and cost estimate.

- *The sponsor's name*: Every project needs a sponsor. Include the name, title, and contact information of the sponsor in the introduction.
- *The names of the project manager and key team members*: The project manager should always be the contact for project information. Depending on the size and nature of the project, names of key team members may also be included.
- *Deliverables of the project*: This section should briefly list and describe the products that will be created as part of the project. Software packages, pieces of hardware, technical reports, and training materials are examples of deliverables.
- *A list of important reference materials*: Many projects have a history that precedes them. Listing important documents or meetings related to a project helps project stakeholders understand that history. This section should reference the plans produced for other knowledge areas. Recall from Chapter 3 that every knowledge area includes some planning processes. Therefore, the project management plan should reference and summarize important parts of the scope management, schedule management, cost management, quality management, human resource management, communications management, risk management, procurement management, and stakeholder management plans.
- *A list of definitions and acronyms, if appropriate*: Many projects, especially IT projects, involve terminology that is unique to a particular industry or technology. Providing a list of definitions and acronyms will help avoid confusion.

The description of how the project is organized should include the following information:

- *Organizational charts*: The description should include an organizational chart for the company sponsoring the project and for the customer's company, if the project is for an external customer. The description should also include a project organizational chart to show the lines of authority, responsibilities, and communication for the project. For example, the Manhattan Project introduced in Chapter 1 had a very detailed organizational chart of all participants.
- *Project responsibilities*: This section of the project plan should describe the major project functions and activities and identify the people responsible for them. A responsibility assignment matrix (described in Chapter 9) is often used to display this information.
- *Other organizational or process-related information*: Depending on the nature of the project, the team might need to document major processes they follow on the project. For example, if the project involves releasing a major software upgrade, team members might benefit from having a diagram or timeline of the major steps involved in the process.

The section of the project management plan that describes management and technical approaches should include the following information:

- *Management objectives*: It is important to understand top management's view of the project, the priorities for the project, and any major assumptions or constraints.

- *Project controls*: This section describes how to monitor project progress and handle changes. Will there be monthly status reviews and quarterly progress reviews? Will there be specific forms or charts to monitor progress? Will the project use earned value management (described in Chapter 7) to assess and track performance? What is the process for change control? What level of management is required to approve different types of changes? (You will learn more about change control later in this chapter.)
- *Risk management*: This section briefly addresses how the project team will identify, manage, and control risks. This section should refer to the risk management plan, if one is required for the project.
- *Project staffing*: This section describes the number and types of people required for the project. It should refer to the human resource plan, if one is required for the project.
- *Technical processes*: This section describes specific methodologies a project might use and explains how to document information. For example, many IT projects follow specific software development methodologies or use particular Computer Aided Software Engineering (CASE) tools. Many companies or customers also have specific formats for technical documentation. It is important to clarify these technical processes in the project management plan.

The next section of the project management plan should describe the work that needs to be performed and reference the scope management plan. It should summarize the following:

- *Major work packages*: A project manager usually organizes the project work into several work packages using a work breakdown structure (WBS) and produces a scope statement to describe the work in more detail. This section should briefly summarize the main work packages for the project and refer to appropriate sections of the scope management plan.
- *Key deliverables*: This section lists and describes the key products created as part of the project. It should also describe the quality expectations for the product deliverables.
- *Other work-related information*: This section highlights key information related to the work performed on the project. For example, it might list specific hardware or software to use on the project or certain specifications to follow. It should document major assumptions made in defining the project work.

The project schedule information section should include the following:

- *Summary schedule*: It is helpful to have a one-page summary of the overall project schedule. Depending on the project's size and complexity, the summary schedule might list only key deliverables and their planned completion dates. For smaller projects, it might include all of the work and associated dates for the entire project in a Gantt chart. For example, the Gantt chart and milestone schedule provided in Chapter 3 for JWD Consulting were fairly short and simple.

- *Detailed schedule*: This section provides more detailed information about the project schedule. It should reference the schedule management plan and discuss dependencies among project activities that could affect the project schedule. For example, this section might explain that a major part of the work cannot start until an external agency provides funding. A network diagram can show these dependencies (see Chapter 6, Project Time Management).
- *Other schedule-related information*: Many assumptions are often made when preparing project schedules. This section should document major assumptions and highlight other important information related to the project schedule.

The budget section of the project management plan should include the following:

- *Summary budget*: The summary budget includes the total estimate of the overall project's budget. It could also include the budget estimate for each month or year by certain budget categories. It is important to provide some explanation of what these numbers mean. For example, is the total budget estimate a firm number that cannot change, or is it a rough estimate based on projected costs over the next three years?
- *Detailed budget*: This section summarizes the contents of the cost management plan and includes more detailed budget information. For example, what are the fixed and recurring cost estimates for the project each year? What are the projected financial benefits of the project? What types of people are needed to do the work, and how are the labor costs calculated? (See Chapter 7, Project Cost Management, for more information on creating cost estimates and budgets.)
- *Other budget-related information*: This section documents major assumptions and highlights other important information related to financial aspects of the project.

4.5b Using Guidelines to Create Project Management Plans

Many organizations use guidelines to create project management plans. Microsoft Project 2013 and other project management software packages come with several template files to use as guidelines. However, do not confuse a project management plan with a Gantt chart. The project management plan is much more than a Gantt chart, as described earlier.

Many government agencies also provide guidelines for creating project management plans. For example, the U.S. Department of Defense (DOD) Standard 2167, Software Development Plan, describes the format for contractors to use when creating a software development plan for DOD projects. The Institute of Electrical and Electronics Engineers (IEEE) Standard 1058–1998 describes the contents of its Software Project Management Plan (SPMP). Table 4-2 provides some of the categories for the IEEE SPMP. Companies that work on software development projects for the Department of Defense must follow this standard or a similar standard.

TABLE 4-2 Sample contents for the IEEE software project management plan (SPMP)

Major Section Headings	Section Topics
Overview	Purpose, scope, and objectives; assumptions and constraints; project deliverables; schedule and budget summary; evolution of the plan
Project Organization	External interfaces; internal structure; roles and responsibilities
Managerial Process Plan	Start-up plans (estimation, staffing, resource acquisition, and project staff training plans); work plan (work activities, schedule, resource, and budget allocation); control plan; risk management plan; closeout plan
Technical Process Plans	Process model; methods, tools, and techniques; infrastructure plan; product acceptance plan
Supporting Process Plans	Configuration management plan; verification and validation plan; documentation plan; quality assurance plan; reviews and audits; problem resolution plan; subcontractor management plan; process improvement plan

Source: IEEE Standard 1058–1998

In many private organizations, specific documentation standards are not as rigorous; however, there are usually guidelines for developing project management plans. It is good practice to follow the organization's standards or guidelines for developing project management plans to facilitate their execution. The organization can work more efficiently if all project management plans follow a similar format. Recall from Chapter 1 that companies that excel in project management develop and deploy standardized project delivery systems.

> The winners clearly spell out what needs to be done in a project, by whom, when, and how. For this they use an integrated toolbox, including PM tools, methods, and techniques. … If a scheduling template is developed and used over and over, it becomes a repeatable action that leads to higher productivity and lower uncertainty. Sure, using scheduling templates is neither a breakthrough nor a feat. But laggards exhibited almost no use of the templates. Rather, in constructing schedules their project managers started with a clean sheet, a clear waste of time.[9]

In the chapter's opening case, Nick Carson's top managers were disappointed because he did not provide the project planning information they needed to make important business decisions. They wanted to see detailed project management plans, including schedules and a means for tracking progress. Nick had never created a project management plan or even a simple progress report before, and the organization did not provide templates or examples to follow. If it had, Nick might have been able to deliver the information top management was expecting.

4.6 DIRECTING AND MANAGING PROJECT WORK

Directing and managing project work involves managing and performing the work described in the project management plan, one of the main inputs for this process. Other inputs include approved change requests, enterprise environmental factors, and organizational process assets. The majority of time on a project is usually spent on execution, as is most of the project's budget.

The application area of the project directly affects project execution because products are created during the execution phase. For example, the next-gen DNA-sequencing instrument from the opening case and all associated software and documentation would be produced during project execution. The project team would need to use its expertise in biology, hardware and software development, and testing to create the product successfully.

The project manager needs to focus on leading the project team and managing stakeholder relationships to execute the project management plan successfully. Project human resource management, communications management, and stakeholder management are crucial to a project's success. See Chapters 9, 10, and 13, respectively, for more information on these knowledge areas. If the project involves a significant amount of risk or outside resources, the project manager also needs to be well versed in project risk management and project procurement management. See Chapters 11 and 12 for details on those knowledge areas. Many unique situations occur during project execution, so project managers must be flexible and creative in dealing with them. Review the situation that Erica Bell faced during project execution in Chapter 3. Also review the ResNet case study (available on the companion website for this text) to understand the execution challenges that project manager Peeter Kivestu and his project team faced.

4.6a Coordinating Planning and Execution

In project integration management, project planning and execution are intertwined and inseparable activities. The main function of creating a project management plan is to guide project execution. A good plan should help produce good products or work results and should document what constitutes good work results. Updates to plans should reflect knowledge gained from completing work earlier in the project. Anyone who has tried to write a computer program from poor specifications appreciates the importance of a good plan. Anyone who has had to document a poorly programmed system appreciates the importance of good execution.

A common-sense approach to improving the coordination between project plan development and execution is to follow this simple rule: Those who will do the work should plan the work. All project personnel need to develop both planning and executing skills, and they need experience in these areas. In IT projects, programmers who have to write detailed specifications and then create the code from them become better at writing specifications. Likewise, most systems analysts begin their careers as programmers, so they understand what type of analysis and documentation they need to write good code. Although project managers are responsible for developing the overall project management plan, they must solicit input from project team members who are developing plans in each knowledge area.

4.6b Providing Strong Leadership and a Supportive Culture

Strong leadership and a supportive organizational culture are crucial during project execution. Project managers must lead by example to demonstrate the importance of creating good project plans and then following them in project execution. Project managers often create plans for things they need to do themselves. If project managers follow through on their own plans, their team members are more likely to do the same.

Good project execution also requires a supportive organizational culture. For example, organizational procedures can help or hinder project execution. If an organization has useful guidelines and templates for project management that everyone in the organization

✓ WHAT WENT RIGHT?

In *Pulse of the Profession®: Capturing the Value of Project Management 2015*, PMI found that organizations that excel in project management are indeed capturing business value. They complete about 80 percent of their projects successfully (defined by meeting the scope on time and on budget) and waste 13 times less money than low-performing counterparts. "Their rigorous approach to project, program and portfolio management **improves their ability to execute strategy** and creates a competitive advantage."[10]

The surprising news in this survey of 2,800 global professionals was that only 12 percent of organizations were considered to be high performers, a percentage that has remained unchanged since 2012. The main industry group surveyed was in IT (19 percent), followed by financial services (11 percent).

In order to improve, organizations must make some major *cultural changes*. They need to make sure that everyone fully understands the value of project management, require that executive sponsors are fully engaged on projects and programs, and align their projects to the organization's strategy.

follows, it will be easier for project managers and their teams to plan and do their work. If the organization uses the project plans as the basis for performing work and monitoring progress during execution, the culture will promote the relationship between good planning and execution. On the other hand, if organizations have confusing or bureaucratic project management guidelines that hinder getting work done or measuring progress against plans, project managers and their teams will be frustrated.

Even with a supportive organizational culture, project managers may sometimes find it necessary to break the rules to produce project results in a timely manner. When project managers break the rules, politics will play a role in the results. For example, if a particular project requires use of nonstandard software, the project manager must use political skills to convince concerned stakeholders that using standard software would be inadequate. Breaking organizational rules—and getting away with it—requires excellent leadership, communication, and political skills.

4.6c Capitalizing on Product, Business, and Application Area Knowledge

In addition to strong leadership, communication, and political skills, project managers need to possess product, business, and application area knowledge to execute projects successfully. It is often helpful for IT project managers to have prior technical experience or at least a working knowledge of IT products. For example, if the project manager were leading a team to help define user requirements, it would be helpful to understand the language of the business and technical experts on the team. See Chapter 5, Project Scope Management, for more information on collecting requirements.

Many IT projects are small, so project managers may be required to perform some technical work or mentor team members to complete the project. For example, a three-month project to develop a web-based application with only three team members would benefit most from a project manager who can complete some of the technical work. On larger projects, however, the project manager's primary responsibility is to lead the team and communicate with key project stakeholders. The project manager does not have time to do the technical work. In this case, it is usually best that the project manager understand the business and application area of the project more than the technology involved.

On very large projects the project manager *must* understand the business and application area of the project. For example, Northwest Airlines completed a series of projects in recent years to develop and upgrade its reservation systems. The company spent millions of dollars and had more than 70 full-time people working on the projects at peak periods. The project manager, Peeter Kivestu, had never worked in an IT department, but he had extensive knowledge of the airline industry and the reservations process. He carefully picked his team leaders, making sure they had the required technical and product knowledge. ResNet was the first large IT project at Northwest Airlines led by a business manager instead of a technical expert, and it was a roaring success. Many organizations have found that large IT projects require experienced general managers who understand the business and application area of the technology, not the technology itself.

4.6d Project Execution Tools and Techniques

Directing and managing project work requires specialized tools and techniques, some of which are unique to project management. Project managers can use specific tools and techniques to perform activities that are part of execution processes. These include:

- *Expert judgment*: Anyone who has worked on a large, complex project appreciates the importance of expert judgment in making good decisions. Project managers should not hesitate to consult experts on different topics, such as what methodology to follow, what programming language to use, and what training approach to follow.
- *Meetings:* Meetings are crucial during project execution. Face-to-face meetings with individuals or groups of people are important, as are phone and virtual meetings. Meetings allow people to develop relationships, pick up on important body language or tone of voice, and have a dialogue to help resolve problems. It is often helpful to establish set meeting times for various stakeholders. For example, Nick could have scheduled a short meeting once a week with senior managers. He could have also scheduled 10-minute stand-up meetings every morning for the project team.
- *Project management information systems*: As described in Chapter 1, hundreds of project management software products are on the market today. Many large organizations use powerful enterprise project management systems that are accessible via the Internet and tie into other systems, such as financial systems. Even in smaller organizations, project managers or other team members can create Gantt charts that include links to other planning documents on an internal network. For example, Nick or his assistant could have created a detailed Gantt chart for their project in Project 2013 and created links to other key planning documents created in Word, Excel, or PowerPoint. Nick could have shown the summary tasks during the progress review meetings, and if top management had questions, Nick could have shown them supporting details. Nick's team could also have set baselines for completing the project and tracked their progress toward achieving those

goals. See Appendix A for details on using Project 2013 to perform these functions, and for samples of Gantt charts and other useful outputs from project management software.

Although project management information systems can aid in project execution, project managers must remember that positive leadership and strong teamwork are critical to successful project management. Project managers should delegate the detailed work involved in using these tools to other team members and focus on providing leadership for the whole project to ensure project success. Stakeholders often focus on the most important output of execution from their perspective: the deliverables. For example, a production version of the next-gen DNA-sequencing instrument was the main deliverable for the project in the opening case. Of course, many other deliverables were created along the way, such as software modules, tests, and reports. Other outputs of project execution include work performance information, change requests, and updates to the project management plan and project documents.

Project managers and their teams are most often remembered for how well they executed a project and handled difficult situations. Likewise, sports teams around the world know that the key to winning is good execution. Team coaches can be viewed as project managers, with each game a separate project. Coaches are often judged on their win-loss record, not on how well they planned for each game. On a humorous note, when one losing coach was asked what he thought about his team's execution, he responded, "I'm all for it!"

4.7 MONITORING AND CONTROLLING PROJECT WORK

On large projects, many project managers say that 90 percent of the job is communicating and managing changes. Changes are inevitable on most projects, so it's important to develop and follow a process to monitor and control changes.

Monitoring project work includes collecting, measuring, and disseminating performance information. It also involves assessing measurements and analyzing trends to determine what process improvements can be made. The project team should continuously monitor project performance to assess the overall health of the project and identify areas that require special attention.

The project management plan, schedule and cost forecasts, validated changes, work performance information, enterprise environmental factors, and organizational process assets are all important inputs for monitoring and controlling project work.

The project management plan provides the baseline for identifying and controlling project changes. A **baseline** is the approved project management plan plus approved changes. For example, the project management plan includes a section that describes the work to perform on a project. This section of the plan describes the key deliverables for the project, the products of the project, and quality requirements. The schedule section of the project management plan lists the planned dates for completing key deliverables, and the budget section of the plan provides the planned cost of these deliverables. The project team must focus on delivering the work as planned. If the project team or someone else causes changes during project execution, the team must revise the project management plan and have it approved by the project sponsor. Many people refer to different types of baselines, such as a cost baseline or schedule baseline, to describe different project goals more clearly and performance toward meeting them.

Schedule and cost forecasts, validated changes, and work performance information provide details on how project execution is going. The main purpose of this information is to alert the project manager and project team about issues that are causing problems or might cause problems in the future. The project manager and project team must continuously monitor and control project work to decide if corrective or preventive actions are needed, what the best course of action is, and when to act.

MEDIA SNAPSHOT

Few events get more media attention than the Olympic Games. Imagine all the work involved in planning and executing an event that involves thousands of athletes from around the world with millions of spectators. The 2002 Olympic Winter Games and Paralympics took five years to plan and cost more than $1.9 billion. PMI presented the Salt Lake Organizing Committee (SLOC) with the Project of the Year award for delivering world-class games that, according to the International Olympic Committee, "made a profound impact upon the people of the world."[11]

Four years before the Games began, the SLOC used a Primavera software-based system with a cascading color-coded WBS to integrate planning. A year before the Games, the team added a Venue Integrated Planning Schedule to help integrate resource needs, budgets, and plans. For example, this software helped the team coordinate different areas involved in controlling access into and around a venue, such as roads, pedestrian pathways, seating and safety provisions, and hospitality areas, saving nearly $10 million.

When the team experienced a budget deficit three years before the Games, it separated "must-have" items from "nice-to-have" items and implemented a rigorous expense approval process. According to Matthew Lehman, SLOC managing director, using classic project management tools turned a $400 million deficit into a $100 million surplus.

The SLOC also used an Executive Roadmap, a one-page list of the top 100 activities during the Games, to keep executives apprised of progress. Activities were tied to detailed project information within each department's schedule. A 90-day highlighter showed which managers were accountable for each integrated activity. Fraser Bullock, SLOC Chief Operating Officer and Chief, said, "We knew when we were on and off schedule and where we had to apply additional resources. The interrelation of the functions meant they could not run in isolation—it was a smoothly running machine."[12]

Important outputs of monitoring and controlling project work include change requests and work performance reports. Change requests include recommended corrective and preventive actions and defect repairs. Corrective actions should result in improvements in project performance. Preventive actions reduce the probability of negative consequences associated with project risks. Defect repairs involve bringing defective deliverables into conformance with requirements. For example, if project team members have not been reporting hours that they worked, a corrective action would show them how to enter the information and let them know that they need to do it. An example of a preventive action might be modifying a time-tracking system screen to avoid common errors people have made in the past. A defect repair might be having someone redo an incorrect entry. Many organizations use a formal change request process and forms to keep track of project changes, as described in the next section. Work performance reports include status reports, progress reports, memos, and other documents used to communicate performance.

4.8 PERFORMING INTEGRATED CHANGE CONTROL

Integrated change control involves identifying, evaluating, and managing changes throughout the project life cycle. The three main objectives of integrated change control are:

- *Influencing the factors that create changes to ensure that changes are beneficial*: To ensure that changes are beneficial and that a project is successful, project managers and their teams must make trade-offs among key project dimensions, such as scope, time, cost, and quality.
- *Determining that a change has occurred*: To determine that a change has occurred, the project manager must know the status of key project areas at all times. In addition, the project manager must communicate significant changes to top management and key stakeholders. Top management and other key stakeholders do not like surprises, especially ones that mean the project might produce less, take longer to complete, cost more than planned, or create products of lower quality.
- *Managing actual changes as they occur*: Managing change is a key role of project managers and their teams. It is important that project managers exercise discipline in managing the project to help minimize the number of changes that occur.

Important inputs to the integrated change control process include the project management plan, work performance information, change requests, enterprise environmental factors, and organizational process assets. Important outputs include approved change requests, a change log, and updates to the project management plan and project documents.

Change requests are common on projects and occur in many different forms. They can be oral or written, formal or informal. For example, a project team member responsible for installing a server might ask the project manager if it is acceptable to order a server with a faster processor than planned. The server is from the same manufacturer and has the same approximate cost. Because this change is positive and should have no negative effects on the project, the project manager might give a verbal approval at the progress review meeting. Nevertheless, it is still important that the project manager document this change to avoid any potential problems. The appropriate team member should update the scope statement to include the new server specifications.

Still, keep in mind that many change requests can have a major impact on a project. For example, customers who change their minds about the number of hardware components they want as part of a project will have a definite impact on its scope and cost. Such a change might also affect the project's schedule. The project team must present such significant changes in written form to the project sponsor, and there should be a formal review process for analyzing and deciding whether to approve these changes.

Change is unavoidable and often expected on most IT projects. Technologies change, personnel change, organizational priorities change, and so on. A good change control system is also important for project success.

4.8a Change Control on IT Projects

From the 1950s to the 1980s, IT was often referred to as data automation or data processing. At that time, a widely held view of project management was that the project team should strive to do exactly what it planned, on time and within budget. The problem with this view was that project teams could rarely meet original project goals, especially for projects that used new technologies. Stakeholders rarely agreed up front on the scope of the project or what the finished product should look like. Time and cost estimates created early in a project were rarely accurate.

Beginning in the 1990s, most project managers and top management realized that project management is a process of constant communication and negotiation about project objectives and stakeholder expectations. This view assumes that changes happen throughout the project life cycle and recognizes that changes are often beneficial to some projects. For example, if a project team member discovers a new hardware or software technology that could satisfy customers' needs for less time and money, the project team and key stakeholders should be open to making major changes in the project.

All projects will have some changes, and managing them is a key issue in project management, especially for IT projects. Many IT projects involve the use of hardware and software that is updated frequently. To continue the example from earlier in this section, the initial plan for ordering the server might have identified a model that used cutting-edge technology at the time. If the actual server order occurred six months later, it is quite possible that a more powerful server could be available at the same cost. This example illustrates a positive change. On the other hand, the server manufacturer specified in the project plan could go out of business, which would result in a negative change. IT project managers should be accustomed to such changes and build some flexibility into their project plans and execution. Customers for IT projects should also be open to meeting project objectives in different ways.

Some changes might make sense but be too large to fit into a current project. Remember that projects have scope, time, cost, and other goals, and changes often affect those goals. If the organization wants to meet time and cost goals, for example, it must control changes to the project's scope. Organizations often decide to document some change requests and include them in an upgrade to the current project.

Even if project managers, project teams, and customers are flexible, it is important that projects have a formal change control system. This formal system is necessary to plan for managing change.

4.8b Change Control System

A **change control system** is a formal, documented process that describes when and how official project documents may be changed. It also describes the people authorized to make changes, the paperwork required for these changes, and any automated or manual tracking systems the project will use. A change control system often includes a change control board, configuration management, and a process for communicating changes.

A **change control board (CCB)** is a formal group of people responsible for approving or rejecting changes to a project. The primary functions of a CCB are to provide guidelines for preparing change requests, evaluating change requests, and managing the implementation of approved changes. An organization could have key stakeholders for the entire organization on this board, and a few members could rotate based on the unique needs of each project. By creating a formal board and a process for managing changes, overall change control should improve.

However, CCBs can have some drawbacks, such as the time it takes to make decisions on proposed changes. CCBs often meet only once a week or once a month and may not make decisions in one meeting. Some organizations have streamlined processes for making quick decisions on smaller project changes. One company created a "48-hour policy," in which task leaders on a large IT project would reach agreements on key decisions or changes within their expertise and authority. The person in the area most affected by this decision or change then had 48 hours to go to top management and seek approval. If the project team's decision could not be implemented for some reason, the top manager consulted would have 48 hours to reverse the decision; otherwise, the project team's decision was approved. This type of process is an effective way to deal with the many time-sensitive decisions or changes that project teams must make on IT projects.

Configuration management is another important part of integrated change control. **Configuration management** ensures that the descriptions of the project's products are correct and complete. It involves identifying and controlling the functional and physical design characteristics of products and their support documentation. Members of the project team, frequently called configuration management specialists, are often assigned to perform configuration management for large projects. Their job is to identify and document the functional and physical characteristics of the project's products, control any changes to such characteristics, record and report the changes, and audit the products to verify conformance to requirements. Visit the Institute of Configuration Management's website (*www.icmhq.com*) for more information on this topic.

 GLOBAL ISSUES

Rapid changes in technology, such as the increased use of mobile roaming for communications, often cause governments around the world to take action. Incompatible hardware, software, and networks can make communications difficult in some regions, and a lack of competition can cause prices to soar. Fortunately, a group called the Organisation for Economic Co-operation and Development (OECD) promotes policies that will improve the economic and social well-being of people around the world. In February 2012, the OECD called upon its members' governments to boost competition in international mobile roaming markets. "The OECD has detailed a series of measures that, if implemented would, it says: 'encourage effective competition, raise consumer awareness and protection and ensure fairer prices.' If these fail to produce results it says: 'Governments should consider price regulation for roaming services,' and that 'Wholesale roaming services could be regulated by means of bilateral or multilateral wholesale agreements with mutually established price caps.'"[13]

OECD also encourages expansion of other technologies. By the end of 2013, wireless broadband penetration grew to 72.4 percent in the 34-country OECD area. Strong demand for smartphones and tablets helped wireless broadband subscriptions grow by 14.6 percent.[14]

Another critical factor in change control is communication. Project managers should use written and oral performance reports to help identify and manage project changes. For example, on software development projects, most programmers must make their edits to a copy of the master file in a database; to ensure version control, programmers must "check out" the file to edit it. If two programmers are allowed to check out the same file, they must coordinate to merge their changes. In addition to written or formal communication methods, oral and informal communications are also important. Some project managers have stand-up meetings once a week or even every morning, depending on the nature of the project. The goal of a stand-up meeting is to quickly communicate what is most important for the project. For example, the project manager might have a stand-up meeting every morning with all of the team leaders. There might be a stand-up meeting every Monday morning with all interested stakeholders. Requiring participants to stand keeps meetings short and forces everyone to focus on the most important project events.

Why is good communication so critical to success? One of the most frustrating aspects of project change is not having everyone coordinated and informed about the latest project information. Again, it is the project manager's responsibility to integrate all project changes so that the project stays on track. The project manager and staff members must develop a system for notifying everyone affected by a change in a timely manner. E-mail, real-time databases, cell phones, and the Web make it easy to disseminate the most current project information. You will learn more about good communication in Chapter 10, Project Communications Management.

Table 4-3 lists suggestions for performing integrated change control. As described earlier, project management is a process of constant communication and negotiation. Project managers should plan for changes and use appropriate tools and techniques, such as a change control board, configuration management, and good communication. It is helpful to define procedures for making timely decisions about small changes, use written and oral performance reports to help identify and manage changes, and use software to assist in planning, updating, and controlling projects.

Project managers must also provide strong leadership to steer the project to successful completion. They must not get too involved in managing project changes. Project managers should delegate much of the detailed work to project team members and focus on

TABLE 4-3   Suggestions for performing integrated change control

View project management as a process of constant communication and negotiation
Plan for change
Establish a formal change control system, including a change control board (CCB)
Use effective configuration management
Define procedures for making timely decisions about smaller changes
Use written and oral performance reports to help identify and manage change
Use project management software and other software to help manage and communicate changes
Focus on leading the project team and meeting overall project goals and expectations

providing overall leadership for the project in general. Remember, project managers must focus on the big picture and perform project integration management well to lead their team and organization to success.

4.9 CLOSING PROJECTS OR PHASES

The last process in project integration management is closing the project or phase, which requires that you finalize all activities and transfer the completed or cancelled work to the appropriate people. The main inputs to this process are the project management plan, accepted deliverables, and organizational process assets. The main tool and technique is again expert judgment. The outputs of closing projects are:

- *Final product, service, or result transition*: Project sponsors are usually most interested in making sure they receive delivery of the final products, services, or results they expected when they authorized the project. For items produced under contract, formal acceptance or handover includes a written statement that the terms of the contract were met. Internal projects can also include some type of project completion form.
- *Organizational process asset updates*: The project team should provide a list of project documentation, project closure documents, and historical information produced by the project in a useful format. This information is considered a process asset. Project teams normally produce a final project report, which often includes a transition plan describing work to be done as part of operations after the project is completed. Teams also often write a lessons-learned report at the end of a project, and this information can be a tremendous asset for future projects. (See Chapter 10, Project Communications Management, for more information on creating final project reports, lessons-learned reports, and other project communications.) Several organizations also conduct a post-implementation review to analyze whether the project achieved what it set out to do. Information from this type of review also becomes an organizational process asset for future projects.

4.10 USING SOFTWARE TO ASSIST IN PROJECT INTEGRATION MANAGEMENT

As described throughout this chapter, project teams can use various types of software to assist in project integration management. Project teams can create documents with word-processing software, give presentations with presentation software, track information with spreadsheets, databases, or customized software, and transmit information using various types of communication software.

Project management software is also an important tool for developing and integrating project planning documents, executing the project management plan and related project plans, monitoring and controlling project activities, and performing integrated change control. Small project teams can use low-end or midrange project management software to coordinate their work. For large projects, such as the Olympic Games described in the Media Snapshot earlier in this chapter, organizations may benefit most from high-end

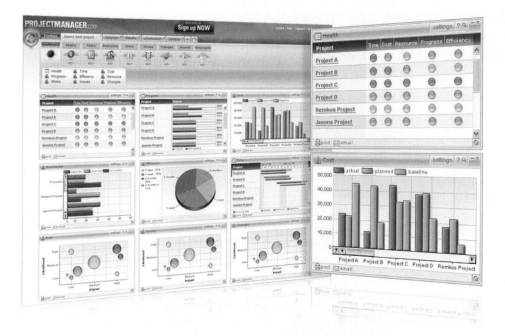

www.projectmanager.com

FIGURE 4-8   Sample portfolio management software screens

tools that provide enterprise project management capabilities and integrate all aspects of project management.

As you learned in Chapter 1, organizations can also use software to assist in project portfolio management and optimization. Portfolio management software often provides many types of charts or dashboards to help managers see the big picture in managing portfolios of projects. For example, Figure 4-8 shows column charts, bar charts, pie charts, and bubble charts from *www.projectmanager.com*. All projects can benefit from using some type of project management information system to coordinate and communicate project information.

In recent years, the growth of cloud computing has transformed how, when, and where people work. Many project management software tools are now available in the cloud, as are other tools and services. Most business professionals and students now store their files using some type of cloud storage (Google Drive, Microsoft OneDrive, DropBox, etc.). Many cloud tools are accessible via smartphones and tablets as well as laptops and desktops. Cloud computing enables users to easily access and share information from any location at any time. Project integration management is not easy, but the cloud has definitely helped provide easier access to important information and applications.

As you can see, a lot of work is involved in project integration management. Project managers and their teams must focus on pulling all the elements of a project together to successfully complete it.

173

CASE WRAP-UP

Without consulting Nick Carson or his team, Nick's CEO hired a new person, Jim Lansing, to act as a middle manager between himself and the people in Nick's department. The CEO and other top managers really liked Jim; he met with them often, shared ideas, and had a great sense of humor. He started developing standards that the company could use to help manage projects in the future. For example, he developed templates for creating plans and progress reports and put them on the company's intranet. However, Jim and Nick did not get along, especially after Jim accidentally sent an e-mail to Nick that was intended for the CEO. In the e-mail, Jim said that Nick was hard to work with and preoccupied with the birth of his son.

Nick was furious when he read the e-mail, and stormed into the CEO's office. The CEO suggested that Nick move to another department, but Nick did not like that option. Without considering the repercussions, the CEO offered Nick a severance package to leave the company. Because of the planned corporate buyout, the CEO knew the company might have to let some people go anyway. Nick talked the CEO into giving him a two-month sabbatical he had earned plus a higher percentage on his stock options. After discussing the situation with his wife and realizing that he would get over $70,000 if he resigned, Nick took the severance package. He had such a bad experience as a project manager that he decided to stick with being a technical expert. Jim, however, thrived in his position and helped the company improve its project management practices and ensure success in a highly competitive market.

Chapter Summary

Project integration management is usually the most important project management knowledge area, because it ties together all the other areas of project management. A project manager's primary focus should be on project integration management.

Before selecting projects to pursue, it is important for organizations to follow a strategic planning process. Many organizations perform a SWOT analysis to help identify potential projects based on their strengths, weaknesses, opportunities, and threats. IT projects should support the organization's overall business strategy. Common techniques for selecting projects include focusing on broad organizational needs, categorizing projects, performing financial analyses, developing weighted scoring models, and using balanced scorecards.

Project integration management includes the following processes:

- Developing the project charter, which involves working with stakeholders to create the document that formally authorizes a project. Project charters can have different formats, but they should include basic project information and signatures of key stakeholders.

- Developing the project management plan, which involves coordinating all planning efforts to create a consistent, coherent document. The main purpose of project plans is to facilitate action.

- Directing and managing project work, which involves carrying out the project plans by performing the activities included in it. Project plan execution usually requires the majority of a project's budget.

- Monitoring and controlling project work, which is necessary to meet the performance objectives of the project. The project team should continuously monitor project performance to assess the overall health of the project.

- Performing integrated change control, which involves identifying, evaluating, and managing changes throughout the project life cycle. A change control system often includes a change control board (CCB), configuration management, and a process for communicating changes.

- Closing the project or phase involves finalizing all project activities. It is important to follow good procedures to ensure that all project activities are completed and that the project sponsor accepts delivery of the final products, services, or results.

Several types of software products are available to assist in project integration management. Other tools can assist in project selection and ensure that projects align with business strategy.

Quick Quiz

1. Which of the following processes is not part of project integration management?
    a. developing the project business case
    b. developing the project charter
    c. developing the project management plan
    d. closing the project or phase
2. What is the last step in the four-stage planning process for selecting IT projects?
    a. IT strategy planning
    b. business area analysis
    c. mind mapping
    d. resource allocation

3. Which of the following is not a best practice for new product development projects?

    a. aligning projects and resources with business strategy

    b. selecting projects that will take less than two years to provide payback

    c. focusing on customer needs in identifying projects

    d. assigning project managers to lead projects

4. A new government law requires an organization to report data in a new way. Which of the following categories would include a new information system project to provide this data?

    a. problem

    b. opportunity

    c. directive

    d. regulation

5. If estimates for total discounted benefits for a project are $120,000 and total discounted costs are $100,000, what is the estimated return on investment (ROI)?

    a. $20,000

    b. $120,000

    c. 20 percent

    d. 120 percent

6. A _____ is a document that formally recognizes the existence of a project and provides direction on the project's objectives and management.

    a. project charter

    b. contract

    c. business case

    d. project management plan

7. Which of the following items is not normally included in a project charter?

    a. the name of the project manager

    b. budget information

    c. stakeholder signatures

    d. a Gantt chart

8. _____ ensures that the descriptions of the project's products are correct and complete.

    a. Configuration management

    b. Integrated change control

    c. Integration management

    d. A change control board

9. Which of the following is not a suggestion for performing integrated change control?

    a. use good configuration management

    b. minimize change

    c. establish a formal change control system

    d. view project management as a process of constant communication and negotiation

10. What tool and technique is used for all processes of project integration management?

    a. project management software

    b. templates

    c. expert judgment

    d. all of the above

Quick Quiz Answers

1. a; 2. d; 3. b; 4. c; 5. c; 6. a; 7. d; 8. a; 9. b; 10. c

Discussion Questions

1. Describe project integration management. How does it relate to the project life cycle, stake-holders, and the other project management knowledge areas?

2. Describe options that organizations have for selecting projects that align with their mission or strategy, and describe how each might work differently in the selection of IT projects.

3. Summarize key work involved in each of the six processes of project integration management.

4. Either from your own experience or by searching the Internet, describe a well-planned and executed project. Describe a failed project. What elements of project integration might have contributed to the success or failure of each?

5. Discuss the importance of following a well-integrated change control process on IT projects. What consequences can result from not following these best practices? What types of change control would be appropriate for small IT projects? What types of change control would be appropriate for large ones?

Exercises

1. Write a short paper based on the chapter's opening case. Answer the following questions:

    a. What do you think the real problem was in this case?

    b. Does the case present a realistic scenario? Why or why not?

    c. Was Nick Carson a good project manager? Why or why not?

    d. What should top management have done to help Nick?

    e. What could Nick have done to be a better project manager?

2. Download a free trial of MindView mind mapping software from *www.matchware.com /itpm* and create a mind map of a SWOT analysis for your organization. Include at least two strengths, weaknesses, opportunities, and threats, and then provide ideas for at least three potential projects. Or, you can use your college or university for the SWOT analysis, focusing on what it can do to improve services for students.

3. Use spreadsheet software to create Figures 4-4 through Figure 4-7 in this text. Make sure your formulas work correctly.

4. Perform a financial analysis for a project using the format provided in Figure 4-5. Assume that the projected costs and benefits for this project are spread over four years as follows: Estimated costs are $200,000 in Year 1 and $30,000 each year in Years 2, 3, and 4. Estimated benefits are $0 in Year 1 and $100,000 each year in Years 2, 3, and 4. Use a 9 percent discount rate, and round the discount factors to two decimal places. Create a spreadsheet or use the business case financials template on the companion website to calculate and clearly display the NPV, ROI, and year in which payback occurs. In addition, write a paragraph explaining whether you would recommend investing in this project, based on your financial analysis.

5. Create a weighted scoring model to determine grades for a course. Final grades are based on three exams worth 20 percent, 15 percent, and 25 percent, respectively; homework is worth 15 percent; and a group project is worth 25 percent. Enter scores for three students. Assume that Student 1 earns 100 percent (or 100) on every item. Assume that Student 2 earns 70 percent on each of the exams, 80 percent on the homework, and 95 percent on the group project. Assume that Student 3 earns 90 percent on Exam 1, 80 percent on Exam 2, 75 percent on Exam 3, 80 percent on the homework, and 70 percent on the group project. You can use the weighted scoring model template, create your own spreadsheet, or make the matrix by hand.

6. Develop an outline (major headings and subheadings only) for a project management plan to create a mobile-friendly website for your class, and then fill in the details for the introduction or overview section. Assume that this website would include a home page with links to a syllabus for the class, lecture notes or other instructional information, links to the website for this textbook, links to other websites with project management information, and links to personal pages for each member of your class and future classes. Also, include a bulletin board and chat room feature where students and the instructor can exchange information. Assume that your instructor is the project sponsor, you are the project manager, your classmates are your project team, and you have three months to complete the project.

7. Research software mentioned in this chapter, such as software for assisting in project selection, enterprise project management software, or cloud-based applications. Find at least two references and summarize your findings in a short memo to senior management.

8. Watch videos and read articles to research how two different organizations did a good job in directing and managing project work. You can search "PMI Project of the Year award" to find examples. Find at least four references and summarize your findings in a short paper.

9. Read the report "2015 Pulse of the Profession®: Capturing the Value of Project Management" by PMI, mentioned in the What Went Right feature. Summarize key points in this study and your opinion of it. Describe some specific steps organizations can take to provide a supportive culture for project management.

Running Case

Note: Additional running cases are provided on the companion website, including the Manage Your Health, Inc. case from the seventh edition of this text. Template files are also available on the companion website. This running case starts here and continues through Chapter 13. Tasks based on this case are explained in the following Tasks section; throughout the book, these tasks will build on work done in previous chapters and scenarios.

Economic inequality is a huge issue. A recent study found that the world's 80 wealthiest individuals own as much as the entire world's poorest 3.5 billion people. The richest 1 percent of the world's population control half of the world's total wealth.[15] Many individuals, corporations, charities, and government agencies have projects and programs in place to attempt to tackle this and other important global issues such as sustainability, but there are many opportunities to do more.

A grassroots group of college students has decided to work together to do their part in making the world a better place. The students are from many different countries, and several of them met at global conferences, through study abroad experiences, or on various Internet groups. Strategic goals of this group include developing skills for both college students and for needy populations, sharing information on existing products and services that promote economic growth and sustainability, and promoting entrepreneurship. Leaders of this group were reviewing some ideas for projects (all with a significant IT component) that they could do to support their strategic goals:

1. *Global Treps:* Many people are familiar with the television show called *Shark Tank* where entrepreneurs (sometimes called "treps") present their business ideas to a group of investors or sharks. Several colleges, high schools, and even elementary schools throughout the world hold unique versions of a shark tank like event. You believe that creating a non-profit organization with one central mobile-friendly website/application to assist groups in organizing these types of events would spark even more entrepreneurs throughout the world. You would plan to hold several shark tank like events during the term of the project and create a site and applications to help continue developing more global treps. This site/application would include the following capabilities:

   • Provide guidelines and templates for running a shark tank type of event

   • Accept donations from potential investors targeted toward specific schools or organizations wishing to host an event (similar to the popular *DonorsChoose.org* site where people can fund teacher's requests)

   • Accept ideas for needed new products or services

   • Provide the ability for organizations to create their own custom site to solicit local participants and sharks, accept applications, and promote the winners as well as losers

   • Research ideas for a mechanism where a certain percentage of all donations and profits earned by contestants are donated back to the Global Treps organization

   • Provide an online version of the events by showing videos of contestants and live reactions of the sharks while also getting live inputs and donations from viewers

2. *Change the Laws Campaign:* Launch a global campaign to change laws to reduce further income inequality and promote social responsibility. This project would also involve creating a mobile-friendly website/application that would include information about current and proposed laws, allow discussions of potential ideas to change laws, organize people to contact appropriate lawmakers, etc.

3. *Wealthy Unite:* Develop a system to enable the richest people in the world to provide their input on how they can make the world a better place. Provide information on what several people are currently doing (i.e., Bill Gates, Warren Buffet, famous celebrities, etc.) to promote philanthropy. Allow others to donate to suggested causes and recommend other ways to reduce economic inequality.

4. *Global Smart Shoppers:* Develop a mobile app and website that recommends products and services produced by organizations that promote social responsibility. Customize the app so it works in any country in the user's desired language. Work with large companies that do not currently sell products or services in certain countries to expand to regions in need. Allow small companies to easily add their products and services to the shopping network.

Tasks

1. Summarize each of the proposed projects using a simple table format suitable for presentation to top management. Include the name of each project, identify how each one supports business strategies, assess the potential financial benefits and other benefits of each project, and provide your initial assessment of the value of each project. Write your results in a one- to two-page memo to top management, including appropriate back-up information and calculations.

2. Evaluate the four projects by preparing a weighted scoring model using the template provided on the companion website for this text. Develop at least four criteria, assign weights to each criterion, assign scores, and then calculate the weighted scores. Print the spreadsheet and bar chart with the results. Also write a one-page paper that describes this weighted scoring model and the results.

3. Prepare a business case for the Global Treps project. Assume that the project will take six months to complete, use many volunteer hours, and cost about $120,000 for hardware, software, travel, and labor. Use the business case template provided on the companion website for this text. Be sure to research information on the television show and events held by colleges and other groups, which have been sparked by the need for more successful entrepreneurs. Also visit *DonorsChoose.org* to see how that site operates and look into steps for forming a non-profit organization.

4. Prepare a draft project charter for the Global Treps project. Assume that the project will take six months to complete and have a budget of $120,000. Use the project charter template provided in this text and the sample project charter provided in Table 4-1 as guides. You will be the project manager, and Dr. K. will be the project sponsor. Other team members will include Bobby, Ashok, Kim, and Alfreda. You plan to hold four shark tank like events plus develop the Global Treps site and application.

5. Prepare a change request for the Global Treps project, using the template provided on the companion website for this text. Assume that you have decided not to provide an online version of the show as it would be too much work for the initial project. Be creative when making up information.

Key Terms

balanced scorecard p.154

baseline p.166

capitalization rate p.148

cash flow p.148

change control board (CCB) p.169

change control system p.169

configuration management p.170

cost of capital p.148

directives p.147

discount factor p.149

discount rate p.148

integrated change control p.168

181

End Notes

[1] BBC, "Siren Police IT project's £15m failure a 'debacle,'" News UK (June 19, 2014).

[2] James Bacon, "The Use of Decision Criteria in Selecting Information Systems/Technology Investments," *MIS Quarterly*, Vol. 16, No. 3 (September 1992), 335–353.

[3] IDG Enterprise, "CIO Magazine Tech Poll Provides Actionable Insight into Tech Spending, Budgets & Objectives," Press Release (July 10, 2014).

[4] *CIO* Magazine, "CIO Magazine Tech Poll Reveals Topline Revenue Growth Is the Top Business Priority" (February 21, 2012).

[5] Louis Columbus, "21 Most Admired Companies Making IT a Competitive Advantage," *Forbes* (April 1, 2013).

[6] Dennis J. Cohen and Robert J. Graham, *The Project Manager's MBA* (San Francisco: Jossey-Bass, 2001), p. 31.

[7] Jake Widman, "Big IT to Small Biz: Listen Up, Little Dudes!" *Computerworld* (January 24, 2008).

[8] Balanced Scorecard Institute, "Balanced Scorecard Basics," *balancedscorecard.org /Resources/About-the-Balanced-Scorecard* (accessed February 4, 2015).

[9] Fragan Milosevic and A. Ozbay, "Delivering Projects: What the Winners Do," *Proceedings of the Project Management Institute Annual Seminars & Symposium* (November 2001).

[10] Project Management Institute, *2015 Pulse of the Profession®: Capturing the Value of Project Management* (February 2015).

[11] Ross Foti, "The Best Winter Olympics, Period," *PM Network* (January 2004), p. 23.

[12] Ibid., 23.

[13] Stuart Corner, "Governments Must Act to Cut Mobile Roaming Costs, Says OECD," ITWire (February 22, 2012).

[14] OECD, "OECD Broadband Statistics Update," (July 22, 2014).

[15] Deborah Hardoon, "Wealth: Having It All and Wanting More," Oxfam International (January 2015).

CHAPTER 5

PROJECT SCOPE MANAGEMENT

LEARNING OBJECTIVES

After reading this chapter, you will be able to:

- Understand the importance of good project scope management
- Describe the process of planning scope management
- Discuss methods for collecting and documenting requirements to meet stakeholder needs and expectations
- Explain the scope definition process and describe the contents of a project scope statement
- Discuss the process for creating a work breakdown structure using the analogy, top-down, bottom-up, and mind-mapping approaches
- Explain the importance of validating scope and how it relates to defining and controlling scope
- Understand the importance of controlling scope and approaches for preventing scope-related problems on information technology (IT) projects
- Describe how software can assist in project scope management

OPENING CASE

Kim Nguyen was leading a meeting to create the work breakdown structure (WBS) for her company's IT upgrade project. This project was necessary because of several high-priority, Internet-based applications the company was developing. The IT upgrade project involved creating and implementing a plan to make all employees' IT assets meet new corporate standards within nine months. These standards specified the minimum requirements for each desktop or laptop computer, including the type of processor, amount of memory, hard disk size, type of network connection, security features, and software. Kim knew that to perform the upgrades, the project team would first have to create a detailed inventory of all the current hardware, networks, and software in the entire company of 2,000 employees.

Kim had worked with other stakeholders to develop a project charter and initial scope statement. The project charter included rough cost and schedule estimates for the project and signatures of key stakeholders; the initial scope statement provided a start in defining the hardware, software, and network requirements as well as other information related to the project scope. Kim called a meeting with her project team and other stakeholders to further define the scope of the project. She wanted to get everyone's ideas on what the project involved, who would do what, and how they could avoid scope creep. The company's new CEO, Walter Schmidt, was known for keeping a close eye on major projects. The company had started using a new project management information system that let everyone know the status of projects at a detailed and high level. Kim knew that a good WBS was the foundation for scope, time, and cost performance, but she had never led a team in creating one or allocating costs based on a WBS. Where should she begin?

5.1 WHAT IS PROJECT SCOPE MANAGEMENT?

Many of the factors associated with project success, such as user involvement, clear business objectives, and optimized scope, are elements of project scope management.

A critically important and difficult aspect of project management is defining the scope of a project. **Scope** refers to *all* the work involved in creating the products of the project and the processes used to create them. Recall from Chapter 2 that a **deliverable** is a product created as part of a project. Deliverables can be product-related, such as a piece of hardware or software, or process-related, such as a planning document or meeting minutes. Project stakeholders must agree what the products of the project are and, to some extent, how they should be produced to define all of the deliverables.

Project scope management includes the processes involved in defining and controlling what work is or is not included in a project. It ensures that the project team and stakeholders have the same understanding of what products the project will produce and what processes the project team will use to produce them. Six main processes are involved in project scope management:

1. *Planning scope management* involves determining how the project's scope and requirements will be managed. The project team works with appropriate stakeholders to create a scope management plan and requirements management plan.
2. *Collecting requirements* involves defining and documenting the features and functions of the products as well as the processes used for creating them. The project team creates requirements documentation and a requirements traceability matrix as outputs of the requirements collection process.

3. *Defining scope* involves reviewing the scope management plan, project charter, requirements documents, and organizational process assets to create a scope statement, adding more information as requirements are developed and change requests are approved. Outputs of scope definition are the project scope statement and updates to project documents.

4. *Creating the WBS* involves subdividing the major project deliverables into smaller, more manageable components. Outputs include a scope baseline (which includes a WBS and a WBS dictionary) and updates to project documents.

5. *Validating scope* involves formalizing acceptance of the project deliverables. Key project stakeholders, such as the customer and sponsor for the project, inspect and then formally accept the deliverables during this process. If the deliverables are not acceptable, the customer or sponsor usually requests changes. The outputs of this process are accepted deliverables, change requests, work performance information, and updates to project documents.

6. *Controlling scope* involves controlling changes to project scope throughout the life of the project—a challenge on many IT projects. Scope changes often influence the team's ability to meet project time and cost goals, so project managers must carefully weigh the costs and benefits of scope changes. The outputs of this process are work performance information, change requests, and updates to the project management plan, project documents, and organizational process assets.

Figure 5-1 summarizes these processes and outputs and shows when they occur in a typical project.

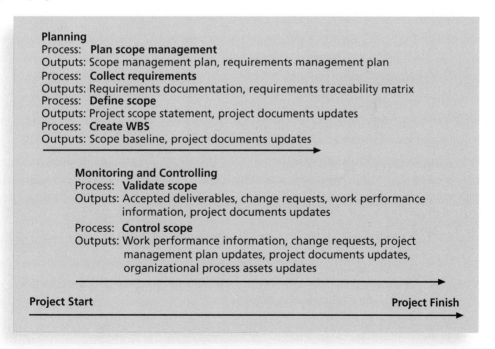

© Cengage Learning 2016

FIGURE 5-1   Project scope management summary

5.2 PLANNING SCOPE MANAGEMENT

The first step in project scope management is planning how the scope will be managed throughout the life of the project. After reviewing the project management plan, project charter, enterprise environmental factors, and organizational process assets, the project team uses expert judgment and meetings to develop two important outputs: the scope management plan and the requirements management plan.

The scope management plan is a subsidiary part of the project management plan, as described in Chapter 4, Project Integration Management. It can be informal and broad or formal and detailed, based on the needs of the project. In fact, small projects may not need a written scope management plan, but large projects or highly technical projects often benefit from one. In general, a scope management plan includes the following information:

- *How to prepare a detailed project scope statement*: For example, are there templates or guidelines to follow? How much detail is needed to describe each deliverable?
- *How to create a WBS*: It is often difficult to create a good WBS. This section of the scope management plan would provide suggestions, samples, and resources for creating a WBS.
- *How to maintain and approve the WBS*: The initial WBS often changes, and project team members disagree on what should be included. The scope management plan describes guidelines for maintaining the WBS and getting approval for it.
- *How to obtain formal acceptance of the completed project deliverables*: It is extremely important to understand the process for obtaining formal acceptance of completed deliverables, especially for projects in which payments are based on formal acceptance.
- *How to control requests for changes to the project scope*: This process is related to performing integrated change control, as described in Chapter 4. Organizations often have guidelines for submitting, evaluating, and approving changes to scope, and this section of the scope management plan would specify how to handle change requests for the project.

Another important output of planning scope management is the requirements management plan. Before you learn about the contents of this document, it is important to understand what requirements are. The 1990 IEEE Standard Glossary of Software Engineering Terminology defines a requirement as follows:

"1. A condition or capability needed by a user to solve a problem or achieve an objective.
2. A condition or capability that must be met or possessed by a system or system component to satisfy a contract, standard, specification, or other formally imposed document.
3. A documented representation of a condition or capability as in 1 or 2."[1]

The *PMBOK® Guide, Fifth Edition*, describes **requirements** as "conditions or capabilities that must be met by the project or present in the product, service, or result to satisfy an agreement or other formally imposed specification." It further explains that requirements "include the quantified and documented needs and expectations of the sponsor, customer, and other stakeholders. These requirements need to be elicited, analyzed, and recorded in enough detail to be included in the scope baseline and be measured once project execution begins."

For example, the chapter's opening case describes a project for upgrading IT assets to meet corporate standards. These standards specify the minimum requirements for each laptop, such as the type of processor, amount of memory, and hard disk size. The documented requirements for this project, therefore, might state that all laptops include an Intel processor, at least 16 GB of memory, and a 2-TB hard drive.

For some IT projects, it is helpful to divide requirements development into categories called *elicitation, analysis, specification,* and *validation.* These categories include all the activities involved in gathering, evaluating, and documenting requirements for a software or software-containing product. It is also important to use an iterative approach to defining requirements because they are often unclear early in a project.

The **requirements management plan** documents how project requirements will be analyzed, documented, and managed. A requirements management plan can include the following information:

- How to plan, track, and report requirements activities
- How to perform configuration management activities
- How to prioritize requirements
- How to use product metrics
- How to trace and capture attributes of requirements

 WHAT WENT RIGHT?

Several studies cite how difficult it is to manage requirements. Finding qualified people—business analysts—to do the job is equally difficult. The U.S. Bureau of Labor Statistics has projected the number of jobs for business analysts to increase 19 percent by 2022.[2] A 2014 PMI survey found that only 49 percent of respondents had the resources in place to do requirements management properly and 53 percent failed to use a formal process to validate requirements.[3]

Fortunately, several organizations have recognized this need and have developed training and certification programs for business analysts.

- The International Institute of Business Analysis (IIBA)® issues both the Certified Business Analysis Professional (CBAP®) and Certification of Competency in Business Analysis (CCBA®) certifications. This organization had about 28,000 members by the end of 2014 and recently published the third edition of the *Guide to Business Analysis Body of Knowledge (BABOK® Guide)*.
- The International Requirements Engineering Board (IREB) provides certification as a Certified Professional for Requirements Engineering (CPRE). Over 19,000 people in 55 countries held this certification by the end of 2014.
- PMI began offering a new certification as a PMI Professional in Business Analysis (PMI-PBA)® in 2014.
- Several colleges and universities are offering majors and minors in business or data analytics at the undergraduate and graduate levels.

5.3 COLLECTING REQUIREMENTS

The second step in project scope management is often the most difficult: collecting requirements. A major consequence of not defining requirements well is rework, which can consume up to half of project costs, especially for software development projects. As illustrated in Figure 5-2, it costs much more (up to 30 times more) to correct a software defect in later development phases than to fix it in the requirements phase. Everyone can cite examples in all types of industries of how important it is to understand requirements as early as possible. For example, if you are designing a house, it is much cheaper to decide where windows and walls will be on paper or a computer screen than after the entire house is framed. New processes and technologies are making it easier to define and implement requirements, but it is still one of the most challenging aspects of project scope management.

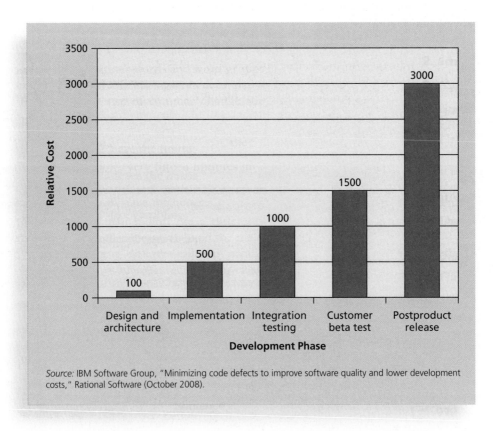

Source: IBM Software Group, "Minimizing code defects to improve software quality and lower development costs," Rational Software (October 2008).

FIGURE 5-2   Relative cost to correct a software defect

BEST PRACTICE

Google continues to be among the most admired companies in the world, well-known for being a great place to work and for being innovative in developing new products. James Whittaker, former engineering director at Google, responsible for testing Chrome, maps, and Google web apps, wrote a book with co-authors Jason Arbon and Jeff Carollo (also former Google employees) called *How Google Tests Software*. Whittaker also worked for Microsoft and as a professor and is one of the best-known names in testing software.

In *How Google Tests Software*, the authors explain that Google used to be like other large companies: testing was not part of the mainstream, and people who did it were underappreciated and overworked. It took Google a long time to develop the people, processes, and technologies it uses today to develop software. A key part of success at Google was changing the culture. Google has fewer dedicated testers than most of its competitors have on a single product team. How is that possible? The authors explain that quality rests on the shoulders of those writing the code. The employees at Google do things the best, fastest way possible for them, knowing that coders are responsible for the quality of their own work. They don't rely on testers to ensure quality.

It is also interesting to note that Google does not believe in fads or buzzwords. In an interview, InfoQ asked the authors how Google's approach fits into the wider Agile community. Their response: "Google doesn't try to be part of the Agile community. We don't use the terminology of scrums or bother with scrum masters and the like. We have crafted our own process of moving fast. It's a very Agile process that doesn't get bogged down with someone else's idea of what it means to be Agile. When you have to stop and define what it means to be Agile and argue what flavor of Agile you are, you just stopped being Agile."[4]

Part of the difficulty is that people often do not have a good process for collecting and documenting project requirements.

There are several ways to collect requirements. Interviewing stakeholders one on one is often very effective, although it can be expensive and time-consuming. Holding focus groups and facilitated workshops, and using group creativity and decision-making techniques to collect requirements, are normally faster and less expensive than one-on-one interviews. Questionnaires and surveys can be efficient ways to collect requirements as long as key stakeholders provide honest and thorough information. Observation can also be a good technique for collecting requirements, especially for projects that involve improving work processes and procedures. For software development projects, prototyping and document analysis are common techniques for collecting requirements, as are context diagrams, which help to clarify the interfaces and boundaries of a project or process. On agile software development projects, the product owner creates the prioritized product backlog for each sprint, as shown in Chapter 3. **Benchmarking**, or generating ideas by comparing specific project practices or product characteristics to those of other projects or products inside or outside the performing organization, can also be used to collect requirements.

Even though there are many ways to collect requirements, people who work on software projects in particular have considerable difficulty defining and managing requirements. A 2011 study revealed some interesting statistics:

- Eighty-eight percent of the software projects involved enhancing existing products instead of creating new ones.

- Eighty-six percent of respondents said that customer satisfaction was the most important metric for measuring the success of development projects, 82 percent said that feedback from customers and partners was the main source of product ideas and requirements, and 73 percent said the most important challenge for their teams was gaining a clear understanding of what customers wanted, followed by documenting and managing requirements.
- Seventy-five percent of respondents were managing projects with at least 100 requirements; 20 percent were managing projects with over 1,000 requirements.
- Seventy percent of respondents spent at least 10 percent of their time managing changes to requirements; 30 percent spent more than 25 percent of their time on such changes.
- The majority of software development teams used a hybrid methodology, 26 percent used waterfall or modified waterfall techniques, and 19 percent used agile techniques.
- Eighty-three percent of software development teams still use Microsoft Office applications such as Word and Excel as their main tools to communicate requirements.
- The respondents listed "requirements collaboration and management software" and "requirements modeling and visualization" as the top two software tools on their wish list, followed by test management and project management.[5]

The project's size, complexity, importance, and other factors affect how much effort is spent on collecting requirements. For example, a team working on a project to upgrade the entire corporate accounting system for a multibillion-dollar company with more than 50 locations should spend a fair amount of time collecting requirements. On the other hand, a project to upgrade the hardware and software for a small accounting firm with only five employees would need a much smaller effort. In any case, it is important for a project team to decide how it will collect and manage requirements. It is crucial to gather inputs from key stakeholders and align the scope with business strategy, as described in Chapter 4.

Just as a project team can collect requirements in several ways, there are several ways to document the requirements. Project teams should first review the project charter because it includes high-level requirements for the project, and they should refer to the scope and requirements management plans. They should also review the stakeholder register and stakeholder management plan to ensure that all key stakeholders have a say in determining requirements. The format for documenting stakeholder requirements can range from a listing of all requirements on a single piece of paper to a room full of notebooks. People who have worked on complex projects, such as building a new airplane, know that the requirements documentation for a plane can weigh more than the plane itself! Requirements documents are often generated by software and include text, images, diagrams, videos, and other media. Requirements are often broken down into different categories such as functional requirements, service requirements, performance requirements, quality requirements, and training requirements.

TABLE 5-1 Sample entry in a requirements traceability matrix

Requirement No.	Name	Category	Source	Status
R32	Laptop memory	Hardware	Project charter and corporate laptop specifications	Complete. Laptops ordered meet requirement by having 16 GB of memory.

© Cengage Learning 2016

In addition to preparing requirements documentation as an output of collecting requirements, project teams often create a requirements traceability matrix. A **requirements traceability matrix (RTM)** is a table that lists requirements, their various attributes, and the status of the requirements to ensure that all are addressed. Table 5-1 provides an example of an RTM entry for the IT upgrade project described in the chapter's opening case. An RTM can have many variations. For example, software requirements are often documented in an RTM that cross-references each requirement with related ones and lists specific tests to verify that they are met. Remember that the main purpose of an RTM is to maintain the linkage from the source of each requirement through its decomposition to implementation and validation. Search the Internet for more detailed examples of an RTM.

5.4 DEFINING SCOPE

The next step in project scope management is to provide a detailed definition of the work required for the project. Good scope definition is very important to project success because it helps improve the accuracy of time, cost, and resource estimates, it defines a baseline for performance measurement and project control, and it aids in communicating clear work responsibilities. The main tools and techniques used in defining scope include expert judgment, product analysis, alternatives generation, and facilitated workshops. For example, a facilitator could have users, developers, and salespeople join a face-to-face meeting or virtual meeting to exchange ideas about developing a new product. The main outputs of scope definition are the project scope statement and project documents updates.

Key inputs for preparing the project scope statement include the project charter, scope management plan, requirements documentation, and organizational process assets such as policies and procedures related to scope statements, as well as project files and lessons learned from previous, similar projects. Table 5-2 shows the project charter for the IT upgrade project described in the opening case. Notice how information from the project charter provides a basis for further defining the project scope. The charter describes the high-level scope, time, and cost goals for the project objectives and success criteria, a general approach to accomplishing the project's goals, and the main roles and responsibilities of important project stakeholders.

Although contents vary, **project scope statements** should include at least a product scope description, product user acceptance criteria, and detailed information on all project deliverables. It is also helpful to document other scope-related information, such as the project boundaries, constraints, and assumptions. The project scope statement should also

TABLE 5-2 Sample project charter

Project Title: Information Technology (IT) Upgrade Project

Project Start Date: March 4   **Projected Finish Date:** December 4

Key Schedule Milestones:
- Inventory update completed April 15
- Hardware and software acquired August 1
- Installation completed October 1
- Testing completed November 15

Budget Information: Budgeted $1,000,000 for hardware and software costs and $500,000 for labor costs.

Project Manager: Kim Nguyen, (310) 555–2784, knguyen@course.com

Project Objectives: Upgrade hardware and software for all employees (approximately 2,000) within nine months based on new corporate standards. See attached sheet describing the new standards. Upgrades may affect servers as well as associated network hardware and software.

Main Project Success Criteria: The hardware, software, and network upgrades must meet all written specifications, be thoroughly tested, and be completed in nine months. Employee work disruptions will be minimal.

Approach:
- Update the IT inventory database to determine upgrade needs
- Develop detailed cost estimate for project and report to CIO
- Issue a request for quote to obtain hardware and software
- Use internal staff as much as possible for planning, analysis, and installation

ROLES AND RESPONSIBILITIES

Name	Role	Responsibility
Walter Schmidt	CEO	Project sponsor, monitor project
Mike Zwack	CIO	Monitor project, provide staff
Kim Nguyen	Project Manager	Plan and execute project
Jeff Johnson	Director of IT Operations	Mentor Kim
Nancy Reynolds	VP, Human Resources	Provide staff, issue memo to all employees about project
Steve McCann	Director of Purchasing	Assist in purchasing hardware and software

Sign-off: (Signatures of all the above stakeholders)

[Handwritten signatures: Walter Schmidt, Steve McCann, Mike Zwack, Nancy Reynolds, Kim Nguyen, Jeff Johnson]

Comments: (Handwritten or typed comments from above stakeholders, if applicable)

"This project must be done within 10 months at the absolute latest." Mike Zwack, CIO

"We are assuming that adequate staff will be available and committed to supporting this project. Some work must be done after hours to avoid work disruptions, and overtime will be provided." Jeff Johnson and Kim Nguyen, IT department

reference supporting documents, such as product specifications that will affect what products are created or purchased, or corporate policies, which might affect how products or services are produced. Many IT projects require detailed functional and design specifications for developing software, which also should be referenced in the detailed scope statement.

As time progresses, the scope of a project should become more clear and specific. For example, the project charter for the IT upgrade project in Table 5-2 includes a short statement about the servers and other computers and software that the project may affect. Table 5-3 provides an example of how the scope becomes progressively more detailed in scope statements labeled Version 1 and Version 2.

Notice in Table 5-3 that the project scope statements often refer to related documents, which can be product specifications, product brochures, or other plans. As more information becomes available and decisions are made related to project scope, such as specific products that will be purchased or changes that have been approved, the project team should update the project scope statement. The team might name different iterations of the scope statement Version 1, Version 2, and so on. These updates may also require changes to other project documents. For example, if the company must purchase servers from a supplier it has never worked with before, the procurement management plan should include information on working with that new supplier.

An up-to-date project scope statement is an important document for developing and confirming a common understanding of the project scope. It describes in detail the work to be accomplished on the project and is an important tool for ensuring customer satisfaction and preventing scope creep, as described later in this chapter.

Recall from Chapter 1 the importance of addressing the triple constraint of project management—meeting scope, time, and cost goals for a project. Time and cost goals are normally straightforward. For example, the time goal for the IT upgrade project is nine months, and the cost goal is $1.5 million. It is much more difficult to describe, agree upon, and meet the scope goal of many projects.

TABLE 5-3   Further defining project scope

Project Charter:
Upgrades may affect servers … (listed under Project Objectives)
Project Scope Statement, Version 1:
Servers: If additional servers are required to support this project, they must be compatible with existing servers. If it is more economical to enhance existing servers, a detailed description of enhancements must be submitted to the CIO for approval. See current server specifications provided in Attachment 6. The CEO must approve a detailed plan describing the servers and their location at least two weeks before installation.
Project Scope Statement, Version 2:
Servers: This project will require purchasing 10 new servers to support web, network, database, application, and printing functions. Virtualization will be used to maximize efficiency. Detailed descriptions of the servers are provided in a product brochure in Attachment 8, along with a plan describing where they will be located.

194

5.5 CREATING THE WORK BREAKDOWN STRUCTURE

After collecting requirements and defining scope, the next step in project scope management is to create a work breakdown structure. A **work breakdown structure (WBS)** is a deliverable-oriented grouping of the work involved in a project that defines its total scope. Because most projects involve many people and many different deliverables, it is important to organize and divide the work into logical parts based on how the work will be performed. The WBS is a foundation document in project management because it provides the basis for planning and managing project schedules, costs, resources, and changes. Because the WBS defines the total scope of the project, some project management experts believe that work should not be done on a project if it is not included in the WBS. Therefore, it is crucial to develop a complete WBS.

The project scope management plan, scope statement, requirements documentation, enterprise environmental factors, and organizational process assets are the primary inputs for creating a WBS. The main tool or technique is **decomposition**—that is, subdividing project deliverables into smaller pieces. The outputs of the process of creating the WBS are the scope baseline and project documents updates. The **scope baseline** includes the approved project scope statement and its associated WBS and WBS dictionary.

What does a WBS look like? A WBS is often depicted as a task-oriented tree of activities, similar to an organizational chart. A project team often organizes the WBS around project products, project phases, or the project management process groups. Many people like to create a WBS in chart form first to help them visualize the whole project and all of

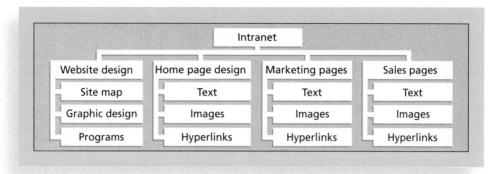

© Cengage Learning 2016

FIGURE 5-3 Sample intranet WBS organized by product

its main parts. Figure 5-3 shows a WBS for an intranet project. Notice that product areas provide the basis for its organization. In this case, there are main boxes or groupings on the WBS for developing the website design, the home page for the intranet, the marketing department's pages, and the sales department's pages.

In contrast, a WBS for the same intranet project can be organized around project phases, as shown in Figure 5-4.[7] Notice that project phases of concept, website design, website development, rollout, and support provide the basis for its organization.

Also note the levels in Figure 5-4. The name of the entire project is in the top box, called Level 1, and the main groupings for the work are listed in the second tier of boxes, called Level 2. This level numbering is based on the Project Management Institute's *Practice Standard for Work Breakdown Structures, Second Edition* (2006). Each of the boxes can be broken down into subsequent tiers of boxes to show the hierarchy of the work. Many people and project management software tools use the term *task* to describe each level of work in the WBS, although PMI does not use that term. For example, in Figure 5-4 the following items can be referred to as tasks: the Level 2 item called "Concept," the Level 3 item called "Define requirements," and the Level 4 item called "Define user requirements." Tasks that are decomposed into smaller tasks are called summary tasks.

Figure 5-4 shows a sample WBS in both chart and tabular form. Notice that both of these formats show the same information. Many documents, such as contracts, use the tabular format. Project management software also uses this format. The WBS becomes the contents of the Task Name column in Microsoft Project, and the hierarchy or level of tasks is shown by indenting and numbering tasks within the software. The numbering shown in the tabular form is based on the *Practice Standard for Work Breakdown Structures, Second Edition*. The automatic numbering feature in Microsoft Project 2013 uses this standard, but not all software does. Be sure to check with your organization to see which numbering scheme it prefers to use for work breakdown structures. To avoid confusion, it is important to decide on a numbering scheme and then use it when referring to WBS items.

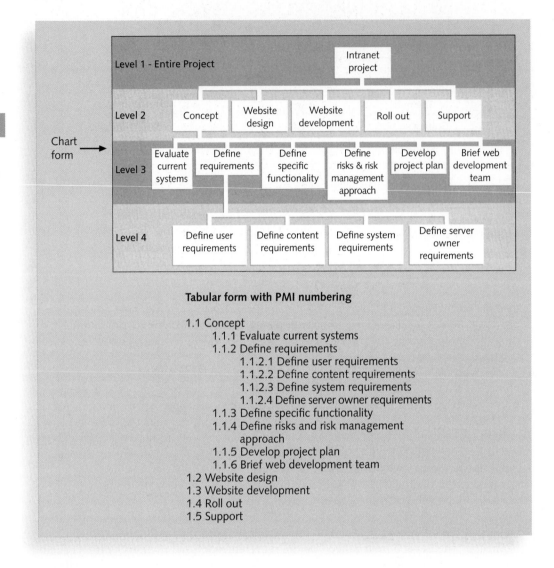

Chart form →

© Cengage Learning 2016

FIGURE 5-4 Sample intranet WBS organized by phase in chart and tabular form

Also determine how you will name WBS items. Some organizations use only nouns to focus on describing deliverables. For example, instead of Define requirements, the WBS would say Requirements definition. Remember that the main purpose of the WBS is to define all of the work required to complete a project, so focus on that while following your organization's structural guidelines.

In Figure 5-4, the lowest level of the WBS is Level 4. A **work package** is a task at the lowest level of the WBS. In Figure 5-4, tasks 1.2.1, 1.2.2, 1.2.3, and 1.2.4 (based on the numbering on the left) are work packages. The other tasks would be broken down further. However, some tasks can remain at Level 2 or 3 in the WBS. Others might be broken down to Level 5 or 6, depending on the complexity of the work.

A work package also represents the level of work that the project manager monitors and controls. You can think of work packages in terms of accountability and reporting. If a project has a relatively short time frame and requires weekly progress reports, a work package might represent work completed in one week or less. If a project has a very long time frame and requires quarterly progress reports, a work package might represent work completed in one month or more. A work package might also be the procurement of a specific product or products, such as an item or items purchased from an outside source. A work package should be defined at the proper level so the project manager can clearly establish an estimate of the effort needed to complete it, estimate the cost of all required resources, and evaluate the quality of the results when the work package is finished.

When using project management software, estimates of work time should be entered only at the work package level. The rest of the WBS items are just groupings or summary tasks for the work packages. The software automatically calculates duration estimates for various WBS levels based on data entered for each work package and the WBS hierarchy.

Figure 5-5 shows the phase-oriented intranet WBS, using the Microsoft Project numbering scheme from Figure 5-4, in the form of a Gantt chart created in Project 2013. You can see from this figure that the WBS is the basis for project schedules. Notice that the WBS is in the left part of the figure in the Task Name column. The resulting schedule is in the right part of the figure. You will learn more about Gantt charts in Chapter 6, Project Time Management.

The example WBSs shown here are simplified so that they are somewhat easy to understand and construct. *Nevertheless, it is very difficult to create a good WBS.* To create a good WBS, you must understand the project and its scope and incorporate the needs and knowledge of the stakeholders. The project manager and the project team must decide as a group how to organize the work and how many levels to include in the WBS.

While many project managers have found that they should focus on doing the top levels well before becoming bogged down in more detailed levels, it is also true that more accurate estimates of scope, time, and cost are obtained when the project is defined appropriately and in sufficient detail. Operating at too high a level increases project risk.

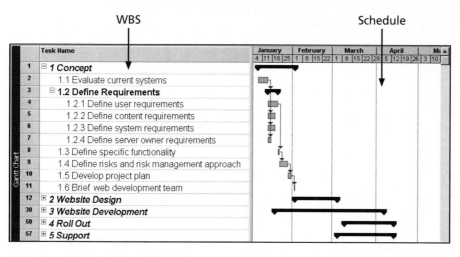

Used with permission from Microsoft Corporation

FIGURE 5-5   Intranet Gantt chart in Microsoft Project

The act of defining the WBS is meant to offset that risk by considering the project's details in advance of their execution.

Many people confuse tasks on a WBS with specifications. Tasks on a WBS represent work that needs to be done to complete the project. For example, if you are creating a WBS to redesign a kitchen, you might have Level 2 categories called design, purchasing, flooring, walls, cabinets, and appliances. Under flooring, you might have tasks to remove the old flooring, install the new flooring, and install the trim. You would not have tasks like "12 ft. by 14 ft. of light oak" or "flooring must be durable"; these are specifications.

Another concern when creating a WBS is how to organize it to provide the basis for the project schedule. You should focus on what work needs to be done and how it will be done, not when it will be done. In other words, the tasks do not have to be developed as a sequential list of steps. If you want some time-based flow for the work, you can create a WBS using the project management process groups of initiating, planning, executing, monitoring and controlling, and closing as Level 2 in the WBS. By doing this, not only does the project team follow good project management practice, the WBS tasks can also be mapped more easily against time. For example, Figure 5-6 shows a WBS and Gantt chart for the intranet project, organized by the five project management process groups. Tasks under initiating include selecting a project manager, forming the project team, and developing the project charter. Tasks under planning include developing a scope statement, creating a WBS, and developing and refining other plans, which would be broken down in more detail for a real project. The tasks of concept, website design, website development, and rollout, which were WBS Level 2 items in Figure 5-4, now become WBS Level 3 items under executing. The executing tasks vary the most from project to project, but many of the tasks under the other project management process groups would be similar for all projects. If you do not use the project management process groups in the WBS, you can have a Level 2 category called "project management" to make sure you account for all tasks

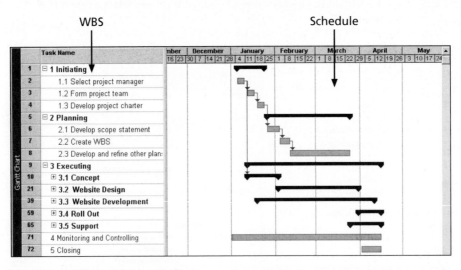

FIGURE 5-6   Intranet project Gantt chart organized by project management process groups

TABLE 5-4   Executing Tasks for JWD Consulting's WBS

3.0 Executing

    3.1 Survey

    3.2 User inputs

    3.3 Intranet site content

        3.3.1 Templates and tools

        3.3.2 Articles

        3.3.3 Links

        3.3.4 Ask the Expert

        3.3.5 User requests

3.4 Intranet site design

3.5 Intranet site construction

3.6 Site testing

3.7 Site promotion

3.8 Site rollout

3.9 Project benefits measurement

© Cengage Learning 2016

related to managing the project. Remember that all work should be included in the WBS, including project management.

Some project teams like to list every deliverable they need to produce and then use those as the basis for creating all or part of their WBS. In Chapter 3, JWD Consulting used the project management process groups for the Level 2 items in its WBS for the project management intranet site project. Then in breaking down the executing task, the project team focused on the product deliverables it had to produce. Table 5-4 shows the categories the team used for that part of the WBS. Recall that the scope statement should list and describe all of the deliverables required for the project. It is very important to ensure consistency between the project charter, scope statement, WBS, and Gantt chart to define the scope of the project accurately.

It is also very important to involve the entire project team and the customer in creating and reviewing the WBS. *People who will do the work should help to plan the work* by creating the WBS. Having group meetings to develop a WBS helps everyone understand *what* work must be done for the entire project and *how* it should be done, given the people involved. It also helps to identify where coordination between different work packages will be required.

5.5a Approaches to Developing Work Breakdown Structures

You can use several approaches to develop a work breakdown structure:

- Using guidelines
- The analogy approach
- The top-down approach
- The bottom-up approach
- The mind-mapping approach

Using Guidelines

If guidelines exist for developing a WBS, it is very important to follow them. Some organizations—the U.S. Department of Defense (DOD), for example—
prescribe the form and content for WBSs for particular projects. Many DOD projects require contractors to prepare their proposals based on the DOD-provided WBS. These proposals must include cost estimates for each task in the WBS at a detailed and summary level. The cost for the entire project must be calculated by summing the costs of all of the lower-level WBS tasks. When DOD personnel evaluate cost proposals, they must compare the contractors' costs with the DOD's estimates. A large variation in costs for a certain WBS task often indicates confusion as to what work must be done.

Consider a large automation project for the U.S. Air Force. In the mid-1980s, the Air Force developed a request for proposals for the Local On-Line Network System (LONS) to automate 15 Air Force Systems Command bases. This $250 million project involved providing the hardware and developing software for sharing documents such as contracts, specifications, and requests for proposals. The Air Force proposal guidelines included a WBS that contractors were required to follow in preparing their cost proposals. Level 2 WBS items included hardware, software development, training, and project management. The hardware item was composed of several Level 3 items, such as servers, workstations, printers, and network hardware. Air Force personnel reviewed the contractors' cost proposals against their internal cost estimate, which was also based on this WBS. Having a prescribed WBS helped contractors to prepare their cost proposals and helped the Air Force to evaluate them.

Many organizations provide guidelines and templates for developing WBSs, as well as examples of WBSs from past projects. Microsoft Project 2013 comes with several templates, and more are available on Microsoft's website and other sites. At the request of many of its members, PMI developed a WBS *Practice Standard* to provide guidance for developing and applying the WBS to project management. The *Practice Standard* includes sample WBSs for a wide variety of projects in various industries, including projects for web design, telecom, service industry outsourcing, and software implementation.

Project managers and their teams should review appropriate information to develop their unique project WBSs more efficiently. For example, Kim Nguyen and key team members from the opening case should review their company's WBS guidelines, templates, and other related information before and during the team meetings to create their WBS.

The Analogy Approach

Another method for constructing a WBS is the analogy approach. In the **analogy approach**, you use a similar project's WBS as a starting point. For example, Kim Nguyen from the opening case might learn that one of her organization's suppliers did a similar IT upgrade project last year. She could ask them to share their WBS for that project to provide a starting point for her own project.

McDonnell Aircraft Company, now part of Boeing, provides an example of using an analogy approach when creating WBSs. McDonnell Aircraft Company designed and manufactured several different fighter aircraft. When creating a WBS for a new aircraft design, it started by using 74 predefined subsystems for building fighter aircraft based on past experience. There was a Level 2 WBS item for the airframe that was composed of Level 3 items such as a forward fuselage, center fuselage, aft fuselage, and wings. This generic, product-oriented WBS provided a starting point for defining the scope of new aircraft projects and developing cost estimates for new aircraft designs.

Some organizations keep a repository of WBSs and other project documentation on file to assist people working on projects. Project 2013 and many other software tools include sample files to assist users in creating a WBS and Gantt chart. Viewing examples of WBSs from similar projects allows you to understand different ways to create a WBS.

The Top-Down and Bottom-Up Approaches

Two other methods of creating WBSs are the top-down and bottom-up approaches. Most project managers consider the top-down approach of WBS construction to be conventional.

To use the **top-down approach**, start with the largest items of the project and break them into subordinate items. This process involves refining the work into greater and greater levels of detail. For example, Figure 5-4 shows how work was broken down to Level 4 for part of the intranet project. After finishing the process, all resources should be assigned at the work package level. The top-down approach is best suited to project managers who have vast technical insight and a big-picture perspective.

In the **bottom-up approach**, team members first identify as many specific tasks related to the project as possible. They then aggregate the specific tasks and organize them into summary activities, or higher levels in the WBS. For example, a group of people might be responsible for creating a WBS to develop an e-commerce application. Instead of looking for guidelines on how to create a WBS or viewing WBSs from similar projects, they could begin by listing detailed tasks they think they would need to perform in order to create the application. After listing these detailed tasks, they would group the tasks into categories. Then they would group these categories into higher-level categories. Some people have found that writing all possible tasks as notes and then placing them on a wall helps the team see all the work required for the project and develop logical groupings for performing the work. For example, a business analyst on the project team might know that it had to define user requirements and content requirements for the e-commerce application. These tasks might be part of the requirements documents the team would have to create as one of the project deliverables. A hardware specialist might know that the team had to define system requirements and server requirements, which would also be part of a requirements document. As a group, they might decide to put all four of these tasks under a higher-level item called "define requirements" that would result in the delivery of a requirements document. Later, they might realize that defining requirements should fall under a broader category of concept design for the e-commerce application, along with other groups of tasks related to the concept design. The bottom-up approach can be very time-consuming, but it can also be a very effective way to create a WBS. Project managers often use the bottom-up approach for projects that represent entirely new systems or approaches to doing a job, or to help create buy-in and synergy with a project team.

Mind Mapping

Some project managers like to use mind mapping to help develop WBSs. As described in Chapter 4 during the discussion of SWOT analysis, mind mapping is a technique that uses branches radiating from a core idea to structure thoughts and ideas. Instead of writing down tasks in a list or immediately trying to create a structure for tasks, mind mapping allows people to write and even draw pictures of ideas in a nonlinear format. This more visual, less structured approach to defining and then grouping tasks can unlock creativity among individuals and increase participation and morale among teams.[8]

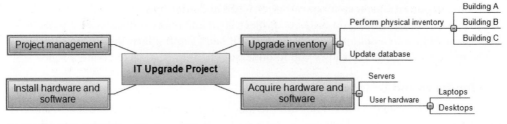

Source: MatchWare's MindView 4 Business Edition

FIGURE 5-7   Sample mind-mapping technique for creating a WBS

Figure 5-7 shows a diagram that uses mind mapping to create a WBS for the IT up-grade project. The rectangle near the center represents the entire project. Each of the four main branches radiating from the center represents the main tasks or Level 2 items for the WBS. Different people at the meeting who are creating this mind map might have different roles in the project, which could help in deciding the tasks and WBS structure. For example, Kim would want to focus on all of the project management tasks, and she might also know that they will be tracked in a separate budget category. People who are familiar with acquiring or installing hardware and software might focus on that work, and so on. Branching off from the main task called "Upgrade inventory" are two subtasks, "Perform physical inventory" and "Update database." Branching off from the "Perform physical inventory" subtask are three further subdivisions labeled Building A, Building B, and Building C. The team would continue to add branches and items until they exhausted ideas for what work needs to be performed.

After discovering WBS items and their structure using the mind-mapping technique, you could then translate the information into chart or tabular form, as described earlier. A feature of MindView 4.0 Business Edition software is that you can click a single icon to convert a mind map into a Gantt chart. The mind map provides the task list based on the WBS. MindView also lets you enter information about tasks, such as dependencies and durations, to generate a complete Gantt chart. You can also export your mind map into Microsoft Project. The WBS is entered in the Task List column, and the structure is created automatically based on the mind map. Figure 5-8 shows the resulting Gantt charts for the IT upgrade project both in MindView 4.0 and Project 2013. See Appendix A for more information on using Project 2013.

Mind mapping can be used for developing WBSs using the top-down or bottom-up approach. For example, you could conduct mind mapping for an entire project by listing the project in the center of a document, adding the main categories on branches radiating from the center, and then adding branches for appropriate subcategories. You could also develop a separate mind-mapping diagram for each deliverable and then merge them to create one large diagram for the entire project. You can also add items anywhere on a mind-mapping document without following a strict top-down or bottom-up approach. After the mind-mapping documents are complete, you can convert them into a chart or tabular WBS form.

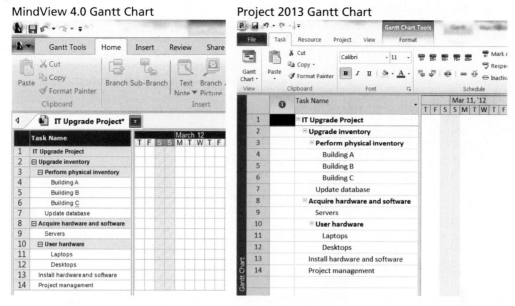

FIGURE 5-8   Gantt charts with WBS generated from a mind map

5.5b The WBS Dictionary

Many of the items listed on the sample WBSs are rather vague. What exactly does "Update database" mean, for example? The person responsible for this task might think that it does not need to be broken down any further, which could be fine. However, the task should be described in more detail so everyone has the same understanding of what it involves. What if someone else has to perform the task? What would you tell that team member to do? What will it cost to complete the task? More detailed information is needed to answer these and other questions.

A **WBS dictionary** is a document that provides detailed information about each WBS item. The term *dictionary* should not be confused with defining terms or acronyms in this case; such definitions belong in a glossary that would be included elsewhere in the project documentation. Instead, the WBS dictionary is a definition of the work involved in the task—a clarification that makes the summary description in the WBS easier to understand in terms of the approach taken to complete the work.

The format of the WBS dictionary can vary based on project needs. It might be appropriate to have a short paragraph describing each work package. For a more complex project, an entire page or more might be needed for each of the work package descriptions. Some projects might require that each WBS item describe the responsible organization, resource requirements, estimated costs, dependencies with other activities, and other information. Project teams often review WBS dictionary entries from similar tasks to get a better idea of how to create their entries.

TABLE 5-5 Sample WBS dictionary entry

WBS Dictionary Entry March 20
Project Title: Information Technology (IT) Upgrade Project
WBS Item Number: 2.2
WBS Item Name: Update Database
Description: The IT department maintains an online database of hardware and software on the corporate intranet. We need to make sure that we know exactly what hardware and software employees are currently using and if they have any unique needs before we decide what to order for the upgrade. This task will involve reviewing information from the current database, producing reports that list each department's employees and location, and updating the data after performing the physical inventory and receiving inputs from department managers. Our project sponsor will send a notice to all department managers to communicate the importance of this project and this particular task. In addition to general hardware and software upgrades, the project sponsors will ask the department managers to provide information for any unique requirements they might have that could affect the upgrades. This task also includes updating the inventory data for network hardware and software. After updating the inventory database, we will send an e-mail to each department manager to verify the information and make changes online as needed. Department managers will be responsible for ensuring that their people are available and cooperative during the physical inventory. Completing this task is dependent on WBS Item Number 2.1, Perform Physical Inventory, and must precede WBS Item Number 3.0, Acquire Hardware and Software.

© Cengage Learning 2016

In the IT upgrade project described in the opening case, Kim should work with her team and sponsor to determine the level of detail needed in the WBS dictionary. They should also decide where this information will be entered and how it will be updated. Kim and her team decided to enter all of the WBS dictionary information into their enterprise project management system, following departmental guidelines. Table 5-5 is an example of one entry.

The approved project scope statement and its associated WBS and WBS dictionary form the scope baseline. Performance in meeting project scope goals is based on this scope baseline.

5.5c Advice for Creating a WBS and WBS Dictionary

As stated previously, creating a good WBS is no easy task and usually requires several iterations. Often, it is best to use a combination of approaches to create a project's WBS. Some basic principles, however, apply to creating any good WBS and its WBS dictionary.

- A unit of work should appear in only one place in the WBS.
- The work content of a WBS item is the sum of the WBS items below it.
- A WBS item is the responsibility of only one person, even though many people might be working on it.
- The WBS must be consistent with the way work actually will be performed; it should serve the project team first, and serve other purposes only if practical.
- Project team members should be involved in developing the WBS to ensure consistency and buy-in.

- Each WBS item must be documented in a WBS dictionary to ensure accurate understanding of the scope of work included and not included in that item.
- The WBS must be a flexible tool to accommodate inevitable changes while properly maintaining control of the work content in the project according to the scope statement.[9]

5.6 VALIDATING SCOPE

It is difficult to create a good project scope statement and WBS for a project. It is even more difficult, especially on IT projects, to verify the project scope and minimize scope changes. Some project teams know from the start that the scope is very unclear and that they must work closely with the project customer to design and produce various deliverables. In this case, the project team must develop a process for scope validation that meets unique project needs. Careful procedures must be developed to ensure that customers are getting what they want and that the project team has enough time and money to produce the desired products and services.

Even when the project scope is fairly well defined, many IT projects suffer from **scope creep**—the tendency for project scope to keep getting bigger and bigger. There are many horror stories about IT projects failing due to problems such as scope creep, including a few classic examples in the following What Went Wrong? feature. For this reason, it is very important to verify the project scope with users throughout the life of the project and develop a process for controlling scope changes.

Scope creep can also be a good thing, if managed well. Later in this chapter, you can see how Northwest Airlines encouraged scope changes on its ResNet project and managed them well.

 WHAT WENT WRONG?

A project scope that is too broad and grandiose can cause severe problems. Scope creep and an overemphasis on technology for technology's sake resulted in the bankruptcy of a large pharmaceutical firm, Texas-based FoxMeyer Drug. In 1994, the CIO was pushing for a $65 million system to manage the company's critical operations. He did not believe in keeping things simple, however. The company spent nearly $10 million on state-of-the-art hardware and software and contracted the management of the project to a prestigious (and expensive) consulting firm. The project included building an $18 million robotic warehouse, which looked like something out of a science fiction movie, according to insiders. The scope of the project kept getting bigger and more impractical. The elaborate warehouse was not ready on time, and the new system generated erroneous orders that cost FoxMeyer Drug more than $15 million in unrecovered excess shipments. In July 1996, the company took a $34 million charge for its fourth fiscal quarter, and by August of that year, FoxMeyer Drug filed for bankruptcy.[10]

Another classic example of scope creep comes from McDonald's Restaurants. In 2001, the fast-food chain initiated a project to create an intranet that would connect its headquarters with all of its restaurants and provide detailed operational information

continued

in real time. For example, headquarters would know if sales were slowing or if the grill temperature was correct in every single store—all 30,000 of them in more than 120 countries. McDonald's would not divulge detailed information, but they admitted that the project was too large in scale and scope. After spending $170 million on consultants and initial implementation planning, McDonald's realized that the project was too much to handle and terminated it.[11]

Another major scope problem on IT projects is a lack of user involvement. A prime example occurred in the late 1980s at Northrop Grumman, which specializes in defense electronics, IT, advanced aircraft, shipbuilding, and space technology. An IT project team there became convinced that it should automate the review and approval process of government proposals. The team implemented a powerful workflow system to manage the whole process. Unfortunately, the end users of the system were aerospace engineers who preferred to work in a more casual, ad hoc fashion. They dubbed the system "Naziware" and refused to use it. This example illustrates an IT project that wasted millions of dollars developing a system that was not in touch with the way end users did their work.[12]

Failing to follow good project management processes and use off-the-shelf software also results in scope problems. 21st Century Insurance Group in Woodland Hills, California, paid Computer Sciences Corporation $100 million to develop a system for managing business applications, including managing insurance policies, billing, claims, and customer service. After five years, the system was still in development and supported less than 2 percent of the company's business. Joshua Greenbaum, an analyst at Enterprise Applications Consulting, called the project a "huge disaster" and questioned the insurance company's ability "to manage a process that is pretty well known these days. ... I'm surprised that there wasn't some way to build what they needed using off-the-shelf components and lower their risk."[13]

Scope validation involves formal acceptance of the completed project deliverables. This acceptance is often achieved by a customer inspection and then sign-off on key deliverables. To receive formal acceptance of the project scope, the project team must develop clear documentation of the project's products and procedures to evaluate whether they were completed correctly and satisfactorily. Recall from Chapter 4 that configuration management specialists identify and document the functional and physical characteristics of the project's products, record and report the changes, and audit the products to verify conformance to requirements. To minimize scope changes, it is crucial to do a good job of configuration management and validating project scope.

The scope management plan, scope baseline, requirements documentation, requirements traceability matrix, validated deliverables, and work performance data are the main inputs for scope validation. The main tools for performing scope validation are inspection and group decision-making techniques. The customer, sponsor, or user inspects the work after it is delivered and decides if it meets requirements. The main outputs of scope validation are accepted deliverables, change requests, work performance information, and project documents updates. For example, suppose that Kim's team members deliver upgraded computers to users as part of the IT upgrade project. Several users might complain because the computers did not include special keyboards they need for medical reasons. Appropriate people would review this change request and take appropriate corrective action, such as getting sponsor approval for purchasing the special keyboards.

🌐 GLOBAL ISSUES

Many countries have had difficulties controlling the scope of large projects, especially those that involve advanced technologies and many different users. For example, the state government of Victoria, Australia, introduced a public transportation smart card, called myki, in 2010. Public Transport Victoria's description of the card included the following information: "Many cities around the world have public transport smart cards. myki has been designed to fit our State's unique needs. myki users enjoy an integrated ticketing system that works across the state on trains, trams and buses."[14]

Unfortunately, there were many problems in developing and implementing the smart cards. The $1.35 billion system became valid on all forms of Melbourne public transportation in July 2010, three years and five months after it was meant to replace the Metcard. Users' initial reactions to the myki smart card were mixed, with several reports of myki readers not working on trams. Many skeptics said they would wait until problems were fixed before trying the new system.[15] Many articles described problems with the myki card, revealing obvious difficulty in validating the scope of this high-visibility project. The Public Transport Users Association (PTUA) compiled a long list of problems with the new card and suggested that people stick to using the old card for a while. Clearly, the new system did not meet user requirements and had major flaws. In January 2012, over 18 months after the myki rollout, 70 percent of users still used the old Metcard. The government decided to keep myki in June 2011 after estimating that it would cost taxpayers more than $1 billion to scrap the troubled system. The Metcard was planned to be phased out for good by the end of 2012. PTUA president Daniel Bowen was not certain that the transition would go smoothly. "To a certain extent it makes sense to bring people across (to myki) because you can't have two systems running at the same time forever. ... Once you get the majority of people using myki though, they'd better make sure it's humming, otherwise there could be chaos."[16] Myki continued to make headlines in 2015, but not in a good way. "Two years after myki became the only ticket in town, frustrated commuters say the system is still riddled with issues."[17]

5.7 CONTROLLING SCOPE

As you learned in Chapter 4 when you studied integrated change control, change is inevitable on projects, especially changes to the scope of IT projects. Scope control involves managing changes to the project scope while keeping project goals and business strategy in mind. Users often are not sure how they want screens to look or what functionality they will need to improve business performance. Developers are not exactly sure how to interpret user requirements, and they also have to deal with constantly changing technologies.

The goal of scope control is to influence the factors that cause scope changes, to ensure that changes are processed according to procedures developed as part of integrated change control, and to manage changes when they occur. You cannot do a good job of controlling scope if you do not first do a good job of collecting requirements, defining scope, and validating scope. How can you prevent scope creep when you have not agreed on the work to be performed and your sponsor has not validated that the proposed work is acceptable? You also need to develop a process for soliciting and monitoring changes to project scope. Stakeholders should be encouraged to suggest changes that will benefit the overall project and discouraged from suggesting unnecessary changes.

The project management plan, requirements documentation, requirements traceability matrix, work performance data, and organizational process assets are the main inputs to scope control. An important tool for performing scope control is variance analysis. **Variance** is the difference between planned and actual performance. For example, if a supplier was supposed to deliver five special keyboards and you received only four, the variance would be one keyboard. The outputs of scope control include work performance information, change requests, project management plan updates, project documents updates, and organizational process assets updates.

Table 1-2 in Chapter 1 lists the top 10 factors that help IT projects succeed. Four of these 10 factors are related to scope validation and control: user involvement, executive support, clear business objectives, and optimizing scope. To avoid project failures, therefore, it is crucial for IT project managers and their teams to improve user input and executive support and reduce incomplete and changing requirements.

The following sections provide more suggestions for improving scope management on IT projects.

5.7a Suggestions for Improving User Input

Lack of user input leads to problems with managing scope creep and controlling change. How can you manage this important issue? The following suggestions can help a project team improve user input:

- Develop a good project selection process for IT projects. Insist that all projects have a sponsor from the user organization. The sponsor should not work in the IT department, nor should the sponsor be the project manager. Project information, including the project charter, project management plan, project scope statement, WBS, and WBS dictionary, should be easily available in the organization. Making basic project information available will help avoid duplication of effort and ensure that the most important projects are the ones on which people are working.
- Have users on the project team. Some organizations require project managers to come from the business area of the project instead of the IT group. Some organizations assign co-project managers to IT projects, one from IT and one from the main business group. Users should be assigned full-time to large IT projects and part-time to smaller projects. A key success factor in Northwest Airlines' ResNet project was training reservation agents—the users—how to write programming code for their new reservation system. (See the companion website for this text to read the entire case study for the ResNet project.) Because the sales agents had intimate knowledge of the business, they provided excellent input and actually created most of the software.
- Have regular meetings with defined agendas. The idea of meeting regularly sounds obvious, but many IT projects fail because the project team members do not have regular interaction with users. They assume that they understand what users need without getting direct feedback. To encourage this interaction, users should sign off on key deliverables presented at meetings.

- Deliver something to project users and sponsors on a regular basis. If the delivered product is hardware or software, make sure it works first.
- Do not promise to deliver what the team cannot deliver in a particular time frame. Make sure the project schedule allows enough time to produce the deliverables.
- Locate users with the developers. People often get to know each other better by being in close proximity. If the users cannot be physically moved to be near developers during the entire project, they should set aside certain days to work in the same location.

5.7b Suggestions for Reducing Incomplete and Changing Requirements

Some requirement changes are expected on IT projects, but many projects have too many changes to their requirements, especially during later stages of the project life cycle when it is more difficult to implement changes. The following suggestions can help improve the requirements process:

- Develop and follow a requirements management process that includes procedures for determining initial requirements.
- Employ techniques such as prototyping, use case modeling, and Joint Application Design to understand user requirements thoroughly. **Prototyping** involves developing a working replica of the system or some aspect of the system. These working replicas may be throwaways or an incremental component of the deliverable system. Prototyping is an effective tool for gaining an understanding of requirements, determining the feasibility of requirements, and resolving user interface uncertainties. **Use case modeling** is a process for identifying and modeling business events, who initiated them, and how the system should respond to them. It is an effective tool for understanding requirements of information systems. **Joint Application Design (JAD)** uses highly organized and intensive workshops to bring together project stakeholders—the sponsor, users, business analysts, programmers, and so on—to jointly define and design information systems. These techniques also help users become more active in defining system requirements. Consult a systems analysis and design text for details on these techniques.
- Put all requirements in writing and keep them current and readily available. Several tools are available to automate this function. For example, a type of software called a requirements management tool aids in capturing and maintaining requirements information, provides immediate access to the information, and assists in establishing necessary relationships between requirements and information created by other tools.
- Create a requirements management database for documenting and controlling requirements. Computer Aided Software Engineering (CASE) tools or other technologies can assist in maintaining a repository for project data. A CASE tool's database can also be used to document and control requirements.
- Provide adequate testing to verify that the project's products perform as expected. Conduct testing throughout the project life cycle. Chapter 8, Project Quality Management, includes more information on testing.

210

- Use a process for reviewing requested requirements changes from a systems perspective. For example, ensure that project scope changes include associated cost and schedule changes. Require approval via signatures of appropriate stakeholders. It is crucial for the project manager to lead the team in its focus on achieving approved scope goals and not getting sidetracked into doing additional work. For example, in his book *Alpha Project Managers*, Andy Crowe tried to uncover what the best or "alpha" project managers do differently from other project managers. One of these alpha project managers explained how he learned an important lesson about scope control:

  > Toward the end of some projects I've worked on, the managers made their teams work these really long hours. After the second or third time this happened, I just assumed that this was the way things worked. Then I got to work with a manager who planned everything out really well and ran the team at a good pace the whole time, and we kept on schedule. When the customer found out that things were on schedule, he kept trying to increase the scope, but we had a good manager this time, and she wouldn't let him do it without adjusting the baselines. That was the first time I was on a project that finished everything on time and on budget, and I was amazed at how easy she made it look.[18]

- Emphasize completion dates. For example, a project manager at Farmland Industries, Inc. in Kansas City, Missouri, kept her 15-month, $7 million integrated supply-chain project on track by setting the project deadline. She said, "May 1 was the drop-dead date, and everything else was backed into it. Users would come to us and say they wanted something, and we'd ask them what they wanted to give up to get it. Sticking to the date is how we managed scope creep."[19]

- Allocate resources specifically for handling change requests. For example, Peeter Kivestu and his ResNet team at Northwest Airlines knew that users would request enhancements to the reservations system they were developing. They provided a special function key on the ResNet screen for users to submit their requests, and the project included three full-time programmers to handle these requests. Users made over 11,000 enhancement requests. The managers who sponsored the four main software applications had to prioritize the software enhancement requests and decide as a group what changes to approve. The three programmers then implemented as many items as they could, in priority order, given the time they had. Although they only implemented 38 percent of the requested enhancements, they were the most important ones, and the users were very satisfied with the system and process.

5.8 USING SOFTWARE TO ASSIST IN PROJECT SCOPE MANAGEMENT

Project managers and their teams can use several types of software to assist in project scope management. As shown in several of the figures and tables in this chapter, you can use word-processing software to create scope-related documents, and most people use spreadsheet or presentation software to develop various charts, graphs, and matrixes related to scope management. Mind-mapping software can be useful in developing a WBS. Project stakeholders also transmit project scope management information using various types of communication software such as e-mail and assorted web-based applications.

Project management software helps you develop a WBS, which serves as a basis for creating Gantt charts, assigning resources, allocating costs, and performing other tasks. You can also use the templates that come with various project management software products to help you create a WBS for your project. (See the section on project scope management in Appendix A for detailed information on using Project 2013, and see the companion website for information on templates related to project scope management.)

You can also use many types of specialized software to assist in project scope management. Many IT projects use special software for requirements management, prototyping, modeling, and other scope-related work. Because scope is such a crucial part of project management, many software products are available to assist in managing project scope. For example, Gartner estimates that the market for requirements definition and management tools was $280 million in 2014 and growing over 3 percent annually. New tools focus on improving collaboration and speed to better address mass market needs.[20]

Project scope management is very important, especially on IT projects. After selecting projects, organizations must plan scope management, collect the requirements and define the scope of the work, break down the work into manageable pieces, validate the scope with project stakeholders, and manage changes to project scope. Using the basic project management concepts, tools, and techniques discussed in this chapter can help you manage project scope successfully.

CASE WRAP-UP

Kim Nguyen reviewed guidelines for creating WBSs that were provided by her company and other sources. She had a meeting with the three team leaders for her project to get their input on how to proceed. They reviewed several sample documents and decided to have major groupings for their project based on updating the inventory database, acquiring the necessary hardware and software, installing the hardware and software, and performing project management. After they decided on a basic approach, Kim led a meeting with the entire project team of 12 people, with some attending virtually. She reviewed the project charter and stakeholder register, described the basic approach they would use to collect requirements and define the project scope, and reviewed sample WBSs. Kim opened the floor for questions, which she answered confidently. She then let each team leader work with his or her people to start writing the detailed scope statement and their sections of the WBS and WBS dictionary. Everyone participated in the meeting, sharing their expertise and openly asking questions. Kim could see that the project was off to a good start.

Chapter Summary

Project scope management includes the processes to ensure that the project addresses all the work required to complete the project successfully. The main processes include planning scope management, collecting requirements, defining scope, creating the WBS, validating scope, and controlling scope.

The first step in project scope management is planning scope management. The project team reviews information and uses expert judgment and meetings to help create a scope management plan and requirements management plan.

The next step is collecting requirements, a crucial part of many IT projects. It is important to review the project charter and meet with key stakeholders listed in the stakeholder register when collecting requirements. The main outputs of this process are requirements documentation and a requirements traceability matrix.

A project scope statement is created in the scope definition process. This document often includes a product scope description, product user acceptance criteria, detailed information on all project deliverables, and information on project boundaries, constraints, and assumptions. There are often several versions of the project scope statement to keep scope information detailed and up to date.

A work breakdown structure (WBS) is a deliverable-oriented grouping of the work involved in a project that defines its total scope. The WBS forms the basis for planning and managing project schedules, costs, resources, and changes. You cannot use project management software without first creating a good WBS. A WBS dictionary is a document that provides detailed information about each WBS item. A good WBS is often difficult to create because of the complexity of the project. There are several approaches for developing a WBS, including using guidelines, the analogy approach, the top-down approach, the bottom-up approach, and mind mapping.

Validating scope involves formal acceptance of the completed project deliverables. Controlling scope involves controlling changes to the project scope.

Poor project scope management is one of the key reasons projects fail. For IT projects, it is important for good project scope management to have strong user involvement, executive support, a clear statement of requirements, and a process for managing scope changes.

Many software products are available to assist in project scope management. The WBS is a key concept in properly using project management software because it provides the basis for entering tasks.

Quick Quiz

1. _____ refer(s) to all the work involved in creating the products of the project and the processes used to create them.
   a. Deliverables
   b. Milestones
   c. Scope
   d. Product development

2. Which tool or technique for collecting requirements is often the most expensive and time consuming?
   a. interviews
   b. focus groups
   c. surveys
   d. observation

3. A _____ is a deliverable-oriented grouping of the work involved in a project that defines its total scope.

   a. scope statement

   b. WBS

   c. WBS dictionary

   d. work package

4. What approach to developing a WBS involves writing down or drawing ideas in a nonlinear format?

   a. top-down

   b. bottom-up

   c. analogy

   d. mind mapping

5. Assume that you have a project with major categories called planning, analysis, design, and testing. What level of the WBS would these items fall under?

   a. 0

   b. 1

   c. 2

   d. 3

6. Which of the following is not a best practice that can help in avoiding scope problems on IT projects?

   a. Keep the scope realistic.

   b. Use off-the-shelf hardware and software whenever possible.

   c. Follow good project management processes.

   d. Don't involve too many users in scope management.

7. Why did McDonald's terminate a large project after spending $170 million on it?

   a. The company found a better technology.

   b. The company decided to outsource the work.

   c. The scope was too much to handle.

   d. The government requirement that prompted the project was repealed.

8. Scope _____ is often achieved by a customer inspection and then sign-off on key deliverables.

   a. acceptance

   b. validation

   c. completion

   d. close-out

9. Which of the following is not a suggestion for improving user input?

   a. Develop a good project selection process for IT projects.

   b. Have users on the project team.

   c. Co-locate users with developers.

   d. Only have meetings as needed, not on a regular basis.

10. Project management software helps you develop a _____, which serves as a basis for creating Gantt charts, assigning resources, and allocating costs.

    a. project plan

    b. schedule

    c. WBS

    d. deliverable

Quick Quiz Answers

1. c; 2. a; 3. b; 4. d; 5. c; 6. d; 7. c; 8. b; 9. d; 10. c

Discussion Questions

1. What is involved in project scope management, and why is good project scope management so important on IT projects?

2. What is involved in collecting requirements for a project? Why is it often difficult to do?

3. Discuss the process of defining project scope in more detail as a project progresses, going from information in a project charter to a project scope statement, WBS, and WBS dictionary.

4. Describe different ways to develop a WBS and explain why it is often so difficult to do.

5. What is the main technique used for validating scope? Give an example of scope validation on a project.

6. Using examples in this book or online, describe a project that suffered from scope creep. Could it have been avoided? How? Can scope creep be a good thing? When? What can organizations do to successfully manage inevitable changes in scope that are good for business?

7. Why do you need a good WBS to use project management software? What other types of software can you use to assist in project scope management?

Exercises

1. You are working on a project to develop a new or enhanced system to help people at your college, university, or organization to find jobs. The system must be tailored to your student or work population and be very easy to use. Write a short paper describing how you would collect requirements for this system, and include at least five requirements in a requirements traceability matrix.

2. Read the report cited in the chapter called PMI's *Pulse of the Profession: Requirements Management—A Core Competency for Project and Program Success*. Find one or two other reports on requirements management written in the past year. Summarize the findings of the reports and your opinion on the topic.

3. Use MindView Business software to develop a WBS in chart form by creating a new file or map in Top Down view. You can download a 30-day trial of MindView Business from

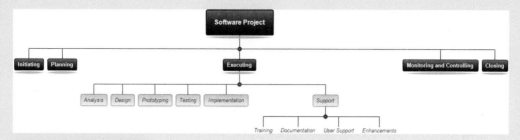

Task Name
Software Project
1. Initiating
2. Planning
⊟ 3. Executing
3.1 Analysis
3.2 Design
3.3 Prototyping
3.4 Testing
3.5 Implementation
⊟ 3.6 Support
3.6.1 Training
3.6.2 Documentation
3.6.3 User Support
3.6.4 Enhancements
4. Monitoring and Controlling
5. Closing

Source: MatchWare's MindView 4 Business Edition

FIGURE 5-9 Top-down WBS and Gantt chart created in MindView Business Software

www.matchware.com/itpm. (The chart should be similar to an organizational chart—see the sample at the top of Figure 5-4). Assume that the Level 1 category is called *Software Project,* and that the Level 2 categories are Initiating, Planning, Executing, Monitoring and Controlling, and Closing. Under the Executing section, include Level 3 categories of Analysis, Design, Prototyping, Testing, Implementation, and Support. Assume that the Support category includes Level 4 items for Training, Documentation, User Support, and Enhancements. Print the WBS in chart form. Show the same information in a Gantt chart by selecting View from the menu bar in MindView Business, then Gantt. Widen the Task Name column and select Number Scheme from the menu bar to add a numbering scheme. Save your file and then print just the Task Name column of the Gantt chart view by taking a screen shot and cropping the screen. Your results should resemble those in Figure 5-9.

4. Create the same WBS described in Exercise 3 using Microsoft Project 2013 and indenting categories appropriately. Use the outline numbering feature to display the outline numbers, or enter the numbers manually. Notice that Project 2013 uses PMI's standard numbering scheme, but MindView does not. You may want to enter the numbers to ensure that they appear as desired and are displayed in all reports. Microsoft Project does not include automatic

numbers in reports. Do not enter any durations or dependencies. See Appendix A or Project 2013's Help for instructions on creating a WBS. Print the resulting Gantt chart on one page, and be sure to display the entire Task Name column.

5. Using the file you created in MindView for Exercise 3, export the WBS into Project 2013. Open the file, select the MindView icon in the upper-left portion of the toolbar, select Export, select Microsoft Project, and name the file. The file opens in Project 2013. Make adjustments as needed and then print the Gantt chart from Project 2013.

6. Create a WBS for one of the following projects:

   • Introducing self-checkout registers at your school's bookstore

   • Providing a new Internet cafe onsite at your organization

   • Developing an app that you and a friend will create and sell online within three months

   • Earning your CAPM or PMP certification

   Decide on all of the Level 2 categories for the WBS. Use your choice of software to create a WBS in chart form and as tasks in a Gantt chart. Do not enter any durations or dependencies. Be sure to include all of the deliverables and work required for the project. Make notes of questions you had while completing this exercise.

7. Review three different template files from Microsoft Project 2013, MindView, or any other project management software tool. What do you think about the WBSs? Write a short paper summarizing your analysis, and provide at least three suggestions for improving one of the WBSs.

8. Research the benefits of and requirements for earning a certification in business analysis, as described in the What Went Right feature in this chapter. Summarize your findings in a short paper.

Running Case

You have been selected as the project manager for the Global Treps project. You helped to run a local shark tank like event at your college last year as part of a class project, so you have a general idea of what is involved. The schedule goal is six months, and the budget is $120,000. Your favorite professor, Dr. K., and a few of her associates have agreed to fund the project. Your strengths are your organizational and leadership skills.

You are a senior, live on-campus, and get free room and board by being a resident assistant in your dorm. Bobby, a computer whiz who funded a lot of his college expenses by building websites, will be your main technical guy on the project. He goes to your college and lives off-campus. Three other people will form your core project team: Kim, a new college grad now working for a non-profit group in Vietnam; Ashok, a business student in India; and Alfreda, a student in the U.S. planning to visit her home town in Ethiopia for two months in a few months. You will hold most meetings virtually, but you can meet face-to-face with Bobby and Dr. K. as needed. You have all known each other for at least a year and are excited to make this project a success.

You and your team members will do the work part-time while you finish school or work at other jobs, but you can use up to $50,000 total to pay yourselves. You estimate that you will need another $30,000 for travel expenses, $20,000 for hardware and software, and the other $20,000 will go toward organizing events, consultants, legal/business fees, etc.

Your goal is to develop a fully functioning website and test it by holding four events in four different countries. You'll make improvements to the site after those events, develop plans to scale it up, and recommend how to transition the project results into a successful business.

Recall from Chapter 4 that this system would include the following capabilities:

- Provide guidelines and templates for running a shark tank type event

- Accept donations from potential investors targeted toward specific schools or organizations wishing to host an event (similar to the popular DonorsChoose.org site, where people can fund teachers' requests)

- Accept ideas for needed new products or services

- Provide the ability for organizations to create their own custom site to solicit local participants and sharks, accept applications, and promote the winners as well as losers.

Note that you decided *not* to include the idea of providing an online version of the event as part of the initial project as your sponsor and team decided that physical events would be most effective. You have also decided to limit the scope of this first project to provide the ability for 20 organizations to create their own custom websites. Your team members will screen the organizations and assist people in using the site to plan their events.

You plan to hold four shark tank like events within four months, using your team members abroad to help organize and run those events, plus one at your college. Your semester has just started, so you plan to hold your event at the end of the term. The project will fund refreshments for the events and prizes for the winners, with a budget of $1,000 for each event. You don't think you'll get any donations via the new website before these events, but you'll try to have it set up to accept donations by the last month.

You will create some short videos to show people how to use the site and provide suggestions for holding the events.

After testing the site and getting customer feedback, you will make some changes and document recommendations for a follow-on project. You will also create a business plan recommending how to transition this project into a real business that can make a profit after two years.

Assume that you would pay for a new website and account through an online provider. Bobby would do most of the customization/programming for the site, but you would consider outsourcing or purchasing services to provide some of the capabilities like accepting donations and developing the short videos on the site. You would also buy a new laptop and Internet access for your three team members abroad so that they could share information with their contacts in those countries.

You and Dr. K. want to attend all of the events as part of the project, and you might include a full face-to-face meeting with the whole team if possible.

Tasks

1. Document your approach for collecting requirements for the project. Include at least five technical requirements and five non-technical requirements in a requirements traceability matrix. Also develop a list of at least five questions you would like to ask the project sponsor. Let your instructor answer them for you, if applicable.

2. Develop a first version of a project scope statement for the project. Use the template provided on the companion website for this text and the example in Chapter 3 as guides. Be as specific as possible in describing product characteristics and requirements, as well as all of the project's deliverables. Be sure to include the Global Treps website, four shark tank like

events, a business plan, and outsourced items (laptops, donation acceptance, video creation, etc.) as part of the project scope.

3. Develop a work breakdown structure for the project. Break down the work to Level 3 or Level 4, as appropriate. Use the template on the companion website and samples in this text as guides. Print the WBS in list form. Be sure the WBS is based on the project charter (created for the Chapter 4 Running Case), the project scope statement created in Task 2 above, and other relevant information.

4. Use the WBS you developed in Task 3 to begin creating a Gantt chart using your choice of software. Do not enter any durations or dependencies. Print the resulting Gantt chart on one page, and be sure to display the entire Task Name column.

5. Develop a strategy for scope validation and change control for this project. Write a short paper summarizing key points of the strategy.

Key Terms

analogy approach p.200

benchmarking p.189

bottom-up approach p.201

decomposition p.194

deliverable p.184

Joint Application Design (JAD) p.209

project scope management p.184

project scope statement p.191

prototyping p.209

requirement p.186

requirements management plan p.187

requirements traceability matrix (RTM) p.191

scope p.184

scope baseline p.194

scope creep p.205

scope validation p.206

top-down approach p.201

use case modeling p.209

variance p.208

WBS dictionary p.203

work breakdown structure (WBS) p.194

work package p.196

End Notes

[1] Karl Wiegers, *Software Requirements*, Second edition (Redmond, WA: Microsoft Press, 2003), p. 7.

[2] Amy Hillman, "The Rise in Business-Analytics Degrees," *Huffington Post* (May 13, 2014).

[3] Project Management Institute, *Pulse of the Profession®: Requirements Management* (August 2014).

[4] Craig Smith, "Interview and Book Review: How Google Tests Software," *InfoQ.com* (September 11, 2012).

[5] John Simpson, "2011: The State of Requirements Management" (2011).

[6] Project Management Institute, *Pulse of the Profession: Requirements Management — A Core Competency for Project and Program Success* (August 2014).

[7] This structure is based on a sample Project 98 file. See *www.microsoft.com* for additional template files.

[8] Mindjet Visual Thinking, "About Mind Maps," *Mindjet.com* (2002).

9 David I. Cleland, *Project Management: Strategic Design and Implementation*, Second edition (New York: McGraw-Hill, 1994).

10 Geoffrey James, "Information Technology Fiascoes … and How to Avoid Them," *Datamation* (November 1997).

11 Paul McDougall, "8 Expensive IT Blunders," *InformationWeek* (October 16, 2006).

12 Geoffrey James, "Information Technology Fiascoes … and How to Avoid Them," *Datamation* (November 1997).

13 Marc L. Songini, "21st Century Insurance Apps in Limbo Despite $100M Investment," *Computerworld* (December 6, 2002).

14 *www.myki.com.au/About-myki/What-is-myki* (accessed March 1, 2012).

15 Megan Levy, "Peak-Hour Test for myki Smartcard System," *The Age* (July 26, 2010).

16 Greg Thom, "When It Comes to myki, Like It or Lump It," *Herald Sun* (January 20, 2012).

17 Alex White, "The $1.5 Billion myki Debacle Labor Doesn't Want to Know About," *Herald Sun* (January 3, 2015).

18 Andy Crowe, *Alpha Project Managers: What the Top 2% Know That Everyone Else Does Not* (Kennesaw, GA: Velociteach Press, 2006), pp. 46–47.

19 Julia King, "IS Reins in Runaway Projects," *Computerworld* (September 24, 1997).

20 Thomas E. Murphy, "Market Guide for Software Requirements Definition and Management Solutions," Gartner (October 7, 2014).

219

PROJECT TIME MANAGEMENT

LEARNING OBJECTIVES

After reading this chapter, you will be able to:

- Understand the importance of project schedules and good project time management
- Discuss the process of planning schedule management
- Define activities as the basis for developing project schedules
- Describe how project managers use network diagrams and dependencies to assist in activity sequencing
- Understand the relationship between estimating resources and project schedules
- Explain how various tools and techniques help project managers perform activity duration estimates
- Use a Gantt chart for planning and tracking schedule information, find the critical path for a project, and describe how critical chain scheduling and the Program Evaluation and Review Technique (PERT) affect schedule development
- Understand how time management is addressed using Agile
- Discuss how reality checks and discipline are involved in controlling and managing changes to the project schedule
- Describe how project management software can assist in project time management and review words of caution before using this software

OPENING CASE

Sue Johnson was the project manager for a consulting company contracted to provide a new online registration system at a local college in nine months or less. This system had to be operational by May 1 so students could use it to register for the fall semester. Her company's contract had a stiff penalty clause if the system was not ready by then, and Sue and her team would get nice bonuses for doing a good job on this project and meeting the schedule. Sue knew that it was her responsibility to meet the schedule and manage scope, cost, and quality expectations. She and her team developed a detailed schedule and network diagram to help organize the project.

Developing the schedule turned out to be the easy part; keeping the project on track was more difficult. Managing personnel issues and resolving schedule conflicts were two of the bigger challenges. Many of the college's employees took unplanned vacations and missed or rescheduled project review meetings. These changes made it difficult for the project team to follow the planned schedule for the system because the team had to have customer sign-off at various stages of the systems development life cycle. One senior programmer on Sue's project team quit, and she knew it would take extra time for a new person to get up to speed, especially since the exiting programmer did a poor job documenting how his code linked to other systems at the college. It was still early in the project, but Sue knew they were falling behind. What could she do to meet the operational date of May 1?

6.1 THE IMPORTANCE OF PROJECT SCHEDULES

Managers often cite the need to deliver projects on time as one of their biggest challenges and the main cause of conflict. Perhaps part of the reason that schedule problems are so common is that time is easily measured and remembered. You can debate scope and cost overruns and make actual numbers appear closer to estimates, but once a project schedule is set, people remember the projected completion date, and anyone can quickly estimate schedule performance by subtracting the original time estimate from how long it really took to complete the project. People often compare planned and actual project completion times without taking into account the approved changes in the project. Time is the variable that has the least amount of flexibility. Time passes no matter what happens on a project.

Individual work styles and cultural differences may also cause schedule conflicts. For example, you will learn in Chapter 9, Project Human Resource Management, about the Myers Briggs Type Indicator. One dimension of this team-building tool deals with attitudes toward structure and deadlines. Some people prefer detailed schedules and emphasize task completion. Others prefer to keep things open and flexible. Different cultures and even entire countries have different attitudes about schedules. For example, in some countries businesses close for several hours every afternoon to have siestas. Countries may have different holidays, which means not much work will be done at certain times of the year. Cultures may also have different perceptions of work ethic—some may value hard work and strict schedules while others may value the ability to remain relaxed and flexible.

With all the possibilities for schedule conflicts, it is important for project managers to use good project time management. **Project time management**, simply defined, involves

MEDIA SNAPSHOT

In contrast to the 2002 Salt Lake City Winter Olympic Games (see Chapter 4's Media Snapshot), planning and scheduling were not well implemented for the 2004 Athens Summer Olympic Games or the 2014 Sochi Winter Olympic Games.

Many articles written before the Athens opening ceremonies predicted that the facilities would not be ready in time. "With just 162 days to go to the opening of the Athens Olympics, the Greek capital is still not ready for the expected onslaught. … By now 22 of the 30 Olympic projects were supposed to be finished. This week the Athens Olympic Committee proudly announced 19 venues would be finished by the end of next month. That's a long way off target."[1] However, many people were pleasantly surprised by the amazing opening ceremonies, beautiful new buildings, and state-of-the-art security and transportation systems in Athens. For example, traffic flow, considered a major pre-Games hurdle, was superb. One spectator at the games commented on the prediction that the facilities would not be ready in time: "Athens proved them all wrong. … It has never looked better."[2] The Greeks even made fun of critics by having construction workers pretend that they were still working as the ceremonies began. Unfortunately, the Greek government suffered a huge financial deficit because the games cost more than twice the planned budget.

The 2014 Winter Olympic Games in Sochi, Russia, suffered even greater financial losses. Originally budgeted at US$12 billion, final costs reached over US$51 billion, making it the most expensive games in history. Unlike Greece's humorous response to challenges at the Athens games, Russian citizens were much more serious. Although in 2006, 86 percent of Sochi residents supported the games, by 2013 only 40 percent supported them. Russian citizens, especially those in Sochi, understood the negative impacts of hosting the games when they heard about the poor planning and huge cost overruns. "… the Sochi Olympics will continue to be a burden for the Russian state, with expenses for operation, maintenance and foregone interest and tax revenue in the order of USD 1.2 billion per year. The event also did not manage to improve the image of Russia in the world and among the domestic population support dropped over the seven years of its implementation, most notably among the local population."[3]

the processes required to ensure timely completion of a project. Seven main processes are involved in project time management:

1. *Planning schedule management* involves determining the policies, procedures, and documentation that will be used for planning, executing, and controlling the project schedule. The main output of this process is a schedule management plan.
2. *Defining activities* involves identifying the specific activities that the project team members and stakeholders must perform to produce the project deliverables. An **activity** or **task** is an element of work normally found on the work breakdown structure (WBS) that has expected duration, cost, and resource requirements. The main outputs of this process are an activity list, activity attributes, a milestone list, and project management plan updates.
3. *Sequencing activities* involves identifying and documenting the relationships between project activities. The main outputs of this process include project schedule network diagrams and project documents updates.

4. *Estimating activity resources* involves estimating how many **resources**—people, equipment, and materials—a project team should use to perform project activities. The main outputs of this process are activity resource requirements, a resource breakdown structure, and project documents updates.

5. *Estimating activity durations* involves estimating the number of work periods that are needed to complete individual activities. Outputs include activity duration estimates and project documents updates.

6. *Developing the schedule* involves analyzing activity sequences, activity resource estimates, and activity duration estimates to create the project schedule. Outputs include a schedule baseline, project schedule, schedule data, project calendars, project management plan updates, and project documents updates.

7. *Controlling the schedule* involves controlling and managing changes to the project schedule. Outputs include work performance information, schedule forecasts, change requests, project management plan updates, project documents updates, and organizational process assets updates.

Figure 6-1 summarizes these processes and outputs, showing when they occur in a typical project.

Planning
Process: **Plan schedule management**
Outputs: Schedule management plan
Process: **Define activities**
Outputs: Activity list, activity attributes, milestone list, project management plan updates
Process: **Sequence activities**
Outputs: Project schedule network diagrams, project documents updates
Process: **Estimate activity resources**
Outputs: Activity resource requirements, resource breakdown structure, project documents updates
Process: **Estimate activity durations**
Outputs: Activity duration estimates, project documents updates
Process: **Develop schedule**
Outputs: Schedule baseline, project schedule, schedule data, project calendars, project management plan updates, project documents updates

Monitoring and Controlling
Process: **Control schedule**
Outputs: Work performance information, schedule forecasts, change requests, project management plan updates, project documents updates, organizational process assets updates

Project Start   **Project Finish**

© Cengage Learning 2016

FIGURE 6-1   Project time management summary

You can improve project time management by performing these processes and by using some basic project management tools and techniques. Every manager is familiar with some form of scheduling, but most managers have not used several of the tools and techniques that are unique to project time management, such as Gantt charts, network diagrams, and critical path analysis.

6.2 PLANNING SCHEDULE MANAGEMENT

The first step in project time management is planning how the schedule will be managed throughout the life of the project. Project schedules grow out of the basic documents that initiate a project. The project charter often mentions planned project start and end dates, which serve as the starting points for a more detailed schedule. After reviewing the project management plan, project charter, enterprise environmental factors, and organizational process assets, the project team uses expert judgment, analytical techniques, and meetings to develop the schedule management plan.

The schedule management plan, like the scope management plan, can be informal and broad or formal and detailed, based on the needs of the project. In general, a schedule management plan includes the following information:

- *Project schedule model development*: Many projects include a schedule model, which contains project activities with estimated durations, dependencies, and other planning information that can be used to produce a project schedule. See Appendix A for information on using Microsoft Project 2013 to create a schedule model.
- *Level of accuracy and units of measure*: This section discusses how accurate schedule estimates should be and determines whether time is measured in hours, days, or another unit.
- *Control thresholds*: Variance thresholds, such as ±10%, are established for monitoring schedule performance.
- *Rules of performance measurement*: For example, if team members are expected to track the percentage of work completed, this section specifies how to determine the percentages.
- *Reporting formats*: This section describes the format and frequency of schedule reports required for the project.
- *Process descriptions*: The schedule management plan also describes how all of the schedule management processes will be performed.

6.3 DEFINING ACTIVITIES

You might think that all project work has been defined in enough detail after planning scope management, but it is often necessary to describe activities in more detail as part of schedule management. Defining activities involves identifying the specific actions that will produce the project deliverables in enough detail to determine resource and schedule estimates. The project team reviews the schedule management plan, scope baseline, enterprise environmental factors, and organizational process assets to begin defining activities. Outputs of this process include an activity list, activity attributes, a milestone list, and project management plan updates.

The **activity list** is a tabulation of activities to be included on a project schedule. The list should include the activity name, an activity identifier or number, and a brief description of the activity. The **activity attributes** provide schedule-related information about each activity, such as predecessors, successors, logical relationships, leads and lags, resource requirements, constraints, imposed dates, and assumptions related to the activity. The activity list and activity attributes should agree with the WBS and WBS dictionary. Information is added to the activity attributes as it becomes available; this information includes logical relationships and resource requirements that are determined in later processes. Many project teams use an automated system to keep track of activity-related information.

A **milestone** on a project is a significant event that normally has no duration. It often takes several activities and a lot of work to complete a milestone, but the milestone itself is a marker to help in identifying necessary activities. Milestones are also useful tools for setting schedule goals and monitoring progress. For example, milestones on a project like the one in the chapter's opening case might include completion and customer sign-off of documents, such as design documents and test plans; completion of specific products, such as software modules or installation of new hardware; and completion of important process-related work, such as project review meetings and tests. Not every deliverable or output created for a project is really a milestone. Milestones are the most important and visible events. For example, in the context of child development, parents and doctors check for *milestones*, such as a child first rolling over, sitting, crawling, walking, and talking. You will learn more about milestones later in this chapter.

Activity information is a required input to the other time management processes. You cannot determine activity sequencing, resources, or durations, develop the schedule, or control the schedule until you have a good understanding of project activities.

Recall the triple constraint of project management—balancing scope, time, and cost goals—and note the order of these items. Ideally, the project team and key stakeholders first define the project scope, then the time or schedule for the project, and then the project's cost. The order of these three items reflects the basic order of the processes in project time management: defining activities (further defining the scope), sequencing activities (further defining the time), and estimating activity resources and activity durations (further defining the time and cost). These project time management processes are the basis for creating a project schedule.

The goal of defining activities is to ensure that the project team completely understands all the work it must do as part of the project scope so they can start scheduling the work. For example, a WBS item might be "Produce study report." The project team must understand what the item means before team members can make schedule-related decisions. How long should the report be? Does it require a survey or extensive research to produce? What skill level does the report writer need to have? Further defining the task will help the project team determine how long it will take to do and who should do it.

The WBS is often dissected further as the project team members continue to define the activities required for performing the work. For example, the task "Produce study report" might be broken down into several subtasks describing the steps of producing the report, such as developing a survey, administering the survey, analyzing the survey results, performing research, writing a draft report, editing the report, and finally producing the report. This process of progressive elaboration, one of the project attributes listed in Chapter 1, is sometimes called "rolling wave planning."

As stated earlier, activities or tasks are elements of work performed during the course of a project; they have expected durations, costs, and resource requirements. Defining activities also results in supporting detail to document important product information as well as assumptions and constraints related to specific activities. The project team should review the activity list and activity attributes with project stakeholders before moving on to the next step in project time management. If the team does not review these items with project stakeholders, it could produce an unrealistic schedule and deliver unacceptable results. For example, if a project manager simply estimated that the "Produce study report" task would take one day and then had an intern or trainee write a 10-page report to complete that task, the result could be a furious customer who expected extensive research, surveys, and a 100-page report. Clearly defining the work is crucial to all projects. If there are misunderstandings about activities, requested changes may be required.

In the opening case of this chapter, Sue Johnson and her project team had a contract and detailed specifications for the college's new online registration system. They also had to focus on meeting the May 1 date for delivering an operational system so the college could start using the new system for the new semester's registration. To develop a project schedule, Sue and her team had to review the contract, detailed specifications, and desired operational date, then create an activity list, activity attributes, and milestone list. After developing more detailed definitions of project activities, Sue and her team would review them with the customers to ensure that the team was on the right track.

 WHAT WENT WRONG?

At the U.S. Federal Bureau of Investigation (FBI), poor time management was one of the reasons behind the failure of Trilogy, a "disastrous, unbelievably expensive piece of vaporware, which was more than four years in the (un)making. The system was supposed to enable FBI agents to integrate intelligence from isolated information silos within the Bureau."[4] In May 2006, the Government Accounting Agency said that the Trilogy project failed at its core mission of improving the FBI's investigative abilities and was plagued with missed milestones and escalating costs.

The FBI rushed to develop the new system beginning in 2001, in response to the attacks on September 11. The need for new software was obvious to former FBI agent David J. Williams, who recalls joining a roomful of agents shortly after 9/11 to help with intelligence. Agents were wearing out the casters on their chairs by sliding back and forth among 20 old computer terminals, many of which were attached to various databases that contained different information.

Congressional hearings revealed numerous problems with the project. Its requirements were very loosely defined, there were many leadership changes throughout the project, and several contracts had no scheduled milestones for completion or penalties if work was late. The new system was finally completed in 2006 and cost more than $537 million—more than a year late and $200 million over budget.

The FBI replaced Trilogy with a new system called Sentinel and began training employees to use it in May 2007.[5] Unfortunately, history repeated itself as troubles still loomed with Sentinel in 2012. According to the FBI's original plan, Sentinel was to be completed by December 2009 at an estimated cost of $425 million. The FBI later

continued

increased the estimated cost to $451 million and extended the project completion date twice, so that the project was now two years behind schedule. During a test exercise in 2011, the system experienced two outages, and the FBI determined that its current hardware structure was inadequate. In 2014, several people complained that the system still wasn't working well. "You can't find what you need most of the time, or you get junk you don't want, but other than that, the FBI's long troubled, half-billion-dollar Sentinel computerized file system is coming along just fine."[6]

6.4 SEQUENCING ACTIVITIES

After defining project activities, the next step in project time management is sequencing them or determining their dependencies. Inputs to the activity sequencing process include the schedule management plan, activity list and attributes, project scope statement, milestone list, and organizational process assets. The sequencing process involves evaluating the reasons for dependencies and the different types of dependencies.

6.4a Dependencies

A **dependency** or **relationship** pertains to the sequencing of project activities or tasks. For example, does a certain activity have to be finished before another can start? Can the project team do several activities in parallel? Can some overlap? Determining these relationships or dependencies among activities is crucial for developing and managing a project schedule.

There are three basic reasons for identifying dependencies among project activities:

- **Mandatory dependencies** are inherent in the nature of the work being performed on a project. They are sometimes referred to as hard logic. For example, you cannot test code until after the code is written.
- **Discretionary dependencies** are defined by the project team. For example, a project team might follow good practice and not start the detailed design of a new information system until the users sign off on all of the analysis work. Discretionary dependencies are sometimes referred to as soft logic and should be used with care because they may limit later scheduling options.
- **External dependencies** involve relationships between project and non-project activities. For example, the installation of a new operating system and other software may depend on delivery of new hardware from an external supplier. Even though delivery of the hardware may not be included in the scope of the project, you should add an external dependency to it because late delivery will affect the project schedule.

As with activity definition, it is important that project stakeholders work together to define the activity dependencies in their project. If you do not define the sequence of activities, you cannot use some of the most powerful scheduling tools available to project managers: network diagrams and critical path analysis.

6.4b Network Diagrams

Network diagrams are the preferred technique for showing activity sequencing. A **network diagram** is a schematic display of the logical relationships among project activities and their sequencing. Some people refer to network diagrams as project schedule network diagrams or PERT charts. PERT is described later in this chapter. Figure 6-2 shows a sample network diagram for Project X.

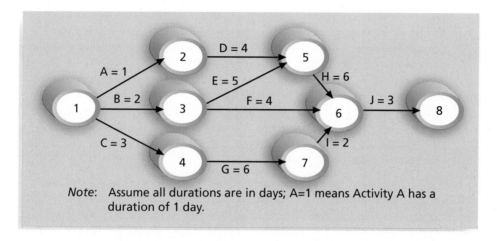

Note: Assume all durations are in days; A=1 means Activity A has a duration of 1 day.

© Cengage Learning 2016

FIGURE 6-2 Network diagram for Project X

Note the main elements on this network diagram. The letters A through J represent activities with dependencies that are required to complete the project. These activities come from the WBS and activity definition process described earlier. The arrows represent the activity sequencing or relationships between tasks. For example, Activity A must be done before Activity D, and Activity D must be done before Activity H.

The format of this network diagram uses the **activity-on-arrow (AOA)** approach or the **arrow diagramming method (ADM)**—a network diagramming technique in which activities are represented by arrows and connected at points called nodes to illustrate the sequence of activities. A **node** is simply the starting and ending point of an activity. The first node signifies the start of a project, and the last node represents the end.

Keep in mind that the network diagram represents activities that must be done to complete the project. It is not a race to get from the first node to the last node. *Every* activity on the network diagram must be completed in order to finish the project. Note also that not every item on the WBS needs to be shown on the network diagram; only activities with dependencies need to be shown. However, some people like to have start and end milestones and to list every activity. It is a matter of preference. For large projects with hundreds of activities, it might be simpler to include only activities with dependencies on a network diagram. Sometimes it is enough to put summary tasks on a network diagram or to break down the project into several smaller network diagrams.

Assuming that you have a list of the project activities and their start and finish nodes, follow these steps to create an AOA network diagram:

1. Find all of the activities that start at Node 1. Draw their finish nodes, and draw arrows between Node 1 and each of the finish nodes. Put the activity letter or name on the associated arrow. If you have a duration estimate, write it next to the activity letter or name, as shown in Figure 6-2. For example, A = 1 means that the duration of Activity A is one day, week, or other standard unit of time. Be sure to put arrowheads on all arrows to signify the direction of the relationships.

2. Continue drawing the network diagram, working from left to right. Look for bursts and merges. **Bursts** occur when two or more activities follow a single node. A **merge** occurs when two or more nodes precede a single node. For example, in Figure 6-2, Node 1 is a burst because it goes into Nodes 2, 3, and 4. Node 5 is a merge preceded by Nodes 2 and 3.

3. Continue drawing the AOA network diagram until all activities are included.

4. As a rule of thumb, all arrowheads should face toward the right, and no arrows should cross on an AOA network diagram. You may need to redraw the diagram to make it look presentable.

Even though AOA or ADM network diagrams are generally easy to understand and create, a different method is more commonly used: the precedence diagramming method. The **precedence diagramming method (PDM)** is a network diagramming technique in which boxes represent activities. It is particularly useful for visualizing certain types of time relationships.

Figure 6-3 illustrates the types of dependencies that can occur among project activities based on a Microsoft Project help screen. After you determine the reason for a dependency between activities (mandatory, discretionary, or external), you must determine the type of

---

Task dependencies

The nature of the relationship between two linked tasks. You link tasks by defining a dependency between their finish and start dates. For example, the "Contact caterers" task must finish before the start of the "Determine menus" task. There are four kinds of task dependencies in Microsoft Project.

Task dependency	Example	Description
Finish-to-start (FS)	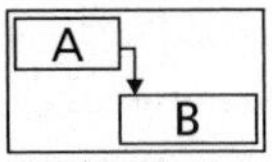 A → B	Task (B) cannot start until task (A) finishes.
Start-to-start (SS)	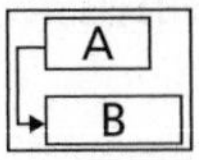 A → B	Task (B) cannot start until task (A) starts.
Finish-to-finish (FF)	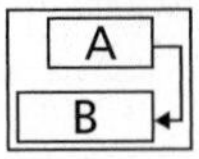 A → B	Task (B) cannot finish until task (A) finishes.
Start-to-finish (SF)	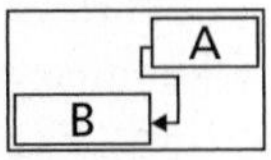 A → B	Task (B) cannot finish until task (A) starts.

FIGURE 6-3 Task dependency types

dependency. Note that the terms *activity* and *task* are used interchangeably, as are *relationship* and *dependency*. See Appendix A to learn how to create dependencies in Microsoft Project 2013. The four types of dependencies or relationships between activities include:

- **Finish-to-start dependency**: A relationship in which the "from" activity or predecessor must finish before the "to" activity or successor can start. For example, you cannot provide user training until after software or a new system has been installed. Finish-to-start is the most common type of relationship or dependency, and AOA network diagrams use only finish-to-start dependencies.

- **Start-to-start dependency**: A relationship in which the "from" activity cannot start until the "to" activity or successor is started. For example, on IT projects, a group of activities might start simultaneously, such as the many tasks that occur when a new system goes live.
- **Finish-to-finish dependency**: A relationship in which the "from" activity must be finished before the "to" activity can be finished. One task cannot finish before another finishes. For example, quality control efforts cannot finish before production finishes, although the two activities can be performed at the same time.
- **Start-to-finish dependency**: A relationship in which the "from" activity must start before the "to" activity can be finished. This type of relationship is rarely used, but it is appropriate in some cases. For example, an organization might strive to stock raw materials just in time for the manufacturing process to begin. A delay in starting the manufacturing process should delay completion of stocking the raw materials. Another example would be a babysitter who wants to finish watching a young child but is dependent on the parent's arrival. The parent must show up or "start" before the babysitter can finish the task.

Figure 6-4 illustrates Project X using the precedence diagramming method. Notice that the activities are placed inside boxes, which represent the nodes on this diagram. Arrows show the relationships between activities. This figure was created using Microsoft Project, which automatically places additional information inside each node. Each task box includes the start and finish dates, which are labeled Start and Finish; the task ID number, labeled ID; the task's duration, labeled Dur; and the names of resources, if any, that are assigned to the task. These resources are labeled Res. The border of boxes for

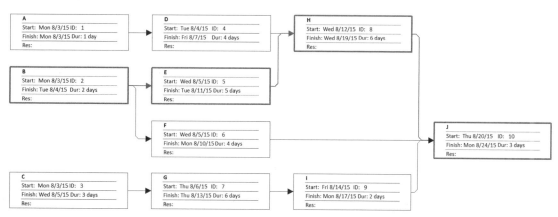

FIGURE 6-4 Precedence diagramming method (PDM) network diagram for Project X

tasks on the critical path appears automatically in red in the Microsoft Project network diagram view. In Figure 6-4, the boxes for critical tasks have a thicker border.

The precedence diagramming method is used more often than AOA network diagrams and offers a number of advantages over the AOA technique. First, most project management software uses the precedence diagramming method. Second, using this method avoids the need to use dummy activities. **Dummy activities** have no duration and no resources, but are occasionally needed on AOA network diagrams to show logical relationships between activities. These activities are represented with dashed arrow lines and have zeros for their duration estimates. Third, the precedence diagramming method shows different dependencies among tasks, whereas AOA network diagrams use only finish-to-start dependencies. You will learn more about activity sequencing using Project 2013 in Appendix A.

6.5 ESTIMATING ACTIVITY RESOURCES

Before you can estimate the duration for each activity, you must have a good idea of the quantity and type of resources (people, equipment, and materials) that will be assigned to each activity. The nature of the project and the organization will affect resource estimates. Expert judgment, an analysis of alternatives, estimating data, and project management software are tools that can assist in resource estimating. The people who help determine what resources are necessary must have experience and expertise in similar projects and with the organization performing the project.

Important questions to answer when estimating activity resources include:

- How difficult will specific activities be on this project?
- Is anything unique in the project's scope statement that will affect resources?
- What is the organization's history in doing similar activities? Has the organization done similar tasks before? What level of personnel did the work?
- Does the organization have people, equipment, and materials that are capable and available for performing the work? Could any organizational policies affect the availability of resources?
- Does the organization need to acquire more resources to accomplish the work? Would it make sense to outsource some of the work? Will outsourcing increase or decrease the amount of resources needed and when they will be available?

Answering these questions requires important inputs such as a project's schedule management plan, activity list, activity attributes, resource calendars, risk register, activity cost estimates, enterprise environmental factors, and organizational process assets such as policies regarding staffing and outsourcing. During the early phases of a project, the project team may not know which specific people, equipment, and materials will be available. For example, the team might know from past projects that a mix of experienced and inexperienced programmers will work on a project. The team might also be able to approximate the number of people or hours needed to perform specific activities.

It is important to thoroughly brainstorm and evaluate alternatives related to resources, especially on projects that involve people from multiple disciplines and companies. Because most projects involve many human resources and the majority of costs are for salaries and benefits, it is often effective to solicit ideas from different people to help develop alternatives and address resource-related issues early in a project. The resource estimates should also be updated as more detailed information becomes available.

The main outputs of the resource estimating process include a list of activity resource requirements, a resource breakdown structure, and project documents updates. A **resource breakdown structure** is a hierarchical structure that identifies the project's resources by category and type. Resource categories might include analysts, programmers, and testers. This information would be helpful in determining resource costs, acquiring resources, and so on. For example, if junior employees will be assigned to many activities, the project manager might request that additional activities, time, and resources be approved to help train and mentor those employees. In addition to providing the basis for estimating activity durations, estimating activity resources provides vital information for project cost estimates (Chapter 7), project human resource management (Chapter 9), project communications management (Chapter 10), project risk management (Chapter 11), and project procurement management (Chapter 12).

6.6 ESTIMATING ACTIVITY DURATIONS

After working with key stakeholders to define activities, determine their dependencies, and estimate their resources, the next process in project time management is to estimate the duration of activities. It is important to note that **duration** includes the actual amount of time worked on an activity *plus* elapsed time. For example, even though it might take one workweek or five workdays to do the actual work, the duration estimate might be two weeks to allow extra time needed to obtain outside information. The people or resources assigned to a task will also affect the task duration estimate. As another example, if someone asked for an estimate of when you plan to finish reading a particular book, you might give an answer of two months. Two months would be the duration estimate, even if you only plan to spend 20 hours actually reading the book.

Do not confuse duration with **effort**, which is the number of workdays or work hours required to complete a task. (Duration is normally entered in the Duration column in software such as Microsoft Project 2013, while effort is entered in a Work column. See Appendix A for more information.) A duration estimate of one day could be based on eight hours of work or 80 hours of work, assuming that multiple people are working on a task that day. Duration relates to the time estimate on a calendar, not the effort estimate. For example, you might plan to spend 20 hours reading a book—the effort estimate—and spread that time out over two months—the duration.

Of course, duration and effort are related, so project team members must document their assumptions when creating duration estimates. The people who will actually do the work, in particular, should have a lot of say in duration estimates because their performances will be evaluated based on their ability to meet the estimates. It is also helpful to review similar projects and seek the advice of experts in estimating activity durations.

Project team members must also update the estimates as the project progresses. If scope changes occur on the project, the duration estimates should be updated to reflect those changes.

There are several inputs to activity duration estimates, including the schedule management plan, activity list, activity attributes, activity resource requirements, resource calendars, project scope statement, risk register, resource breakdown structure, enterprise environmental factors, and organizational process assets. In addition to reviewing past project information, the team should review the accuracy of the duration estimates thus far on the project. For example, if team members find that all of their estimates have been much too long or short, they should update the estimates to reflect what they have learned.

One of the most important considerations in making activity duration estimates is the availability of resources, especially human resources. What specific skills do people need to do the work? What are the skill levels of the people assigned to the project? How many people are expected to be available to work on the project at any one time?

The outputs of activity duration estimates include the estimates themselves and project documents updates. Duration estimates are often provided as a discrete number, such as four weeks; as a range, such as three to five weeks; or as a three-point estimate. A **three-point estimate** includes an optimistic, most likely, and pessimistic estimate, such as three weeks for the optimistic scenario, four weeks for the most likely scenario, and five weeks for the pessimistic scenario. The optimistic estimate is based on a best-case scenario, while the pessimistic estimate is based on a worst-case scenario. The most likely estimate, as you might expect, is based on a most likely or expected scenario. A three-point estimate is required for performing PERT estimates, as described later in this chapter, and for performing Monte Carlo simulations, as described in Chapter 11, Project Risk Management. Other duration estimating techniques include analogous and parametric estimating and reserve analysis, as described in Chapter 7, Project Cost Management. Expert judgment is also an important tool for developing good activity duration estimates.

6.7 DEVELOPING THE SCHEDULE

Schedule development uses the results of all the preceding project time management processes to determine the start and end dates of the project and its activities. Project time management processes often go through several iterations before a project schedule is finalized. The ultimate goal of developing a realistic project schedule is to provide a basis for monitoring project progress for the time dimension of the project. The main outputs of this process are the project schedule, a schedule baseline, schedule data, project calendars, project management plan updates, and project documents updates. Some project teams create a computerized model to create a network diagram, enter resource requirements and availability by time period, and adjust other information to quickly generate alternative schedules. See Appendix A for information on using Project 2013 to assist in schedule development.

Several tools and techniques assist in schedule development:

- A Gantt chart is a common tool for displaying project schedule information.
- Critical path analysis is a very important tool for developing and controlling project schedules.
- Critical chain scheduling is a technique that focuses on limited resources when creating a project schedule.
- PERT analysis is a means for considering schedule risk on projects.

The following sections provide samples of each of these tools and techniques and discuss their advantages and disadvantages.

6.7a Gantt Charts

Gantt charts provide a standard format for displaying project schedule information by listing project activities and their corresponding start and finish dates in calendar form. Gantt charts are sometimes referred to as bar charts because the activities' start and end dates are shown as horizontal bars. Figure 6-5 shows a simple Gantt chart for Project X created with Microsoft Project. Figure 6.6 shows a Gantt chart that is more sophisticated and is based on a software launch project from a template provided by Microsoft. The activities on the Gantt chart are driven by the deliverables on the WBS, and should coincide in turn with the activity list and milestone list. Notice that the Gantt chart for the software launch project contains milestones, summary tasks, individual task durations, and arrows showing task dependencies.

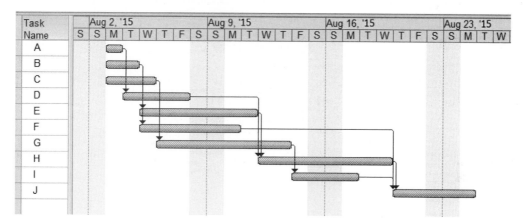

FIGURE 6-5   Gantt chart for Project X

Notice the different symbols on the Gantt chart for the software launch project (see Figure 6-6):

- The black diamond represents a milestone. In Figure 6-6, Task 1, "Marketing Plan distributed," is a milestone that occurs on March 17. Tasks 3, 4, 8, 9, 14, 25, 27, 43, and 45 are also milestones. For very large projects, top managers might want to see only milestones on a Gantt chart. Microsoft Project allows you to filter information displayed on a Gantt chart so you can easily show specific tasks, such as milestones.

- The thick black bars with arrows at the beginning and end represent summary tasks. For example, Activities 12 through 15—"Develop creative briefs," "Develop concepts," "Creative concepts," and "Ad development"—are all subtasks of the summary task called "Advertising," Task 11. WBS activities are referred to as tasks and subtasks in most project management software.

- The light gray horizontal bars for Tasks 5, 6, 7, 10, 12, 13, 15, 22, 24, 26, and 44 represent the duration of each individual task. For example, the light gray bar for Subtask 5, "Packaging," starts in mid-February and extends until early May.

- Arrows connecting these symbols show relationships or dependencies between tasks. Gantt charts often do not show dependencies, which is their major disadvantage. If dependencies have been established in Microsoft Project, they are automatically displayed on the Gantt chart.

WBS hierarchy shown
by indentations

Summary
task

Milestone

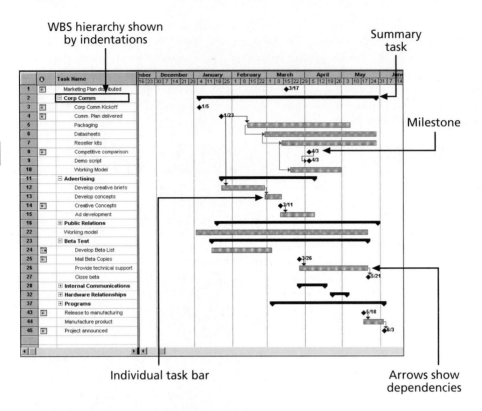

Individual task bar

Arrows show
dependencies

FIGURE 6-6   Gantt chart for software launch project

6.7b Adding Milestones to Gantt Charts

Milestones can be a particularly important part of schedules, especially for large projects. Many people like to focus on meeting milestones, so you can create them to emphasize important events or accomplishments on projects. Normally, you create milestones by entering tasks with zero duration. In Microsoft Project, you can mark any task as a milestone by checking the appropriate box in the Advanced tab of the Task Information dialog box. The duration of the task will not change to zero, but the Gantt chart will show the milestone symbol to represent that task based on its start date. See Appendix A for more information.

To make milestones meaningful, some people use the SMART criteria to help define them. The **SMART criteria** are guidelines suggesting that milestones should be:

- Specific
- Measurable
- Assignable
- Realistic
- Time-framed

For example, distributing a marketing plan is specific, measurable, and assignable if everyone knows what should be in the marketing plan, how it should be distributed, how many copies should be distributed and to whom, and who is responsible for the actual delivery. Distributing the marketing plan is realistic and able to be time-framed if it is an achievable event and scheduled at an appropriate time.

BEST PRACTICE

In his book, *The Happiness Advantage*, Shawn Achor shares principles of positive psychology that can fuel success at work. One problem many people have at work is feeling overwhelmed. They complain that they are working all the time, but they cannot get their work done. Achor suggests that the 20-second rule can help people improve their focus by minimizing barriers to change.

The 20-second rule capitalizes on people's preference for taking the path of least resistance. For example, you can more easily resist having an extra scoop of ice cream if you have to wait 20 seconds in line for it rather than have it served to you. Many people have trouble focusing on work because they are easily distracted by checking their e-mail, stocks, news, social media, etc. Achor recommends making it more difficult for yourself to be distracted. For example, keep e-mail closed while you are working. Don't leave your favorite non-work-related websites open or have your passwords saved in them. You can actually "save time by adding time"—but only to the distracting behaviors at work.[7]

6.7c Using Tracking Gantt Charts to Compare Planned and Actual Dates

You can use a special form of a Gantt chart to evaluate progress on a project by showing actual schedule information. Figure 6-7 shows a **Tracking Gantt chart**—a Gantt chart that compares planned and actual project schedule information. The planned schedule dates

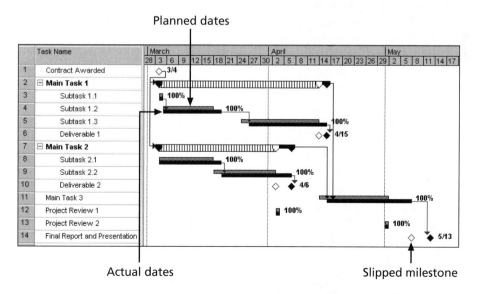

Used with permission from Microsoft Corporation

FIGURE 6-7 Sample Tracking Gantt chart

for activities are called the **baseline dates**, and the entire approved planned schedule is called the **schedule baseline**. The Tracking Gantt chart includes columns labeled "Start" and "Finish" to represent actual start and finish dates for each task, as well as columns labeled "Baseline Start" and "Baseline Finish" to represent planned start and finish dates for each task. (These columns are hidden in Figure 6-7.) In this example, the project is completed, but several tasks missed their planned start and finish dates.

To serve as a progress evaluation tool, a Tracking Gantt chart uses a few additional symbols:

- Notice that the Gantt chart in Figure 6-7 often shows two horizontal bars for tasks. The top horizontal bar represents the planned or baseline duration for each task. The bar below it represents the actual duration. Subtasks 1.2 and 1.3 illustrate this type of display. If these two bars are the same length, meaning they start and end on the same dates, then the actual schedule was the same as the planned schedule for that task. This scheduling occurred for Subtask 1.1, in which the task started and ended as planned on March 4. If the bars do not start and end on the same dates, then the actual schedule differed from the planned or baseline schedule. If the top horizontal bar is shorter than the bottom one, the task took longer than planned, as you can see for Subtask 1.2. If the top horizontal bar is longer than the bottom one, the task took less time than planned. A striped horizontal bar, as illustrated by Main Tasks 1 and 2, represents the planned duration for summary tasks. The black bar adjoining it shows progress for summary tasks. For example, Main Task 2 clearly shows that the actual duration took longer than planned.
- A white diamond on the Tracking Gantt chart represents a **slipped milestone**. A slipped milestone means the milestone activity was completed later than originally planned. The last task provides an example of a slipped milestone because the final report and presentation were completed later than planned.
- Percentages to the right of the horizontal bars display the percentage of work completed for each task. For example, 100 percent means the task is finished, and 50 percent means the task is still in progress but is 50 percent completed.

A Tracking Gantt chart is based on the percentage of work completed for project tasks or the actual start and finish dates. It allows the project manager to monitor schedule progress on individual tasks and the whole project. For example, Figure 6-7 shows that the project is completed. It started on time, but it finished a little late, on May 13 (5/13) instead of May 8.

The main advantage of using Gantt charts is that they provide a standard format for displaying planned and actual project schedule information. In addition, they are easy to create and understand. The main disadvantage of Gantt charts is that they do not *usually* show relationships or dependencies between tasks. If Gantt charts are created using project management software and tasks are linked, then the dependencies *will* be displayed, but differently than they would be displayed on a network diagram. Whether you view dependencies on a Gantt chart or network diagram is a matter of personal preference.

6.7d Critical Path Method

Many projects fail to meet schedule expectations. **Critical path method (CPM)**—also called **critical path analysis**—is a network diagramming technique used to predict total project duration. This important tool helps you combat project schedule overruns. A **critical path** for a project is the series of activities that determine the *earliest* time by which the project can be completed. It is the *longest* path through the network diagram and has the least amount of slack or float. **Slack** or **float** is the amount of time an activity may be delayed without delaying a succeeding activity or the project finish date. Normally, several tasks are done in parallel on projects, and most projects have multiple paths through a network diagram. The longest path or the path that contains the critical tasks is what drives the completion date for the project. You are not finished with the project until you have finished *all* the tasks.

6.7e Calculating the Critical Path

To find the critical path for a project, you must first develop a good network diagram, which in turn requires a good activity list based on the WBS. Once you create a network diagram, you must also estimate the duration of each activity to determine the critical path. Calculating the critical path involves adding the durations for all activities on each path through the network diagram. The longest path is the critical path.

Figure 6-8 shows the AOA network diagram for Project X again. Note that you can use either the AOA or precedence diagramming method to determine the critical path on projects. Figure 6-8 shows all of the paths—a total of four—through the network diagram. Note that each path starts at the first node (1) and ends at the last node (8) on the AOA network diagram. This figure also shows the length or total duration of each path through the network diagram. These lengths are computed by adding the durations of each activity on the path. Because path B-E-H-J has the longest duration at 16 days, it is the critical path for the project.

What does the critical path really mean? Even though the critical path is the *longest* path, it represents the *shortest* time required to complete a project. If one or more

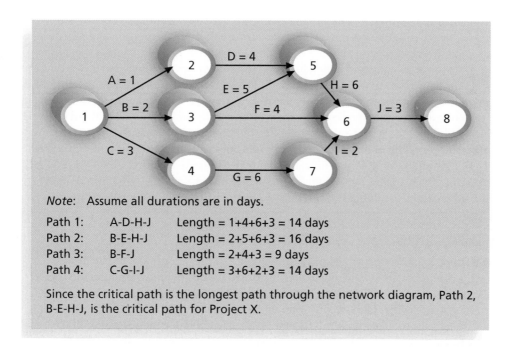

Note: Assume all durations are in days.

Path 1:	A-D-H-J	Length = 1+4+6+3 = 14 days
Path 2:	B-E-H-J	Length = 2+5+6+3 = 16 days
Path 3:	B-F-J	Length = 2+4+3 = 9 days
Path 4:	C-G-I-J	Length = 3+6+2+3 = 14 days

Since the critical path is the longest path through the network diagram, Path 2, B-E-H-J, is the critical path for Project X.

FIGURE 6-8 Determining the critical path for Project X

activities on the critical path take longer than planned, the whole project schedule will slip *unless* the project manager takes corrective action.

Project teams can be creative in managing the critical path. For example, Joan Knutson, a well-known author and speaker in the project management field, often describes how a gorilla helped Apple Inc. complete a project on time. Team members worked in an area with cubicles, and whoever was in charge of the current task on the critical path had a stuffed gorilla on top of his or her cubicle. Everyone knew that person was under the most time pressure and did not need distractions. When a critical task was completed, the person in charge of the next critical task received the gorilla.

6.7f Growing Grass Can Be on the Critical Path

People are often confused about what a project's critical path really means. Some people think the critical path includes the most critical activities, but it is concerned only with the time dimension of a project. The fact that its name includes the word *critical* does not mean that it includes all critical activities. For example, Frank Addeman, Executive Project Director at Walt Disney Imagineering, explained in a keynote address at a PMI-ISSIG Professional Development Seminar that growing grass was on the critical path for building Disney's Animal Kingdom theme park! The 500-acre park required special grass for its animal inhabitants, and some of the grass took years to grow. Another misconception is that the critical path is the shortest path through the network diagram. In some areas, such as transportation modeling, identifying the shortest path in network diagrams is the goal. For a project, however, each task or activity on the critical path must be done in order to complete the project. It is not a matter of choosing the shortest path.

Other aspects of critical path analysis may cause confusion. Can there be more than one critical path on a project? Does the critical path ever change? In the Project X example, suppose that Activity A has a duration estimate of three days instead of one day. This new duration estimate would make the length of Path 1 equal to 16 days. Now the project has two longest paths of equal duration, so there are two critical paths. Therefore, a project *can* have more than one critical path. Project managers should closely monitor performance of activities on the critical path to avoid late project completion. If there is more than one critical path, project managers must keep their eyes on all of them.

The critical path on a project can change as the project progresses. For example, suppose everything is going as planned at the beginning of the project. Suppose that Activities A, B, C, D, E, F, and G all start and finish as planned. Then suppose that Activity I runs into problems. If Activity I takes more than four days, it will cause path C-G-I-J to be longer than the other paths, assuming they progress as planned. This change would cause path C-G-I-J to become the new critical path. Therefore, the critical path can change on a project.

6.7g Using Critical Path Analysis to Make Schedule Trade-Offs

It is important to know the critical path throughout the life of a project so the project manager *can* make trade-offs. If a task on the critical path is behind schedule, the project manager must be aware of the problem and decide what to do about it. Should the schedule be renegotiated with stakeholders? Should more resources be allocated to other items on the critical path to make up for that time? Is it acceptable for the project to finish behind schedule? By keeping track of the critical path, the project manager and the team take a proactive role in managing the project schedule.

A technique that can help project managers make schedule trade-offs is determining the free slack and total slack for each project activity. **Free slack** or **free float** is the amount of time an activity can be delayed without delaying the early start date of any immediately following activities. The **early start date** is the earliest possible time an activity can start based on the project network logic. **Total slack** or **total float** is the amount of time an activity can be delayed from its early start without delaying the planned project finish date.

Project managers calculate free slack and total slack by doing a forward and backward pass through a network diagram. A **forward pass** determines the early start and early finish dates for each activity. The **early finish date** is the earliest possible time an activity can finish based on the project network logic. The project start date is equal to the early start date for the first network diagram activity. The early start plus the duration of the first activity is equal to the early finish date of the first activity. It is also equal to the early start date of each subsequent activity unless an activity has multiple predecessors. When an activity has multiple predecessors, its early start date is the latest of the early finish dates of those predecessors. For example, Tasks D and E immediately precede Task H in Figure 6-8. The early start date for Task H, therefore, is the early finish date of Task E, because it occurs later than the early finish date of Task D. A **backward pass** through the network diagram determines the late start and late finish dates for each activity in a similar fashion. The **late start date** is the latest possible time an activity might begin without delaying the project finish date. The **late finish date** is the latest possible time an activity can be completed without delaying the project finish date.

Project managers can determine the early and late start and finish dates of each activity by hand. For example, Figure 6-9 shows a simple network diagram with three tasks, A, B, and C. Tasks A and B both precede Task C. Assume that all duration estimates are in days. Task A has an estimated duration of 5 days, Task B has an estimated duration of

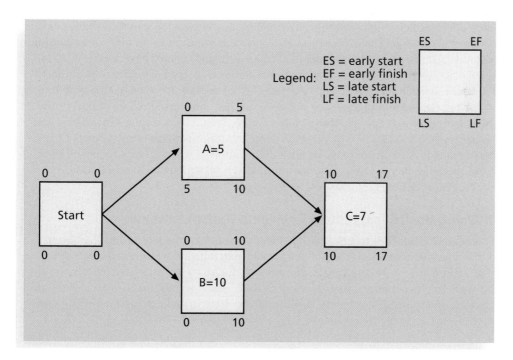

© Cengage Learning 2016

FIGURE 6-9 Calculating early and late start and finish dates

TABLE 6-1 Free and total float or slack for Project X

Task Name	Start	Finish	Late Start	Late Finish	Free Slack	Total Slack
A	8/3/15	8/3/15	8/5/15	8/5/15	0d	2d
B	8/3/15	8/4/15	8/3/15	8/4/15	0d	0d
C	8/3/15	8/5/15	8/5/15	8/7/15	0d	2d
D	8/4/15	8/7/15	8/6/15	8/11/15	2d	2d
E	8/5/15	8/11/15	8/5/15	8/11/15	0d	0d
F	8/5/15	8/10/15	8/14/15	8/17/15	7d	7d
G	8/6/15	8/13/15	8/10/15	8/17/15	0d	2d
H	8/12/15	8/19/15	8/12/15	8/19/15	0d	0d
I	8/14/15	8/17/15	8/18/15	8/19/15	2d	2d
J	8/20/15	8/24/15	8/20/15	8/24/15	0d	0d

© Cengage Learning 2016

10 days, and Task C has an estimated duration of 7 days. There are only two paths through this small network diagram: Path A-C has a duration of 12 days (5+7), and path B-C has a duration of 17 days (10+7). Because path B-C is longer, it is the critical path. There is no float or slack on this path, so the early and late start and finish dates are the same. However, Task A has 5 days of float or slack. Its early start date is day 0, and its late start date is day 5. Its early finish date is day 5, and its late finish date is day 10. Both the free and total float amounts for Task A are 5 days.

Using project management software is a much faster and easier way to determine early and late start and finish dates and free and total slack amounts for activities. Table 6-1 shows the free and total slack for all activities on the network diagram for Project X using the data from Figure 6-8 and assuming that Tasks A, B, and C started on August 3, 2015. (The network diagram is shown in Figure 6-4, which was created with Microsoft Project.) The data in this table was created by selecting the Schedule Table view in Microsoft Project.

Knowing the amount of float or slack allows project managers to know whether the schedule is flexible and how flexible it might be. For example, at 7 days (7d), Task F has the most free and total slack. The most slack on any other activity is only 2 days (2d). Understanding how to create and use slack information provides a basis for negotiating project schedules. See the Help information in Microsoft Project or research other resources for more detailed information on calculating slack.

6.7h Using the Critical Path to Shorten a Project Schedule

It is common for stakeholders to want to shorten a project schedule estimate. A project team may have done its best to develop a project schedule by defining activities, determining sequencing, and estimating resources and durations for each activity. The results of this work may have shown that the project team needs 10 months to complete the project, but the sponsor might ask if the project can be done in eight or nine months. (Rarely do people ask the project team to take longer than suggested.) By knowing the critical path, the project manager and the team can use several duration compression techniques to shorten the project schedule. One technique is to reduce the duration of activities on the critical path. The project manager can shorten the duration of critical-path activities by allocating more resources to those activities or by changing their scope.

Recall that Sue Johnson in the opening case was having schedule problems with the online registration project because several users missed important project review meetings and one of the senior programmers quit. If Sue and her team created a realistic project schedule, produced accurate duration estimates, and established dependencies between tasks, they could analyze their status in terms of meeting the May 1 deadline. If some activities on the critical path had already slipped and they did not build in extra time at the end of the project, then they would have to take corrective actions to finish the project on time. Sue could request that her company or the college provide more people to work on the project in an effort to make up time. She could also request that the scope of activities be reduced to complete the project on time. Sue could also use project time management techniques, such as crashing or fast tracking, to shorten the project schedule.

Crashing is a technique for making cost and schedule trade-offs to obtain the greatest amount of schedule compression for the least incremental cost. For example, suppose that one of the items on the critical path for the online registration project was entering course data for the new semester into the new system. If this task has not yet been done and was originally estimated to take two weeks based on the college providing a part-time data entry clerk, Sue could suggest that the college have the clerk work full time to finish the task in one week instead of two. This change would not cost Sue's company more money, and it could shorten the project end date by one week. If the college could not meet this request, Sue could consider hiring a temporary data entry person for one week to help get the task done faster. By focusing on tasks on the critical path that could be done more quickly for no extra cost or a small cost, the project schedule can be shortened.

The main advantage of crashing is shortening the time needed to finish a project. The main disadvantage of crashing is that it often increases total project costs. You will learn more about project costs in Chapter 7, Project Cost Management.

Another technique for shortening a project schedule is fast tracking. **Fast tracking** involves doing activities in parallel that you would normally do in sequence. For example, Sue Johnson's project team may have planned not to start any of the coding for the online registration system until *all* of the analysis was done. Instead, they could consider starting some coding activity before the analysis is completed. The main advantage of fast tracking, like crashing, is that it can shorten the time needed to finish a project. The main disadvantage is that it can lengthen the project schedule because starting some tasks too soon often increases project risk and results in rework.

6.7i Importance of Updating Critical Path Data

In addition to finding the critical path at the beginning of a project, it is important to update the schedule with actual data. After the project team completes activities, the project manager should document the actual durations of those activities. The project manager should also document revised estimates for activities in progress or yet to be started. These revisions often cause a project's critical path to change, resulting in a new estimated completion date for the project. Again, proactive project managers and their teams stay on top of changes so they can make informed decisions and keep stakeholders involved in major project decisions.

6.7j Critical Chain Scheduling

Another technique that addresses the challenge of meeting or beating project finish dates is an application of the Theory of Constraints called critical chain scheduling. The **Theory of Constraints (TOC)** is a management philosophy developed by Eliyahu M. Goldratt and discussed in his books *The Goal* and *Critical Chain*. The Theory of Constraints is based on the metaphor of a chain and its weakest link: Any complex system at any point in time often has only one aspect or constraint that limits the ability to achieve more of the system's goal. For the system to attain any significant improvements, that constraint must be identified, and the whole system must be managed with it in mind. **Critical chain scheduling** is a method that considers limited resources when creating a project schedule and includes buffers to protect the project completion date.

An important concept in critical chain scheduling is the availability of scarce resources. Some projects cannot be done unless a particular resource is available to work on one or several tasks. For example, if a television network wants to produce a show centered around a particular celebrity, it must first check the availability of that celebrity. As another example, if a particular piece of equipment is needed full time to complete each of two tasks that were originally planned to occur simultaneously, critical chain scheduling acknowledges that you must either delay one of those tasks until the equipment is available or find another piece of equipment in order to meet the schedule. Other important concepts related to critical chain scheduling include multitasking and time buffers.

Although many people are proud to say they are good at multitasking, multitasking is not a good thing to do if you want to finish a project in a timely manner. **Multitasking** occurs when a resource works on more than one task at a time. This situation occurs frequently on projects. People are assigned to multiple tasks within the same project or different tasks on multiple projects. For example, suppose someone is working on three different tasks—Task 1, Task 2, and Task 3—for three different projects, and each task takes 10 days to complete. If the person did not multitask, and instead completed each task sequentially starting with Task 1, then Task 1 would be completed after day 10, Task 2 would be completed after day 20, and Task 3 would be completed after day 30, as shown in Figure 6-10a. However, because many people in this situation try to please all three parties who need their tasks completed, they often work on the first task for some time, then the second, then the third, then go back to the first task, and so on, as shown in Figure 6-10b. In this example, the tasks were all half-done one at a time, then completed one at a time. Task 1 is now completed at the end of day 20 instead of day 10, Task 2 is completed at the end of day 25 instead of day 20, and Task 3 is still completed on day 30. This example illustrates how multitasking can delay task completion. Multitasking also often involves wasted setup time, which increases total duration.

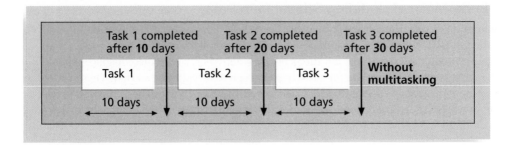

FIGURE 6-10a   Three tasks without multitasking

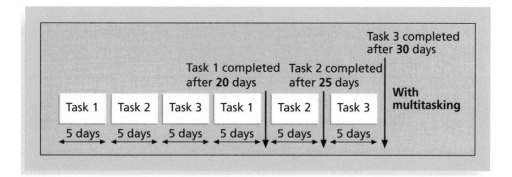

© Cengage Learning 2016

FIGURE 6-10b   Three tasks with multitasking

Critical chain scheduling assumes that resources do not multitask or at least minimize multitasking. Someone should not be assigned to two tasks simultaneously on the same project when critical chain scheduling is in effect. Likewise, critical chain theory suggests that projects be prioritized so that people who are working on more than one project at a time know which tasks take priority. Preventing multitasking avoids resource conflicts and wasted setup time caused by shifting between multiple tasks over time.

An essential concept to improving project finish dates with critical chain scheduling is to change the way people make task estimates. Many people add a safety or **buffer**—additional time to complete a task—to an estimate to account for various factors. These factors include the negative effects of multitasking, distractions, and interruptions, fear that estimates will be reduced, and Murphy's Law. **Murphy's Law** states that if something can go wrong, it will. Critical chain scheduling removes buffers from individual tasks and instead creates a **project buffer**, which is time added before the project's due date. Critical chain scheduling also protects tasks on the critical chain from being delayed by using **feeding buffers**, which consist of time added before tasks on the critical chain if they are preceded by other tasks that are not on the critical path.

Figure 6-11 provides an example of a network diagram constructed using critical chain scheduling. Note that the critical chain accounts for a limited resource, X, and the schedule includes use of feeding buffers and a project buffer in the network diagram. The tasks marked with an X are part of the critical chain, which can be interpreted as being the critical path using this technique. The task estimates in critical chain scheduling should be shorter than traditional estimates because they do not include their own buffers. Not having task buffers should mean fewer occurrences of **Parkinson's Law**, which states that work expands to fill the time allowed. The feeding and project buffers protect the date that really needs to be met—the project completion date.

Several organizations have reported successes with critical chain scheduling. For example, the What Went Right feature shows how the healthcare industry is learning to think differently by using the Theory of Constraints.

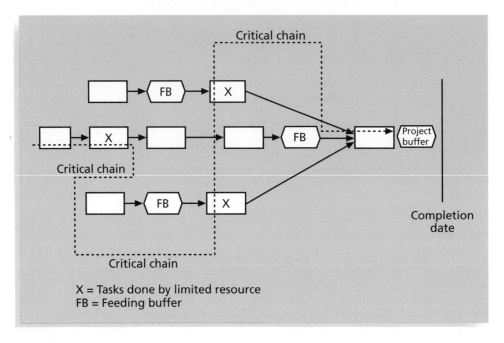

Source: Eliyahu Goldratt, *Critical Chain*

FIGURE 6-11   Example of critical chain scheduling[8]

 **WHAT WENT RIGHT?**

Experts in healthcare quality management have thought carefully about how scheduling works at a doctor's office or healthcare clinic and have considered how it might be improved:

> Consider a relatively simple system of a physician's office or clinic. The steps in the process could be patients checking in, filling out forms, having vital signs taken by a nurse, seeing the physician, seeing the nurse for a prescribed procedure such as vaccination, and so forth. These steps could take place in a simple linear sequence or chain. ... Each link in this chain has the ability to perform its tasks at different average rates. In this example, the first resource can process 13 patients, charts, or blood samples per hour; the second can process 17, and so forth. One may think that this process can produce 13 per hour, the average of all resources. In fact, this process or chain only can produce an average of eight per hour. The chain is only as strong as its weakest link and the rate of the slowest resource in this example, the weakest link, is eight. This is true regardless of how fast each of the other resources can process individually, how much work is stuffed into the pipeline, or how complex the process or set of interconnected processes is to complete. Moreover, improving the performance of any link besides the constraint does nothing to improve the system as a whole.[9]

In fact, the Avraham Y. Goldratt Institute (*www.goldratt.com*) applied this thinking at a client's site and showed just how well critical chain scheduling can work. The National University Hospital in Singapore decreased patient admission times by more

continued

than 50 percent. Improved scheduling lowered average wait times, which went from 6 to 8 hours to less than three hours. By applying critical chain techniques, the hospital admitted 63 percent of patients in less than 1.5 hours. Although these times still seem long, they show significant improvement.[10]

As you can see, critical chain scheduling is a fairly complicated yet powerful tool that involves critical path analysis, resource constraints, and changes in how buffers are used as part of task estimates. Some people consider critical chain scheduling one of the most important new concepts in the field of project management.

6.7k Program Evaluation and Review Technique (PERT)

When there is a high degree of uncertainty about the individual activity duration estimates, the network analysis **Program Evaluation and Review Technique (PERT)** can be used to estimate project duration. PERT applies the critical path method (CPM) to a weighted average duration estimate. This approach was developed at about the same time as CPM, in the late 1950s, and it also uses network diagrams, which are still sometimes referred to as PERT charts.

PERT uses **probabilistic time estimates**—duration estimates based on using optimistic, most likely, and pessimistic estimates of activity durations—instead of one specific or discrete duration estimate, as CPM does. To use PERT, you calculate a weighted average for the duration estimate of each project activity using the following formula:

$$\text{PERT weight average} = \frac{\text{optimistic time} + 4 * \text{most likely time} + \text{pessimistic time}}{6}$$

By using the **PERT weighted average** for each activity duration estimate, the total project duration estimate takes into account the risk or uncertainty in the individual activity estimates.

Suppose that Sue Johnson's project team in the opening case used PERT to determine the schedule for the online registration system project. The team would have to collect numbers for the optimistic, most likely, and pessimistic duration estimates for each project activity. Suppose that one of the activities was to design an input screen for the system. Someone might estimate that it would take about two weeks or 10 workdays to do this activity. Without using PERT, the duration estimate for that activity would be 10 workdays. Using PERT, the project team would also need to estimate the pessimistic and optimistic times for completing this activity. Suppose an optimistic estimate is that the input screen can be designed in eight workdays, and a pessimistic time estimate is 24 workdays. Applying the PERT formula, you get the following:

$$\text{PERT weight average} = \frac{8 \text{ workdays} + 4 * 10 \text{ workdays} + 24 \text{ workdays}}{6}$$

$$= 12 \text{ workdays}$$

Instead of using the most likely duration estimate of 10 workdays, the project team would use 12 workdays when doing critical path analysis. These additional two days could help the project team get the work completed on time.

The main advantage of PERT is that it attempts to address the risk associated with duration estimates. Because many projects exceed schedule estimates, PERT may help in developing schedules that are more realistic. PERT's main disadvantages are that it involves more work than CPM because it requires several duration estimates, and there are better probabilistic methods for assessing schedule risk. (See the information on Monte Carlo simulations in Chapter 11, Project Risk Management.)

6.7l Agile and Time Management

Recall from Chapter 2 that two of the core values of the Manifesto for Agile Software Development are "customer collaboration over contract negotiation" and "responding to change over following a plan." These values seem to contradict some of the structured project time management processes and tools described in this chapter. Agile methods like Scrum were designed to address collaboration and flexibility, especially on projects with a complex scope of work. For example, the product owner defines and prioritizes the work to be done within a sprint, so customer collaboration is designed into the process. The short period of each sprint (normally two to four weeks) and daily Scrum meetings provide an environment where team members collaborate to focus on completing specific tasks.

An adaptive or agile approach can be used on large projects, even after they are started using a more prescriptive approach. For example, the FBI says that switching to an agile approach is what helped them complete the Sentinel project described in the What Went Wrong? feature earlier in the chapter. The system went live "thanks to the fact that it was rescued by following an agile software development methodology... The primary lesson? Agile actually works. It's not perfect, and many people in government and in the contractor community still struggle with it, but it's succeeding where it counts—enabling the rollout of large-scale IT projects that are on time, on budget and actually do what stakeholders want them to do. Imagine that."[11]

How was project time management different after moving to an agile approach? After changing to a Scrum method in 2010, the work for the Sentinel project was organized into user stories based on the original systems requirements specifications. Each user story was allocated a number of story points based on difficulty. At the beginning of each two-week sprint, the development team identified which user stories to do during each sprint. At the end of each sprint the team demonstrated the system, regardless of whether all of the work was completed, but only the user stories that passed tests (approved by the customers) were reported as complete. If user stories were not complete, they were moved to the product backlog. This approach helped the team focus on delivering a working system that met customer needs in a specified timeframe. In other words, the emphasis was on completing some useful work for the customer in short time increments versus trying to define all the work required first and then scheduling when it could be done.[12]

6.8 CONTROLLING THE SCHEDULE

The final process in project time management is controlling the schedule. Like scope control, schedule control is a portion of the integrated change control process in project integration management. The goal of schedule control is to know the status of the schedule, influence the factors that cause schedule changes, determine that the schedule has changed, and manage changes when they occur.

The main inputs to schedule control are the project management plan, project schedule, work performance data, project calendars, schedule data, and organizational process assets. Some of the tools and techniques include:

- Performance reviews, where progress reports are often provided
- A schedule change control system, operated as part of the integrated change control system described in Chapter 4, Project Integration Management
- A scheduling tool and/or project management software, such as Project 2013 or similar software
- Variance analysis, such as analyzing float or slack and using earned value, as described in Chapter 7, Project Cost Management
- What-if scenario analysis, which can be done manually or with the aid of software
- Adjusting leads and lags
- Schedule compression, such as crashing and fast tracking, as described earlier in this chapter
- Resource optimization techniques, such as resource leveling, as described in Chapter 9, Project Human Resource Management

The main outputs of schedule control include work performance measurements, organizational process assets updates such as lessons-learned reports related to schedule control, change requests, project management plan updates, and project documents updates.

Many issues are involved in controlling changes to project schedules. It is important first to ensure that the project schedule is realistic. Many projects, especially in IT, have very unrealistic schedule expectations. It is also important to use discipline and leadership to emphasize the importance of following and meeting project schedules. Although the various tools and techniques assist in developing and managing project schedules, project managers must handle several personnel-related issues to keep projects on track. "Most projects fail because of people issues, not from failure to draw a good PERT chart."[13] Project managers can perform a number of reality checks that will help them manage changes to project schedules. Several soft skills can help project managers to control schedule changes.

6.8a Reality Checks on Scheduling and the Need for Discipline

It is important for projects to have realistic schedule goals and for project managers to use discipline to help meet those goals. One of a project manager's first reality checks is to review the draft schedule that is usually included in the project charter. Although this draft schedule might include only a project start and end date, the project charter sets some initial schedule expectations for the project. Next, the project manager and project team should prepare a more detailed schedule and get stakeholders' approval. To establish the schedule, it is critical to get involvement and commitment from all project team members, top management, the customer, and other key stakeholders.

Another type of reality check comes from progress meetings with stakeholders. The project manager is responsible for keeping the project on track, and key stakeholders like to stay informed, often through high-level periodic reviews. Project managers often illustrate progress with a Tracking Gantt chart that shows key deliverables and activities. The project manager needs to understand the schedule, including why activities are or are not on track, and take a proactive approach to meeting stakeholder expectations. It is also important to verify schedule progress, as Sue Johnson from the opening case discovered (see the Case Wrap-Up later in this chapter). Just because a team member says a task was completed on time does not always mean that it was. Project managers must review the actual work and develop a good relationship with team members to ensure that work is completed as planned or changes are reported as needed.

Top management hates surprises, so the project manager must be clear and honest in communicating project status. By no means should project managers create the illusion that the project is going fine when it is actually having serious problems. When serious conflicts arise that could affect the project schedule, the project manager must alert top management and work with them to resolve the conflicts.

Project managers must also use discipline to control project schedules. Several IT project managers have discovered that setting firm dates for key project milestones helps minimize schedule changes. It is very easy for scope creep to raise its ugly head on IT projects. Insisting that important schedule dates be met and that proper planning and analysis be completed up front helps everyone focus on doing what is most important for the project. This discipline results in meeting project schedules.

6.9 USING SOFTWARE TO ASSIST IN PROJECT TIME MANAGEMENT

Several types of software are available that assist with project time management. Software for facilitating communications helps project managers exchange schedule-related information with project stakeholders. Decision support models can help project managers analyze various trade-offs that can be made to address schedule issues.

However, project management software was designed specifically for performing project management tasks. You can use project management software to draw network diagrams, determine the critical path for a project, create Gantt charts, and report, view, and filter specific project time management information. For example, Figures 6-4, 6-5, 6-6, 6-7, and Table 6-1 were all created using Microsoft Project; Appendix A shows many more examples of using this software to assist in project time management.

Many projects involve hundreds of tasks with complicated dependencies. After you enter the necessary information, project management software automatically generates a network diagram and calculates the critical path(s) for the project. It also highlights the critical path in red on the network diagram.

Project management software also calculates the free and total float or slack for all activities. Using project management software eliminates the need to perform cumbersome calculations manually and allows for "what if" analysis as activity duration estimates or dependencies change. Recall that knowing which activities have the most slack allows the project manager to reallocate resources or make other changes to compress the schedule or help keep it on track.

Project 2013 easily creates Gantt charts and Tracking Gantt charts, which make it easier for project teams to track actual schedule performance versus the planned or baseline schedule. However, for a project to benefit from using Tracking Gantt charts, actual schedule information must be entered in a timely manner. Some organizations use e-mail or other communications software to send updated task and schedule information to the person responsible for updating the schedule. He or she can then quickly authorize these updates and enter them directly into the project management software. This process provides an accurate and up-to-date project schedule in Gantt chart form.

Project 2013 also includes many built-in reports, views, and filters to assist in project time management. For example, a project manager can quickly run a report to list all tasks that are scheduled to start soon, and then send a reminder to the people responsible for these tasks. A project manager who was presenting project schedule information to top management could create a Gantt chart showing only summary tasks or milestones. You can also create custom reports, views, tables, and filters. See Appendix A to learn how to use the project time management features of Project 2013.

 GLOBAL ISSUES

Most software companies use case studies or customer testimonials to showcase how their software helps customers solve business problems. Microsoft tells the customer story of Mexico's Secretary of Economy, who wanted to ensure that IT initiatives aligned with business goals and improved project management efficiency. Internal IT project requests often took several weeks to fulfill because the organization lacked a centralized method of capturing project information and used several diagramming tools.

The Director General of Information Technology decided to establish an Office of Project Management and search for a solution that combined professional diagramming capabilities with project management and collaboration tools. Assistant Director General of the Office of Information Technology, Carlos Benítez Gonzales, worked with other agencies to find the best solution. After deploying several of Microsoft's tools (Visio, Project, and SharePoint), the organization was able to handle more internal IT projects without adding staff, while fulfilling requests 60 percent faster.

"By documenting and incorporating governance procedures and project lifecycle stages into a standardized workflow process, the Secretary's IT team can finish projects in less time. Benítez estimates that it previously took an average of five business days to fulfill requests. The team can now complete the same work in two business days on average … 'We now have a single platform for managing process information that used to be scattered throughout the organization and inaccessible because it was stored on local computers,' says Benítez. The IT team can now handle four times the number of concurrent projects without the need to hire additional staff."[14]

Words of Caution on Using Project Management Software

Many people misuse project management software because they do not understand the concepts behind creating a network diagram, determining the critical path, or setting a schedule baseline. They might also rely too heavily on sample files or templates in developing their own project schedules. Understanding the underlying concepts (or even being able to work with the tools manually) is critical to successful use of project management software, as is understanding the specific needs of your project.

Many top managers, including software professionals, have made blatant errors using various versions of Microsoft Project and similar tools. For example, one top manager did not know how to establish dependencies among project activities and entered every single start and end date for hundreds of activities. When asked what would happen if the project started a week or two late, she responded that she would have to reenter all of the dates.

This manager did not understand the importance of establishing relationships among the tasks, which allows the software to update formulas automatically when the inputs change. If the project start date slips by one week, the project management software will update all the other dates automatically, as long as they are not hard-coded into the software. (Hard-coding involves entering all activity dates manually instead of letting the software calculate them based on durations and relationships.) If one activity cannot start before another ends, and the first activity's actual start date is two days late, the start date for the succeeding activity will automatically be moved back two days. To achieve this type of functionality, tasks that have relationships must be linked in project management software.

Another top manager on a large IT project did not know how to set a baseline in Microsoft Project. He spent almost one day every week copying and pasting information from Microsoft Project into a spreadsheet and using complicated "IF" statements to figure out what activities were behind schedule. He had never received training on Microsoft Project and did not know about many of its capabilities. To use any software effectively, users must have adequate training in the software and an understanding of its underlying concepts.

Many project management software programs also come with templates or sample files. It is very easy to use these files without considering unique project needs. For example, a project manager for a software development project can use the Microsoft Project Software Development template file, the files from similar projects done in the past, or sample files purchased from other companies. All of these files include suggested tasks, durations, and relationships. There are benefits to using templates or sample files, such as less setup time and a reality check if the project manager has never led a certain type of project before. However, there are drawbacks to this approach. Many assumptions made in these template files might not apply to the project, such as a design phase that takes three months to complete or the performance of certain types of testing. Project managers and their teams should be careful not to rely too much on templates or sample files and ignore the unique concerns of their particular projects.

CASE WRAP-UP

It was now March 15, just a month and a half before the new online registration system was supposed to go live. The project was in total chaos. Sue Johnson thought she could handle all of the conflicts that kept occurring on the project, and she was too proud and scared to admit to her top management or the college president that things were not going well. She spent a lot of time preparing a detailed schedule for the project, and she thought she was using the project management software well enough to keep up with project status. However, the five main programmers on the project all figured out a way to generate automatic updates for their tasks every week, saying that everything was completed as planned. They paid very little attention to the actual plan and hated filling out status information. Sue did not check most of their work to verify that it was actually completed. In addition, the head of the Registrar's Office was uninterested in the project and delegated sign-off responsibility to one of his clerks, who did not completely understand the registration process. When Sue and her team started testing the new system, she learned they were using last year's course data, which caused additional problems because the college was moving from quarters to semesters in the new term. How could they have missed that requirement? Sue hung her head in shame and anguish as she walked into a meeting with her manager to ask for help. She learned the hard way how difficult it was to keep a project on track. She wished she had spent more time talking face to face with key project stakeholders, especially her programmers and the Registrar's Office representatives, to verify that the project was on schedule and that the schedule was updated accurately.

Chapter Summary

Project time management is often cited as the main source of conflict on projects. Most IT projects exceed time estimates. The main processes involved in project time management include planning schedule management, defining activities, sequencing activities, estimating activity resources, estimating activity durations, developing the schedule, and controlling the schedule.

Planning schedule management involves determining the policies, procedures, and documentation that will be used for planning, executing, and controlling the project schedule. The main output is a schedule management plan.

Defining activities involves identifying the specific activities that must be completed to produce the project deliverables. It usually results in a more detailed WBS.

Sequencing activities determines the relationships or dependencies between activities. Three reasons for creating relationships are that they are mandatory based on the nature of the work, discretionary based on the project team's experience, or external based on non-project activities. Activity sequencing must be done in order to use critical path analysis.

Network diagrams are the preferred technique for showing activity sequencing. The two methods used to create these diagrams are the arrow diagramming method and the precedence diagramming method. There are four types of relationships between tasks: finish-to-start, finish-to-finish, start-to-start, and start-to-finish.

Estimating activity resources involves determining the quantity and type of resources (people, equipment, and materials) that will be assigned to each activity. The nature of the project and the organization will affect resource estimates.

Estimating activity durations creates estimates for the amount of time it will take to complete each activity. These time estimates include the actual amount of time worked plus elapsed time.

Developing the schedule uses results from all of the other project time management processes to determine the start and end dates for the project. Project managers often use Gantt charts to display the project schedule. Tracking Gantt charts show planned and actual schedule information.

The critical path method predicts total project duration. The critical path for a project is the series of activities that determines the earliest completion date for the project. It is the longest path through a network diagram. If any activity on the critical path slips, the whole project will slip unless the project manager takes corrective action.

Crashing and fast tracking are two techniques for shortening project schedules. Project managers and their team members must be careful about accepting unreasonable schedules, especially for IT projects.

Critical chain scheduling is an application of the Theory of Constraints (TOC) that uses critical path analysis, resource constraints, and buffers to help meet project completion dates.

The Program Evaluation and Review Technique (PERT) is a network analysis technique used to estimate project duration when there is a high degree of uncertainty about the individual activity duration estimates. PERT uses optimistic, most likely, and pessimistic estimates of activity durations. PERT is seldom used today.

Agile methods like Scrum take a different approach to project time management by providing more flexibility. The short time period of each sprint (normally two to four weeks) and daily Scrum meetings provide an environment where team members collaborate to focus on completing specific tasks within that time period. The product owner identifies and prioritizes tasks to be done during each sprint.

Controlling the schedule is the final process in project time management. Even though scheduling techniques are very important, most projects fail because of personnel issues, not from a poor network diagram. Project managers must involve all stakeholders in the schedule development process. It is critical to set realistic project schedules and use discipline to meet schedule goals.

Project management software can assist in project scheduling if used properly. With project management software, you can avoid the need to perform cumbersome calculations manually and perform "what if" analysis as activity duration estimates or dependencies change. Many people misuse project management software because they do not understand the concepts behind creating a network diagram, determining the critical path, or setting a schedule baseline. Project managers must also avoid relying too much on sample files or templates when creating their unique project schedules.

Quick Quiz

1. Which of the following processes involves determining the policies, procedures, and documentation that will be used for planning, executing, and controlling the project schedule?

   a. planning schedule management

   b. defining activities

   c. estimating activity resources

   d. activity sequencing

2. Predecessors, successors, logical relationships, leads and lags, resource requirements, constraints, imposed dates, and assumptions are all examples of _____.

   a. items in an activity list

   b. items on a Gantt chart

   c. milestone attributes

   d. activity attributes

3. As the project manager for a software development project, you are helping to develop the project schedule. You decide that writing code for a system should not start until users sign off on the analysis work. What type of dependency is this?

   a. technical

   b. mandatory

   c. discretionary

   d. external

4. You cannot start editing a technical report until someone else completes the first draft. What type of dependency does this represent?

    a. finish-to-start

    b. start-to-start

    c. finish-to-finish

    d. start-to-finish

5. Which of the following statements is false?

    a. A resource breakdown structure is a hierarchical structure that identifies the project's resources by category and type.

    b. Duration and effort are synonymous terms.

    c. A three-point estimate includes an optimistic, most likely, and pessimistic estimate.

    d. A Gantt chart is a common tool for displaying project schedule information.

6. What symbol on a Gantt chart represents a slipped milestone?

    a. a black arrow

    b. a white arrow

    c. a black diamond

    d. a white diamond

7. What type of diagram shows planned and actual project schedule information?

    a. a network diagram

    b. a Gantt chart

    c. a Tracking Gantt chart

    d. a milestone chart

8. _____ is a network diagramming technique used to predict total project duration.

    a. PERT

    b. A Gantt chart

    c. Critical path method

    d. Crashing

9. Which of the following statements is false?

    a. Growing grass was on the critical path for a large theme park project.

    b. The critical path is the series of activities that determine the earliest time by which a project can be completed.

    c. A forward pass through a project network diagram determines the early start and early finish dates for each activity.

    d. Fast tracking is a technique for making cost and schedule trade-offs to obtain the greatest amount of schedule compression for the least incremental cost.

10. _____ is a method of scheduling that considers limited resources when creating a project schedule and includes buffers to protect the project completion date.

   a. Parkinson's Law

   b. Scrum

   c. Critical path analysis

   d. Critical chain scheduling

Quick Quiz Answers

1. a; 2. d; 3. c; 4. a; 5. b; 6. d; 7. c; 8. c; 9. d; 10. d

Discussion Questions

1. Why do you think schedule issues often cause the most conflicts on projects?

2. Why is defining activities a process of project time management instead of project scope management?

3. Why is it important to determine activity sequencing on projects? Discuss diagrams you have seen that are similar to network diagrams. Describe their similarities and differences.

4. How does activity resource estimating affect estimating activity durations?

5. Explain the difference between estimating activity durations and estimating the effort required to perform an activity.

6. Explain the following schedule development tools and concepts: Gantt charts, critical path method, PERT, critical chain scheduling, and sprints.

7. What do you think about adding slack to individual task estimates (sometimes called *padding estimates*)? What do you think about adding a project buffer for the entire project, as critical chain scheduling suggests? What are some ethical considerations when using slack and buffers?

8. How can you minimize or control changes to project schedules?

9. List some of the reports you can generate with Project 2013 to assist with project time management.

10. Why is it difficult to use project management software well?

Exercises

1. Using Figure 6-2, enter the activities, their durations (in days), and their relationships in Project 2013. Use a project start date of August 3, 2016. View the network diagram. Does it look like Figure 6-4? Print the network diagram on one page. Return to the Gantt chart view. Click View on the menu bar, select Table: Entry, and then click Schedule to re-create Table 6-1. You may need to move the split bar to the right to reveal all of the table columns. (See Appendix A for detailed information on using Project 2013.) Write a few paragraphs explaining what the network diagram and schedule table show about Project X's schedule.

2. Consider Table 6-2. All duration estimates or estimated times are in days, and the network proceeds from Node 1 to Node 9. (Note that you can easily change this table to create multiple exercises.)

TABLE 6-2 Network diagram data for a small project

Activity	Initial Node	Final Node	Estimated Duration
A	1	2	2
B	2	3	2
C	2	4	3
D	2	5	4
E	3	6	2
F	4	6	3
G	5	7	6
H	6	8	2
I	6	7	5
J	7	8	1
K	8	9	2

© Cengage Learning 2016

a. Draw an AOA network diagram representing the project. Put the node numbers in circles and draw arrows from node to node, labeling each arrow with the activity letter and estimated time.

b. Identify all of the paths on the network diagram and note how long they are, using Figure 6-8 as a guide for how to represent each path.

c. What is the critical path for this project and how long is it?

d. What is the shortest possible time needed to complete this project?

3. Consider Table 6-3. All duration estimates or estimated times are in weeks, and the network proceeds from Node 1 to Node 8. (Note that you can easily change this table to create multiple exercises.)

a. Draw an AOA network diagram representing the project. Put the node numbers in circles and draw arrows from node to node, labeling each arrow with the activity letter and estimated time.

b. Identify all of the paths on the network diagram and note how long they are, using Figure 6-8 as a guide for how to represent each path.

c. What is the critical path for this project and how long is it?

d. What is the shortest possible time needed to complete this project?

TABLE 6-3 Network diagram data for a large project

Activity	Initial Node	Final Node	Estimated Duration
A	1	2	10
B	1	3	12
C	1	4	8
D	2	3	4
E	2	5	8
F	3	4	6
G	4	5	4
H	4	6	8
I	5	6	6
J	5	8	12
K	6	7	8
L	7	8	10

© Cengage Learning 2016

4. Enter the information from Exercise 2 into Project 2013. View the network diagram and task schedule table to see the critical path and float or slack for each activity. Print the Gantt chart and network diagram views and the task schedule table. Write a short paper that interprets this information for someone unfamiliar with project time management.

5. Enter the information from Exercise 3 into Project 2013. View the network diagram and task schedule table to see the critical path and float or slack for each activity. Print the Gantt chart and network diagram views and the task schedule table. Write a short paper that interprets this information for someone unfamiliar with project time management.

6. Create a scenario and schedule for a 6-month or 12-month project. Include the five process groups, but focus on key tasks for executing the project. For example, you could develop a schedule for starting a business, renovating a house, developing an app, or writing a book. Give only your scenario information to a classmate to work on, and compare the results. Create a schedule based on your classmate's scenario. Write a short paper summarizing the similarities and differences in what each of you created and the challenges you faced.

7. Find at least three different sample schedules created in Microsoft Project, MindView Business, or other project management software. Analyze the schedules, focusing on how complete the task lists are, how realistic the durations are, whether dependencies are included, and so on. Document your results in a short paper, including screen shots of the schedules and references. You can download a 60-day free trial of Microsoft Project from *www.microsoft.com /project* and a 30-day free trial of MindView Business from *www.matchware.com*.

8. Interview someone who uses some of the techniques discussed in this chapter. How does the person feel about network diagrams, critical path analysis, Gantt charts, critical chain scheduling, Scrum, using project management software, and managing the personnel issues involved in project time management? Write a short paper describing the responses.

9. Review two different articles about critical chain scheduling. Write a short paper describing how this technique can help improve project schedule management.

10. Search for videos that explain how and why you would want to find the critical path for a project. Write a short paper describing your findings. Summarize the best two videos; provide screen shots and explain why you liked the videos. (Note: Instructors can change the topic from critical path to other concepts in this chapter as well.)

Running Case

You are the project manager for the Global Treps Project, sponsored by Dr. K. Team members include Bobby, your IT guy; Kim, a new college grad now working for a non-profit group in Vietnam; Ashok, a business student in India; and Alfreda, a student in the U.S. originally from Ethiopia. You plan to outsource some of the work (for example, purchasing laptops, developing a website feature for accepting donations, and creating videos for the website). Recall that your schedule and cost goals are to complete the project in six months for under $120,000.

Tasks

1. Review the WBS and Gantt chart you created for Tasks 3 and 4 in Chapter 5. Propose three to five additional activities that would help you estimate resources and durations. Write a one-page paper describing these new activities.

2. Identify at least five milestones for the Global Treps Project. Write a short paper describing each milestone using the SMART criteria. Discuss how determining the details of these milestones might add activities or tasks to the Gantt chart. Remember that milestones normally have no duration, so you must have tasks that will lead to completing them.

3. Using the Gantt chart you created for Task 4 in Chapter 5 and the new activities and milestones you proposed in Tasks 1 and 2 above, create a new Gantt chart using Project 2013 or another tool. Estimate the task durations and enter dependencies as appropriate. Remember that your schedule goal for the project is six months. Print the Gantt chart and network diagram, each on one page.

4. Write a short paper summarizing how you would assign people and/or dollars to each activity from Tasks 1, 2, and 3. Include a table or matrix listing how many hours each person would work (or how many dollars you would assign) for each task. These resource assignments should make sense given the duration estimates made in Task 3 above. Remember that duration estimates are not the same as effort estimates because they include elapsed time.

Key Terms

activity p.223

activity attributes p.226

activity list p.226

activity-on-arrow (AOA) p.229

arrow diagramming method (ADM) p.229

backward pass p.241

baseline dates p.238

buffer p.245

burst p.230

crashing p.243

critical chain scheduling p.244

critical path p.238

critical path method (CPM) or critical path analysis p.238

End Notes

1 Fran Kelly, "The World Today—Olympic planning schedule behind time," *ABC Online* (March 4, 2004).

2 Jay Weiner and Rachel Blount, "Olympics are safe but crowds are sparse," *Minneapolis Star Tribune* (August 22, 2004), A9.

3 Martin Muller, "After Sochi 2014: Costs and Impacts of Russia's Olympic Games", Social Science Research Network (February 2015).

4 Paul Roberts, "Frustrated contractor sentenced for hacking FBI to speed deployment," *InfoWorld Tech Watch* (July 6, 2006).

5 Stephen Losey, "FBI to begin training employees on Sentinel case management system," *FederalTimes.com* (April 26, 2007).

[6] Jeff Stein, "FBI's Expensive Sentinel Computer System Still Isn't Working, Despite Report," *Newsweek* (September 24, 2014).

[7] Shawn Achor, *The Happiness Advantage* (New York: Crown Business, 2010).

[8] Eliyahu Goldratt, *Critical Chain* (Great Barrington, MA: The North River Press, 1997), p. 218.

[9] Anne M. Breen, Tracey Burton-Houle, and David C. Aron, "Applying the Theory of Constraints in Health Care: Part 1—The Philosophy," *Quality Management in Health Care*, Volume 10, Number 3 (Spring 2002).

[10] Avraham Y. Goldratt Institute (AGI), "A Sampling of Client Results" (*www.goldratt.com /resultsoverview*) (accessed April 29, 2015).

[11] Jason Bloomberg, "How the FBI Proves Agile Works for Government Agencies," *CIO.com* (August 22, 2012).

[12] Brian Wernham, "FBI Sentinel Programme Saved by Agile?," brianwernham.wordpress.com (May 31, 2012)

[13] Bart Bolton, "IS Leadership," *Computerworld* (May 19, 1997).

[14] Microsoft, "Secretary of Economy of Mexico: Agency Uses Diagramming, Collaboration Tools to Complete Projects 60 Percent Faster," Microsoft Customer Stories (November 19, 2014).

CHAPTER 7

PROJECT COST MANAGEMENT

LEARNING OBJECTIVES

After reading this chapter, you will be able to:

- Understand the importance of project cost management
- Explain basic project cost management principles, concepts, and terms
- Describe the process of planning cost management
- Discuss different types of cost estimates and methods for preparing them
- Understand the processes of determining a budget and preparing a cost estimate for an information technology (IT) project
- Understand the benefits of using earned value management and project portfolio management to assist in cost control
- Describe how project management software can assist in project cost management

OPENING CASE

Juan Gonzales was a systems analyst and network specialist for the waterworks department of a major Mexican city. He enjoyed helping the city develop its infrastructure. His next career objective was to become a project manager so he could have even more influence. One of his colleagues invited him to attend an important project review meeting for large government projects, including the Surveyor Pro project, in which Juan was most interested. The Surveyor Pro project was a concept for developing a sophisticated information system that included expert systems, object-oriented databases, and wireless communications. The system would provide instant, graphical information to help government surveyors do their jobs. For example, after a surveyor touched a map on the screen of a handheld device, the system would prompt the surveyor to enter the type of information needed for that area. This system would help in planning and implementing many projects, from laying fiber-optic cable to installing water lines.

Juan was very surprised, however, that the majority of the meeting was spent discussing cost-related issues. The government officials were reviewing many existing projects to evaluate their performance and the potential impact on the government's budget before discussing funding for any new projects. Juan did not understand many of the terms and charts being presented. What was this "earned value" they kept referring to? How were they estimating what it would cost to complete projects or how long it would take? Juan thought he would learn more about the new technologies the Surveyor Pro project would use, but he discovered that the cost estimates and projected benefits were of most interest to the government officials at the meeting. It also seemed that considerable effort would go toward detailed financial studies before any technical work could even start. Juan wished he had taken some accounting and finance courses so he could understand the acronyms and concepts people were discussing. Although Juan had a degree in electrical engineering, he had no formal education in finance and little experience with it. However, if Juan could understand information systems and networks, he was confident that he could understand financial issues on projects as well. He jotted down questions to discuss with his colleagues after the meeting.

7.1 THE IMPORTANCE OF PROJECT COST MANAGEMENT

IT projects have a poor track record in meeting budget goals. A 2011 study published in the *Harvard Business Review* examined IT change initiatives in almost 1,500 projects and reported an average cost overrun of 27 percent. Cost **overrun** is the additional percentage or dollar amount by which actual costs exceed estimates. The study was considered the largest ever to analyze IT projects. The projects ranged from enterprise resource planning to management information and customer relationship management systems. Most projects incurred high expenses, with an average cost of $167 million; the largest project cost $33 billion.[1]

The most important finding in the study, however, was the discovery of a large number of gigantic overages when analyzing the project overrun data. One in six of all projects studied contained a "black swan": a high-impact event that is rare and unpredictable, but not improbable in retrospect. These IT black swan projects had an average cost overrun of 200 percent and a schedule overrun of almost 70 percent. "This highlights the true pitfall of IT change initiatives: It's not that they're particularly prone to high cost overruns on average, as management consultants and academic studies have previously suggested.

It's that an unusually large proportion of them incur massive overages—that is, there are a disproportionate number of black swans. By focusing on averages instead of the more damaging outliers, most managers and consultants have been missing the real problem."[2]

Obviously, IT projects have room for improvement in meeting cost goals. This chapter describes important concepts in project cost management, particularly planning cost management, creating good estimates, and using earned value management (EVM) to assist in cost control.

 WHAT WENT WRONG?

The United Kingdom's National Health Service (NHS) IT modernization program was called "the greatest IT disaster in history" by one London columnist. This 10-year program, which started in 2002, was created to provide an electronic patient records system, appointment booking, and a prescription drug system in England and Wales. Britain's Labor government estimates that the program will eventually cost more than $55 billion, *a $26 billion overrun*. The program has been plagued by technical problems due to incompatible systems, resistance from physicians who say they were not adequately consulted about system features, and arguments among contractors about who's responsible for what.[3] A government audit in June 2006 found that the program, one of the largest civilian IT projects undertaken worldwide, was progressing despite high-profile problems. In an effort to reduce cost overruns, the NHS program would no longer pay for products until delivery, shifting some financial responsibility to prime contractors, including BT Group, Accenture, and Fujitsu Services.[4] On September 22, 2011, government officials in the United Kingdom announced that they were scrapping the National Programme for Health IT. Health Secretary Andrew Lansley said that the program "let down the NHS and wasted taxpayers' money."[5]

7.1a What Is Cost?

A popular cost accounting textbook states, "Accountants usually define cost as a resource sacrificed or foregone to achieve a specific objective."[6] Webster's dictionary defines cost as "something given up in exchange." Costs are often measured in monetary amounts, such as dollars, that must be paid to acquire goods and services. (For convenience, the examples in this chapter use dollars for monetary amounts.) Because projects cost money and consume resources that could be used elsewhere, it is very important for project managers to understand project cost management.

Many IT professionals, however, often react to cost overrun information with a smirk. They know that many of the original cost estimates for IT projects are low or based on unclear project requirements, so naturally there will be cost overruns. Not emphasizing the importance of realistic project cost estimates from the outset is only one part of the problem. In addition, many IT professionals think that preparing cost estimates is a job for accountants. On the contrary, preparing good cost estimates is a demanding, important skill that many professionals need to acquire.

Another perceived reason for cost overruns is that many IT projects involve new technology or business processes. Any new technology or business process is untested and has inherent risks. Thus, costs grow and failures are to be expected, right? Wrong. Using good project cost management can change this false perception.

7.1b What Is Project Cost Management?

Recall from Chapter 1 that the triple constraint of project management involves balancing scope, time, and cost goals. Chapters 5 and 6 discuss project scope and time management, and this chapter describes project cost management. **Project cost management** includes the processes required to ensure that a project team completes a project within an approved budget. Notice two crucial phrases in this definition: "a project" and "approved budget." Project managers must make sure *their* projects are well defined, have accurate time and cost estimates, and have a realistic budget that *they* were involved in approving.

It is the project manager's job to satisfy project stakeholders while continuously striving to reduce and control costs. There are four processes for project cost management:

1. *Planning cost management* involves determining the policies, procedures, and documentation that will be used for planning, executing, and controlling project cost. The main output of this process is a cost management plan.
2. *Estimating costs* involves developing an approximation or estimate of the costs of the resources needed to complete a project. The main outputs of the cost estimating process are activity cost estimates, basis of estimates, and project documents updates.
3. *Determining the budget* involves allocating the overall cost estimate to individual work items to establish a baseline for measuring performance. The main outputs of the cost budgeting process are a cost baseline, project funding requirements, and project documents updates.
4. *Controlling costs* involves controlling changes to the project budget. The main outputs of the cost control process are work performance information, cost forecasts, change requests, project management plan updates, project documents updates, and organizational process assets updates.

Figure 7-1 summarizes these processes and outputs, showing when they occur in a typical project.

To understand each of the project cost management processes, you must first understand the basic principles of cost management. Many of these principles are not unique to project management; however, project managers need to understand how these principles relate to their specific projects.

7.2 BASIC PRINCIPLES OF COST MANAGEMENT

Many IT projects are never initiated because IT professionals do not understand the importance of basic accounting and finance principles. Important concepts such as net present value analysis, return on investment, and payback analysis were discussed in Chapter 4, Project Integration Management. Likewise, many projects that are started never finish because of cost management problems. Most members of an executive board have a better understanding of financial terms than IT terms, and are more interested in finance. Therefore, IT project managers need to be able to present and discuss project information both in financial terms and technical terms. In addition to net present value analysis, return on investment, and payback analysis, project managers must understand several other cost management principles, concepts, and terms. This section describes general topics such as profits, life cycle costing, cash flow analysis, tangible and intangible costs and benefits,

Planning
Process: **Plan cost management**
Outputs: Cost management plan
Process: **Estimate costs**
Outputs: Activity cost estimates, basis of estimates, project documents updates
Process: **Determine budget**
Outputs: Cost baseline, project funding requirements, project documents updates

Monitoring and Controlling
Process: **Control costs**
Outputs: Work performance information, cost forecasts, change requests, project management plan updates, project documents updates, organizational process assets updates

Project Start   **Project Finish**

© Cengage Learning 2016

FIGURE 7-1   Project cost management summary

direct costs, sunk costs, learning curve theory, and reserves. Another important topic—earned value management—is one of the key tools and techniques for controlling project costs; it is described in detail in the section on cost control.

Profits are revenues minus expenditures. To increase profits, a company can increase revenues, decrease expenses, or try to do both. Most executives are more concerned with profits than with other issues. When justifying investments in new information systems and technology, it is important to focus on the impact on profits, not just revenues or expenses. Consider an e-commerce application that you estimate will increase revenues for a $100 million company by 10 percent. You cannot measure the potential benefits of the application without knowing the profit margin. **Profit margin** is the ratio of profits to revenues. If revenues of $100 generate $2 in profits, there is a 2 percent profit margin. If the company loses $2 for every $100 in revenue, there is a −2 percent profit margin.

Life cycle costing provides a big-picture view of the cost of a project throughout its life cycle. This helps you develop an accurate projection of a project's financial costs and benefits. Life cycle costing considers the total cost of ownership, or development plus support costs, for a project. For example, a company might complete a project to develop and implement a new customer service system in 1 or 2 years, but the new system could be in place for 10 years. Project managers, with assistance from financial experts in their organizations, should create estimates of the costs and benefits of the project for its entire life cycle (10 years in the preceding example). Recall from Chapter 4 that the net present value analysis for the project would include the entire 10-year period of costs and benefits. Top management and project managers need to consider the life cycle costs of projects when they make financial decisions.

MEDIA SNAPSHOT

A primary goal of many projects is to achieve some type of financial benefits, measured using life cycle costing. Project success criteria often include reaching a certain return on investment (ROI) over the life cycle. You cannot measure ROI for projects if you do not have a benefits measurement process in place. How do you know if you earned or saved a certain amount each year after the project was completed if you do not have a way to measure it? According to a 2015 report by PMI:

- Many organizations do not have a benefits measurement process at all.
- Only twenty percent of organizations report having a high level of benefits realization maturity.
- Thirty-nine percent of high-performing organizations report high benefits realization maturity compared to nine percent of low performers.

"Organizations with mature benefits realization processes can benefit from:

- Clearly identifying the strategic rewards prior to starting a project
- Effectively assessing and monitoring risks to project success
- Proactively planning for making necessary changes in the organization
- Explicitly defining accountability for project success
- Routinely extending responsibility for integration to the project team."[7]

Organizations have a history of not spending enough money in the early phases of IT projects, which affects total cost of ownership. For example, it is much more cost-effective to spend money on defining user requirements and doing early testing on IT projects than to wait for problems to appear after implementation. Recall from Chapter 5 that correcting a software defect late in a project costs much more than fixing the defect early.

Because organizations depend on reliable IT, huge costs are associated with downtime.

- When Facebook was down for 20 minutes on September 3, 2014, they lost a little more than $22,453 for every minute or more than $500,000.[8]
- On August 19, 2013, Amazon.com went down for about 30 minutes, costing them $66,240 per minute or nearly $2 million.[9]
- For Fortune 1000 companies, the average cost of an infrastructure failure is $100,000 per hour; the average cost of a critical application failure is $500,000 to $1 million per hour, or $8,300 to $16,600 per minute.[10]
- In 2014, the average annual cost of unplanned application downtime in Fortune 1000 companies was $1.25 billion to $2.5 billion.[11]

WHAT WENT RIGHT?

An important cost-cutting strategy has been inspired by the global emphasis on improving the environment. Investing in green IT and other initiatives has helped both the environment and companies' bottom lines. Michael Dell, CEO of Dell, said he aimed to make

continued

his company "carbon neutral" in 2008. "The computer giant is looking to zero-out its carbon emissions through a number of initiatives, such as offering small businesses and consumers curbside recycling of their old computers, stuffing small recycling bags with free postage into new printer-ink cartridge boxes, and operating a 'Plant a Tree for Me' program."[12] Dell did reach his goal; as of March 2012, Dell had helped its customers save almost $7 billion in energy costs.

Dell continues to practice corporate responsibility by helping the environment. In 2014, they reported the following progress:

- Recovered 230.9 million pounds of used electronics and are on track to reach our goal of 2 billion pounds by 2020
- Reduced the average energy intensity of our product line by 23.2 percent compared to FY12
- Decreased operational emissions by 10 percent
- Used more than 10 million pounds of post-consumer recycled plastics in our products[13]

Cash flow analysis is a method for determining the estimated annual costs and benefits for a project and the resulting annual cash flow. Project managers must conduct cash flow analysis to determine net present value. Most consumers understand the basic concept of cash flow: If they do not have enough money in their wallets or bank accounts, they cannot purchase something. Top management must consider cash flow concerns when selecting projects in which to invest. If top management selects too many projects that have high cash flow needs in the same year, the company will not be able to support all of its projects and maintain its profitability. It is also important to clarify the year used to analyze dollar amounts. For example, if a company bases all costs on 2012 estimates, it would need to account for inflation and other factors when projecting costs and benefits in future-year dollars.

Tangible and intangible costs and benefits are categories for determining how well an organization can define the estimated costs and benefits for a project. **Tangible costs or benefits** are easy to measure in dollars. For example, suppose that the Surveyor Pro project described in the chapter's opening case included a preliminary feasibility study. If a company completed this study for $100,000, its tangible cost is $100,000. If a government agency estimated that it could have done the study for $150,000, the tangible benefits of the study would be $50,000 to the government: It could pay for the study and then assign the government workers who would have done the study to other projects.

In contrast, **intangible costs or benefits** are difficult to measure in dollars. Suppose that Juan and a few other people spent their own personal time using government-owned computers, books, and other resources to research areas related to the study. Although their hours and the government-owned materials would not be billed to the project, they could be considered intangible costs. Intangible benefits for projects often include items like goodwill, prestige, and general statements of improved productivity that an organization cannot easily translate into dollar amounts. Because intangible costs and benefits are difficult to quantify, they are often harder to justify.

Direct costs can be directly related to creating the products and services of the project. You can attribute direct costs to a particular project. For example, direct costs include the salaries of people working full time on the project and the cost of hardware and software purchased specifically for the project. Project managers should focus on direct costs because they can be controlled.

Indirect costs are not directly related to the products or services of the project, but are indirectly related to performing work on the project. For example, indirect costs would include the cost of electricity, paper towels, and other necessities in a large building that houses 1,000 employees who work on many projects. Indirect costs are allocated to projects, and project managers have very little control over them.

Sunk cost is money that has been spent in the past. Consider it gone, like a sunken ship that can never be raised. When deciding what projects to invest in or continue, you should not include sunk costs. For example, in the chapter's opening case, suppose that Juan's office had spent $1 million on a project over the past three years to create a geographic information system, but had never produced anything valuable. If his government were evaluating what projects to fund next year and an official suggested continuing to fund the geographic information system project because $1 million had been spent on it already, the official would incorrectly be making sunk cost a key factor in the project selection decision. Many people fall into the trap of continuing to spend money on a failing project because so much money has been spent on it already. This trap is similar to gamblers who continue betting because they have already lost money. Sunk costs should be forgotten, even though it is often difficult to think that way.

Learning curve theory states that when many items are produced repetitively, the unit cost of those items decreases in a regular pattern as more units are produced. For example, suppose that the Surveyor Pro project would potentially produce 1,000 handheld devices that could run the new software and access information via satellite. The cost of the first handheld unit would be much higher than the cost of the thousandth unit. Learning curve theory can help estimate costs on projects that involve the production of large quantities of items.

Learning curve theory also applies to the amount of time required to complete some tasks. For example, the first time a new employee performs a specific task, it will probably take longer than the tenth time that employee performs a very similar task. Effort estimates, therefore, should be lower for more experienced workers.

Reserves are dollar amounts included in a cost estimate to mitigate cost risk by allowing for future situations that are difficult to predict. **Contingency reserves** allow for future situations that may be partially planned for (sometimes called **known unknowns**) and are included in the project cost baseline. For example, if an organization knows it has a 20 percent rate of turnover for IT personnel, it should include contingency reserves to pay for recruiting and training costs of IT personnel. **Management reserves** allow for future situations that are unpredictable (sometimes called **unknown unknowns**). For example, if a project manager gets sick for two weeks or an important supplier goes out of business, management reserve could be set aside to cover the resulting costs. Management reserves are not included in a cost baseline, as you will learn later in this chapter.

7.3 PLANNING COST MANAGEMENT

The first step in project cost management is planning how the costs will be managed throughout the life of the project. Project costs, like project schedules, grow out of the basic documents that initiate a project, like the project charter. The project manager and other stakeholders use expert judgment, analytical techniques, and meetings to produce the cost management plan.

The cost management plan, like the scope and schedule management plans, can be informal and broad or formal and detailed, based on the needs of the project. In general, a cost management plan includes the following information:

- *Level of accuracy*: Activity cost estimates normally have rounding guidelines, such as rounding to the nearest $100. There may also be guidelines for the amount of contingency funds to include, such as 10 or 20 percent.
- *Units of measure*: Each unit used in cost measurements, such as labor hours or days, should be defined.
- *Organizational procedures links*: Many organizations refer to the work breakdown structure (WBS) component used for project cost accounting as the control account (CA). Each control account is often assigned a unique code that is used in the organization's accounting system. Project teams must understand and use these codes properly.
- *Control thresholds*: Similar to schedule variance, costs often have a specified amount of variation allowed before action needs to be taken, such as ±10 percent of the baseline cost.
- *Rules of performance measurement*: If the project uses earned value management (EVM), as described later in this chapter, the cost management plan would define measurement rules, such as how often actual costs will be tracked and to what level of detail.
- *Reporting formats*: This section would describe the format and frequency of cost reports required for the project.
- *Process descriptions*: The cost management plan would also describe how to perform all of the cost management processes.

7.4 ESTIMATING COSTS

Project managers must take cost estimates seriously if they want to complete projects within budget constraints. After developing a good resource requirements list, project managers and their project teams must develop several estimates of the costs for these resources. Recall from Chapter 6 that an important process in project time management is estimating activity resources, which provides a list of activity resource requirements. For example, if an activity for a project is to perform a particular type of test, the list of activity resource requirements would describe the skill level of the people needed to perform the test, the number of people and hours suggested to perform the test, the need for special software or equipment, and other requirements. All of this information is required to develop a good cost estimate. This section describes various types of cost estimates, tools and techniques for estimating costs, typical problems associated with IT cost estimates, and a detailed example of a cost estimate for an IT project.

7.4a Types of Cost Estimates

One of the main outputs of project cost management is a cost estimate. Project managers normally prepare several types of cost estimates for most projects. Three basic types of estimates include the following:

- A **rough order of magnitude (ROM) estimate** provides an estimate of what a project will cost. A ROM estimate can also be referred to as a ballpark estimate, a guesstimate, a swag, or a broad gauge. This type of estimate is done very early in a project or even before a project is officially started. Project managers and top management use this estimate to help make project selection decisions. The time frame for this type of estimate is often three or more years prior to project completion. A ROM estimate's accuracy is typically −50 percent to +100 percent, meaning the project's actual costs could be 50 percent below the ROM estimate or 100 percent above. For example, the actual cost for a project with a ROM estimate of $100,000 could range from $50,000 to $200,000. For IT project estimates, this accuracy range is often much wider. Many IT professionals automatically double estimates for software development because of the history of cost overruns on IT projects.

- A **budgetary estimate** is used to allocate money into an organization's budget. Many organizations develop budgets at least two years into the future. Budgetary estimates are made one to two years prior to project completion. The accuracy of budgetary estimates is typically −10 percent to +25 percent, meaning the actual costs could be 10 percent less or 25 percent more than the budgetary estimate. For example, the actual cost for a project with a budgetary estimate of $100,000 could range from $90,000 to $125,000.

- A **definitive estimate** provides an accurate estimate of project costs. Definitive estimates are used for making many purchasing decisions for which accurate estimates are required and for estimating final project costs. For example, if a project involves purchasing 1,000 personal computers from an outside supplier in the next three months, a definitive estimate would be required to aid in evaluating supplier proposals and allocating the funds to pay the chosen supplier. Definitive estimates are made one year or less prior to project completion. A definitive estimate should be the most accurate of the three types of estimates. The accuracy of this type of estimate is normally −5 percent to +10 percent, meaning the actual costs could be 5 percent less or 10 percent more than the definitive estimate. For example, the actual cost for a project with a definitive estimate of $100,000 could range from $95,000 to $110,000. Table 7-1 summarizes the three basic types of cost estimates.

TABLE 7-1 Types of cost estimates

Type of Estimate	When Done	Why Done	How Accurate
Rough order of magnitude (ROM)	Very early in the project life cycle, often 3–5 years before project completion	Provides estimate of cost for selection decisions	−50% to +100%
Budgetary	Early, 1–2 years out	Puts dollars in the budget plans	−10% to +25%
Definitive	Later in the project, less than 1 year out	Provides details for purchases, estimates actual costs	−5% to +10%

TABLE 7-2   Maximum FTE by department by year

Department	Year 1	Year 2	Year 3	Year 4	Year 5	Totals
Information systems	24	31	35	13	13	116
Marketing systems	3	3	3	3	3	15
Reservations	12	29	33	9	7	90
Contractors	2	3	1	0	0	6
Totals	41	66	72	25	23	227

© Cengage Learning 2016

The number and type of cost estimates vary by application area. For example, the Association for the Advancement of Cost Engineering (AACE) International identifies five types of cost estimates for construction projects: order of magnitude, conceptual, preliminary, definitive, and control. The main point is that estimates are usually done at various stages of a project and should become more accurate as time progresses.

In addition to creating cost estimates for the entire project and activity cost estimates, it is also important to provide supporting details for the estimates and updates to project documents. The supporting details include the ground rules and assumptions used in creating the estimate, a description of the project (such as scope statement and WBS) used as a basis for the estimate, and details on the cost estimation tools and techniques used to create the estimate. These supporting details should make it easier to prepare an updated estimate or similar estimate as needed.

Another important consideration in preparing cost estimates is labor costs, because a large percentage of total project costs are often labor costs. Many organizations estimate the number of people or hours they need by department or skill over the life cycle of a project. For example, when Northwest Airlines developed initial cost estimates for its reservation system project, ResNet, it determined the maximum number of full-time equivalent (FTE) staff it could assign to the project each year by department. Table 7-2 shows this information. Note the small number of contractors that Northwest Airlines planned to use. Labor costs are often much higher for contractors, so it is important to distinguish between internal and external resources. (See the companion website for this text to read the detailed case study on ResNet, including cost estimates.)

7.4b Cost Estimation Tools and Techniques

As you can imagine, developing a good cost estimate is difficult. Fortunately, several tools and techniques are available to assist in creating one. These tools and techniques include expert judgment, analogous cost estimating, bottom-up estimating, three-point estimating, parametric estimating, the cost of quality, project management estimating software, vendor bid analysis, and reserve analysis.

Analogous estimates, also called **top-down estimates**, use the actual cost of a previous, similar project as the basis for estimating the cost of the current project. This technique requires a good deal of expert judgment and is generally less costly than other techniques, but it is also less accurate. Analogous estimates are most reliable when the previous projects are similar in fact, not just in appearance. In addition, the groups preparing cost estimates must have the needed expertise to determine whether certain parts of the project will be more or less expensive than analogous projects. For example, estimators often try to find a similar project and then customize or modify it for known differences. However, if the project to be estimated involves a new programming language or working with a new type of hardware or network, the analogous estimate technique could easily result in too low an estimate.

Bottom-up estimates involve estimating the costs of individual work items or activities and summing them to get a project total. This approach is sometimes referred to as activity-based costing. The size of the individual work items and the experience of the estimators drive the accuracy of the estimates. If a detailed WBS is available for a project, the project manager could require each person who is responsible for a work package to develop a cost estimate for that work package, or at least an estimate of the amount of resources required. Someone in the financial area of an organization often provides resource cost rates, such as labor rates or costs per pound of materials, which can be entered into project management software to calculate costs. The software automatically calculates information to create cost estimates for each level of the WBS and finally for the entire project. Using smaller work items increases the accuracy of the cost estimate because the people assigned to do the work develop the cost estimate instead of someone unfamiliar with the work. The drawback with bottom-up estimates is that they are usually time-intensive and therefore expensive to develop.

Three-point estimates involve estimating the most likely, optimistic, and pessimistic costs for items. You can use a formula like the PERT weighted average described in Chapter 6, Project Time Management, to calculate cost estimates or use a Monte Carlo simulation, described in Chapter 11, Project Risk Management.

Parametric estimating uses project characteristics (parameters) in a mathematical model to estimate project costs. For example, a parametric model might provide an estimate of $50 per line of code for a software development project based on the programming language the project is using, the level of expertise of the programmers, the size and complexity of the data involved, and so on. Parametric models are most reliable when the historical information used to create the model is accurate, the parameters are readily quantifiable, and the model is flexible in terms of the project's size. Many projects involving building construction use parametric estimates based on cost per square foot. The costs vary based on the quality of construction, location, materials, and other factors. In practice, many people find that using a combination or hybrid approach with analogous, bottom-up, three-point, and parametric estimating provides the best cost estimates.

Other considerations when preparing cost estimates are how much to include in reserves, as described earlier; the cost of quality, as described in Chapter 8, Project Quality Management; and other cost estimating methods such as vendor bid analysis, as described in Chapter 12, Project Procurement Management. Using software to assist in cost estimating is described later in this chapter.

7.4c Typical Problems with IT Cost Estimates

Although many tools and techniques can assist in creating project cost estimates, many IT project cost estimates are still very inaccurate, especially those for new technologies or software development. Tom DeMarco, a well-known author on software development, suggests four reasons for these inaccuracies and some ways to overcome them.[14]

- *Estimates are done too quickly.* Developing an estimate for a large software project is a complex task that requires significant effort. Many estimates must be done quickly and before clear system requirements have been produced. For example, the Surveyor Pro project described in the opening case involves a lot of complex software development. Before fully understanding what information surveyors need in the system, someone would have to create a ROM estimate and budgetary estimates for this project. Rarely are the more precise, later cost estimates less than the earlier estimates for IT projects. It is important to remember that estimates are done at various stages of the project, and project managers need to explain the rationale for each estimate.

- *People lack estimating experience.* The people who develop software cost estimates often do not have much experience with cost estimation, especially for large projects. They also do not have enough accurate, reliable project data on which to base estimates. If an organization uses good project management techniques and develops a history of keeping reliable project information, including estimates, the organization's estimates should improve. Enabling IT people to receive training and mentoring on cost estimating will also improve cost estimates.

- *Human beings are biased toward underestimation.* For example, senior IT professionals or project managers might make estimates based on their own abilities and forget that many younger people will be working on a project. Estimators might also forget to allow for extra costs needed for integration and testing on large IT projects. It is important for project managers and top management to review estimates and ask important questions to make sure the estimates are not biased.

- *Management desires accuracy.* Management might ask for an estimate but really want a more accurate number to help them create a bid to win a major contract or get internal funding. This problem is similar to the situation discussed in Chapter 6, Project Time Management, in which top managers or other stakeholders want project schedules to be shorter than the estimates. It is important for project managers to help develop good cost and schedule estimates and to use their leadership and negotiation skills to stand by those estimates.

It is also important to be cautious with initial estimates. Top management never forgets the first estimate and rarely, if ever, remembers how approved changes affect the estimate. It is a never-ending and crucial process to keep top management informed about revised cost estimates. It should be a formal process, albeit a possibly painful one.

7.4d How to Develop a Cost Estimate

One of the best ways to learn how the cost estimating process works is by studying sample cost estimates. Every cost estimate is unique, just as every project is unique. You can see a short sample cost estimate in Chapter 3 for JWD Consulting's project management intranet site project. You can also view the ResNet cost estimate on the companion website for this text.

This section includes a step-by-step approach for developing a cost estimate for the Surveyor Pro project described in the opening case. Of course, it is much shorter and simpler than a real cost estimate, but it illustrates a process to follow and uses several of the tools and techniques described earlier.

Before beginning a cost estimate, you must gather as much information as possible about the project and ask how the organization plans to use the cost estimate. If the cost estimate will be the basis for contract awards and performance reporting, it should be a definitive estimate and as accurate as possible, as described earlier.

It is also important to clarify the ground rules and assumptions for the estimate. The Surveyor Pro project cost estimate includes the following ground rules and assumptions:

- This project was preceded by a detailed study and proof of concept to show that it was possible to develop the hardware and software needed by surveyors and link the new devices to existing information systems. The proof of concept project produced a prototype handheld device and much of the software to provide basic functionality and link to the Global Positioning System (GPS) and other government databases used by surveyors. Some data is available to help estimate future labor costs, especially for the software development, and to help estimate the cost of the handheld devices.
- The main goal of this project is to produce 100 handheld devices, continue developing the software (especially the user interface), test the new system in the field, and train 100 surveyors in selected cities to use the new system. A follow-up contract is expected for a much larger number of devices based on the success of this project.
- The project has the following WBS:
  1. Project management
  2. Hardware
     - 2.1 Handheld devices
     - 2.2 Servers
  3. Software
     - 3.1 Licensed software
     - 3.2 Software development
  4. Testing
  5. Training and support
  6. Reserves
- Costs must be estimated by WBS and by month. The project manager will report progress on the project using earned value analysis, which requires this type of estimate.
- Costs will be provided in U.S. dollars. Because the project length is one year, inflation will not be included.
- The project will be managed by the government's project office. The project will require a part-time project manager and four team members. The team members will help manage various parts of the project and provide their expertise in the areas of software development, training, and support. Their total hours will be allocated as follows: 25 percent to project management, 25 percent to software development, 25 percent to training and support, and 25 percent to non-project work.
- The project involves purchasing the handheld devices from the same company that developed the prototype device. Based on producing 100 devices,

the cost rate is estimated to be $600 per unit. The project will require four additional servers to run the software required for the devices and for managing the project.

- The project requires purchased software licenses for accessing the GPS and three other external systems. Software development includes developing a graphical user interface for the devices, an online help system, and a new module for tracking surveyor performance using the device.
- Testing costs should be low due to the success of the prototype project. An estimate based on multiplying the total hardware and software estimates by 10 percent should be sufficient.
- Training will include instructor-led classes in five different locations. The project team believes it will be best to outsource most of the training, including developing course materials, holding the sessions, and providing help desk support for three months as the surveyors start using their devices in the field.
- Because several risks are related to this project, include 20 percent of the total estimate as reserves.
- You must develop a computer model for the estimate so that you can easily change several inputs, such as the number of labor hours for various activities or labor rates.

Fortunately, the project team can easily access cost estimates and actual information from similar projects. A great deal of information is available from the proof of concept project, and the team can also talk to contractors from the past project to help them develop the estimate. Computer models are also available, such as a software-estimating tool based on function points. **Function points** are a means of measuring software size based on what the software does for end users. Function points are comprised of inputs, outputs, inquiries, internal data, and external interface data. Allen Albrecht initially defined this metric in the 1970s, and today it is the international standard used to measure software size. It is the most commonly used software size metric, followed by lines of code.[15]

Because the estimate must be provided by WBS and by month, the team first reviews a draft of the project schedule. The team decides to begin by estimating the cost of each WBS item and then determine when the work will be performed, even though costs may be incurred at different times than when the work is performed. The team's budget expert has approved this approach for the estimate. The team has further assumptions and information for estimating the costs for each WBS category:

1. *Project management*: Estimate based on compensation for the part-time project manager and 25 percent of the four team members' time. The budget expert for this project suggested using a labor rate of $100/hour for the project manager and $75/hour for each team member, based on working an average of 160 hours per month, full time. Therefore, the total hours for the project manager under this category are 960 (160/2 * 12 = 960). Costs are also included for the four project team members who are each working 25 percent of their time: a total of 160 hours per month for all project personnel (160 * 12 = 1920). An additional amount for all contracted labor is estimated by multiplying 10 percent of the total estimates for software development and testing costs (10% * ($594,000 + $69,000)).

2. *Hardware*
   2.1 *Handheld devices*: 100 devices estimated by contractor at $600 per unit.
   2.2 *Servers*: Four servers estimated at $4,000 each, based on recent server purchases.
3. *Software*
   3.1 *Licensed software:* License costs will be negotiated with each supplier. Because there is a strong probability of large future contracts and great publicity if the system works well, costs are expected to be lower than usual. A cost of $200/handheld device will be used.
   3.2 *Software development:* This estimate will include two approaches: a labor estimate and a function point estimate. The higher estimate will be used. If the estimates differ by more than 20 percent, the project will require a third estimation approach. The supplier who developed the proof of concept project will provide the labor estimate input, and local technical experts will make the function point estimates.
4. *Testing*: Based on similar projects, testing will be estimated as 10 percent of the total hardware and software cost.
5. *Training and support*: Based on similar projects, training will be estimated on a per-trainee basis, plus travel costs. The cost per trainee (100 total) will be $500, and travel will cost $700/day/person for the instructors and project team members. The team estimates that the project will require a total of 12 travel days. Labor costs for the project team members will be added to this estimate because they will assist in training and providing support after the training. The labor hours estimate for team members is 1,920 hours total.
6. *Reserves*: As directed, reserves will be estimated at 20 percent of the total estimate.

The project team then develops a cost model using the preceding information. Figure 7-2 shows a spreadsheet that summarizes the costs by WBS item. Notice that the WBS items are listed in the first column, and some are broken down into more detail based on how the costs are estimated. For example, the project management category is broken down into three subcategories because the project manager, team members, and contractors will each perform project management activities that must be accounted for in the costs. Also notice the columns for entering the number of units or hours and the cost per unit or hour. Several items are estimated using this approach. The estimate includes some short comments, such as reserves being 20 percent of the total estimate. Also notice that you can easily change several input variables, such as number of hours or cost per hour, to revise the estimate.

The asterisk by the software development item in Figure 7-2 provides reference for detailed information on how this more complicated estimate was made. Recall the assumption that software development must be estimated using two approaches, and that the higher estimate would be used as long as both estimates differed by no more than 20 percent. The labor estimate was used in this case because it was slightly higher than the function point estimate ($594,000 versus $567,000). Figure 7-3 shows how the function point estimate was made, and the Best Practice feature provides more information on function point estimates. As you can see, many assumptions were made in producing the function point estimate. By putting the information into a cost model, you can easily change several inputs to adjust the estimate.

Surveyor Pro Project Cost Estimate Created October 5

WBS Items	# Units/Hrs.	Cost/Unit/Hr.	Subtotals	WBS Level 2 Totals	% of Total
1. Project Management				**$306,300**	**20%**
Project manager	960	$100	$96,000		
Project team members	1920	$75	$144,000		
Contractors (10% of software development and testing)			$66,300		
2. Hardware				**$76,000**	**5%**
2.1 Handheld devices	100	$600	$60,000		
2.2 Servers	4	$4,000	$16,000		
3. Software				**$614,000**	**40%**
3.1 Licensed software	100	$200	$20,000		
3.2 Software development*			$594,000		
4. Testing (10% of total hardware and software costs)			$69,000	**$69,000**	**5%**
5. Training and Support				**$202,400**	**13%**
Trainee cost	100	$500	$50,000		
Travel cost	12	$700	$8,400		
Project team members	1920	$75	$144,000		
Subtotal			$1,267,700		
6. Reserves (20% of total estimate)			$253,540	**$253,540**	**17%**
Total project cost estimate				**$1,521,240**	

*See software development estimate.

© Cengage Learning 2016

FIGURE 7-2   Surveyor Pro project cost estimate

Surveyor Pro Software Development Estimate Created October 5

1. Labor Estimate	# Units/Hrs.	Cost/Unit/Hr.	Subtotals	Calculations
Contractor labor estimate	3000	$150	$450,000	3000*150
Project team member estimate	1920	$75	$144,000	1920*75
Total labor estimate			**$594,000**	Sum above two values
2. Function point estimate	Quantity	Conversion Factor	Function Points	Calculations
External inputs	10	4	40	10*4
External interface files	3	7	21	3*7
External outputs	4	5	20	4*5
External queries	6	4	24	6*4
Logical internal tables	7	10	70	7*10
Total function points			175	Sum above function point values
Java 2 language equivalency value			46	Assumed value from reference
Source lines of code (SLOC) estimate			8,050	175*46
Productivity×KSLOC^Penalty (in months)			29.28	3.13*8.05^1.072 (see reference)
Total labor hours (27 hours/function point)*			4,725	27*175
Cost/labor hour ($120/hour)			$120	Assumed value from budget expert
Total function point estimate			**$567,000**	4,725*120

* Based on historical data

© Cengage Learning 2016

FIGURE 7-3   Surveyor Pro software development estimate

#1 BEST PRACTICE

Software expert and author Alvin Alexander shared his knowledge on the challenging topic of estimating software development costs in several presentations and a book called *Cost Estimating in an Agile Development Environment* (2015). Alexander describes how to use Function Point Analysis (FPA) techniques based on his personal experience working on a multimillion dollar software project over five years. (Recall that function points are a means of measuring software size in terms that are meaningful to end users.) The project initially used a more traditional, waterfall approach but later moved to a more agile approach.

Alexander explained that at the beginning of the project, when requirements documents were very long and detailed, the programming work took about three times the amount of time that was required to create the requirements (a ratio of 3:1). Later in the project, after their client trusted them more and actually knew the developers by name, the requirements were much shorter (more like user stories), and the ratio of programming work to requirements work was much higher—6:1 to 9.5:1. User stories describe what users do or need to do as part of their job function, focusing on the "who," "what," and "why" of a requirement in a simple, concise way. Developers can analyze user stories to estimate the number of internal logical files (ILFs)—a group of logically related data that resides entirely within the application boundary and is maintained through external inputs. You can then use the ILFs to approximate the number of function points, and then multiply by a certain number of hours/function point to estimate the person-hours needed to develop the software.[16]

World class organizations take about half as long as average organizations (19 versus 35 hours) to develop one function point. They use consistent documentation (for requirements, analysis, and use cases), they follow consistent processes for developing software, and their technical staff focus on business instead of technology. "It is impossible to separate world-class organizations from world-class metrics organizations."[17]

It is very important to have several people review the project cost estimate. It is also helpful to analyze the total dollar value as well as the percentage of the total amount for each major WBS category. For example, a senior executive could quickly look at the Surveyor Pro project cost estimate and decide if the numbers are reasonable and the assumptions are well documented. In this case, the government had budgeted $1.5 million for the project, so the estimate was in line with that amount. The WBS Level 2 items, such as project management, hardware, software, and testing, also seemed to be at appropriate percentages of the total cost based on similar past projects. In some cases, a project team might also be asked to provide a range estimate for each item instead of one discrete amount. For example, the team might estimate that the testing costs will be between $60,000 and $80,000 and document their assumptions in determining those values. It is also important to update cost estimates, especially if any major changes occur on a project.

After the total cost estimate is approved, the team can then allocate costs for each month based on the project schedule and when costs will be incurred. Many organizations also require that the estimated costs be allocated into certain budget categories, as described in the next section.

7.5 DETERMINING THE BUDGET

Determining the budget involves allocating the project cost estimate to individual material resources or work items over time. These material resources or work items are based on the activities in the work breakdown structure for the project. The cost management plan, scope baseline, activity cost estimates, basis of estimates, project schedule, resource calendars, risk register, agreements, and organizational process assets are all inputs for determining the budget. The main goal of the cost budgeting process is to produce a cost baseline for measuring project performance and to determine project funding requirements. The process may also result in project documents updates, such as items being added, removed, or modified in the scope statement or project schedule.

The Surveyor Pro project team would use the cost estimate from Figure 7-2 along with the project schedule and other information to allocate costs for each month. Figure 7-4 provides an example of a cost baseline for this project. A **cost baseline** is a time-phased budget that project managers use to measure and monitor cost performance. Again, it's important for team members to document assumptions they made when developing the cost baseline and have several experts review it.

Most organizations have a well-established process for preparing budgets. For example, many organizations require budget estimates to include the number of FTE for each month of the project. One FTE normally means 40 hours of work. One person could be assigned full-time to a project to provide one FTE, or two people could be assigned half-time to provide one FTE. This number provides the basis for estimating total compensation costs each year. Many organizations also want to know the amount of money projected to be paid to suppliers for their labor costs or other purchased goods and services. Other common budget categories include travel, depreciation, rents and leases, and other supplies and expenses. It is important to understand these budget categories before developing an estimate to make sure data is collected accordingly. Organizations use this information to track costs across projects and non-project work and to look for ways to reduce costs. They also use the information for legal and tax purposes.

Surveyor Pro Project Cost Baseline Created October 10*

WBS Items	1	2	3	4	5	6	7	8	9	10	11	12	Totals
1. Project Management													
1.1 Project manager	8,000	8,000	8,000	8,000	8,000	8,000	8,000	8,000	8,000	8,000	8,000	8,000	96,000
1.2 Project team members	12,000	12,000	12,000	12,000	12,000	12,000	12,000	12,000	12,000	12,000	12,000	12,000	144,000
1.3 Contractors		6,027	6,027	6,027	6,027	6,027	6,027	6,027	6,027	6,027	6,027	6,027	66,300
2. Hardware													
2.1 Handheld devices				30,000	30,000								60,000
2.2 Servers				8,000	8,000								16,000
3. Software													
3.1 Licensed software				10,000	10,000								20,000
3.2 Software development		60,000	60,000	80,000	127,000	127,000	90,000	50,000					594,000
4. Testing			6,000	8,000	12,000	15,000	15,000	13,000					69,000
5. Training and Support													
5.1 Trainee cost									50,000				50,000
5.2 Travel cost									8,400				8,400
5.3 Project team members							24,000	24,000	24,000	24,000	24,000	24,000	144,000
6. Reserves				10,000	10,000	30,000	30,000	60,000	40,000	40,000	30,000	3,540	253,540
Totals	20,000	86,027	92,027	172,027	223,027	198,027	185,027	173,027	148,427	90,027	80,027	53,567	1,521,240

*See the lecture slides for this chapter on the companion website for a larger view of this and other figures in this chapter. Numbers are rounded, so some totals appear to be off.

© Cengage Learning 2016

FIGURE 7-4 Surveyor Pro project cost baseline

In addition to providing a cost baseline, estimating costs for each major project activity over time provides project managers and top management with a foundation for project cost control, as described in the next section. Cost budgeting, as well as requested changes or clarifications, may result in updates to the cost management plan, which is a subsidiary part of the project management plan. See Appendix A for information on using Project 2013 for cost control.

Cost budgeting also provides information for project funding requirements. Some projects have all funds available when the project begins, but others must rely on periodic funding to avoid cash flow problems. If the cost baseline shows that more funds are required in certain months than are expected to be available, the organization must make adjustments to avoid financial problems.

7.6 CONTROLLING COSTS

Controlling project costs includes monitoring cost performance, ensuring that only appropriate project changes are included in a revised cost baseline, and informing project stakeholders of authorized changes to the project that will affect costs. The project management plan, project funding requirements, work performance data, and organizational process assets are inputs for controlling costs. Outputs of this process are work performance information, cost forecasts, change requests, project management plan updates, project documents updates, and organizational process asset updates.

Several tools and techniques assist in project cost control. As shown in Appendix A, Project 2013 has many cost management features to help you enter budgeted costs, set a baseline, enter actuals, calculate variances, and run various cost reports.

In addition to using software, however, you need a change control system to define procedures for changing the cost baseline. This cost control change system is part of the integrated change control system described in Chapter 4, Project Integration Management. Because many projects do not progress exactly as planned, new or revised cost estimates are often required, as are estimates to evaluate alternate courses of action.

Performance review meetings can be a powerful tool for helping to control project costs. People often perform better when they know they must report on their progress. Another very important tool for cost control is performance measurement. Although many general accounting approaches are available for measuring cost performance, earned value management (EVM) is a powerful cost control technique that is unique to the field of project management.

7.6a Earned Value Management

Earned value management (EVM) is a project performance measurement technique that integrates scope, time, and cost data. Given a cost performance baseline, project managers and their teams can determine how well the project is meeting scope, time, and cost goals by entering actual information and then comparing it to the baseline. A **baseline** is the budget figure in the original project plan plus approved changes. Actual information includes whether or not a WBS item was completed, approximately how much of the work was completed, when the work actually started and ended, and how much the completed work actually cost.

In the past, earned value management was used primarily on large government projects. Today, however, more and more companies are realizing the value of using this tool to help control costs. Moreover, a discussion by several academic experts in earned value management and a real practitioner revealed the need to clarify how to calculate earned value. Brenda Taylor, a senior project manager for P2 Project Management Solutions in Johannesburg, South Africa, questioned the accuracy of calculating earned value simply by multiplying the planned value to date by a percentage complete value. She suggested using the rate of performance instead, as described below.

Earned value management involves calculating three values for each activity or summary activity from a project's WBS.

1. The **planned value (PV)**, also called the budget, is the portion of the approved total cost estimate planned to be spent on an activity during a given period. Table 7-3 shows an example of earned value calculations. Suppose that a project included a summary activity of purchasing and installing a new web server. Suppose further that, according to the plan, it would take one week and cost a total of $10,000 for the labor hours, hardware, and software. Therefore, the planned value (PV) for the activity that week is $10,000.

2. The **actual cost (AC)** is the total direct and indirect costs incurred in accomplishing work on an activity during a given period. For example, suppose that it actually took two weeks and cost $20,000 to purchase and install the new web server. Assume that $15,000 of these actual costs were incurred during Week 1 and $5,000 was incurred during Week 2. These amounts are the actual cost (AC) for the activity each week.

3. The **earned value (EV)** is an estimate of the value of the physical work actually completed. EV is based on the original planned costs for the project or activity and the rate at which the team is completing work on the project or activity to date. The **rate of performance (RP)** is the ratio of actual work completed to the percentage of work planned to have been completed at any given time during the life of the project or activity. For example, suppose that the server installation was halfway completed by the end of Week 1. The rate of performance would be 50 percent because by the end of Week 1, the planned schedule reflects that the task should be complete but only 50 percent of the work has been completed. In Table 7-3, the earned value estimate after one week is therefore $5,000.[18]

TABLE 7-3 Earned value calculations for one activity after Week 1

Activity	Week 1
Earned value (EV)	5,000
Planned value (PV)	10,000
Actual cost (AC)	15,000
Cost variance (CV)	−10,000
Schedule variance (SV)	−5,000
Cost performance index (CPI)	33%
Schedule performance index (SPI)	50%

TABLE 7-4 Earned value formulas

Term	Formula
Earned value (EV)	EV = PV to date * RP
Cost variance (CV)	CV = EV − AC
Schedule variance (SV)	SV = EV − PV
Cost performance index (CPI)	CPI = EV/AC
Schedule performance index (SPI)	SPI = EV/PV
Estimate at completion (EAC)	EAC = BAC/CPI
Estimated time to complete	Original time estimate/SPI

© Cengage Learning 2016

The earned value calculations in Table 7-4 are carried out as follows:

$$EV = 10{,}000 * 50\% = 5{,}000$$
$$CV = 5{,}000 - 15{,}000 = -10{,}000$$
$$SV = 5{,}000 - 10{,}000 = -5{,}000$$
$$CPI = 5{,}000/15{,}000 = 33\%$$
$$SPI = 5{,}000/10{,}000 = 50\%$$

Table 7-4 summarizes the formulas used in earned value management. Note that the formulas for variances and indexes start with EV, the earned value. Variances are calculated by subtracting the actual cost or planned value from EV, and indexes are calculated by dividing EV by the actual cost or planned value. After you total the EV, AC, and PV data for all activities on a project, you can use the CPI and SPI to project how much it will cost and how long it will take to finish the project based on performance to date. Given the budget at completion and original time estimate, you can divide by the appropriate index to calculate the estimate at completion (EAC) and estimated time to complete, assuming that performance remains the same. There are no standard acronyms for the terms *estimated time to complete* or *original time estimate*.

Cost variance (CV) is the earned value minus the actual cost. If cost variance is a negative number, it means that performing the work cost more than planned. If cost variance is a positive number, performing the work cost less than planned.

Schedule variance (SV) is the earned value minus the planned value. A negative schedule variance means that it took longer than planned to perform the work, and a positive schedule variance means that the work took less time than planned.

The **cost performance index (CPI)** is the ratio of earned value to actual cost; it can be used to estimate the projected cost of completing the project. If the CPI is equal to one, or 100 percent, then the planned and actual costs are equal—the costs are exactly as budgeted. If the CPI is less than one or less than 100 percent, the project is over budget. If the CPI is greater than one or more than 100 percent, the project is under budget.

The **schedule performance index (SPI)** is the ratio of earned value to planned value; it can be used to estimate the projected time to complete the project. Similar to the cost performance index, an SPI of one, or 100 percent, means the project is on schedule. If the SPI is greater than one or 100 percent, then the project is ahead of schedule. If the SPI is less than one or 100 percent, the project is behind schedule.

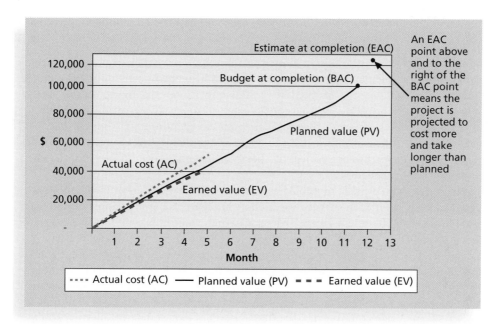

© Cengage Learning 2016

FIGURE 7-5   Earned value chart for project after five months

Note that in general, *negative numbers for cost and schedule variance indicate problems in those areas.* Negative numbers mean the project is costing more than planned or taking longer than planned. Likewise, *a CPI and SPI of less than one or less than 100 percent also indicate problems.*

The cost performance index can be used to calculate the **estimate at completion (EAC)**—an estimated cost of completing a project based on performance to date. Similarly, the schedule performance index can be used to calculate an estimated time to complete the project.

You can graph earned value information to track project performance. Figure 7-5 shows an earned value chart for a one-year project after five months. Note that the actual cost and earned value lines end at five months because the data was collected or estimated at that point. The chart includes three lines and two points, as follows:

- Planned value (PV), the cumulative planned amounts for all activities by month. Note that the planned value line extends for the estimated length of the project and ends at the BAC point.
- Actual cost (AC), the cumulative actual amounts for all activities by month.
- Earned value (EV), the cumulative earned value amounts for all activities by month.
- **Budget at completion (BAC)**, the original total budget for the project, or $100,000 in this example. The BAC point is plotted on the chart at the original time estimate of 12 months.
- Estimate at completion (EAC), estimated to be $122,308 in this example. This number is calculated by taking the BAC, or $100,000 in this case, and dividing by the CPI, which was 81.761 percent. This EAC point is plotted on the chart at the estimated time to complete of 12.74 months. This number

is calculated by taking the original time estimate, or 12 months in this case, and dividing by the SPI, which in this example was 94.203 percent.

Viewing earned value information in chart form helps you visualize how the project is performing. For example, you can see the planned performance by looking at the planned value line. If the project goes as planned, it will finish in 12 months and cost $100,000. Notice in the example in Figure 7-5 that the actual cost line is always on or above the earned value line, which indicates that costs are equal to or more than planned. The planned value line is close to the earned value line and is slightly higher in the last month. This relationship means that the project has been on schedule until the last month, when the project fell behind schedule.

Top managers who oversee multiple projects often like to see performance information in a graphical form, such as the earned value chart in Figure 7-5. For example, in the opening case, the government officials were reviewing earned value charts and EACs for several different projects. Earned value charts allow you to see quickly how projects are performing. If there are serious cost and schedule performance problems, top management may decide to terminate projects or take other corrective action. The EACs are important inputs to budget decisions, especially if total funds are limited. Earned value management is an important technique when used effectively, because it helps top management and project managers evaluate progress and make sound management decisions. Consult the *PMBOK® Guide* and other resources for more information and calculations about earned value.

If earned value management is such a powerful cost control tool, then why doesn't every organization use it? Why do many government projects require it, but many commercial projects don't? Two reasons are EVM's focus on tracking actual performance versus planned performance and the importance of percentage completion data in making calculations. Many projects, particularly IT projects, do not have good planning information, so tracking performance against a plan might produce misleading information. Several cost estimates are usually made on IT projects, and keeping track of the most recent cost estimate and the associated actual costs could be cumbersome. In addition, estimating percentage completion of tasks might produce misleading information. What does it mean to say that a task is actually 75 percent complete after three months? Such a statement is often not synonymous with saying the task will be finished in one more month or after spending an additional 25 percent of the planned budget.

To make earned value management simpler to use, organizations can modify the level of detail and still reap the benefits of the technique. For example, you can use percentage completion data such as 0 percent for items not yet started, 50 percent for items in progress, and 100 percent for completed tasks. As long as the project is defined in enough detail, this simplified percentage completion data should provide enough summary information to allow managers to see how well a project is doing overall. You can get very accurate total project performance information using these simple percentage complete amounts. For example, using simplified percentage complete amounts for a one-year project with weekly reporting and an average task size of one week, you can expect about a 1 percent error rate.[19]

You can enter and collect earned value data only at summary levels of the WBS. Quentin Fleming, author of the book *Earned Value Project Management*,[20] often gives presentations about earned value management. Many people express their frustration in trying to collect such detailed information. Fleming explains that you do not have to collect information at the work package level to use earned value management. It is most important to have a deliverable-oriented WBS, and many WBS items can summarize several subdeliverables. For example, you might have a WBS for a house that includes items for each room in the house. Collecting earned value data for each room would provide meaningful information instead of trying to collect detailed information for each component in the room, such as flooring, furniture, and lighting.

It is important to remember that the heart and soul of EVM are estimates. The entire EVM process begins with an estimate; when the estimate is off, all the calculations will be off. Before an organization attempts to use EVM, it must learn to develop good estimates.

Earned value management is the primary method available for integrating performance, cost, and schedule data. It can be a powerful tool for project managers and top management to use in evaluating project performance. Project management software, such as Project 2013, includes tables for collecting earned value data and reports that calculate variance information. Project 2013 also allows you to easily produce an earned value chart, similar to the one in Figure 7-5, without importing the data into Microsoft Excel. See the project cost management section of Appendix A for an example of using earned value management.

Another approach to evaluating the performance of multiple projects is project portfolio management, as described in the following section.

GLOBAL ISSUES

The Project Management Institute conducted a major study in 2011 to help understand and gauge the current level of EVM practice. The researchers surveyed more than 600 project management practitioners in 61 countries, providing a cross-sectional view of the most current EVM practices. Respondents were classified by industry sector, motivation for EVM usage, organizational role, and geographic location. The study included the following key findings:

- EVM is used worldwide, and it is particularly popular in the Middle East, South Asia, Canada, and Europe.
- Most countries require EVM for large defense or government projects, as shown in Figure 7-6.
- EVM is also used in such private-industry sectors as IT, construction, energy, and manufacturing. However, most private companies have not yet applied EVM to their projects because management does not require it, feeling it is too complex and not cost effective.
- The level of EVM use and maturity varies among organizations and projects, but budget size appears to be the most important decision factor.
- EVM's contributions and cost effectiveness are widely recognized; most respondents said they agree or strongly agree that EVM provides early warning signs, helping them to control project scope, time, and cost. EVM's contribution to cost performance was ranked higher than schedule performance, and the difference was statistically significant.
- Top barriers to enhanced use of EVM were lack of motivation and lack of expertise.
- Top management support, buy-in of project staff, training, organizational culture and leadership, and maturity of the project management system were the most important factors in successful use of EVM.[21]

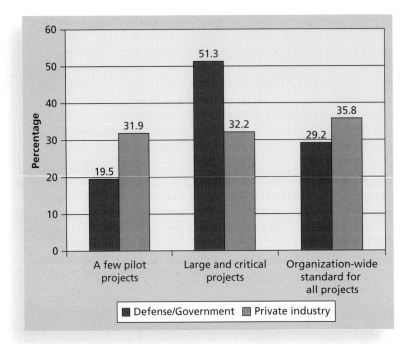

Source: Lingguang Song, "Earned Value Management: A Global and Cross-Industry Perspective on Current EVM Practice," PMI (2011).

FIGURE 7-6   Earned value usage

7.6b Project Portfolio Management

As you saw in Chapter 1, many organizations now collect and control an entire suite of projects or investments as one set of interrelated activities in one place—a portfolio. Several software tools provide graphics to summarize performance on a portfolio of projects, as shown in Chapter 4. Key metrics, including cost performance, are often shown in green, yellow, or red, indicating that things are going as planned, that problems exist, or that major problems exist, respectively. Project managers need to understand how their projects fit into the bigger picture. For example, there can be a portfolio for IT projects and portfolios for other types of projects. Looking at broad categories of similar projects enables project managers to help their organizations make wise investment decisions.

An organization can view project portfolio management as having five levels, from simplest to most complex, as follows:

1. Put all your projects in one database.
2. Prioritize the projects in your database.
3. Divide your projects into two or three budgets based on type of investment, such as utilities or required systems to keep things running, incremental upgrades, and strategic investments.
4. Automate the repository.
5. Apply modern portfolio theory, including risk-return tools that map project risk on a curve.

Many project managers also want to move on to manage larger projects, become program managers, then vice presidents, and eventually CEOs. Understanding project portfolio management, therefore is important for both project and organizational success.

Jane Walton, the project portfolio manager for IT projects at Schlumberger, saved the company $3 million in one year by organizing the organization's 120 IT projects into a portfolio. Manufacturing companies have used project portfolio management since the 1960s, and Walton anticipated the need to justify investments in IT projects just as managers have to justify capital investment projects. She found that 80 percent of the organization's projects overlapped, and that 14 separate projects were trying to accomplish the same thing. Other managers, such as Douglas Hubbard, president of a consulting firm, see the need to use project portfolio management, especially for IT projects. Hubbard suggests, "IT investments are huge, risky investments. It's time we do this."[22]

Project portfolio managers can start by using spreadsheet software to develop and manage project portfolios, or they can use sophisticated software designed to help manage project portfolios. Several software tools available today help project portfolio managers summarize earned value and project portfolio information, as described in the following section.

7.7 USING PROJECT MANAGEMENT SOFTWARE TO ASSIST IN PROJECT COST MANAGEMENT

Most organizations use software to assist with project cost management. Spreadsheets are a common tool for cost estimating, cost budgeting, and cost control. Many companies also use more sophisticated and centralized financial software to provide important cost-related information to accounting and finance personnel. This section focuses on how you can use project management software in cost management. Appendix A includes a section on using the cost management features in Project 2013.

Project management software can increase a project manager's effectiveness during each process of project cost management. It can help you study overall project information or identify and focus on tasks that are over a specified cost limit. You can use the software to assign costs to resources and tasks, prepare cost estimates, develop cost budgets, and monitor cost performance. Project 2013 has several standard cost reports: cash flow, budget, over-budget tasks, over-budget resources, and earned value reports. For several of these reports, you must enter percentage completion information and actual costs, just as you do when manually calculating earned value or other analyses.

Many IT project managers use other tools to manage cost information because they do not know that they can use project management software, or they do not track costs based on a WBS, as most project management software does. Instead of using dedicated project management software for cost management, some IT project managers use company accounting systems; others use spreadsheet software to achieve more flexibility. Project managers who use other software often do so because these other systems are more generally accepted in their organizations and more people know how to use them. To improve project cost management, several companies have developed methods to link data between their project management software and their main accounting software. Regardless, users need training to use dedicated project management software and understand the available features.

Many organizations are using software to organize and analyze all types of project data into project portfolios and across the entire enterprise. Enterprise or project portfolio management (PPM) tools integrate information from multiple projects to show the projects' status and health. In 2012, over half of the respondents in two different studies (PMI's PMI Pulse of the Profession™ and a PricewaterhouseCoopers survey) reported frequent use of PPM. The highest adoption rates were reported by organizations in retail, insurance, auto, banking and capital markets, telecommunications, manufacturing, energy, and defense. The main reasons organizations use project portfolio management included customer satisfaction, cost reduction, and revenue growth.[23]

More recently, a 2014 report from Gartner says the market for PPM software continues to grow, with annual sales over $1.65 billion. "Demand for IT PPM applications has not wavered in more than 13 years, but, rather, increased exponentially over the past 10 years. The pace of change… is driving continued demand for enterprise software products that can help with the effective planning, execution, and management of projects and programs materializing from the need for today's enterprises to change and adapt quickly to shifts in the business climate."[24]

A study by Forrester estimates that companies are achieving returns of 250 percent from their investments in PPM tools. At a Planisware PPM Solutions Summit in 2014, customers shared examples of their success stories in achieving even higher returns:

- Pfizer uses PPM software to accelerate innovation and improve transparency and accountability of resources to deliver scientific excellence. Pfizer can quickly access trusted data analytics to make strategic resource allocations that maximize portfolio value.
- Ford uses Planisware to gain greater transparency over their portfolio of projects. Greater transparency gives management a better understanding of resources shared across projects, and enhances communication about statuses. They can quickly alert affected program managers and product development teams of potential risks so they can implement risk management strategies.[25]

As with using any software, however, managers must make sure that the data is accurate and up to date, and ask pertinent questions before making any major decisions.

CASE WRAP-UP

After talking to his colleagues about the meeting, Juan had a better idea about the importance of project cost management. He understood the value of doing detailed studies before making major expenditures on new projects, especially after learning about the high cost of correcting defects late in a project. He also learned the importance of developing good cost estimates and keeping costs on track. He enjoyed seeing how the cost estimate was developed for the Surveyor Pro project, and was eager to learn more about various estimating tools and techniques.

At the meeting, government officials cancelled several projects when the project managers showed how poorly the projects were performing and admitted that they did not do much planning and analysis early in the projects. Juan knew that he could not focus on just the technical aspects of projects if he wanted to move ahead in his career. He began to wonder whether several projects the city was considering were really worth the taxpayers' money. Issues of cost management added a new dimension to Juan's job.

Chapter Summary

Project cost management is traditionally a weak area of IT projects. IT project managers must acknowledge the importance of cost management and take responsibility for understanding basic cost concepts, cost estimating, budgeting, and cost control.

Project managers must understand several basic principles of cost management to be effective in managing project costs. Important concepts include profits and profit margins, life cycle costing, cash flow analysis, sunk costs, and learning curve theory.

Planning cost management involves determining the policies, procedures, and documentation that will be used for planning, executing, and controlling project cost. The main output of this process is a cost management plan.

Estimating costs is a very important part of project cost management. There are several types of cost estimates, including rough order of magnitude (ROM), budgetary, and definitive. Each type of estimate is done during different stages of the project life cycle, and each has a different level of accuracy. Several tools and techniques can help you develop cost estimates, including analogous estimating, bottom-up estimating, parametric estimating, and computerized tools. Function point analysis can also be used to estimate software development costs.

Determining the budget involves allocating costs to individual work items over time. It is important to understand how particular organizations prepare budgets so estimates are made accordingly.

Controlling costs includes monitoring cost performance, reviewing changes, and notifying project stakeholders of changes related to costs. Many basic accounting and finance principles relate to project cost management. Earned value management is an important method used for measuring project performance. Earned value management integrates scope, cost, and schedule information. Project portfolio management allows organizations to collect and control an entire suite of projects or investments as one set of interrelated activities.

Several software products can assist with project cost management. Project 2013 has many cost management features, including earned value management. Enterprise project management software and portfolio management software can help managers evaluate data on multiple projects.

Quick Quiz

1. Accountants usually define _____ as a resource sacrificed or foregone to achieve a specific objective.

    a. money

    b. liability

    c. trade

    d. cost

2. What is the main goal of project cost management?

    a. to complete a project for as little cost as possible

    b. to complete a project within an approved budget

    c. to provide truthful and accurate cost information on projects

    d. to ensure that an organization's money is used wisely

3. Which of the following is not an output of the project cost management process called estimating costs, according to the *PMBOK* *Guide?*

   a. activity cost estimates

   b. a cost baseline

   c. basis of estimates

   d. project documents updates

4. If a company loses $5 for every $100 in revenue for a certain product, what is the profit margin for that product?

   a. −5 percent

   b. 5 percent

   c. −$5

   d. $5

5. _____ reserves allow for future situations that are unpredictable.

   a. Contingency

   b. Financial

   c. Management

   d. Baseline

6. You are preparing a cost estimate for a building based on its location, purpose, number of square feet, and other characteristics. What cost-estimating technique are you using?

   a. parametric

   b. analogous

   c. bottom-up

   d. top-down

7. _____ involves allocating the project cost estimate to individual material resources or work items over time.

   a. Reserve analysis

   b. Life cycle costing

   c. Project cost budgeting

   d. Earned value analysis

8. _____ is a project performance measurement technique that integrates scope, time, and cost data.

   a. Reserve analysis

   b. Life cycle costing

   c. Project cost budgeting

   d. Earned value management

9. If the actual cost for a WBS item is $1,500 and its earned value is $2,000, what is its cost variance, and is it under or over budget?

    a. The cost variance is –$500, which is over budget.

    b. The cost variance is –$500, which is under budget.

    c. The cost variance is $500, which is over budget.

    d. The cost variance is $500, which is under budget.

10. If a project is halfway completed, its schedule performance index is 110 percent, and its cost performance index is 95 percent, how is it progressing?

    a. It is ahead of schedule and under budget.

    b. It is ahead of schedule and over budget.

    c. It is behind schedule and under budget.

    d. It is behind schedule and over budget.

Quick Quiz Answers

1. d; 2. b; 3. b; 4. a; 5. c; 6. a; 7. c; 8. d; 9. d; 10. b

Discussion Questions

1. Discuss why many IT professionals may overlook project cost management and how this might affect the ability to complete projects within budget.

2. Explain some of the basic principles of cost management, such as profits, life cycle costs, tangible and intangible costs and benefits, direct and indirect costs, and reserves.

3. What is meant by a sunk cost? Give examples of typical sunk costs for an IT project as well as examples from your personal life. Why is it difficult for people to ignore them when they should?

4. Give examples of when you would prepare rough order of magnitude (ROM), budgetary, and definitive cost estimates for an IT project. Give an example of how you would use each of the following techniques for creating a cost estimate: analogous, parametric, and bottom-up.

5. Explain what happens during the process to determine the project budget.

6. Explain how earned value management (EVM) can be used to control costs and measure project performance, and explain why you think it is not used more often. What are some general rules of thumb for deciding if numbers for cost variance, schedule variance, cost performance index, and schedule performance index are good or bad?

7. What is project portfolio management? Can project managers use it with earned value management?

8. Describe several types of software that project managers can use to support project cost management.

Exercises

1. Given the following information for a one-year project, answer the following questions. Recall that PV is the planned value, EV is the earned value, AC is the actual cost, and BAC is the budget at completion.

    $$PV = \$23,000$$
    $$EV = \$20,000$$
    $$AC = \$25,000$$
    $$BAC = \$120,000$$

    a. What is the cost variance, schedule variance, cost performance index (CPI), and schedule performance index (SPI) for the project?

    b. How is the project doing? Is it ahead of schedule or behind schedule? Is it under budget or over budget?

    c. Use the CPI to calculate the estimate at completion (EAC) for this project. Is the project performing better or worse than planned?

    d. Use the SPI to estimate how long it will take to finish this project.

    e. Sketch the earned value chart for this project, using Figure 7-5 as a guide.

2. Create a cost estimate and model for building a new, state-of-the-art multimedia classroom for your organization within the next six months. The classroom should include 20 high-end personal computers with appropriate software for your organization, a network server, Internet access for all machines, an instructor station, and a projection system. Be sure to include personnel costs associated with the project management for this project. Document the assumptions you made in preparing the estimate and provide explanations for key numbers.

3. Research using the cost management features of Project 2013 or other software tools, including project portfolio management software. Also review the project cost management section of Appendix A. Ask three people in different IT organizations that use project management software if they use the cost management features of the software and in what ways. Write a brief report on what you learned from your research.

4. Read the free ebook *Cost Estimating in an Agile Development Environment* by Alvin Alexander, which discusses estimating software costs. Find one or two other references on ways to measure software development costs. In your own words, write a two-page paper that explains how to estimate software development costs using at least two different approaches.

5. Create a spreadsheet to calculate your projected total costs, total revenues, and total profits for giving a seminar on cost estimating. Make the following assumptions:

    - You will charge $600 per person for a two-day class.

    - You estimate that 30 people will attend the class, but you want to change this input.

    - Your fixed costs include $500 total to rent a room for both days, setup fees of $400 for registration, and $300 for designing a postcard for advertising.

    - You will not include your labor costs for this estimate, but you estimate that you will spend at least 150 hours developing materials, managing the project, and giving the actual class. You would like to know what your time is worth given different scenarios.

- You will order 5,000 postcards, mail 4,000, and distribute the rest to friends and colleagues.
- Your variable costs include the following:
    a. $5 per person for registration plus four percent of the class fee per person to handle credit card processing; assume that everyone pays by credit card
    b. $.40 per postcard for printing if you order 5,000 or more
    c. $.35 per postcard for mailing and postage
    d. $25 per person for beverages and lunch
    e. $30 per person for class handouts

Be sure to have input cells for any variables that might change, such as the cost of postage and handouts. Calculate your profits based on each of the following numbers of people who might attend: 10, 20, 30, 40, 50, and 60. In addition, calculate what your time would be worth per hour based on the number of students. Try to use the Excel data table feature to show the profits based on the number of students. If you are unfamiliar with data tables, just repeat the calculations for each possibility of 10, 20, 30, 40, 50, and 60 students. Print your results on one page, highlighting the profits for each scenario and what your time is worth.

6. Read the study by Lingguang Song cited in the End Notes or a similar study about the use of earned value management. Summarize the findings and your opinions of the study and the use of earned value management. Why do you think it is still used mostly on large government or defense projects?

Running Case

You and your team are continuing your work on the Global Treps Project. Your project sponsor, Dr. K., has asked you to refine the existing cost estimate for the project so you can evaluate supplier bids and have a solid cost baseline for evaluating project performance. Recall that your schedule and cost goals are to complete the project in six months for under $120,000. You planned to use up to $50,000 total to pay yourself and your team members, and your initial estimates were $30,000 for travel expenses, $20,000 for hardware and software, and $20,000 for organizing four events, including consultants, legal/business fees, etc.

Tasks

1. Prepare and print a one-page cost model for the project, similar to the model provided in Figure 7-2. Use the following WBS or the WBS you developed in Chapter 5, and be sure to document your assumptions in preparing the cost model. Assume a labor rate of $20/hour for yourself (the project manager) and team members (Kim, Ashok, and Alfreda). You will pay Bobby, your IT guy, $30/hour. The project will fund refreshments for the four shark tank like events and prizes for the winners, at a cost of $1,000 for each event.

    1.1 Project management
    1.2 Hardware (3 laptops and Internet access for Kim, Ashok, and Alfreda)

1.3 Software

    1.3.1 Outsourced

        1.3.1.1 Domain name and site hosting

        1.3.1.2 Donation acceptance feature of website

        1.3.1.3 Video creation for website

    1.3.2 In-house Development

        1.3.2.1 Guidelines and templates for events

        1.3.2.2 Acceptance of ideas for needed new products or services

        1.3.2.3 Custom site for 20 events

    1.3.3 Testing

1.4 Business Plan

    1.4.1 Internal labor

    1.4.2 Legal information/assistance

1.5 Travel

1.6 Events

    1.6.1 Internal labor

    1.6.2 Consultant labor

    1.6.3 Refreshments

    1.6.4 Prizes

2. Using the cost model you created in Task 1, prepare a cost baseline by allocating the costs by WBS for each month of the project.

3. Assume that you have completed three months of the project. The BAC was $120,000 for this six-month project. You can also make the following assumptions:

$$PV = \$60,000$$
$$EV = \$55,000$$
$$AC = \$50,000$$

    a.   What is the cost variance, schedule variance, cost performance index (CPI), and schedule performance index (SPI) for the project?

    b.   How is the project doing? Is it ahead of schedule or behind schedule? Is it under budget or over budget?

    c.   Use the CPI to calculate the estimate at completion (EAC) for this project. Is the project performing better or worse than planned?

    d.   Use the SPI to estimate how long it will take to finish this project.

    e.   Sketch an earned value chart using the information from your answers to parts a through d. Use Figure 7-5 as a guide.

Key Terms

actual cost (AC) p.283
analogous estimates p.273
baseline p.282
bottom-up estimates p.274
budget at completion (BAC) p.285
budgetary estimate p.272
cash flow analysis p.269
contingency reserves p.270
cost baseline p.281
cost performance index (CPI) p.284
cost variance (CV) p.284
definitive estimate p.272
direct costs p.269
earned value (EV) p.283
earned value management (EVM) p.282
estimate at completion (EAC) p.285
function points p.277
indirect costs p.270
intangible costs or benefits p.269
known unknowns p.270

learning curve theory p.270
life cycle costing p.267
management reserves p.270
overrun p.264
parametric estimating p.274
planned value (PV) p.283
profit margin p.267
profits p.267
project cost management p.266
rate of performance (RP) p.283
reserves p.270
rough order of magnitude (ROM)
    estimate p.272
schedule performance index (SPI) p.284
schedule variance (SV) p.284
sunk cost p.270
tangible costs or benefits p.269
top-down estimates p.273
unknown unknowns p.270

End Notes

[1] Bent Flyvbjerg and Alexander Budzier, "Why Your IT Project May Be Riskier Than You Think," *Harvard Business Review*, *hbr.org/2011/09/why-your-it-project-may-be-riskier-than-you-think/* (September 2011).

[2] Ibid.

[3] Paul McDougall, "U.K. Health System IT Upgrade Called a 'Disaster,'" *InformationWeek*, *www.informationweek.com/uk-health-system-it-upgrade-called-a-disaster/d/d-id/1043912?* (June 5, 2006).

[4] Jeremy Kirk, "Datacenter Failure Pinches U.K. Health Service," *IDG News Service*, *www.infoworld.com/article/2655787/database/datacenter-failure-pinches-uk-health-service.html* (August 1, 2006).

[5] Press Association, "U.K. Health Service to Dismantle Nationwide Health IT Program," *iHealthBeat*, *www.ihealthbeat.org/articles/2011/9/23/uk-health-service-to-dismantle-nationwide-health-it-program* (September 23, 2011).

[6] Charles T. Horngren, George Foster, and Srikanti M. Datar, *Cost Accounting*, Eighth edition (Englewood Cliffs, NJ: Prentice-Hall, 1994).

[7] Project Management Institute, "Pulse of the Profession®: Capturing the Value of Project Management," *www.pmi.org/~/media/PDF/learning/pulse-of-the-profession-2015.ashx* (February 2015).

[8] Dominique Levin, "Facebook's 20 Minute Downtime Costs More Than $500,000," *AgileOne*, *www.agilone.com/blog/facebook-downtime-costs-them-more* (September 3, 2014).

[9] Kelly Clay," Amazon.com Goes Down, Loses $66,240 Per Minute," *Forbes*, *www.forbes.com/sites/kellyclay/2013/08/19/amazon-com-goes-down-loses-66240-per-minute/* (August 19, 2013).

[10] Alan Shimel, "The real cost of downtime," *Blogs, Business of DevOps*, *devops.com/2015/02/11/real-cost-downtime/* (Feb 11, 2015).

[11] IDC, *DevOps and the Cost of Downtime: Fortune 1000 Best Practice Metrics Quantified* (2014).

[12] Dawn Kawamoto, "Dell's Green Goal for 2008," *Tech Culture* (blog), *CNET*, *www.cnet.com/news/dells-green-goal-for-2008/* (September 27, 2007).

[13] Dell, *FY 2014 Corporate Responsibility Report: A Progress Report on Our 2020 Legacy of Good Plan*, *i.dell.com/sites/doccontent/corporate/corp-comm/en/Documents/fy14-cr-report.pdf* (2014).

[14] Tom DeMarco, *Controlling Software Projects* (New York: Yourdon Press, 1982).

[15] International Function Point User Group, "What Are Function Points—Fact Sheet," *www.ifpug.org/publications-products/what-are-function-points-fact-sheet* (accessed April 28, 2015).

[16] Alvin Alexander, *Cost Estimating in an Agile Development Environment* (2014). *alvinalexander.com/downloads/Book3-EstimatingInAnAgileEnvironment.pdf.*

[17] David Longstreet, "Function Points?," *www.softwaremetrics.com/files/OneHour.pdf,* p. 16 (accessed March 13, 2015).

[18] Brenda Taylor, P2 Senior Project Manager, P2 Project Management Solutions, Johannesburg, South Africa, E-mail, 2004.

[19] Daniel M. Brandon, Jr., "Implementing Earned Value Easily and Effectively," *Project Management Journal* (June 1998) 29 (2), p. 11–18.

[20] Quentin W. Fleming and Joel M. Koppelman, *Earned Value Project Management,Third Edition* (NewTown Square, PA: Project Management Institute, 2006).

[21] Lingguang Song, *Earned Value Management: A Global and Cross-Industry Perspective on Current EVM Practice* (NewTown Square, PA: Project Management Institute, 2010).

[22] Scott Berinato, "Do the Math," *CIO Magazine* (October 1, 2001), p. 52.

[23] Project Management Institute, Inc. *Pulse of the Profession® In-Depth Report: Portfolio Management* (2012).

[24] Daniel B. Stang and Robert A. Handler, *MarketScope for IT Project and Portfolio Management Software Applications*, Gartner (May 19, 2014).

[25] Planisware Press Release, "Leaders in Innovation Divulge Best Practices at Planisware's User Summit" (May 15, 2014). *www.planisware.com/news/leaders-innovation-divulge-best-practices-planiswares-user-summit.*

PROJECT QUALITY MANAGEMENT

LEARNING OBJECTIVES

After reading this chapter, you will be able to:

- Understand the importance of project quality management for information technology (IT) products and services

- Define project quality management and understand how quality relates to various aspects of IT projects

- Describe quality management planning and how quality and scope management are related

- Discuss the importance of quality assurance

- Explain the main outputs of the quality control process

- Understand the tools and techniques for quality control, such as the Seven Basic Tools of Quality, statistical sampling, Six Sigma, and testing

- Summarize the contributions of noteworthy quality experts to modern quality management

- Describe how leadership, the cost of quality, organizational influences, expectations, cultural differences, and maturity models relate to improving quality in IT projects

- Discuss how software can assist in project quality management

> ## OPENING CASE
>
> A large medical instruments company just hired Scott Daniels, a senior consultant from a large consulting firm, to lead a project to resolve the quality problems with the company's new Executive Information System (EIS). A team of internal programmers and analysts worked with several company executives to develop this new system. Many executives were hooked on the new, user-friendly EIS. They loved the way the system allowed them to track sales of various medical instruments quickly and easily by product, country, hospital, and sales representative. After successfully testing the new EIS with several executives, the company decided to make the system available to all levels of management.
>
> Unfortunately, several quality problems developed with the new EIS after a few months of operation. People complained that they could not get into the web-based system. The system started going down a couple of times a month, and the response time was reportedly getting slower. Users complained when they could not access information within a few seconds. Several people kept forgetting how to log in to the system, thus increasing the number of calls to the company's help desk. There were complaints that some of the reports in the system gave inconsistent information. How could a summary report show totals that were not consistent with a detailed report on the same information? The executive sponsor of the EIS wanted the problems fixed quickly and accurately, so he decided to hire an expert in quality from outside the company whom he knew from past projects. Scott Daniels' job was to lead a team of people from both the medical instruments company and his own firm to identify and resolve quality-related issues with the EIS and to develop a plan to help prevent quality problems on future projects.

8.1 THE IMPORTANCE OF PROJECT QUALITY MANAGEMENT

Most people have heard jokes about how cars would work if they followed a development history similar to that of computers. A well-known Internet joke goes as follows:

> At the COMDEX computer exposition, Bill Gates, the founder and CEO of Microsoft Corporation, stated: "If General Motors had kept up with technology like the computer industry has, we would all be driving $25 cars that got 1,000 miles to the gallon." In response to Gates' comments, General Motors issued a press release stating: "If GM had developed technology like Microsoft, we would all be driving cars with the following characteristics:
>
> - For no reason whatsoever your car would crash twice a day.
> - Every time they repainted the lines on the road, you would have to buy a new car.
> - Macintosh would make a car that was powered by the sun, reliable, five times as fast, and twice as easy to drive, but would run on only five percent of the roads.
> - New seats would force everyone to have the same size hips.
> - The airbag system would say "Are you sure?" before going off.
> - Occasionally, for no reason whatsoever, your car would lock you out and refuse to let you in until you simultaneously lifted the door handle, turned the key, and grabbed hold of the radio antenna."[1]

Most people simply accept poor quality from many IT products. So what if your computer crashes a couple of times a month? Just make sure you back up your data. So what if you cannot log in to the corporate intranet or the Internet right now? Just try a little later when it is less busy. So what if the latest update of your word-processing software has several known bugs? You like the software's new features, and all new software has bugs. Is quality a real problem with IT projects?

Yes, it is! IT is not just a luxury available in some homes, schools, or offices. Companies throughout the world provide employees with access to computers. The majority of people in the United States use the Internet, and usage in other countries continues to grow rapidly. Many aspects of our daily lives depend on high-quality IT products. Food is produced and distributed with the aid of computers; cars have computer chips to track performance; children use computers to help them learn in school; corporations depend on technology for many business functions; and millions of people rely on technology for entertainment and personal communications. Computing everywhere and the Internet of things, as described in Chapter 1, are expanding our reliance on IT to smart appliances and devices (TVs, refrigerators, thermostats, etc.), pay-as-you-go services, and much more. Many IT projects develop mission-critical systems that are used in life-and-death situations, such as navigation systems on aircraft and computer components built into medical equipment. Financial institutions and their customers also rely on high-quality information systems. Customers get very upset when systems provide inaccurate financial data or reveal information to unauthorized users that could lead to identity theft. When one of these systems does not function correctly, it is much more than a slight inconvenience, as described in the following "What Went Wrong?" examples.

 WHAT WENT WRONG?

- In 1981, a small timing difference caused by a computer program change created a 1-in-67 chance that the space shuttle's five onboard computers would not synchronize. The error caused a launch abort.[2]
- In 1986, two hospital patients died after receiving fatal doses of radiation from a Therac 25 machine. A software problem caused the machine to ignore calibration data.[3]
- In one of the biggest software errors in banking history, Chemical Bank mistakenly deducted about $15 million from more than 100,000 customer accounts. The problem resulted from a single line of code in an updated computer program that caused the bank to process every withdrawal and transfer at its automated teller machines (ATMs) twice. For example, a person who withdrew $100 from an ATM had $200 deducted from his or her account, though the receipt indicated only a withdrawal of $100. The mistake affected 150,000 transactions.[4]
- In 2015, The United States Department of Justice unsealed indictments in what it described as "the largest data breach of names and e-mail addresses in the history of the internet." Two people hacked into at least eight e-mail service providers, stealing more than a billion e-mail addresses. They allegedly used the data to send spam, making millions of dollars from an affiliate marketing arrangement with another individual.[5]

Before you can improve the quality of IT projects or any type of project, it is important to understand the basic concepts of project quality management.

8.2 WHAT IS PROJECT QUALITY MANAGEMENT?

Project quality management is a difficult knowledge area to define. The International Organization for Standardization (ISO) defines **quality** as "the totality of characteristics of an entity that bear on its ability to satisfy stated or implied needs" (ISO8042:1994) or "the degree to which a set of inherent characteristics fulfils requirements" (ISO9000:2000). Many people spent many hours developing these definitions, yet they are still vague. Other experts define quality based on conformance to requirements and fitness for use. **Conformance to requirements** means that the project's processes and products meet written specifications. For example, if the project scope statement requires delivery of 100 computers with specific processors and memory, you could easily check whether suitable computers had been delivered. **Fitness for use** means that a product can be used as it was intended. If these computers were delivered without monitors or keyboards and were left in boxes on the customer's shipping dock, the customer might not be satisfied because the computers would not be fit for use. The customer may have assumed that the delivery included monitors and keyboards, unpacking the computers, and installation so they would be ready to use.

The purpose of **project quality management** is to ensure that the project will satisfy the needs for which it was undertaken. Recall that project management involves meeting or exceeding stakeholder needs and expectations. The project team must develop good relationships with key stakeholders, especially the main customer for the project, to understand what quality means to them. *After all, the customer ultimately decides if quality is acceptable.* Many technical projects fail because the project team focuses only on meeting the written requirements for the main products being created and ignores other stakeholder needs and expectations for the project. For example, the project team should know what successfully delivering 100 computers means to the customer.

Quality, therefore, must be on an equal level with project scope, time, and cost. If a project's stakeholders are not satisfied with the quality of the project management or the resulting products of the project, the project team will need to adjust scope, time, and cost to satisfy the stakeholder. Meeting only written requirements for scope, time, and cost is not sufficient. To achieve stakeholder satisfaction, the project team must develop a good working relationship with all stakeholders and understand their stated or implied needs.

Project quality management involves three main processes:

1. *Planning quality management* includes identifying which quality requirements and standards are relevant to the project and how to satisfy them. Incorporating quality standards into project design is a key part of quality planning. For an IT project, quality standards might include allowing for system growth, planning a reasonable response time for a system, or ensuring that the system produces consistent and accurate information. Quality standards can also apply to IT services. For example, you can set standards for how long it should take to get a reply from a help desk or how long it should take to ship a replacement part for a hardware item under warranty. The main outputs of planning quality management are a quality management plan, a process improvement plan, quality metrics, quality checklists,

and project documents updates. A **metric** is a standard of measurement. Examples of common metrics include failure rates of products, availability of goods and services, and customer satisfaction ratings.

2. *Performing quality assurance* involves periodically evaluating overall project performance to ensure that the project will satisfy the relevant quality standards. The quality assurance process involves taking responsibility for quality throughout the project's life cycle. Top management must take the lead in emphasizing the roles all employees play in quality assurance, especially senior managers' roles. The main outputs of this process are change requests, project management plan updates, project documents updates, and organizational process asset updates.

3. *Controlling quality* involves monitoring specific project results to ensure that they comply with the relevant quality standards while identifying ways to improve overall quality. This process is often associated with the technical tools and techniques of quality management, such as Pareto charts, quality control charts, and statistical sampling. You will learn more about these tools and techniques later in this chapter. The main outputs of quality control include quality control measurements, validated changes, validated deliverables, work performance information, change requests, project management plan updates, project documents updates, and organizational process asset updates.

Figure 8-1 summarizes these processes and outputs, showing when they occur in a typical project.

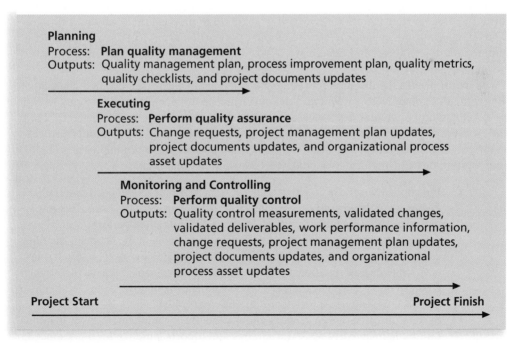

Planning
Process: **Plan quality management**
Outputs: Quality management plan, process improvement plan, quality metrics, quality checklists, and project documents updates

Executing
Process: **Perform quality assurance**
Outputs: Change requests, project management plan updates, project documents updates, and organizational process asset updates

Monitoring and Controlling
Process: **Perform quality control**
Outputs: Quality control measurements, validated changes, validated deliverables, work performance information, change requests, project management plan updates, project documents updates, and organizational process asset updates

Project Start   **Project Finish**

© Cengage Learning 2016

FIGURE 8-1 Project quality management summary

8.3 PLANNING QUALITY MANAGEMENT

Project managers today have a vast knowledge base of information related to quality, and the first step to ensuring project quality management is planning. Planning quality management implies the ability to anticipate situations and prepare actions that bring about the desired outcome. The current thrust in modern quality management is the prevention of defects through a program of selecting the proper materials, training and indoctrinating people in quality, and planning a process that ensures the appropriate outcome. In project quality management planning, it is important to identify relevant quality standards for each unique project and to design quality into the products of the project and the processes involved in managing the project.

Several tools and techniques are available for planning quality management. For example, **design of experiments** is a technique that helps identify which variables have the most influence on the overall outcome of a process. Understanding which variables affect outcome is a very important part of quality planning. For example, computer chip designers might want to determine which combination of materials and equipment will produce the most reliable chips at a reasonable cost. You can also apply design of experiments to project management issues such as cost and schedule trade-offs. Junior programmers or consultants cost less than senior programmers or consultants, but you cannot expect them to complete the same level of work in the same amount of time. An appropriately designed experiment to compute project costs and durations for various combinations of junior and senior programmers or consultants can allow you to determine an optimal mix of personnel, given limited resources. Refer to the section on the Taguchi method later in this chapter for more information.

Quality planning also involves communicating the correct actions for ensuring quality in a format that is understandable and complete. In quality planning for projects, it is important to describe key factors that directly contribute to meeting the customer's requirements. Organizational policies related to quality, the particular project's scope statement and product descriptions, and related standards and regulations are all important input to the quality planning process.

As mentioned in the discussion of project scope management (see Chapter 5), it is often difficult to completely understand the performance dimension of IT projects. Even if the development of hardware, software, and networking technology would stand still for a while, customers often have difficulty explaining exactly what they want in an IT project. Important scope aspects of IT projects that affect quality include functionality and features, system outputs, performance, and reliability and maintainability.

- **Functionality** is the degree to which a system performs its intended function. **Features** are the system's special characteristics that appeal to users. It is important to clarify what functions and features the system *must* perform, and what functions and features are *optional*. In the EIS example in the chapter's opening case, the mandatory functionality of the system might allow users to track sales of specific medical instruments by predetermined categories such as the product group, country, hospital, and sales representative. Mandatory features might be a graphical user interface with icons, menus, and online help.
- **System outputs** are the screens and reports the system generates. It is important to define clearly what the screens and reports look like for a system. Can the users easily interpret these outputs? Can users get all of the reports they need in a suitable format?

- **Performance** addresses how well a product or service performs the customer's intended use. To design a system with high-quality performance, project stakeholders must address many issues. What volumes of data and transactions should the system be capable of handling? How many simultaneous users should the system be designed to handle? What is the projected growth rate in the number of users? What type of equipment must the system run on? How fast must the response time be for different aspects of the system under different circumstances? For the EIS in the opening case, several of the quality problems appear to relate to performance issues. The system is failing a couple of times a month, and users are unsatisfied with the response time. The project team may not have had specific performance requirements or tested the system under the right conditions to deliver the expected performance. Buying faster hardware might address these performance issues. Another performance problem that might be more difficult to fix is that some reports are generating inconsistent results. This could be a software quality problem that is difficult and costly to correct because the system is already in operation.
- **Reliability** is the ability of a product or service to perform as expected under normal conditions. In discussing reliability for IT projects, many people use the term *IT service management.*
- **Maintainability** addresses the ease of performing maintenance on a product. Most IT products cannot reach 100 percent reliability, but stakeholders must define their expectations. For the EIS, what are the normal conditions for operating the system? Should reliability tests be based on 100 people accessing the system at once and running simple queries? Maintenance for the EIS might include uploading new data into the system or performing maintenance procedures on the system hardware and software. Are the users willing to have the system be unavailable several hours a week for system maintenance? Providing help desk support could also be a maintenance function. How fast a response do users expect for help desk support? How often can users tolerate system failure? Are the stakeholders willing to pay more for higher reliability and fewer failures?

These aspects of project scope are just a few of the requirement issues related to quality management planning. Project managers and their teams need to consider all of these project scope issues in determining quality goals for the project. The main customers for the project must also realize their role in defining the most critical quality needs for the project and constantly communicate these needs and expectations to the project team. Because most IT projects involve requirements that are not set in stone, it is important for all project stakeholders to work together to balance the quality, scope, time, and cost dimensions of the project. *Project managers, however, are ultimately responsible for quality management on their projects.*

Project managers should be familiar with basic quality terms, standards, and resources. For example, the ISO provides information based on inputs from 163 different countries. The ISO has an extensive website (*www.iso.org*), which is the source of ISO 9000 and more than 19,500 international standards for business, government, and society as of May 2015. If you're curious where the acronym came from, the word "iso" comes from the Greek language, meaning "equal." IEEE also provides many standards related to quality and has detailed information on its website (*www.ieee.org*).

8.4 PERFORMING QUALITY ASSURANCE

It is one thing to develop a plan for ensuring the quality of a project; it is another to ensure delivery of high-quality products and services. **Quality assurance** includes all of the activities related to satisfying the relevant quality standards for a project. Another goal of quality assurance is continuous quality improvement. Important inputs for performing quality assurance are the quality management plan, process improvement plan, quality metrics, quality control measurements, and project documents.

Many companies understand the importance of quality assurance and have entire departments dedicated to it. They have detailed processes in place to make sure their products and services conform to various quality requirements. They also know they must offer those products and services at competitive prices. To be successful in today's competitive business environment, good companies develop their own best practices and evaluate other organizations' best practices to continuously improve the way they do business. The Japanese word for improvement or change for the better is **kaizen**; a kaizen approach has been used in many organizations since the end of World War II. Another popular term, **lean**, involves evaluating processes to maximize customer value while minimizing waste. Kanban, as described briefly in Chapter 2, is a technique often used in lean. See the following What Went Right? for more information, and consult other texts, articles, and websites for more detailed information on kaizen, lean, kanban, and other aspects of quality assurance.

Several tools used in quality planning can also be used in quality assurance. Design of experiments, as described under quality planning, can also help ensure and improve product quality. **Benchmarking** generates ideas for quality improvements by comparing

---

✓ WHAT WENT RIGHT?

In 2005 David J. Anderson, a founder of the Agile movement and author of several books, visited Tokyo's Imperial Palace gardens during a trip to Japan. He noticed that kanban was used at the gardens to manage the flow of visitors and realized that it could be applied to many processes, including software development.

Kanban uses five core properties:

1. Visual workflow
2. Limit work-in-progress
3. Measure and manage flow
4. Make process policies explicit
5. Use models to recognize improvement opportunities

In his book *Kanban*, Anderson explains that the application of kanban is different for every team. Visitors to his company saw that no set of kanban boards were alike, and all of their teams used a different process to develop software. Anderson explains that kanban requires some type of process to already be in place, and it is used to incrementally improve the process. It gives teams permission to be different. "Each team's situation is different. They evolve their process to fit their context ... The simple act of limiting work-in-progress with kanban encourages higher quality and greater performance."[6]

specific project practices or product characteristics to those of other projects or products within or outside the performing organization. For example, if a competitor has an EIS with an average downtime of only one hour a week, that might be a benchmark for which to strive.

An important tool for quality assurance is a quality audit. A **quality audit** is a structured review of specific quality management activities that help identify lessons learned and that could improve performance on current or future projects. In-house auditors or third parties with expertise in specific areas can perform quality audits; these quality audits can be scheduled or random. Industrial engineers often perform quality audits by helping to design specific quality metrics for a project and then applying and analyzing the metrics throughout the project. For example, the Northwest Airlines Resnet project (which is available on the companion website for this text) provides an excellent example of using quality audits to emphasize the main goals of a project and then track progress in reaching those goals. The main objective of the Resnet project was to develop a new reservation system to increase direct airline ticket sales and reduce the time it took for sales agents to handle customer calls. The measurement techniques for monitoring these goals helped Resnet's project manager and project team supervise various aspects of the project by focusing on meeting those goals. Measuring progress toward increasing direct sales and reducing call times also helped the project manager justify continued investments in Resnet.

8.5 CONTROLLING QUALITY

Many people only think of quality control when they think of quality management, perhaps because there are many popular tools and techniques in this area. Before you learn about these tools and techniques, it is important to distinguish quality control from quality planning and quality assurance.

Although one of the main goals of **quality control** is to improve quality, the main outcomes of this process are acceptance decisions, rework, and process adjustments.

- **Acceptance decisions** determine if the products or services produced as part of the project will be accepted or rejected. If they are accepted, they are considered to be validated deliverables. If project stakeholders reject some of the project's products or services, there must be rework. For example, the executive who sponsored development of the EIS in the chapter's opening case was obviously not satisfied with the system and hired an outside consultant, Scott Daniels, to lead a team to address and correct the quality problems.
- **Rework** is action taken to bring rejected items into compliance with product requirements, specifications, or other stakeholder expectations. Rework often results in requested changes and validated defect repair, and it results from recommended defect repair or corrective or preventive actions. Rework can be very expensive, so the project manager must strive to do a good job of quality planning and quality assurance to avoid this need. Because the EIS did not meet all of the stakeholders' expectations for quality in the opening case, the medical instruments company was spending additional money for rework.

307

- **Process adjustments** correct or prevent further quality problems based on quality control measurements. Process adjustments often result in updates to organization process assets and the project management plan. For example, Scott Daniels, the consultant in the opening case, might recommend that the medical instruments company purchase a faster server for the EIS to correct the response-time problems. This change would require changes to the project management plan because it would require more project-related work. The company also hired Scott to develop a plan to help prevent future IT project quality problems.

8.6 TOOLS AND TECHNIQUES FOR QUALITY CONTROL

Quality control includes many general tools and techniques. This section describes the Seven Basic Tools of Quality, statistical sampling, and Six Sigma and discusses how they can be applied to IT projects. The section concludes with a discussion of testing, because IT projects use testing extensively to ensure quality.

The designation of the Seven Basic Tools of Quality arose in postwar Japan, supposedly inspired by the seven famous weapons of Benkei. The following seven tools are listed in the *PMBOK® Guide, Fifth Edition*:

1. **Cause-and-effect diagrams** trace complaints about quality problems back to the responsible production operations. In other words, they help you find the root cause of a problem. They are also known as **fishbone** or **Ishikawa diagrams**, named after their creator, Kaoru Ishikawa. You can also use the technique known as the **5 whys**, in which you repeatedly ask the question "Why?" to help peel away the layers of symptoms that can lead to the root cause of a problem. (Using five questions is a good rule of thumb, although other numbers can be used.) These symptoms can be branches on the cause-and-effect diagram.

   Figure 8-2 provides an example of a cause-and-effect diagram that Scott Daniels, the consultant in the opening case, might create to discover why users cannot log in to the EIS. Notice that it resembles the skeleton of a fish, hence the name *fishbone diagram*. This diagram lists the main areas that could be the cause of the problem: the EIS system's hardware, the user's hardware or software, or the user's training. The figure describes two of these areas, the individual user's hardware and training, in more detail.

   Using the 5 whys, you could first ask why users cannot get into the system, then why they keep forgetting their passwords, why they did not reset their passwords, and why they did not check a box to save a password. The root cause of the problem would have a significant impact on actions taken to solve the problem. If many users could not get into the system because their computers did not have enough memory, the solution might be to upgrade memory for those computers. If many users could not get into the system because they forgot their passwords, there might be a much quicker, less expensive solution.

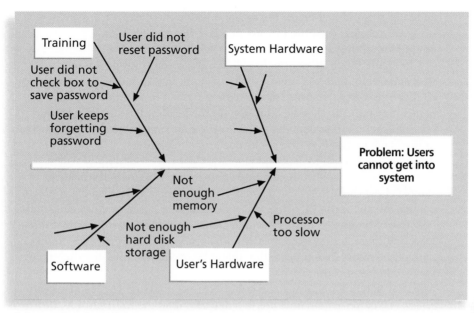

Training

User did not
reset password

System Hardware

User did not
check box to
save password

User keeps
forgetting
password

**Problem: Users
cannot get into
system**

Not
enough
memory

Processor
too slow

Not enough
hard disk
storage

Software

User's Hardware

FIGURE 8-2 Sample cause-and-effect diagram

2. A **control chart** is a graphic display of data that illustrates the results of a process over time. Control charts allow you to determine whether a process is in control or out of control. When a process is in control, any variations in the results of the process are created by random events. Processes that are in control do not need to be adjusted. When a process is out of control, variations in the results of the process are caused by nonrandom events. When a process is out of control, you need to identify the causes of those nonrandom events and adjust the process to correct or eliminate them.

Figure 8-3 provides an example of a control chart for a process that manufactures 12-inch wood rulers by machines on an assembly line. Each point on the chart represents a length measurement for a ruler that comes off the assembly line. The customer has specified that all rulers it purchases must be between 11.90 and 12.10 inches long, or 12 inches plus or minus 0.10 inches. The scale on the vertical axis goes from 11.90, the lower specification limit, to 12.10, the upper specification limit. The lower and upper control limits on the quality control chart are 11.91 and 12.09 inches, respectively. This means the manufacturing process is designed to produce rulers between 11.91 and 12.09 inches long.

Looking for and analyzing patterns in process data is an important part of quality control. You can use quality control charts and the seven run rule to look for patterns in data. The **seven run rule** states that if seven data points in a row are all below the mean or above the mean, or are all increasing or decreasing, then the process needs to be examined for nonrandom problems.

In Figure 8-3, data points that violate the seven run rule are marked with stars. Note that you include the first point in a series of points that are all increasing or decreasing. In the ruler manufacturing process, these data points may indicate that a calibration device needs adjustment. For example, the machine that cuts the wood for the rulers might need to be adjusted or the blade on the machine might need to be replaced.

3. A **checksheet** is used to collect and analyze data. It is sometimes called a tally sheet or checklist, depending on its format. Figure 8-4 provides a sample checksheet that Scott Daniels could use to track the media source of complaints about the EIS. Note that tally marks are used to enter each data occurrence manually. In this example, most complaints arrive via text message, and there are more complaints on Monday and Tuesday than on other days of the week. This information might be useful in improving the process for handling complaints.

4. A **scatter diagram** helps to show if there is a relationship between two variables. The closer data points are to a diagonal line, the more closely the two variables are related. For example, Figure 8-5 provides a sample scatter diagram that Scott Daniels might create to compare user satisfaction ratings of the EIS system to the age of respondents to see if there is a relationship. Scott might find that younger users are less satisfied with the system, for example, and make decisions based on that finding.

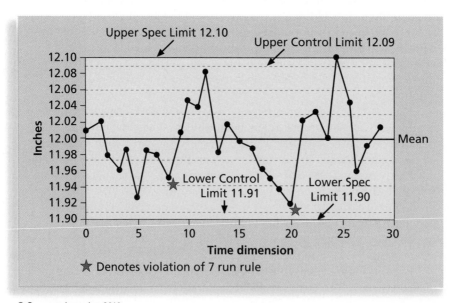

© Cengage Learning 2016

FIGURE 8-3 Sample control chart

System Complaints	Day							
Source	Monday	Tuesday	Wednesday	Thursday	Friday	Saturday	Sunday	Total
E-mail	|||	||||			||						12
Text	⦀⦀ ||	||||	⦀⦀		|||	||||	||	|||	29
Phone call			||					||				8
Total	11	10	8	6	7	3	4	49

© Cengage Learning 2016

FIGURE 8-4 Sample checksheet

© Cengage Learning 2016

FIGURE 8-5 Sample scatter diagram

5. A **histogram** is a bar graph of a distribution of variables. Each bar represents an attribute or characteristic of a problem or situation, and the height of the bar represents its frequency. For example, Scott Daniels might ask the Help Desk to create a histogram to show how many total complaints they received each week about the EIS system. Figure 8-6 shows a sample histogram.

6. A **Pareto chart** is a histogram that can help you identify and prioritize problem areas. The variables described by the histogram are ordered by frequency of occurrence. Pareto charts help you identify the vital few contributors that account for most quality problems in a system. **Pareto analysis** is sometimes referred to as the 80-20 rule, meaning that 80 percent of problems are often due to 20 percent of the causes.

For example, suppose there was a detailed history of user complaints about the EIS. The project team could create a Pareto chart based on that data, as shown in Figure 8-7.

Notice that login problems are the most frequent user complaint, followed by the system locking up, the system being too slow, the system being hard to use, and the reports being inaccurate. The first complaint accounts for 55 percent of the total complaints. The first and second complaints together account for almost 80 percent of the total complaints. Therefore, the

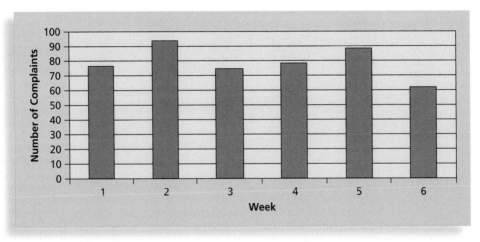

© Cengage Learning 2016

FIGURE 8-6 Sample histogram

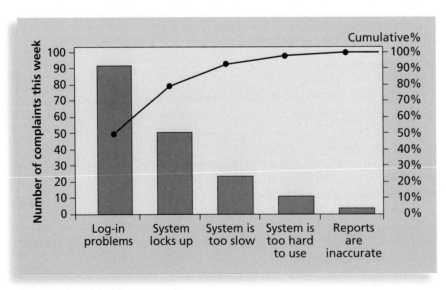

© Cengage Learning 2016

FIGURE 8-7 Sample Pareto chart

company should focus on making it easier to log in to the system to improve quality, because most complaints fall under that category. The company should also address why the system locks up.

Because Figure 8-7 shows that inaccurate reports are rarely mentioned, the project manager should investigate who made this complaint before spending a lot of effort on addressing the problem. The project manager should also find out if complaints about the system being too slow were actually due to the user not being able to log in or the system locking up. You can use the template file for this chart and other charts on the companion website for this text, and you can find videos and articles that explain how to create the charts.

7. **Flowcharts** are graphic displays of the logic and flow of processes that help you analyze how problems occur and how processes can be improved. They show activities, decision points, and the order of how information is processed.

Figure 8-8 provides a simple example of a flowchart that shows the process a project team might use for accepting or rejecting deliverables. The American Society for Quality (ASQ) calls this basic quality tool *stratification*, a technique that shows data from a variety of sources to see if a pattern emerges.

In addition to flowcharts, run charts are also used for stratification. A **run chart** displays the history and pattern of variation of a process over time. It is a line chart that shows data points plotted in the order of occurrence. You can use run charts to perform trend analysis and forecast future outcomes based on historical results. For example, trend analysis can help you analyze how many defects have been identified over time and see if

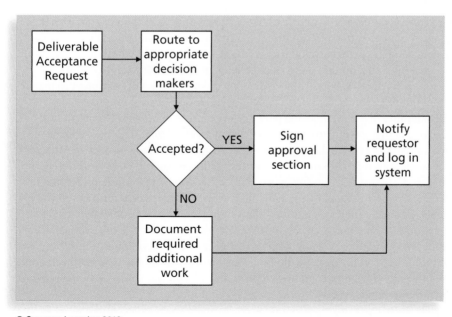

© Cengage Learning 2016

FIGURE 8-8 Sample flowchart

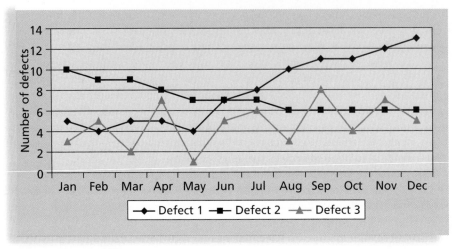

© Cengage Learning 2016

FIGURE 8-9 Sample run chart

there are trends. Figure 8-9 shows a sample run chart of the number of defects each month for three different types of defects. You can easily see the patterns of Defect 1 increasing over time, Defect 2 decreasing the first several months and then holding steady, and Defect 3 fluctuating each month.

8.6a Statistical Sampling

Statistical sampling is a key concept in project quality management. Members of a project team who focus on quality control must have a strong understanding of statistics, but other project team members need to understand only the basic concepts. These concepts include statistical sampling, certainty factor, standard deviation, and variability. Standard deviation and variability are fundamental concepts for understanding quality control charts. This section briefly describes these concepts and describes how a project manager might apply them to IT projects. Refer to statistics texts for additional details.

Statistical sampling involves choosing part of a population of interest for inspection. For example, suppose that a company wants to develop an electronic data interchange (EDI) system for handling invoice data from all of its suppliers. Assume also that in the past year, the company received 50,000 invoices from 200 different suppliers. It would be very time consuming and expensive to review every invoice to determine data requirements for the new system. Even if the system developers did review all 200 invoice forms from the different suppliers, the data might be entered differently on every form. Statisticians have developed techniques to determine an appropriate sample size when it is impractical or impossible to study every member of a population. Using statistical techniques, the system developers might find that 100 invoices would be enough to determine the data requirements.

The size of the sample depends on how representative you want it to be. A simple formula for determining sample size is:

$$\text{Sample size} = 0.25 * (\text{certainty factor/acceptable error})^2$$

The certainty factor denotes how confident you want to be that the sampled data includes only variations that naturally exist in the population. You calculate the certainty

TABLE 8-1 Commonly used certainty factors

Desired Certainty	Certainty Factor
95%	1.960
90%	1.645
80%	1.281

© Cengage Learning 2016

factor from tables that are available in statistics books. Table 8-1 shows some commonly used certainty factors. The acceptable error is related to the desired certainty and is 1 – percent certainty/100. So if you set your desired certainty to 95 percent, then the acceptable error value is 1 – 95/100 = .05.

For example, suppose that the developers of the EDI system would accept a 95 percent certainty that a sample of invoices would contain no variation unless it was present in the population of total invoices. They would then calculate the sample size as:

$$\text{Sample size} = 0.25 * (1.960/.05)^2 = 384$$

If the developers would accept 90 percent certainty, they would calculate the sample size as:

$$\text{Sample size} = 0.25 * (1.645/.10)^2 = 68$$

If the developers would accept 80 percent certainty, they would calculate the sample size as:

$$\text{Sample size} = 0.25 * (1.281/.20)^2 = 10$$

Assume that the developers decide on 90 percent for the certainty factor. Then they would need to examine 68 invoices to determine the type of data the EDI system would need to capture. As stated earlier, even if they reviewed all 200 invoices, some data could be entered differently. Additional means of data collection should be used to ensure that important user requirements are met.

8.6b Six Sigma

The work of many project quality experts contributed to the development of today's Six Sigma principles. There has been some confusion in the past few years about the term *Six Sigma*. This section summarizes recent information about this important concept and explains how organizations worldwide use Six Sigma principles to improve quality, decrease costs, and better meet customer needs.

In their book *The Six Sigma Way*, authors Peter Pande, Robert Neuman, and Roland Cavanagh define **Six Sigma** as "a comprehensive and flexible *system* for achieving, sustaining and maximizing business success. Six Sigma is uniquely driven by close understanding of customer needs, disciplined use of facts, data, and statistical analysis, and diligent attention to managing, improving, and reinventing business processes."[7]

Six Sigma's target for quality is no more than 3.4 defects, errors, or mistakes per million opportunities. This target number is explained in more detail later in this section. An organization can apply Six Sigma principles to the design and production of a product, a help desk, or other customer-service process.

Projects that use Six Sigma principles for quality control normally follow a five-phase improvement process called **DMAIC** (pronounced *de-MAY-ick*), which stands for Define, Measure, Analyze, Improve, and Control. DMAIC is a systematic, closed-loop process for continued improvement that is scientific and fact based. The following are brief descriptions of each phase of the DMAIC improvement process:

1. *Define*: Define the problem/opportunity, process, and customer requirements. Important tools used in this phase include a project charter, a description of customer requirements, process maps, and Voice of the Customer (VOC) data. Examples of VOC data include complaints, surveys, comments, and market research that represent the views and needs of the organization's customers.

2. *Measure*: Define measures and then collect, compile, and display data. Measures are defined in terms of defects per opportunity.

3. *Analyze*: Scrutinize process details to find improvement opportunities. A project team working on a Six Sigma project, normally referred to as a Six Sigma team, investigates and verifies data to prove the suspected root causes of quality problems and substantiates the problem statement. An important tool in this phase is the fishbone or Ishikawa diagram, described earlier in this chapter.

4. *Improve*: Generate solutions and ideas for improving the problem. A final solution is verified with the project sponsor, and the Six Sigma team develops a plan to pilot test the solution. The Six Sigma team reviews the results of the pilot test to refine the solution, if needed, and then implements the solution where appropriate.

5. *Control*: Track and verify the stability of the improvements and the predictability of the solution. Control charts are one tool used in the control phase.

How Is Six Sigma Quality Control Unique?

How does using Six Sigma principles differ from using previous quality control initiatives? Many people remember other quality initiatives from the past few decades, such as Total Quality Management (TQM) and Business Process Reengineering (BPR). The origins of many Six Sigma principles and tools are found in these previous initiatives; however, several new ideas are included in Six Sigma principles that help organizations improve their competitiveness and bottom-line results:

- Using Six Sigma principles is an organization-wide commitment. CEOs, top managers, and all levels of employees in an organization that embraces Six Sigma principles have seen remarkable improvements due to its use. There are often huge training investments, but they pay off as employees practice Six Sigma principles and produce higher-quality goods and services at lower costs.
- Six Sigma training normally follows the "belt" system, similar to a martial arts class in which students receive different-color belts for each training level. In Six Sigma training, those in the Yellow Belt category receive the minimum level of training, which is normally two to three full days for project team members who work on Six Sigma projects on a part-time basis. Those in the Green Belt category usually participate in two to three full weeks of training. Those in the Black Belt category normally work on Six Sigma projects full-time

and attend four to five full weeks of training. Project managers are often Black Belts. The Master Black Belt category describes experienced Black Belts who act as technical resources and mentors to people with lower-level belts.

- Organizations that successfully implement Six Sigma principles have the ability and willingness to adopt two seemingly contrary objectives at the same time. For example, Six Sigma organizations believe that they can be creative *and* rational, focus on the big picture *and* minute details, reduce errors *and* get things done faster, and make customers happy *and* make a lot of money. Authors James Collins and Jerry Porras describe this as the "We can do it all" or "Genius of the And" approach in their book, *Built to Last*.[8]

- Six Sigma is not just a program or a discipline to organizations that have benefited from it. Six Sigma is an operating philosophy that is customer-focused and strives to drive out waste, raise levels of quality, and improve financial performance at *breakthrough* levels. A Six Sigma organization sets high goals and uses the DMAIC improvement process to achieve extraordinary quality improvements.

Many organizations do some of what now fits under the definition of Six Sigma, and many Six Sigma principles are not brand-new. What *is* new is its ability to bring together many different themes, concepts, and tools into a coherent management process that can be used on an organization-wide basis.

Six Sigma and Project Selection and Management

Organizations implement Six Sigma by selecting and managing projects. An important part of project management is good project selection.

Joseph M. Juran stated, "All improvement takes place project by project, and in no other way."[9] This statement is especially true for Six Sigma projects. Pande, Neuman, and Cavanagh conducted an informal poll to find out the most critical and most commonly mishandled activity in launching Six Sigma, and the unanimous answer was project selection. "It's a pretty simple equation, really: Well-selected and -defined improvement projects equal better, faster results. The converse equation is also simple: Poorly selected and defined projects equal delayed results and frustration."[10]

Organizations must be careful to apply higher quality where it makes sense. An article in *Fortune* stated that companies that have implemented Six Sigma have not necessarily boosted their stock values. Although GE boasted savings of more than $2 billion in 1999 due to its use of Six Sigma, other companies, such as Whirlpool, could not clearly demonstrate the value of their investments. Why can't all companies benefit from Six Sigma? Because minimizing defects does not matter if an organization makes a product that people do not want. As one of Six Sigma's biggest supporters, Mikel Harry, put it, "I could genetically engineer a Six Sigma goat, but if a rodeo is the marketplace, people are still going to buy a Four Sigma horse."[11]

What makes a project a potential Six Sigma project? First, there must be a quality problem or gap between the current and desired performance. This first criterion does not apply to many projects, such as building a house, merging two corporations, or providing an IT infrastructure for a new organization. Second, the project should not have a clearly understood problem. Third, the solution should not be predetermined, and an optimal solution should not be apparent.

317

Once a project is selected as a good candidate for Six Sigma, many project management concepts, tools, and techniques described in this text come into play. For example, Six Sigma projects usually have a business case, a project charter, requirements documents, a schedule, and a budget. Six Sigma projects are done in teams and have sponsors called champions. There are also project managers, although they are often called *team leaders* in Six Sigma organizations. In other words, Six Sigma projects are simply types of projects that focus on supporting the Six Sigma philosophy by being customer-focused and striving to drive out waste, raise levels of quality, and improve financial performance at breakthrough levels.

Six Sigma and Statistics

An important concept in Six Sigma is improving quality by reducing variation. The term *sigma* means standard deviation. **Standard deviation** measures how much variation exists in a distribution of data. A small standard deviation means that data clusters closely around the middle of a distribution and there is little variability among the data. A large standard deviation means that data is spread around the middle of the distribution and there is relatively greater variability. Statisticians use the Greek symbol σ (sigma) to represent the standard deviation.

Figure 8-10 provides an example of a **normal distribution**—a bell-shaped curve that is symmetrical around the **mean** or average value of the population (the data being analyzed). In any normal distribution, 68.3 percent of the population is within one standard deviation (1σ) of the mean, 95.5 percent of the population is within two standard deviations (2σ), and 99.7 percent of the population is within three standard deviations (3σ) of the mean.

Standard deviation is a key factor in determining the acceptable number of defective units in a population. Table 8-2 illustrates the relationship between sigma, the

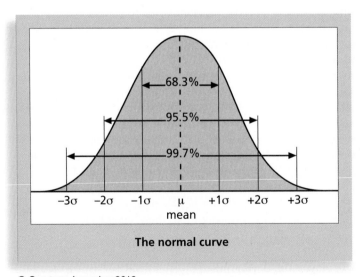

The normal curve

© Cengage Learning 2016

FIGURE 8-10 Normal distribution and standard deviation

percentage of the population within that sigma range, and the number of defective units per billion. Note that this table shows that being plus or minus six sigma in pure statistical terms means only *two* defective units per *billion*. Why, then, is the target for Six Sigma programs 3.4 defects per million opportunities, as stated earlier in this chapter?

Based on Motorola's original work on Six Sigma in the 1980s, the convention used for Six Sigma is a scoring system that accounts for more variation in a process than you would typically find in a few weeks or months of data gathering. In other words, time is an important factor in determining process variations. Table 8-3 shows a Six Sigma conversion table applied to Six Sigma projects. The **yield** represents the number of units handled correctly through the process steps. A **defect** is any instance in which the product or service fails to meet customer requirements. Because most products or services have multiple customer requirements, there can be several opportunities to have a defect. For example, suppose that a company is trying to reduce the number of errors on customer billing statements. There could be several errors on a billing statement due to a misspelled name, incorrect address, wrong date of service, or calculation error. There might be 100 opportunities for a defect to occur on one billing statement. Instead of measuring the number of defects per unit or billing statement, Six Sigma measures the number of defects based on the number of opportunities.

TABLE 8-2   Sigma and defective units

Specification Range (in ± Sigmas)	Percent of Population within Range	Defective Units per Billion
1	68.27	317,300,000
2	95.45	45,400,000
3	99.73	2,700,000
4	99.9937	63,000
5	99.999943	57
6	99.9999998	2

© Cengage Learning 2016

TABLE 8-3   Six Sigma conversion table

Sigma	Yield	Defects per Million Opportunities (DPMO)
1	31.0%	690,000
2	69.2%	308,000
3	93.3%	66,800
4	99.4%	6,210
5	99.97%	230
6	99.99966%	3.4

© Cengage Learning 2016

As you can see, the Six Sigma conversion table shows that a process operating at six sigma means there are no more than 3.4 defects per million opportunities. However, most organizations today use the term *six sigma project* in a broad sense to describe projects that will help them in achieving, sustaining, and maximizing business success through better business processes.

A term you may hear in the telecommunications industry is **six 9s of quality**, which is a measure of quality control equal to 1 fault in 1 million opportunities. In the telecommunications industry, it means 99.9999 percent service availability or *30 seconds of downtime a year*. This level of quality has also been stated as the target goal for the number of errors in a communications circuit, system failures, or errors in lines of code. Achieving six 9s of quality requires continual testing to find and eliminate errors or enough redundancy and backup equipment in systems to reduce the overall system failure rate to the required level.

8.6c Testing

Many IT professionals think of testing as a stage that comes near the end of IT product development. Instead of putting serious effort into proper planning, analysis, and design of IT projects, some organizations rely on testing just before a product ships to ensure some degree of quality. In fact, testing needs to be done during almost every phase of the systems development life cycle, not just before the organization ships or hands over a product to the customer.

Figure 8-11 shows one way of portraying the systems development life cycle. This example includes 17 main tasks involved in a software development project and shows their relationship to each other. Every project should start by initiating the project, conducting a feasibility study, and then performing project planning. The figure then shows that preparing detailed requirements and the detailed architecture for the system can be performed simultaneously. The oval-shaped phases represent actual tests or tasks, which will include test plans to help ensure quality on software development projects.[12]

Several of the phases in Figure 8-11 include specific work related to testing.

- A **unit test** is done to test each individual component (often a program) to ensure that it is as defect-free as possible. Unit tests are performed before moving on to the integration test.
- **Integration testing** occurs between unit and system testing to test functionally grouped components. It ensures that a subset or subsets of the entire system work together.
- **System testing** tests the entire system as one entity. It focuses on the big picture to ensure that the entire system is working properly.
- **User acceptance testing** is an independent test performed by end users prior to accepting the delivered system. It focuses on the business fit of the system to the organization, rather than technical issues.

Other types of testing include alpha and beta testing, performance testing, and scalability testing. For example, several companies, including Amazon and Target, have suffered serious consequences when their websites crashed because they could not handle demand due to inadequate scalability testing. To help improve the quality of software development projects, it is important for organizations to follow a thorough and disciplined

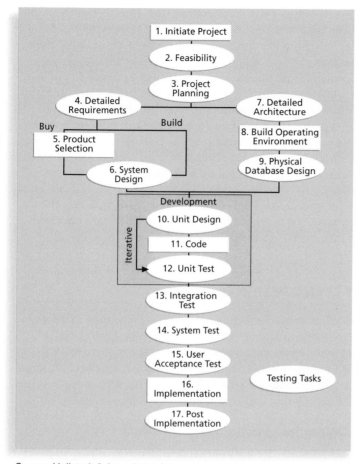

Source: Hollstadt & Associates, Inc.

FIGURE 8-11   Testing Tasks in the Software Development Life Cycle

testing methodology. System developers and testers must also establish a partnership with all project stakeholders to make sure the system meets their needs and expectations and the tests are done properly. As described in the next section, tremendous costs are involved in failure to perform proper testing.

Testing alone, however, cannot always solve software defect problems, according to Watts S. Humphrey, a renowned expert on software quality and Fellow at Carnegie Mellon's Software Engineering Institute. He believes that the traditional code/test/fix cycle for software development is not enough. As code gets more complex, the number of defects missed by testing increases and becomes the problem not just of testers, but also of paying customers. Humphrey says that, on average, programmers introduce a defect for every nine or 10 lines of code, and the finished software, after all testing, contains about five to six defects per thousand lines of code.

Although there are many different definitions, Humphrey defines a **software defect** as anything that must be changed before delivery of the program. Testing does not sufficiently prevent software defects because the number of ways to test a complex system is huge. In addition, users will continue to invent new ways to use a system that its developers never considered, so certain functionalities may never have been tested or even included in the system requirements.

Humphrey suggests that people rethink the software development process to provide *no* potential defects when you enter system testing. This means that developers must be responsible for providing error-free code at each stage of testing. Humphrey teaches a development process in which programmers measure and track the kinds of errors they commit so they can use the data to improve their performance. He also acknowledges that top management must support developers by letting them self-direct their work. Programmers need to be motivated and excited to do high-quality work and have some control over how they do it.[13]

For additional information on software testing, you can visit *www.ISTQB.org*, the website for the International Software Testing Qualifications Board. The board offers a testing certification scheme that is known around the world, with more than 354,000 certified testers in over 100 countries.

8.7 MODERN QUALITY MANAGEMENT

Modern quality management requires customer satisfaction, prefers prevention to inspection, and recognizes management responsibility for quality. Several noteworthy people helped develop the following theories, tools, and techniques that define modern quality management.[14] The suggestions from these quality experts led to many projects to improve quality and provided the foundation for today's Six Sigma projects. This section summarizes major contributions made by Deming, Juran, Crosby, Ishikawa, Taguchi, and Feigenbaum.

8.7a Deming and His 14 Points for Management

Dr. W. Edwards Deming is known primarily for his work on quality control in Japan. Deming went to Japan after World War II at the request of the Japanese government to assist in improving productivity and quality. Deming, a statistician and former professor at New York University, taught Japanese manufacturers that higher quality meant greater productivity and lower cost. American industry did not recognize Deming's theories until Japanese manufacturers started creating products that seriously challenged American products, particularly in the auto industry. Ford Motor Company then adopted Deming's quality methods and experienced dramatic improvement in quality and sales thereafter. By the 1980s, after seeing the excellent work coming out of Japan, several U.S. corporations vied for Deming's expertise to help them establish quality improvement programs in their own factories.

Many people are familiar with the Deming Prize, an award given to recognize high-quality organizations, and Deming's Cycle for Improvement: plan, do, check, and act. Most Six Sigma principles are based on the plan-do-check-act model created by Deming.

Many people are also familiar with Deming's 14 Points for Management, summarized below from his text book *Out of the Crisis*[15]:

1. Create constancy of purpose for improvement of product and service.
2. Adopt the new philosophy.
3. Cease dependence on inspection to achieve quality.

4. End the practice of awarding business based on price tag alone. Instead, minimize total cost by working with a single supplier.
5. Improve constantly and forever every process for planning, production, and service.
6. Institute training on the job.
7. Adopt and institute leadership.
8. Drive out fear.
9. Break down barriers between staff areas.
10. Eliminate slogans, exhortations, and targets for the workforce.
11. Eliminate numerical quotas for the workforce and numerical goals for management.
12. Remove barriers that rob people of workmanship. Eliminate the annual rating or merit system.
13. Institute a vigorous program of education and self-improvement for everyone.
14. Put everyone in the company to work to accomplish the transformation.

8.7b Juran and the Importance of Top Management Commitment to Quality

Joseph M. Juran, like Deming, taught Japanese manufacturers how to improve their productivity. U.S. companies later discovered him as well. He wrote the first edition of the *Quality Control Handbook* in 1974, stressing the importance of top management commitment to continuous product quality improvement. In 2000, at the age of 94, Juran published the fifth edition of this famous handbook.[16] He also developed the Juran Trilogy: quality improvement, quality planning, and quality control. Juran stressed the difference between the manufacturer's view of quality and the customer's view. Manufacturers often focus on conformance to requirements, but customers focus on fitness for use. Most definitions of quality now use fitness for use to stress the importance of satisfying stated or implied needs and not just meeting stated requirements or specifications. Juran developed 10 steps to quality improvement:

1. Build awareness of the need and opportunity for improvement.
2. Set goals for improvement.
3. Organize to reach the goals (establish a quality council, identify problems, select projects, appoint teams, designate facilitators).
4. Provide training.
5. Carry out projects to solve problems.
6. Report progress.
7. Give recognition.
8. Communicate results.
9. Keep score.
10. Maintain momentum by making annual improvement part of the regular systems and processes of the company.

8.7c Crosby and Striving for Zero Defects

Philip B. Crosby wrote *Quality Is Free* in 1979 and is best known for suggesting that organizations strive for zero defects.[17] He stressed that the costs of poor quality should include all the costs of not doing the job right the first time, such as scrap, rework, lost labor hours and machine hours, customer ill will and lost sales, and warranty costs. Crosby suggested that the cost of poor quality is so understated that companies can profitably spend unlimited amounts of money on improving quality. Crosby developed the following 14 steps for quality improvement:

1. Make it clear that management is committed to quality.
2. Form quality improvement teams with representatives from each department.
3. Determine where current and potential quality problems lie.
4. Evaluate the cost of quality and explain its use as a management tool.
5. Raise the quality awareness and personal concern of all employees.
6. Take actions to correct problems identified through previous steps.
7. Establish a committee for the zero-defects program.
8. Train supervisors to actively carry out their part of the quality improvement program.
9. Hold a "zero-defects day" to let all employees realize that there has been a change.
10. Encourage individuals to establish improvement goals for themselves and their groups.
11. Encourage employees to communicate to management the obstacles they face in attaining their improvement goals.
12. Recognize and appreciate those who participate.
13. Establish quality councils to communicate on a regular basis.
14. Do it all over again to emphasize that the quality improvement program never ends.

Crosby developed the Quality Management Process Maturity Grid in 1978. This grid can be applied to an organization's attitude toward product usability. For example, the first stage in the grid is ignorance, where people might think they don't have any problems with usability. The final stage is wisdom, where people have changed their attitudes so that usability defect prevention is a routine part of their operation.

8.7d Ishikawa's Guide to Quality Control

Kaoru Ishikawa is best known for his 1972 book *Guide to Quality Control*.[18] He developed the concept of quality circles and pioneered the use of cause-and-effect diagrams, as described earlier in this chapter. **Quality circles** are groups of nonsupervisors and work leaders in a single company department who volunteer to conduct group studies on how to improve the effectiveness of work in their department. Ishikawa suggested that Japanese managers and workers were totally committed to quality, but that most U.S. companies delegated the responsibility for quality to a few staff members.

8.7e Taguchi and Robust Design Methods

Genichi Taguchi is best known for developing the Taguchi methods for optimizing the process of engineering experimentation. Key concepts in the Taguchi methods are that quality should be designed into the product and not inspected into it, and that quality is best achieved by minimizing deviation from the target value. For example, if the target response time for accessing the EIS described in the opening case is half a second, there should be little deviation from this time. By the late 1990s, Taguchi had become, in the words of *Fortune* magazine, "America's new quality hero."[19] Many companies, including Xerox, Ford, Hewlett-Packard, and Goodyear, have recently used Taguchi's Robust Design methods to design high-quality products. **Robust Design methods** focus on eliminating defects by substituting scientific inquiry for trial-and-error methods.

8.7f Feigenbaum and Workers' Responsibility for Quality

Armand V. Feigenbaum developed the concept of total quality control (TQC) in his 1983 book *Total Quality Control: Engineering and Management*.[20] He proposed that the responsibility for quality should rest with the people who do the work. In TQC, product quality is more important than production rates, and workers are allowed to stop production whenever a quality problem occurs.

8.7g Malcolm Baldrige National Quality Award

The **Malcolm Baldrige National Quality Award** originated in 1987 in the United States to recognize companies that have achieved a level of world-class competition through quality management. The award was started in honor of Malcolm Baldrige, who was the U.S. Secretary of Commerce from 1981 until his death in a rodeo accident in July 1987. Baldrige was a proponent of quality management as a key element in improving the prosperity and long-term strength of U.S. organizations. The Malcolm Baldrige National Quality Award is given by the president of the United States to U.S. businesses and organizations. Organizations must apply for the award, and they must be judged outstanding in seven areas: leadership, strategic planning, customer and market focus, information and analysis, human resource focus, process management, and business results. Three awards may be given annually in each of the categories of manufacturing, service, small business, and education/healthcare. The awards recognize achievements in quality and performance and raise awareness about the importance of quality as a competitive edge; the award is not given for specific products or services.

8.7h ISO Standards

The International Organization for Standardization (ISO) is a network of national standards institutes that work in partnership with international organizations, governments, industries, businesses, and consumer representatives. **ISO 9000**, a quality system standard developed by the ISO, is a three-part, continuous cycle of planning, controlling, and documenting quality in an organization. According to the ISO website (*www.iso.org*) in March 2015, "The ISO 9000 family addresses various aspects of quality management and contains some of ISO's best known standards. The standards provide guidance and tools for companies and organizations who want to ensure that their products and services consistently meet customer's requirements, and that quality is consistently improved." The ISO quality management standards and guidelines have earned a global reputation as the basis for establishing quality management systems.

Standards continue to be updated, and new standards are developed as needed. For example, in 2013, ISO collaborated with the International Electrotechnical Commission (IEC) to publish a standard to help organizations integrate information security and service management.[21]

ISO continues to offer standards to provide a framework for the assessment of software processes. The overall goals of a standard are to encourage organizations that are interested in improving quality of software products to employ proven, consistent, and reliable methods for assessing the state of their software development processes. They can also use their assessment results as part of coherent improvement programs. One of the outcomes of assessment and consequent improvement programs is reliable, predictable, and continuously improving software processes.

 GLOBAL ISSUES

In 2015, 15 electric cars were introduced throughout the world, including the Tesla Model X, BMW X5 eDrive, VW Passat GTE Plug-in, Audi A3 e-Tron, Chevy Volt, and three different Mercedes-Benz models. Fortunately, ISO provided standards to make them safe.

An even more impressive technology for automobiles—driverless cars—is sparking new safety concerns. In a well-publicized event in March 2015, the Delphi car, a modified Audi SQ5 equipped with radar, high-end microprocessors, and software, completed a trip across the United States. A person did have to sit in the driver's seat to comply with state laws.

Chris Urmson, the director of self-driving cars at Google, is committed to ensuring that driverless vehicles are standard within five years. Google began testing them in 2009. About 33,000 people die on America's roads every year, and drivers are the least reliable part of the car. Urmson and his team at Google are using several quality tools and techniques to improve the quality of driverless cars to reduce accident rates. "As we continue to work toward our vision of fully self-driving vehicles that can take anyone from point A to point B at the push of a button, we're thinking a lot about how to measure our progress and our impact on road safety."[22]

The contributions of quality experts, quality awards, and quality standards are important parts of project quality management. The Project Management Institute was proud to announce in 1999 that its certification department had become the first in the world to earn ISO 9000 certification, and that the *PMBOK® Guide* had been recognized as an international standard. Emphasizing quality in project management helps ensure that projects create products or services that meet customer needs and expectations.

8.8 IMPROVING IT PROJECT QUALITY

In addition to some of the suggestions provided for using good quality planning, quality assurance, and quality control, other important issues are involved in improving the quality of IT projects. Strong leadership, understanding the cost of quality, providing a good workplace to enhance quality, and working toward improving the organization's overall maturity level in software development and project management can all help improve quality.

8.8a Leadership

As Joseph M. Juran said in 1945, "It is most important that top management be quality-minded. In the absence of sincere manifestation of interest at the top, little will happen below."[23] Juran and many other quality experts argue that the main cause of quality problems is a lack of leadership.

As globalization continues to increase and customers become more and more demanding, creating high-quality products quickly at a reasonable price is essential for staying in business. Having good quality programs in place helps organizations remain competitive. To establish and implement effective quality programs, top management must lead the way. A large percentage of quality problems are associated with management, not technical issues. Therefore, top management must take responsibility for creating, supporting, and promoting quality programs.

Motorola provides an excellent example of a high-technology company that truly emphasizes quality. Leadership is one of the factors that helped Motorola achieve its great success in quality management and Six Sigma. Top management emphasized the need to improve quality and helped all employees take responsibility for customer satisfaction. Strategic objectives in Motorola's long-range plans included managing quality improvement in the same way that new products or technologies were managed. Top management stressed the need to develop and use quality standards and provided resources such as staff, training, and customer inputs to help improve quality.

Leadership provides an environment conducive to producing quality. Management must publicly declare the company's philosophy and commitment to quality, implement company-wide training programs in quality concepts and principles, implement measurement programs to establish and track quality levels, and actively demonstrate the importance of quality. When every employee insists on producing high-quality products, then top management has done a good job of promoting the importance of quality.

8.8b The Cost of Quality

The **cost of quality** is the cost of conformance plus the cost of nonconformance. **Conformance** means delivering products that meet requirements and fitness for use. Examples include the costs associated with developing a quality plan, costs for analyzing and managing product requirements, and costs for testing. The **cost of nonconformance** means taking responsibility for failures or not meeting quality expectations.

The five major cost categories related to quality include:

1. **Prevention cost**: The cost of planning and executing a project so that it is error-free or within an acceptable error range. Preventive actions such as training, detailed studies related to quality, and quality surveys of suppliers and subcontractors fall under this category. Recall from the discussion of cost management (see Chapter 7) that detecting defects in information systems during the early phases of the systems development life cycle is much less expensive than during the later phases. One hundred dollars spent refining user requirements could save millions by finding a defect before implementing a large system. The Year 2000 (Y2K) issue provided a good example of these costs. If organizations had decided during the 1960s, 1970s, and 1980s that all dates would need four computer characters to represent the year instead of two, they would have saved billions of dollars.

2. **Appraisal cost**: The cost of evaluating processes and their outputs to ensure that a project is error-free or within an acceptable error range. Activities such as inspection and testing of products, maintenance of inspection and

test equipment, and processing and reporting inspection data all contribute to appraisal costs of quality.

3. **Internal failure cost**: A cost incurred to correct an identified defect before the customer receives the product. Items such as scrap and rework, charges related to late payment of bills, inventory costs that are a direct result of defects, costs of engineering changes related to correcting a design error, premature failure of products, and correcting documentation all contribute to internal failure cost.

4. **External failure cost**: A cost that relates to all errors not detected and corrected before delivery to the customer. Items such as warranty cost, field service personnel training cost, product liability suits, complaint handling, and future business losses are examples of external failure costs.

5. **Measurement and test equipment costs**: The capital cost of equipment used to perform prevention and appraisal activities.

Many industries tolerate a very low cost of nonconformance, but not the IT industry. Tom DeMarco is famous for several studies he conducted on the cost of nonconformance in the IT industry. In the early 1980s, DeMarco found that the average large company devoted more than 60 percent of its software development efforts to maintenance. Around 50 percent of development costs were typically spent on testing and debugging software.[24] Although these percentages may have improved some since the 1980s, they remain very high especially in light of the need to address computer security issues.

Top management is primarily responsible for the high cost of nonconformance in IT. Top managers often rush their organizations to develop new systems and do not give project teams enough time or resources to do a project right the first time. To correct these quality problems, top management must create a culture that embraces quality.

MEDIA SNAPSHOT

Computer viruses and malware software have been a quality concern for years. In a new twist, consumers are now being warned that e-cigarettes, though better for health, can be bad for computers.

According to the social media forum Reddit, an executive at a large corporation found a malware infection on his computer. His IT staff investigated the problem, and after looking at all traditional means of infection, they started looking at other possibilities. The executive said he had recently quit smoking and started using an e-cigarette made in China. IT found that the e-cigarette charger had malware hardcoded on it that phoned home and infected the computer after it was plugged into the USB port.

Technical security experts confirmed that anything, including e-cigarette chargers, can infect your computer if it can be inserted into a USB port. Dmitri Alperovitch, co-founder and chief technology officer of Crowd Strike, a cyber threat research firm, said the malware can then steal your files, capture your keystrokes, or turn on your web cam. He also said that if possible, use an electrical outlet instead of a USB port to charge devices, because you can't infect an outlet.[25]

continued

Although it is difficult to find reputable sources that confirm the problem-cigarette charger story, there are many other quality concerns with new consumer products. For example, several news agencies ran stories showing smart phone users that their whereabouts were being tracked if they did not turn off a certain feature. Owners of smart TVs are advised to turn off the voice recognition feature so manufacturers cannot eavesdrop on them. As you can see, IT can be used to create many innovative products that people want, but as the saying goes, "Let the buyer beware!"

8.8c The Impact of Organizational Influences, and Workplace Factors on Quality

A study by Tom DeMarco and Timothy Lister produced interesting results related to organizations and relative productivity. Starting in 1984, DeMarco and Lister conducted "Coding War Games" over several years; more than 600 software developers from 92 organizations participated. The games were designed to examine programming quality and productivity over a wide range of organizations, technical environments, and programming languages. The study demonstrated that organizational issues had a much greater influence on productivity than the technical environment or programming languages.

For example, DeMarco and Lister found that productivity varied by a factor of about one to 10 across all participants. That is, one team may have finished a coding project in one day while another team took 10 days to finish the same project. In contrast, productivity varied by an average of only 21 percent between pairs of software developers from the same organization. If one team from an organization finished a coding project in one day, the longest it took another team from the same organization to finish the project was 1.21 days.

DeMarco and Lister also found *no correlation* between productivity and programming language, years of experience, or salary. Furthermore, the study showed that providing a dedicated workspace and a quiet work environment were key factors in improving productivity. The results of the study suggested that top managers must focus on workplace factors to improve productivity and quality.[26]

In their book *Peopleware* DeMarco and Lister argue that major problems with work performance and project failures are not technological but sociological in nature.[27] They suggest minimizing office politics and giving smart people physical space, intellectual responsibility, and strategic direction—and then just *letting* them work. The manager's function is not to *make* people work but to make it possible for people to work by removing political roadblocks. The Agile Manifesto described in Chapter 2 reiterates this concept of focusing on individuals and interactions over processes and tools.

8.8d Expectations and Cultural Differences in Quality

Many experienced project managers know that a crucial aspect of project quality management is managing expectations. Although many aspects of quality can be clearly defined and measured, many cannot. Different project sponsors, customers, users, and other stakeholders have different expectations about various aspects of projects.

It's very important to understand these expectations and manage conflicts that might occur due to differences in expectations. For example, in the opening case, several users were upset when they could not access information within a few seconds. In the past, it may have been acceptable to wait two or three seconds for a system to load, but many of today's computer users expect systems to run much faster. Project managers and their teams must consider quality-related expectations as they define the project scope.

Expectations can also vary based on an organization's culture or geographic region. Anyone who has traveled to different parts of an organization, a country, or the world understands that expectations are not the same everywhere. For example, one department in a company might expect workers to be in their work areas most of the workday and to dress a certain way. Another department in the same company might focus on whether workers produce expected results, no matter where they work or how they dress.

People who work in other countries for the first time are often amazed at different quality expectations. Visitors to other countries may complain about things they once took for granted, such as easily making cell phone calls, using a train or subway instead of relying on a car for transportation, or getting up-to-date maps. It's important to realize that different countries are at different stages of development in terms of quality.

8.8e Maturity Models

Another approach to improving quality in software development projects and project management in general is the use of **maturity models**, which are frameworks for helping organizations improve their processes and systems. Maturity models describe an evolutionary path of increasingly organized and systematically more mature processes. Many maturity models have five levels, with the first level describing characteristics of the least organized or mature organizations and the fifth level describing characteristics of the most organized or mature organizations. Three popular maturity models include the Software Quality Function Deployment (SQFD) model, the Capability Maturity Model Integration (CMMI), and project management maturity models.

Software Quality Function Deployment Model

The **Software Quality Function Deployment (SQFD) model** is an adaptation of the quality function deployment model suggested in 1986 as an implementation vehicle for Total Quality Management (TQM). SQFD focuses on defining user requirements and planning software projects. The result of SQFD is a set of measurable technical product specifications and their priorities. Having clearer requirements can lead to fewer design changes, increased productivity, and, ultimately, software products that are more likely to satisfy stakeholder requirements. The idea of introducing quality early in the design stage was based on Taguchi's emphasis on Robust Design methods.[28]

Capability Maturity Model Integration

Another popular maturity model is in continuous development at the Software Engineering Institute (SEI) at Carnegie Mellon University. The SEI is a federally funded research and development center established in 1984 by the U.S. Department of Defense with a broad mandate to address the transition of software engineering technology. The **Capability Maturity Model Integration (CMMI)** is "a process improvement approach that provides organizations with the essential elements of effective processes. It can be used to guide process improvement across a project, a division, or an entire organization. CMMI helps integrate traditionally separate organizational functions, set process improvement goals and priorities, provide guidance for quality processes, and provide a point of reference for appraising current processes."

The capability levels of the CMMI are:

0. *Incomplete*: At this level, a process is either not performed or partially performed. No generic goals exist for this level, and one or more of the specific goals of the process area are not satisfied.

1. *Performed*: A performed process satisfies the specific goals of the process area and supports and enables the work needed to produce work products. Although this capability level can result in improvements, those improvements can be lost over time if they are not institutionalized.

2. *Managed*: At this level, a process has the basic infrastructure in place to support it. The process is planned and executed based on policies and employs skilled people who have adequate resources to produce controlled outputs. The process discipline reflected by this level ensures that existing practices are retained during times of stress.

3. *Defined*: At this maturity level, a process is rigorously defined. Standards, process descriptions, and procedures for each project are tailored from the organization's set of standard processes.

4. *Quantitatively managed*: At this level, a process is controlled using statistical and other quantitative techniques. The organization establishes quantitative objectives for quality and process performance that are used as criteria in managing the process.[29]

5. *Optimizing*: An optimizing process is improved based on an understanding of the common causes of variation inherent in the process. The focus is on continually improving the range of process performance through incremental and innovative improvements.[30]

Many companies that want to work in the government market have realized that they will not get many opportunities even to bid on projects unless they have a CMMI Level 3. According to one manager, "CMMI is really the future. People who aren't on the bandwagon now are going to find themselves falling behind."[31]

Project Management Maturity Models

In the late 1990s, several organizations began developing project management maturity models based on the CMMI. Just as organizations realized the need to improve their software development processes and systems, they also realized the need to enhance their project management processes and systems for all types of projects.

The PMI Standards Development Program published the first edition of the Organizational Project Management Maturity Model (OPM3) in December 2003 and the third edition was released in September 2013. More than 200 volunteers from around the world were part of the initial OPM3 team. The model is based on market research surveys that were sent to more than 30,000 project management professionals, and it incorporates

180 best practices and more than 2,400 capabilities, outcomes, and key performance indicators.[32] According to John Schlichter, the OPM3 program director, "The standard would help organizations to assess and improve their project management capabilities as well as the capabilities necessary to achieve organizational strategies through projects. The standard would be a project management maturity model, setting the standard for excellence in project, program, and portfolio management best practices, and explaining the capabilities necessary to achieve those best practices."[33]

BEST PRACTICE

OPM3 provides the following example to illustrate a best practice, capability, outcome, and key performance indicator:

- *Best practice*: Establish internal project management communities
- *Capability*: Facilitate project management activities
- *Outcome*: Establish local initiatives, meaning the organization develops pockets of consensus around areas of special interest
- *Key performance indicator*: The community addresses local issues

Best practices are organized into three levels: project, program, and portfolio. Within each of those categories, best practices are categorized by four stages of process improvement: standardize, measure, control, and improve. For example, the following list contains several best practices listed in OPM3:

- Project best practices:
  - Project Initiation Process Standardization
  - Project Plan Development Process Measurement
  - Project Scope Planning Process Control
  - Project Scope Definition Process Improvement
- Program best practices:
  - Program Activity Definition Process Standardization
  - Program Activity Sequencing Process Measurement
  - Program Activity Duration Estimating Process Control
  - Program Schedule Development Process Improvement
- Portfolio best practices:
  - Portfolio Resource Planning Process Standardization
  - Portfolio Cost Estimating Process Measurement
  - Portfolio Cost Budgeting Process Control
  - Portfolio Risk Management Planning Process Improvement[34]

Several other companies provide similar project management maturity models. The International Institute for Learning, Inc., has five levels in its model called common language, common processes, singular methodology, benchmarking, and continuous improvement. ESI International Inc.'s model has five levels called ad hoc, consistent, integrated, comprehensive, and optimizing. Regardless of the names of each level, the goal is clear: Organizations want to improve their ability to manage projects. Many organizations are assessing where they stand in terms of project management maturity, just as they did for software development maturity with the SQFD and CMMI maturity models. Organizations are recognizing that they must make a commitment to the discipline of project management to improve project quality.

8.9 USING SOFTWARE TO ASSIST IN PROJECT QUALITY MANAGEMENT

This chapter provides examples of several tools and techniques used in project quality management. Software can be used to assist with several of these tools and techniques. For example, you can use spreadsheet and charting software to create charts and diagrams from many of the Seven Basic Tools of Quality. You can use statistical software packages to help you determine standard deviations and perform many types of statistical analyses. You can create Gantt charts using project management software to help you plan and track work related to project quality management. Specialized software products can assist people with managing Six Sigma projects, creating quality control charts, and assessing maturity levels. Project teams need to decide what types of software will help them manage their particular projects.

As you can see, quality is a very broad topic, and it is only one of the 10 project management knowledge areas. Project managers must focus on defining how quality relates to their specific projects and ensure that those projects satisfy the needs for which they were undertaken.

CASE WRAP-UP

Scott Daniels assembled a team to identify and resolve quality-related issues with the EIS and to develop a plan to help the medical instruments company prevent future quality problems. The team's first task was to research the problems with the EIS. The team created a cause-and-effect diagram similar to the one in Figure 8-2. The team also created a Pareto chart (see Figure 8-7) to help analyze the many complaints the Help Desk received and documented about the EIS. After further investigation, Scott and his team found that many managers using the system were very inexperienced in using computers beyond basic office automation systems. They also found that most users received no training on how to properly access or use the new EIS. The team found no major problems with the EIS hardware or the users' individual computers. The complaints about reports not giving consistent information all came from one manager, who had actually misread the reports, so there were no problems with the software design. Scott was very impressed with the quality of the entire project, except for the training. Scott reported his team's findings to the project sponsor of the EIS, who was relieved to find out that the quality problems were not as serious as many people feared.

Chapter Summary

Quality is a serious issue. Mistakes in several mission-critical IT systems have caused deaths, and quality problems in many business systems have resulted in major financial losses.

Customers are ultimately responsible for defining quality. Important quality concepts include satisfying stated or implied stakeholder needs, conforming to requirements, and delivering items that are fit for use.

Project quality management includes planning quality management, performing quality assurance, and controlling quality. Planning quality management identifies which quality standards are relevant to the project and how to satisfy them. Performing quality assurance involves evaluating overall project performance to ensure that the project will satisfy the relevant quality standards. Controlling quality includes monitoring specific project results to ensure that they comply with quality standards and identifying ways to improve overall quality.

Many tools and techniques are related to project quality management. The Seven Basic Tools of Quality include cause-and-effect diagrams, control charts, checksheets, scatter diagrams, histograms, Pareto charts, and flowcharts. Statistical sampling helps define a realistic number of items to include when analyzing a population. Six Sigma helps companies improve quality by reducing defects. Standard deviation measures the variation in data. Testing is very important in developing and delivering high-quality IT products.

Many people made significant contributions to the development of modern quality management, including Deming, Juran, Crosby, Ishikawa, Taguchi, and Feigenbaum. Many organizations today use their ideas, which also influenced Six Sigma principles. The Malcolm Baldrige National Quality Award and ISO 9000 have also helped organizations emphasize the importance of improving quality.

There is much room for improvement in IT project quality. Strong leadership helps emphasize the importance of quality. Understanding the cost of quality provides an incentive for its improvement. Providing a good workplace can improve quality and productivity. Understanding stakeholders' expectations and cultural differences are also related to project quality management. Developing and following maturity models can help organizations systematically improve their project management processes to increase the quality and success rate of projects.

Several types of software are available to assist in project quality management. It is important for project teams to decide which software will be most helpful for their particular projects.

Quick Quiz

1. _____ is the degree to which a set of inherent characteristics fulfills requirements.
   a. Quality
   b. Conformance to requirements
   c. Fitness for use
   d. Reliability

2. What is the purpose of project quality management?
   a. to produce the highest-quality products and services possible
   b. to ensure that appropriate quality standards are met
   c. to ensure that the project will satisfy the needs for which it was undertaken
   d. all of the above

3. _____ generates ideas for quality improvements by comparing specific project practices or product characteristics to those of other projects or products within or outside the performing organization.

    a. Quality audits

    b. Design of experiments

    c. Six Sigma

    d. Benchmarking

4. What does the term *kaizen* mean?

    a. minimize waste

    b. maximize value

    c. do it right the first time

    d. improvement

5. What tool can you use to determine whether a process is in control or out of control?

    a. a cause-and-effect diagram

    b. a control chart

    c. a run chart

    d. a control panel diagram

6. Six Sigma's target for perfection is the achievement of no more than _____ defects, errors, or mistakes per million opportunities.

    a. 6

    b. 9

    c. 3.4

    d. 1

7. The seven run rule states that if seven data points in a row on a control chart are all below the mean, above the mean, or all increasing or decreasing, then the process needs to be examined for _____ problems.

    a. random

    b. nonrandom

    c. Six Sigma

    d. quality

8. What is the preferred order for performing testing on IT projects?

    a. unit testing, integration testing, system testing, user acceptance testing

    b. unit testing, system testing, integration testing, user acceptance testing

    c. unit testing, system testing, user acceptance testing, integration testing

    d. unit testing, integration testing, user acceptance testing, system testing

9. _____ is known for his work on quality control in Japan, and he developed the 14 Points for Management in his text *Out of the Crisis*.

    a. Juran

    b. Deming

    c. Crosby

    d. Ishikawa

10. PMI's OPM3 is an example of a _____ model or framework for helping organizations improve their processes and systems.

    a. benchmarking

    b. Six Sigma

    c. maturity

    d. quality

Quick Quiz Answers

1. a; 2. c; 3. d; 4. d; 5. b; 6. c; 7. b; 8. a; 9. b; 10. c

Discussion Questions

1. Discuss some of the examples of poor quality in IT projects presented in the "What Went Wrong?" section. Could most of these problems have been avoided? Why do you think there are so many examples of poor quality in IT projects?

2. What are the main processes in project quality management?

3. Why is quality assurance becoming more important? What does it mean to use lean in quality assurance?

4. How do functionality, system outputs, performance, reliability, and maintainability requirements affect quality planning?

5. What are benchmarks, and how can they assist in performing quality assurance? Describe typical benchmarks associated with a college or university.

6. What are the three main categories of outputs for quality control?

7. Provide examples of when you would use at least three of the Seven Basic Tools of Quality on an IT project.

8. Discuss the history of modern quality management. How have experts such as Deming, Juran, Crosby, and Taguchi affected the quality movement and today's use of lean and Six Sigma?

9. Discuss three suggestions for improving IT project quality that were not made in this chapter.

10. Describe three types of software that can assist in project quality management.

Exercises

1. Assume that your organization wants to hire new instructors for your project management course. Develop a list of quality standards that you could use in making this hiring decision. Suppose that some current instructors do not meet these standards. Provide suggestions for how you would handle this situation.

2. Create a Pareto chart based on the information in the following table. First, create a spreadsheet in Excel using the data in the table. List the most frequent customer problems first. Use the Excel template called pareto_chart.xls on the text's companion website and check your entries so your resulting chart looks similar to the one in Figure 8-7. If you need assistance creating the chart, search for videos describing how to create Pareto charts using Excel.

Customer Complaints	Frequency/Week
Customer is on hold too long	90
Customer gets transferred to wrong area or cut off	20
Service rep cannot answer customer's questions	120
Service rep does not follow through as promised	40

3. To illustrate a normal distribution, roll a pair of dice 30 times and graph the results. You are more likely to roll a 6, 7, or 8 than a 2 or 12. To create the graph, use Excel or draw one by hand. Label the x-axis with the numbers 2 through 12. Label the y-axis with the numbers 1 through 10. Fill in the appropriate grid for each roll of the dice. Do your results resemble a normal distribution? Why or why not?

4. Research the criteria for the Malcolm Baldrige National Quality Award or a similar quality award provided by another organization. Investigate a company that has received this award. What steps did the company take to earn it? What are the benefits of earning a quality award? Summarize your findings in a short paper to management.

5. Review the information in this chapter about Six Sigma principles and Six Sigma organizations. Brainstorm ideas for a potential Six Sigma project that could improve quality on your campus, at your workplace, or in your community. Write a short paper describing one project idea and explain why it would be a Six Sigma project. Review and discuss how you could use the DMAIC process on this project.

6. Research information on performing quality assurance using lean. How can lean be used on IT projects? How can you use kanban cards, a lean tool, to maximize customer value while minimizing waste?

7. Review the concepts in this chapter that are related to improving the quality of software. Write a short paper describing how you could apply these concepts to software development projects.

Running Case

Part 5: Project Quality Management

The Global Treps Project team is working hard to ensure they meet expectations, especially for the people who will be holding and participating in the four events. The team has a detailed scope statement, but you want to make sure you are not forgetting requirements that might affect how people view the quality of the project. You knows that the project's sponsor and other key stakeholders are most concerned with getting people to use the new website, having successful events, and helping promote entrepreneurship across the globe. You also know that various geographic and cultural issues will need to be addressed.

Tasks

1. Develop a list of quality standards or requirements related to meeting the stakeholder expectations described in the running case. Provide a brief description of each requirement. For example, two requirements related to the new website might be that users can read the content in several different languages and that users provide good ratings for the online video training.

2. Based on the list you created for Task 1, determine how you will measure progress on meeting the requirements. For example, you might have people take a survey after they view the online training videos to collect feedback.

3. After analyzing survey information, you decide to create a Pareto chart to see which types of guidelines for running an event generated the most interest. First, create a spreadsheet in Excel using the data in the following table. List the most frequently requested guidelines first. Use the Excel template called pareto_chart.xls on the text's companion website and check your entries so the resulting chart looks similar to the one in Figure 8-7.

Requested Guidelines	# of Times Requested
How to find good participants	24
How participants should present their ideas	20
How to find local sharks	15
How to select participants	12
How to manage and engage the audience	7
How to set up the facilities	3

Key Terms

5 whys p.308

acceptance decisions p.307

appraisal cost p.327

benchmarking p.306

Capability Maturity Model Integration (CMMI) p.331

cause-and-effect diagram p.308

checksheet p.310

End Notes

[1] This joke was found on hundreds of websites and printed in the *Consultants in Minnesota Newsletter*, Independent Computer Consultants Association (December 1998).

[2] *Design News* (February 1988).

[3] *Datamation* (May 1987).

[4] *New York Times* (February 18, 1994).

5 Lee Munson, "Three Charged over Largest Email Hack 'in the History of the Internet'," *Naked Security* (March 9, 2015).

6 David J. Anderson, *Kanban* (Seattle WA: Blue Hole Press Inc, 2013).

7 Peter S. Pande, Robert P. Neuman, and Roland R.Cavanagh, *The Six Sigma Way* (New York: McGraw-Hill, 2000), p. xi.

8 James C. Collins and Jerry I. Porras, *Built to Last: Successful Habits of Visionary Companies* (New York: Harper Business, 1994).

9 "What You Need to Know About Six Sigma," *Productivity Digest* (December 2001), p. 38.

10 Peter S. Pande, Robert P. Neuman, and Roland R. Cavanagh, *The Six Sigma Way* (New York: McGraw-Hill, 2000), p. 137.

11 Lee Clifford, "Why You Can Safely Ignore Six Sigma," *Fortune* (January 22, 2001), p. 140.

12 Hollstadt & Associates, Inc., *Software Development Project Life Cycle Testing Methodology User's Manual* (Burnsville: MN, August 1998), p. 13.

13 Bart Eisenberg, "Achieving Zero-Defects Software," *Pacific Connection* (January 2004).

14 Harold Kerzner, *Project Management*, sixth edition (New York: Van Nostrand Reinhold, 1998), p. 1048.

15 W. Edwards Deming, *Out of the Crisis* (Boston: MIT Press, 1986).

16 Joseph M. Juran and A. Blanton Godfrey, *Juran's Quality Handbook*, fifth edition (New York: McGraw-Hill Professional, 2000).

17 Philip B. Crosby, *Quality Is Free: The Art of Making Quality Certain* (New York: McGraw-Hill, 1979).

18 Kaoru Ishikawa, *Guide to Quality Control*, second edition (Asian Productivity Organization, 1986).

19 Gene Bylinsky, "How to Bring Out Better Products Faster," *Fortune* (November 23, 1998), p. 238[B].

20 Armand V. Feigenbaum, *Total Quality Control: Engineering and Management*, third rev. edition (New York: McGraw-Hill, 1991).

21 Elizabeth Gasiorowski Denis, "Integrating Information Security and Service management—A New ISO/IEC Standard Tells How," *www.iso.org/iso/news.htm?refid=Ref1696* (January 16, 2013).

22 Chris Urmson, "The View from the Front Seat of the Google Self-Driving Car," *Back Channel* (May 11, 2015).

23 American Society for Quality (ASQ), "About ASQ: Joseph M. Juran," *ASQ.com* (*www.asq.org/about-asq/who-we-are/bio_juran.html*).

24 Tom DeMarco, *Quality Controlling Software Projects: Management, Measurement and Estimation* (New Jersey: Prentice Hall PTR Facsimile Edition, 1986).

25 Ellen Nakashima, "Are E-Cigs Bad for Your Computer?" *The Washington Post* (November 24, 2014).

26 Tom DeMarco and Timothy Lister, *Peopleware: Productive Projects and Teams* (New York: Dorset House, 1987).

27 Tom DeMarco and Timothy Lister, *Peopleware: Productive Projects and Teams*, second edition (New York: Dorset House, 1999).

28 R. R.Yilmaz and Sangit Chatterjee, "Deming and the Quality of Software Development," *Business Horizons* [Foundation for the School of Business at Indiana University] 40, no. 6 (November–December 1997), pp. 51–58.

29 Software Engineering Institute, Carnegie Mellon, "What is CMMI," *www.sei.cmu.edu/cmmi/general/index.html* (January 2007).

30 CMMI Product Team, "CMMI® for Development, Version 1.2," CMU/SEI–2006–TR–008 ESC–TR–2006–008 (August 2006).

31 Michael Hardy, "Strength in Numbers: New Maturity Ratings Scheme Wins Support Among Systems Integrators," *FCW.com* (March 28, 2004).

32 John Schlichter, "The Project Management Institute's Organizational Project Management Maturity Model: An Update on the PMI's OPM3® Program," *PMForum.com* (September 2002).

33 John Schlichter, "The History of OPM3®," *Project Management World Today* (June 2003).

34 Project Management Institute, *Organizational Project Management Maturity Model (OPM3®)*, Third Edition (2013).

CHAPTER **9**

PROJECT HUMAN RESOURCE MANAGEMENT

OPENING CASE

This was the third time someone from the Information Technology (IT) department tried to work with Ben, the head of the F-44 radar upgrade project. The F-44 was one of five aircraft programs in the company. The company had program managers in charge of each aircraft program, with several project managers reporting to them. Workers supporting each project were part of a matrix organization, with people from engineering, IT, manufacturing, sales, and other departments allocated as needed to each project.

Ben had been with the company for almost 30 years, and was known for being "rough around the edges" and very demanding. The company was losing money on the F-44 radar upgrade project because the upgrade kits were not being delivered on time. The Canadian government had written severe late-penalty fees into its contract, and other customers were threatening to take their business elsewhere. Ben blamed it all on the IT department for not letting his staff access the upgrade project's information system directly so they could work with their customers and suppliers more effectively. The information system was based on very old technology that only a couple of people in the company knew how to use. It often took days or even weeks for Ben's group to get the information they needed.

Ed Davidson, a senior programmer, attended a meeting with Sarah Ellis, an internal IT business consultant. Sarah was in her early thirties and had advanced quickly in her company, primarily due to her keen ability to work well with all types of people. Sarah's job was to uncover the real problems with IT support for the F-44 radar upgrade project, and then develop a solution with Ben and his team. If she found it necessary to invest in more IT hardware, software, or staff, Sarah would write a business case to justify these investments and then work with Ed, Ben, and his group to implement the suggested solution as quickly as possible.

Ben and three of his project team members entered the conference room. Ben threw his books on the table and started yelling at Ed and Sarah. Ed could not believe his eyes or ears when Sarah stood nose to nose with Ben and started yelling right back at him.

9.1 THE IMPORTANCE OF HUMAN RESOURCE MANAGEMENT

Many corporate executives have said, "People are our most important asset." People determine the success and failure of organizations and projects. Most project managers agree that managing human resources effectively is one of the toughest challenges they face. Project human resource management is a vital component of project management, especially in the IT field—in which qualified people are often hard to find and keep. It is important to understand global IT workforce issues and their implications for the future.

9.1a The Global IT Workforce

Although the IT labor market has had its ups and down, there will always be a need for people to develop and maintain IT hardware, software, networks, and applications. The global job market for IT workers is expanding, and the demand for project managers continues to increase:

- By the end of 2014, there were almost 3 billion Internet users and 2.3 billion mobile-broadband subscriptions. Two-thirds of Internet users were from developing countries, as were 55 percent of mobile-broadband subscriptions. Mobile-cellular subscriptions reached almost 7 billion, and over half were from the Asia-Pacific region.[1] By 2025, 100 billion connections will be generated globally, and 90 percent will come from intelligent sensors.[2]

- By 2020, global information and communications technology (ICT) spending is projected to grow to nearly $5 trillion.[3] A survey of IT executives showed that IT budgets were expected to increase by 4.3%. "IT is expected to again kick up spending on security tools, customer-facing technologies and information exchange/collaboration technologies that comprise the so-called SMAC stack — social and mobile tools, analytic systems and cloud computing. Meanwhile, it's likely that hardware spending will continue to drop and services budgets will continue to rise."[4]

- Project management was number two on *Computerworld*'s hottest skill list for 2015, moving up from number five in 2014 and just behind programming/application development.[5]

- PMI estimates demand for 15.7 million project management jobs from 2010 to 2020, with 6.2 million of those jobs in the United States.[6]

These studies highlight the need for skilled IT workers and project managers. As the economy changes and technology progresses, however, people need to continually upgrade their skills to remain marketable and flexible. Negotiation and presentation skills are also crucial to finding and keeping a good job. Workers need to know how they personally contribute to an organization's bottom line and how they can continue to do so.

9.1b Implications for the Future of IT Human Resource Management

It is crucial for organizations to practice what they preach about human resources. If people truly are their greatest asset, organizations must work to fulfill their human resource needs *and* the needs of individual people in their organizations, regardless of the job market. If organizations want to implement IT projects successfully, they need to understand the importance of project human resource management and make effective use of people.

Proactive organizations address current and future human resource needs by improving benefits, redefining work hours and incentives, and finding future workers. Many organizations have changed their benefits policies to meet worker needs. Most workers assume that companies provide some perks, such as casual dress codes, flexible work hours, on-the-job training, continuing education, and tuition assistance. Other companies might provide on-site day care, fitness club discounts, or matching contributions to retirement savings. Google, the winner of *Fortune*'s 100 Best Companies award six times in recent years, provides employees with free gourmet meals, on-site doctors, a swimming spa and corporate gym, beach volleyball, Foosball, video games, pool tables, ping-pong, roller hockey, and weekly Thank Goodness It's Friday (TGIF) parties! Google built a large, outdoor sports complex in 2011 to help keep its employees in shape. The company also provides indoor recreation with bowling alleys and a dance studio, and offers a generous amount of leave for new parents (regardless of gender, including dads, domestic partners, adoptive parents, and surrogate parents)—twelve weeks of fully paid "baby bonding" plus $500.[7] With an average of 130 applicants per hire, it's almost ten times harder to get a job at Google than it is to get into Harvard.

Other trends affecting the future of human resource management relate to the hours that organizations expect many IT professionals to work and how they reward performance. Today people are happier when they can work *less* than 40 hours a week or work from home. If companies plan their projects well, they can avoid the need for overtime, or they can make it clear that overtime is optional. Many companies also outsource more of their project work to manage the fluctuating demand for workers, as described in Chapter 12, Project Procurement Management.

Companies can also provide incentives that use performance, not hours worked, as the basis of rewards. If performance can be measured objectively, as it can in many aspects of IT jobs, then it should not matter where employees do their work or how long it takes. For example, if a technical writer can produce a high-quality publication at home in one week, the company should accept the arrangement instead of insisting that the writer come to the office and take two weeks to produce the publication. Objective measures of work performance and incentives based on meeting those criteria are important considerations.

 GLOBAL ISSUES

In early 2013, Marissa Meyer, Yahoo's CEO, issued a memo stating that Yahoo employees could no longer work from home. She believed that people needed to work side-by-side to have the best communication and collaboration. This new policy caused quite a stir throughout the world as workers and managers discussed the pros and cons of working from home.

Another CEO, Andy Mattes at Diebold, which makes ATMs, took the exact opposite approach as Meyer and started recruiting employees who wanted to work from home. He told *The Huffington Post* that he wanted to lure the best and brightest workers away from Yahoo, HP, Oracle, and other companies cutting back on telecommuting.

Which CEO has the right approach? *The Huffington Post* would vote for Andy Mattes. "Now, two years later, it's clear: Telecommuting has won. Even Yahoo seems to have softened its stance. Workers inside the company told HuffPost that some employees still do occasionally work from home, depending on their job, and some do not have a desk in the office. Yahoo declined to comment for this article."[8]

The need to develop future talent in IT has important implications for everyone. Who will maintain the systems we have today when the last of the "baby boomer" generation retires? Who will continue to develop new technologies and innovative products based on them? Some schools require all students to take computer literacy courses, although most teenagers today already know how to use computers, iPods, iPads, cell phones, and other technologies. But are today's children learning the skills they'll need to develop new technologies and work on global teams? As the workforce becomes more diverse, will more women and minorities be ready and willing to enter IT fields? Several colleges, government agencies, and private groups have programs to help recruit more women and minorities into technical fields. Some companies provide options to assist employees who desire work-life integration. Today's efforts to come up with innovative ways to address these issues will help to develop the human resources needed for future IT projects.

⊗ WHAT WENT WRONG?

A 2014 report by CompTIA found a gap between skills that employers wanted and what they actually found in the IT workforce.

- Even with 5.73 million people working in the U.S. IT industry, 68 percent of IT firms report having a "very challenging" time finding new staff.
- Fifty-two percent of organizations report having job openings, and 33 percent say they are understaffed, while 42 percent say they are fully staffed but want to hire more people in order to expand.
- Fifty-eight percent of businesses are concerned about the quality and quantity of IT talent available for hire.
- Top technology priorities in this survey included security, data storage, and network infrastructure.
- The number one strategy to handle understaffing is requiring workers to put in more hours.
- Ninety-four percent of IT professionals plan to pursue more training.[9]

9.2 WHAT IS PROJECT HUMAN RESOURCE MANAGEMENT?

Project human resource management includes the processes required to make the most effective use of the people involved with a project. Human resource management includes all project stakeholders: sponsors, customers, project team members, support staff, suppliers supporting the project, and so on. Human resource management includes the following four processes:

1. *Planning human resource management* involves identifying and documenting project roles, responsibilities, and reporting relationships. The main output of this process is a human resource plan.
2. *Acquiring the project team* involves assigning the needed personnel to work on the project. Key outputs of this process are project staff assignments, resource calendars, and project management plan updates.
3. *Developing the project team* involves building individual and group skills to enhance project performance. Team-building skills are often a challenge for many project managers. The main outputs of this process are team performance assessments and enterprise environmental factors updates.
4. *Managing the project team* involves tracking team member performance, motivating team members, providing timely feedback, resolving issues and conflicts, and coordinating changes to help enhance project performance. Outputs of this process include change requests, project management plan updates, project documents updates, enterprise environmental factors updates, and organizational process assets updates.

Figure 9-1 summarizes these processes and outputs, showing when they occur in a typical project.

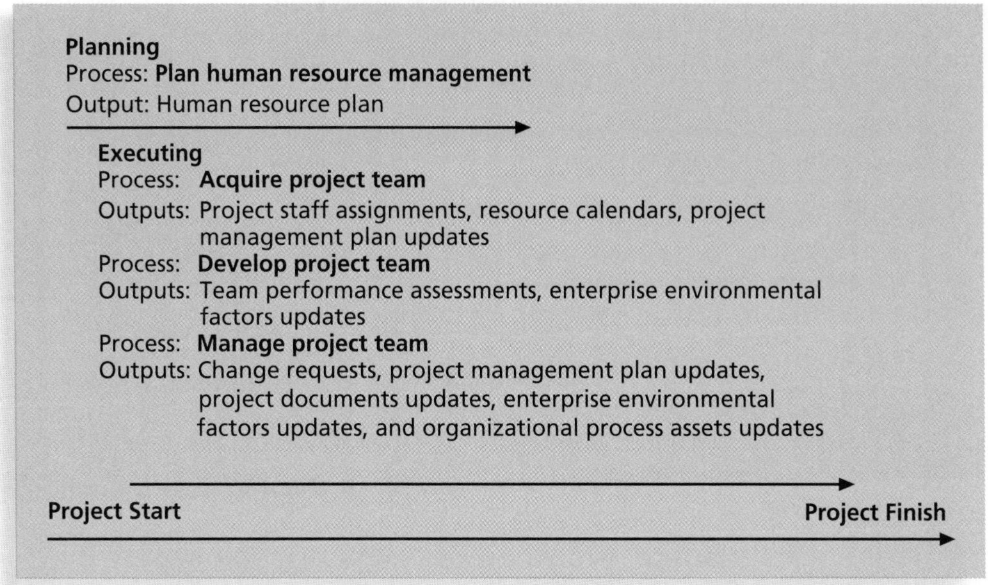

Planning
Process: **Plan human resource management**
Output: Human resource plan

Executing
Process: **Acquire project team**
Outputs: Project staff assignments, resource calendars, project
management plan updates
Process: **Develop project team**
Outputs: Team performance assessments, enterprise environmental
factors updates
Process: **Manage project team**
Outputs: Change requests, project management plan updates,
project documents updates, enterprise environmental
factors updates, and organizational process assets updates

Project Start   **Project Finish**

© Cengage Learning 2016

FIGURE 9-1   Project human resource management summary

You were introduced to several topics related to human resource management, including understanding organizations, stakeholders, and different organizational structures, in Chapter 2, The Project Management and Information Technology Context. You will learn about other related issues in Chapter 13, Project Stakeholder Management. This chapter expands on some of those topics and introduces other important concepts in project human resource management, including theories about managing and leading people, resource loading, and resource leveling. You also learn how to use software to assist in project human resource management.

9.3 KEYS TO MANAGING AND LEADING PEOPLE

Industrial-organizational psychologists and management theorists have devoted extensive research and thought to the field of managing and leading people at work. Psychosocial issues that affect how people work and how well they work include motivation, influence and power, effectiveness, emotional intelligence, and leadership. This section reviews the contributions of Abraham Maslow, Frederick Herzberg, David McClelland, and Douglas McGregor to an understanding of motivation; the work of H. J. Thamhain and D. L. Wilemon on influencing workers and reducing conflict; the effect of power on project teams; Stephen Covey's work on how people and teams can become more effective; Howard Gardner and Daniel Goleman's focus on emotional intelligence; and recent research on leadership. The final part of this section looks at some implications and recommendations for project managers.

9.3a Motivation Theories

Psychologists, managers, coworkers, teachers, parents, and most people in general struggle to understand what motivates people to do what they do. **Intrinsic motivation** causes people to participate in an activity for their own enjoyment. For example, some people love to read, write, or play an instrument because it makes them feel good. **Extrinsic motivation** causes people to do something for a reward or to avoid a penalty. For example, some young children would prefer *not* to play an instrument, but they do because they receive a reward or avoid a punishment for doing so. Why do some people require no external motivation to produce high-quality work while others require significant external motivation to perform routine tasks? Why can't you get someone who is extremely productive at work to do simple tasks at home? Humankind is fascinated with asking and trying to answer these types of questions. A basic understanding of motivational theory will help anyone who works or lives with other people to understand themselves and others. Keep in mind that the following are brief summaries, and you are encouraged to research these topics further, especially as they relate to working with people on projects.

Maslow's Hierarchy of Needs

Abraham Maslow, a highly respected psychologist who rejected the dehumanizing negativism of psychology in the 1950s, is best known for developing a hierarchy of needs. In the 1950s, proponents of Sigmund Freud's psychoanalytic theory promoted the idea that human beings were not the masters of their destiny and that all their actions were governed by unconscious processes dominated by primitive sexual urges. During the same period, behavioral psychologists saw human beings as controlled by the environment. Maslow argued that both schools of thought failed to recognize unique qualities of human behavior: love, self-esteem, belonging, self-expression, and creativity. He argued that these unique qualities enable people to make independent choices, which gives them full control of their destiny.

Figure 9-2 shows the basic pyramid structure of Maslow's **hierarchy of needs**, which states that people's behaviors are guided or motivated by a sequence of needs. At the bottom of the hierarchy are physiological needs. Once physiological needs are satisfied, safety needs guide behavior. Once safety needs are satisfied, social needs come to the forefront, and so on up the hierarchy. The order of these needs and their relative sizes in the pyramid are significant. Maslow suggests that each level of the hierarchy is a prerequisite for the levels above. A person cannot consider self-actualization without first addressing basic needs of security and safety. For example, people in an emergency, such as a flood or hurricane, do not worry about personal growth. Personal survival will be their main motivation. Once a particular need is satisfied, however, it no longer serves as a potent motivator of behavior.

The bottom four needs in Maslow's hierarchy—physiological, safety, social, and esteem—are referred to as deficiency needs, and the highest level, self-actualization, is considered a growth need. Only after meeting deficiency needs can people act upon growth needs. Self-actualized people are problem-focused, have an appreciation for life, are concerned about personal growth, and are able to have peak experiences.

Most people working on an IT project probably have their basic physiological and safety needs met. If someone has a sudden medical emergency or is laid off from work, however, physiological and safety needs will move to the forefront. The project manager needs to understand each team member's motivation, especially with regard to social, esteem, and self-actualization or growth needs. Team members who are new to a company

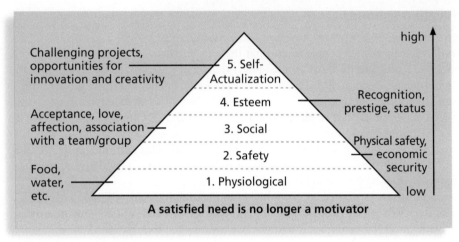

© Cengage Learning 2016

FIGURE 9-2   Maslow's hierarchy of needs

and city might be motivated by social needs. To address social needs, some companies organize gatherings and social events for new workers. Other project members may find these events to be an invasion of personal time that they would rather spend with their friends and family, or working on an advanced degree.

Maslow's hierarchy conveys a message of hope and growth. People can work to control their own destinies and naturally strive to satisfy higher needs. Successful project managers know they must focus on meeting project goals, but they also must understand team members' personal goals and needs to provide appropriate motivation and maximize team performance.

Herzberg's Motivation-Hygiene Theory

Frederick Herzberg is best known for distinguishing between motivational factors and hygiene factors when considering motivation in work settings. He referred to factors that cause job satisfaction as motivators and factors that could cause dissatisfaction as hygiene factors.

Herzberg was the head of Case Western University's psychology department, and he wrote the book *Work and the Nature of Man* in 1966 and a famous *Harvard Business Review* article, "One More Time: How Do You Motivate Employees?" in 1968.[10] Herzberg analyzed the factors that affected productivity among a sample of 1,685 employees. Popular beliefs at the time were that work output was most improved through larger salaries, more supervision, or a more attractive work environment. According to Herzberg, these hygiene factors would cause dissatisfaction if not present, but would not motivate workers to do more if present. Today, professionals might also expect employers to provide health benefits, training, and a computer or other equipment required to perform their jobs. Herzberg found that people were motivated to work mostly by feelings of personal achievement and recognition. Motivators, Herzberg concluded, included achievement, recognition, the work itself, responsibility, advancement, and growth, as shown in Table 9-1.

TABLE 9-1 Examples of Herzberg's Hygiene Factors and Motivators

Hygiene Factors	Motivators
Larger salaries	Achievement
More supervision	Recognition
More attractive work environment	Work itself
Computer or other required equipment	Responsibility
Health benefits	Advancement
Training	Growth

© Cengage Learning 2016

In his books and articles, Herzberg explained why companies could not instill motivation by attempting to use positive factors such as reducing time spent at work, increasing wages, offering fringe benefits, and providing human relations and sensitivity training. He argued that people want to actualize themselves by being able to use their creativity and work on challenging projects. They need stimuli to grow and advance, in accordance with Maslow's hierarchy of needs. Factors such as achievement, recognition, responsibility, advancement, and growth produce job satisfaction and are work motivators.

MEDIA SNAPSHOT

Books and articles are written every year on the topic of human motivation. Videos are also popular on this subject, especially one by Daniel Pink. RSA Animate used its popular whiteboard drawing technique to summarize key points from Pink's book in a YouTube video called "Drive: The surprising truth about what motivates us." Pink narrates the video, summarizing several studies that suggest money often causes people to perform *worse* on tasks that involve cognitive skills. He suggests that organizations should pay people enough to eliminate resentments over money and stop using the carrot-and-stick approach to motivation. Pink also suggests that managers focus on the following three motivators:

- *Autonomy*: People like to be self-directed and have freedom in their work. Maslow, Herzberg, and other researchers also found that people are motivated by autonomy. Pink gives an example of how an Australian software company called Atlassian lets people decide what they want to work on, and with whom, for one day every quarter. Workers show the results of their work that day in a fun meeting. This one day of total autonomy has produced a large number of new products and fixes to problems.
- *Mastery*: People like to improve their skills, such as playing an instrument, participating in a sport, writing software, and mastering work-related activities. Pink states that several products like UNIX, Apache, and Wikipedia were created because people enjoyed the challenge and mastery involved.

continued

> • *Purpose:* People want to work for a good purpose. When the profit motive is separated from the purpose motive, people notice and do not perform as well. Many great products were created for a purpose. For example, the founder of Skype wanted to make the world a better place, and Steve Jobs, the co-founder of Apple, wanted to put a "ding in the universe."[11]

McClelland's Acquired-Needs Theory

David McClelland proposed that a person's specific needs are acquired or learned over time and shaped by life experiences. The main categories of acquired needs include achievement, affiliation, and power.[12] Normally, one or two of these needs are dominant in people.

- *Achievement:* People who have a high need for achievement (nAch) seek to excel, and tend to avoid both low-risk and high-risk situations to improve their chances for achieving something worthwhile. Achievers need regular feedback and often prefer to work alone or with other high achievers. Managers should give high achievers challenging projects with achievable goals. Achievers should receive frequent performance feedback, and although money is not an important motivator to them, it is an effective form of feedback.
- *Affiliation:* People with a high need for affiliation (nAff) desire harmonious relationships with other people and need to feel accepted by others. They tend to conform to the norms of their work group and prefer work that involves significant personal interaction. Managers should try to create a cooperative work environment to meet the needs of people with a high need for affiliation.
- *Power:* People with a need for power (nPow) desire either personal power or institutional power. People who need personal power want to direct others and can be seen as bossy. People who need institutional power or social power want to organize others to further the goals of the organization. Management should provide such employees with the opportunity to manage others, emphasizing the importance of meeting organizational goals.

The Thematic Apperception Test (TAT) is a tool to measure the individual needs of different people using McClelland's categories. The TAT presents subjects with a series of ambiguous pictures and asks them to develop a spontaneous story for each picture, assuming they will project their own needs into the story.

McGregor's Theory X and Theory Y

Douglas McGregor was one of the great popularizers of a human relations approach to management, and he is best known for developing Theory X and Theory Y. In his research, documented in his 1960 book *The Human Side of Enterprise*, McGregor found that although many managers spouted the right ideas, they actually followed a set of assumptions about worker motivation that he called *Theory X* (sometimes referred to as classical systems theory).[13] People who believe in Theory X assume that workers dislike and avoid work if possible, so managers must use coercion, threats, and various control schemes to have workers make adequate efforts to meet objectives. They assume that the average worker wants to be directed and prefers to avoid responsibility, has little ambition, and wants security above all else. Research clearly demonstrated that these assumptions were not valid. McGregor suggested a different series of assumptions about human behavior that he called *Theory Y* (sometimes referred to as human relations theory). Managers who believe in Theory Y assume that employees do not inherently dislike work, but consider it as natural as play or rest. The most significant rewards are the satisfaction of esteem and self-actualization needs, as described by Maslow. McGregor urged managers to motivate people based on Theory Y notions.

In 1981, William Ouchi introduced another approach to management in his book *Theory Z: How American Business Can Meet the Japanese Challenge*.[14] Theory Z is based on the Japanese approach to motivating workers, which emphasizes trust, quality, collective decision making, and cultural values. Whereas Theory X and Theory Y emphasize how management views employees, Theory Z also describes how workers perceive management. Theory Z workers, it is assumed, can be trusted to do their jobs to their utmost ability, as long as management can be trusted to support them and look out for their well-being. Theory Z emphasizes job rotation, broadening of skills, generalization versus specialization, and the need for continuous training of workers.

9.3b Influence and Power

Many people working on a project do not report directly to project managers, and project managers often do not have control over project staff who report to them. For example, if they are given work assignments they do not like, many workers will simply quit or transfer to other departments or projects. People are free to change jobs when they like.

H. J. Thamhain and D. L. Wilemon investigated the approaches that project managers use to deal with workers and how those approaches relate to project success. They identified nine influence bases that are available to project managers:

1. *Authority*: the legitimate hierarchical right to issue orders
2. *Assignment*: the project manager's perceived ability to influence a worker's later work assignments
3. *Budget*: the project manager's perceived ability to authorize others' use of discretionary funds
4. *Promotion*: the ability to improve a worker's position
5. *Money*: the ability to increase a worker's pay and benefits
6. *Penalty*: the project manager's perceived ability to dispense or cause punishment
7. *Work challenge*: the ability to assign work that capitalizes on a worker's enjoyment of doing a particular task, which taps an intrinsic motivational factor
8. *Expertise*: the project manager's perceived special knowledge that others deem important
9. *Friendship*: the ability to establish friendly personal relationships between the project manager and others[15]

Top management grants authority to the project manager. However, assignment, budget, promotion, money, and penalty influence bases are not automatically available to project managers as part of their position. Others' perceptions are important in establishing the usefulness of these influence bases. For example, any manager can influence workers by providing challenging work; the ability to provide challenging work (or take it away) is not a special ability of project managers. In addition, project managers must earn the ability to influence by using expertise and friendship.

Thamhain and Wilemon found that projects were more likely to fail when project managers relied too heavily on using authority, money, or penalty to influence people. *When project managers used work challenge and expertise to influence people, projects were more likely to succeed.* The effectiveness of work challenge in influencing people is consistent with Maslow's and Herzberg's research on motivation. The importance of expertise as a means of influencing people makes sense on projects that involve special knowledge, as in most IT projects.

In 2013, Thamhain published a study of 72 global project teams, and the results again showed that people issues have the strongest impact on project performance. Managers cannot succeed by simply issuing work orders, preparing plans, or providing guidelines. They must emphasize common values and goals to focus and unify global teams. "In particular, the field study shows that certain conditions related to the people side, such as personal interest, pride and satisfaction with the work, professional work challenge, accomplishments and recognition, appear most favorable toward unifying culturally diverse project teams and their work processes. These conditions serve as a bridging mechanism between organizational goals and personal interests, between central control and local management norms, and between following a project plan and adaptive problem solving. These are some of the conditions crucial to project success in complex multi-cultural organizations."[16]

Influence is related to **power**, which is the ability to influence behavior to get people to do things they would not otherwise do. Power is much stronger than influence, because it is often used to force people to change their behavior. There are five main types of power, according to French and Raven's classic study, "The Bases of Social Power."[17]

- **Coercive power** involves using punishment, threats, or other negative approaches to get people to do things they do not want to do. This type of power is similar to Thamhain and Wilemon's influence category called *penalty*. For example, a project manager can threaten to fire workers or subcontractors to try to get them to change their behavior. If the project manager really has the power to fire people, he or she could follow through on the threat. Recall, however, that influencing by using penalties is correlated with unsuccessful projects. Still, coercive power can be very effective in stopping negative behavior. For example, if students tend to hand in assignments late, an instructor can have a policy in the syllabus for late penalties, such as a 20 percent grade reduction for each day an assignment is late. Workers' pay can be docked if they arrive late for work, or they might be fired if they arrive late more than once.
- **Legitimate power** is getting people to do things based on a position of authority. This type of power is similar to the authority basis of influence. If top management gives project managers organizational authority, they can use legitimate power in several situations. They can make key decisions without involving the project team, for example. Overemphasis on legitimate power or authority also correlates with project failure.

- **Expert power** involves using personal knowledge and expertise to get people to change their behavior. People who perceive that project managers are experts in certain situations will follow their suggestions. For example, if a project manager has expertise in working with a particular IT supplier and its products, the project team will be more likely to follow the project manager's suggestions on how to work with that vendor and its products.
- **Reward power** involves using incentives to induce people to do things. Rewards can include money, status, recognition, promotions, and special work assignments. Many motivation theorists suggest that only certain types of rewards, such as work challenge, achievement, and recognition, truly induce people to change their behavior or work hard.
- **Referent power** is based on a person's own charisma. People who have referent power are held in very high regard; others will do what they say based on that regard. People such as Martin Luther King, Jr., John F. Kennedy, and Bill Clinton had referent power. Very few people possess the natural charisma that underlies referent power.

It is important for project managers to understand what types of influence and power they can use in different situations. New project managers often overemphasize their position—their legitimate power or authority influence—especially when dealing with project team members or support staff. They also neglect the importance of reward power or work challenge influence. People often respond much better to a project manager who motivates them with challenging work and provides positive reinforcement for doing a good job. Project managers should understand the basic concepts of influence and power, and should practice using them to their own advantage and to help their teams.

9.3c Covey and Improving Effectiveness

Stephen Covey, author of *The 7 Habits of Highly Effective People: Powerful Lessons in Personal Change*,[18] expanded on the work done by Maslow, Herzberg, and others to develop an approach for helping people and teams become more effective. Covey's first three habits of effective people—be proactive, begin with the end in mind, and put first things first—help people achieve a private victory by becoming independent. After achieving independence, people can then strive for interdependence by developing the next three habits—think win/win, seek first to understand then to be understood, and synergize. (**Synergy** is the concept that the whole is equal to more than the sum of its parts.) Finally, everyone can work on Covey's seventh habit—sharpen the saw—to develop and renew their physical, spiritual, mental, social, and emotional selves.

Project managers can apply Covey's seven habits to improve effectiveness on projects, as follows:

1. *Be proactive.* Covey, like Maslow, believes that people have the ability to be proactive and choose their responses to different situations. Project managers must be proactive in anticipating and planning for problems and inevitable changes on projects. They can also encourage their team members to be proactive in working on their project activities.
2. *Begin with the end in mind.* Covey suggests that people focus on their values, what they want to accomplish, and how they want to be remembered in

their lives. He suggests writing a mission statement to help achieve this habit. Many organizations and projects have mission statements that help them focus on their main purpose.

3. *Put first things first.* Covey developed a time management system and matrix to help people prioritize their time. He suggests that most people need to spend more time doing things that are important, but not urgent. Such activities include planning, reading, and exercising. Project managers need to spend a lot of time working on important but not urgent activities, such as developing various project plans, building relationships with major project stakeholders, and mentoring project team members. They also need to avoid focusing only on important and urgent activities—putting out fires.

4. *Think win/win.* Covey presents several paradigms of interdependence; think win/win is the best choice in most situations. When you use a win/win paradigm, parties in potential conflict work together to develop new solutions that benefit all parties. Project managers should strive to use a win/win approach in making decisions, but in competitive situations they sometimes must use a win/lose paradigm.

5. *Seek first to understand, then to be understood.* **Empathic listening** is listening with the intent to understand. It is more powerful than active listening because you set aside your personal interests and focus on truly understanding the other person. When you practice empathic listening, you can begin two-way communication. This habit is critical for project managers so they can understand their stakeholders' needs and expectations.

6. *Synergize.* A project team can synergize by creating collaborative products that are much better than a collection of individual efforts. Covey also emphasizes the importance of valuing differences in others to achieve synergy. Synergy is essential to many highly technical projects; in fact, several major breakthroughs in IT occurred because of synergy. For example, in his Pulitzer Prize-winning book, *The Soul of a New Machine*, Tracy Kidder documented the synergistic efforts of a team of Data General researchers to create a new 32-bit superminicomputer during the 1970s.[19]

7. *Sharpen the saw.* When you practice sharpening the saw, you take time to renew yourself physically, spiritually, mentally, and socially. The practice of self-renewal helps people avoid burnout. Project managers must make sure that they and their project teams have time to retrain, reenergize, and occasionally even relax to avoid burnout. A simple technique like encouraging people to stand up and walk around for a brief time every hour can improve physical health and mental performance.

Douglas Ross, author of *Applying Covey's Seven Habits to a Project Management Career*, related Covey's habits to project management. Ross suggests that Habit 5—Seek first to understand, then to be understood—differentiates good project managers from average or poor ones. People have a tendency to focus on their own agendas instead of first trying to understand other people's points of view. Empathic listening can help project managers and team members find out what motivates different people. Understanding what motivates key stakeholders and customers can mean the difference between a project's success or failure. Once project managers and team members begin to practice empathic listening, they can communicate and work together to tackle problems more effectively.[20]

Before you can practice empathic listening, you first have to get people to talk to you. In many cases, you must work on developing a rapport with the other person. **Rapport** is a relation of harmony, conformity, accord, or affinity. Without rapport, people cannot begin to communicate. For example, in the chapter's opening case, Ben was not ready to talk to anyone from the IT department, even if Ed and Sarah were ready to listen. Ben was angry about the lack of support he received from the IT department and bullied anyone who reminded him of that group. Before Sarah could begin to communicate with Ben, she had to establish rapport.

One technique for establishing rapport is mirroring. **Mirroring** is matching certain behaviors of the other person. People tend to like others who are like themselves, and mirroring helps you take on some of the other person's characteristics. It also helps them realize if they are behaving unreasonably, as in the chapter's opening case. You can mirror someone's tone and tempo of voice, breathing, movements, or body postures. After Ben started yelling at her, Sarah quickly decided to mirror his voice tone, tempo, and body posture. She stood nose to nose with Ben and started yelling back at him. This action made Ben realize what he was doing, and it also made him notice and respect his colleague from the IT department. Once Ben overcame his anger, he could start communicating his needs. In most cases, however, such extreme measures are not needed, and mirroring must be used with caution. When done improperly or with the wrong person, it could result in very negative consequences.

Recall the importance of getting users involved in IT projects. For organizations to be truly effective in IT project management, they must find ways to help users and developers of information systems work together. It is widely accepted that organizations make better project decisions when business professionals and IT staff collaborate. It is also widely accepted that this task is easier said than done. Many companies have been very successful in integrating technology and business departments, but many other companies continue to struggle with this issue.

9.3d Emotional Intelligence

As the title suggests, Howard Gardner's book *Frames of Mind: The Theory of Multiple Intelligences*, introduced the concept of using more than one way to think of and measure human intelligence. Gardner suggested the need to develop both interpersonal intelligence (the capacity to understand the motivations, intentions, and desires of others) and intrapersonal intelligence (the capacity to understand oneself, one's feelings, and motivations). Empathic listening is an example of interpersonal intelligence, while knowing that you have a high need for achievement is an example of intrapersonal intelligence. The concept **emotional intelligence**—knowing and managing one's own emotions and understanding the emotions of others for improved performance—became popular in 1995 when Daniel Goleman's book, *Emotional Intelligence*, became a best-seller.

Several articles and books have been written on the need for project managers to develop their emotional intelligence (EI). For example, Anthony C. Mersino, PMP, author of *Emotional Intelligence for Project Managers: The People Skills You Need to Achieve Outstanding Results*, says that EI comes into play as project managers work on team building, collaboration, negotiation, and relationship development. EI is also becoming a more sought after characteristic. According to a *CareerBuilder.com* survey of over 2,600 U.S. hiring managers and human resource professionals:

- 71 percent said they value EI in an employee more than IQ.
- 59 percent said they would not hire someone who has a high IQ but low EI.
- 75 percent said they are more likely to promote an employee with high EI than an employee with a high IQ.[21]

9.3e Leadership

As defined in Chapter 1, a leader focuses on long-term goals and big-picture objectives while inspiring people to reach those goals. Leadership is a soft skill, and there is no one best way to be a leader. Peter Northouse, author of a popular textbook called *Leadership: Theory and Practice*, says, "In the past 60 years, as many as 65 different classification systems have been developed to define the dimensions of leadership."[22] Some classification systems focus on group processes, while others focus on personality traits or behaviors. People discuss transformational leaders, transactional leaders, and servant leaders, to name a few. There are many different leadership styles, and the one thing most experts agree on is that the best leaders are able to adapt their style to needs of the situation.

Daniel Goleman, author of *Emotional Intelligence*, also wrote a book called *Primal Leadership*, which describes six different styles of leadership and situations where they are most appropriate:

1. *Visionary*: Needed when an organization needs a new direction, and the goal is to move people towards a new set of shared dreams. The leader articulates where the group is going, but lets them decide how to get there by being free to innovate, experiment, and take calculated risks.
2. *Coaching*: One-on-one style that focuses on developing individuals, showing them how to improve their performance. This approach works best with workers who show initiative and request assistance.
3. *Affiliative*: Emphasizes the importance of team work and creating harmony by connecting people to each other. This approach is effective when trying to increase morale, improve communication, or repair broken trust.
4. *Democratic*: Focuses on people's knowledge and skills and creates a commitment to reaching shared goals. This leadership style works best when the leader needs the collective wisdom of the group to decide on the best direction to take for the organization.
5. *Pacesetting*: Used to set high standards for performance. The leader wants work to be done better and faster and expects everyone to put forth their best effort.
6. *Commanding*: Most often used, also called autocratic or military style leadership. This style is most effective in a crisis or when a turnaround is needed.

Goleman points out that "The goal for leaders should be to develop a solid understanding of the different styles of leadership and their implications, and reach the point where choosing the right one for the situation becomes second nature to them."[23]

✓ WHAT WENT RIGHT?

It's important for professional societies to stay abreast of skills needed in their profession. In 2015, PMI acknowledged that project management professionals need to be continually updating their skills by developing a new Continuing Certification Requirements (CCR) program. Applicants who want to renew a PMI certification must now demonstrate ongoing professional development that meets the new PMI Talent Triangle. The Talent Triangle includes:

- Technical project management: Knowledge, skills, and behaviors related to specific domains of project, program, and portfolio management
- Strategic and business management: Knowledge of and expertise in the industry or organization that enhances performance and better delivers business outcomes
- Leadership: Knowledge, skills, and behaviors specific to leadership-oriented, cross-cutting skills that help an organization achieve its business goals.

PMI has always emphasized the need to stay abreast of technical project management, but now it is placing more emphasis on strategic and business management as well as leadership skills. PMI often surveys individuals and organizations, and in a recent report, 75 percent of organizations ranked leadership skills as most important for successful navigation of complexity in projects. "Managing complex projects requires project managers who are able to establish the vision, mission and expected outcomes in a way that is broad enough to be complete yet simple enough to understand. It also requires the skill to align the team to that vision. These are project managers who have become project executives with the leadership skill and business acumen to drive success.[24]

It is important to understand and pay attention to concepts of motivation, influence, power, effectiveness, emotional intelligence, and leadership in all project processes. It is also important to remember that projects operate within an organizational environment. The challenge comes from applying the preceding theories to the many unique people involved in particular projects.

Many important topics related to motivation, influence, power, effectiveness, emotional intelligence, and leadership are relevant to project management. Projects are done by and for people, so it is important for project managers and team members to understand and practice key concepts related to these topics. Remember that everyone prefers to work with people they like and respect, and it is important to treat others with respect, regardless of their title or position. This is especially true for people in support roles, such as administrative assistants, security guards, or members of the cleaning crew. You never know when you may need their help at a critical point in a project.

9.4 DEVELOPING THE HUMAN RESOURCE PLAN

To develop a human resource plan for a project, you must identify and document project roles, responsibilities, skills, and reporting relationships. The human resource plan often includes an organizational chart for the project, detailed information on roles and responsibilities, and a staffing management plan.

Before creating an organizational chart or any part of the human resource plan for a project, top management and the project manager must identify what types of people the project needs to ensure success. If the key to success lies in having the best Java programmers you can find, planning should reflect that need. If the real key to success is having a top-notch project manager and respected team leaders, that need should drive human resource planning.

9.4a Project Organizational Charts

Recall from Chapter 2 that the nature of IT projects often means that project team members come from different backgrounds and possess a wide variety of skills. It can be very difficult to manage such a diverse group of people, so it is important to provide a clear organizational structure for a project. After identifying important skills and the types of people needed to staff a project, the project manager should work with top management and project team members to create an organizational chart for the project. Figure 9-3 provides part of an organizational chart for a large project that involves hardware and software development. For example, in the chapter's opening case, a program manager might be in charge of every project related to the F-44 aircraft, and each major component of the aircraft, like the radar system, might have its own dedicated project manager. Note that the project personnel include a deputy project manager, subproject managers, and teams. Other boxes on the chart represent each functional department supporting the project, such as systems engineering, quality assurance, and configuration management, as well as an external independent test group. **Deputy project managers** fill in for project managers in their absence and assist them as needed. **Subproject managers** are responsible for managing the subprojects into which a large project might be divided.

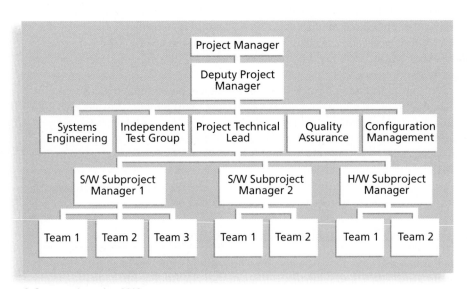

© Cengage Learning 2016

FIGURE 9-3 Sample organizational chart for a large IT project

For example, an aircraft radar upgrade project could involve several major software (S/W) upgrades as well as hardware (H/W) upgrades, so a subproject manager could be in charge of each upgrade. This structure is typical for large projects that use a matrix organizational structure. When many people work on a project, clearly defining and allocating project work is essential. (For example, visit the companion website for this text to see the project organizational chart that Northwest Airlines used for its large Resnet project.) Smaller projects usually do not have deputy project managers or subproject managers. On smaller projects, the project managers might have team leaders reporting directly to them.

In addition to defining an organizational structure for a project, it is also important to follow a work definition and assignment process. Figure 9-4 provides a framework for defining and assigning work that consists of four steps:

1. Finalizing the project requirements
2. Defining how the work will be accomplished
3. Breaking down the work into manageable elements
4. Assigning work responsibilities

The work definition and assignment process is carried out during the proposal and startup phases of a project. Note that the process is iterative, often taking more than one pass. A Request for Proposal (RFP) or draft contract often provides the basis for defining and finalizing work requirements, which are then documented in a final contract and technical baseline. If the project does not require an RFP, then the internal project charter and scope statement would provide the basis for defining and finalizing work requirements, as described in Chapter 5, Project Scope Management. The project team leaders then decide on a technical approach for how to do the work. Should work be broken down using a product-oriented approach or a phased approach? Will the project

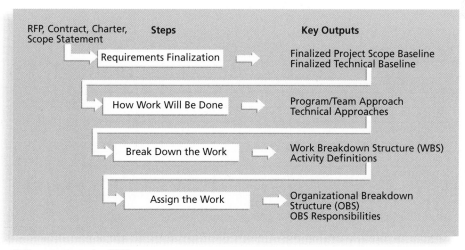

© Cengage Learning 2016

FIGURE 9-4 Work definition and assignment process

team outsource some of the work or subcontract to other companies? Once the project team has decided on a technical approach, it develops a work breakdown structure (WBS) to establish manageable elements of work, as described in Chapter 5. The team then develops activity definitions for the work involved in each activity on the WBS, as you learned in Chapter 6, Project Time Management. The last step is assigning the work.

Once the project manager and project team have broken down the work into manageable elements, the project manager assigns work to organizational units. The project manager often bases these work assignments on where the work fits in the organization and uses an organizational breakdown structure to conceptualize the process. An **organizational breakdown structure (OBS)** is a specific type of organizational chart that shows which organizational units are responsible for which work items. The OBS can be based on a general organizational chart and then broken down into more detail, based on specific units within departments in the company or units in any subcontracted companies. For example, OBS categories might include software development, hardware development, and training.

9.4b Responsibility Assignment Matrices

After developing an OBS, the project manager can develop a responsibility assignment matrix. A **responsibility assignment matrix (RAM)** maps the work of the project, as described in the WBS, to the people responsible for performing the work, as described in the OBS. Figure 9-5 shows an example of a RAM. The RAM allocates work to responsible and performing organizations, teams, or individuals, depending on the desired level of detail. For smaller projects, it is best to assign individual people to WBS activities. For very large projects, it is more effective to assign the work to organizational units or teams, as shown in Figure 9-5.

In addition to using a RAM to assign detailed work activities, you can use it to define general roles and responsibilities on projects. This type of RAM can include the

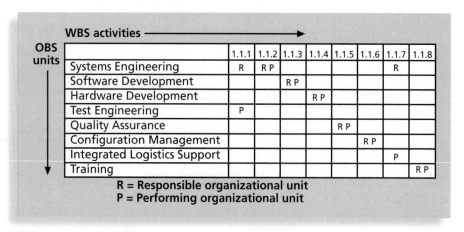

OBS units \ WBS activities	1.1.1	1.1.2	1.1.3	1.1.4	1.1.5	1.1.6	1.1.7	1.1.8
Systems Engineering	R	R P					R	
Software Development			R P					
Hardware Development				R P				
Test Engineering	P							
Quality Assurance					R P			
Configuration Management						R P		
Integrated Logistics Support							P	
Training								R P

R = Responsible organizational unit
P = Performing organizational unit

© Cengage Learning 2016

FIGURE 9-5 Sample responsibility assignment matrix (RAM)

stakeholders in the project. Some organizations use **RACI charts** to show four key roles for project stakeholders:

- Responsibility: Who does the task?
- Accountability: Who signs off on the task or has authority for it?
- Consultation: Who has information necessary to complete the task?
- Informed: Who needs to be notified of task status and results?

As shown in Table 9-2, a RACI chart lists tasks vertically and lists individuals or groups horizontally. Each intersecting cell contains an R, A, C, or I. A task may have multiple R, C, or I entries, but there can be only one A entry per row to clarify who is accountable for each task. For example, a mechanic is responsible for repairing a car, but the shop owner is accountable for the repairs being made properly. The car owner and parts supplier would be other stakeholders with various roles for different work activities, as shown in Table 9-2. Project managers can use the RACI codes or any other codes to help clarify the roles that different organizational units or specific stakeholders have in getting the work done.

TABLE 9-2   Sample RACI chart

	Car Owner	Shop Owner	Mechanic	Parts Supplier
Pay for parts and services	A, R	C		
Determine parts and services needed	C		A, R	C
Supply parts		C	C	A, R
Install parts	I	A	R	

© Cengage Learning 2016

9.4c Staffing Management Plans and Resource Histograms

A **staffing management plan** describes when and how people will be added to the project team and taken off it. The level of detail may vary based on the type of project. For example, if an IT project is expected to need 100 people on average over a year, the staffing management plan would describe the types of people needed to work on the project, such as Java programmers, business analysts, and technical writers, and the number of each type of person needed each month. The plan would also describe how these resources would be acquired, trained, rewarded, and reassigned after the project. All of these issues are important to meeting the needs of the project, the employees, and the organization.

The staffing management plan often includes a **resource histogram**, which is a column chart that shows the number of resources assigned to a project over time. Figure 9-6 provides an example of a histogram that might be used for a six-month IT project. Notice that the columns represent the number of people needed in each area—managers, business analysts, programmers, and technical writers. By stacking the columns, you can see the total number of people needed each month. After determining the project staffing needs, the next steps in project human resource management are to acquire the necessary staff and then develop the project team.

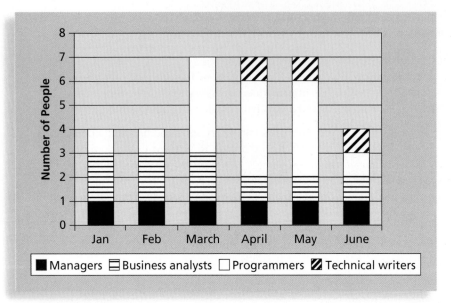

FIGURE 9-6   Sample resource histogram

9.5 ACQUIRING THE PROJECT TEAM

During the late 1990s, the IT job market became extremely competitive. It was a seller's market with corporations competing fiercely for a shrinking pool of qualified, experienced IT professionals. In the early 2000s, the market declined tremendously, so employers could be very selective in recruiting. Today, many organizations again face a shortage of IT staff. Regardless of the current job market, however, acquiring qualified IT professionals is critical. There is a saying that the project manager who is the smartest person on the team has done a poor job of recruiting. In addition to recruiting team members, it is also important to assign the appropriate type and number of people to work on projects at the appropriate times. This section addresses important topics related to acquiring the project team: resource assignment, resource loading, and resource leveling.

9.5a Resource Assignment

After developing a staffing management plan, project managers must work with other people in their organizations to assign personnel to their projects or to acquire additional human resources needed to staff the project. Project managers with strong influencing and negotiating skills are often good at getting internal people to work on their projects. However, the organization must ensure that people are assigned to the projects that best fit their skills and the needs of the organization. The main outputs of this process are project staff assignments, resource availability information, and updates to the staffing management plan. Many project teams also find it useful to create a project team directory.

Organizations that do a good job of staff acquisition have good staffing plans. These plans describe the number and type of people who are currently in the organization and the number and type of people anticipated to be needed for the project based on current and upcoming activities. An important component of staffing plans is maintaining a complete and accurate inventory of employees' skills. If there is a mismatch between the current mix of people's skills and needs of the organization, it is the project manager's job to work with top management, human resource managers, and other people in the organization to address staffing and training needs.

It is also important to have good procedures in place for hiring subcontractors and recruiting new employees. Because the Human Resource department is normally responsible for hiring people, project managers must work with their human resource managers to address any problems in recruiting appropriate people. It is also a priority to address retention issues, especially for IT professionals.

One innovative approach to hiring and retaining IT staff is to offer existing employees incentives for helping recruit and retain personnel. For example, several consulting companies give their employees one dollar for every hour worked by a new person they helped recruit. This provides an incentive for current employees to help attract new people and to keep all of them working at the company. Another approach to attract and retain IT professionals is to provide benefits based on personal need. For example, some people might want to work only four days a week or have the option of working a couple of days a week from home. As it becomes more difficult to find good IT professionals, organizations must become more innovative and proactive in addressing this issue.

It is very important to consider the needs of individuals and the organization when making recruiting and retention decisions and to study the best practices of leading companies in these areas. It is also important to address a growing trend in project teams—many team members work in a virtual environment. See the section on managing the project team for suggestions on working with virtual team members.

BEST PRACTICE

Best practices can also include the best places for people to work. *Fortune* magazine publishes a list of the "100 Best Companies to Work For" in the United States every year, with Google taking top honors for the sixth time in 2015. Companies want to make the list and be known for being a great place to work, and people are drawn to work for companies on the list. *Working Mothers* magazine lists the best companies in the United States for women based on benefits for working families. The *Times online* (*www.time-sonline.co.uk*) provides the London *Sunday Times* list of the "100 Best Companies to Work For," a key benchmark against which U.K. companies can judge their performance as employers. The Great Place to Work Institute, which produces *Fortune* magazine's "100 Best Companies to Work For," uses the same selection methodology for more than 20 international lists, including all 15 countries of the European Union, Brazil, Korea, and a number of other countries throughout Latin America and Asia. Companies make these lists based on feedback from their best critics: their own employees. Quotes from employees often show why their companies made the lists:

continued

- "Working here can make you feel that you've made it into the technical equivalent of Major League Baseball or the NFL—you're at the top of your field." #1: Google
- "Although people come from across the world, from different cultures, and from different life experiences," one employee says, "everyone shares a passion for problem-solving and a positive attitude about teamwork." #2: Boston Consulting Group
- "Our health insurance benefits are awesome, our schedules are flexible and we can keep our bodies healthy at our gym," says one team member. "ACUITY takes not only good care of me, but also my family." #3: ACCUITY
- "SAS has provisions to support you at whatever stage of life you are in – child care for your newborn to preschooler, resources for dealing with your teenager and college planning, help with your elderly parent," says one employee. "More importantly, a real sense of community is built when people work together for so long." #4 SAS[25]

9.5b Resource Loading

Chapter 6, Project Time Management, described using network diagrams to help manage a project's schedule. One of the problems or dangers inherent in scheduling processes is that they often do not address the issues of resource utilization and availability. This is why the development of critical chain scheduling is so important. Schedules tend to focus primarily on time rather than both time and resources, which includes people. An important measure of a project manager's success is how well he or she balances the trade-offs among performance, time, and cost. During a period of crisis, it is occasionally possible to add resources—such as additional staff—to a project at little or no cost. Most of the time, however, resolving performance, time, and cost trade-offs entails additional costs to the organization. The project manager's goal must be to achieve project success without increasing the costs or time required to complete the project. The key to accomplishing this goal is effectively managing human resources on the project.

Once people are assigned to projects, two techniques are available to project managers that help them use project staff most effectively: resource loading and resource leveling. **Resource loading** refers to the amount of individual resources that an existing schedule requires during specific time periods. Resource loading helps project managers understand the demands of a project on the organization's resources and on individual people's schedules. Project managers often use resource histograms, like the one shown in Figure 9-6, to depict period-by-period variations in resource loading. A resource histogram can be very helpful in determining staffing needs or in identifying staffing problems.

A resource histogram can also show when work is being overallocated to a certain person or group. **Overallocation** means that not enough resources are available to perform the assigned work during a given time period. Figure 9-7 shows a sample resource histogram created in Microsoft Project. This histogram illustrates how much one person, Joe Franklin, is assigned to work on the project each week. The numbers on the vertical axis represent the percentage of Joe's available time that is allocated for him to work on the project. The top horizontal axis represents time in weeks. Note that Joe Franklin is overallocated most of the time. For example, for most of March and April and part of May, Joe's

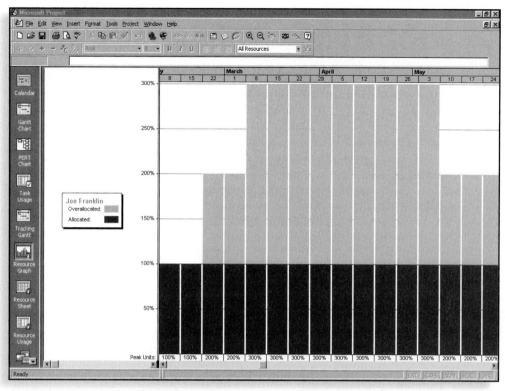

Used with permission from Microsoft Corporation

FIGURE 9-7 Sample histogram showing an overallocated person

work allocation is 300 percent of his available time. If Joe is normally available eight hours per day, this means he would have to work 24 hours a day to meet this staffing projection!

Overallocation can happen for many reasons. Many people don't use the resource assignment features of project management software properly. (See Appendix A for detailed information on using Microsoft Project 2013.) You also need to provide good estimates of how many hours are required to accomplish work. As mentioned in Chapter 6, Project Time Management, a typical worker does productive work between 70 and 80 percent of the time. If people are assigned to work for 40 hours in a week, you should estimate that they will accomplish 28 to 32 hours of productive work. Of course, there are exceptions to this rule of thumb, but it is unrealistic to assume that all workers are productive 100 percent of the time.

9.5c Resource Leveling

Resource leveling is a technique for resolving resource conflicts by delaying tasks. It is a form of network analysis in which resource management concerns drive scheduling decisions (start and finish dates). The main purpose of resource leveling is to create a smoother distribution of resource usage. Project managers examine the network diagram for areas of slack or float, and to identify resource conflicts. For example, you can sometimes remove overallocations by delaying noncritical tasks, which does not result in an overall schedule delay. At other times, you will need to delay the project completion date to reduce or remove overallocations. Appendix A explains how to use Microsoft Project 2013 to level resources using both of these approaches. You can also view resource leveling as addressing the resource constraints described in critical chain scheduling (see Chapter 6, Project Time Management).

Overallocation is one type of resource conflict. If a certain resource is overallocated, the project manager can change the schedule to remove resource overallocation. If a certain resource is underallocated, the project manager can change the schedule to try to improve the use of the resource. Resource leveling, therefore, aims to minimize period-by-period variations in resource loading by shifting tasks within their slack allowances.

Figure 9-8 illustrates a simple example of resource leveling. The network diagram at the top of this figure shows that Activities A, B, and C can all start at the same time. Activity A has a duration of two days and will take two people to complete; Activity B has a duration of five days and will take four people to complete; and Activity C has a duration of three days and will take two people to complete. The histogram in the lower-left corner of this figure shows the resource usage if all activities start on day one. The histogram in

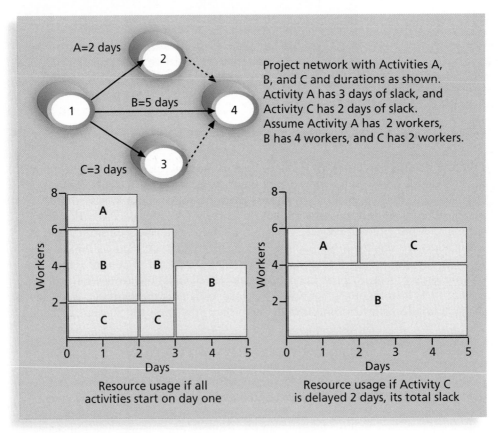

© Cengage Learning 2016

FIGURE 9-8 Resource leveling example

the lower-right corner shows the resource usage if Activity C is delayed two days, its total slack allowance. Notice that the lower-right histogram is flat or leveled; that is, its activities are arranged to take up the least space, saving days and numbers of workers. You may recognize this strategy from the computer game Tetris, in which you earn points for keeping the falling shapes as level as possible. In the same way, resources are used best when they are leveled.

Resource leveling has several benefits. First, when resources are used on a more constant basis, they require less management. For example, it is much easier to manage someone who is scheduled to work 20 hours per week on a project for the next three months than it is to manage the same person for 10 hours one week, 40 the next, 5 the next, and so on.

Second, resource leveling may enable project managers to use a just-in-time inventory type of policy for subcontractors or other expensive resources. For example, a project manager might want to level resources for work that must be done by particular subcontractors such as testing consultants. This leveling might allow the project to use four outside consultants full-time to perform testing for four months instead of spreading out the work over more time or using more than four people. The latter approach is usually more expensive. Recall from Chapter 6 that crashing and fast tracking can also be used along with resource allocation to improve a project schedule.

Third, resource leveling results in fewer problems for project personnel and accounting departments. Increasing and decreasing labor levels and human resources often produce additional work and confusion. For example, if people with expertise in the same area are only assigned to a project two days a week and they need to work together, then the schedule needs to reflect this need. The Accounting department might complain when subcontractors charge a higher rate for billing less than 20 hours a week on a project. The accountants will remind project managers to strive to get the lowest rates possible.

Finally, resource leveling often improves morale. People like to have stability in their jobs. It is very stressful for people not to know what projects they will be working on from week to week or even from day to day.

Project management software can automatically level resources. However, the project manager must be careful in using the results without making adjustments. Automatic leveling often pushes out the project's completion date. Resources may also be reallocated to work at times that are inappropriate with other constraints. To ensure that the leveling is done appropriately, a wise project manager would have his or her work checked by a team member who is proficient in using the project management software.

9.6 DEVELOPING THE PROJECT TEAM

Even if a project manager has successfully recruited enough skilled people to work on a project, the project manager must ensure that people can work together as a team to achieve project goals. Many IT projects have talented people working on them, but it takes teamwork to complete most projects successfully. The main goal of **team development** is to help people work together more effectively to improve project performance.

First published in 1965 and modified in the 1970s, Dr. Bruce Tuckman's model of team development remains relevant today. The **Tuckman model** describes five stages of team development:

1. *Forming* involves the introduction of team members, either at the initiation of the team or as new members are introduced. This stage is necessary, but little work is actually achieved.
2. *Storming* occurs when team members have different opinions for how the team should operate. People test each other, and there is often conflict within the team.
3. *Norming* is achieved when team members have developed a common working method, and cooperation and collaboration replace the conflict and mistrust of the previous phase.
4. *Performing* occurs when the emphasis is on reaching the team's goals rather than working on team process. Relationships are settled, and team members are likely to build loyalty toward each other. At this stage, the team is able to manage tasks that are more complex and cope with greater change.
5. *Adjourning* involves the break-up of the team after it successfully reaches its goals and completes the work.[26]

There is an extensive body of literature on team development. This section highlights a few important tools and techniques for team development, including training, team-building activities, and reward and recognition systems.

9.6a Training

Project managers often recommend that people take specific training courses to improve individual and team development. For example, Sarah from the opening case had gone through training in emotional intelligence and dealing with difficult people. She was familiar with the mirroring technique and felt comfortable using that approach with Ben. Many other people would not have reacted so quickly and effectively in the same situation. If Ben and Sarah did reach agreement on what actions they could take to resolve the F-44 aircraft program's IT problems, it might result in a new project to develop and deliver a new system for Ben's group. If Sarah became the project manager for this new project, she would understand the need for special training in interpersonal skills for specific people in her department and Ben's. Individual team members could take special training classes to improve their interpersonal skills. If Sarah thought the whole project team could benefit from taking training together to learn to work as a team, she could arrange for a special team-building session for the entire project team and key stakeholders.

It is very important to provide training in a just-in-time fashion. For example, if Sarah were preparing for a technical assignment that required her to learn a new programming language, training to deal with difficult people would not help her much. However, the training was very timely for her new consulting position. Many organizations provide e-learning opportunities for their employees so they can learn specific skills at any time and any place. They have also found that e-learning is sometimes more cost-effective than traditional instructor-led training courses. It is important to make sure that the timing and delivery method for the training is appropriate for specific situations and individuals. Organizations have also found that it is often more economical to train current employees in particular areas than it is to hire new people who already possess those skills.

Several organizations that have successfully implemented Six Sigma principles have taken a unique and effective approach to training. They only let high-potential employees attend Six Sigma Black Belt training, which is a substantial investment of time and money. In addition, they do not let employees into a particular Black Belt course until the employees have had a potential Six Sigma project approved that relates to their current job. Attendees can then apply the new concepts and techniques they learn in the classes to their jobs. High-potential employees feel rewarded by being picked to take this training, and the organization benefits by having these employees implement high-payoff projects because of the training.

9.6b Team-Building Activities

Many organizations provide in-house team-building training activities, and many also use services provided by external companies that specialize in this area. It is important to understand individual needs, including learning styles, past training, and physical limitations, when determining team-building training options. Two common approaches to team-building activities are physical challenges and psychological preference indicator tools.

Several organizations have teams go through physically challenging activities to help them develop as a team. Military basic training or boot camps provide one example. Men and women who want to join the military must first finish basic training, which often involves strenuous physical activities such as rappelling off towers, running and marching in full military gear, going through obstacle courses, passing marksmanship training, and mastering survival training. Many organizations use a similar approach by sending teams to special locations where they work together to navigate white water rapids, climb mountains or rocks, and participate in rope courses. Research shows that physical challenges often help teams of strangers to work together more effectively, but it can cause already dysfunctional teams to have even more problems.

Even more organizations have teams participate in mental team-building activities in which they learn about themselves, each other, and how to work as a group most effectively. It is important for people to understand and value each other's differences to work effectively as a team. Three common exercises used in mental team building include the Myers-Briggs Type Indicator, Wilson Learning Social Styles Profile, and the DISC Profile.

The Myers-Briggs Type Indicator

The **Myers-Briggs Type Indicator (MBTI)** is a popular tool for determining personality preferences. During World War II, Isabel B. Myers and Katherine C. Briggs developed the first version of the MBTI based on psychologist Carl Jung's theory of psychological type. The four dimensions of psychological type in the MBTI include:

- *Extrovert/Introvert (E/I)*: This first dimension determines if you are generally extroverted or introverted, which signifies whether you draw energy from other people (extrovert) or from yourself (introvert).
- *Sensation/Intuition (S/N)*: This second dimension relates to the manner in which you gather information. Sensation (or Sensing) type people take in facts, details, and reality and describe themselves as practical. Intuitive type people are imaginative, ingenious, and attentive to hunches or intuition. They describe themselves as innovative and conceptual.

- *Thinking/Feeling (T/F)*: Thinking judgment is objective and logical, and feeling judgment is subjective and personal.
- *Judgment/Perception (J/P)*: This fourth dimension concerns people's attitudes toward structure. Judgment type people like closure and task completion. They tend to establish deadlines and take them seriously, expecting others to do the same. Perceiving types prefer to keep things open and flexible. They regard deadlines more as a signal to start rather than complete a project and do not feel that work must be done before play or rest begins.[27]

Much more than this simple sketch is involved in determining personality types, and many books are available on this topic. In 1998, David Keirsey published *Please Understand Me II: Temperament, Character, Intelligence*.[28] This book includes a test called the *Keirsey Temperament Sorter*, which is a personality type preference test based on the work of Jung, Myers, and Briggs. The test is easy to take and interpret.

An interesting study of the MBTI types within the general population of the United States and information systems (IS) developers revealed some significant contrasts.[29] The two groups of people were most similar in the judgment/perception dimension, with slightly more than half of each group preferring the judgment type (J). There were significant differences, however, in the other three dimensions. Most people would not be surprised to learn that most IS developers are introverts. This study found that 75 percent of IS developers were introverts, and only 25 percent of the general population were introverts. This personality type difference might help explain some of the problems users have communicating with developers. Another sharp contrast found in the study was that almost 80 percent of IS developers were thinking types compared to 50 percent of the general population. IS developers were also much more likely to be intuitive (about 55 percent) than the general population (about 25 percent). These results fit with Keirsey's classification of NT (Intuitive/Thinking types) people as *rationals*. Educationally, they tend to study the sciences, enjoy technology as a hobby, and pursue systems work. Keirsey also suggests that no more than 7 percent of the general population are NTs. Would you be surprised to know that Bill Gates is classified as a rational?[30]

Project managers can often benefit from knowing their team members' MBTI profiles by adjusting their management styles for each person. For example, if the project manager is a strong N and one of the team members is a strong S, the project manager should provide more concrete, detailed explanations for that person's task assignments. Project managers may also want to make sure they have a variety of personality types on their teams. For example, if all team members are strong introverts, it may be difficult for them to work well with users and other important stakeholders who are extroverts.

Like any test, you should use the MBTI with caution. Several studies argue that the lack of progress in improving software development teams and other teams is due in part to the inappropriate use of psychological tests and basic misunderstandings of personality theory. "Software engineers often complain about those who, in the course of their work, do some programming in support of their professional activities: the claim being that such individuals are not professionals and do not understand the discipline. The same can be said of those who adopt psychological approaches without the relevant qualifications and background."[31]

The Social Styles Profile

Many organizations also use the Social Styles Profile in team-building activities. Psychologist David Merril, who helped develop the Wilson Learning Social Styles Profile, describes people as falling into four approximate behavioral profiles, or zones, based on their assertiveness and responsiveness:

- *Drivers* are proactive and task-oriented. They are firmly rooted in the present, and they strive for action. Adjectives to describe drivers include pushy, severe, tough, dominating, harsh, strong-willed, independent, practical, decisive, and efficient.
- *Expressives* are proactive and people-oriented. They are future-oriented and use their intuition to look for fresh perspectives on the world around them. Adjectives to describe expressives include manipulating, excitable, undisciplined, reacting, egotistical, ambitious, stimulating, wacky, enthusiastic, dramatic, and friendly.
- *Analyticals* are reactive and task-oriented. They are past-oriented and strong thinkers. Adjectives to describe analyticals include critical, indecisive, stuffy, picky, moralistic, industrious, persistent, serious, expecting, and orderly.
- *Amiables* are reactive and people-oriented. They think in terms of the present, past, or future depending on the situation, and they strongly value relationships. Adjectives to describe amiables include conforming, unsure, ingratiating, dependent, awkward, supportive, respectful, willing, dependable, and agreeable.[32]

Figure 9-9 shows these four social styles and their two main determinants: assertiveness and responsiveness. To determine your level of assertiveness, ask if you are more

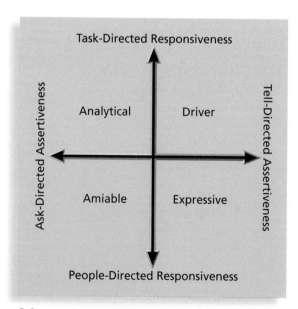

FIGURE 9-9 Social styles

373

likely to tell people what to do or ask them what should be done. To determine your responsiveness to tasks, ask whether you focus on the task itself or on the people involved in performing the task.

Knowing the social styles of project stakeholders can help project managers understand why certain people may have problems working together. For example, drivers are often very impatient working with amiables, and analyticals often have difficulties understanding expressives.

DISC Profile

Similar to the Social Styles Profile, the DISC Profile uses a four-dimensional model of normal behavior. The four dimensions—Dominance, Influence, Steadiness, and Compliance—provide the basis for the name DISC. Note that other, similar, terms are sometimes used for some of these letters, such as stability for steadiness or conscientiousness for compliance. The DISC Profile is based on the 1928 work of psychologist William Moulton Marston. The DISC Profile reveals people's behavioral tendencies under certain situations. For example, it reveals how you tend to behave under stress, in conflict, when communicating, and when avoiding certain activities. According to *www.onlinediscprofile.com*, "over 5 million people have taken various forms of the DISC Profile throughout the world. Marston's original work continues to be enhanced by ongoing behavioral research and profiles can be found in more than 50 languages by various publishers of the disc assessment."[33]

Figure 9-10 shows the four dimensions of the DISC Profile model and describes key characteristics of each dimension. Notice that each dimension is also associated with a color and emphasis, such as I, We, You, or It:

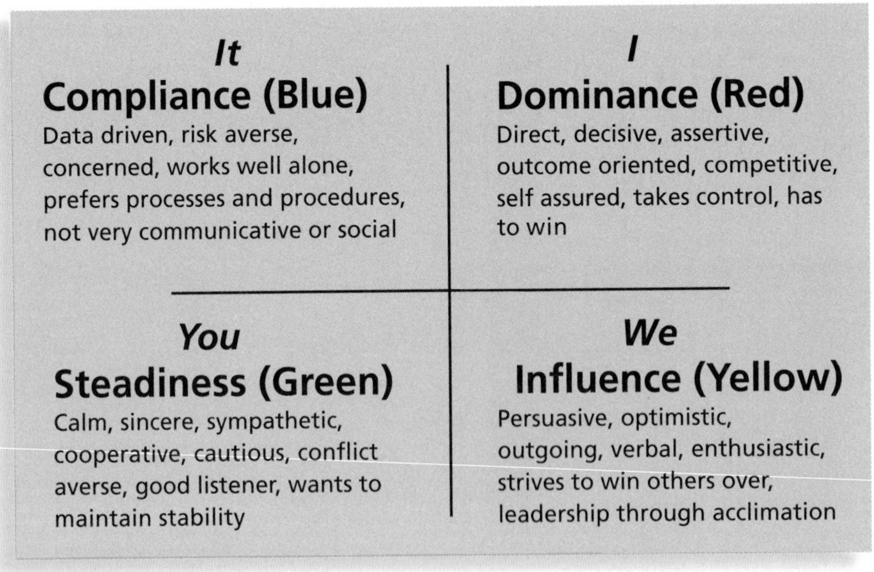

It **Compliance (Blue)** Data driven, risk averse, concerned, works well alone, prefers processes and procedures, not very communicative or social	*I* **Dominance (Red)** Direct, decisive, assertive, outcome oriented, competitive, self assured, takes control, has to win
You **Steadiness (Green)** Calm, sincere, sympathetic, cooperative, cautious, conflict averse, good listener, wants to maintain stability	*We* **Influence (Yellow)** Persuasive, optimistic, outgoing, verbal, enthusiastic, strives to win others over, leadership through acclamation

© Cengage Learning 2016

FIGURE 9-10 The DISC profile

- *Dominance*: Represented by red and emphasizing "I," dominance traits include being direct, decisive, assertive, outcome-oriented, competitive, self-assured, controlling, and wanting to win.
- *Influence*: Represented by yellow and emphasizing "We," influence traits include being persuasive, optimistic, outgoing, verbal, enthusiastic, striving to win others over, and practicing leadership through acclimation.
- *Steadiness*: Represented by green and emphasizing "You," steadiness traits include being calm, sincere, cautious, conflict averse, a good listener, and wanting to maintain stability.
- *Compliance*: Represented by blue and emphasizing "It," compliance traits include being data driven, risk averse, concerned, working well alone, preferring processes and procedures, and not being very communicative or social.

375

Like the Social Styles Profile, people in opposite quadrants, such as Dominance and Steadiness or Influence and Compliance, can have problems understanding each other.

Many other team-building activities and tests are available. For example, some people take Dr. Meredith Belbin's test to help determine which of nine team roles they might prefer. Again, professionals should use any team-building or personality tool with caution. In reality, most professionals must be flexible and do whatever is needed for their teams to succeed. Project managers can use their leadership and coaching skills to help all types of people communicate better with each other and focus on meeting project goals.

9.6c Reward and Recognition Systems

Another important tool for promoting team development is the use of team-based reward and recognition systems. If management rewards teamwork, they will promote or reinforce the philosophy that people work more effectively in teams. Some organizations offer bonuses, trips, or other rewards to workers that meet or exceed company or project goals. In a project setting, project managers can recognize and reward people who willingly work overtime to meet an aggressive schedule objective or go out of their way to help a teammate. Project managers should not reward people who work overtime just to get extra pay or because of their own poor work or planning.

Project managers must continually assess their team's performance. When they find areas in which individuals or the entire team can improve, it's their job to find the best way to develop their people and improve performance.

9.7 MANAGING THE PROJECT TEAM

In addition to developing the project team, the project manager must lead it in performing various project activities. (Note that PMI uses the word *managing* the project team as the third process for human resource management versus *leading,* so that wording is used here as well.) After assessing team performance and related information, the project manager must decide if changes should be requested to the project, or if updates are needed to enterprise environmental factors, organizational process assets, or the project management plan. Project managers must use their soft skills to find the best way to motivate and manage each team member.

9.7a Tools and Techniques for Managing Project Teams

Several tools and techniques are available to assist in managing project teams:

- *Observation and conversation*: Project managers need to observe team members at work to assess how they are performing and ask team members how they feel about their work. Many project managers like to practice "management by walking around" (MBWA) to physically see and hear their team members at work. Informal or formal conversations about how a project is going can provide crucial information. For virtual workers, project managers can observe and discuss work and personal issues via e-mail, telephone, web conference, or other media.
- *Project performance appraisals*: Just as managers provide performance appraisals for their workers, so can project managers. The need for project performance appraisals and the types required vary depending on the length of the project, its complexity, organizational policies, contract requirements, and related communications. Even if a project manager does not provide official project performance appraisals for team members, it is still important to provide timely performance feedback. If a team member hands in sloppy or late work, the project manager should determine the reason and take appropriate action. Perhaps the team member had a death in the family and could not concentrate. Perhaps the team member was planning to leave the project. The reasons for the behavior should have a strong impact on the action the project manager takes.
- *Interpersonal skills*: As you learned in Chapter 1, project managers must possess several interpersonal skills. To be effective, it is especially important to focus on leadership, influencing, and decision-making skills.
- *Conflict management*: Few projects are completed without conflicts. Some types of conflict are actually desirable on projects, but many are not. It's important for project managers to understand strategies for handling conflicts and to proactively manage conflict.

Blake and Mouton (1964) delineated five basic modes or strategies for handling conflicts in their popular managerial grid. Each strategy has high, medium, or low importance on two levels: importance of the task or goal (or concern for production), and importance of the relationship between the conflicting parties (concern for people). These modes are shown in Figure 9-11.

1. *Confrontation*: When using the **confrontation mode**, project managers face a conflict directly using a problem-solving approach that allows affected parties to work through their disagreements. This approach is also called the problem-solving mode or win/win using Covey's terminology. When the task and relationship are both of high importance, this mode is usually the most effective.
2. *Compromise*: With the **compromise mode**, project managers use a give-and-take approach to resolving conflicts. They bargain and search for solutions that bring some degree of satisfaction to all the parties in a dispute. This mode works best when both the task and relationship are of medium importance.

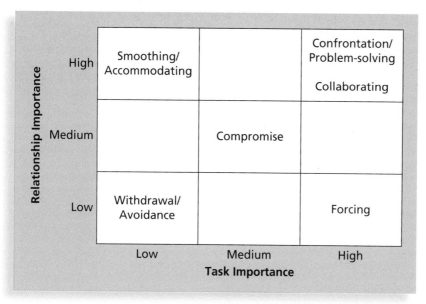

Source: Kathy Schwalbe, *An Introduction to Project Management, Fourth Edition* (July 2012)

FIGURE 9-11   Conflict handling modes

3. *Smoothing*: When using the **smoothing mode**, the project manager deemphasizes or avoids areas of differences and emphasizes areas of agreement. This approach is also called accommodating, and it is best used when the relationship is of high importance and the task is of low importance.

4. *Forcing*: The **forcing mode** can be viewed as the win/lose approach to conflict resolution. Project managers exert their viewpoint at the potential expense of another viewpoint. If the task is of high importance and the relationship is of low importance, this mode can be very effective.

5. *Withdrawal*: When using the **withdrawal mode**, project managers retreat or withdraw from an actual or potential disagreement. This approach is also called avoiding, and is normally the least desirable conflict-handling mode, unless the task and relationship are both of low importance.

More recent studies recognize a sixth conflict-handling mode:

6. *Collaborating*: Using the **collaborating mode**, decision makers incorporate different viewpoints and insights to develop consensus and commitment. Even though managers might not agree on a decision, they commit to following it in the best interests of the organization.

Project managers must also realize that not all conflict is bad. Conflict often produces important results, such as new ideas, better alternatives, and motivation to work harder and more collaboratively. Project team members may become stagnant or develop **groupthink**—conformance to the values or ethical standards of a group—if there are no conflicting viewpoints on various aspects of a project. Research by Karen Jehn, Professor of Management at the University of Melbourne, suggests that task-related conflict, which is derived from differences over team objectives and how to achieve them, often improves team performance. Emotional conflict, however, stems from personality clashes and misunderstandings, and often depresses team performance. Project managers should create an environment that encourages and maintains the positive and productive aspects of conflict.[34]

9.7b General Advice on Managing Teams

According to Patrick Lencioni, a well-known author and consultant on teams, "Teamwork remains the one sustainable competitive advantage that has been largely untapped … teamwork is almost always lacking within organizations that fail, and often present within those that succeed."[35] However, teamwork is challenging to create, and because teams are subject to dysfunction, maintaining teamwork is equally challenging. The five dysfunctions of teams are:

1. Absence of trust
2. Fear of conflict
3. Lack of commitment
4. Avoidance of accountability
5. Inattention to results

Lencioni's books provide suggestions for overcoming each of these dysfunctions. For example, he suggests that team members take the Myers-Briggs Type Indicator, as described earlier in this chapter, to help people open up to each other and build trust. To master conflict, he suggests that teams practice having unfiltered, passionate debates about important issues. To achieve commitment, he stresses the importance of expressing all possible ideas and getting people to agree to disagree, but then having them commit to decisions. To embrace accountability, Lencioni emphasizes the importance of clarifying and focusing on everyone's top priorities. He also suggests that peer pressure and the distaste for letting down a colleague are often better motivators than authoritative intervention. Finally, using some type of scoreboard to focus on team results helps eliminate ambiguity so everyone knows what it means to achieve positive results.

Additional suggestions for ensuring that teams are productive include the following:

- Be patient and kind with your team. Assume the best about people; do not assume that your team members are lazy and careless.
- Fix the problem instead of blaming people. Help people work out problems by focusing on behaviors.
- Establish regular, effective meetings. Focus on meeting project objectives and producing positive results.
- Allow time for teams to go through Tuckman's basic team-building stages of forming, storming, norming, performing, and adjourning. Don't expect teams to work at the highest performance level right away.
- Limit the size of work teams to three to seven members.
- Plan some social activities to help project team members and other stakeholders get to know each other better. Make the social events fun and not mandatory.
- Stress team identity. Create traditions that team members enjoy.

- Nurture team members and encourage them to help each other. Identify and provide training that will help individuals and the team as a whole become more effective.
- Acknowledge individual and group accomplishments.
- Take additional actions to work with virtual team members. If possible, have a face-to-face or phone meeting at the start of a virtual project or when introducing a virtual team member. Screen people carefully to make sure they can work effectively in a virtual environment. Clarify how virtual team members will communicate.

As you can imagine, team development, leadership, and management are critical concerns on many IT projects. To paraphrase Keirsey, many IT project managers must break out of their rational/NT preference and focus on empathically listening to other people to address their concerns and create an environment in which individuals and teams can grow and prosper.

9.8 USING SOFTWARE TO ASSIST IN HUMAN RESOURCE MANAGEMENT

Earlier in this chapter, you read that a simple responsibility assignment matrix or resource histograms are useful tools that can help you effectively manage human resources on projects. You can use several different software packages, including spreadsheets or project management software such as Microsoft Project 2013, to create matrixes and histograms. Many people do not realize that Project 2013 provides a variety of human resource management tools, some of which include assigning and tracking resources, resource leveling, resource usage reports, overallocated resource reports, and to-do lists. You can learn how to use many of these functions and features in Appendix A.

You can use Project 2013 to assign resources such as equipment, materials, facilities, and people to tasks. It enables you to allocate individual resources to individual projects or to pool resources and share them across multiple projects. By defining and assigning resources in Project 2013, you can:

- Keep track of resources through stored information and reports on resource assignments.
- Identify potential resource shortages that could cause a project to miss scheduled deadlines and possibly extend the duration of a project.
- Identify underutilized resources and reassign them, which may enable you to shorten a project's schedule and reduce costs.
- Use automated leveling to make level resources easier to manage.

Just as many project management professionals are unaware of the powerful cost-management features of Project 2013, many are unaware of its powerful human resource management features. The Microsoft Enterprise Project Management Solution provides additional human resource management capabilities. You can also purchase add-in software for Microsoft products or purchase software from other companies to manage your project's human resources. With the aid of this software, project managers can have more information available in useful formats to help them decide how to manage human resources most effectively.

Project resource management involves much more than using software to assess and track resource loading and to level resources. People are the most important asset on most projects, and human resources are very different from other resources. You cannot simply replace people in the same way that you replace a piece of equipment. It is essential to treat people with consideration and respect, to understand what motivates them, and to communicate carefully with them. What makes good project managers great is not their use of tools, but their ability to enable project team members to deliver their best work on a project.

CASE WRAP-UP

After Sarah yelled back at Ben, he said, "You're the first person who's had the guts to stand up to me." After that brief introduction, Sarah, Ben, and the other meeting participants had a good discussion about what was happening on the F-44 upgrade project. Sarah was able to write a justification to get Ben's group special software and support to download key information from the old system so they could manage their project better. When Sarah stood nose to nose with Ben and yelled at him, she used a technique for establishing rapport called mirroring. Although Sarah was not a loud and obnoxious person, she saw that Ben was and decided to mirror his behavior and attitude. She put herself in his shoes for a while, which helped break the ice so Sarah, Ben, and the other people at the meeting could start communicating and working together as a team to solve their problems.

Chapter Summary

People are the most important assets in organizations and on projects. Therefore, it is essential for project managers to be good human resource managers.

The major processes of project human resource management include planning human resources, acquiring the project team, developing the project team, and managing the project team.

Psychosocial issues that affect how people work and how well they work include motivation, influence and power, and effectiveness.

Maslow developed a hierarchy of needs that suggests physiological, safety, social, esteem, and self-actualization needs motivate behavior. Once a need is satisfied, it no longer serves as a motivator.

Herzberg distinguished between motivators and hygiene factors. Hygiene factors such as larger salaries or a more attractive work environment will cause dissatisfaction if not present, but do not motivate workers to do more if present. Achievement, recognition, the work itself, responsibility, and growth are factors that contribute to work satisfaction and motivating workers.

McClelland proposed the acquired-needs theory, suggesting that a person's needs are acquired or learned over time and shaped by their life experiences. The three types of acquired needs are a need for achievement, a need for affiliation, and a need for power.

McGregor developed Theory X and Theory Y to describe different approaches to managing workers, based on assumptions of worker motivation. Research supports the use of Theory Y, which assumes that people see work as natural and indicates that the most significant rewards are the satisfaction of esteem and self-actualization needs that work can provide. According to Ouchi's Theory Z, workers can be trusted to do their jobs to their utmost ability as long as management supports them and looks out for their well-being. Theory Z emphasizes job rotation, broadening of skills, generalization versus specialization, and the need for continuous training of workers.

Thamhain and Wilemon identified nine influence bases available to project managers: authority, assignment, budget, promotion, money, penalty, work challenge, expertise, and friendship. Their research found that project success is associated with project managers who use work challenge and expertise to influence workers. Project failure is associated with placing too much emphasis on authority, money, or penalty.

Power is the ability to influence behavior to get people to do things they would not otherwise do. The five main types of power are coercive power, legitimate power, expert power, reward power, and referent power.

Project managers can use Stephen Covey's seven habits of highly effective people to help themselves and project teams become more effective. The seven habits include being proactive; beginning with the end in mind; putting first things first; thinking win/win; seeking first to understand, then to be understood; achieving synergy; and sharpening the saw. Using empathic listening is a key skill of good project managers.

Emotional intelligence is also an important concept. It involves knowing and managing one's own emotions and those of others for improved performance.

Project managers must also develop leadership skills. The best leaders understand and apply different leadership styles appropriate to the situation at hand.

Developing the human resource plan involves identifying, assigning, and documenting project roles, responsibilities, and reporting relationships. A responsibility assignment matrix (RAM), staffing management plans, resource histograms, and RACI charts are key tools for defining roles and responsibilities on projects. The main output is a human resource plan.

Acquiring the project team means assigning the appropriate staff to work on the project. This is an important issue in today's competitive environment. Companies must use innovative approaches to find and retain good IT staff.

Resource loading shows the amount of individual resources that an existing schedule requires during specific time frames. Histograms show resource loading and identify overallocation of resources.

Resource leveling is a technique for resolving resource conflicts, such as overallocated resources, by delaying tasks. Leveled resources require less management, lower costs, produce fewer personnel and accounting problems, and often improve morale.

Two crucial skills of a good project manager are team development and team management. Teamwork helps people work more effectively to achieve project goals. Project managers can recommend individual training to improve skills related to teamwork, organize team-building activities for the entire project team and key stakeholders, and provide reward and recognition systems that encourage teamwork. Project managers can use several tools and techniques, including observation and conversation, project performance appraisals, interpersonal skills, and conflict management, to effectively manage their teams. There are several conflict-handling modes, and they can be viewed based on two dimensions: task importance and relationship importance.

Spreadsheets and project management software such as Microsoft Project 2013 can help project managers in project human resource management. Software makes it easy to produce responsibility assignment matrixes, create resource histograms, identify overallocated resources, level resources, and provide various views and reports related to project human resource management.

Project human resource management involves much more than using software to facilitate organizational planning and assign resources. What makes good project managers great is their ability to enable project team members to deliver their best work on a project.

Quick Quiz

1. Which of the following is not part of project human resource management?
   a. resource estimating
   b. acquiring the project team
   c. developing the project team
   d. managing the project team

2. _____ causes people to participate in an activity for their own enjoyment.
   a. Intrinsic motivation
   b. Extrinsic motivation
   c. Self motivation
   d. Social motivation

3. At the bottom of Maslow's pyramid or hierarchy of needs are _____ needs.
   a. self-actualization
   b. esteem
   c. safety
   d. physiological

4. According to McClelland's acquired-needs theory, people who desire harmonious relations with other people and need to feel accepted have a high _____ need.

   a. social

   b. achievement

   c. affiliation

   d. extrinsic

5. _____ power is based on a person's individual charisma.

   a. Affiliation

   b. Referent

   c. Personality

   d. Legitimate

383

6. A _____ maps the work of a project, as described in the WBS, to the people responsible for performing the work.

   a. project organizational chart

   b. work definition and assignment process

   c. resource histogram

   d. responsibility assignment matrix

7. A staffing management plan often includes a resource _____, which is a column chart that shows the number of resources assigned to the project over time.

   a. chart

   b. graph

   c. histogram

   d. timeline

8. What technique can you use to resolve resource conflicts by delaying tasks?

   a. resource loading

   b. resource leveling

   c. critical path analysis

   d. overallocation

9. What are the five stages in Tuckman's model of team development, in chronological order?

   a. forming, storming, norming, performing, and adjourning

   b. storming, forming, norming, performing, and adjourning

   c. norming, forming, storming, performing, and adjourning

   d. forming, storming, performing, norming, and adjourning

10. Which of the following is not a tool or technique for managing project teams?

   a. observation and conversation

   b. project performance appraisals

   c. conflict management

   d. Social Styles Profile

Quick Quiz Answers

1. a; 2. a; 3. d; 4. c; 5. b; 6. d; 7. c; 8. b; 9. a; 10. d

Discussion Questions

1. Discuss changes in the job market for IT workers. How do the job market and current state of the economy affect human resource management?

2. Summarize the processes involved in project human resource management.

3. Briefly summarize the works of Maslow, Herzberg, McClelland, McGregor, Ouchi, Thamhain and Wilemon, and Covey. How do their theories relate to project management?

4. What is emotional intelligence (EI)? Why is it important to develop EI skills?

5. Describe a situation where it would be appropriate to use each of the six leadership styles described by Daniel Goleman.

6. Describe situations in which it would be appropriate to create a project organizational chart, a responsibility assignment matrix, a RACI chart, and a resource histogram. Describe what these charts or matrices look like.

7. Discuss the difference between resource loading and resource leveling, and provide an example of when you would use each technique.

8. Explain two types of team-building activities described in this chapter and discuss their advantages and disadvantages.

9. Summarize the different ways that project managers can address conflicts to help them manage project teams. What can they do to manage virtual team members successfully?

10. How can you use Project 2013 to assist in project human resource management?

Exercises

1. Watch a video about a famous company, such as Google, Apple, or Walmart, that focuses on its treatment of workers and customers. (Netflix has several videos about companies, and you can find several documentaries on the Internet or through your school's library.) How do these organizations manage their human resources? How do they treat customers and suppliers? Do they treat people differently in different parts of the world or in different positions? What perks do they provide? Which perks would be most important to you, and why? Summarize your findings and opinions in a one- or two-page paper, and cite the references you use.

2. Research recent books, articles, and videos on motivation, including work by Daniel Pink. (He has a popular YouTube video created by RSA Animate.) Do you think there are any new insights in the information you found? Are managers trying to focus on what really motivates people to do project work better? Summarize your findings and opinions in a one- or two-page paper, and cite the references you use.

3. Your company is planning to launch an important new project that starts on January 1 and lasts one year. You estimate that you will need one full-time project manager, two full-time business analysts for the first six months, two full-time senior programmers for the whole year, four full-time junior programmers for the months of July, August, and September, and

one full-time technical writer for the last three months. Use the resource_histogram template file from the companion website to create a stacked column chart showing a resource histogram for this project, similar to the example in Figure 9-6. Be sure to include a legend to label the types of resources needed. Use appropriate titles and axis labels.

4. Take the MBTI test and research information about this tool. Several websites have different versions of the test, including *www.humanmetrics.com*, *www.personalitytype.com*, and *www.keirsey.com*. Write a short paper describing your MBTI type and your thoughts on this test as a team-building tool. If you are working on a team project, compare your results and discuss how they might affect team dynamics.

5. Summarize three of Covey's habits in your own words and give examples of how these habits would apply to project management. Document your ideas in a short paper, and include at least two references.

6. Research different tools for assessing leadership styles. Summarize at least three tools and the styles they mention. Do you believe that it's best for leaders to use different styles in different situations? Why or why not?

7. Research recruiting and retention strategies at three different companies. Make sure that the strategies use contrasting approaches. For example, find out how Google treats its workers, and compare the approach with that of Foxconn or another company in the news. What distinguishes one company from another in this area? Are strategies such as signing bonuses, tuition reimbursement, and business casual dress codes standard for new IT workers? What strategies appeal most to you? Summarize your ideas in a short paper that cites at least three references.

8. Write a short paper summarizing the main features of Microsoft Project 2013 that can assist project managers in human resource management. In addition, interview someone who uses Project 2013. Ask if his or her organization uses any of the project human resource management features described in this chapter and Appendix A, and document the reasons given for using or not using certain features.

9. Developing good IT project managers is an important issue. Review several of the studies cited in this chapter that are related to the IT and project management job markets and required skills for these markets. Also review requirements at your college or university for people entering these fields. Summarize your findings and opinions on this issue in a short paper.

Running Case

Several people working on the Global Treps Project are confused about their responsibilities for providing content for the new website. Recall that the team members include you, the project manager, Bobby, the IT guy, and three people who will run shark-tank-like events in Vietnam, India, and Ethiopia (Kim, Ashok, and Alfreda). Recall that the activities in the WBS for the in-house development include the following:

    1.3.2.1   Guidelines and templates for events

    1.3.2.2   Acceptance of ideas for needed new products or services

    1.3.2.3   Custom site for 20 events

You and your team also need to provide information for the videos that you are outsourcing. Recall that the purpose of these short videos is to show people how to use the site and provide suggestions for holding the events. That activity is 1.3.1.3 Video creation for website in the WBS. You have selected the company that will do the outsourced video creation, and their main contact person is Angela.

1. Prepare a RACI chart for the four WBS activities listed. You decide that one person should be accountable for each of these four activities, spreading the work between you, Kim, Ashok, and Alfreda. Bobby will be informed on each activity, and you will be consulted on the ones you are not accountable for. Document key assumptions you make in preparing the chart.

2. You realize that all of your team members have different personality types, and you believe you could work better as a team if you understood each other better. You asked everyone to take an MBTI-based assessment (a free one you found at *www.humanmetrics.com*). You are an ENTJ, Bobby is an INTJ, Kim is an ISFP, Ashok is an ESTJ, and Alfreda is an ISFJ. Find information about each of these MBTI types and summarize their traits as well as suggestions for improving teamwork.

3. Angela, the person in charge of the company preparing the short videos for you website, has suggested that you work together to prepare a detailed list of resources available to help prepare scripts and edit the videos they will create. You decide to use animations instead of real people in the videos, and Angela's company has a lot of experience in that area. Together, you decide that you will need someone to take on the roles of script writers, script editors, animators, sound experts, content editors, and technical editors. Angela and her team will do all of the animating, sound, and technical work and will provide guidance for you and your team to do the other work. To keep costs down and stay on schedule, you decide to plan for all of the video work to be done in 20 days, using no more than 240 total hours of effort, with about half of the effort from Angela's company. Prepare a resource histogram to estimate the number of hours by role for each of the 20 days. Document key assumptions you make in preparing the histogram.

Key Terms

coercive power p.354

collaborating mode p.377

compromise mode p.376

confrontation mode p.376

deputy project managers p.360

emotional intelligence p.357

empathic listening p.356

expert power p.355

extrinsic motivation p.349

forcing mode p.377

groupthink p.377

hierarchy of needs p.349

intrinsic motivation p.349

legitimate power p.354

mirroring p.357

Myers-Briggs Type Indicator (MBTI) p.371

organizational breakdown structure (OBS) p.362

overallocation p.366

power p.354

RACI charts p.363

rapport p.357

referent power p.355

Endnotes

1. International Telecommunication Union, "ICT Facts and Figures" (April 2014).

2. Huawei Technologies Co., Ltd, "Global ICT Spending to Jump to USD 5 tln by 2020—Huawei," *telecompaper.com* (September 29, 2014).

3. Ibid.

4. Stacy Collet, "Forecast 2015: IT Spending on an Upswing," *Computerworld* (November 3, 2014).

5. Mary K. Pratt, "10 Hottest IT Skills for 2015," *Computerworld* (November 18, 2014).

6. Project Management Institute, "Project Management Talent Gap" (March, 2013).

7. Fortune, "100 Best Companies to Work For, 2015," *Fortune* (January 30, 2015), *fortune.com/best-companies/*.

8. Emily Peck, "Proof That Working From Home Is Here To Stay: Even Yahoo Still Does It," *The Huffington Post* (March 18, 2015).

9. CompTIA, "State of the IT Skills Gap," *CompTIA* (2014), *www.comptia.org/resources/state-of-the-it-skills-gap-2014*.

10. Frederick Herzberg, "One More Time: How Do You Motivate Employees?" *Harvard Business Review* (February 1968), pp. 51–62.

11. RSA Animate, "Drive: The Surprising Truth about What Motivates Us," YouTube video, 10:48, from a talk given by Dan Pink at RSA: 21st Century Enlightenment on February 27, 2013, uploaded April 1, 2010 by RSA, *www.youtube.com/watch?v=u6XAPnuFjJc*.

12. David C. McClelland, *The Achieving Society* (New York: Free Press, 1961).

13. Douglas McGregor, *The Human Side of Enterprise* (New York: McGraw-Hill, 1960).

14. William Ouchi, *Theory Z: How American Business Can Meet the Japanese Challenge* (New York: Avon Books, 1981).

15. H. J. Thamhain and D. L. Wilemon, "Building Effective Teams for Complex Project Environments," *Technology Management* 5, no. 2 (May 1999).

16. Hans J. Thamhain, "Changing Dynamics of Team Leadership in Global Project Environments," *American Journal of Industrial and Business Management*, 3 (2013), pp. 146–156, *dx.doi.org/10.4236/ajibm.2013.32020* (published online April 2013).

17. John R. French and Bertram H. Raven, "The Bases of Social Power," in *Studies in Social Power*, D. Cartwright (Ed.) (Ann Arbor: University of Michigan Press, 1959).

18. Stephen Covey, *The 7 Habits of Highly Effective People: Powerful Lessons in Personal Change* (New York: Simon & Schuster, 1990).

19. Tracy Kidder, *The Soul of a New Machine* (New York: Modern Library, 1997).

20. Douglas Ross, "Applying Covey's Seven Habits to a Project Management Career," *PM Network* (April 1996), pp. 26–30.

21. PMI, "Must-Have Career Skill: Emotional Intelligence" (October 18, 2011).

22. Peter Northouse, *Leadership: Theory and Practice*, Seventh Edition (Thousand Oaks, CA: SAGE Publications, Inc., 2015), p. 5.

23. Bendelta, "Goleman's 6 Leadership Styles–and When to Use Them" (December 9, 2014).

24. PMI, "Pulse of the Profession In-Depth Report: Navigating Complexity" (2013).

25. Great Rated!™, "2015 Fortune 100 Best Companies to Work For® List" (2015), *us.greatrated.com/rankings/2015-fortune-100-best-companies-to-work-for-list*.

26. Bruce Tuckman and Mary Ann Jensen, "Stages of Small-Group Development Revisited," *Group Organization Management*, 2 (1977), pp. 419–427.

27. Isabel Myers Briggs, with Peter Myers, *Gifts Differing: Understanding Personality Type* (Palo Alto, CA: Consulting Psychologists Press, 1995).

28. David Keirsey, *Please Understand Me II: Temperament, Character, Intelligence* (Del Mar, CA: Prometheus Nemesis Book Company, 1998).

29. Michael L. Lyons, "The DP Psyche," *Datamation* (August 15, 1985).

30. The information provided about the Keirsey Temperament Sorter and Keirsey Temperament Theory was compiled from *Keirsey.com*.

31. Sharon McDonald and Helen M. Edwards, "Who Should Test Whom? Examining the Use and Abuse of Personality Tests in Software Engineering," *Communications of the ACM* 50, no. 1 (January 2007).

32. Harvey A. Robbins and Michael Finley, *The New Why Teams Don't Work: What Goes Wrong and How to Make It Right* (San Francisco, CA: Berrett-Koehler Publishers, 1999).

33. John C. Goodman, "DISC, What Is It? Who Created the DISC Model?" *OnlineDiscProfile.com* (2004–2008).

34. "Constructive Team Conflict," *Wharton Leadership Digest* 1, no. 6 (March 1997).

35. Patrick Lencioni, *Overcoming the Five Dysfunctions of a Team: A Field Guide for Leaders, Managers, and Facilitators* (San Francisco, CA: Jossey-Bass, 2005), p. 3.

CHAPTER 10

PROJECT COMMUNICATIONS MANAGEMENT

LEARNING OBJECTIVES

After reading this chapter, you will be able to:

- Understand the importance of good communications on projects and the need to develop soft skills, especially for IT project managers and their teams

- Review key concepts related to communications

- Explain the elements of planning project communications and how to create a communications management plan

- Describe how to manage communications, including communication technologies, media, and performance reporting

- Discuss methods for controlling communications to ensure that information needs are met throughout the life of the project

- List various methods for improving project communications, such as running effective meetings, using various technologies effectively, and using templates

- Describe how software can enhance project communications management

> ## OPENING CASE
>
> Peter Gumpert worked his way up the corporate ladder in a large telecommunications company. He was intelligent, competent, and a strong leader, but the company's new fiber-optic undersea telecommunications program was much larger and more complicated than anything he had previously worked on, let alone managed. This program consisted of several distinct projects, and Peter was in charge of overseeing them all. The changing marketplace for undersea telecommunications systems and the large number of projects involved made communications and flexibility critical concerns for Peter. For missing milestone and completion dates, his company would suffer financial penalties ranging from thousands of dollars per day for smaller projects to more than $250,000 per day for larger projects. Many projects depended on the success of other projects, so Peter had to understand and actively manage those critical interfaces.
>
> Peter held several informal and formal discussions with the project managers who reported to him on the program. He worked with them and his project executive assistant, Christine Braun, to develop a communications plan for the program. He was still unsure, however, about the best way to distribute information and manage all of the inevitable changes that would occur. He also wanted to develop consistent ways for project managers to develop their plans and track performance without stifling their creativity and autonomy. Christine suggested that they consider using some new communications technologies to keep important project information up to date and synchronized. Although Peter knew a lot about telecommunications and laying fiber-optic lines, he was not an expert in using information technology (IT) to improve the communication process. In fact, that was part of the reason he had asked Christine to be his assistant. Could they really develop a process for communicating that would be flexible and easy to use? Time was of the essence, as more projects were being added to the fiber-optic undersea telecommunications program every week.

10.1 THE IMPORTANCE OF PROJECT COMMUNICATIONS MANAGEMENT

Many experts agree that the greatest threat to the success of any project, especially IT projects, is a failure to communicate. Many problems in other knowledge areas, such as an unclear scope or unrealistic schedules, indicate problems with communication. It is crucial for project managers and their teams to make good communication a priority, especially with top management and other key stakeholders.

The IT field is constantly changing, and these changes come with a great deal of technical jargon. When computer professionals communicate with people who aren't as proficient with or knowledgeable about computers—a group that includes many business professionals and senior managers—technical jargon can often complicate matters and create confusion. Even though most people use computers today, the gap between users and developers increases as technology advances. This gap in knowledge and experience causes some of the communication problems between technical professionals and their business colleagues. Of course, not every computer professional is a poor communicator, but most people in any field can improve their communication skills.

In addition, many educational systems for IT graduates promote strong technical skills over strong communication and social skills. Most IT-related degree programs have many technical requirements, but few require courses in communications (speaking, writing, listening), psychology, sociology, and the humanities. People often assume that learning these soft skills is easy, but they *are* important skills, so people must learn and develop them.

Many studies have shown that IT professionals need these soft skills just as much or even more than other skills. You cannot totally separate technical skills and soft skills when working on IT projects. For projects to succeed, every project team member needs both types of skills, and needs to develop them continuously through formal education and on-the-job training.

Studies continue to show a high demand for IT professionals and the importance of good communication and business skills. According to a 2014 article in the *International Journal of Business and Social Science*:

- Organizations are looking for workers with the correct mix of technical, soft, and business skills.
- The most important non-technical skills are problem solving, team work, listening, the ability to adapt to new technologies and languages, time management, the ability to transfer knowledge to application, multitasking, verbal communication, the ability to visualize and conceptualize, "be the customer" mentality, interpersonal skills, understanding business culture, inter-team communication, and give and receive constructive criticism.
- "The need for these non-technical skills is so great that some IT companies indicate that they will hire individuals with minimum technical skills so long as they demonstrate solid soft and business skills."[1]

This chapter highlights keys to good communications, describes the processes of project communications management, provides suggestions for improving communications, and describes how software can assist in project communications management.

The goal of project communications management is to ensure timely and appropriate generation, collection, dissemination, storage, and disposition of project information. There are three main processes in project communications management:

1. *Planning communications management* involves determining the information and communications needs of the stakeholders. Who needs what information? When will they need it? How will the information be given to them? The outputs of this process include a communications management plan and project documents updates.
2. *Managing communications* involves creating, distributing, storing, retrieving, and disposing of project communications based on the communications management plan. The main outputs of this process are project communications, project documents updates, project management plan updates, and organizational process assets updates. Recall from Chapter 4 that organizational process assets include formal and informal plans, policies, procedures, guidelines, information systems, financial systems, management systems, lessons learned, and historical information. These assets help people understand, follow, and improve business processes in an organization.
3. *Controlling communications* involves monitoring and controlling project communications to ensure that stakeholder communication needs are met.

Figure 10-1 summarizes these processes and outputs, showing when they occur in a typical project.

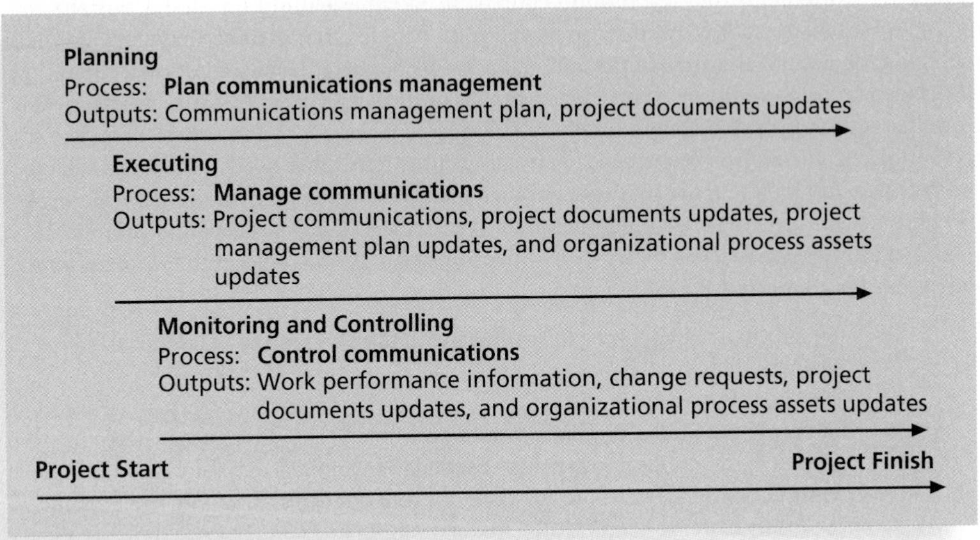

Planning
Process: **Plan communications management**
Outputs: Communications management plan, project documents updates

Executing
Process: **Manage communications**
Outputs: Project communications, project documents updates, project
management plan updates, and organizational process assets
updates

Monitoring and Controlling
Process: **Control communications**
Outputs: Work performance information, change requests, project
documents updates, and organizational process assets updates

Project Start   **Project Finish**

© Cengage Learning 2016

FIGURE 10-1   Project communications management summary

10.2 KEYS TO GOOD COMMUNICATIONS

Project managers say they spend as much as 90 percent of their time communicating. Just as it is difficult to understand people and their motivations, it is also difficult to communicate with people effectively. Several important concepts can help, such as focusing on individual and group communication needs, using formal and informal methods for communicating, providing important information in an effective and timely manner, setting the stage for communicating bad news, and understanding communication channels.

10.2a   Focusing on Group and Individual Communication Needs

Many top managers think they can just add more people to a project that is falling behind schedule. Unfortunately, this approach often causes more setbacks because of the increased complexity of communications. In his popular book *The Mythical Man-Month*, Frederick Brooks illustrates this concept very clearly.[2] People are not interchangeable parts. You cannot assume that a task scheduled to take two months of one person's time can be done in one month by two people. A popular analogy is that you cannot take nine women and produce a baby in one month!

It is important to understand individual and group preferences for communications. As you learned in Chapter 9, people have different personality traits that often affect their communication preferences. For example, if you want to praise a project team member for doing a good job, most introverts would be more comfortable receiving that praise in private, while most extroverts would like everyone to hear about their good work. An intuitive person would want to understand how something fits into the big picture, while a sensing person would prefer to have more focused, step-by-step details. Strong thinkers would want to know the logic behind information, while feeling people would want to know how the information affects them personally as well as other people. A judging person would be very driven to meet deadlines with few reminders, while a perceiving person would need more assistance in developing and following plans.

However, every person is unique, so you cannot simply generalize based on a personality profile or other traits. You need to seek first to understand, as author Stephen Covey suggests in *The 7 Habits of Highly Effective People*, and put yourself in someone else's shoes before you can truly communicate.

It is important for project managers and their team members to be aware of their own communication styles. As you learned in the previous chapter, many IT professionals have different personality traits than the general population, such as being more introverted, intuitive, and oriented to thinking (as opposed to feeling). These personality differences can lead to miscommunication with people who are extroverted, sensation-oriented, and feeling-oriented. For example, a user guide written by an IT professional might not provide the detailed steps most users need. Many users also prefer face-to-face meetings or short videos to learn how to use a new system instead of trying to follow a written guide. They might prefer to have a two-way conversation in which they can get hands-on experience and ask questions on the spot.

Also, the receiver of information rarely interprets it exactly as the sender intended. Therefore, it is important to provide several methods of communication, such as written words, visuals, videos, and meetings, and an environment that promotes open dialogue. Instead of assuming that the receiver understands, you can build in a feedback loop to make sure. For example, several teachers use clickers or similar tools to quickly gauge how well their students understand a concept. Many are surprised at the difference in what they think people understand and what they really do. It is also difficult for many people to admit that they do not understand something. Project managers and their teams must be patient and flexible when communicating information and focus on making sure their messages are understood. You cannot overcommunicate!

 WHAT WENT WRONG?

Amusing examples of miscommunications are common, especially when they involve the use of new technologies. For example, I was teaching an introductory course in information systems several years ago. Other instructors would often sit in on the course to learn how to use the latest software applications. One day, students were learning how to adjust settings and use short cuts on their computers. I would tell the students to "right-click" and then select Properties, or "right-click" and then select Copy. At the end of the class, an instructor quietly approached, waited until the other students were gone, and then said, "I don't know what I'm doing wrong." She held up a piece of paper

continued

on which she had written the word "click" about a dozen times. In other words, she literally did write "click" when told to do so instead of right-clicking. I asked, "Are you a Mac user?" Macintosh computers do not normally have a mouse with two buttons, so users never have to right-click. I showed the instructor how to right-click with a mouse, and in future classes made sure to point out operations that were different on PCs than Macs.

Geographic location and cultural background also affect the complexity of project communications. If project stakeholders are in different countries, it is often difficult or impossible to schedule times for two-way communication during normal working hours. Language barriers can also cause communication problems; the same word may have very different meanings in different languages. Times, dates, and other units of measure are also interpreted differently. People from some cultures also communicate in ways that might make others uncomfortable. For example, managers in some countries still do not allow women or workers of lower ranks to give formal presentations. Some cultures also reserve written documents for binding commitments. Taking the time to research and understand these nuances of communications early in a project can help tremendously.

10.2b Formal and Informal Methods for Communicating

It is not enough for project team members to submit reports to their project managers and other stakeholders and then assume that everyone who needs to know the information will read the reports. Occasionally, that approach might work, but many people prefer informal communications. About half the general population are extroverts, so they enjoy talking to other people. Often, many nontechnical professionals—from colleagues to managers—prefer to have a two-way conversation about a project rather than reading detailed reports, e-mails, or web pages to try to find pertinent information.

Many colleagues and managers want to know the people working on their projects and develop a trusting relationship with them. They use informal discussions about the project to develop these relationships. Therefore, project managers must be good at nurturing relationships through good communication. Many experts believe that the difference between good project managers and excellent project managers is their ability to nurture relationships and use empathic listening skills, as described in Chapter 9, Project Human Resource Management.

Oral communication also helps build stronger relationships among project personnel and project stakeholders. People like to interact with each other to get a true feeling for how a project is going. Research conducted by Albert Mehrabian and discussed in his book *Silent Messages* indicated that in face-to-face interactions information is communicated through body language, tone of voice, and the spoken content.[3] The lesson for project communications today is that it is important to pay attention to more than someone's actual words. A person's tone of voice and body language say a lot about how they feel.

Effective creation and distribution of information depends on project managers and project team members having good communication skills. Communicating includes many different dimensions such as writing, speaking, and listening, and project personnel need to use all of these dimensions in their daily routines. In addition, different people respond positively to different levels or types of communication. For example, a project sponsor may prefer to stay informed through informal discussions held once a week over coffee. The project manager needs to be aware of this preference and take advantage of it. The project sponsor will give better feedback about the project during these informal talks than through some other form of communication. Informal conversations allow the project sponsor to exercise a leadership role and provide insights and information that are critical to the success of the project and the organization as a whole. Short face-to-face meetings are often more effective than electronic communications, particularly for sensitive information.

10.2c Distributing Important Information in an Effective and Timely Manner

It is important to include detailed technical information that affects critical performance features of products or services developed in a project. It is even more important to document any changes in technical specifications that might affect product performance. For example, if the fiber-optic undersea telecommunications program described in the chapter's opening case included a project to purchase and provide special diving gear, and the supplier of the oxygen tanks enhanced the tanks so divers could stay under water longer, other people would need to know about this important new capability. The information should not be buried in an attachment with the supplier's new product brochure.

People have a tendency to avoid reporting bad news. If the oxygen tank vendor was behind on production, the person in charge of the project to purchase the tanks might wait until the last minute to report this critical information. This news could be delivered quickly via text through a website, e-mail, text message, or similar means. However, people tend to become overwhelmed by too much information, and they might not understand what it means to them on their particular project.

Oral communication via meetings and informal talks helps bring important information—positive or negative—into the open. Because IT projects often require a lot of coordination, it is a good idea to have short, frequent meetings. For example, some IT project managers require all project personnel to attend a "stand-up" meeting every week or even every morning, depending on project needs. Stand-up meetings have no chairs, which forces people to focus on what they need to communicate. Recall that projects using an agile approach have daily meetings to make sure everyone is on the same page. If people can't meet face to face, they can have virtual meetings instead.

10.2d Setting the Stage for Communicating Bad News

It is important to put information in context, especially if it's bad news. If there is a problem, know how it will affect the whole project and the organization. Bad news might seem like a major setback, but you can recommend steps to take to mitigate a problem. Project sponsors and other senior managers want to know that you have evaluated the impact of the situation, considered alternatives, and made a recommendation based on your expertise. Project managers should know how a major problem might affect the bottom line of the organization and be able to use their leadership skills to handle the challenge.

An amusing example of how to mitigate bad news is provided in the following letter from a college student to her parents. Variations of this letter can be found on many websites.

> *Dear Mom and Dad, or should I say Grandma & Grandpa,*
>
> *Yes, I am pregnant. No, I'm not married yet since Larry, my boyfriend, is out of a job. Larry's employers just don't seem to appreciate the skills he has learned since he quit high school. Larry looks much younger than you, Dad, even though he is three years older. I'm quitting college and getting a job so we can get an apartment before the baby is born. I found a beautiful apartment above a 24-hour auto repair garage with good insulation so the exhaust fumes and noise won't bother us.*
>
> *I'm very happy. I thought you would be too.*
>
> *Love, Ashley*
>
> *P.S. There is no Larry. I'm not pregnant. I'm not getting married. I'm not quitting school, but I am getting a "D" in Chemistry. I just wanted you to have some perspective.*

10.2e Determining the Number of Communication Channels

Another important aspect of communications is the number of people involved in a project. As the number increases, the complexity of communication increases because there are more channels or pathways through which people can communicate. You can use the following simple formula to determine the number of communication channels as the number of people involved in a project increases:

$$\text{number of communication channels} = \frac{n(n-1)}{2}$$

where n is the number of people involved.

For example, two people have one communication channel: $(2(2-1))/2 = 1$. Three people have three channels: $(3(3-1))/2 = 3$. Four people have six channels, five people have 10, and so on. Figure 10-2 illustrates this concept. You can see that as the number of people increases above three, the number of communication channels increases rapidly. Project managers should try to limit the size of teams or subteams to avoid making communications too complex. For example, if three people are working together on a particular project task, they have three communication channels. If you added two more people to their team, you would have 10 communication channels, an increase of seven. If you added three more people instead of two, you'd have 12 communication channels. You can see how quickly communication becomes more complex as you increase team size.

Good communicators consider many factors before deciding how to distribute information, including the size of the group, the type of information, and the appropriate communication medium. People often send e-mail messages that are quickly written and therefore not as carefully planned as they should be. While this can be a problem even with a small group of five recipients, the negative effects multiply many times when sending such a message to a group of 500 people or more. When asked why you cannot always

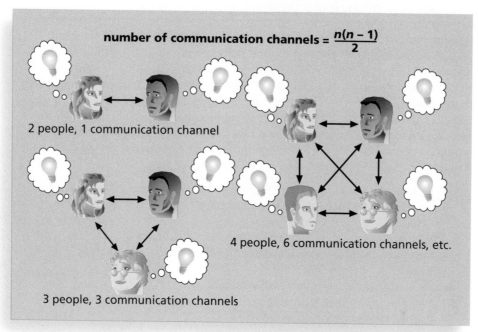

number of communication channels = $\dfrac{n(n-1)}{2}$

2 people, 1 communication channel

4 people, 6 communication channels, etc.

3 people, 3 communication channels

© Cengage Learning 2016

FIGURE 10-2   The impact of the number of people on communication channels

send an e-mail to a very large team of people just as you could to a small one, one CIO answered, "As a group increases in size, you have a whole slew of management challenges. Communicating badly exponentially increases the possibility of making fatal mistakes. A large-scale project has a lot of moving parts, which makes it that much easier to break down. Communication is the oil that keeps everything working properly. It's much easier to address an atmosphere of distrust among a group of five team members than it is with a team of 500 members."[4]

However, in some situations you cannot have face-to-face meetings and must e-mail a large group of people. Many IT professionals work on virtual projects in which they never meet their project sponsors, other team members, or other project stakeholders. In a virtual project environment, it is crucial for project managers to develop clear communication procedures. They must use e-mail, web conferencing, instant messaging, discussion threads, project websites, and other technologies to communicate most information. They might be able to use phone calls or other media occasionally, but in general, they must rely on good written communications.

As you can see, project communication involves more than creating and sending status reports or holding periodic meetings. Many good project managers know their personal strengths and weaknesses in this area and surround themselves with people who complement their skills, just as Peter Gumpert did in the opening case by asking Christine to be his assistant. It is good practice to share the responsibility for project communications management with the entire project team.

10.3 PLANNING COMMUNICATIONS MANAGEMENT

Because communication is so important on projects, every project should include a **communications management plan**—a document that guides project communications. This plan should be part of the overall project management plan, as you learned in Chapter 4, Project Integration Management. The communications management plan varies with the needs of the project, but some type of written plan should always be prepared. For small projects, such as the project management intranet site project described in Chapter 3, the communications management plan can be part of the team contract. For large projects, it should be a separate document. The communications management plan should address the following items:

1. Stakeholder communications requirements
2. Information to be communicated, including format, content, and level of detail
3. Who will receive the information and who will produce it
4. Suggested methods or technologies for conveying the information
5. Frequency of communication
6. Escalation procedures for resolving issues
7. Revision procedures for updating the communications management plan
8. A glossary of common terminology

It is important to know what kinds of information will be distributed to particular stakeholders. By analyzing stakeholder communication needs, you can avoid wasting time or money on creating or disseminating unnecessary information.

Table 10-1 provides part of a sample stakeholder communications analysis that shows which stakeholders should get particular written communications. Note that the stakeholder communications analysis includes columns that list the contact person for the information, when the information is due, and the preferred format for the information. Notice that the first stakeholder, customer management, wants a hard copy of the monthly status reports plus a meeting to talk about them. You can create a similar table to show which stakeholders should attend particular formal project meetings. It is always a good idea to include comment sections with these types of tables to record special considerations or details related to each stakeholder, document, meeting, or other component. Have stakeholders review and approve the stakeholder communications analysis to ensure that the information is correct and useful.

Many projects do not include enough initial information on communications. Project managers, top management, and project team members often assume that using existing communication channels to relay project information is sufficient. The problem with using existing channels is that each group (as well as other stakeholders) has different communication needs. Creating some sort of communications management plan and reviewing it with project stakeholders early in a project helps prevent or reduce later communication problems. If an organization works on many projects, developing some consistency in handling project communications helps the organization run smoothly.

Consistent communication helps organizations improve project communications, especially for programs composed of multiple projects. For example, Peter Gumpert, the program manager in the opening case, would benefit greatly from having a communications management plan that all of his project managers help develop and follow. Because

TABLE 10-1 Sample stakeholder communications analysis

Stakeholders	Document Name	Document Format	Contact Person	Due
Customer management	Monthly status report	Hard copy and meeting	Tina Erndt, Tom Silva	First of month
Customer business staff	Monthly status report	Hard copy	Julie Grant, Sergey Cristobal	First of month
Customer technical staff	Monthly status report	E-mail	Li Chau, Nancy Michaels	First of month
Internal management	Monthly status report	Hard copy and meeting	Bob Thomson	First of month
Internal business and technical staff	Monthly status report	Intranet	Angie Liu	First of month
Training subcontractor	Training plan	Hard copy	Jonathan Kraus	November 1
Software subcontractor	Software implementation plan	E-mail	Najwa Gates	June 1

Comments: Put the titles and dates of documents in e-mail headings and have recipients acknowledge receipt.

© Cengage Learning 2016

several of the projects have some of the same stakeholders, it is even more important to develop a coordinated communications management plan. For example, if customers receive status reports from Peter's company that have totally different formats and do not coordinate information from related projects within the same company, they will question the ability of Peter's company to manage large programs.

Information about the content of essential project communications comes from the work breakdown structure (WBS). In fact, many WBSs include a section for project communications to ensure that reporting key information is a project deliverable. If reporting essential information is an activity defined in the WBS, it becomes even more important to know what project information to report, when to report it, how to report it, and who is responsible for generating the report.

10.4 MANAGING COMMUNICATIONS

Managing communications is a large part of a project manager's job. Getting project information to the right people at the right time and in a useful format is just as important as developing the information in the first place. The stakeholder communications analysis serves as a good starting point for managing communications. Project managers and their teams must decide who receives particular information, but they must also determine the best way to create and distribute the information. Is it sufficient to send written reports for project information? Is text appropriate, or would visuals or even videos communicate the information better? Are meetings alone effective in distributing some project information? Are meetings and written communications both required for project information? What is the best way to provide information to virtual team members?

During project execution, project teams must address important considerations for managing information, and they often end up updating business processes through improved communications. For example, they might modify policies and procedures, modify information systems, or incorporate new technologies to improve information distribution. For example, Peter Gumpert, the program manager in the opening case, might decide that providing key project members with special apps on smartphones would enhance communications. He would need to request additional funds to provide these devices and apps, and training on how to use them.

After answering key questions related to project communications, project managers and their teams must decide on the best way to create and distribute the information. Important considerations include the use of technology, the appropriate methods and media to use, and performance reporting.

10.4a Using Technology to Enhance Information Creation and Distribution

Technology can facilitate the process of creating and distributing information, when used effectively. Most people and businesses rely on e-mail, instant messaging, websites, telephones, cell phones, texting, and other technologies to communicate. Using a project management information system, you can create and organize project documents, schedules, meeting minutes, and customer requests, and make them available in an electronic format. You can store this information locally or in the cloud. Storing templates and samples of project documents electronically can make accessing standard forms easier, thus making information distribution easier. It is also important to have backup procedures in place in case something goes wrong with normal communications technologies, as described in the following "Global Issues" feature. Two important considerations in deciding which technologies to use include the communication method and media, as described in the next sections. You will learn more about using software to assist in project communications management later in this chapter.

 GLOBAL ISSUES

Natural disasters often disrupt communications around the world. For example, the scale of the damage to Japan's communications infrastructure after a 9.0 magnitude earthquake in March 2011 was unprecedented. Fortunately, thousands of employees from NTT East worked around the clock to restore communications. As a result of their efforts, 4.75 million public phone calls were made *on the day after the disaster*. The following list summarizes some facts and figures about the damage and the recovery efforts:

- Approximately 90 trunk lines were severed as a result of damage to bridges and railways.
- 990 exchange buildings were left without power.
- 1.5 million lines were damaged.
- 16 exchange buildings were destroyed.
- 2,700 km of aerial cables were damaged.

continued

- 3,930 emergency-use public phone lines were set up.
- NTT East donated 30,000 telephones to local authorities.
- 450 emergency Internet access points were created.[5]

It's great that communications can be restored a day after a disaster, but often that's too late. The April 2015 Nepal earthquake killed over 8,800 people and injured more than 23,000. After cell phone and internet connections disappeared, several people turned to older technology, like ham radios, to communicate information about missing victims quickly.

To improve communications when the next disaster hits, researchers have been working on a better solution. Danish designers Pernille Skjødt and Ida Stougaard created a device called Reachi, which was a finalist in the 2015 Global Social Venture Competition. It uses a technology called mesh-networking that sends a signal from person to person—the same technology used in the smartphone app called FireChat. The Reachi is a single-function device that is sturdier than a phone, can survive immersion in water, and runs on solar power. "The designers are currently finishing their final proof of concept and coordinating with the Philippines Red Cross to plan a rollout across the country. Eventually, they hope to bring it to other countries as well. It's something that could be useful anywhere; even the most-connected places on Earth can't easily communicate when standard infrastructure breaks."[6]

10.4b Selecting the Appropriate Communication Methods and Media

There are three broad classifications for communication methods:

1. *Interactive communication*: As the name implies, two or more people interact to exchange information via meetings, phone calls, or video conferencing. This method is usually the most effective way to ensure common understanding.
2. *Push communication*: Information is sent or pushed to recipients without their request via reports, e-mails, faxes, voice mails, and other means. This method ensures that the information is distributed, but does not ensure that it was received or understood.
3. *Pull communication*: Information is sent to recipients at their request via websites, bulletin boards, e-learning, knowledge repositories like blogs and wikis, and other means.

In addition to determining the appropriate method or methods for communicating specific project information, it is important to consider which media to use. For example, if you know that you must use interactive communication to review an important topic with the project sponsor, you still need to determine which media to use. Table 10-2 provides guidelines from Practical Communications, Inc., a communications consulting firm, about how well different types of media are suited to different communication needs. These media include hard copy, phone calls, voice mail, e-mail, meetings, and websites. For example, if you were trying to assess commitment of project stakeholders, a meeting would be the most appropriate medium to use. (A face-to-face meeting would be preferable, but a web conference, in which participants could see and hear each other, would also qualify as a meeting.) A phone call would be adequate, but the other media would not be appropriate. Project managers must assess the needs of the organization, the project, and individuals in determining which communication medium to use and when. They must also be aware of new technologies that can enhance communications and collaboration, as described in the following What Went Right? feature.

TABLE 10-2 Media choice table

Key: 1 = Excellent, 2 = Adequate, 3 = Inappropriate						
How Well Medium Is Suited to:	Hard Copy	Phone Call	Voice Mail	E-mail	Meeting	Website
Assessing commitment	3	2	3	3	1	3
Building consensus	3	2	3	3	1	3
Mediating a conflict	3	2	3	3	1	3
Resolving a misunderstanding	3	1	3	3	2	3
Addressing negative behavior	3	2	3	2	1	3
Expressing support or appreciation	1	2	2	1	2	3
Encouraging creative thinking	2	3	3	1	3	3
Making an ironic statement	3	2	2	3	1	3
Conveying a reference document	1	3	3	3	3	2
Reinforcing one's authority	1	2	3	3	1	1
Providing a permanent record	1	3	3	1	3	3
Maintaining confidentiality	2	1	2	3	1	3
Conveying simple information	3	1	1	1	2	3
Asking an informational question	3	1	1	1	3	3
Making a simple request	3	1	1	1	3	3
Giving complex instructions	3	3	2	2	1	2
Addressing many people	2	3 or 1*	2	2	3	1

*Depends on system functionality

Source: Tess Galati, *Email Composition and Communication (EmC2)*, Practical Communications, Inc., *www.praccom.com* (2001)

✓ WHAT WENT WRONG?

A Frost & Sullivan study sponsored by Verizon Business and Microsoft Corp., called "Meetings Around the World: The Impact of Collaboration on Business Performance," found that collaboration is a key driver of overall performance of companies around the world. The impact of collaboration is twice as significant as a company's aggressiveness in pursuing new market opportunities and five times as significant as the external market environment. The study defines collaboration as an interaction between culture and technology, such as audio and web conferencing, e-mail, and instant messaging. The researchers also created a method to measure how collaboration affects business performance.

continued

Of all the collaboration technologies that were studied, three were more commonly present in high-performing companies than in low-performing ones: web conferencing, audio conferencing, and meeting-scheduler technologies. "This study reveals a powerful new metric business leaders can use to more successfully manage their companies and achieve competitive advantage," said Brian Cotton, a vice president at Frost & Sullivan. "Measuring the quality and capability of collaboration in a given organization presents an opportunity for management to prioritize technology investments, encourage adoption of new tools and open up communications lines for improved collaboration."[7]

The study also revealed regional differences in how people in various countries prefer to communicate with one another. These differences highlight an opportunity for greater cultural understanding to improve collaborative efforts around the world. For example:

- American professionals are more likely to enjoy working alone, and they prefer to send e-mail rather than call a person or leave a voice mail message. They are also more comfortable with audio, video, and web conferencing technologies than people from other regions. In addition, they tend to multitask the most when on conference calls.
- Europeans thrive on teamwork more than their counterparts elsewhere and prefer to interact in real time with other people. They are more likely to feel that it is irresponsible not to answer the phone, and they want people to call them back rather than leave a voice mail message.
- Professionals in the Asia-Pacific region, more than anywhere else, want to be in touch constantly during the workday. As a result, they find the phone to be an indispensable tool and prefer instant messaging to e-mail.

In a follow-up study sponsored by Verizon and Cisco, Frost & Sullivan examined the role that collaboration solutions play in enabling high levels of organizational performance and developed a model for measuring return on collaboration (ROC). Surveys from 3,662 managers across the globe were analyzed to estimate the return generated from deploying collaboration technology in critical business activities from six functional areas: innovations and new product development (Research & Development), employee retention and churn/attrition (Human Resources), sales performance (Sales), customer acquisition (Marketing), shareholder value (Investor Relations), and corporate reputation (Public Relations). The study results show the highest returns in the areas of sales performance and innovations and new product development. "Our main finding was striking: As organizations deploy and use IP-enabled, advanced collaboration tools in their operations, they are able to perform better on business critical activities, and realize a higher return on their collaboration.[8]

10.4c Reporting Performance

Another important tool for managing project communications is performance reporting. Performance reporting keeps stakeholders informed about how resources are being used to achieve project objectives. It also motivates workers to have some progress to report. Recall from Chapter 1 that progress reports are considered to be a super tool—a tool that is extensively used and has been found to improve project performance. Performance reports are normally provided as progress reports or status reports.

Many people use the two terms interchangeably, but some people distinguish between them as follows:

- **Progress reports** describe what the project team has accomplished during a certain period. Many projects have each team member prepare a monthly report or sometimes a weekly progress report. Team leaders often create consolidated progress reports based on the information received from team members. A sample template for a monthly progress report is provided later in this chapter.
- **Status reports** describe where the project stands at a specific point in time. Status reports address where the project stands in terms of the triple constraint, meeting scope, time, and cost goals. How much money has been spent to date? How long did it take to do certain tasks? Is work being accomplished as planned? Status reports can take various formats depending on the stakeholders' needs. As described in Chapter 2, when using agile project management, progress is communicated via daily Scrum meetings and burndown charts.

Forecasts predict future project status and progress based on past information and trends. How long will it take to finish the project based on how things are going? How much more money will be needed to complete the project? Project managers can use earned value management (see Chapter 7, Project Cost Management) to answer these questions by estimating the budget at completion and projected completion date based on how the project is progressing.

An important technique for performance reporting is the status review meeting. Status review meetings, as described in Chapter 4, Project Integration Management, are a good way to highlight information provided in important project documents, empower people to be accountable for their work, and have face-to-face discussions about important project issues. Many program and project managers hold periodic status review meetings to exchange important project information and motivate people to make progress on their parts of the project. Likewise, many top managers hold monthly or quarterly status review meetings in which program and project managers must report overall status information.

Status review meetings sometimes become battlegrounds where conflicts between different parties come to a head. Project managers or higher-level top managers should set ground rules for status review meetings to control the amount of conflict and should work to resolve any potential problems. It is important to remember that project stakeholders should work together to address performance problems.

10.5 CONTROLLING COMMUNICATIONS

The main goal of controlling communications is to ensure the optimal flow of information throughout the entire project life cycle. The main inputs are the project management plan, project communications, issue logs, work performance data, and organizational process assets. (Issue logs are described in Chapter 13, Project Stakeholder Management.) The project manager and project team should use their various reporting systems, expert judgment, and meetings to assess how well communications are working. If communication problems exist, the project manager and team need to take action, which often requires changes to the earlier processes of planning and managing project communications. The main outputs of controlling communications are work performance information, change requests, project documents updates, and organizational process assets updates.

It is often beneficial to have a facilitator from outside the project team assess how well communications are working. A facilitator can also help the team solve any communication problems. Many project teams need help in improving communications, and many internal and external experts are available to help. The following section also provides suggestions for improving project communications.

10.6 SUGGESTIONS FOR IMPROVING PROJECT COMMUNICATIONS

Good communication is vital to the management and success of IT projects. So far in this chapter, you have learned that project communications management can ensure that essential information reaches the right people at the right time, that feedback and reports are appropriate and useful, and that there are formalized processes for planning, managing, and controlling communications. This section highlights a few areas that all project managers and project team members should consider in their quests to improve project communications. This section provides guidelines for developing better communication skills, running effective meetings, using e-mail, instant messaging, texting, kanban boards, and collaborative tools effectively, and using templates for project communications.

10.6a Developing Better Communication Skills

Some people seem to be born with great communication skills. Others seem to have a knack for picking up technical skills. It is rare to find someone with a natural ability for both. Both types of skills, however, can be developed. Most IT professionals enter the field because of their technical skills. Most find, however, that communication skills are the key to advancing in their careers, especially if they want to become good project managers.

Most companies spend a lot of money on technical training for their employees, even when employees might benefit more from communications training. Individuals are also more likely to enroll voluntarily in classes to learn the latest technology than in classes that develop soft skills.

Communication skills training usually includes role-playing activities in which participants learn concepts such as building rapport, as described in Chapter 9, Project Human Resource Management. Training sessions also give participants a chance to develop specific skills in small groups. Sessions that focus on presentation skills typically use video to record the participants' presentations. Most people are surprised to see some of their mannerisms and enjoy the challenge of improving their skills. A minimal investment in communication and presentation training can have a tremendous payback to individuals, their projects, and their organizations.

As organizations become more global, they realize that they must also invest in ways to improve communication with people from different countries and cultures. For example, Apple released their new 2015 operating system, which included hundreds of diverse emojis to appeal to users all over the world.

Many Americans are raised to speak their minds, while in some other cultures people are offended by outspokenness. Decision makers from several countries, such as China, focus on building personal relationships and trust rather than on facts and quick responses, like Americans. Not understanding how to communicate effectively with people of other cultures and diverse backgrounds hurts projects and businesses. Many training courses are available to educate people in cultural awareness, international business, and international team building. Workers also need to learn how to participate in virtual meetings and conference calls. Some people take these skills for granted, but many people need assistance in becoming comfortable and productive in new work environments.

It takes leadership to help improve communication. If top management lets employees give poor presentations, write sloppy reports, offend people from different cultures, or behave poorly at meetings, the employees will not want to improve their communication skills. Top management must set high expectations and lead by example. Some organizations send all IT professionals to training that includes development of technical *and* communication skills. Successful organizations allocate time in project schedules for preparing drafts of important reports and presentations and incorporating feedback on the drafts. It is good practice to include time for informal meetings with customers to help develop relationships and provide staff to assist in relationship management. As with any other goal, communication can be improved with proper planning, support, and leadership from top management.

MEDIA SNAPSHOT

Many readers of this book grew up using social media sites like Facebook and Twitter. You may be surprised to learn that 93 percent of recruiters check out social media profiles of prospective hires. A 2014 article in *Money* magazine provides a list of "10 Social Media Blunders That Cost a Millennial a Job—or Worse," as follows:

1. Posting something embarrassing on the corporate Twitter feed.
2. Sexual oversharing.
3. Revealing company secrets.
4. Blowing your own cover.
5. Talking smack about a job before you've even accepted it.
6. Making fun of clients or donors.
7. Making fun of your boss/team.
8. Posting while you're supposed to be working.
9. Complaining about your job.
10. Drinking in a photo—even if you're over 21.[9]

10.6b Running Effective Meetings

A well-run meeting can be a vehicle for fostering team building and reinforcing expectations, roles, relationships, and commitment to the project. However, a poorly run meeting can have a detrimental effect on a project. For example, a terrible kick-off meeting may cause important stakeholders to decide not to support the project further.

Many people complain about the time they waste in unnecessary or poorly planned and poorly executed meetings. The following guidelines can help improve time spent at meetings:

- *Determine if a meeting can be avoided.* Do not have a meeting if there is a better way to achieve the objective at hand. For example, a project manager might need approval from a top manager to hire another person for the project team. It could take a week or longer to schedule even a 10-minute meeting on the top manager's calendar. Instead, an e-mail or phone call describing the situation and justifying the request is a faster, more effective approach than having a meeting. However, you often do need a face-to-face meeting in certain situations because using e-mail or a phone call would be inappropriate. Consider which medium would be most effective.

- *Define the purpose and intended outcome of the meeting.* Be specific about what should happen as a result of the meeting. Is the purpose to brainstorm ideas, provide status information, or solve a problem? Make the purpose of a meeting very clear to all meeting planners and participants. For example, if a project manager calls a meeting of all project team members without knowing the true purpose of the meeting, everyone will focus on their own agendas and very little will be accomplished. All meetings should have a purpose and intended outcome.

- *Determine who should attend the meeting.* Do certain stakeholders have to be at a meeting to make it effective? Should only the project team leaders attend a meeting, or should the entire project team be involved? Many meetings are most effective with the minimum number of participants possible, especially if decisions must be made. Other meetings require many attendees. It is important to determine who should attend a meeting based on its purpose and intended outcome.

- *Provide an agenda to participants before the meeting.* Meetings are most effective when the participants come prepared. Did they read reports before the meeting? Did they collect necessary information? Some professionals refuse to attend meetings if they do not have an agenda ahead of time. Insisting on an agenda forces meeting organizers to plan the meeting and gives potential participants the chance to decide whether they need to attend.

- *Prepare handouts and visual aids, and make logistical arrangements ahead of time.* By creating handouts and visual aids, you must organize thoughts and ideas. This usually helps the entire meeting run more effectively. It is also important to make logistical arrangements by booking an appropriate room, having necessary equipment available, and providing refreshments or entire meals, if appropriate. It takes time to plan for effective meetings. Project managers and their team members must take time to prepare for meetings, especially important ones with key stakeholders.

- *Run the meeting professionally.* Introduce people, restate the purpose of the meeting, and state any ground rules that attendees should follow. Have someone facilitate the meeting to make sure that important items are discussed, watch the time, encourage participation, summarize key issues, and clarify decisions and action items. Designate someone to take minutes and then send them to all participants soon after the meeting. Minutes should be short and focus on the crucial decisions and action items from the meeting.

- *Set the ground rules for the meeting.* State up front how the meeting will be run. For example, can people speak at will, or will the facilitator lead discussions? Can attendees use their laptops or other electronic devices during the meeting? Don't assume that all meetings are run in the same way. Do what works best in each specific case.

- *Build relationships.* Depending on the culture of the organization and project, it may help to build relationships by making meetings fun experiences. For example, it may be appropriate to use humor, refreshments, or prizes for good ideas to keep meeting participants actively involved. If used effectively, meetings are a good way to build relationships.

10.6c Using E-Mail, Instant Messaging, Texting, Kanban Boards, and Collaborative Tools Effectively

Because most people use e-mail and other electronic communication tools now, communications should improve, right? Not necessarily. In fact, few people have received any training or guidelines on when or how to use e-mail, instant messaging, texting, kanban boards, or other collaborative tools, such as Microsoft SharePoint portals, Google Docs, or wikis. A **SharePoint portal** allows users to create custom websites to access documents and applications stored on shared devices. **Google Docs** allows users to create, share, and edit

---

#1 BEST PRACTICE

One of the main features of kanban is visualizing workflow, which is often done by using kanban boards. Figure 10-3 provides a very simple example of a kanban board. Notice that the main categories where tasks are placed include To Do, In Progress, and Done. Team members work together to complete all of the tasks, clearly showing which ones need to be done (in the To Do section), which ones are being worked on (in the In Progress section), and which ones are completed (in the Done section). People using kanban boards can tailor the concept to meet their needs. For example, they could create a physical board or use a wall in their office environment, write the names of tasks on sticky notes, and physically move the sticky notes along the board or wall. Or, a team could use an online tool to enter and track their workflow. They could add people's names to each task, color code tasks, include a calendar, or use whatever approach helps the team improve their performance.

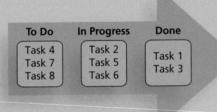

Source: Kathy Schwalbe, *An Introduction to Project Management*, Fifth Edition (2015)

FIGURE 10-3 Sample kanban board

documents, spreadsheets, and presentations online. A **wiki** is a website that enables any-one who accesses it to contribute to or modify its content. Kanban boards visually show tasks that need to be done, are in progress, or are completed. They have become a popular tool to improve communications, as described in the Best Practice feature.

Even if people do know when to use e-mail or other tools for project communications, they also need to know how to use the tools. New features are added to software programs with every release, but often users are unaware of these features and do not receive train-ing on how to use them. Do you know how to organize and file your e-mail messages, or do you have hundreds of them in your inbox? Do you know how to use your address book or how to create distribution lists? Have you ever used sorting features to find e-mail mes-sages or documents by date, author, or key words? Do you use filtering software to prevent spam? Do you know how to share your desktop with instant messaging to teach some-one how to use software on your computer? Do you know how to track and incorporate changes in Google Docs to create reports and spreadsheets as a collaborative effort? Does everyone on your project team know how to use important features of your SharePoint portal or wiki? Are you using a software tool for creating kanban boards that is tailored to meet your needs? Project teams and organizations that emphasize using a shared reposi-tory for good communications are often more productive. Many project management soft-ware tools include the ability to share project documents and other communications, but processes must be established first and followed.

Something as simple as a standard college course illustrates these issues. Many college courses now use online course management software like Moodle or Blackboard. Instruc-tors have learned to post the course syllabus, handouts, lecture notes, and other docu-ments for the entire class to share. Students are often required to take quizzes, participate in discussions, and post their own files on a central site. Posting all information in one location enhances communications. If the instructor states in the syllabus that students must check their e-mail frequently for course information, they will do so, even though they might prefer to use text messaging. If they fail to check their e-mail, participate in discussions, or generally use the online course tools, the consequences will affect their grades.

Even if you know how to use all the features of these communication systems, you will likely still need to learn how to put ideas into words clearly and effectively. For exam-ple, the subject line for any e-mail message you write should clearly state the intention of the e-mail. Folder and file names for collaborative projects should be clear and follow file naming conventions, if provided. A business professional who does not write well might prefer to talk to people than to send an e-mail or instant message. Poor writing often leads to misunderstandings and confusion.

Project managers should do whatever they can to help their project stakeholders use e-mail, instant messaging, texting, and other tools effectively and not waste time with poor or unclear communications. Information sent via e-mail, instant messaging, texting, or a collaborative tool should be appropriate for that medium. If you can communicate the information better with a phone call or meeting, for example, then do so. If you introduce a new technique, such as kanban boards, be sure to tailor it to meet your needs. Do not use new tools because they are the latest fad. Use them because they improve commu-nications and productivity. Learn how to use important features of your e-mail, texting, instant messaging, and collaborative software, and make sure that everyone on your team also learns.

The following guidelines can help you use e-mail as a more effective communication tool:

- Be sure to send e-mail to the right people. Do not automatically "reply to all" on an e-mail, for example, if it is not necessary.
- Use meaningful subject lines in e-mails so readers can quickly see what information the message contains. If the entire message can fit in the subject line, put it there. For example, if a meeting is cancelled, just enter that message in the subject line. Also, do not continue replying to an e-mail thread when the subject has changed without changing the subject line. The subject line should always relate to the latest topic.
- Limit the content of the e-mail to one main subject. Send a second or third e-mail if it relates to a different subject.
- The body of the e-mail should be as clear and concise as possible. Use as few words as possible while maintaining a clear and friendly tone. If three questions need to be answered, number them as questions 1, 2, and 3 and put each on a separate line.
- Always reread your e-mail before you send it. Also, be sure to check your spelling using the spell-check function.
- Limit the number and size of e-mail attachments. If you can include a link to an online version of a document instead of attaching a file, do so.
- Delete e-mail that you do not need to save or that does not require a response. Do not even open e-mail that you know is not important, such as spam. Use the e-mail blocking feature of the software, if available, to block unwanted junk mail.
- Make sure that your virus protection software is up to date. Never open e-mail attachments if you do not trust the source.
- Respond to e-mail quickly, if possible. It will take you longer to open and read the e-mail again later. In addition, if you send an e-mail that does not require a response, make that clear as well.
- If you need to keep e-mail, file each message appropriately. Create folders with meaningful names to file the e-mail messages you want to keep. File them as soon as possible.

Most people are comfortable with using e-mail, but some may not be familiar with other technologies. Develop a strategy for getting users up to date, and discuss when it's best to use other technologies versus e-mail. The following additional guidelines can help you use other communication tools more effectively:

- Collaborative tools continue to advance. Make sure that your team is using a good tool. Many, like Google Docs and several wikis, are available for free.
- Be sure to authorize the right people to share your collaborative documents. Also ensure that other security is in place. Confidential project documents should probably not be stored on Google Docs. Use more secure tools when needed.
- Make sure that the right person can authorize changes to shared documents and that you back up files.
- Develop a logical structure for organizing and filing shared documents. Use good file-naming conventions for folder and document names.

10.6d Using Templates for Project Communications

Many intelligent people have a hard time writing a performance report or preparing a 10-minute technical presentation for a customer review. Some people in these situations are too embarrassed to ask for help. To make it easier to prepare project communications, project managers need to provide examples and templates for common project communications such as project descriptions, project charters, monthly performance reports, and issue logs. Good documentation from past projects can be an ample source of examples. Samples and templates of both written and oral reports are particularly helpful for people who have never had to write project documents or give project presentations. Finding, developing, and sharing relevant templates and sample documents are important tasks for many project managers. Several examples of project documentation are provided throughout this text, including a business case, project charter, scope statement, stakeholder analysis, WBS, Gantt chart, and cost estimate. The companion website for this text includes the actual files used to create the templates for these sample documents. A few of these templates and guidelines for preparing them are provided in this section.

Figure 10-4 shows a sample template for a brief project description. This form could be used to show a snapshot of an entire project on one page. For example, top managers

Project X Description

Objective: Describe the objective of the project in one or two sentences. Focus on the business benefits of doing the project.

Scope: Briefly describe the scope of the project. What business functions are involved, and what are the main products the project will produce?

Assumptions: Summarize the most critical assumptions for the project.

Cost: Provide the total estimated cost of the project. If desired, list the total cost each year.

Schedule: Provide summary information from the project's Gantt chart, as shown. Focus on summary tasks and milestones.

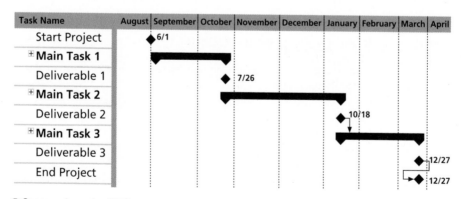

© Cengage Learning 2016

FIGURE 10-4 Sample template for a project description

might require that all project managers provide a brief project description as part of a quarterly management review meeting. Peter Gumpert, the program manager in the opening case, might request this type of document from all of his project managers to get an overall picture of what each project involves. A project description should include the project objective, scope, assumptions, cost information, and schedule information. This template suggests including information from the project's Gantt chart to highlight key deliverables and other milestones.

Table 10-3 shows a template for a monthly progress report. Sections of the progress report include accomplishments from the current period, plans for the next period, issues, and project changes. Recall that progress reports focus on accomplishments during a specific time period, while status reports focus on where the project stands at a certain point in time. Because progress and status reports are effective ways to communicate project information, it is important for project teams to tailor the reports to meet their specific needs. Some organizations, such as JWD Consulting from Chapter 3, combine both progress and status information on the same template.

Table 10-4 provides a list of all of the documentation that should be organized and filed at the end of a major project. From this list, you can see that a large project can generate a lot of documentation. In fact, some project professionals have observed that documentation for designing an airplane seems to weigh more than the airplane itself. (Smaller projects usually generate much less documentation!)

The project manager and project team members should prepare a **lessons-learned report**—a reflective statement that documents important information they have learned from working on the project. The project manager often combines information from all of the lessons-learned reports into a project summary report. See Chapter 3 for an example of this type of lessons-learned report. Some items discussed in lessons-learned reports include reflections on whether project goals were met, whether the project was successful or not, the causes of variances on the project, the reasoning behind corrective

TABLE 10-3   Sample template for a monthly progress report

I.	**Accomplishments for January (or appropriate month):**
	• Describe most important accomplishments. Relate them to project's Gantt chart.
	• Describe other important accomplishments, one bullet for each. If any issues were resolved from the previous month, list them as accomplishments.
II.	**Plans for February (or following month):**
	• Describe most important items to accomplish in the next month. Again, relate them to project's Gantt chart.
	• Describe other important items to accomplish, one bullet for each.
III.	**Issues:** Briefly list important issues that surfaced or are still important. Managers hate surprises and want to help the project succeed, so be sure to list issues.
IV.	**Project Changes (Dates and Description):** List any approved or requested changes to the project. Include the date of the change and a brief description.

TABLE 10-4   Final project documentation items

I.	Project description
II.	Project proposal and backup data (request for proposal, statement of work, proposal correspondence, and so on)
III.	Original and revised contract information and client acceptance documents
IV.	Original and revised project plans and schedules (WBS, Gantt charts and network diagrams, cost estimates, communications management plan, etc.)
V.	Design documents
VI.	Final project report
VII.	Deliverables, as appropriate
VIII.	Audit reports
IX.	Lessons-learned reports
X.	Copies of all status reports, meeting minutes, change notices, and other written and electronic communications

© Cengage Learning 2016

actions chosen, the use of different project management tools and techniques, and personal words of wisdom based on team members' experiences. On some projects, all project members are required to write a brief lessons-learned report; on other projects, just the team leads or project manager writes the report. These reports provide valuable reflections by people who know what worked or did not work on the project. Everyone learns in different ways and has different insights into a project, so it is helpful to have more than one person provide inputs on the lessons-learned reports. These reports can be an excellent resource and can help future projects run more smoothly. To reinforce the benefits of lessons-learned reports, some companies require new project managers to read past lessons-learned reports and discuss how they will incorporate some of the ideas into their own projects. It is also important to organize and prepare project archives. **Project archives** are a complete set of organized project records that provide an accurate history of the project. These archives can provide valuable information for future projects as well.

In the past few years, more and more project teams have started putting all or part of their project information on project websites, including various templates and lessons-learned reports. Project websites provide a centralized way of delivering project documents and other communications. Project teams can develop project websites using wikis, web authoring tools, or by using free or paid sites available from Google, Basecamp, and many other companies. The project team should be sure to address important issues in creating and using a project website, such as security, access, and the type of content that should be included.

Project teams can use one of the many software products available to assist in project communications through the web. These products vary considerably in price and

Used with permission from Basecamp

FIGURE 10-5 Basecamp used on several devices

functionality, as you learned in Chapter 1. For example, Figure 10-5 shows examples of using Basecamp on various devices. Many project teams want to access project information on mobile devices, so many tools now include this capability.

When the project team develops its project communications management plan, it should determine what templates to use for key documentation. To make it more convenient to use templates, the organization should make project templates readily available online. The project team should also understand what types of documents are expected by top management and customers for each project. For example, if a project sponsor or customer wants a one-page monthly progress report for a specific project, but the project team delivers a 20-page report, there are communication problems. In addition, if particular customers or top managers want specific items to be included in all final project reports, they should make sure that the project team is aware of those expectations and modifies templates for those reports to account for the requirements.

10.7 USING SOFTWARE TO ASSIST IN PROJECT COMMUNICATIONS

Many organizations are discovering how valuable project management software can be in communicating project information across the organization. Project management software can provide different views of information to help meet various communication needs. For example, senior managers might only need to see summary screens with colors indicating the overall health of all projects. Middle managers often want to see the status of milestones for all of the projects in their area. Project team members often need to see all project documentation. Often, one of the biggest communication problems on projects is providing the most recent project plans, Gantt charts, specifications, meeting information, and change requests to stakeholders in a timely fashion. Most project management software allows users to insert hyperlinks to other project-related files. In Project 2013, you can insert a hyperlink from a task or milestone listed in a Gantt chart to another file that contains relevant information. For example, there might be a milestone that the project charter was signed. You can insert a hyperlink from the Gantt chart to the Word file that contains the project charter. You could also link appropriate tasks or milestones to Excel files that contain a staffing management plan or cost estimate or to Microsoft PowerPoint files with important presentations or other information. The Project 2013 file and all associated hyperlinked files could then be placed on a local area network server or web server, allowing all project stakeholders easy access to important project information. (See Appendix A for more information on using Microsoft Project 2013 to assist in project communications management.)

Even though organizations routinely use many types of hardware and software to enhance communications, they need to take advantage of new technologies and adjust existing systems to serve the special communications needs of customers and project teams. In addition to diverse customer and project needs, they have to address the changing expectations of consumers and the workforce. For example, several television shows have harnessed communications technology to engage their audiences by letting them vote online or via cell phone for their favorite singers, e-mail or tweet celebrities, or access information on their websites or Facebook pages. Many people, especially younger people, use instant messaging or text messages every day to communicate with friends. Some business and technical professionals also find instant messaging and text messaging to be useful tools for quickly communicating with colleagues, customers, suppliers, and others. **Blogs** are journals on the web that allow users to write entries, respond to another poster's comments, create links, upload pictures, and post comments to journal entries. Blogs have also become popular as a communication technology. If television shows and nontechnical people can use advanced communications technologies, why can't project stakeholders?

Employers have made changes to meet changing expectations and needs in communications. On several IT projects, project managers have found that their team members can be more productive when they are allowed to work from home. Other project managers have no choice in the matter when some or all of their project team members work remotely. As you learned in Chapter 9, Project Human Resource Management, studies show that providing a quiet work environment and a dedicated workspace increases programmer productivity. Most people who work from home have well-equipped, comfortable offices with fewer distractions and more space than corporate offices. Workers also appreciate the added bonus of avoiding traffic and having more flexible work schedules. However, it is important to make sure that work is well defined and that communications are in place to allow remote workers to work effectively.

Several products are available to assist individual consumers and organizations with communications. Many products were developed or enhanced in recent years to address the issue of providing fast, convenient, consistent, and up-to-date project information. Webcasts are now a common tool for presenting video, graphics, sound, voice, and participant feedback live over the web. Podcasts and YouTube videos have also become popular tools for providing various types of audio and video information, from exercise instructions to class lectures. Most working adults and students have cell phones that they use to take and send pictures or send and receive text messages or e-mail. Many high school or college students text or tweet their friends to plan social activities or discuss academic topics.

These same technologies can enhance project communications. For even more powerful and integrated communications, enterprise project management software provides many workgroup functions that allow a team of people at different locations to work together on projects and share project information. Workgroup functions allow the exchange of messages through e-mail, an intranet, wireless devices, or the web. For example, you can use Project 2013 to alert members about new or changed task assignments, and members can return status information and notify other workgroup members about changes in the schedule or other project parameters.

Microsoft Office Enterprise Project Management (EPM) Solution and similar products also provide the following tools to enhance communications:

- *Portfolio management*: By providing a centralized and consolidated view of programs and projects, the user can evaluate and prioritize activities across the organization. This feature makes it possible to maximize productivity, minimize costs, and keep activities aligned with strategic objectives.
- *Resource management*: Maximizing human resources is often the key to minimizing project costs. This feature enables the user to maximize resource use across the organization to help plan and manage the workforce effectively.
- *Project collaboration*: Sharing project information is often a haphazard endeavor. Project collaboration enables an organization to share knowledge immediately and consistently to improve communications and decision making,

CASE WRAP-UP

Christine Braun worked closely with Peter Gumpert and his project managers to develop a communications management plan for all of the fiber-optic undersea telecommunications projects. Peter was very skilled at running effective meetings, so everyone focused on meeting specific objectives. Peter emphasized the importance of keeping himself, the project managers, and other major stakeholders informed about the status of all projects. He emphasized that the project managers were in charge of their projects, and that he did not intend to tell them how to do their jobs. He just wanted to have accurate and consistent information to help coordinate all of the projects and make everyone's jobs easier. When some of the project managers balked at the additional work of providing more project information in different formats, Peter openly discussed the issues with them in more detail. He then authorized each project manager to use additional staff to help develop and follow standards for all project communications.

Christine used her strong technical and communications skills to create a website that included samples of important project documents, presentations, and templates for other people to download and use on their own projects. After determining the need for more remote communications and collaboration between projects, Christine and other staff members researched the latest hardware and software products. Peter authorized funds for a new project led by Christine to evaluate and then purchase smartphones, apps, and enterprise project management (EPM) software with wiki capability that could be accessed via the web. All managers and technical staff, including Peter, received their own devices, and any project stakeholder could request one and get one-on-one training for how to use it with the new apps and EPM software.

eliminate redundancies, and take advantage of best practices for project management.

Communication is among the more important factors for success in project management. While technology can aid in the communications process and be the easiest aspect of the process to address, it is not the most important. Far more important is improving an organization's ability to communicate. Improving this ability often requires a cultural change in an organization that takes a lot of time, hard work, and patience. IT personnel, in particular, often need special coaching to improve their communications skills. The project manager's chief role in the communications process is that of facilitator. Project managers must educate all stakeholders—management, team members, and customers—on the importance of good project communications and ensure that the project has a good communications management plan.

Chapter Summary

Failure to communicate is often the greatest threat to the success of any project, especially IT projects. Communication is the oil that keeps a project running smoothly. Project communications management involves planning communications management, managing communications, and controlling communications.

Project managers can spend as much as 90 percent of their time on communicating. Several keys to good communications include focusing on individual and group communication needs, using formal and informal methods for communicating, providing important information in an effective and timely manner, setting the stage for communicating bad news, and understanding communication channels.

A communications management plan of some type should be created for all projects to help ensure good communications. Contents of this plan will vary based on the needs of the project.

Managing communication includes creating and distributing project information. The various methods for distributing project information include formal, informal, written, and verbal. It is important to determine the most appropriate means for distributing different types of project information. Project managers and their teams should focus on the importance of building relationships as they communicate project information. As the number of people that need to communicate increases, the number of communication channels also increases.

Reporting performance involves collecting and disseminating information about how well a project is moving toward meeting its goals. Project teams can use earned value charts and other forms of progress information to communicate and assess project performance. Status review meetings are an important part of communicating, monitoring, and controlling projects.

The main goal of controlling communications is to ensure the optimal flow of information throughout the entire project life cycle. Project managers and their teams should consider using facilitators and other experts to provide assistance.

To improve project communications, project managers and their teams must develop their communication skills. Suggestions for improving project communications include learning how to run more effective meetings, how to use e-mail, instant messaging, texting, kanban boards, and collaborative software more effectively, and how to use templates for project communications.

New hardware and software continue to become available to help improve communications. As more people work remotely, it is important to make sure they have the necessary tools to be productive. Enterprise project management software provides many features to enhance communications across the organization.

Quick Quiz

1. What do many experts agree is the greatest threat to the success of any project?

    a. lack of proper funding

    b. a failure to communicate

    c. poor listening skills

    d. inadequate staffing

2. In face-to-face interactions, how is most information conveyed?

   a. by the tone of voice

   b. by the words spoken

   c. by body language

   d. by the location

3. Which of the following is not a process in project communications management?

   a. planning communications management

   b. controlling communications

   c. managing communications

   d. managing stakeholders

4. What strategy can a project manager use to deliver bad news?

   a. Tell a joke first.

   b. Tell senior management as soon as possible so they can develop alternatives and recommendations.

   c. Ask the project champion to deliver the news.

   d. Set the stage by putting the news into context, emphasizing the impact on the bottom line.

5. If you add three more people to a project team of five, how many more communication channels will you add?

   a. 2

   b. 12

   c. 15

   d. 18

6. A(n) _____ report describes where a project stands at a specific point in time.

   a. status

   b. performance

   c. forecast

   d. earned value

7. What term describes information that is sent to recipients at their request via websites, bulletin boards, e-learning, knowledge repositories like blogs, and other means?

   a. push communications

   b. pull communications

   c. interactive communications

   d. customer communications

8. Which of the following is not a recommendation for improving project communications?

   a. You cannot overcommunicate.

   b. Project managers and their teams should take time to develop their communications skills.

c. Do not use facilitators or experts outside of the project team to communicate important information.

d. Use templates to help prepare project documents.

9. Which of the following is not a guideline to help improve time spent at meetings?

a. Determine if a meeting can be avoided.

b. Invite extra people who support your project to make the meeting run more smoothly.

c. Define the purpose and intended outcome of the meeting.

d. Build relationships.

10. A _____ report is a reflective statement that documents important information learned from working on the project.

a. kanban

b. lessons-learned

c. project archive

d. progress

Quick Quiz Answers

1. b; 2. c; 3. d; 4. d; 5. d; 6. a; 7. b; 8. c; 9. b; 10. b

Discussion Questions

1. Think of examples in the media that poke fun at the communications skills of technical professionals, such as Dilbert® or xkcd.com cartoons. How does this satire influence the industry and educational programs?

2. What courses in your educational program address the development of communications skills? What skills do you think employers are looking for? Do you think there should be more emphasis on communications skills in your degree program?

3. Discuss the importance of understanding tone of voice and body language in comprehending the meaning of what people say. Give examples of how the same words said in different ways have totally different meanings.

4. What items should a communications management plan address? How can a stakeholder analysis assist in preparing and implementing parts of this plan?

5. Discuss the advantages and disadvantages of different ways of distributing project information.

6. What are some of the ways to create and distribute project performance information?

7. Discuss advantages and disadvantages of telecommuting.

8. Explain why you agree or disagree with some of the suggestions in this chapter for improving project communications, such as creating a communications management plan, stakeholder analysis, or performance reports. What other suggestions do you have?

9. How can software assist in project communications? How can it hurt project communications?

Exercises

1. Research the topic of understanding body language. What are some common body movements that can help you understand how people are really feeling? What does it mean if someone looks up a lot when talking versus looking down or side to side? What does it mean when people cross their arms, touch their noses, or make other common gestures with their bodies? Perform a role-play of common project scenarios, and have people take turns saying something that does not match their body language. For example, someone might say that work is going well on a particular task when it is not.

2. Find examples of how project teams use new technologies to communicate project information. Which technologies seem to be most effective? Document your findings in a short paper, citing at least three references.

3. Review the following scenarios, and then write a paragraph for each one describing what media you think would be most appropriate to use and why. See Table 10-2 for suggestions.

    a. Many of the technical staff on the project arrive at work from 9:30 a.m. to 10:00 a.m., while the business users always arrive before 9:00 a.m. The business users have been making comments. The project manager wants to have the technical people come in by 9:00, although many of them leave late.

    b. Your company is bidding on a project for the entertainment industry. You know that you need new ideas on how to put together the proposal and communicate your approach in a way that will impress the customer.

    c. Your business has been growing successfully, but you are becoming inundated with phone calls and e-mails asking similar types of questions.

    d. You need to make a general announcement to a large group of people and you want to make sure they receive the information.

4. How many different communication channels does a project team with six people have? How many more communication channels would there be if the team grew to 10 people?

5. Review the templates for various project documents provided in this chapter. Pick one of them and apply it to a project of your choice. Make suggestions for improving the template.

6. Research examples of project teams using kanban boards to improve workflow and communications. Write a short paper or create a short presentation summarizing your findings.

7. Write a lessons-learned report for a project of your choice, using the template provided on the companion website and the sample in Chapter 3 as guides. Do you think it is important for all project managers and team members to write lessons-learned reports? Would you take the time to read them if they were available in your organization? Why or why not?

8. Research new software products that assist in communications management for large projects. Write a short paper summarizing your findings. Include websites for software vendors and your opinion of some of the products.

Running Case

Part 7: Project Communications Management

Several issues have arisen on the Global Treps Project. Ashok, your team member in India, broke his wrist playing tennis yesterday and cannot work on the project at all for three weeks. His work, which involves helping to edit the videos, starts in one week, so you need to reassign it to others.

Bobby suggests you use Kanban boards to list all of the tasks for editing the videos and to track where they are in the work flow. Bobby, a techie and not known for being a good communicator, is the only person who's ever used Kanban boards. You have not yet broken down the tasks into much detail and need more information from Angela, the contractor in charge of creating the videos.

Alfreda is having difficulties communicating with her main contact in Ethiopia, Dr. B. He is very busy all the time and does not use texting, Alfreda's preferred communications medium. He has also not communicated key information with students who could be candidates for their event, which is only a month away. Alfreda is not sure if he booked a room for the event yet.

1. Describe how you would communicate to Ashok and the rest of the team about Ashok's injury. What actions would you take? What communications medium would you use with different stakeholders?

2. Prepare a partial communications management plan to address some of the challenges mentioned in Part 7 of the case.

3. Research free, online tools for using Kanban boards and choose one to use. Prepare a list of at least ten tasks that would be done in editing the videos and enter them into your tool of choice. Prepare or find a short guide or video explaining how to use the Kanban boards.

4. Write a one-page paper describing options for communicating with Dr. B. and making sure students at his university get information about your event.

Key Terms

blogs p.415

communications management plan p.398

forecasts p.404

Google Docs p.408

lessons-learned report p.413

progress reports p.404

project archives p.413

SharePoint portal p.408

status reports p.404

wiki p.408

End Notes

1. Janet L Bailey, Non-Technical Skills for Success in a Technical World, *International Journal of Business and Social Science*, Vol. 5 No. 4 Special Issue (March 2014).

2. Frederick P. Brooks, *The Mythical Man-Month*, second edition (Boston: Addison-Wesley, 1995).

3. Albert Mehrabian, *Silent messages: Implicit communication of emotions and attitudes*, second edition (Belmont, CA: Wadsworth, 1981).

4. Carol Hildenbrand, "Loud and Clear," *CIO Magazine* (April 15, 1996).

5. NTT Communications, "Great East Japan Earthquake: Shinsai Recovery in Numbers," NTTCOM.TV (March 13, 2012).

6. Adele Peters, "In a Disaster, This Device Lets People Communicate Without a Cell Signal, Wi-Fi, or Power," *Co.Exist, Fast Company* (April 30, 2015).

7. "New Research Reveals Collaboration Is a Key Driver of Business Performance Around the World: Verizon Business, Microsoft sponsor international study; create first-of-its-kind collaboration index to measure impact of communications culture, technologies," *Microsoft Press Pass* (June 5, 2006).

8. Frost & Sullivan, "Meetings Around the World II: Charting the Course of Advanced Collaboration" (October 14, 2009).

9. Susie Poppick, "10 Social Media Blunders That Cost a Millennial a Job—or Worse," *Money, http://time.com/money/3019899/10-facebook-twitter-mistakes-lost-job-millennials-viral/ (September 5, 2014).*

CHAPTER 11

PROJECT RISK MANAGEMENT

OPENING CASE

Cliff Branch was the president of a small IT consulting firm that specialized in developing Internet and mobile applications and providing full-service support. The staff consisted of programmers, business analysts, database specialists, web designers, project managers, and others. The firm had 50 full-time people and planned to hire at least 10 more in the next year. The firm also planned to increase the number of part-time consultants it used. The company had done very well during the past few years, but it was recently having difficulty winning contracts. Spending time and resources to respond to various requests for proposals from prospective clients was becoming expensive. Many clients were starting to require presentations and even some prototype development before awarding a contract.

Cliff knew he had an aggressive approach to risk and liked to bid on the projects with the highest payoff. He did not use a systematic approach to evaluate the risks involved in various projects before bidding on them. He focused on the profit potentials and on how challenging the projects were. His strategy was now causing problems for the company because it was investing heavily in the preparation of proposals, yet winning few contracts. Several employees who were not currently working on projects were still on the payroll, and some of their part-time consultants were actively pursuing other opportunities because they were being underutilized. What could Cliff and his company do to better understand project risks? Should Cliff adjust his strategy for deciding what projects to pursue? How?

11.1 THE IMPORTANCE OF PROJECT RISK MANAGEMENT

Project risk management is the art and science of identifying, analyzing, and responding to risk throughout the life of a project and in the best interests of meeting project objectives. A frequently overlooked aspect of project management, risk management can often result in significant improvements in the ultimate success of projects. Risk management can have a positive impact on selecting projects, determining their scope, and developing realistic schedules and cost estimates. It helps project stakeholders understand the nature of the project, involves team members in defining strengths and weaknesses, and helps to integrate the other project management knowledge areas.

Good project risk management often goes unnoticed, unlike crisis management, which indicates an obvious danger to the success of a project. The crisis, in turn, receives the intense interest of the entire project team. Resolving a crisis has much greater visibility, often accompanied by rewards from management, than successful risk management. In contrast, when risk management is effective, it results in fewer problems, and for the few problems that exist, it results in more expeditious resolutions. It may be difficult for outside observers to tell whether risk management or luck was responsible for the smooth development of a new system, but project teams always know that their projects worked out better because of good risk management. Managing project risks takes dedicated, talented professionals. In response to this need, PMI introduced the PMI Risk Management Professional (PMI-RMP)[SM] credential in 2008. (Consult PMI's website for further information.)

All industries, especially the software development industry, tend to underestimate the importance of project risk management. William Ibbs and Young H. Kwak studied project management maturity in 38 organizations in different industries. The organizations were divided into four industry groups: engineering and construction, telecommunications, information systems/software development, and high-tech manufacturing. Survey participants answered 148 multiple-choice questions to assess how mature their organization was in the project management knowledge areas of scope, time, cost, quality, human resources, communications, risk, and procurement. The rating scale ranged from 1 to 5, with 5 being the highest maturity rating. Table 11-1 shows the results of the survey. Notice that risk management was the only knowledge area for which all ratings were less than 3. This study showed that all organizations should put more effort into project risk management, especially companies in the information systems and software development industry, which had the lowest rating of 2.75.[1]

TABLE 11-1   Project Management Maturity by Industry Group and Knowledge Area

KEY: 1 = Lowest Maturity Rating, 5 = Highest Maturity Rating				
Knowledge Area	Engineering/ Construction	Telecommunications	Information Systems	High-Tech Manufacturing
Scope	3.52	3.45	3.25	3.37
Time	3.55	3.41	3.03	3.50
Cost	3.74	3.22	3.20	3.97
Quality	2.91	3.22	2.88	3.26
Human resources	3.18	3.20	2.93	3.18
Communications	3.53	3.53	3.21	3.48
Risk	2.93	2.87	2.75	2.76
Procurement	3.33	3.01	2.91	3.33

Source: Ibbs and Kwak

A similar survey was completed with software development companies in Mauritius, South Africa. The average maturity rating was only 2.29 for all knowledge areas on a scale of 1 to 5, with 5 being the highest maturity rating. The lowest average maturity rating, 1.84, was also in the area of project risk management, like the study by Ibbs and Kwak. Cost management had the highest maturity rating of 2.5, and the survey authors noted that organizations in the study were often concerned with cost overruns and had metrics in place to help control costs. The authors also found that maturity rating was closely linked to the success rate of projects, and that the poor rating for risk management was a likely cause of project problems and failures.[2]

KLCI Research Group surveyed 260 software organizations worldwide to study software risk management practices. The following points summarize some of their findings:

- Ninety-seven percent of the participants said they had procedures in place to identify and assess risk.
- Eighty percent identified anticipating and avoiding problems as the primary benefit of risk management.

- Seventy percent of the organizations had defined software development processes.
- Sixty-four percent had a Project Management Office.

Figure 11-1 shows the main benefits from software risk management practices cited by survey respondents. In addition to anticipating and avoiding problems, risk management practices helped software project managers prevent surprises, improve negotiations, meet customer commitments, and reduce schedule slips and cost overruns.[3]

Although many organizations know that they do not do a good job of managing project risk, little progress seems to have been made over the past decade in improving risk management on a project level or an enterprise level. Several books and articles have been written on the topic. For example shortly after the fall 2008 stock market crash, Dr. David Hillson, PMP, wrote about the importance of project risk management. Hillson said:

> There is no doubt that all sectors of industry and society are facing real challenges in coping with the current fallout from the credit crunch. But risk management should not be regarded as a nonessential cost to be cut in these difficult times. Instead, organisations should use the insights offered by the risk process to ensure that they can handle the inevitable uncertainties and emerge in the best possible position in [the] future. With high levels of volatility surrounding us on all sides, risk management is more

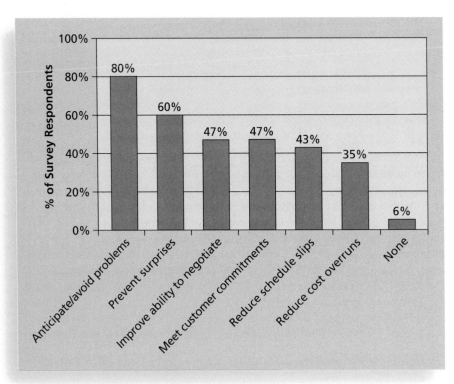

Source: Kulik and Weber, KLCI Research Group

FIGURE 11-1 Benefits from software risk management practices

needed now than ever, and cutting it would be a false economy. Rather than treating risk management as part of the problem, we should see it as a major part of the solution.[4]

Hillson continues to write articles and books, give presentations, and provide videos on his website at *www.risk-doctor.com*.

 GLOBAL ISSUES

Many people around the world suffered losses as various financial markets dropped in the fall of 2008, even after the $700 billion economic stabilization act was passed by the U.S. Congress. According to a survey of 316 global financial services executives conducted in July 2008, over 70 percent of respondents believed that the losses during the financial crisis were largely due to failures to address risk management issues. The executives identified several challenges in implementing risk management, including data and company culture issues. For example, access to relevant, timely, and consistent data continues to be a major obstacle in many organizations. Many respondents also said that fostering a culture of risk management was a major challenge.

Executives and lawmakers finally started paying attention to risk management. Fifty-nine percent of survey respondents said the financial crisis prompted them to scrutinize their risk management practices in greater detail, and many institutions are revisiting their risk management practices. The Financial Stability Forum (FSF) and the Institute for International Finance (IIF) called for closer scrutiny of the risk management process.[5]

Risk continues to be an important issue in the financial industry, and organizations are taking a more proactive approach by investing in IT such as cloud computing, big data, and analytics to help them identify and mitigate risk. "Worldwide, the capital markets, banking and insurance sectors will spend roughly $78.6 billion on risk information technologies and services (RITS) in 2015, according to a new study. What's more, that figure is expected to grow to $96.3 billion by 2018."[6]

Before you can improve project risk management, you must understand what risk is. A basic dictionary definition states that risk is "the possibility of loss or injury." This definition highlights the negativity often associated with risk and points out that uncertainty is involved. Project risk management involves understanding potential problems that might occur on the project and how they might impede project success. The *PMBOK® Guide, Fifth Edition* refers to this type of risk as a negative risk or threat. However, there are also positive risks or opportunities, which can result in good outcomes for a project. A general definition of a project **risk**, therefore, is an uncertainty that can have a negative or positive effect on meeting project objectives.

Managing negative risks involves a number of possible actions that project managers can take to avoid, lessen, change, or accept the potential effects of risks on their projects. Positive risk management is like investing in opportunities. It is important to note that risk management *is* an investment—costs are associated with it. The investment that an organization is willing to make in risk management activities depends on the nature of the project, the experience of the project team, and the constraints imposed on both. In any case, the cost for risk management should not exceed the potential benefits.

If there is so much risk in IT projects, why do organizations pursue them? Many companies are in business today because they took risks that created great opportunities. Organizations survive over the long term when they pursue opportunities. IT is often a key part of a business's strategy; without it, many businesses might not survive. Given that all projects involve uncertainties that can have negative or positive outcomes, the question is how to decide which projects to pursue and how to identify and manage project risk throughout a project's life cycle.

BEST PRACTICE

Some organizations make the mistake of addressing only tactical and negative risks when performing project risk management. David Hillson (*www.risk-doctor.com*) suggests overcoming this problem by widening the scope of risk management to encompass both *strategic risks* and *upside opportunities,* which he refers to as integrated risk management. Benefits of this approach include:

- Bridging the strategy and tactics gap to ensure that project delivery is tied to organizational needs and vision
- Focusing projects on the benefits they exist to support, rather than producing a set of deliverables
- Managing opportunities proactively as an integral part of business processes at both strategic and tactical levels
- Providing useful information to decision makers at all levels when the environment is uncertain
- Allowing an appropriate level of risk to be taken intelligently with full awareness of the degree of uncertainty and its potential effects on objectives[7]

In a 2014 paper, Hilson also described the importance of good working relationships as a best practice in managing project risk. "... management of overall project risk becomes a shared duty of both project sponsor and project manager, acting in partnership to ensure that the project has the optimal chance of achieving its objectives within the allowable risk threshold. Successful management of risk at this whole-project level therefore depends largely on the effectiveness of the working relationship between these two key players."[8]

Several risk experts suggest that organizations and individuals should strive to find a balance between risks and opportunities in all aspects of projects and their personal lives. The idea of striving for balance suggests that different organizations and people have different attitudes toward risk. The *PMBOK® Guide, Fifth Edition,* states that these attitudes are based on two themes: "One is **risk appetite**, which is the degree of uncertainty an entity is willing to take on, in anticipation of a reward. The other is **risk tolerance**, which is the maximum acceptable deviation an entity is willing to accept on the project or business objectives as the potential impact.... The project may be accepted if the risks are within tolerances and are in balance with the rewards that may be gained by taking the risks."[9] Some organizations or people have a neutral tolerance for risk, some have an aversion to risk, and others are risk-seeking. These three preferences are part of the utility theory of risk.

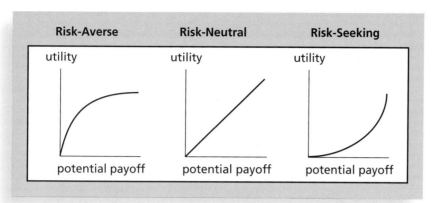

Risk-Averse   **Risk-Neutral**   **Risk-Seeking**

© Cengage Learning 2016

FIGURE 11-2   Risk utility function and risk preference

Risk utility is the amount of satisfaction or pleasure received from a potential payoff. Figure 11-2 shows the basic difference between risk-averse, risk-neutral, and risk-seeking preferences. The y-axis represents utility, or the amount of pleasure received from taking a risk. The x-axis shows the amount of potential payoff or dollar value of the opportunity at stake. Utility rises at a decreasing rate for a **risk-averse** person. In other words, when more payoff or money is at stake, a person or organization that is risk-averse gains less satisfaction from the risk, or has lower tolerance for the risk. Those who are **risk-seeking** have a higher tolerance for risk, and their satisfaction increases when more payoff is at stake. A risk-seeking person prefers outcomes that are more uncertain and is often willing to pay a penalty to take risks. A **risk-neutral** person achieves a balance between risk and payoff. For example, a risk-averse organization might not purchase hardware from a vendor who has not been in business for a specified period of time. A risk-seeking organization might deliberately choose start-up vendors for hardware purchases to gain new products with unusual features that provide an advantage. A risk-neutral organization might perform a series of analyses to evaluate possible purchase decisions. This type of organization evaluates decisions using a number of factors—risk is just one of them.

The goal of project risk management can be viewed as minimizing potential negative risks while maximizing potential positive risks. The term **known risks** is sometimes used to describe risks that the project team has identified and analyzed. Known risks can be managed proactively. However, **unknown risks**, or risks that have not been identified and analyzed, cannot be managed.

As you can imagine, good project managers know it is good practice to take the time to identify and manage project risks. Six major processes are involved in risk management:

1. *Planning risk management* involves deciding how to approach and plan risk management activities for the project. By reviewing the project management plan, project charter, stakeholder register, enterprise environmental factors, and organizational process assets, project teams can discuss and analyze risk management activities for their particular projects. The main output of this process is a risk management plan.

2. *Identifying risks* involves determining which risks are likely to affect a project and documenting the characteristics of each. The main output of this process is the start of a risk register, which you will learn about later in this chapter.

3. *Performing qualitative risk analysis* involves prioritizing risks based on their probability of occurrence and impact. After identifying risks, project teams can use various tools and techniques to rank risks and update information in the risk register. The main outputs are project documents updates.

4. *Performing quantitative risk analysis* involves numerically estimating the effects of risks on project objectives. The main outputs of this process are project documents updates.

5. *Planning risk responses* involves taking steps to enhance opportunities and reduce threats to meeting project objectives. Using outputs from the preceding risk management processes, project teams can develop risk response strategies that often result in updates to the project management plan and other project documents.

6. *Controlling risk* involves monitoring identified and residual risks, identifying new risks, carrying out risk response plans, and evaluating the effectiveness of risk strategies throughout the life of the project. The main outputs of this process include work performance information, change requests, and updates to the project management plan, other project documents, and organizational process assets.

Figure 11-3 summarizes these processes and outputs, showing when they occur in a typical project.

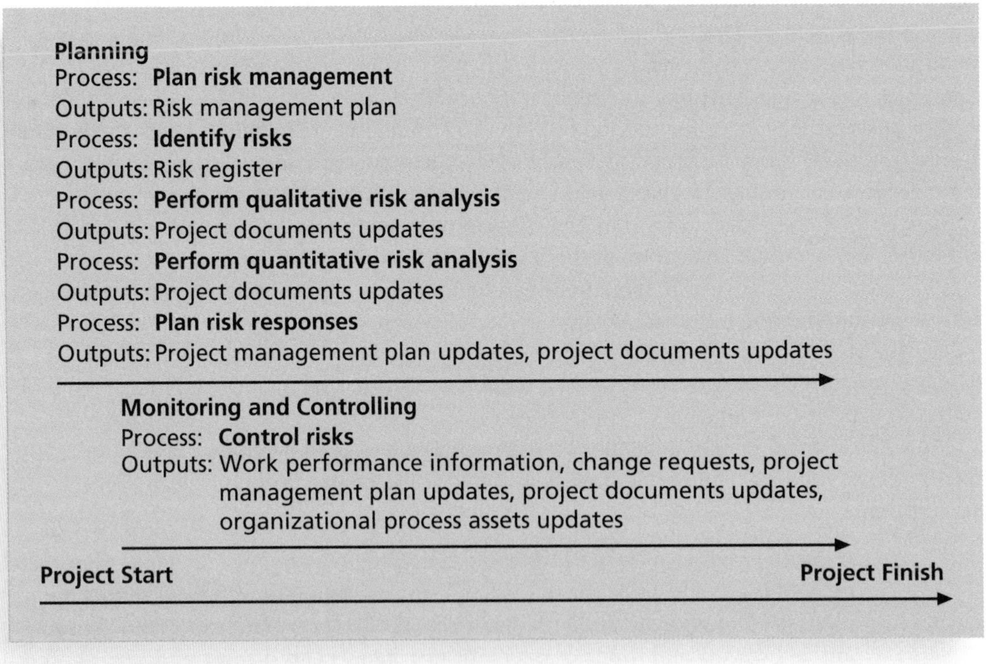

Planning
Process: **Plan risk management**
Outputs: Risk management plan
Process: **Identify risks**
Outputs: Risk register
Process: **Perform qualitative risk analysis**
Outputs: Project documents updates
Process: **Perform quantitative risk analysis**
Outputs: Project documents updates
Process: **Plan risk responses**
Outputs: Project management plan updates, project documents updates

Monitoring and Controlling
Process: **Control risks**
Outputs: Work performance information, change requests, project management plan updates, project documents updates, organizational process assets updates

Project Start   **Project Finish**

© Cengage Learning 2016

FIGURE 11-3 Project risk management summary

The first step in project risk management is determining how to address this knowledge area for a particular project by performing risk management planning.

11.2 PLANNING RISK MANAGEMENT

Planning risk management is the process of deciding how to approach risk management activities and plan for them in a project; the main output of this process is a risk management plan. A **risk management plan** documents the procedures for managing risk throughout the project. Project teams should hold several planning meetings early in the project's life cycle to help develop the risk management plan. The project team should review project documents as well as corporate risk management policies, risk categories, lessons-learned reports from past projects, and templates for creating a risk management plan. It is also important to review the risk tolerances of various stakeholders. For example, if the project sponsor is risk-averse, the project might require a different approach to risk management than if the project sponsor were a risk seeker.

A risk management plan summarizes how risk management will be performed on a particular project. Like plans for other knowledge areas, it becomes a subset of the project management plan. Table 11-2 lists the general topics that a risk management plan should address. It is important to clarify roles and responsibilities, prepare budget and schedule estimates for risk-related work, and identify risk categories for consideration. It is also important to describe how risk management will be done, including assessment

433

TABLE 11-2 Topics addressed in a risk management plan

Topic	Questions to Answer
Methodology	How will risk management be performed on this project? What tools and data sources are available and applicable?
Roles and responsibilities	Which people are responsible for implementing specific tasks and providing deliverables related to risk management?
Budget and schedule	What are the estimated costs and schedules for performing risk-related activities?
Risk categories	What are the main categories of risks that should be addressed on this project? Is there a risk breakdown structure for the project? (See the information on risk breakdown structures later in this chapter.)
Risk probability and impact	How will the probabilities and impacts of risk items be assessed? What scoring and interpretation methods will be used for the qualitative and quantitative analysis of risks? How will the probability and impact matrix be developed?
Revised stakeholders' tolerances	Have stakeholders' tolerances for risk changed? How will those changes affect the project?
Tracking	How will the team track risk management activities? How will lessons learned be documented and shared? How will risk management processes be audited?
Risk documentation	What reporting formats and processes will be used for risk management activities?

of risk probabilities and impacts as well as the creation of risk-related documentation. The level of detail included in the risk management plan can vary with the needs of the project.

In addition to a risk management plan, many projects also include contingency plans, fallback plans, contingency reserves, and management reserves.

- **Contingency plans** are predefined actions that the project team will take if an identified risk event occurs. For example, if the project team knows that a new release of a software package may not be available in time to use for the project, the team might have a contingency plan to use the existing, older version of the software.
- **Fallback plans** are developed for risks that have a high impact on meeting project objectives and are put into effect if attempts to reduce the risk do not work. For example, a new college graduate might have a main plan and several contingency plans for where to live after graduation, but if these plans do not work out, a fallback plan might be to live at home for a while. Sometimes the terms *contingency plan* and *fallback plan* are used interchangeably.
- **Contingency reserves** or **contingency allowances** are funds included in the cost baseline that can be used to mitigate cost or schedule overruns if known risks occur. For example, if a project appears to be off course because the staff is not experienced with a new technology and the team had identified that as a risk, the contingency reserves could be used to hire an outside consultant to train and advise the project staff in using the new technology.
- **Management reserves** are funds held for unknown risks that are used for management control purposes. They are not part of the cost baseline, but they are part of the project budget and funding requirements. If the management reserves are used for unforeseen work, they are added to the cost baseline after the change is approved.

Contingency plans, fallback plans, and reserves show the importance of taking a proactive approach to managing project risks.

Before you can really understand and use project risk management processes on IT projects, it is necessary to recognize and understand the common sources of risk.

11.3 COMMON SOURCES OF RISK ON IT PROJECTS

Several studies have shown that IT projects share some common sources of risk. For example, the Standish Group did a follow-up study to its CHAOS research called Unfinished Voyages. This study brought together 60 IT professionals to elaborate on how to evaluate a project's overall likelihood of being successful. Table 11-3 shows the Standish Group's success potential scoring sheet and the relative importance of the project success criteria. User involvement was cited as being the most important criterion for successful projects. If a potential project does not receive a minimum score, the organization might decide not to work on it or to reduce the risks before the project invests too much time or money.[10]

TABLE 11-3 IT success potential scoring sheet

Success Criterion	Relative Importance
User involvement	19
Executive management support	16
Clear statement of requirements	15
Proper planning	11
Realistic expectations	10
Smaller project milestones	9
Competent staff	8
Ownership	6
Clear vision and objectives	3
Hard-working, focused staff	3
Total	100

Source: The Standish Group

The Standish Group provides specific questions for each success criterion to help decide how many points to assign to a project. For example, the following five questions are related to user involvement:

- Do I have the right users?
- Did I involve the users early and often?
- Do I have a quality relationship with the users?
- Do I make involvement easy?
- Did I find out what the users need?

The number of questions corresponding to each success criterion determines the number of points each positive response is assigned. For example, the topic of user involvement includes five questions. For each positive reply, you would get 3.8 (19/5) points; 19 represents the weight of the criterion, and 5 represents the number of questions. Therefore, you would assign a value to the user involvement criterion by adding 3.8 points to the score for each question you can answer positively.

Many organizations develop their own risk questionnaires. Broad categories of risks described on these questionnaires might include:

- *Market risk*: If the IT project will create a new product or service, will it be useful to the organization or marketable to others? Will users accept and use the product or service? Will someone else create a better product or service faster, making the project a waste of time and money?
- *Financial risk*: Can the organization afford to undertake the project? How confident are stakeholders in the financial projections? Will the project meet NPV, ROI, and payback estimates? If not, can the organization afford to continue the project? Is this project the best way to use the organization's financial resources?
- *Technology risk*: Is the project technically feasible? Will it use mature, leading-edge, or bleeding-edge technologies? When will decisions be made

on which technology to use? Will hardware, software, and networks function properly? Will the technology be available in time to meet project objectives? Could the technology be obsolete before a useful product can be created? You can also break down the technology risk category into hardware, software, and network technology, if desired.

- *People risk*: Does the organization have people with appropriate skills to complete the project successfully? If not, can the organization find such people? Do people have the proper managerial and technical skills? Do they have enough experience? Does senior management support the project? Is there a project champion? Is the organization familiar with the sponsor or customer for the project? How good is the relationship with the sponsor or customer?

- *Structure/process risk*: What degree of change will the new project introduce into user areas and business procedures? How many distinct user groups does the project need to satisfy? With how many other systems does the new project or system need to interact? Does the organization have processes in place to complete the project successfully?

✓ WHAT WENT WRONG?

Performing risk management is important to improving the likelihood of project success. But in1995, more than half of projects with significant cost or schedule overruns had no risk management in place, according to a study conducted by KPMG, a large consulting firm.[11] Nearly 20 years later, the situation was much the same. In a 2013 KPMG survey of over 1,000 executives, although risk management was a high priority, only 66 percent of companies said they often or constantly build it into their strategic planning decisions. A key observation in the survey report is that "Risk management is at the top of the global executive agenda...those companies that fail to manage them well imperil their future."[12] Only 44 percent of executives believed their organizations were effective at developing stakeholders' understanding of risk. The executives also said challenges are growing faster than they can handle them. The top three risks reported were growing regulatory pressure from governments, reputational risk, and market risk.

Airline incidents cause concerns, especially when lives are lost. The Germanwings crash in 2015 resulted in 150 deaths, allegedly due to the co-pilot's poor mental state. Senior managers are reviewing policies related to risk management to help prevent future tragedies. Some changes can take place immediately, while others will take more time. For example, the German air traffic control authority suggested investing in new technologies like remote command of passenger planes, an approach that will take a fair amount of time and money to implement. Other policy changes have already been made. "Since the Germanwings crash, European airlines have implemented a rule that two people must be in the cockpit at all times and Germany has set up a task force with the aviation industry to consider changes to medical and psychological tests for pilots."[13]

Reviewing a proposed project in terms of the Standish Group's success criteria, a risk questionnaire, or another similar tool is a good method for understanding common sources of risk on IT projects. It is also useful to review the work breakdown structure (WBS) for a project to see if there might be specific risks by WBS categories. For example, if an item on the WBS involves preparing a press release and no one on the project team has ever written one, it could be a negative risk if the release is not handled professionally.

A risk breakdown structure is a useful tool to help project managers consider potential risks in different categories. Similar in form to a work breakdown structure, a **risk breakdown structure** is a hierarchy of potential risk categories for a project. Figure 11-4 shows a sample risk breakdown structure that might apply to many IT projects. The highest-level categories are business, technical, organizational, and project management. Competitors, suppliers, and cash flow are categories that fall under business risks. Under technical risks are the categories of hardware, software, and network. Hardware could be broken down further to include malfunctions, availability, and cost. Notice how the risk breakdown structure provides a simple, one-page chart to help ensure that a project team considers important risk categories related to all IT projects. For example, Cliff and his managers in the chapter's opening case could have benefited from considering several of the categories listed under project management—estimates, communication, and resources. They could have discussed these risks and other types of risks related to the projects their company bid on, and then developed appropriate strategies for optimizing positive risks and minimizing negative ones.

In addition to identifying risk based on the nature of the project or products created, it is also important to identify potential risks according to project management knowledge areas, such as scope, time, cost, and quality. Notice that a major category in the risk breakdown structure in Figure 11-4 is project management. Table 11-4 lists potential negative risk conditions that can exist within each knowledge area.[14]

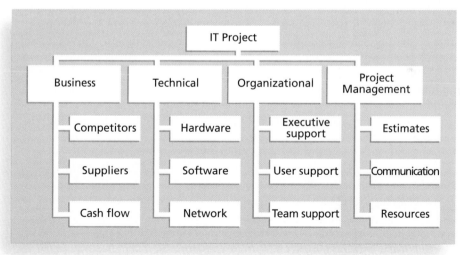

© Cengage Learning 2016

FIGURE 11-4 Sample risk breakdown structure

TABLE 11-4   Potential negative risk conditions associated with each knowledge area

Knowledge Area	Risk Conditions
Integration	Inadequate planning; poor resource allocation; poor integration management; lack of post-project review
Scope	Poor definition of scope or work packages; incomplete definition
Time	Errors in estimating time or resource availability; errors in determining the critical path; poor allocation and management of float; early release of competitive products
Cost	Estimating errors; inadequate productivity, cost, change, or contingency
Quality	Poor attitude toward quality; substandard design, materials, and workmanship; inadequate quality assurance program
Human resource	Poor conflict management; poor project organization and definition of responsibilities; absence of leadership
Communications	Carelessness in planning or communicating
Risk	Ignoring risk; unclear analysis of risk; poor insurance management
Procurement	Unenforceable conditions or contract clauses; adversarial relations
Stakeholders	Lack of consultation with key stakeholder, poor sponsor engagement

Source: R.M. Wideman

Understanding common sources of risk is very helpful in risk identification, which is the next step in project risk management.

11.4 IDENTIFYING RISKS

Identifying risks is the process of understanding what potential events might hurt or enhance a particular project. It is important to identify potential risks early, but you must also continue to identify risks based on the changing project environment. Also remember that you cannot manage risks if you do not identify them first. By understanding common sources of risks and reviewing a project's planning documents (for risk, cost, schedule, quality, and human resource management), activity cost and duration estimates, the scope baseline, stakeholder register, project documents, procurement documents, enterprise environmental factors, and organizational process assets, project managers and their teams can identify many potential risks.

Another consideration for identifying risks is the likelihood of advanced discovery, which is often viewed at a program level rather than a project level. The *Risk Management Guide for DOD Acquisition, Sixth Edition*, addresses this concept and emphasizes the need to establish high-level indicators for an entire program. For example, several experts track asteroids to enable a response in case one threatens our planet. Although the likelihood of a deadly asteroid is very low, the impact is extremely high. For IT programs, advanced discovery could involve monitoring an important supplier who might remove support for software used on several projects. Some suppliers provide early warning for this possibility, while others do not. It is important for organizations to identify these advanced discovery risks early and track their status in case time is needed to develop responses.

11.4a Suggestions for Identifying Risks

There are several tools and techniques for identifying risks. Project teams often begin this process by reviewing project documentation, recent and historical information related to the organization, and assumptions that might affect the project. Project team members and outside experts often hold meetings to discuss this information and ask important questions about it as they relate to risk. After identifying potential risks at the initial meeting, the project team might then use different information-gathering techniques to further identify risks. Four common techniques include brainstorming, the Delphi technique, interviewing, and root cause analysis.

Brainstorming is a technique by which a group attempts to generate ideas or find a solution for a specific problem by amassing ideas spontaneously and without judgment. This approach can help the group create a comprehensive list of risks to address later during qualitative and quantitative risk analysis. An experienced facilitator should run the brainstorming session and introduce new categories of potential risks to keep the ideas flowing. After the ideas are collected, the facilitator can group and categorize the ideas to make them more manageable. Care must be taken, however, not to overuse or misuse brainstorming. Although businesses use brainstorming widely to generate new ideas, the psychology literature shows that individual people working alone produce a greater number of ideas than they produce through brainstorming in small, face-to-face groups. Group effects, such as fear of social disapproval, the effects of authority hierarchy, and domination of the session by one or two vocal people, often inhibit idea generation for many participants.[15]

439

The Delphi technique is an approach to gathering information that helps prevent some of the negative group effects found in brainstorming. The basic concept of the **Delphi technique** is to derive a consensus among a panel of experts who make predictions about future developments. Developed by the Rand Corporation for the U.S. Air Force in the late 1960s, the Delphi technique is a systematic, interactive forecasting procedure based on independent and *anonymous* input regarding future events. The Delphi technique uses repeated rounds of questioning and written responses, including feedback to responses in earlier rounds, to take advantage of group input while avoiding the possible biasing effects of oral panel deliberations. To use the Delphi technique, you must select a panel of experts for the particular area in question. For example, Cliff Branch from the opening case could use the Delphi technique to help him understand why his company is no longer winning many contracts. Cliff could assemble a panel of people with knowledge in his business area. Each expert would answer questions related to Cliff's situation, and then Cliff or a facilitator would evaluate their responses, together with opinions and justifications, and provide that feedback to each expert in the next iteration. Cliff would continue this process until the group responses converge to a specific solution. If the responses diverge, the facilitator of the Delphi technique needs to determine if there is a problem with the process.

Interviewing is a fact-finding technique for collecting information in face-to-face, phone, e-mail, or virtual discussions. Interviewing people with similar project experience is an important tool for identifying potential risks. For example, if a new project involves using a particular type of hardware or software, people who had recent experience with that hardware or software could describe their problems on a past project. If people have worked with a particular customer, they might provide insight into the potential risks of working for that customer again. It is important to be well prepared for leading interviews; it often helps to create a list of questions to use as a guide during the interview.

It is not uncommon for people to identify problems or opportunities without really understanding them. Before suggesting courses of action, it is important to identify the root cause of a problem or opportunity. Root cause analysis (as you learned in Chapter 8, Project Quality Management) often results in identifying even more potential risks for a project.

Another technique is a SWOT analysis of strengths, weaknesses, opportunities, and threats, which is often used in strategic planning. SWOT analysis can also be used during risk identification by having project teams focus on the broad perspectives of potential risks for particular projects. (You first learned about SWOT analysis in Chapter 4, Project Integration Management.) For example, before writing a particular proposal, Cliff Branch could have a group of his employees discuss in detail their company's strengths, their weaknesses for the project, and what opportunities and threats exist. Do they know that several competing firms are much more likely to win a certain contract? Do they know that winning a particular contract will likely lead to future contracts and help expand their business? Applying SWOT to specific potential projects can help identify the broad risks and opportunities that apply in that scenario.

Three other techniques for risk identification include the use of checklists, analysis of assumptions, and creation of diagrams:

- Checklists that are based on risks encountered in previous projects provide a meaningful template for understanding risks in a current project. You can use checklists similar to those developed by the Standish Group and other IT research consultants to help identify risks on IT projects.
- It is important to analyze project assumptions to make sure they are valid. Incomplete, inaccurate, or inconsistent assumptions might lead to identifying more risks.
- Diagramming techniques include using cause-and-effect diagrams or fishbone diagrams, flowcharts, and influence diagrams. Recall from Chapter 8, Project Quality Management, that fishbone diagrams help you trace problems back to their root cause. System or process **flowcharts** are diagrams that show how different parts of a system interrelate. For example, many programmers create flowcharts to show programming logic. (A sample flowchart is provided in Chapter 8.) Another type of diagram, an **influence diagram**, represents decision problems by displaying essential elements, including decisions, uncertainties, causality, and objectives, and how they influence each other. (See other references, such as *www.lumina.com/software/influencediagrams.html*, for detailed information on influence diagrams.)

11.4b The Risk Register

The main output of risk identification is a list of identified risks and other information needed to begin creating a risk register. A **risk register** is a document that contains results of various risk management processes; it is often displayed in a table or spreadsheet format. A risk register is a tool for documenting potential risk events and related information. **Risk events** refer to specific, uncertain events that may occur to the detriment or enhancement of the project. For example, negative risk events might include the performance failure of a product created as part of a project, delays in completing work as scheduled, increases in estimated costs, supply shortages, litigation against the company, and strikes. Examples of positive risk events include completing work sooner or cheaper than planned, collaborating with suppliers to produce better products, and good publicity resulting from the project.

Table 11-5 provides a sample of the format for a risk register that Cliff and his managers from the opening case might use on a new project. Actual data that might be entered for one of the risks is included below the table. Notice the main headings often included in the register. Many of these items are described in more detail later in this chapter. Elements of a risk register include:

- *An identification number for each risk event*: The project team may want to sort by risk events or quickly search for specific risk events, so they need to identify each risk with a unique descriptor, such as an identification number.
- *A rank for each risk event*: The rank is usually a number, with 1 representing the highest risk.
- *The name of the risk event*: Example names include *defective server, late completion of testing, reduced consulting costs*, and *good publicity*.
- *A description of the risk event*: Because the name of a risk event is often abbreviated, it helps to provide a more detailed description. Consider using a risk statement format similar to the following: "Because of <one or more causes>, <risk event> might occur, which would lead to <one or more effects>." For example, reduced consulting costs might be expanded to: "Because this particular consultant enjoys working for our company and is open to negotiating her rates, reduced consulting costs might occur, which could lead to saving money on the project."
- *The category under which the risk event falls*: For example, *defective server* might fall under the broader category of technology or hardware technology.
- *The root cause of the risk*: The root cause of the defective server might be a defective power supply.
- *Triggers for each risk*: **Triggers** are indicators or symptoms of actual risk events. For example, cost overruns on early activities may be symptoms of poor cost estimates. Defective products may be symptoms of a low-quality supplier. Documenting potential risk symptoms for projects also helps the project team identify more potential risk events.
- *Potential responses to each risk*: A potential response to the defective server might be to include a clause in the supplier's contract to replace the server within a certain time period at a negotiated cost.

441

TABLE 11-5 Sample risk register

No.	Rank	Risk	Description	Category	Root Cause	Triggers	Potential Responses	Risk Owner	Probability	Impact	Status
R44	1										
R21	2										
R7	3										

© Cengage Learning 2016

- *The **risk owner** or person who will take responsibility for the risk*: For example, a certain person might be in charge of any server-related risk events and managing response strategies.
- *The probability of the risk occurring*: There might be a high, medium, or low probability of a certain risk event. For example, the risk might be low that the server would actually be defective.
- *The impact to the project if the risk occurs*: There might be a high, medium, or low impact to project success if the risk event actually occurs. A defective server might have a high impact on successfully completing a project on time.
- *The status of the risk*: Did the risk event occur? Was the response strategy completed? Is the risk no longer relevant to the project? For example, a contract clause may have been completed to address the risk of a defective server.

For example, the following data might be entered for the first risk in the register. Notice that Cliff's team is taking a proactive approach in managing this risk.

- *No.*: R44
- *Rank*: 1
- *Risk*: New customer
- *Description*: We have never done a project for this organization before and don't know too much about them. One of our company's strengths is building good customer relationships, which often leads to further projects with that customer. We might have trouble working with this customer because they are new to us.
- *Category*: People risk
- *Root cause*: We won a contract to work on a project without really getting to know the customer.
- *Triggers*: The new customer asked a lot of questions in person and via e-mail that our existing customers would not, so we could easily misunderstand their needs and expectations.
- *Potential responses*: Make sure the project manager is sensitive to the fact that this is a new customer and takes the time to understand them. Have the PM set up a meeting to get to know the customer and clarify their expectations. Have Cliff attend the meeting, too.
- *Risk owner*: Project manager
- *Probability*: Medium
- *Impact*: High
- *Status*: PM will set up the meeting within the week.

After identifying risks, the next step is to understand which risks are most important by performing qualitative risk analysis.

11.5 PERFORMING QUALITATIVE RISK ANALYSIS

Qualitative risk analysis involves assessing the likelihood and impact of identified risks to determine their magnitude and priority. This section describes how to use a probability/impact matrix to produce a prioritized list of risks. It also provides examples of using the

Top Ten Risk Item Tracking technique to produce an overall ranking for project risks and to track trends in qualitative risk analysis. Finally, this section discusses the importance of expert judgment in performing risk analysis.

11.5a Using Probability/Impact Matrixes to Calculate Risk Factors

People often describe a risk probability or consequence as being high, medium or moderate, or low. For example, a meteorologist might predict a high probability or likelihood of severe rain showers on a certain day. If that day happens to be your wedding day and you are planning a large outdoor ceremony, the consequences or impact of severe showers might also be high.

A project manager can chart the probability and impact of risks on a **probability/ impact matrix or chart**, which lists the relative probability of a risk occurring and the relative impact of the risk occurring. Many project teams would benefit from using this simple technique to help them identify risks that need attention. To use this approach, project stakeholders list the risks they think might occur on their projects. They then label a risk as having a high, medium, or low probability of occurrence and a high, medium, or low impact if it does occur.

The project manager then summarizes the results in a probability/impact matrix or chart, as shown in Figure 11-5. For example, Cliff Branch and some of his project managers in the opening case could each identify three negative and positive potential risks for a particular project. They could then label the probability of occurrence and impact of each risk as being high, medium, or low. For example, one project manager might list a severe market downturn as a negative risk that is low in probability but high in impact. Cliff may have listed the same risk as being medium in both probability and impact. The team could

443

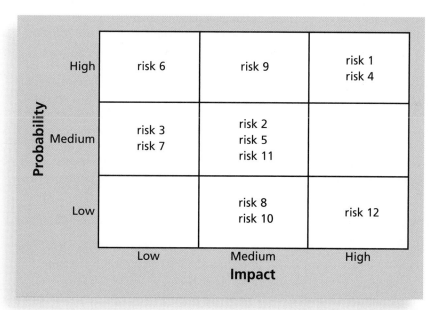

© Cengage Learning 2016

FIGURE 11-5   Sample probability/impact matrix

then plot all of the risks on a matrix or chart, combine common risks, and decide where those risks should be on the matrix or chart. The team should then focus on risks that fall in the high sections of the probability/impact matrix or chart. For example, Risks 1 and 4 are listed as high in both probability and impact. Risk 6 is high in probability but low in impact. Risk 9 is high in probability and medium in impact, and so on. The team should then discuss how it plans to respond to the risks if they occur, as you will learn later in this chapter in the section on risk response planning.

It may be useful to create a separate probability/impact matrix or chart for negative risks and positive risks to make sure that both types are adequately addressed. Some project teams also collect data on the probability of risks and the negative or positive impact they could have on scope, time, and cost goals. Qualitative risk analysis is normally done quickly, so the project team has to decide what type of approach makes the most sense for its project.

Some project teams develop a single number for a risk score simply by multiplying a numeric score for probability by a numeric score for impact. A more sophisticated approach to using probability/impact information is to calculate risk factors. To quantify risk probability and consequence, the U.S. Defense Systems Management College (DSMC) developed a technique for calculating **risk factors**—numbers that represent the overall risk of specific events, based on their probability of occurring and the consequences to the project if they do occur. The technique makes use of a probability/impact matrix that shows the probability of risks occurring and the impact or consequences of the risks.

Probabilities of a risk occurring can be estimated based on several factors determined by the unique nature of each project. For example, factors to evaluate for potential hardware or software technology risks could include the technology not being mature, the technology being too complex, and an inadequate support base for developing the technology. The impact of a risk occurring could include factors such as the availability of fallback solutions or the consequences of not meeting performance, cost, and schedule estimates.

Figure 11-6 provides an example of how risk factors were used to graph the probability of failure and consequence of failure in a research study on proposed technologies for designing more reliable aircraft. The figure classifies potential technologies (dots on the chart) as high, medium, or low risk, based on the probability of failure and consequences of failure. The researchers strongly recommended that the U.S. Air Force invest in the low- to medium-risk technologies and suggested that it not pursue the high-risk technologies.[16] The rigor involved in using the probability/impact matrix and risk factors can provide a much stronger argument than simply stating that risk probabilities or consequences are high, medium, or low.

11.5b Top Ten Risk Item Tracking

Top Ten Risk Item Tracking is a qualitative risk analysis tool. In addition to identifying risks, it maintains an awareness of risks throughout the life of a project by helping to monitor risks. Using this tool involves establishing a periodic review of the project's most significant risk items with management; similar reviews can also occur with the customer. The review begins with a summary of the status of the top ten sources of risk on the project. The summary includes each item's current ranking, previous ranking, number of times it appears on the list over a period of time, and a summary of progress made

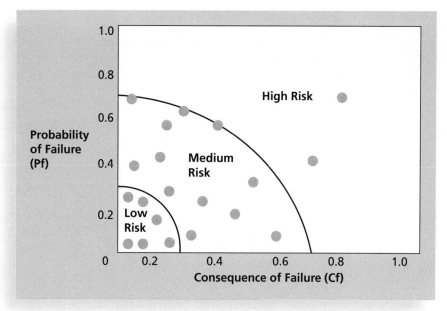

© Cengage Learning 2016

FIGURE 11-6 Chart showing high-, medium-, and low-risk technologies

in resolving the risk item since the previous review. The Microsoft Solution Framework (MSF), the methodology Microsoft uses for managing projects, is an example of how one company tracks risk items. It uses a risk management model that includes developing and monitoring a top ten master list of risks. The methodology combines aspects of software design and development, and building and deploying infrastructure, into a single-project life cycle for guiding technology solutions of all kinds. (Consult Microsoft's website for more information on MSF.)

Table 11-6 provides an example of a Top Ten Risk Item Tracking chart that could be used at a management review meeting for a project. This example includes only the top five negative risk events. Notice that each risk event is ranked based on the current month, previous month, and how many months it has been in the top ten. The last column briefly describes the progress for resolving each risk item. You can have separate charts for negative and positive risks or combine them into one chart.

A risk management review accomplishes several objectives. First, it keeps management and the customer (if included) aware of major influences that could prevent or enhance the project's success. Second, by involving the customer, the project team may be able to consider alternative strategies for addressing the risks. Third, the review promotes confidence in the project team by demonstrating to management and the customer that the team is aware of significant risks, has a strategy in place, and is effectively carrying out that strategy.

The main output of qualitative risk analysis is updating the risk register. The ranking column of the risk register should be filled in, along with a numeric value or rating of high, medium, or low for the probability and impact of the risk event. Additional information

TABLE 11-6 Example of top ten risk item tracking

	MONTHLY RANKING			
Risk Event	Rank This Month	Rank Last Month	Number of Months in Top Ten	Risk Resolution Progress
Inadequate planning	1	2	4	Working on revising the entire project management plan
Poor definition	2	3	3	Holding meetings with project customer and sponsor to clarify scope
Absence of leadership	3	1	2	Assigned a new project manager to lead the project after the previous one quit
Poor cost estimates	4	4	3	Revising cost estimates
Poor time estimates	5	5	3	Revising schedule estimates

© Cengage Learning 2016

is often added for risk events, such as identification of risks that need more attention in the near term or those that can be placed on a watch list. A **watch list** is a list of risks that have low priority but are still identified as potential risks. Qualitative analysis can also identify risks that should be evaluated quantitatively, as you learn in the next section.

MEDIA SNAPSHOT

Even more than 100 years after the Titanic sank on April 15, 1912, people mark the anniversary on which more than 1,500 of the ship's passengers and crew died. A recent article in PMI's Virtual Library explains how to avoid "the Titanic factor" in your projects by analyzing the interdependence of risks. For example, the probability of one risk event occurring might change if another one materializes, and the response to one risk event might affect another. The article's author addresses the issue of how project risks interact and how project teams can address those risks. Some of the interdependent risk events on the Titanic included the following:

- The design of the bulkheads, rudder, and engines were integrated. As six of the 16 watertight compartments were breached and began flooding, the weight of the water in the bow pulled the ship under until the bulkheads overtopped. The rudder design was considered adequate for use on the open seas, but it was undersized for the tight maneuvers required that fateful night. The central propeller had a steam turbine as its power source, but this engine could not be reversed and was stopped during the run up to the iceberg. This stopped the water flow past the rudder and became a critical problem for the ship.
- Several procedures were not followed, which had the cumulative effect of creating other major problems. Iceberg reports from two other ships were not passed on to the bridge. The wireless radio did not work most of the day, so

continued

another critical iceberg warning failed to reach the Titanic's captain. The ship was traveling too fast for the amount of ice in the area, and visibility was terrible that night.

- Unknown risk events also contributed to the sinking of the Titanic. For example, the steel in the hull could not withstand the cold temperatures, causing it to break without bending. Iron rivet heads also burst due to the cold.[17]

11.6 PERFORMING QUANTITATIVE RISK ANALYSIS

Quantitative risk analysis often follows qualitative risk analysis, yet both processes can be done together or separately. On some projects, the team may only perform qualitative risk analysis. The nature of the project and availability of time and money affect which risk analysis techniques are used. Large, complex projects involving leading-edge technologies often require extensive quantitative risk analysis. The main techniques for quantitative risk analysis include data gathering, analysis and modeling techniques, and expert judgment. Data gathering often involves interviewing experts and collecting probability distribution information. This section focuses on using the quantitative risk analysis and modeling techniques of decision tree analysis, simulation, and sensitivity analysis.

11.6a Decision Trees and Expected Monetary Value

A **decision tree** is a diagramming analysis technique used to help select the best course of action when future outcomes are uncertain. A common application of decision tree analysis involves calculating expected monetary value. **Expected monetary value (EMV)** is the product of a risk event probability and the risk event's monetary value. To illustrate this concept, Figure 11-7 uses the issue of which project(s) an organization might pursue. Suppose Cliff Branch's firm was trying to decide if it should submit a proposal for Project 1, Project 2, both projects, or neither project. The team could draw a decision tree with two branches, one for Project 1 and one for Project 2. The firm could then calculate the expected monetary value to help make this decision.

To create a decision tree, and to calculate expected monetary value specifically, you must estimate the probabilities or chances of certain events occurring. For example, Figure 11-7 shows a 20 percent probability ($P = .20$) that Cliff's firm will win the contract for Project 1, which is estimated to be worth $300,000 in profits—the outcome of the top branch in the figure. There is an 80 percent probability ($P = .80$) that the firm will not win the contract for Project 1, and the outcome is estimated to be –$40,000, meaning that the firm will have invested $40,000 into Project 1 with no reimbursement if it does not win the contract. The sum of the probabilities for outcomes for each project must equal one (for Project 1, .20 plus .80). Probabilities are normally determined based on expert judgment. Cliff or other people in his firm should have a sense of the likelihood of winning certain projects.

Figure 11-7 also shows probabilities and outcomes for Project 2. Suppose there is a 20 percent probability that Cliff's firm will lose $50,000 on Project 2, a 10 percent probability that it will lose $20,000, and a 70 percent probability that it will earn $60,000. Again, experts would need to estimate these dollar amounts and probabilities.

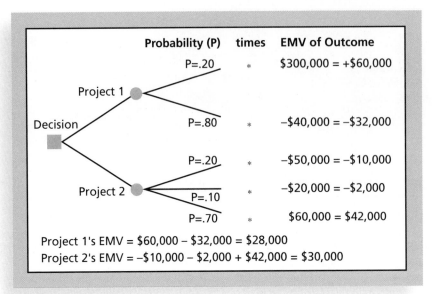

Project 1's EMV = $60,000 – $32,000 = $28,000
Project 2's EMV = –$10,000 – $2,000 + $42,000 = $30,000

FIGURE 11-7   Expected monetary value (EMV) example

To calculate the EMV for each project, multiply the probability by the outcome value for each potential outcome for each project and sum the results. To calculate EVM for Project 1, going from left to right, multiply the probability by the outcome for each branch and sum the results. In this example, the EMV for Project 1 is $28,000.

.2($300,000) + .8(– $40,000) = $60,000 – $32,000 = $28,000

The EMV for Project 2 is $30,000.

.2(– $50,000) + .1(– $20,000) + .7($60,000) = – $10,000 – $2,000 + $42,000 = $30,000

Because the EMV provides an estimate for the total dollar value of a decision, you want to have a positive number; the higher the EMV, the better. Because the EMV is positive for both Projects 1 and 2, Cliff's firm would expect a positive outcome from each and could bid on both projects. If it had to choose between the two projects, perhaps because of limited resources, Cliff's firm should bid on Project 2 because it has a higher EMV.

Notice in Figure 11-7 that if you just look at the potential outcome of the two projects, Project 1 looks more appealing. You could earn $300,000 in profits from Project 1, but you could only earn $60,000 for Project 2. If Cliff were a risk seeker, he would naturally want to bid on Project 1. However, there is only a 20 percent chance of earning the $300,000 on Project 1, as opposed to a 70 percent chance of earning $60,000 on Project 2. Using EMV helps account for all possible outcomes and their probabilities of occurrence, thereby reducing the tendency to pursue overly aggressive or conservative risk strategies.

11.6b Simulation

A more sophisticated technique for quantitative risk analysis is simulation, which uses a representation or model of a system to analyze its expected behavior or performance. Most simulations are based on some form of Monte Carlo analysis. **Monte Carlo analysis** simulates a model's outcome many times to provide a statistical distribution of the calculated results. For example, Monte Carlo analysis can determine that a project will finish by a certain date only 10 percent of the time, and determine another date for which the project will finish 50 percent of the time. In other words, Monte Carlo analysis can predict the probability of finishing by a certain date or the probability that the cost will be equal to or less than a certain value.

You can use several different types of distribution functions when performing a Monte Carlo analysis. The following example is a simplified approach. The basic steps of a Monte Carlo analysis are:

1. Collect the most likely, optimistic, and pessimistic estimates for the variables in the model. For example, if you are trying to determine the likelihood of meeting project schedule goals, the project network diagram would be your model. You would collect the most likely, optimistic, and pessimistic time estimates for each task. Notice that this step is similar to collecting data for performing PERT estimates. However, instead of applying the same PERT weighted average formula, you perform the following steps in a Monte Carlo simulation.

2. Determine the probability distribution of each variable. What is the likelihood of a variable falling between the optimistic and most likely estimates? For example, if an expert assigned to a particular task provides a most likely estimate of 10 weeks, an optimistic estimate of eight weeks, and a pessimistic estimate of 15 weeks, you then ask about the probability of completing that task between 8 and 10 weeks. The expert might respond that there is a 20 percent probability.

3. For each variable, such as the time estimate for a task, select a random value based on the probability distribution for the occurrence of the variable. For example, using the preceding scenario, you would randomly pick a value between 8 weeks and 10 weeks 20 percent of the time and a value between 10 weeks and 15 weeks 80 percent of the time.

4. Run a deterministic analysis or one pass through the model using the combination of values selected for each of the variables. For example, one task described in the preceding scenario might have a value of 12 on the first run. All of the other tasks would also have one random value assigned to them on the first run, based on their estimates and probability distributions.

5. Repeat Steps 3 and 4 many times to obtain the probability distribution of the model's results. The number of iterations depends on the number of variables and the degree of confidence required in the results, but it typically lies between 100 and 1,000. Using the project schedule as an example, the final simulation results will show you the probability of completing the entire project within a certain time period.

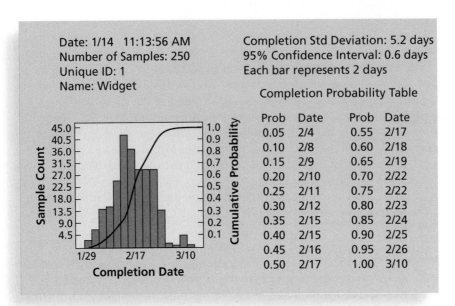

Date: 1/14   11:13:56 AM
Number of Samples: 250
Unique ID: 1
Name: Widget

Completion Std Deviation: 5.2 days
95% Confidence Interval: 0.6 days
Each bar represents 2 days

Completion Probability Table

Prob	Date	Prob	Date
0.05	2/4	0.55	2/17
0.10	2/8	0.60	2/18
0.15	2/9	0.65	2/19
0.20	2/10	0.70	2/22
0.25	2/11	0.75	2/22
0.30	2/12	0.80	2/23
0.35	2/15	0.85	2/24
0.40	2/15	0.90	2/25
0.45	2/16	0.95	2/26
0.50	2/17	1.00	3/10

FIGURE 11-8   Sample monte carlo-based simulation results for project schedule

Figure 11-8 illustrates the results from a Monte Carlo-based simulation of a project schedule. The simulation was done using Microsoft Project and Risk+ software. On the left side of Figure 11-8 is a chart displaying columns and an S-shaped curve. The height of each column indicates how many times the project was completed in a given time interval during the simulation run, which is the sample count. In this example, the time interval was two working days, and the simulation was run 250 times. The first column shows that the project was completed by January 29 only two times during the simulation. The S-shaped curve shows the cumulative probability of completing the project on or before a given date. The right side of Figure 11-8 shows the information in tabular form. For example, there is a 10 percent probability that the project will be completed by 2/8 (February 8), a 50 percent chance of completion by 2/17 (February 17), and a 90 percent chance of completion by 2/25 (February 25).

Several PC-based software packages that perform Monte Carlo simulations are available. Many products display the major risk drivers for a project based on the simulation results. This enables you to identify the chief source of uncertainty in a project schedule. For example, a wide range for a certain task estimate might cause most of the uncertainty in the project schedule. You will learn more about using simulation software and other software related to project risk management later in this chapter.

WHAT WENT RIGHT?

Microsoft Excel is a common tool for performing quantitative risk analysis. Microsoft provides examples of how to use Excel to perform Monte Carlo simulation on its website, and explains how several companies use Monte Carlo simulation as an important tool for decision making:

- General Motors uses simulation for forecasting its net income, predicting structural costs and purchasing costs of vehicles, and determining the company's susceptibility to different kinds of risk, such as interest rate changes and exchange rate fluctuations.
- Eli Lilly uses simulation to determine the optimal plant capacity that should be built for developing each drug.
- Procter & Gamble uses simulation to model and optimally hedge foreign exchange risk.[18]

Monte Carlo simulation can also help reduce schedule risk on agile projects. For example, instead of using linear techniques, which assume a fixed future velocity and a discrete completion date, you can use Monte Carlo simulation to estimate a range of completion dates. "Consider a simple scenario where two teams both have an average velocity of 7.5. Using this average, either team could deliver the next 45 points in 6 iterations. However, suppose Team A's historical velocity values were 10, 4, 5, and 11, and Team B's historical velocity values were 7, 8, 8, and 7. The average is the same, but because the velocity values for Team A have a higher variance, there is greater risk when predicting future results."[19]

11.6c Sensitivity Analysis

Many people are familiar with using **sensitivity analysis** to see the effects of changing one or more variables on an outcome. For example, many people perform a sensitivity analysis to determine their monthly payments for a loan given different interest rates or periods of the loan. What will your monthly mortgage payment be if you borrow $100,000 for 30 years at a 6 percent rate? What will the payment be if the interest rate is 7 percent? What will the payment be if you decide to pay off the loan in 15 years at 5 percent?

Many professionals use sensitivity analysis to help make several common business decisions, such as determining break-even points based on different assumptions. People often use spreadsheet software like Microsoft Excel to perform sensitivity analysis. Figure 11-9 shows an example Excel file created to quickly show the break-even point for a product based on various inputs: the sales price per unit, the manufacturing cost per unit, and fixed monthly expenses. The current inputs result in a break-even point of 6,250 units sold. Users of this spreadsheet can change inputs and see the effects on the break-even point in chart format. Project teams often create similar models to determine the sensitivity of various project variables. For example, Cliff's team could develop sensitivity analysis models to estimate their profits on jobs by varying the number of hours required to do the jobs or by varying costs per hour.

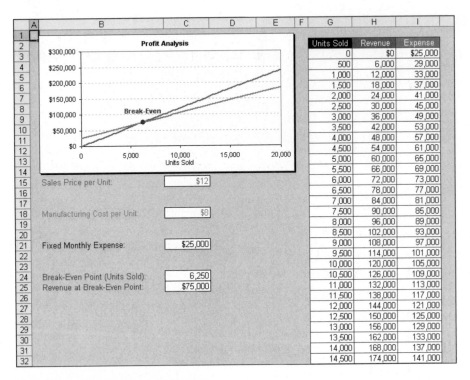

	Units Sold	Revenue	Expense
	0	$0	$25,000
	500	6,000	29,000
	1,000	12,000	33,000
	1,500	18,000	37,000
	2,000	24,000	41,000
	2,500	30,000	45,000
	3,000	36,000	49,000
	3,500	42,000	53,000
	4,000	48,000	57,000
	4,500	54,000	61,000
	5,000	60,000	65,000
	5,500	66,000	69,000
	6,000	72,000	73,000
	6,500	78,000	77,000
	7,000	84,000	81,000
	7,500	90,000	85,000
	8,000	96,000	89,000
	8,500	102,000	93,000
	9,000	108,000	97,000
	9,500	114,000	101,000
	10,000	120,000	105,000
	10,500	126,000	109,000
	11,000	132,000	113,000
	11,500	138,000	117,000
	12,000	144,000	121,000
	12,500	150,000	125,000
	13,000	156,000	129,000
	13,500	162,000	133,000
	14,000	168,000	137,000
	14,500	174,000	141,000

Sales Price per Unit: $12

Manufacturing Cost per Unit: $8

Fixed Monthly Expense: $25,000

Break-Even Point (Units Sold): 6,250
Revenue at Break-Even Point: $75,000

FIGURE 11-9 Sample sensitivity analysis for determining break-even point

The main outputs of quantitative risk analysis are updates to the risk register, such as revised risk rankings or detailed information behind those rankings. The quantitative analysis also provides high-level information about the probabilities of achieving certain project objectives. This information might cause the project manager to suggest changes in contingency reserves. In some cases, projects may be redirected or canceled based on the quantitative analysis, or the quantitative analysis might be used to help initiate new projects to help the current one succeed.

11.7 PLANNING RISK RESPONSES

After an organization identifies and quantifies risks, it must develop an appropriate response to them. Developing a response to risks involves developing options and defining strategies for reducing negative risks and enhancing positive risks.

The four basic response strategies for negative risks are:

- **Risk avoidance** or eliminating a specific threat, usually by eliminating its causes. Of course, not all risks can be eliminated, but specific risk events can be. For example, a project team may decide to continue using a specific piece of hardware or software on a project because the team knows it works. Other products that could be used on the project may be available, but if the project team is unfamiliar with them, they could cause significant risk. Using familiar hardware or software eliminates this risk.

- **Risk acceptance** or accepting the consequences if a risk occurs. For example, a project team planning a big project review meeting could take an active approach to risk by having a contingency or backup plan and contingency reserves if the team cannot get approval for a specific meeting site. On the other hand, the team could take a passive approach and accept whatever facility the organization provides.
- **Risk transference** or shifting the consequence of a risk and responsibility for its management to a third party. For example, risk transference is often used in dealing with financial risk exposure. A project team may purchase special insurance or warranty protection for specific hardware needed for a project. If the hardware fails, the insurer must replace it within a specified period of time.
- **Risk mitigation** or reducing the impact of a risk event by reducing the probability of its occurrence. Suggestions for reducing common sources of risk on IT projects were provided at the beginning of this chapter. Other examples of risk mitigation include using proven technology, having competent project personnel, using various analysis and validation techniques, and buying maintenance or service agreements from subcontractors.

Table 11-7 provides general mitigation strategies for technical, cost, and schedule risks on projects.[20] Note that increasing the frequency of project monitoring and using a work breakdown structure (WBS) and Critical Path Method (CPM) are strategies for all three areas. Increasing the project manager's authority is a strategy for mitigating technical and cost risks, and selecting the most experienced project manager is recommended for reducing schedule risks. Improving communication is also an effective strategy for mitigating risks.

The four basic response strategies for positive risks are:

- **Risk exploitation** or doing whatever you can to make sure the positive risk happens. For example, suppose that Cliff's company funded a project to provide

TABLE 11-7 General risk mitigation strategies for technical, cost, and schedule risks

Technical Risks	Cost Risks	Schedule Risks
Emphasize team support and avoid stand-alone project structure	Increase the frequency of project monitoring	Increase the frequency of project monitoring
Increase project manager authority	Use WBS and CPM	Use WBS and CPM
Improve problem handling and communication	Improve communication, understanding of project goals, and team support	Select the most experienced project manager
Increase the frequency of project monitoring	Increase project manager authority	
Use WBS and CPM		

source: J. Couillard

new computer classrooms for a nearby school in need. They might select one of their top project managers to organize news coverage of the project, write a press release, or hold some other public event to ensure that the project produces good public relations for the company, which could lead to more business.

- **Risk sharing** or allocating ownership of the risk to another party. Using the same example of implementing new computer classrooms, the project manager could form a partnership with the school's principal, school board, or parent-teacher organization to share responsibility for achieving good public relations for the project. On the other hand, the company might partner with a local training firm that agrees to provide free training for all of the teachers on how to use the new computer classrooms.

- **Risk enhancement** or changing the size of the opportunity by identifying and maximizing key drivers of the positive risk. For example, an important driver of getting good public relations for the computer classrooms project might be to generate awareness and excitement about it among students, parents, and teachers. These groups might then do their own formal or informal advertising of the project and Cliff's company, which in turn might interest other groups and generate more business.

- **Risk acceptance** also applies to positive risks when the project team does not take any actions toward a risk. For example, the computer classrooms project manager might assume that the project will result in good public relations for the company and not feel compelled to do anything extra.

The main outputs of risk response planning include risk-related contractual agreements, updates to the project management plan and other project documents, and updates to the risk register. For example, if Cliff's company decided to partner with a local training firm on the computer classrooms project to share the opportunity of achieving good public relations, it could write a contract with that firm. The project management plan and its related plans might need to be updated if the risk response strategies require additional tasks, resources, or time to accomplish. Risk response strategies often result in changes to the WBS and project schedule, so plans that contain this information must be updated as well. The risk response strategies also provide updated information for the risk register by describing the risk responses, risk owners, and status information.

Risk response strategies often include identification of residual and secondary risks as well as contingency plans and reserves, as described earlier. **Residual risks** are risks that remain after all of the response strategies have been implemented. For example, even though a stable hardware product may have been used on a project, there may still be a risk that it fails to function properly. **Secondary risks** are a direct result of implementing a risk response. For example, using the more stable hardware may have caused a risk of peripheral devices failing to function properly.

11.8 CONTROLLING RISKS

Controlling risks involves executing the risk management processes to respond to risk events and ensuring that risk awareness is an ongoing activity performed by the entire project team throughout the entire project. Project risk management does not stop with the initial risk analysis. Identified risks may not materialize, or their probabilities of occurrence or loss may diminish. Previously identified risks may be determined to have a greater probability of occurrence or a higher estimated loss value. Similarly, new risks will be identified as the project progresses. Newly identified risks need to go through the same process as those identified during the initial risk assessment. A redistribution of resources devoted to risk management may be necessary because of relative changes in risk exposure.

Carrying out individual risk management plans involves monitoring risks based on defined milestones and making decisions regarding risks and their response strategies. It may be necessary to alter a strategy that becomes ineffective, implement a planned contingency activity, or eliminate a risk from the list of potential risks when it no longer exists. Project teams sometimes use **workarounds**—unplanned responses to risk events— when they do not have contingency plans in place.

Tools and techniques for performing risk control include risk reassessment, risk audits, variance and trend analysis, technical performance measurements, reserve analysis, and status meetings or periodic risk reviews such as the Top Ten Risk Item Tracking method. Outputs of this process are work performance information, change requests, and updates to the project management plan, other project documents, and organizational process assets.

11.9 USING SOFTWARE TO ASSIST IN PROJECT RISK MANAGEMENT

As you saw in several parts of this chapter, you can use a variety of software tools to enhance various risk management processes. Most organizations use software to create, update, and distribute information in their risk registers. The risk register is often a simple Microsoft Word or Excel file, but it can also be part of a more sophisticated database. Spreadsheets can aid in tracking and quantifying risks, preparing charts and graphs, and performing sensitivity analysis. Software can be used to create decision trees and estimate expected monetary value.

More sophisticated risk management software, such as Monte Carlo simulation software, can help you develop models and use simulations to analyze and respond to various risks. Several high-end project management tools include simulation capabilities. You can also purchase add-on software to perform Monte Carlo simulations using Excel (such as Oracle's Crystal Ball or Palisade's @Risk for Excel) or Project 2013 (such as Deltek's Risk+ or Palisade's @Risk for Project). Several software packages have also been created specifically for project risk management. Although it has become easier to do sophisticated risk analysis with new software tools, project teams must be careful not to rely too heavily on software when performing project risk management. If a risk is not identified, it cannot be managed, and intelligent, experienced people are needed to do a good job of identifying risks. It also takes hard work to develop and implement good risk response strategies. Software should be used as a tool to help make good decisions in project risk management, not as a scapegoat when things go wrong.

Well-run projects, like a master violinist's performance, an Olympic athlete's gold medal win, or a Pulitzer Prize-winning book, appear to be almost effortless. Those on the outside—whether audiences, customers, or managers—cannot observe the effort that goes into a superb performance. They cannot see the hours of practice, the edited drafts, or the planning, management, and foresight that create the appearance of ease. To improve IT project management, project managers should strive to make their jobs look easy—it reflects the results of a well-run project.

CASE WRAP-UP

Cliff Branch and two of his senior people attended a seminar on project risk management where the speaker discussed several techniques, such as estimating the expected monetary value of projects and Monte Carlo simulations. Cliff asked the speaker how these techniques could help his company decide which projects to bid on, because bidding on projects often required up-front investments with the possibility of no payback. The speaker walked through an example of EMV and then ran a quick Monte Carlo simulation. Cliff did not have a strong math background and had a hard time understanding the EMV calculations. He thought the simulation was much too confusing to have any practical use for him. He believed in his gut instincts much more than any math calculation or computer output.

The speaker finally sensed that Cliff was not impressed, so she explained the importance of looking at the odds of winning project awards and not just at the potential profits. She suggested using a risk-neutral strategy by bidding on projects that the company had a good chance of winning (50 percent or so) and that had a good profit potential, instead of focusing on projects that they had a small chance of winning and that had a larger profit potential. Cliff disagreed with this advice, and he continued to bid on high-risk projects. The two other managers who attended the seminar now understood why the firm was having problems—their leader loved taking risks, even if it hurt the company. They soon found jobs with competing companies, as did several other employees.

Chapter Summary

Risk is an uncertainty that can have a negative or positive effect on meeting project objectives. Many organizations do a poor job of project risk management, if they do any at all. Successful organizations realize the value of good project risk management.

Risk management is an investment; in other words, costs are associated with identifying risks, analyzing those risks, and establishing plans to address them. Those costs must be included in cost, schedule, and resource planning.

Risk utility or risk tolerance is the amount of satisfaction or pleasure received from a potential payoff. Risk seekers enjoy high risks, risk-averse people do not like to take risks, and risk-neutral people seek to balance risks and potential payoff.

Project risk management is a process in which the project team continually assesses what risks may negatively or positively affect the project, determines the probability of such events occurring, and determines the impact if such events occur. Risk management also involves analyzing and determining alternate strategies to deal with risks. The six main processes of risk management are planning risk management, identifying risks, performing qualitative risk analysis, performing quantitative risk analysis, planning risk responses, and controlling risks.

Planning risk management is the process of deciding how to approach risk management activities and plan for them in a project. A risk management plan is a key output of risk management planning, and a risk register is a key output of the other risk management processes. Contingency plans are predefined actions that a project team will take if an identified risk event occurs. Fallback plans are developed for risks that have a high impact on meeting project objectives and are implemented if attempts to reduce the risk are not effective. Contingency reserves or contingency allowances are provisions held by the project sponsor or organization to reduce the risk of cost or schedule overruns to an acceptable level.

IT projects often involve several risks, including lack of user involvement, lack of executive management support, unclear requirements, and poor planning. Lists developed by the Standish Group and other organizations can help you identify potential risks on IT projects. A risk breakdown structure is a useful tool that can help project managers consider potential risks in different categories. Lists of common risk conditions in project management knowledge areas can also be helpful in identifying risks, as can information-gathering techniques such as brainstorming, the Delphi technique, interviewing, and SWOT analysis. A risk register is a document that contains results of various risk management processes; it is often displayed in a table or spreadsheet format. A risk register is a tool for documenting potential risk events and related information. Risk events refer to specific, uncertain events that may occur to the detriment or enhancement of the project.

Risks can be assessed qualitatively and quantitatively. Tools for qualitative risk analysis include a probability/impact matrix and the Top Ten Risk Item Tracking technique. Tools for quantitative risk analysis include decision trees and Monte Carlo simulation. Expected monetary value (EMV) uses decision trees to evaluate potential projects based on their expected value. Simulations are a more sophisticated method for creating estimates to help you determine the likelihood of meeting specific project schedule or cost goals. Sensitivity analysis is used to show the effects of changing one or more variables on an outcome.

The four basic responses to negative risks are avoidance, acceptance, transference, and mitigation. Risk avoidance involves eliminating a specific threat or risk. Risk acceptance means accepting the consequences of a risk if it occurs. Risk transference is shifting the consequence of a risk and responsibility for its management to a third party. Risk mitigation is reducing the impact of a risk event by reducing the probability of its occurrence. The four basic response strategies for positive risks are risk exploitation, risk sharing, risk enhancement, and risk acceptance.

Controlling risks involves executing the risk management processes and the risk management plan to respond to risks. Outputs of this process include work performance information, change requests, and updates to the project management plan, other project documents, and organizational process assets.

Several types of software can assist in project risk management. Monte Carlo-based simulation software is a particularly useful tool to help you get a better idea of project risks and top sources of risk or risk drivers.

Quick Quiz

1. _____ is an uncertainty that can have a negative or positive effect on meeting project objectives.

    a. Risk utility

    b. Risk tolerance

    c. Risk management

    d. Risk

2. A person who is risk- _____ receives greater satisfaction when more payoff is at stake and is willing to pay a penalty to take risks.

    a. averse

    b. seeking

    c. neutral

    d. aware

3. Which risk management process involves prioritizing risks based on their probability and impact of occurrence?

    a. planning risk management

    b. identifying risks

    c. performing qualitative risk analysis

    d. performing quantitative risk analysis

4. Your project involves using a new release of a common software application, but if that release is not available, your team has _____ plans to use the current release.

    a. contingency

    b. fallback

    c. reserve

    d. mitigation

5. Which risk identification tool involves deriving a consensus among a panel of experts by using anonymous input regarding future events?

    a.   risk breakdown structure

    b.   brainstorming

    c.   interviewing

    d.   Delphi technique

6. A risk _____ is a document that contains results of various risk management processes, and is often displayed in a table or spreadsheet format.

    a.   management plan

    b.   register

    c.   breakdown structure

    d.   probability/impact matrix

7. _____ are indicators or symptoms of actual risk events, such as a cost overrun on early activities being a symptom of poor cost estimates.

    a.   Probabilities

    b.   Impacts

    c.   Watch list items

    d.   Triggers

8. Suppose there is a 30 percent chance that you will lose $10,000 and a 70 percent chance that you will earn $100,000 on a particular project. What is the project's estimated monetary value?

    a.   −$30,000

    b. $70,000

    c. $67,000

    d.   −$67,000

9. _____ is a quantitative risk analysis tool that uses a model of a system to analyze its expected behavior or performance.

    a.   Simulation

    b.   Sensitivity analysis

    c.   Monte Carlo analysis

    d.   EMV

10. Your project team has decided not to use an upcoming release of software because it might cause your schedule to slip. Which negative risk response strategy are you using?

    a.   avoidance

    b.   acceptance

    c.   transference

    d.   mitigation

Quick Quiz Answers

1. d; 2. b; 3. c; 4. a; 5. d; 6. b; 7. d; 8. c; 9. a; 10. a

Discussion Questions

1. Discuss the risk utility function and risk preference chart in Figure 11-2. Would you rate yourself as being risk-averse, risk-neutral, or risk-seeking? Give examples of each approach from different aspects of your life, such as your current job, your personal finances, romances, and eating habits.

2. What are some questions that should be addressed in a risk management plan?

3. Discuss the common sources of risk on IT projects and suggestions for managing them. Which suggestions do you find most useful? Which do you feel would not work in your organization? Why?

4. What is the difference between using brainstorming and the Delphi technique for risk identification? What are some of the advantages and disadvantages of each approach? Describe the contents of a risk register and how it is used in several risk management processes.

5. Describe how to use a probability/impact matrix and the Top Ten Risk Item Tracking approaches for performing qualitative risk analysis. How could you use each technique on a project?

6. Explain how to use decision trees and Monte Carlo analysis for quantifying risk. Give an example of how you could use each technique on an IT project.

7. Provide realistic examples of each of the risk response strategies for both negative and positive risks.

8. List the tools and techniques for performing risk control.

9. How can you use Excel to assist in project risk management? What other software can help project teams make better risk management decisions?

Exercises

1. Suppose your college or organization is considering a project to develop an information system that would allow all employees, students, and customers to access and maintain their own human resources information, such as address, marital status, and tax information. The main benefits of the system would be a reduction in human resources personnel and more accurate information. For example, if an employee, student, or customer had a new telephone number or e-mail address, he or she would be responsible for entering the data in the new system. The new system would also allow employees to change their tax withholdings or pension plan contributions. Identify five potential risks for this new project, and be sure to list some negative and positive risks. Provide a detailed description of each risk and propose strategies for addressing each risk. Document your results in a short paper.

2. Review a document related to risk management, such as the Microsoft *Security Risk Management Guide*. Does this guide address most of the topics related to risk management planning, as described in this text? Document your analysis in a short paper.

3. Research risk management software. Are many products available? What are the main advantages of using them in managing projects? What are the main disadvantages? Write a short paper to discuss your findings, and include at least three references.

4. Suppose that your organization is deciding which of four projects to bid on, as summarized in the following table. Assume that all up-front investments are not recovered, so they are shown as negative profits. Draw a diagram and calculate the EMV for each project. Write a few paragraphs explaining which projects you would bid on. Be sure to use the EMV information and your personal risk tolerance to justify your answer.

Project	Chance of Outcome	Estimated Profits
Project 1	50 percent	$120,000
	50 percent	-$50,000
Project 2	30 percent	$100,000
	40 percent	$ 50,000
	30 percent	-$60,000
Project 3	70 percent	$ 20,000
	30 percent	-$ 5,000
Project 4	30 percent	$ 40,000
	30 percent	$ 30,000
	20 percent	$ 20,000
	20 percent	-$50,000

5. Open the template file called breakeven using Microsoft Excel. Examine the formulas in the file to understand the relationships between the variables (such as sales price per unit, manufacturing cost per unit, and fixed monthly expenses) and the outputs (such as break-even point and revenue at break-even point). Run at least three different scenarios, changing the inputs as desired and noting the outputs. Write a short paper to summarize the results, including screen shots of the three scenarios and your opinions on sensitivity analysis in general and in this example.

6. Find an example of a company that took a big risk on an IT project and succeeded. In addition, find an example of a company that took a big risk and failed. Summarize each project and situation in a short paper. In the paper, you should also discuss whether you believe that anything besides luck makes a difference between success and failure.

Running Case

You and your team identified some risks during the first week of the Global Treps Project. However, you never ranked the risks or developed any response strategies. Because several negative risk events have already occurred (such as Ashok breaking his wrist and poor communications with a key stakeholder in Ethiopia, as described in Chapter 10), you have decided to be more proactive in managing risks. You also want to address positive risks as well as negative risks.

1. Create a risk register for the project, using Table 11-5 and the data after it as a guide. Identify six potential risks, including risks related to the problems described in the preceding paragraph. Include three negative and three positive risks. Describe the risks using the format: "Because of <one or more causes>, <risk event> might occur, which would lead to <one or more effects>."

2. Plot the six risks on a probability/impact matrix, using Figure 11-5 as a guide. Also assign a numeric value for the probability that a risk will occur and the impact of each risk on meeting

the main project objectives. Use a scale of 1 to 10 to assign the values, with 1 representing the lowest value. For a simple risk factor calculation, multiply the probability score and the impact score. Add a column called Risk Score to your risk register to the right of the impact column. Enter the new data in the risk register. Write your rationale for how you determined the scores for one of the negative risks and one of the positive risks.

3. Develop a response strategy for one of the negative risks and one of the positive risks. Enter the information in the risk register. Also write a separate paragraph describing what specific tasks would be required to implement the strategy. Include time and cost estimates for each strategy as well.

Key Terms

Endnotes

1. C. William Ibbs and Young Hoon Kwak, "Assessing Project Management Maturity," *Project Management Journal* 31, no. 1 (March 2000), pp. 32–43.

2. Aneerav Sukhoo, Andries Barnard, Mariki M. Eloff, and John A. Van der Poll, "An Assessment of Software Project Management Maturity in Mauritius," *Issues in Informing Science and Information Technology* 2 (May 2003), pp. 671–690.

3. Peter Kulik and Catherine Weber, "Software Risk Management Practices—2001," KLCI Research Group (August 2001).

4. David Hillson, "Boom, bust, and risk management," *Project Manager Today* (September 2008).

5. SAS, "Survey: Better risk management would have lessened credit crisis," SAS Press Release (September 18, 2008).

6. Michael Versace, "Forecast: Financial Services Industry Will Continue to Spend Big on Risk IT," Global Association of Risk Professionals (May 15, 2015).

7. David Hillson, "Integrated Risk Management as a Framework for Organisational Success," *PMI Global Congress Proceedings (2006).*

8. Hilson, David, "Managing Overall Project Risk," *PMI Global Congress Proceedings* (2014).

9. Project Management Institute, *A Guide to the Project Management Body of Knowledge (PMBOK® Guide),* Fifth Edition (2012).

10. The Standish Group, "Unfinished Voyages," *StandishGroup.com* (1996).

11. Andy Cole, "Runaway Projects—Cause and Effects," *Software World* 26, no. 3 (1995), pp. 3–5.

12. KPMG International, "Expectation of Risk Management Outpacing Capabilities – It's Time for Action," (2013).

13. The Guardian, "Germanwings crash: call for technology to enable remote command of plane," *The Guardian* (April 15, 2015).

14. R. Max Wideman, "Project and Program Risk Management: A Guide to Managing Project Risks and Opportunities," (Upper Darby, PA: Project Management Institute, 1992), II–4.

15. J. Daniel Couger, *Creative Problem Solving and Opportunity Finding* (New York: Boyd & Fraser Publishing Company (1995).

16. McDonnell Douglas Corporation, "Hi-Rel Fighter Concept," Report MDC B0642 (1988).

17. Bruce J. Weeks, "Risk Determination in Highly Interactive Environments: How to Avoid the Titanic Factor in Your Project," PMI Virtual Library (2010).

18. Microsoft Corporation, "Introduction to Monte Carlo simulation," *support.office.com/en-ca/article/Introduction-to-Monte-Carlo-simulation-64c0ba99-752a-4fa8-bbd3-4450d8db16f1* (accessed June 18, 2015).

19. Jerry Odenwelder, "How to Reduce Agile Risk with Monte Carlo Simulation," VersionOne (March 21, 2015).

20. Jean Couillard, "The Role of Project Risk in Determining Project Management Approach," *Project Management Journal* 25, no. 4 (December 1995), pp. 3–15.

PROJECT PROCUREMENT MANAGEMENT

LEARNING OBJECTIVES

After reading this chapter, you will be able to:

- Understand the importance of project procurement management and the increasing use of outsourcing for information technology (IT) projects

- Describe the work involved in planning procurements for projects, including determining the proper type of contract to use and preparing a procurement management plan, statement of work, source selection criteria, and make-or-buy analysis

- Discuss how to conduct procurements and strategies for obtaining seller responses, selecting sellers, and awarding contracts

- Understand the process of controlling procurements by managing procurement relationships and monitoring contract performance

- Describe the process of closing procurements

- Discuss types of software that are available to assist in project procurement management

OPENING CASE

Marie McBride could not believe how much money her company was paying for outside consultants to help finish an important system conversion project. The consulting company's proposal said it would provide experienced professionals who had completed similar conversions, and that the job would be finished in six months or less with four consultants working full time. Nine months later her company was still paying high consulting fees, and half of the original consultants on the project had been replaced with new people. One new consultant had graduated from college only two months before and had extremely poor communications skills. Marie's internal staff complained that they were wasting time training some of these "experienced professionals." Marie talked to her company's purchasing manager about the contract, fees, and special clauses that might be relevant to the problems they were having.

Marie was dismayed at how difficult it was to interpret the contract. It was very long and obviously written by someone with a legal background. When she asked what her company could do because the consulting firm was not following its proposal, the purchasing manager stated that the proposal was not part of the official contract. Marie's company was paying for time and materials, not specific deliverables. There was no clause stating the minimum experience level required for the consultants, nor were there penalty clauses for not completing the work on time. There was a termination clause, however, meaning that the company could terminate the contract. Marie wondered why her company had signed such a poor contract. Was there a better way to procure services from outside the company?

12.1 THE IMPORTANCE OF PROJECT PROCUREMENT MANAGEMENT

Procurement means acquiring goods and services from an outside source. The term *procurement* is widely used in government; many private companies use the terms *purchasing* and *outsourcing*. Organizations or individuals who provide procurement services are referred to as suppliers, vendors, contractors, subcontractors, or sellers; of these terms, *suppliers* is the most widely used. Many IT projects involve the use of goods and services from outside the organization. The Project Management Institute defines an outside source as a source outside the project team, so the same organization can be a supplier to the project team, or the project team can be a supplier to another group in the organization. In fact, many IT departments in organizations are in direct competition with outside vendors, and they are subject to the same kind of requirements definition, statements of work, and bids. The rules and methods of sound project procurement practices are good to follow regardless of who provides the services to whom.

As you learned in Chapter 2, outsourcing is a hot topic for research and debate, especially the implications of outsourcing to other countries, which is called offshoring. Gartner estimated the value of the global IT industry in 2014 at $3.8 trillion, an increase of about 3.2 percent from 2013. The largest spending category is telecommunication services at 45 percent of the total or about $1.7 trillion.[1] According to a study by the Center for International Business Education (CIBER) and the International Offshoring Research Network's (ORN) Project at Duke University, the outsourcing market continues to grow:

- U.S. companies are transferring more work abroad, especially in the areas of IT infrastructure, application development and maintenance, and innovation processes.

- India, China, and the Philippines are the preferred locations for outsourcing, and Latin America is growing in popularity.
- A shortage of qualified personnel, not cost savings, is the top reason for global outsourcing of IT services.
- According to Arie Lewin, director of CIBER, "For companies that are engaged in offshoring, we've seen a significant jump in the number of respondents who say offshoring activities have led to improved organizational flexibility."[2]

 GLOBAL ISSUES

A recent approach to bringing IT jobs back to the U.S. is called urban onshoring. Software testing in particular has sparked several organizations to work together to meet the need for jobs in low income, high unemployment urban areas, improve quality and efficiency, and reduce overseas costs. For example, Doran Jones Inc., a startup consulting firm that does testing work for banks and media companies in Manhattan, partnered with Per Scholas to create the first Urban Development Center (UDC) for software testing projects. The UDC model develops the infrastructure, resources, and jobs in low-income urban neighborhoods as part of a company's Corporate Social Responsibility strategy. Per Scholas is the oldest and largest professional IT workforce development program in New York City. They provide technology education, training, and job placement services for over 4,500 unemployed and low-income adults.

Several start-up companies are applying similar models in an effort to improve bleak neighborhoods, like Hunts Point in the South Bronx. Startup Box, founded by husband and wife team Majora Carter and James Chase, is initially focusing on quality assurance testing for games and apps like Game Chaser. To recruit testers, they hold gaming tournaments in and around Hunts Point and provide feedback on the games to developers, similar to a focus group.

Doran Jones Inc. and Startup Box do not want their work to be viewed as charity projects. "As offshoring becomes more and more problematic in the ever-changing tech world… on-shoring is a major market opportunity. They can make outsourcing more efficient and diversify the talent pipeline in tech, in addition to bringing some much needed jobs back to the US. Both Startup Box and Doran Jones have plans to replicate this urban on shoring thing in other cities."[3]

Politicians debate whether offshoring helps their own country or not. Andy Bork, chief operating officer of a computer network service provider, described outsourcing as an essential part of a healthy business diet. He described the idea of good versus bad outsourcing as something like good versus bad cholesterol. He said that most people view offshoring as being bad because it takes jobs away from domestic workers. However, many companies are realizing that they can use offshoring *and* create more jobs at home. For example, Atlanta-based Delta Air Lines created 1,000 call-center jobs in India in 2003, saving $25 million, which enabled it to add 1,200 jobs for reservations and sales agents in the United States.[4] Other companies, like Walmart, successfully manage the majority of their IT projects in-house with very little commercial software and no outsourcing at all. Other organizations are moving IT services back in-house, such as General Motors (GM). Randy Mott, the CIO of GM and former CIO of Walmart, Dell, and Hewlett-Packard, overhauled GM's IT operations and switched from outsourcing 90 percent of its IT services to only 10 percent from 2012–2015. See the What Went Right? feature for a description of how Zulily uses in-house software development to provide a competitive advantage.

✓ WHAT WENT RIGHT?

Retailer Zulily is one of a growing number of organizations developing software in-house to meet their need for speed and innovation. CIO Luke Friang said it would be nearly impossible for off-the-shelf software to keep up with their pace. Zulily offers flash sales where items are available for limited times only, and its website technology to track and customize the shopping experience are an essential part of their business strategy. Other companies gaining competitive advantages by developing innovative, in-house software include General Motors and Tesla Motors Inc.

Zulily developed proprietary algorithms that track customers throughout the site and quickly make adjustments to meet changing consumer preferences. The retailer, based in Seattle, sends customers emails containing deals targeted to what they've bought from the site and to their page viewing patterns. Zulily is also working on software to more efficiently route merchandise within its fulfillment centers, and they are upgrading an internal website it uses to exchange order information with vendors.

"'You almost have to build the technology... from scratch because there won't be something out there on the market that fits perfectly,' said Mr. Friang. Zulily's sales soared 97 percent to $285 million in one quarter, enabling the company to slightly raise its forecast for 2014 sales to at least $1.2 billion, which would represent 74 percent growth from last year. Zulily's net income rose 94 percent to $7.8 million."[5]

Deciding whether to outsource, what to outsource, and how to outsource are important topics for many organizations throughout the world. Organizations are turning to outsourcing to accomplish the following:

- *Access skills and technologies*. Organizations can gain access to specific skills and technologies when they are required by using outside resources. As mentioned earlier, a shortage of qualified personnel is the main reason that companies outsource IT services. A project may require experts in a particular field for several months, or it might require specific technologies from an outside source. Planning for this procurement ensures that the needed skills and technologies will be available for the project.
- *Reduce both fixed and recurrent costs*. Outsourcing suppliers often can use economies of scale that may not be available to the client alone, especially for hardware and software. It can also be less expensive to outsource some labor costs to other organizations in the same country or offshore. Companies can use outsourcing to reduce labor costs on projects by avoiding the costs of hiring, firing, and reassigning people to projects or paying their salaries when they are between projects.

- *Allow the client organization to focus on its core business.* Most organizations are not in business to provide IT services, yet many have spent valuable time and resources on IT functions when they should have focused on core competencies such as marketing, customer service, and new product design. By outsourcing many IT functions, employees can focus on jobs that are critical to the success of the organization.
- *Provide flexibility.* Outsourcing to provide extra staff during periods of peak workloads can be much more economical than trying to staff entire projects with internal resources. Many companies cite better flexibility in staffing as a key reason for outsourcing. As you learned in Chapter 2, Apple says it could not produce several of its products fast enough without outsourcing.
- *Increase accountability.* A well-written **contract**—a mutually binding agreement that obligates the seller to provide specified products or services and obligates the buyer to pay for them—can clarify responsibilities and sharpen focus on key deliverables of a project. Because contracts are legally binding, there is more accountability for delivering the work as stated in the contract.

Organizations must also consider reasons they might *not* want to outsource. When an organization outsources work, it often does not have as much control over the aspects of projects that suppliers carry out. In addition, an organization could become too dependent on particular suppliers. If those suppliers went out of business or lost key personnel, it could cause great damage to a project. Organizations must also be careful to protect strategic information that could become vulnerable in the hands of suppliers. According to Scott McNealy, co-founder and former CEO of Sun Microsystems, Inc., "What you want to handle in-house is the stuff that gives you an edge over your competition—your core competencies. I call it your 'secret sauce.' If you're on Wall Street and you have your own program for tracking and analyzing the market, you'll hang onto that. At Sun, we have a complex program for testing microprocessor designs, and we'll keep it."[6] Project teams must think carefully about procurement issues and make wise decisions based on the unique needs of their projects and organizations. They must also be aware of political issues, as described in the following example.

469

 WHAT WENT WRONG?

In 2011, New York City's mayor, Michael Bloomberg, acknowledged that City Hall had mismanaged its major IT projects and vowed to improve their oversight. He even said that city administrators would not oppose legislation requiring them to alert the City Council when projects ran into serious problems. These statements were made at a Council hearing called in response to reports of troubled technology projects. For example, prosecutors said the $700 million price tag for the CityTime payroll system was inflated by fraud, and the mayor demanded $600 million back from the main contractor. The automated personnel system, Nycaps, suffered significant delays and cost overruns due to leadership issues, increasing from an original estimate of $66 million to over $363 million.

Caswell F. Holloway, the deputy mayor for operations, testified at the hearing that the administration had begun an overhaul of how it manages complex technology projects. He said it would seek more use of off-the-shelf software and avoid paying

continued

consultants by the hour when it could specify completion of key deliverables for payment. He also said the city would stop letting individual agencies negotiate their own contracts and bring in the city's Law Department and the Mayor's Office of Contract Services to negotiate IT contracts worth more than $5 million.

"Other speakers at the hearing said that much of what Mr. Holloway was promising to do was already written into city policy, to little effect. Henry Garrido, research director for District Council 37, the municipal workers' union, said a standard clause in the city's IT contracts allowed the city to sue contractors for damages. 'But the city doesn't exercise it,' he said."[7]

Outsourcing can also cause problems in other areas for companies and nations as a whole. For example, in 2004 many people in Australia were concerned about outsourcing software development. "The Australian Computer Society says sending work offshore may lower the number of students entering IT courses, deplete the number of skilled IT professionals, and diminish the nation's strategic technology capability. Another issue is security, which encompasses the protection of intellectual property, integrity of data, and the reliability of infrastructure in offshore locations."[8] A 2015 article stated that the job market for IT workers in Australia did improve as several companies brought jobs back to the country. The only downside was that pay increases were declining.[9]

The success of many IT projects that use outside resources is often due to good project procurement management. **Project procurement management** includes the processes required to acquire goods and services for a project from outside the performing organization. Organizations can be either the buyer or seller of products or services under a contract or other agreement.

There are four main processes in project procurement management:

1. *Planning procurement management* involves determining what to procure and when and how to do it. In procurement planning, one must decide what to outsource, determine the type of contract, and describe the work for potential sellers. **Sellers** are providers, contractors, or suppliers who provide goods and services to other organizations. Outputs of this process include a procurement management plan, procurement statements of work, procurement documents, source selection criteria, make-or-buy decisions, change requests, and project documents updates.

2. *Conducting procurements* involves obtaining seller responses, selecting sellers, and awarding contracts. Outputs include selected sellers, agreements, resource calendars, change requests, and updates to the project management plan and other project documents.

3. *Controlling procurements* involves managing relationships with sellers, monitoring contract performance, and making changes as needed. The main outputs of this process include work performance information, change requests, and updates to the project management plan, project documents, and organizational process assets.

4. *Closing procurements* involves completion and settlement of each contract or agreement, including resolution of any open items. Outputs include closed procurements and organizational process assets updates.

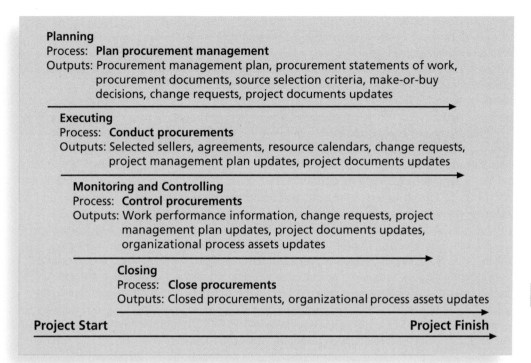

Planning
Process: **Plan procurement management**
Outputs: Procurement management plan, procurement statements of work,
procurement documents, source selection criteria, make-or-buy
decisions, change requests, project documents updates

Executing
Process: **Conduct procurements**
Outputs: Selected sellers, agreements, resource calendars, change requests,
project management plan updates, project documents updates

Monitoring and Controlling
Process: **Control procurements**
Outputs: Work performance information, change requests, project
management plan updates, project documents updates,
organizational process assets updates

Closing
Process: **Close procurements**
Outputs: Closed procurements, organizational process assets updates

Project Start   **Project Finish**

© Cengage Learning 2016

FIGURE 12-1   Project procurement management summary

Figure 12-1 summarizes these processes and outputs, showing when they occur in a typical project.

12.2 PLANNING PROCUREMENT MANAGEMENT

Planning procurements involves identifying which project needs can best be met by using products or services outside the organization. It involves deciding whether to procure, how to procure, what to procure, how much to procure, and when to procure. An important output of this process is the **make-or-buy decision**, in which an organization decides whether it should make certain products and perform certain services inside the organization, or if it is better to buy those products and services from an outside organization. If there is no need to buy products or services from outside the organization, then further procurement management is not needed.

Inputs needed for planning procurements include the project management plan, requirements documentation, the risk register, activity resource requirements, the project schedule, activity cost estimates, the stakeholder register, enterprise environmental factors, and organizational process assets, such as types of contracts.

12.2a Types of Contracts

Contract type is an important consideration in procurement management. Different types of contracts can be used in different situations. Three broad categories of contracts are fixed price or lump sum, cost reimbursable, and time and material. A single contract can actually include all three of these categories if it makes sense for a particular procurement. For example, you could have a contract with a seller that includes purchasing specific hardware for a fixed price or lump sum, some services that are provided on a cost-reimbursable basis, and other services that are provided on a time-and-material basis. Project managers and their teams must understand and decide which approaches to use to meet their project needs. It is also important to understand when and how to take advantage of unit pricing in contracts.

Fixed-price or **lump-sum contracts** involve a fixed total price for a well-defined product or service. The buyer incurs little risk in this situation because the price is predetermined. The sellers often pad their estimate to reduce their risk, although they realize their price must still be competitive. For example, a company could award a fixed-price contract to purchase 100 laser printers with a certain print resolution and print speed to be delivered to one location within two months. In this example, the product and delivery date are well defined. Several sellers could create fixed-price estimates for completing the job. Fixed-price contracts may also include incentives for meeting or exceeding selected project objectives. For example, the contract could include an incentive fee paid if the laser printers are delivered within one month. A firm-fixed-price (FFP) contract has the least amount of risk for the buyer, followed by a fixed-price incentive fee (FPIF) contract. A fixed-price with economic price adjustment contract (FP-EPA) includes a special provision for predefined final adjustments to the contract price due to changes in conditions such as inflation or the cost of specific commodities. An FP-EPA contract is intended to protect both the buyer and seller from external conditions beyond their control.

Contracts can also include incentives to prevent or reduce cost overruns. For example, according to the U.S. Federal Acquisition Regulation (FAR) 16.4, fixed-price incentive fee contracts can include a **Point of Total Assumption (PTA)**, which is the cost at which the contractor assumes total responsibility for each additional dollar of contract cost. Contractors do not want to reach the PTA because it hurts them financially, so they have an incentive to prevent cost overruns. The PTA is calculated with the following formula:

$$\text{PTA} = (\text{ceiling price} - \text{target price})/\text{government share} + \text{target cost}$$

For example, given the following information, and assuming that all dollar amounts are in millions, the PTA will be $1.2 million:

Ceiling price = $1,250
Target price = $1,100
Target cost = $1,000
Government share: 75percent

$$\text{PTA} = (\$1,250 - \$1,100)/.75 + \$1,000 = \$1,200 [10]$$

Contracts for the U.S. federal government can be very complex. Consult FAR 16.4 and similar references for more details.

Cost-reimbursable contracts involve payment to the supplier for direct and indirect actual costs. Recall from Chapter 7 that direct costs can be directly related to producing a project's products and services. Normally, these costs can be traced back to a project in a cost-effective way. Indirect costs are not directly related to the products or services of the project, but they are indirectly related to performing the project. Normally, these costs cannot be traced back to the project in a cost-effective way. For example, direct costs include the salaries for people working directly on a project and hardware or software purchased for a specific project. Indirect costs include the cost of providing a work space with electricity and an employee cafeteria. Indirect costs are often calculated as a percentage of direct costs. Cost-reimbursable contracts often include fees, such as a profit percentage or incentives for meeting or exceeding selected project objectives. These contracts are often used for projects that include providing goods and services that involve new technologies. The buyer absorbs more of the risk with cost-reimbursable contracts than with fixed-price contracts. Three types of cost-reimbursable contracts, in order of lowest to highest risk to the buyer, include cost plus incentive fee, cost plus fixed fee, and cost plus percentage of costs.

- With a **cost plus incentive fee (CPIF) contract**, the buyer pays the supplier for allowable costs (as defined in the contract) along with a predetermined fee and an incentive bonus. See the Media Snapshot for an example of providing financial incentives to complete an important construction project ahead of schedule. Also, incentives are often provided to suppliers for reducing contract costs. If the final cost is less than the expected cost, both the buyer and the supplier benefit from the cost savings, according to a negotiated share formula. For example, suppose that the expected cost of a project is $100,000, the fee to the supplier is $10,000, and the share formula is 85/15, meaning that the buyer absorbs 85 percent of the uncertainty and the supplier absorbs 15 percent. If the final cost is $80,000, the cost savings are $20,000. The supplier would be paid the final cost and the fee plus an incentive of $3,000 (15 percent of $20,000), for a total reimbursement of $93,000.

MEDIA SNAPSHOT

Contract incentives can be extremely effective. On August 1, 2007, tragedy struck Minneapolis, Minnesota, when an Interstate bridge over the Mississippi River suddenly collapsed, killing 13 motorists and injuring 150 people. The Minnesota Department of Transportation (MnDOT) acted quickly to find a contractor to rebuild the bridge. MnDOT also provided a strong incentive to finish the bridge as quickly as possible, ensuring quality and safety along the way.

Peter Sanderson, project manager for the joint venture of Flatiron-Manson, led his team in completing the rebuilding project three months ahead of schedule, and the new bridge opened on September 18, 2008. The contractors earned $25 million in incentive fees on top of their $234 million contract for completing the bridge ahead of schedule.

Why did MnDOT offer such a large incentive fee for finishing the project early? "I-35W in Minneapolis is a major transportation artery for the Twin Cities and entire state. Each day this bridge has been closed, it has cost road users more than $400,000," MnDOT Commissioner Tom Sorel remarked. "Area residents, business owners, motorists, workers and others have been affected by this corridor's closure. The opening of this bridge reconnects our community."[11]

- With a **cost plus fixed fee (CPFF) contract**, the buyer pays the supplier for allowable costs (as defined in the contract) plus a fixed fee payment that is usually based on a percentage of estimated costs. This fee does not vary, however, unless the scope of the contract changes. For example, suppose that the expected cost of a project is $100,000 and the fixed fee is $10,000. If the actual cost of the contract rises to $120,000 and the scope of the contract remains the same, the contractor will still receive the fee of $10,000.

- With a **cost plus award fee (CPAF) contract**, the buyer pays the supplier for allowable costs (as defined in the contract) plus an award fee based on the satisfaction of subjective performance criteria. A tip or gratuity that you would give a server in a restaurant would qualify as a simple example, as long as there is no set gratuity percentage. You still pay for the cost of your meal, but you can decide on the tip amount based on your satisfaction with the food, drinks, and service provided. This type of contract is not usually subject to appeals.

- With a **cost plus percentage of costs (CPPC) contract**, the buyer pays the supplier for allowable costs (as defined in the contract) along with a predetermined percentage based on total costs. From the buyer's perspective, this is the least desirable type of contract because the supplier has no incentive to decrease costs. In fact, the supplier may be motivated to increase costs, because doing so will automatically increase profits based on the percentage of costs. This type of contract is prohibited for U.S. government use, but it is sometimes used in private industry, particularly in the construction industry. All of the risk is borne by the buyer.

Time and material (T&M) contracts are a hybrid of fixed-price and cost-reimbursable contracts. For example, an independent computer consultant might have a contract with a company based on a fee of $80 per hour for services, plus a fixed price of $10,000 for providing specific project materials. The materials fee might also be based on approved receipts for purchasing items, with a ceiling of $10,000. The consultant would send an invoice to the company each week or month; the invoice would list the materials fee, the number of hours worked, and a description of the work produced. This type of contract is often used for required services when the work cannot be specified clearly and total costs cannot be estimated in a contract. Many contract programmers and consultants, such as those Marie's company hired in the chapter's opening case, prefer time and material contracts.

Unit pricing can also be used in various types of contracts to require the buyer to pay the supplier a predetermined amount per unit of product or service. The total value of the contract is a function of the quantities needed to complete the work. Consider an IT department that might have a unit price contract for purchasing computer hardware. If the company purchases only one unit, the cost might be $1,000. If the company purchases 10 units, the cost might be $10,000. This type of pricing often involves volume discounts. For example, if the company purchases between 10 and 50 units, the contracted cost might be $900 per unit. If the company purchases more than 50 units, the cost might go down to $800 per unit. This flexible pricing strategy is often advantageous to both the buyer and the seller.

Any type of contract should include specific clauses that account for unique project issues. For example, if a company uses a time and material contract for consulting services, the contract should stipulate different hourly rates based on the level of experience of the individual contractors. The services of a junior programmer with no Bachelor's degree and less than three years' experience might be billed at $40 per hour, whereas the services of a senior programmer with a Bachelor's degree and more than 10 years of experience might be billed at $80 per hour.

Figure 12-2 summarizes the spectrum of risk to the buyer and supplier for different types of contracts. Buyers have the least risk with firm-fixed price contracts, because they know exactly what they must pay the supplier. Buyers have the most risk with cost plus percentage of costs (CPPC) contracts because they do not know the supplier's costs in advance, and the suppliers may be motivated to keep increasing costs. From the supplier's perspective, a CPPC contract carries the least risk and a firm-fixed price contract carries the most risk.

Time and material contracts and unit-price contracts can be high- or low-risk, depending on the nature of the project and other contract clauses. For example, if an organization is unclear in describing the work that needs to be done, it cannot expect a supplier to sign a firm-fixed price contract. However, the buyer could find a consultant or group of consultants to work on specific tasks based on a predetermined hourly rate. The buying organization could evaluate the work produced each day or week to decide if it wants to continue using the consultants. In this case, the contract would include a **termination clause**—a contract clause that allows the buyer or supplier to end the contract. Some termination clauses state that the buyer can terminate a contract for any reason and give the supplier only 24 hours' notice. Suppliers, by contrast, must often give a one-week notice to terminate a contract and must have sufficient reasons for the termination. The buyer could also include a contract clause that specifies hourly rates based on the education and experience of consultants. These contract clauses reduce the risk incurred by the buyer while providing flexibility for accomplishing the work.

It is important to understand why a company would want to procure goods or services and what inputs are needed to plan purchases and acquisitions. In the opening case, Marie's company hired outside consultants to help complete an operating system conversion project because it needed people with specialized skills for a short period of time. This is a common occurrence in many IT projects. It can be more effective to hire skilled consultants to perform specific tasks for a short period of time than to hire or keep employees on staff full time.

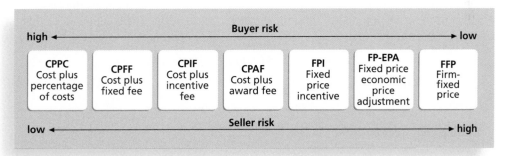

FIGURE 12-2 Contract Types versus risk

However, it is also important to define clearly the scope of the project, the products, services, or results required, market conditions, and constraints and assumptions. In Marie's case, the scope of the project and services required were relatively clear, but her company may not have adequately defined the market conditions or constraints and assumptions involved in using outside consultants. Could other companies provide consultants to help with similar conversion projects? Did the project team investigate the background of the company that provided the consultants? Did the team list important constraints and assumptions for using the consultants, such as limiting the time that the consultants had to complete the conversion project or the minimum years of experience for any consultant assigned to the project? It is important to answer these types of questions before signing an outsourcing agreement.

12.2b Tools and Techniques for Planning Procurement Management

Several tools and techniques are available to help project managers and their teams in planning procurement management, including make-or-buy analysis, expert judgment, and market research.

Make-or-Buy Analysis

Make-or-buy analysis is a general management technique used to determine whether an organization should make a product or perform a service inside the organization or buy it from someone else. This form of analysis involves estimating the internal costs of providing a product or service and comparing the estimate to the cost of outsourcing. Consider a company that has 1,000 international salespeople with laptops. Using make-or-buy analysis, the company could compare the cost of providing those services using internal resources to the cost of buying the same services from an outside source. If supplier quotes were less than the company's internal estimates, the company would have to consider outsourcing the training and user support services. Another common make-or-buy decision, though more complex, is whether a company should develop an application itself or purchase software from an outside source and customize it to the company's needs.

Many organizations also use make-or-buy analysis to decide whether to purchase or lease items for a project. For example, suppose that a project requires a piece of equipment that has a purchase price of $12,000 and daily operating costs of $400. Suppose that you could lease the same piece of equipment for $800 per day, including the operating costs. You can set up an equation so that you can see when the purchase cost equals the lease cost and determine when it makes sense financially to lease or buy the equipment. In this example, d is the number of days you need the piece of equipment. The equation would be:

$$\$800/\text{day} = \$12,000 + \$400/\text{day}$$

Subtracting $400/day from both sides, you get:

$$\$400/\text{day} = \$12,000$$

Dividing both sides by $400, you get:

$$d = 30$$

In other words, the purchase cost would equal the lease cost in 30 days. So, if you need the equipment for less than 30 days, leasing would be more economical. If you need the equipment for more than 30 days, you should purchase it. In general, leasing is often cheaper for meeting short-term needs, but more expensive for long-term needs.

Expert Judgment

Experts both from inside and outside an organization can provide excellent advice in planning purchases and acquisitions. Project teams often need to consult experts within their organization as part of good business practice. Internal experts might suggest that the company in the preceding example could not provide training and support for the 1,000 laptop users because the service involves so many people with different skill levels in so many different locations. Experts in the company might also know that most of their competitors outsource this type of work and know who the qualified outside suppliers are. It is also important to consult legal experts because contracts for outsourced work are legal agreements.

Experts outside the company, including potential suppliers themselves, can also provide expert judgment. For example, suppliers might suggest an option for salespeople to purchase the laptops themselves at a reduced cost. This option would solve problems that would otherwise be created during employee turnover—exiting employees would own their laptops and new employees would purchase a laptop through the program. An internal expert might then suggest that employees receive a technology bonus to help offset what they might view as an added expense. Expert judgment, both internal and external, is an asset in making many procurement decisions.

477

Market Research

Market research is very important in planning procurements. Many potential suppliers are often available for goods and services, so the project team must choose suppliers carefully. Some organizations have a preferred vendor list and detailed information about them. A wealth of information is also available online, and numerous conferences are held where attendees can see and discuss new products.

In addition to make-or-buy decisions, change requests, and project documents updates, important outputs of planning procurements are a procurement management plan, statement of work, procurement documents such as requests for proposals or quotes, and source selection criteria.

12.2c Procurement Management Plan

As you have learned, every project management knowledge area includes some planning. The procurement management plan is a document that describes how the procurement processes will be managed, from developing documentation for making outside purchases or acquisitions to contract closure. Like other project plans, contents of the procurement management plan will vary with project needs. The following materials can be included in a procurement management plan:

- Guidelines for types of contracts to be used in different situations
- Standard procurement documents or templates to be used, if applicable
- Guidelines for creating contract work breakdown structures, statements of work, and other procurement documents
- Roles and responsibilities of the project team and related departments, such as the purchasing or legal department

- Guidelines for using independent estimates to evaluate sellers
- Suggestions for managing multiple providers
- Processes for coordinating procurement decisions with other project areas, such as scheduling and performance reporting
- Constraints and assumptions related to purchases and acquisitions
- Lead times for purchases and acquisitions
- Risk mitigation strategies for purchases and acquisitions, such as insurance contracts and bonds
- Guidelines for identifying prequalified sellers and organizational lists of preferred sellers
- Procurement metrics to assist in evaluating sellers and managing contracts

12.2d Statement of Work

The **statement of work (SOW)** is a description of the work required for the procurement. Some organizations use the term *statement of work* for a document that describes internal work as well. If a SOW is used to describe only the work required for a particular contract, it is called a *contract statement of work*. The contract SOW is a type of scope statement that describes the work in sufficient detail to allow prospective suppliers to determine if they can provide the required goods and services and to determine an appropriate price. A contract SOW should be clear, concise, and as complete as possible. It should describe all services required and include performance reporting. It is important to use appropriate wording in a contract SOW, such as *must* instead of *may*. For example, *must* means that something has to be done; *may* implies that a choice is involved in doing something or not. The contract SOW should specify the products and services required for the project, use industry terms, and refer to industry standards.

Many organizations use samples and templates to generate SOWs. Figure 12-3 provides a basic outline or template for a contract SOW that Marie's organization could use when hiring outside consultants or purchasing other goods or services. For example, for the operating system conversion project, Marie's company should specify the manufacturer and model number for the hardware involved, the former operating systems and new ones for the conversion, and the number of pieces of each type of hardware involved. The contract SOW should also specify the location of the work, the expected period of performance, specific deliverables and when they are due, applicable standards, acceptance criteria, and special requirements. A good contract SOW gives bidders a better understanding of the buyer's expectations. A contract SOW should become part of the official contract to ensure that the buyer gets what the supplier bid on.

12.2e Procurement Documents

Planning procurements also involves preparing the documents needed for potential sellers to bid on a project and determining the evaluation criteria for the contract award. The project team often uses standard forms and expert judgment as tools to help create relevant procurement documents and evaluation criteria.

Two common examples of procurement documents include a Request for Proposal (RFP) and a Request for Quote (RFQ). A **Request for Proposal (RFP)** is a document used to solicit proposals from prospective suppliers. A **proposal** is a document prepared by a seller when there are different approaches for meeting buyer needs. For example, if an organization wants to automate its work practices or solve a business problem, it can

---

Statement of Work (SOW)

I. **Scope of Work:** Describe the work to be done in detail. Specify the hardware and software involved and the exact nature of the work.

II. **Location of Work:** Describe where the work must be performed. Specify the location of hardware and software and where the people must perform the work.

III. **Period of Performance:** Specify when the work is expected to start and end, working hours, number of hours that can be billed per week, where the work must be performed, and related schedule information.

IV. **Deliverables Schedule:** List specific deliverables, describe them in detail, and specify when they are due.

V. **Applicable Standards:** Specify any company or industry-specific standards that are relevant to performing the work.

VI. **Acceptance Criteria:** Describe how the buyer organization will determine if the work is acceptable.

VII. **Special Requirements:** Specify any special requirements such as hardware or software certifications, minimum degree or experience level of personnel, travel requirements, and so on.

FIGURE 12-3   Statement of Work (SOW) Template

write and issue an RFP so suppliers can respond with proposals. Suppliers might propose various hardware, software, and networking solutions to meet the organization's need. Selections of winning sellers are often made on a variety of criteria, not just the lowest price. Developing an RFP is often a time-consuming process. Organizations must plan properly to ensure that they adequately describe what they want to procure, what they want sellers to include in their proposals, and how they will evaluate proposals.

Although RFPs have been used for many years, outsourcing experts say the process is becoming less appealing in several IT procurement processes. "In today's dynamic era of technology change, the traditional RFP simply takes too long and costs too much. By the time the proposals come in, the business requirements have often changed."[12] Enterprise marketplaces, such as app stores that provide a collection of software and services for sale (i.e., Google Play, App Store, and IBM Cloud Marketplace) and other new purchasing processes will emerge as companies collaborate with service providers to figure out better IT solutions.

A **Request for Quote (RFQ)** is a document used to solicit quotes or bids from prospective suppliers. A **bid**, also called a *tender* or *quote* (short for *quotation*), is a document prepared by sellers to provide pricing for standard items that the buyer has clearly defined. Organizations often use an RFQ for solicitations that involve specific items. For example, if a company wanted to purchase 100 personal computers with specific features, it might issue an RFQ to potential suppliers. RFQs usually do not take nearly as long to prepare as RFPs, nor do responses to RFQs. Selections are often based on the lowest bid.

Writing a good RFP is a critical part of project procurement management, but many people have never had to write or respond to one. To generate a good RFP, expertise is invaluable. Many examples of RFPs are available within different companies, from potential contractors, and from government agencies. Legal requirements are often involved in issuing RFPs and reviewing proposals, especially for government projects. It is important to consult with experts who know the contract planning process for particular organizations. To make sure that an RFP has enough information to provide the basis for a good proposal, the buying organization should try to put itself in the suppliers' shoes. Could the organization develop a good proposal based on the information it provided in the RFP? Could it determine detailed pricing and schedule information based on the RFP? Developing a good RFP is difficult, as is writing a good proposal.

Figure 12-4 provides a basic outline or template for an RFP. The main sections of an RFP usually include its statement of purpose, background information on the organization

Request for Proposal Template

I. Purpose of RFP

II. Organization's Background

III. Basic Requirements

IV. Hardware and Software Environment

V. Description of RFP Process

VI. Statement of Work and Schedule Information

VII. Possible Appendices

    A. Current System Overview

    B. System Requirements

    C. Volume and Size Data

    D. Required Contents of Vendor's Response to RFP

    E. Sample Contract

© Cengage Learning 2016

FIGURE 12-4 Request for Proposal (RFP) template

issuing the RFP, the basic requirements for the products and services being proposed, the hardware and software environment (which is usually important for IT-related proposals), a description of the RFP process, the statement of work and schedule information, and possible appendices. A simple RFP might be three to five pages long, but an RFP for a larger, more complicated procurement might take hundreds of pages.

Other terms used for RFQs and RFPs include *invitations for bid*, *invitations for negotiation*, and *initial contractor responses*. Regardless of what they are called, all procurement documents should be written to facilitate accurate and complete responses from prospective sellers. Procurement documents should include background information on the organization and project, a relevant statement of work, a schedule, a description of the desired form of response, evaluation criteria, pricing forms, and any required contractual provisions. The documents should also be rigorous enough to ensure consistent, comparable responses, but flexible enough to allow consideration of sellers' suggestions for better ways to satisfy the requirements.

12.2f Source Selection Criteria

It is very important for organizations to prepare some form of evaluation criteria for source selection, preferably before they issue a formal RFP. Organizations use criteria to rate or score proposals, and they often assign a weight to each criterion to indicate its importance. Some examples of criteria and weights include the technical approach (30 percent weight), management approach (30 percent weight), past performance (20 percent weight), and price (20 percent weight). The criteria should be specific and objective. For example, if the buyer wants the supplier's project manager to be a certified Project Management Professional (PMP), the procurement documents should state that requirement clearly and follow it during the award process. Losing bidders may pursue legal recourse if the buyer does not follow a fair and consistent evaluation process.

Organizations should heed the saying, "Let the buyer beware." It is critical to evaluate proposals based on more than the professionalism of the paperwork submitted. A key factor in evaluating bids, particularly for projects involving IT, is the past performance record of the bidder. The RFP should require bidders to list other similar projects they have worked on and provide customer references for those projects. Reviewing performance records and references reduces the risk of selecting a supplier with a poor track record. Suppliers should also demonstrate their understanding of the buyer's need, their technical and financial capabilities, their management approach to the project, and their price for delivering the desired goods and services. It is also crucial to write the contract to protect the buyer's interests.

Some IT projects also require potential sellers to deliver a technical presentation as part of their proposal. The proposed project manager should lead the potential seller's presentation team. When the outside project manager leads the proposal presentation, the organization can build a relationship with the potential seller from the beginning. Visits to contractor sites can also help the buyer get a better feeling for the seller's capabilities and management style.

12.3 CONDUCTING PROCUREMENTS

After planning for procurement management, the next process involves deciding whom to ask to do the work, sending appropriate documentation to potential sellers, obtaining proposals or bids, selecting a seller, and awarding a contract. Prospective sellers do some of the work in this process, normally at no cost to the buyer or project. The buying organization is responsible for advertising the work, and for large procurements, the organization often holds some sort of bidders' conference to answer questions about the job. Two of the main outputs of this process are a selected seller and procurement contract award.

Organizations can advertise to procure outside goods and services in many different ways. Sometimes a specific supplier might be the top choice for the buyer. In this case, the buyer gives procurement information just to that company. If the preferred supplier responds favorably, the organizations proceed to work together. Many organizations have formed good working relationships with certain suppliers.

In many cases, however, more than one supplier might be qualified to provide the goods and services. Providing information to multiple sources and receiving bids from them often takes advantage of the competitive business environment. Offshore outsourcing, as you learned earlier, has increased tremendously as organizations find suitable sellers around the globe. As a result of pursuing a competitive bidding strategy, the buyer can receive better goods and services than expected at a lower price.

A bidders' conference, also called a *supplier conference* or *pre-bid conference*, is a meeting with prospective sellers prior to preparation of their proposals or bids. These conferences help ensure that everyone has a clear, common understanding of the buyer's desired products or services. In some cases, the bidders' conference might be held online via a webcast or using other communications technology. Buyers will also post procurement information on a website and post answers to frequently asked questions. Before, during, or after the bidders' conference, the buyer may incorporate responses to questions into the procurement documents as amendments.

Once buyers receive proposals or bids, they can select a supplier or decide to cancel the procurement. Selecting suppliers or sellers, often called *source selection*, involves evaluating proposals or bids from sellers, choosing the best one, negotiating the contract, and awarding the contract. It can be a long, tedious process, especially for large procurements. Several stakeholders in the procurement process should be involved in selecting the best supplier for the project. Often, teams of people are responsible for evaluating various sections of the proposals. There might be a technical team, a management team, and a cost team to focus on each major area. Buyers typically develop a short list of the top three to five suppliers to reduce the work involved in selecting a source.

Experts in source selection highly recommend that buyers use formal proposal evaluation sheets during source selection. Figure 12-5 provides a sample proposal evaluation sheet that the project team might use to help create a short list of the best three to five proposals. Notice that this example is a form of a weighted scoring model, as described in Chapter 4, Project Integration Management. To calculate the score for a criterion, multiply the weight of the criterion by the rating for the proposal. Add the scores to provide the total weighted score for each proposal. The proposals with the highest weighted scores should be included in the short list of possible sellers. Experts also recommend that technical criteria should not be given more weight than management or cost criteria. Many organizations have suffered the consequences of paying too much attention to the technical aspects of proposals. For example, the project might cost much more than expected or take longer to complete because the source selection team focused only on technical aspects of proposals. Paying too much attention to these technical aspects is especially likely to occur on IT projects. However, it is often the supplier's management team—not the technical team—that makes procurement successful.

Criteria	Weight	Proposal 1		Proposal 2		Proposal 3, etc.	
		Rating	Score	Rating	Score	Rating	Score
Technical approach	30%						
Management approach	30%						
Past performance	20%						
Price	20%						
Total score	100%						

© Cengage Learning 2016

FIGURE 12-5 Sample Proposal Evaluation Sheet

After developing a short list of possible sellers, organizations often follow a more detailed proposal evaluation process. For example, they might list more detailed criteria for important categories, such as the management approach. They might assign points for the potential project manager's educational background and PMP certification, the seller's formal presentation if it was part of the evaluation process, top management support for the project, and the organization's project management methodologies. If the criteria and evaluation are done well, the seller with the most points based on all of the criteria should be offered the contract.

It is customary to have contract negotiations during the source selection process. Sellers on the short list are often asked to prepare a best and final offer (BAFO). In addition, top managers from both the buying and selling organizations usually meet before making final decisions. The final output is a contract that obligates the seller to provide the specified products or services and obligates the buyer to pay for them. For some projects, it is also appropriate to prepare a contract management plan that describes how the contract will be managed.

12.4 CONTROLLING PROCUREMENTS

Controlling procurements ensures that the seller's performance meets contractual requirements. The contractual relationship is a legal relationship, which means it is subject to state and federal contract laws. It is very important that appropriate legal and contracting professionals be involved in writing and administering contracts.

Ideally, the project manager, a project team member, or an active user in the project should help write and administer the contract, so that everyone understands the importance of good procurement management. The project team should also seek expert advice when working with contractual issues. Project team members must be aware of potential legal problems they might cause by not understanding a contract. For example, most projects involve changes, and these changes must be handled properly for items under contract. Without understanding the provisions of the contract, a project manager may unknowingly authorize a contractor to do additional work at greater costs. Therefore, change control is an important part of the contract administration process.

It is critical that project managers and team members watch for constructive change orders. **Constructive change orders** are oral or written acts or omissions by someone with actual or apparent authority that can be construed to have the same effect as a written change order. For example, if a member of the buyer's project team has met with the contractor on a weekly basis for three months to provide guidelines for performing work, the team member can be viewed as an apparent authority. If the team member tells the contractor to redo part of a report that has already been delivered and accepted by the project manager, the action can be viewed as a constructive change order and the contractor can legally bill the buyer for the additional work. Likewise, if the apparent authority tells the contractor to skip parts of a critical review meeting in the interests of time, the omission of that information is not the contractor's fault.

It is important to follow other good practices related to project procurement:

- Changes to any part of the project need to be reviewed, approved, and documented by the same people in the same way they approved the original part of the plan.
- Evaluation of any change should include an impact analysis. How will the change affect the scope, time, cost, and quality of the goods or services being provided? There must also be a baseline to understand and analyze changes.
- Changes must be documented in writing. Project team members should document all important meetings and telephone calls.
- When procuring complex information systems, project managers and their teams must stay closely involved to make sure the new system will meet business needs and work in an operational environment. Do not assume that everything will go well because you hired a reputable supplier. The buying organization needs to provide expertise as well.
- Have backup plans in case the new system does not work as planned.
- Several tools and techniques can help in contract administration, such as a formal contract change control system, buyer-conducted procurement performance reviews, inspections and audits, performance reporting, payment systems, claims administration, and records management systems.

12.5 CLOSING PROCUREMENTS

The final process in project procurement management is closing procurements, which is sometimes referred to as contract closure. Contract closure involves completion and settlement of contracts and resolution of any open items. The project team should determine if all work required in each contract was completed correctly and satisfactorily. The contract itself should include requirements for formal acceptance and closure. The team should also update records to reflect final results and archive information for future use.

Tools to assist in contract closure include procurement audits, negotiated settlements, and a records management system. Procurement audits are often done during contract closure to identify lessons learned in the entire procurement process. A records management system provides the ability to easily organize, find, and archive procurement-related documents. It is often an automated system, or at least partially automated, because a large amount of information can be related to project procurement.

BEST PRACTICE

In today's fast-changing competitive environment, it isn't enough to follow traditional procurement best practices. Instead, find innovative ways to improve the procurement process. Mining completely different functional areas and technologies is a great way to discover ideas that can be used to improve procurement. "Supply market intelligence starts from procurement being intelligent about how business requirements can be matched intelligently to what supply markets can offer. So, the greater your diversity of knowledge of solutions from far flung areas, the better you'll be able to match supply [solutions] to demand [requirements]." The following examples illustrate some ideas of how to make procurement more intelligent:

- Data scientists build predictive models to analyze big data related to finance, marketing, etc. Why not model procurement processes?
- Behavioral economists know that people do not act rationally. Why not apply irrationality to your advantage in negotiations?
- Quality control/assurance departments encourage employees to suggest quality improvements all the time. Why not enable your workers to be on the lookout for additional new and innovative suppliers?
- Crowdsourcing solicits ideas from a large group of people. Can it apply to some of your organization's procurements?[13]

Ideally, all procurements should end in a negotiated settlement between the buyer and seller. If negotiation is not possible, then some type of alternate dispute resolution such as mediation or arbitration can be used; if all else fails, litigation in courts can be used to settle contracts.

Archiving information for future use is particularly important. Organizations should strive to improve all of their business processes, including procurement management. Archiving information, particularly in an automated records management system, supports efforts to improve procurement management.

Outputs from contract closure include closed procurements and updates to organizational process assets. The buying organization often provides the seller with formal written notice that the contract has been completed.

12.6 USING SOFTWARE TO ASSIST IN PROJECT PROCUREMENT MANAGEMENT

Over the years, organizations have used various types of productivity software to assist in project procurement management. For example, most organizations use word-processing software to write proposals or contracts, spreadsheet software to create proposal evaluation worksheets, databases to track suppliers, and presentation software to present procurement-related information.

Many companies are now using more advanced software to assist in procurement management. The term *e-procurement* often describes various procurement functions that are now done electronically, as follows:

- *Web-based ERP (Electronic Resource Planning)*: Creating and approving purchasing requisitions, placing purchase orders, and receiving goods and services by using a software system based on Internet technology.
- *E-MRO (Maintenance, Repair, and Overhaul)*: The same as web-based ERP, except that the goods and services ordered are MRO supplies that are not related to a particular product.
- *E-sourcing*: Identifying new suppliers for a specific category of purchasing requirements using Internet technology.
- *E-tendering*: Sending requests for information and prices to suppliers and receiving the responses of suppliers using Internet technology.
- *E-reverse auctioning*: Using Internet technology to buy goods and services from a number of known or unknown suppliers.
- *E-informing*: Gathering and distributing purchasing information with internal and external parties using Internet technology.
- *E-marketsites*: Expands on web-based ERP to open up value chains. Buying communities can access preferred suppliers' products and services, add to shopping carts, create requisitions, seek approval, receive purchase orders, and process electronic invoices with integration to suppliers' supply chains and buyers' financial systems.

Many websites and software tools can assist in procurement functions. For example, most business travelers use the web to purchase airline tickets and to reserve rental cars and hotel rooms for business trips. With the rise of applications for smartphones, shoppers can even take pictures of barcodes on all types of products and compare prices of competing stores to confirm that they are getting the best deal. Likewise, many organizations can purchase items online, or they can buy specialized software to help streamline their procurement activities.

One type of software that is particularly useful for streamlining procurement is the procure-to-pay suite, which provides support for indirect procurements. Unlike direct procurement, where procurement experts in organizations acquire raw materials and goods for production or services related to their organization's primary business, indirect procurement involves acquiring supplies and services required to keep the day-to-day business functioning, such as equipment repairs, office supplies, and services related to keeping business processes running. According to Gartner, the procurement process has evolved from paper-intensive order processing to a strategic enterprise function. Their qualitative analysis of the procure-to-pay suites market makes the point that because self-service software tools are available, employees at all levels of an organization can buy goods and services without the need for professional procurement expertise. This streamlines the process for indirect procurements, so that procurement experts can focus on the more strategic direct procurements. The four main capabilities of procure-to-pay suites for indirect procurements include:

- E-purchasing functionality: Provides a self-service solution to requisition and order goods and services through the use of catalogs, e-forms, or free-text orders (for when users cannot find items in a structured format).
- Catalog management capabilities: Includes catalog content upload, content update evaluation tools, and catalog search tools.

- E-invoicing: Enables the interchange and storage of legally valid invoices in electronic format.
- Accounts Payable Invoice Automation (APIA): Allows approval and control of incoming invoices through either automatic or manual approvals by automatic workflows.

At current software suite prices, organizations with annual revenues of $800 million or more usually realize a good return on investment from using these tools. Gartner's research identified Ariba (SAP), Coupa, Basware, and SciQuest as market leaders in 2015.[14]

Organizations can also take advantage of information available on the web, in industry publications, or in various discussion groups offering advice on selecting suppliers. For example, many organizations invest millions of dollars in enterprise project management software. Before deciding which seller's software to use, organizations use the Internet to find product information provided by various suppliers, prices, case studies, and current customers to assist in making procurement decisions. Buyers can also use the Internet to hold bidders' conferences, as you learned earlier in this chapter, or to communicate procurement-related information.

As with any information or software tool, organizations must focus on using the information and tools to meet project and organizational needs. Many nontechnical issues are often involved in getting the most value out of new technologies, especially new e-procurement software. For example, organizations must often develop partnerships and strategic alliances with other organizations to take advantage of potential cost savings. Organizations should practice good procurement management in selecting new software tools and managing relationships with the chosen suppliers.

The processes of project procurement management follow a clear, logical sequence. However, many project managers are not familiar with the issues involved in purchasing goods and services from other organizations. If projects will benefit by procuring goods or services, then project managers and their teams must follow good project procurement management. As outsourcing for IT projects increases, it is important for all project managers to have a fundamental understanding of this knowledge area.

CASE WRAP-UP

After reading the contract for her company's consultants carefully, Marie McBride found a clause giving her company the right to terminate the contract with a one-week notice. She met with her project team to get suggestions. The team still needed help completing the system conversion project. One team member had a friend who worked for a competing consulting firm. The competing firm had experienced people available, and their fees were lower than those in the current contract. Marie asked this team member to help her research other consulting firms that could work on the conversion project. She then requested bids from these companies. She personally interviewed people from the top three suppliers' management teams and checked their references for similar projects.

Marie worked with the purchasing department to terminate the original contract and issue a new one with a new consulting firm that had a much better reputation and lower hourly rates. This time, she made certain the contract included a statement of work, specific deliverables, and requirements for the minimum experience level of consultants provided. The contract also included incentive fees for completing the conversion work within a certain time period. Marie had learned the importance of good project procurement management.

Chapter Summary

Procurement, purchasing, or outsourcing is the acquisition of goods and services from an outside source. IT outsourcing continues to grow, both within an organization's own country and offshore. Organizations outsource to reduce costs, focus on their core business, access skills and technologies, provide flexibility, and increase accountability. It is becoming increasingly important for IT professionals to understand project procurement management.

Project procurement management includes planning procurement management and then conducting, controlling, and closing procurements.

Planning procurement management involves deciding what to procure or outsource, what type of contract to use, and how to describe the effort in a statement of work. Make-or-buy analysis helps an organization determine whether it can procure a product or service at a reasonable cost. Project managers should consult with internal and external experts to assist them with procurement planning because many legal, organizational, and financial issues are often involved.

The basic types of contracts are fixed price, cost reimbursable, and time and material. Fixed-price contracts involve a fixed total price for a well-defined product and entail the least risk to buyers. Cost-reimbursable contracts involve payments to suppliers for direct and indirect actual costs and require buyers to absorb some of the risk. Time and material contracts are a hybrid of fixed-price and cost-reimbursable contracts, and are commonly used by consultants. Unit pricing involves paying suppliers a predetermined amount per unit of service and imposes different levels of risk on buyers, depending on how the contract is written. It is important to decide which contract type is most appropriate for a particular procurement. All contracts should include specific clauses that address unique aspects of a project and that describe termination requirements.

A statement of work (SOW) describes the work required for the procurement in enough detail to allow prospective suppliers to determine if they can provide the goods and services and to determine an appropriate price.

Conducting procurements involves obtaining seller responses, selecting sellers, and awarding contracts. Organizations should use a formal proposal evaluation form when evaluating suppliers. Technical criteria should not be given more weight than management or cost criteria during evaluation.

Controlling procurements involves managing relationships with sellers, monitoring contract performance, and making changes as needed. The project manager and key team members should be involved in writing and administering the contract. Project managers must be aware of potential legal problems they might cause if they do not understand a contract. Project managers and teams should use change control procedures when working with outside contracts and should be especially careful about constructive change orders.

Closing procurements involves completion and settlement of each contract, including resolution of any open items. Procurement audits, negotiated settlements, and records management systems are tools and techniques for closing procurements.

Several types of software can assist in project procurement management. E-procurement software helps organizations save money in procuring various goods and services. Organizations can also use the web, industry publications, and discussion groups to research and compare various suppliers.

Quick Quiz

1. What is the top reason for global outsourcing of IT services?

   a. cost reduction

   b. a shortage of qualified personnel

   c. decreasing time to market

   d. increasing revenues

2. Your organization hired a specialist in a certain field to provide training for a short period of time. Which reason for outsourcing would this example fall under?

   a. reducing costs

   b. allowing the client organization to focus on its core business

   c. accessing skills and technologies

   d. providing flexibility

3. In which project procurement management process is an RFP often written?

   a. planning procurement management

   b. conducting procurements

   c. controlling procurements

   d. selecting sellers

4. An item you need for a project has a daily lease cost of $200. If you decide to purchase the item, the investment cost is $6,000 and the daily cost is $100. After how many days will the lease cost be the same as the purchase cost?

   a. 30

   b. 40

   c. 50

   d. 60

5. Which type of contract has the least amount of risk for the buyer?

   a. fixed-price

   b. cost plus incentive fee (CPIF)

   c. time and material

   d. cost plus fixed fee (CPFF)

6. The _____ is the point at which the contractor assumes total responsibility for each additional dollar of contract cost.

   a. breakeven point

   b. Share Ratio Point

   c. Point of Reconciliation

   d. Point of Total Assumption

7. If your college or university wanted to get information from potential sellers for providing a new sports stadium, what type of document would be required of the potential sellers?

   a. RFP

   b. RFQ

   c. proposal

   d. quote

8. Buyers often prepare a _____ list when selecting a seller to make the process more manageable.

   a. preferred

   b. short

   c. qualified suppliers

   d. BAFO

9. A proposal evaluation sheet is an example of a(n) _____.

   a. RFP

   b. NPV analysis

   c. earned value analysis

   d. weighted scoring model

10. _____ is a term used to describe various procurement functions that are now done electronically.

   a. E-procurement

   b. eBay

   c. E-commerce

   d. EMV

Quick Quiz Answers

1. b; 2. c; 3. a; 4. d; 5. a; 6. d; 7. c; 8. b; 9. d; 10. a

Discussion Questions

1. List five reasons why organizations outsource. When should an organization choose not to outsource? Why are some organizations moving their software development work back in-house? Why are some organizations beginning to use onshoring?

2. Explain the make-or-buy decision process and describe how to perform the financial calculations in the simple lease-or-buy example provided in this chapter.

3. What are the main types of contracts if you decide to outsource? What are the advantages and disadvantages of each?

4. Do you think many IT professionals have experience writing RFPs and evaluating proposals for IT projects? What skills would be useful for these tasks?

5. How do organizations decide whom to send RFPs or RFQs?

6. How can organizations use a weighted scoring model to evaluate proposals as part of seller selection?

7. List two suggestions for ensuring adequate change control on projects that involve outside contracts.

8. What is the main purpose of a procurement audit?

9. How can software assist in procuring goods and services? What is e-procurement software? Do you see any ethical issues with e-procurement? For example, should stores be able to block people with smartphones from taking pictures of barcodes to do comparison shopping?

Exercises

1. Search the Internet for the term *IT outsourcing* and find at least two articles that discuss outsourcing. Summarize the articles and answer the following questions:

   - What are the main types of goods and services being outsourced?
   - Why are the organizations in the articles choosing to outsource?
   - Have the organizations in the articles benefited from outsourcing? Why or why not?

2. Interview someone who was involved in an IT procurement process, such as a manager in your organization's IT department, and have the person explain the process that was followed. Alternatively, find an article describing an IT procurement in an organization. Write a paper describing the procurement and any lessons learned by the organization.

3. Suppose that your company is trying to decide whether it should buy special equipment to prepare high-quality publications itself or lease the equipment from another company. Suppose that leasing the equipment costs $240 per day. If you decide to purchase the equipment, the initial investment is $6,800, and operations will cost $70 per day. After how many days will the lease cost be the same as the purchase cost for the equipment? Assume that your company would only use this equipment for 30 days. Should your company buy the equipment or lease it?

4. Search online for samples of IT contracts. Use search phrases like "IT contract" or "sample contract." Analyze the key features of the contract. What type of contract was used, and why? Review the language and clauses in the contract. What are some of the key clauses? List questions you have about the contract and try to get answers from someone who is familiar with contracts.

5. Review a sample RFP for an IT project. Write a paper summarizing the purpose of the RFP and how well you think it describes the work required.

6. Draft the source selection criteria that might be used for evaluating proposals to provide smartphones with wireless plans for all students, faculty, and staff at your college or university or to all business professionals in your organization. Use Figure 12-5 as a guide. Include at least five criteria, and make the total weights add up to 100. Write a paper explaining and justifying the criteria and their weights.

Running Case

As described in earlier chapters, your Global Treps team would pay for a new website and account through an online provider. Bobby would do most of the customization and programming for the site, but you would consider outsourcing or purchasing services to provide some of the capabilities like accepting donations and developing the short videos on the site. You would also buy a new laptop and Internet access for your three team members abroad, which they could share with their contacts in those countries. You have budgeted $20,000 for outsourced hardware and software. The activities listed in your WBS for outsourced software development include:

1.3.1.1   Domain name and site hosting

1.3.1.2   Donation acceptance feature of website

1.3.1.3   Video creation for website

1. Bobby is very familiar with purchasing domain names and site hosting and has already looked into options for providing the donation acceptance feature. However, you all agree that you need professionals to create the videos for the website. Brainstorm options for this procurement, and research potential suppliers. Summarize your findings in a short paper, and include at least three references.
2. Draft a contract statement of work for creating the videos for the website. Use the outline provided in Figure 12-3.
3. Assume that the source selection criteria for creating the videos for the website are as follows:

   - Management approach, 15 percent
   - Technical approach, 25 percent
   - Past performance, 10 percent
   - Price, 20 percent
   - Sample videos, 30 percent

   Using Figure 12-5 and the weighted scoring model template as guides, create a spreadsheet that could be used to enter ratings and calculate scores for each criterion and total weighted scores for three proposals. Enter scores for Proposal 1 as 80, 75, 70, 90, and 85, respectively. Enter scores for Proposal 2 as 90, 50, 95, 80, and 75. Enter scores for Proposal 3 as 80, 90, 95, 80, and 75. Add a paragraph to the spreadsheet that summarizes the results and your recommendation. Print your results on one page.
4. Draft potential clauses that you could include in the contract to provide incentives and/or penalties for on-time and within-budget delivery of high-quality videos that users would enjoy watching. Be creative in your response, and document your ideas in a short paper. Be sure to describe how you will measure if the criteria were met and what the incentives and/or penalties would be.

Key Terms

bid p.479

constructive change orders p.484

contract p.469

cost plus award fee (CPAF) contract p.474

cost plus fixed fee (CPFF) contract p.474

End Notes

1 Gartner, Inc., "Gartner Says Worldwide IT Spending on Pace to Grow 3.2 Percent in 2014" (April 2, 2014).

2 Duke University, "Survey: Organizational Flexibility a New Benefit of Global Outsourcing," Duke News Release (February 13, 2012).

3 Issie Lapowsky, "Urban Onshoring: The Movement to Bring Tech Jobs Back to America," *wired.com* (November 4, 2014).

4 Andy Bork, "Soft Skills Needed in a Hard World," *Minneapolis Star Tribune* (May 24, 2004).

5 Clint Boulton, "Zulily Calls In-House Software a 'Differentiator for Competitive Advantage,'" *CIO Journal* (blog), *Wall Street Journal* (August 8, 2014), *blogs.wsj.com/cio/2014/08/08/ zulily-calls-in-house-software-a-differentiator-for-competitive-advantage/*.

6 Scott McNealy, "The Future of the Net: Why We Don't Want You to Buy Our Software," *Sun Executive Perspectives, www.sun.com/dot-com/perspectives/stop.html* (Sun Microsystems, Inc., 1999): 1.

7 David M. Halbfinger, "City Hall Admits Mishandling Technology Projects," *The New York Times* (October 31, 2011).

8 Stan Beer, "Is going offshore good for Australia?" *The Age* (September 21, 2004).

9 Chris Pash, "The Market for IT Jobs in Australia Is Improving but the Pay Rates Aren't," *Business Insider Australia* (January 22, 2015).

10 Robert Antonio, "The Fixed-Price Incentive Firm Target Contract: Not As Firm As the Name Suggests," *WIFCON.com* (November 2003).

11 Dick Rohland, "I-35W Bridge Completion Brings Closure to Minneapolis," *ConstructionEquipmentGuide.com* (October 4, 2008).

12 Stephanie Overby, "10 Outsourcing Trends to Watch in 2015," *CIO.com* (January 5, 2015).

13 Pierre Mitchell, "Procurement Must Stretch Beyond 'Procurement Best Practices'," *Chief Procurement Officer* (January 21, 2015), *spendmatters.com/cpo/procurement-must -stretch-beyond-procurement-best-practices/*.

14 Magnus Bergfors, Paolo Malinverno, and Deborah R Wilson, "Magic Quadrant for Procure-to-Pay Suites for Indirect Procurement," Gartner (March 24, 2015).

CHAPTER 13

PROJECT STAKEHOLDER MANAGEMENT

LEARNING OBJECTIVES

After reading this chapter, you will be able to:

- Understand the importance of project stakeholder management throughout the life of a project
- Discuss the process of identifying stakeholders, how to create a stakeholder register, and how to perform a stakeholder analysis
- Describe the contents of a stakeholder management plan
- Understand the process of managing stakeholder engagement and how to use an issue log effectively
- Explain methods for controlling stakeholder engagement
- Discuss types of software available to assist in project stakeholder management

OPENING CASE

Debra Hughes took the risk of becoming an independent consultant after working her way up the corporate ladder for 10 years. Her last firm was downsizing and cut her entire strategic IT consulting department, but the firm offered her a transfer that would require her to travel about 80 percent of the time. With two small children, she did not want to travel, so she jumped at the chance to work independently. One of her colleagues knew an IT director at a local oil company, and he offered her a contract that paid three times what she received as an employee. The problem was that the initial contract was only for two weeks. However, after she proved her value by successfully managing the first project, the company kept her on, giving her bigger and bigger projects to manage. Her current project was to evaluate and then implement a project management software solution so the new VP of Operations, Stephen, could oversee the upgrade of oil refineries in several countries. The refinery upgrades were estimated to cost over $200 million. Debra worked with an internal analyst, Ryan, and Stephen to determine requirements and their approach to choosing a new software solution. They needed to award a contract to a supplier within two months and then integrate the new system with their other systems, especially the accounting systems, as quickly as possible.

Unfortunately, Chien, the IT director who hired Debra and authorized her paycheck every week, was very upset with her recommendation. He called her into his office and started yelling at her. "How could you make this recommendation? You know it goes against what I think is best for IT at this company. Ryan made a totally different recommendation than you did. You consultants think you can come in and shake things up, not worrying about what happens to us after you're gone. Get out of here before I say something I shouldn't!" Debra quietly left Chien's office, worrying about what to do next. She knew that her recommendation would please Stephen and be in the best interest of the entire company, even though it was not the choice that Chien and Ryan were promoting.

13.1 THE IMPORTANCE OF PROJECT STAKEHOLDER MANAGEMENT

As you learned in Chapter 1, stakeholders are an important part of the project management framework. Stakeholders request projects, approve them, reject them, support them, and oppose them. Because stakeholder management is so important to project success, the Project Management Institute decided to create an entire knowledge area devoted to it as part of the Fifth Edition of the *PMBOK® Guide* in 2013. Many of the concepts related to communications and human resource management also apply to stakeholder management, but unique activities are required to perform good stakeholder management. The purpose of project stakeholder management is to identify all people or organizations affected by a project, to analyze stakeholder expectations, and to effectively engage stakeholders in project decisions throughout the life of a project. Project managers and their teams must have a good dialogue with stakeholders and address issues as they occur to ensure stakeholder satisfaction.

Projects often cause changes in organizations, and some people may lose their jobs when a project is completed. For example, a project might create a new system that makes some jobs obsolete, or a project might result in outsourcing work to an external group to make the organization more efficient. The project managers might be viewed as enemies by these stakeholders and other negatively affected stakeholders. By contrast, some people may view project managers as allies if they lead a project that increases profits, produces new jobs, or increases pay for certain stakeholders. In any case, project managers must learn to identify, understand, and work with a variety of stakeholders.

 WHAT WENT WRONG?

Changing the way work is done can send a shock wave through an organization, leaving many people afraid and even thinking about ways to stop or sabotage a project. Donald White, founder and program manager at Defense Systems Leaders in Washington, D.C., described situations that can lead to project sabotage:

- *Buy-in blues*: Top-down support and early buy-in for projects is crucial. Allowing negativity to fester will decrease the likelihood of project success. Deal with protesters early.
- *Short-term profits*: Cutting costs by any means possible for immediate payoff will sacrifice the future health of an organization and its employees. Avoid projects that focus only on the short term.
- *Overachieving*: Trying to do too many things at the same time introduces waste and significantly slows down progress. Focus on the most important projects first.
- *Lack of respect*: "Disrespect people, and they will retaliate with apathy, boredom, absenteeism, make-work [performing tasks of little importance to keep busy], outright sabotage and other maladies. Disrespect customers, and they'll find someone who will treat them better."[1]

497

The four processes in project stakeholder management include the following:

1. *Identifying stakeholders* involves identifying everyone involved in the project or affected by it and determining the best ways to manage relationships with them. The main output of this process is a stakeholder register.
2. *Planning stakeholder management* involves determining strategies to effectively engage stakeholders in project decisions and activities based on their needs, interests, and potential impact. Outputs of this process are a stakeholder management plan and project documents updates.
3. *Managing stakeholder engagement* involves communicating and working with project stakeholders to satisfy their needs and expectations, resolving issues, and fostering engagement in project decisions and activities. The outputs of this process are issue logs, change requests, project management plan updates, project documents updates, and organizational process assets updates.
4. *Controlling stakeholder engagement* involves monitoring stakeholder relationships and adjusting plans and strategies for engaging stakeholders as needed. Outputs of this process are work performance information, change requests, project documents updates, and organizational process assets updates.

Figure 13-1 summarizes these processes and outputs, showing when they occur in a typical project.

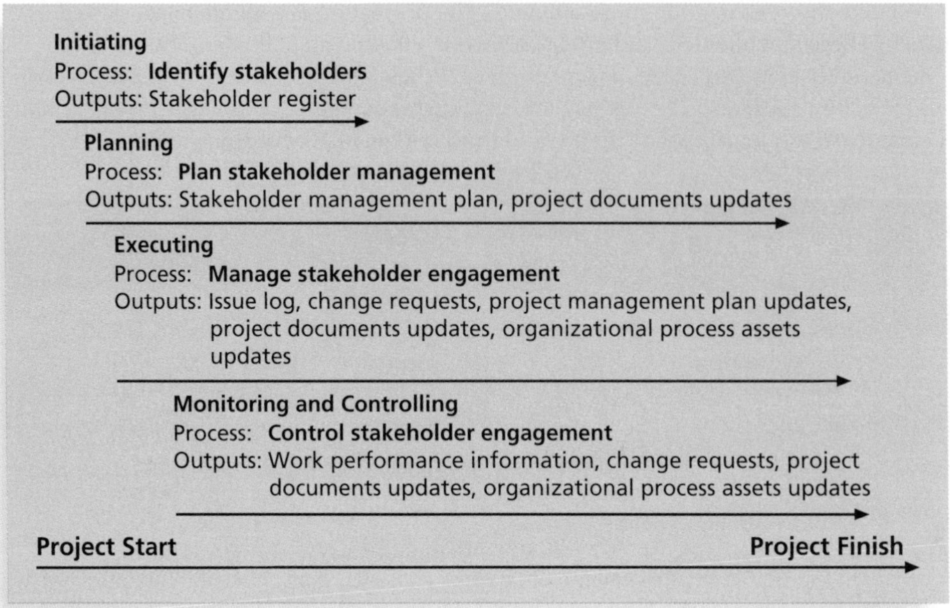

> **Initiating**
> Process: **Identify stakeholders**
> Outputs: Stakeholder register
>
> **Planning**
> Process: **Plan stakeholder management**
> Outputs: Stakeholder management plan, project documents updates
>
> **Executing**
> Process: **Manage stakeholder engagement**
> Outputs: Issue log, change requests, project management plan updates, project documents updates, organizational process assets updates
>
> **Monitoring and Controlling**
> Process: **Control stakeholder engagement**
> Outputs: Work performance information, change requests, project documents updates, organizational process assets updates
>
> **Project Start**   **Project Finish**

FIGURE 13-1   Project stakeholder management summary

13.2 IDENTIFYING STAKEHOLDERS

Recall from Chapter 1 that stakeholders are the people involved in project activities or affected by them. The *PMBOK® Guide, Fifth Edition*, expands on this definition as follows: "Project stakeholders are individuals, groups, or organizations who may affect, be affected by, or perceive themselves to be affected by a decision, activity, or outcome of a project." Stakeholders can be internal to the organization or external.

- Internal project stakeholders generally include the project sponsor, project team, support staff, and internal customers for the project. Other internal stakeholders include top management, other functional managers, and other project managers because organizations have limited resources.
- External project stakeholders include the project's customers (if they are external to the organization), competitors, suppliers, and other external groups that are potentially involved in the project or affected by it, such as government officials and concerned citizens.

The website *www.projectstakeholder.com* offers an even more detailed list of potential stakeholders for a project:

- Program director
- Program manager
- Project manager
- Project manager's family
- Sponsor

- Customer
- Performing organization
- Other employees of the organization
- Labor unions
- Project team members
- Project management office
- Governance board
- Suppliers
- Governmental regulatory agencies
- Competitors
- Potential customers with an interest in the project
- Groups representing consumer, environmental, or other interests
- Groups or individuals who are competing for limited resources
- Groups or individuals who are pursuing goals that conflict with those of the project[2]

Recall that the ultimate goal of project management is to meet or exceed stakeholder needs and expectations for a project. To do that, you must first identify your particular project stakeholders. Identifying some stakeholders is obvious, but others might be more difficult to identify. For example, some competitors outside the organization or even inside it might be opposed to the project without the project manager's knowledge. Stakeholders also might change during a project due to employee turnover, partnerships, and other events. It is important to use formal and informal communications networks to make sure that all key stakeholders are identified.

It is also necessary to focus on stakeholders with the most direct ties to the project. For example, if you listed every single supplier for goods and services used on a project, you would be wasting precious time and resources. If a supplier is just providing an off-the-shelf product, it should need little if any attention. However, if a supplier is providing a customized product or service that is critical to the project's success, the supplier deserves much more attention.

A simple way to document basic information on project stakeholders is by creating a **stakeholder register**. This document can take various forms and include the following information:

- *Identification information*: The stakeholders' names, positions, locations, roles in the project, and contact information
- *Assessment information*: The stakeholders' major requirements and expectations, potential influences, and phases of the project in which stakeholders have the most interest
- *Stakeholder classification*: Is the stakeholder internal or external to the organization? Is the stakeholder a supporter of the project or resistant to it?

Table 13-1 provides an example of part of the stakeholder register for the project described in the chapter's opening case. Notice that it includes only basic stakeholder information, such as name, position, whether stakeholders are internal or external to the organization, their role on the project, and contact information. Because this document is available to other people in the organization, the project manager must be careful not to include

TABLE 13-1   Sample stakeholder register

Name	Position	Internal/ External	Project Role	Contact Information
Stephen	VP of Operations	Internal	Project sponsor	stephen@globaloil.com
Betsy	CFO	Internal	Senior manager, approves funds	betsy@globaloil.com
Chien	CIO	Internal	Senior manager, PM's boss	chien@globaloil.com
Ryan	IT analyst	Internal	Team member	ryan@globaloil.com
Lori	Director, Accounting	Internal	Senior manager	lori@globaloil.com
Sanjay	Director, Refineries	Internal	Senior manager of largest refinery	sanjay@globaloil.com
Debra	Consultant	External	Project manager	debra@gmail.com
Suppliers	Suppliers	External	Supply software	suppliers@gmail.com

© Cengage Learning 2016

sensitive information, such as how strongly the stakeholders support the project or how much power they have. Also notice that some stakeholders, like the project manager's husband and children, are not included on this list, even though they are important stakeholders to Debra!

A **stakeholder analysis** is a technique for analyzing information to determine which stakeholders' interests to focus on and how to increase stakeholder support throughout the project. After identifying key project stakeholders, you can use different classification models to determine an approach for managing stakeholder relationships. For example, you can create a **power/interest grid** to group stakeholders based on their level of authority (power) and their level of concern (interest) for project outcomes, as shown in Figure 13-2. You should manage relationships very closely with stakeholders 1 and 2 in this example because they have high interest and high power, especially stakeholder 1. You should keep stakeholders 3 and 4 informed because they have high interest but low power. Stakeholders 5 and 6 should be kept satisfied, perhaps by brief updates on the project, because they have low interest but high power. You should spend the least amount of effort by simply monitoring stakeholders 7 and 8, who both have low interest and low power.

It is also important to measure the engagement level of stakeholders throughout the project. You can categorize stakeholders as being one of the following:

- *Unaware*: Unaware of the project and its potential impacts on them
- *Resistant*: Aware of the project yet resistant to change
- *Neutral*: Aware of the project yet neither supportive nor resistant
- *Supportive*: Aware of the project and supportive of change
- *Leading*: Aware of the project and its potential impacts and actively engaged in helping it succeed

The project team should take corrective action if stakeholders with high interest and high power are also categorized as resistant or unaware. If they are unaware, setting up a short meeting to discuss the importance of the project would be appropriate. The project

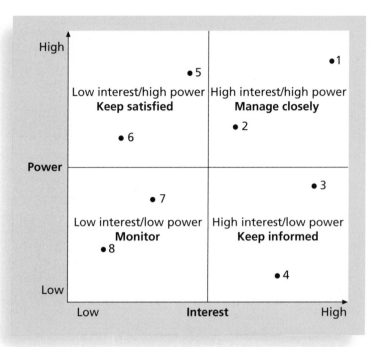

Source: Kathy Schwalbe, *An Introduction to Project Management,* Fourth Edition (2012)

FIGURE 13-2   Power/interest grid[3]

manager could ask the project sponsor or another senior manager to participate in the meeting. If stakeholders are resistant to the project, you would definitely want a senior-level manager to talk to them directly to understand the reasons for their resistance and develop a strategy to handle potential conflicts. Another common problem with stakeholders, especially project sponsors, is that they support a project but have unreasonable expectations. It can be difficult to say "no" to them, as described in the following What Went Right? feature.

✓ **WHAT WENT RIGHT?**

Instead of just saying "no" when your project sponsor asks for something unreasonable, it is better to explain what is wrong with the request and then present a realistic way to solve the problem at hand. For example, Christa Ferguson, a PMP and independent program manager in San Francisco, described how she handled a request from a project sponsor to deliver a new tablet device in two months when she knew she would need more time. Based on her experience, she knew the Request for Quote for the effort alone would take almost a month. Christa quickly researched the facts to propose a realistic delivery schedule.

continued

"I created a timeline for the request for quotation and requested the companies quoting the job to include a breakdown of the work required with a high-level schedule. Then we could see the project was going to take at least six months to complete. By creating a factual, data-driven picture of the situation, I didn't have to explain anything other than what work had to be done and how long it would take. Our sponsor reset expectations once he learned what it took to produce the tablets."[4]

13.3 PLANNING STAKEHOLDER MANAGEMENT

After identifying and analyzing stakeholders, the project manager and team should develop a stakeholder management plan to help them effectively engage stakeholders and make sure that good decisions are made throughout the life of the project. This plan may be formal or informal, based on the needs of the project.

In addition to information found in the stakeholder register, such as stakeholder identification information, assessment information, and classification, a stakeholder management plan can include the following:

- *Current and desired engagement levels*: If these levels are not the same, the project team should develop a strategy to align engagement levels.
- *Interrelationships between stakeholders*: As you learned in earlier chapters, there are many interrelationships between project activities and stakeholders. The project manager must be in tune with the politics of the organization.
- *Communication requirements*: The communications management plan should specify stakeholder requirements, and the stakeholder register can expand on unique requests from specific people.
- *Potential management strategies for each stakeholder*: This critical section can contain very sensitive information.
- *Methods for updating the stakeholder management plan*: All plans need some process for handling changes and updates. Flexibility would be important as stakeholders change on the project.

Because a stakeholder management plan often includes sensitive information, it should *not* be part of the official project documents, which are normally available for all stakeholders to review. In many cases, only project managers and a few other team members should prepare the stakeholder management plan. In many cases, parts of the stakeholder management plan are not written down, and if they are, distribution is strictly limited.[5]

Table 13-2 provides an example of parts of a stakeholder management plan that Debra could use to help manage project stakeholders in the opening case. It is important for project managers to take the time to develop this plan, which helps them meet stakeholder needs and expectations. In addition, as new stakeholders are added to the project and more information is provided, the plan should be updated. For example, once a supplier is selected for a project, specific supplier names and other information can be added to the list.

TABLE 13-2 Sample stakeholder analysis

Name	Power/ Interest	Current Engagement	Potential Management Strategies
Stephen	High/high	Leading	Stephen can seem intimidating due to his physical stature and deep voice, but he has a great personality and sense of humor. He previously led a similar refinery upgrade program at another company and knows what he wants. Manage closely and ask for his advice as needed. He likes short, frequent updates in person.
Chien	High/ medium	Resistant	Chien is a very organized yet hardheaded man. He has been pushing corporate IT standards, and the system the PM and sponsor (Debra and Stephen) like best goes against those standards, even though it's the best solution for this project and the company as a whole. Need to convince him that this is okay and that people still respect his work and position.
Ryan	Medium/ high	Supportive	Ryan has been with the company for several years and is well respected, but he feels threatened by Debra. He also resents her getting paid more than he does. He wants to please his boss, Chien, first and foremost. Need to convince him that the suggested solution is in everyone's best interest.
Betsy	High/low	Neutral	Very professional, logical person. Gets along well with Chien. She has supported Debra in approving past projects with strong business cases. Provide detailed financial justification for the suggested solution to keep her satisfied. Also ask her to talk to Chien on Debra's behalf.

© Cengage Learning 2016

13.4 MANAGING STAKEHOLDER ENGAGEMENT

Project managers must understand and work with various stakeholders; therefore, they should specifically address how to use various communications methods and their interpersonal and management skills to engage stakeholders. Recall that project success is often measured in different ways, such as meeting scope, time, and cost goals. Many practitioners, however, define project success as satisfying the customer or sponsor, knowing that it's rare to meet scope, time, and cost goals without modifying at least one goal.

Project sponsors can usually rank scope, time, and cost goals in order of importance and provide guidelines on how to balance the triple constraint. This ranking can be shown in an **expectations management matrix**, which can help clarify expectations. For example, Table 13-3 shows part of an expectations management matrix that Debra could use to help manage key stakeholders from the opening case. The expectations management matrix includes a list of measures of success as well as priorities, expectations, and guidelines related to each measure. You could add other measures of success, such as meeting quality expectations, achieving a certain customer satisfaction rating, and meeting ROI projections after the project is completed, to meet individual project needs. The challenge comes when key stakeholders disagree on priorities. For example, Stephen wants a system that will meet his requirements, so scope is most important to him. Chien wants to enforce corporate standards, so technology/standards are most important to him. Project managers must acknowledge these different priorities and make the tough decisions about what to do. In this example, Debra believes that Stephen's

TABLE 13-3 Expectations management matrix

Measure of Success	Priority	Expectations	Guidelines
Scope	1	The scope statement clearly defines mandatory requirements and optional requirements.	Focus on meeting mandatory requirements before considering optional ones. In this case, following corporate IT standards is optional.
Time	1	There is little give in the project completion date. The schedule is very realistic.	The project sponsor must be alerted if any issues might affect meeting schedule goals.
Cost	3	This project is crucial to the organization. If you can clearly justify the need for more funds, they can be made available.	There are strict rules for project expenditures and escalation procedures. Cost is very important, but it takes a back seat to meeting schedule and then scope goals.
Technology/ standards	2	There are several potential solutions available, but only one that meets all of the sponsor's technical requirements, especially for accounting.	While corporate IT standards are important, an exception makes sense in this case.

priorities are most important to the company as a whole, even though it might hurt her relationship with Chien.

Understanding the stakeholders' expectations can help in managing issues. If the project manager knows that cost is not as high a priority as the schedule, it shouldn't be difficult to ask the project sponsor for needed funds, as long as the request makes sense.

Issues should be documented in an **issue log**, a tool used to document, monitor, and track issues that need resolution. Unresolved issues can be a major source of conflict and result in stakeholder expectations not being met. Note that PMI lists issue logs as a tool for stakeholder management, even though they can be used to address issues related to other knowledge areas. For example, issues can be documented for requirements, procurement, staffing, and other areas, but stakeholders must be informed about these issues and engaged in the process of addressing them.

Table 13-4 provides a sample issue log that Debra could use to help document and manage issues on her project. The issue log includes columns for the issue number, the issue description, the impact of the issue on the project, the date the issue was reported, who reported the issue, the person assigned to resolve the issue, the priority of the issue (high, medium, or low), the due date for reporting back on the issue, the status of the issue, and comments related to the issue. Some project management software includes the ability to track issues, or a simple spreadsheet can be used. Many project managers sort issues by priority and focus on resolving the high-priority issues first.

In addition to an issue log, other outputs of managing stakeholder engagement include change requests and updates to the project management plan, project documents, and organizational process assets. For example, after Stephen clarified which

TABLE 13-4 Sample issue log

Issue #	Description	Impact	Date Reported	Reported By	Assigned To	Priority (H/M/L)	Due Date	Status	Comments
1	Need requirements categorized as mandatory and optional	Cannot do much without it	Feb. 4	Ryan	Stephen	H	Feb. 8	Closed	Requirements clearly labeled
2	Need shorter list of potential suppliers – no more than 10	Will delay evaluation without it	Feb. 6	Debra	Ryan	H	Feb. 12	Open	Almost finished; needed requirements categorized first
Etc.									

© Cengage Learning 2016

requirements were mandatory for the project management system needed to upgrade the oil refineries, it would probably affect which suppliers would meet the criteria for potential selection. If the project included visiting potential suppliers, the schedule and cost might be affected depending on the location of the top suppliers. In addition, Debra might be able to use these mandatory requirements to argue for using nonstandard technology when talking to Chien. Debra would still need to address this issue carefully with him, and she could benefit from using some of the ideas described in the following Best Practice feature.

BEST PRACTICE

Project managers are often faced with challenges, especially in managing stakeholders. Sometimes they simply cannot meet requests from important stakeholders. Suggestions for handling these situations include the following:

- *Be clear from the start.* Project managers should emphasize the importance of their projects to the entire organization. For example, in the opening case, the company had to upgrade several oil refineries to stay in business. IT standards are important, but when a powerful new VP is hired and wants software with specific requirements to get an important job done, you have to consider all options.
- *Explain the consequences.* Project managers have to be able to explain the consequences of various decisions. Senior managers may not like a decision, but if you present the logic behind it, they are more open to accepting it.
- *Have a contingency plan.* There are many forms of contingency plans. If a project manager cannot reason with an important stakeholder, a more senior person might be asked to help, for example. In extreme cases, project managers might even move on to other jobs if they feel their work is not appreciated.

continued

- *Avoid surprises.* It is much better to be honest about project challenges so that actions can be taken. One of the worst situations project managers face is telling sponsors something cannot be done after assuring them that it could.
- *Take a stand.* Project managers do make a difference in leading their projects, and part of the job is acknowledging the need for a change in course. "If you don't step it up and say, 'We cannot get this done and this is the way it is,' then what are you there for? … If a sponsor wants a good, seasoned project manager, that's what you must do."[6]

13.5 CONTROLLING STAKEHOLDER ENGAGEMENT

You cannot control stakeholders, but you can control their level of engagement. Engagement involves a dialogue in which people seek understanding and solutions to issues of mutual concern. Many teachers are familiar with various techniques for engaging students. It is important to set the proper tone at the start of a class or project. For example, if a

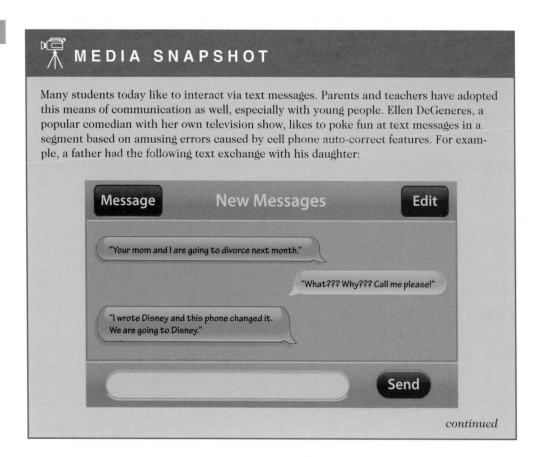

MEDIA SNAPSHOT

Many students today like to interact via text messages. Parents and teachers have adopted this means of communication as well, especially with young people. Ellen DeGeneres, a popular comedian with her own television show, likes to poke fun at text messages in a segment based on amusing errors caused by cell phone auto-correct features. For example, a father had the following text exchange with his daughter:

continued

In addition to watching out for auto-correct errors when messaging, users must also be careful who they reply to and what they say in reply. The following example comes from an actual college student who forgot about an exam. The professor called the student's cell phone shortly after the exam started. Her policy was to assign a grade of zero if students did not show up without a valid excuse. The student did not answer the phone call, but he sent the following texts:

Message	**New Messages**

Student: "Who is this?"

Professor: "Where are you?"

Student: "In class. Who is this?"

Professor: "Did you drop MIS101? Professor Smith"

Student: "No. I had to give my sister's fiancé a ride to the veteran's hospital because he doesn't have a car and my sister was at work."

Professor: "You are missing exam 1 right now."

Student: "Okay. Is it possible to do it during your office hours?"

Professor: "No. Now."

Send

The professor was surprised when the student walked into her classroom a few seconds later. Apparently he was down the hall working on a campus computer. Even though he lied twice (about being in class and about taking someone to the hospital), the professor let him take the exam and tried not to give him a hard time about his lies. The student was on time for future exams.

teacher does nothing but lecture on the first day of class or criticizes the first student who offers a comment, students will quickly decide that their best strategy is to keep quiet and maybe not even attend class. On the other hand, if the teacher uses a lot of activities to get all students to speak or use technology to participate, students will expect to be active participants in future classes.

Just like teachers, project managers need to set the stage for engaging project stakeholders early in the project. For example, key stakeholders should be invited to actively participate in a kick-off meeting rather than merely attend it. The project manager should emphasize that a dialogue is expected at the meeting, using whatever means of communication the stakeholders prefer. It is also helpful for the project manager to meet with important stakeholders before the kick-off meeting.

The project schedule should include activities and deliverables related to stakeholder engagement. Surveys, reviews, demonstrations, sign-offs, and other items require stakeholder engagement.

On some IT projects, important stakeholders are invited to be members of the project teams. For example, when Northwest Airlines (now Delta) was developing a new reservation system called ResNet, it interviewed reservation agents for positions as programmers on the project team. Northwest made sure that user needs were understood by having them actually develop the system's user interface. See the companion website for detailed information about how the ResNet team engaged with users.

13.6 USING SOFTWARE TO ASSIST IN PROJECT STAKEHOLDER MANAGEMENT

As in the other knowledge areas, software can also assist in project stakeholder management. Productivity software like word processors, spreadsheets, and presentation software can aid in creating various documents related to stakeholder management. Communications software like e-mail, blogs, websites, texts, and tweets can aid in stakeholder communications. Collaboration tools like Google docs, wikis, and virtual meeting software can also promote stakeholder engagement in projects.

A very popular software category today—social media—can also help engage stakeholders. For example, many professionals use LinkedIn to connect with other professionals. Several project management groups are on LinkedIn and other sites where people can share ideas about various topics. In fact, searching LinkedIn groups for the term *project management* in May 2015 yielded over 7,000 results, including the following:

- *The Project Manager Network*: With over 705,000 members, this group says it is the "#1 Project Manager Social Media Group & Community on LinkedIn." It was created by *ProjectManagers.net*.
- *Project Manager Community*: This group claims to be the "best group for project management" with over 288,000 members. This community was created by *ProjectManager.com*.
- *PMI Project, Program and Portfolio Management*: With over 156,000 members, this official PMI group claims to be #1 for career advancement.
- *PMO—Project Management Office*: This virtual community has over 79,000 members around the globe.

Although many organizations do not promote the use of Facebook at work, several project management software tools include functionality like Facebook's to encourage relationship building on projects. For example, some tools allow people to give each other "high fives" for a job well done. Many include photos of project team members and other stakeholders. Users can also have conversation threads within the tools. In fact, several books and articles are available about using social media to help manage projects.

Elizabeth Harrin, Director of the Otobos Group in London, is the author of *Social Media for Project Managers*. In the book, Harrin describes the pros and cons of several social media tools, including blogs, collaboration tools, instant messaging, microblogs like Twitter and Facebook, podcasts, RSS, social networks, vodcasts (video podcasts), webinars, and wikis. In the foreword of the book, Len O'Neal, Online Content and Strategy Manager for PMI, stated: "Making social media work on your projects can be a project in itself ... Individual, team, organizational, and cultural biases and influences can play a significant part in how far you explore the road to project-based social media efforts and how successful you are."[7] Harrin provides advice for when to use social media and when not to use it.

As the saying goes, "A fool with a tool is still just a fool." It is crucial that project managers and their teams focus on controlling stakeholder management to meet their needs and expectations, not to show off the latest technology. A lot of stakeholder engagement requires old-fashioned techniques like talking to someone!

 GLOBAL ISSUES

Not all software implementations go well, and managing stakeholders is a major challenge. The U.K. government scrapped its £11.4 billion national healthcare IT initiative in September 2011 after it failed to deliver the promised benefits. Unfortunately, this project was just one in a series of high-profile failures in the U.K.

In response, the government decided to send its project managers back to school! The government partnered with the University of Oxford and the Deloitte consulting firm to establish the Major Projects Leadership Academy in Oxford, England. Currently, 300 people are categorized as major project leaders in the British government. The goal of the new academy is to reduce the overreliance on expensive external consultants and build expertise within the civil service. In the future, "no one will be able to lead a major government project without completing the Academy."[8] Project leaders working on the 2012 Olympics and the High Speed Two railway system were the first to benefit from the new program.

As of spring 2015, about 120 people have graduated and another 200 have enrolled. Has it made a difference? According to Paul Chapman, EngD, the head of the academy, it certainly has. "Three years ago, about one-third of the government's major projects were delivered on time and to budget.... now this is nearly two-thirds."[9] You can find more details on the Major Projects Leadership Academy website.

The processes involved in project stakeholder management, like the other knowledge areas, follow a clear, logical sequence. However, this may be the most difficult area to master for many project managers. As you learned in this and previous chapters, understanding a wide variety of people and getting them to work together to meet project goals is not an easy undertaking.

CASE WRAP-UP

Debra let Chien cool down a while before entering his office again. She realized that she needed his signature on an important document.

"Are you going to yell at me again?" she asked.

Chien smiled and apologized for being so upset earlier. He was very happy with Debra's performance and knew that she was an asset to the company. He explained how hard it was for him to try to develop and enforce IT standards, especially when a new VP like Stephen comes in and gets what he wants so easily.

Debra explained that the software solution she recommended was the only one that would integrate well with the various accounting systems at refineries in other countries. She described some of the technical details she learned after meeting with the Director of Accounting, and Stephen knew it was essential to keep track of costs well on such a huge project. Chien agreed that upgrading the oil refineries quickly and cost-effectively was the top priority for the company now. He told Debra that he trusted her objective analysis in making the best recommendation. He also told her that it took a lot of guts to go against him and Ryan, but he knew now that it was best for the company as a whole.

Chapter Summary

Managing stakeholders is the tenth knowledge area in the *PMBOK® Guide*. Project stakeholder management includes identifying stakeholders, planning stakeholder management, managing stakeholder engagement, and controlling stakeholder engagement.

You cannot perform the other stakeholder management processes until you first identify project stakeholders. Stakeholders can be internal or external to the organization, and they might support or oppose your project. The main output of this process is a stakeholder register.

A stakeholder analysis is a key technique used in planning stakeholder engagement. Some information, such as how to manage relationships with stakeholders, might be sensitive, so it must be handled carefully. A stakeholder management plan describes stakeholder engagement levels, interrelationships, communication requirements, management strategies, and a process for updating the plan.

When managing stakeholder engagement, project managers and their teams must understand various expectations of stakeholders and use their communications and interpersonal skills. It is important to encourage engagement early in a project and have deliverables that require engagement. An important output of this process is an issue log—a document used to help track and resolve issues on projects.

It is important to control stakeholder engagement by having an open dialogue and tracking deliverables related to engagement.

Several types of software can assist in project stakeholder management. In addition to technologies mentioned in other chapters to improve communications and collaboration, social media can also help in developing relationships with stakeholders. Some project management software applications include features inspired by social media, such as giving "high fives" and posting comment threads.

511

Quick Quiz

1. Which knowledge area was first introduced in the *PMBOK® Guide* in 2013?
    a. project engagement management
    b. project consulting management
    c. project stakeholder engagement
    d. project stakeholder management

2. Suppliers and concerned citizens are examples of which type of stakeholders?
    a. internal
    b. external
    c. supportive
    d. unsupportive

3. What type of information about stakeholders is not included in a stakeholder register?
    a. identification
    b. classification

    c.   assessment

    d.   engagement level

4. What type of grid can categorize stakeholders based on their level of authority and concern?

    a.   a power/interest grid

    b.   an authority/concern grid

    c.   an authority/interest grid

    d.   a resistance/support grid

5. One of your project stakeholders has a high amount of authority and a high amount of interest. How should you manage that relationship?

    a.   keep informed

    b.   keep satisfied

    c.   manage closely

    d.   monitor

6. Which type of matrix can help clarify which knowledge areas are most important to stakeholders on a project?

    a.   a knowledge area matrix

    b.   a prioritization matrix

    c.   an expectations management matrix

    d.   a stakeholder management matrix

7. What tool can you use to document, monitor, and track items that need resolution on a project?

    a.   an issue log

    b.   a risk register

    c.   an issue register

    d.   a resolution log

8. When should you start controlling stakeholder engagement on a project?

    a.   in the early phases

    b.   in the middle phases

    c.   in the latter phases

    d.   none of the above; you cannot control stakeholder engagement

9. Which of the following statements is false about software that can assist in project stakeholder management?

    a.   Social media tools can assist in stakeholder management.

    b.   Some project management software includes features like giving "high fives."

    c.   Texting is an example of a microblog that can keep stakeholders informed about project work.

    d.   A vodcast is a video podcast that can inform and engage stakeholders.

10. After a series of large project disasters, what country is requiring people to complete a new academic program in project management before leading a large government project?

   a. Australia

   b. U.K.

   c. India

   d. Japan

Quick Quiz Answers

1. d; 2. b; 3. d; 4. a; 5. c; 6. c; 7. a; 8. a; 9. c; 10. b

Discussion Questions

1. Why do you think PMI created a separate knowledge area for stakeholder management?

2. What are some ways to identify project stakeholders? Which stakeholders do you think are often not identified when they should be?

3. What are some ways to manage a stakeholder relationship closely? Give examples of how you might manage relationships differently based on the unique personalities of different people.

4. Discuss ways that you have seen people manage stakeholder engagement in your classroom or work environments. Which approaches seem to work the best?

5. Describe the type of information that is documented in an issue log. How can you avoid spending too much time documenting and tracking issues?

6. How can software assist in project stakeholder management? Do you think social media tools are more likely to help or hinder projects?

Exercises

1. Review the chapter's opening case and some of the sample documents related to it. How do you think Debra handled the various stakeholders? Offer at least two suggestions for what she might have done to avoid being yelled at by a senior manager. Summarize your answers in a short memo to Debra.

2. Search the Internet for articles related to dealing with project sponsors. Summarize two good articles in a memo that you could send to a new project manager, offering advice on how to effectively engage sponsors.

3. Interview someone who worked on an information technology project that involved several difficult stakeholders. Ask what they did that worked well and what did not work well. Summarize the interview results in a thank-you e-mail to the person you interviewed, highlighting important lessons you learned from them.

4. Review the information for using a power/interest grid. Find at least two articles that describe this grid or a similar one to help categorize stakeholders and how to manage them. Summarize your results in a memo to a new project manager who is interested in this tool.

5. Go to *www.linkedin.com.* If you do not have an account, set one up. Search for groups related to project management and topics related to stakeholder management. Join at least two groups and read some of the discussion topics. Post one good question to each of the groups and wait at least two days for responses. Summarize what you learned and post the summary on both sites.

6. Search for articles related to the importance of keeping certain stakeholder information confidential. What types of information should be confidential? Describe two examples of actual problems that occurred when confidential information was leaked. Summarize your findings in a short paper or presentation.

Running Case

Recall that the following people are involved in the Global Treps Project:

- You, the project manager
- Dr. K., the project sponsor
- Bobby, team member/technical specialist
- Alfreda, Kim, and Ashok, team members organizing events in other countries
- Suppliers for the domain name and site hosting, the donation acceptance feature of the website, and the video creation for the website (including Angela, the contact person at the video supplier)
- Instructors at each site helping to organize the events (including Dr. B. in Ethiopia)

1. Prepare a stakeholder register using the preceding information. Make up other information as needed.

2. Create a stakeholder management strategy for the project, focusing on members who are not on the project team, such as Angela and Dr. B. Make up names and personalities for the other two instructor contacts in India and Vietnam. Be creative in developing potential management strategies.

3. Prepare an issue log for the project. Include issues discussed in prior chapters, such as Ashok breaking his wrist, Bobby's desire to use Kanban boards, and Alfreda's difficulties communicating with Dr. B. Make up three additional potential issues.

Key Terms

expectations management matrix p.503

issue log p.504

power/interest grid p.500

stakeholder analysis p.500

stakeholder register p.499

End Notes

[1] Peter Fretty, "Most Valuable Players," *PM Network* (May 2012).

[2] Peter Gilliland, "List of Project Stakeholders," *www.projectstakeholder.com* (accessed May 1, 2012).

3 Kathy Schwalbe, *An Introduction to Project Management, Fourth Edition* (2012).

4 Denene Brox, "Say No," *PM Network* (May 2012).

5 Kathy Schwalbe, *An Introduction to Project Management, Fourth Edition* (2012).

6 Denene Brox, "Say No," *PM Network* (May 2012).

7 Elizabeth Harrin, *Social Media for Project Managers*, Project Management Institute (2010).

8 University of Oxford, "Oxford Teams Up with Cabinet Office to Teach Leadership," *PM Network* (February 7, 2012).

9 Steve Hendershot, "Facing Up to Government IT Project Failures," *PM Network* (May 2015), *www.pmi.org/Learning/PM-Network/2015/facing-government-it-project-failures.aspx*.

GUIDE TO USING MICROSOFT PROJECT 2013

Note 1: This Appendix is used with permission from Schwalbe Publishing. It was published as a stand-alone book on May 2, 2013, and as an appendix in Kathy Schwalbe's *Healthcare Project Management* (co-authored with Dan Furlong) and *Revised An Introduction to Project Management, Fourth Edition.*

Note 2: This guide was written using the free trial of Microsoft Office Project 2013 Professional and Windows 7. Your screens may appear slightly different. You can download a free trial of Project 2013 Professional from the Microsoft website. You can access updated information as well as the older version of this guide based on Project 2010 at *www. intropm.com.* You can purchase just this new Appendix from *www.intropm.com* in Kindle or hard-copy format. Also note that Microsoft now provides a cloud-based tool called Project Online, available for a monthly fee.

INTRODUCTION

There are hundreds of project management software products on the market today. Gartner estimated the project and portfolio management (PPM) software market to be over $1 billion in 2011, and it continues to grow. Unfortunately, many people who own PPM software have no idea how to use it. It is important to understand the basic concepts of project management, such as creating a work breakdown structure, determining task dependencies, and so on before making effective use of this software. Many project teams still use spreadsheets or other familiar software to help manage projects. However, if you can master a good project management software tool, it can really help in managing projects. This appendix summarizes basic information on project management software in general. It also provides a brief guide to using Microsoft Office Project 2013 Professional (often referred to as Project 2013), the latest version of the most widely used PPM software.

PROJECT MANAGEMENT SOFTWARE REVIEWS

Figure A-1 provides a screen shot showing the top ten project management software products based on a June 2009 review by TopTenREVIEWS™. That was the last year that a review was provided of non-online PPM software. Most PPM tools now offer totally online versions, including Project 2013.

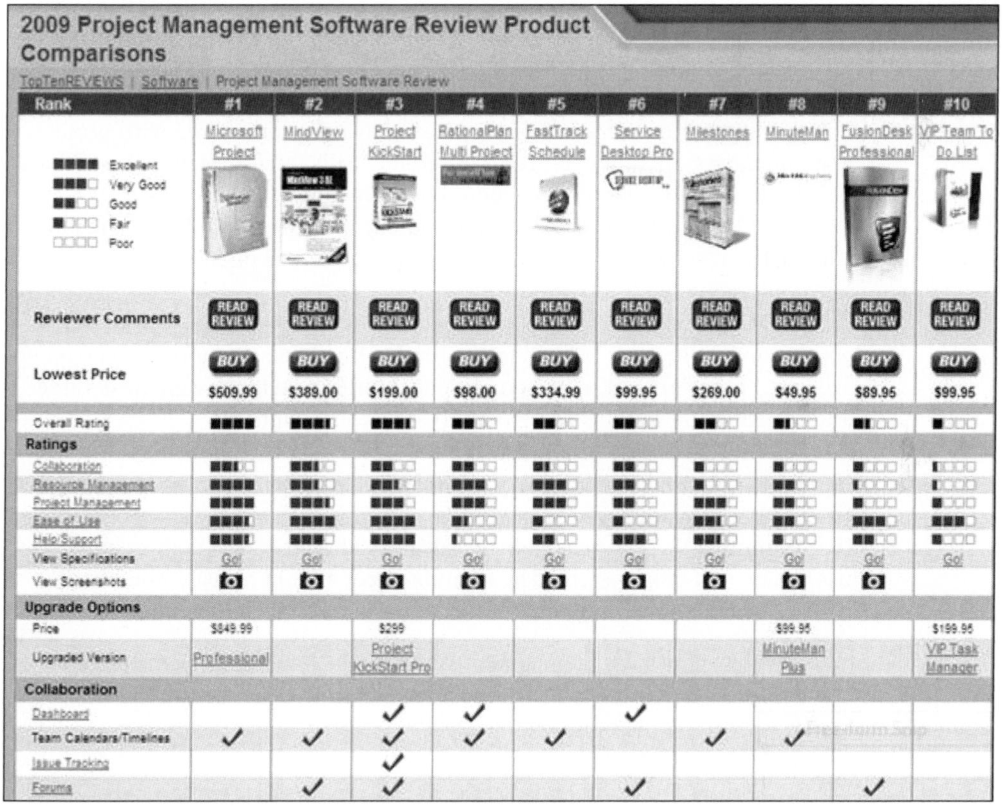

Rank	#1	#2	#3	#4	#5	#6	#7	#8	#9	#10
	Microsoft Project	MindView	Project KickStart	RationalPlan Multi Project	FastTrack Schedule	Service Desktop Pro	Milestones	MinuteMan	FusionDesk Professional	VIP Team To Do List
Reviewer Comments	READ REVIEW	READ REVIEW	READ REVIEW	READ REVIEW	READ REVIEW	READ REVIEW	READ REVIEW	READ REVIEW	READ REVIEW	READ REVIEW
Lowest Price	BUY $509.99	BUY $389.00	BUY $199.00	BUY $98.00	BUY $334.99	BUY $99.95	BUY $269.00	BUY $49.95	BUY $89.95	BUY $99.95
Overall Rating										
Ratings										
Collaboration										
Resource Management										
Project Management										
Ease of Use										
Help/Support										
View Specifications	Go!	Go!	Go!	Go!	Go!	Go!	Go!	Go!	Go!	Go!
View Screenshots	📷	📷	📷	📷	📷	📷	📷	📷	📷	
Upgrade Options										
Price	$849.99		$299					$99.95		$199.95
Upgraded Version	Professional		Project KickStart Pro					MinuteMan Plus		VIP Task Manager
Collaboration										
Dashboard			✓	✓		✓				
Team Calendars/Timelines	✓	✓	✓	✓	✓		✓	✓		
Issue Tracking			✓							
Forums		✓	✓			✓			✓	

2009 Project Management Software Review Product Comparisons

TopTenREVIEWS | Software | Project Management Software Review

Excellent
Very Good
Good
Fair
Poor

[1]TopTenREVIEWS™, "Project Management Software," (*project-management-software-review.toptenreviews.com*) (accessed June 17, 2009).

FIGURE A-1 Top ten project management software product comparisons

The products listed in the top ten include:

1. Microsoft Project
2. MindView
3. Project KickStart
4. RationalPlan Multi Project
5. FastTrack Schedule
6. Service Desktop Pro
7. Milestones
8. MinuteMan
9. FusionDesk Professional
10. VIP Team To Do List

Notice that Microsoft Project is number one on the list. Also notice its steep price back in 2009 of over $500 for a single user. Remember that students can purchase Microsoft Project and other software at greatly reduced rates from sites such as *www.journeyed.com*. You can also download a free trial of Project 2013 Professional (not Project Online, which cost $45 per user per month without an annual subscription, as of April 2013) and other software products or access them remotely via the Internet with your school's software license. Check with your school's IT department for more information.

Below are descriptions of the criteria for comparing the software products:

- **Collaboration:** How information and issues are communicated with project team members, including e-mail, conference calls, meetings, web-based locations, and more. Collaboration should be easy to use.
- **Resource Management:** Project management software should manage and control the resources needed to run a project, such as people, money, time, and equipment.
- **Project Management:** The process, practice, and activities needed to perform continuous evaluation, prioritization, budgeting, and selection of investments are key. Proper project management capabilities provide the greatest value and contribution to the strategic interest of your company.
- **Ease of Use:** All project management software has a learning curve, but the best have functions that are easy to find and simple enough for anyone to use from Day 1, Project 1.
- **Help/Support:** Project management software should offer a comprehensive user guide and help system. The manufacturer should provide e-mail addresses or telephone numbers for direct answers to technical questions.[1]

In addition to reviewing project management software in general, TopTenREVIEWS™ also compared online products in a separate category. These products require an Internet connection for use. Figure A-2 lists the top ten results for 2013.

The top ten products listed include:

1. Clarizen
2. Genius Project
3. Daptiv
4. Tenrox

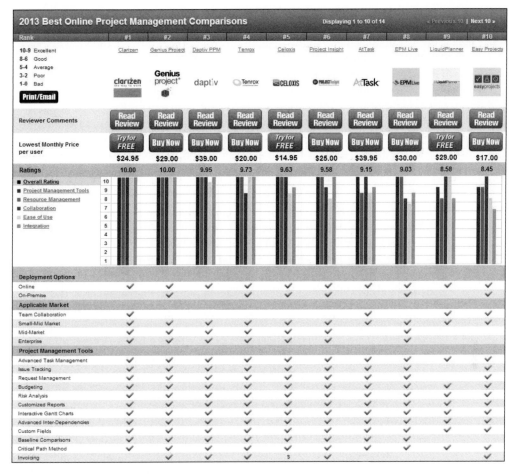

²TopTenREVIEWS™, "Best Online Project Management Comparisons," (*online-project-management-review. toptenreviews.com/*) (accessed April 7, 2013).

FIGURE A-2   Top ten online project management product comparisons[2]

    5. Celoxis
    6. Project Insight
    7. AtTask
    8. EPM Live
    9. Liquid Planner
    10. Easy Projects.net

TopTenREVIEWS™ only listed online project management tools in 2013, and their review was done before Microsoft's Project Online was released. Tools in this list provide the ability to create Gantt charts, numerous reports and views, project dashboards, and integrate with Microsoft Project files. See End Note 2 or visit the websites for any of these products and use a free trial version. Also note that there are many other tools available.

BASIC FEATURES OF PROJECT MANAGEMENT SOFTWARE

What makes project management software different from other software tools? Why not just use a spreadsheet or database to help manage projects?

You can do a lot of project management planning and tracking using non-project management software. You could use a simple word processor to list tasks, resources, dates, and so on. If you put that information into a spreadsheet, you can easily sort it, graph it, and perform other functions. A relational database tool could provide even more manipulation of data. You can use e-mail and other tools to collaborate with others.

However, project management software is designed specifically for managing projects, so it normally includes several distinct and important features not found in other software products:

- *Creating work breakdown structures, Gantt charts, and network diagrams*: A fundamental concept of project management is breaking down the scope of the project into a work breakdown structure (WBS). The WBS is the basis for creating the project schedule, normally shown as a Gantt chant. The Gantt chart shows start and end dates of tasks as well as dependencies between tasks, which are more clearly shown in a network diagram. Project management software makes it easy to create a WBS, Gantt chart, and network diagram. These features help the project manager and team visualize the project at various levels of detail.
- *Integrating scope, time, and cost data*: The WBS is a key tool for summarizing the scope of a project, and the Gantt chart summarizes the time or schedule for a project. Project management software allows you to assign cost and other resources to tasks on the WBS, which are tied to the schedule. This allows you to create a cost baseline and use earned value management to track project performance in terms of scope, time, and cost in an integrated fashion.
- *Setting a baseline and tracking progress*: Another important concept of project management is preparing a plan and measuring progress against the plan. Project management software lets you track progress for each task. The tracking Gantt chart is a nice tool for easily seeing the planned and actual schedule, and other views and reports show progress in other areas.
- *Providing other advanced project management features*: Project management software often provides other advanced features, such as setting up different types of scheduling dependencies, determining the critical path and slack for tasks, working with multiple projects, and leveling resources. For example, you can easily set up a task to start when its predecessor is halfway finished. After entering task dependencies, the software should easily show you the critical path and slack for each task. You can also set up multiple projects in a program and perform portfolio management analysis with some products. Many project management software products also allow you to easily adjust resources within their slack allowances to create a smoother resource distribution. These advanced features unique to project management are rarely found in other software tools.

As you can see, there are several important features that are unique to project management software that make them worth using. Next you'll learn what's new in Project 2013 and how to use its basic features.

WHAT'S NEW IN PROJECT 2013

If you are familiar with Project 2010 or an earlier version, it may be helpful to review some of the new features in Project 2013.

- *Improved reports*: With Project 2013, you can create professional reports and add pictures, charts, animation, and links to clearly share project status information. An entirely new set of pre-installed reports are available, including burn down reports, a popular chart used for agile projects. The earned value chart is also much easier to create.
- *New collaboration features*: You can stay in touch with team members by getting progress updates, asking questions, or having strategy discussions, all without leaving Project 2013. You can hover over a name and start an IM session, video chat, e-mail, or phone call. You must have Lync 2010 or later installed to take advantage of this feature.
- *Task paths*: You can now highlight any task and see its task path. All of the task's predecessor tasks show up in one color, and all of its successor tasks show up in another color.
- *Extended dates*: You can set task and project dates up to 12/31/2149.
- *Shared meetings*: If you export Project 2013 reports, timelines, or data to other Office programs, you can use the new sharing feature to join online meetings, share your PowerPoint slides, Word documents, Excel spreadsheets, and OneNote notes from any supported device, even if Office isn't installed.
- *Cloud storage*: You can easily save files to your own SkyDrive or to your organization's shared site. From there you can access and share your files from Project 2013 and other Office applications. Note that Project Online is delivered through Office 365 and used totally online.
- *Easy access*: If you have Project Online, Windows 7 (or later), and an Internet connection, you can access a full version of Project from any location, similar to the new Office applications.

Next, you will learn some basic information about Project 2013 and explore the main screen elements and Help facility.

USING PROJECT 2013

Before you can use Project 2013 or any project management software effectively, you must understand the fundamental concepts of project management, such as creating work breakdown structures (WBS), linking tasks, entering duration estimates, assigning resources, and so on. The purpose of this text is to provide specific instructions for using Project 2013 Professional. Consult Microsoft's website for detailed information on other products and other resources to help you understand project management concepts.

Before You Begin

This appendix assumes you are using Project 2013 with Windows 7 (or later) and are familiar with other Windows-based applications. Check your work by reviewing the many screen shots included in the steps, or by using the solution files that are available for download from the companion website or from your instructor.

> **N O T E**
>
> *You need to be running Windows 7 or later to use Project 2013, a 1 Ghz or greater x86/x64 processor with SSE2 instruction set, 1 GB RAM (32 Bit) / 2 GB RAM (64 Bit), and an up-to-date browser. Certain features require Internet connectivity.* You can read more detailed system requirements and download a free trial from Microsoft's website. Students can purchase a full version from sites like *www. journeyed.com* at a discount. Many colleges and universities provide the software to students either on campus or through remote access. If you can use remote access, the main requirement is Internet connectivity. Check with your instructor for details. You might also want to pay for monthly access to Project Online.

This appendix uses a fictitious project—Project A+—to illustrate how to use the software. The WBS for Project A+ uses the five project management process groups as level 2 items (initiating, planning, executing, monitoring and controlling, and closing). Standard deliverables under each of those process groups are included. Each section of the appendix includes hands-on activities for you to perform.

> **N O T E**
>
> To complete some of the hands-on activities in the appendix, you will need to download files from the companion website (*www.intropm.com*) to your computer. When you begin each set of steps, make sure you are using the correct file. Save the files you create yourself in a different folder so you do not write over the ones you download.

In addition, you will create the following files from scratch as you work through the steps:

- mywbs.mpp
- myschedule.mpp

You will also use the following file to create a hyperlink:

- stakeholder register.doc

Using the 60-Day Trial of Project 2013

If you plan to download the free trial, perform the following steps:

1. Search for Microsoft's site for downloading a free trial of Project 2013 (the site address changes periodically) and click the **Try on** button under Project Professional 2013.
2. Enter your account information. You do need a Microsoft account. It used to be called a Windows Live account, so you may already have one if you set it up for Xbox 360, SkyDrive, Office 2013, Office 365 or other items. If you do not have a Microsoft account, set one up for free.
3. Install Project 2013. The installation for Project 2013 is a bit different from past installations. Follow the instructions from Microsoft. The trial software is run through Microsoft's online environment, similar to Office 365.

Next you will learn how to start Project 2013, review the Help facility and a template file, and begin to plan Project A+.

Overview of Project 2013

The first step to mastering Project 2013 is to become familiar with the major screen elements and the Help facility. This section describes each of these features.

Starting Project 2013 and Getting Started

To start Project 2013:

1. *Open Project 2013.* There are slightly different methods for opening Project 2013 depending on your operating system. For example, in Windows 7, click the **Start** button on the taskbar, and then click **Project 2013 or type it in the search bar**. Alternatively, a shortcut or icon might be available on the desktop; in this case, double-click the icon to start the software.
2. *Review the Get Started feature.* Click **Get Started**, as shown in the upper right section of Figure A-3.

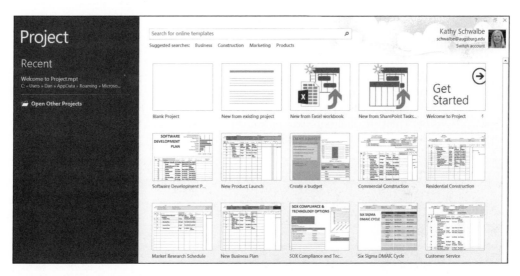

Created using Microsoft Project, used with permission from Microsoft.

FIGURE A-3   Project 2013 initial options – access Get Started

3. *Start the introduction.* Click **Create**, and then click **Start**, as shown in Figure A-4.

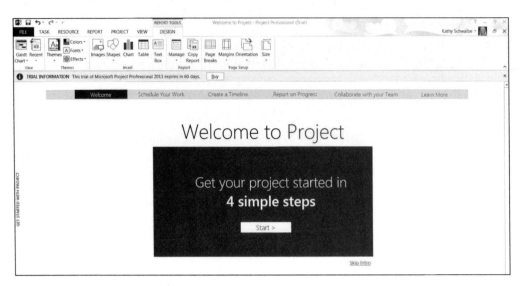

Created using Microsoft Project, used with permission from Microsoft.

FIGURE A-4   Project 2013 Get Started introductory screen

4. *Review the "4 simple steps" Microsoft lists for using Project 2013.* Review the first step, called Schedule your work, as shown in Figure A-5. Review the other steps by clicking **Next**, as shown in Figures A-6–A-8.

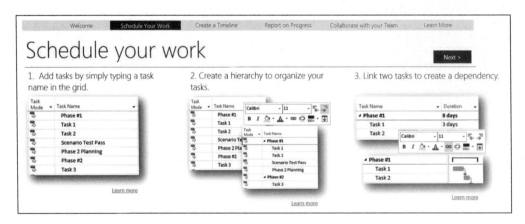

Created using Microsoft Project, used with permission from Microsoft.

FIGURE A-5   Schedule your work screen

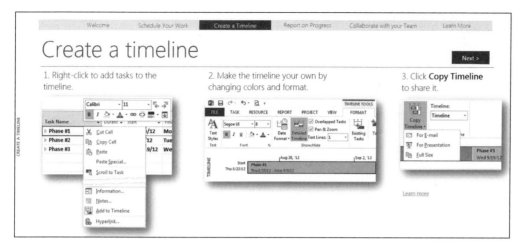

Created using Microsoft Project, used with permission from Microsoft.

FIGURE A-6 Create a timeline screen

Created using Microsoft Project, used with permission from Microsoft.

FIGURE A-7 Report on progress screen

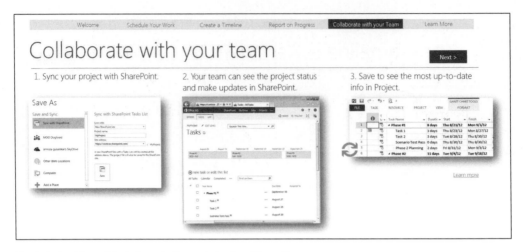

Created using Microsoft Project, used with permission from Microsoft.

FIGURE A-8   Collaborate with your team screen

5. *Explore Help features*. The last screen of Getting Started, **Learn More**, as shown in Figure A-9, provides links to the Project 2013 Getting Started Center (which includes a short video on what's new that is worth watching) and the Project blog. The help feature (question mark in the upper right of the screen) also includes a lot of helpful resources.

Created using Microsoft Project, used with permission from Microsoft.

FIGURE A-9   Learn More screen

Understanding the Main Screen Elements

To open a blank file:

1. *Open a blank file*. Click the **File** tab, **New**, and then click the first option, **Blank Project.**
2. *Examine the main screen*. Review the main screen elements, as shown in Figure A-10. Look at some of the elements of the screen.

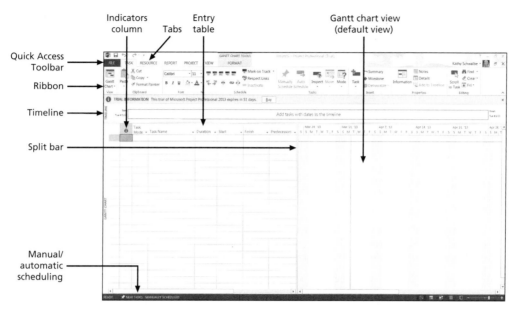

Created using Microsoft Project, used with permission from Microsoft.

FIGURE A-10   Project 2013 main screen

- The Ribbon, tabs, and Quick Access toolbar are similar to other Office applications.
- The timeline view is displayed below the ribbon.
- The default manual scheduling for new tasks is on the lower left of the screen. You can click that option to switch to automatic scheduling.
- The default view is the Gantt chart view, which shows tasks and other information as well as a calendar display. You can access other views by clicking the View icon on the far left side of the ribbon.
- The areas where you enter information in a spreadsheet-like table are part of the Entry table. For example, you can see entry areas for Task Name, Duration, Start, Finish, and Predecessors.
- You can make the Entry table more or less wide by using the Split bar. When you move the mouse over the split bar, your cursor changes to the resize pointer. Clicking and dragging the split bar to the right reveals columns for Resource Names and Add New columns.
- The first column in the Entry table is the Indicators column. The Indicators column displays indicators or symbols related to items associated with each task, such as task notes or hyperlinks to other files. The second column displays if a task is manually or automatically scheduled, as described later in this appendix.
- The file name displays centered at the top of the screen. When you open a Blank Project after starting Project 2013, it opens a new file named Project1, which is shown in the title bar. If you open a second Blank Project, the name will be Project2, and so on, until you save and rename the file.

Using Project Help and the Project Website

To access information to help you learn how to use Project 2013:

> 1. *Access Project Help.* Click the **question mark/help icon** on the upper side of the ribbon. The Project Help screen displays, as shown in Figure A-11. Remember that this feature requires an Internet connection.

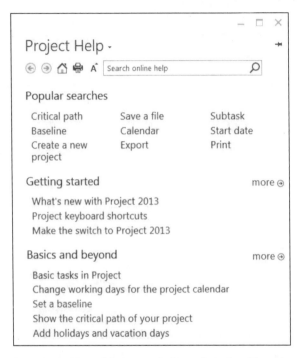

Created using Microsoft Project, used with permission from Microsoft.

FIGURE A-11   Topics under Project help

> 2. *Explore various help topics.* Click the Project Help link called **"What's new with Project 2013."** Microsoft provides short videos, steps, templates, articles, and other features to help you learn to use this powerful software. Watch the short video, read the other information on the page, and explore links for more help.
>
> 3. *Close Project 2013.* Click the **Close icon** (X in the upper right of the screen) to exit Project 2013.

Many features in Project 2013 are similar to ones in other Windows programs. For example, to collapse or expand tasks, click the appropriate symbols to the left of the task name. To access shortcut items, right-click in either the Entry table area or the Gantt chart. Many of the Entry table operations in Project 2013 are very similar to operations in Excel. For example, to adjust a column width, click and drag between the column heading titles.

Next, you will get some hands-on experience by opening an existing file to explore various screen elements. Project 2013 comes with several template files, and you can also access templates from Microsoft Office Online or other websites.

EXPLORING PROJECT 2013 USING AN EXISTING FILE

To open a template file and adjust Project 2013 screen elements:

1. *Open Project 2013 and select the Customer Service template file.* Click the **Start** button on the taskbar, select **Project 2013, click Customer Service, and then click Create. These screen shots were taken on April 3, 2013, so you can enter that date if you like. Your screen should resemble** Figure A-12. **(Note: If you cannot find the template, you can download it from** *www. intropm.com* **and open it. To open an existing file,** click the **File tab, then** select **Open,** and browse to find the file.)

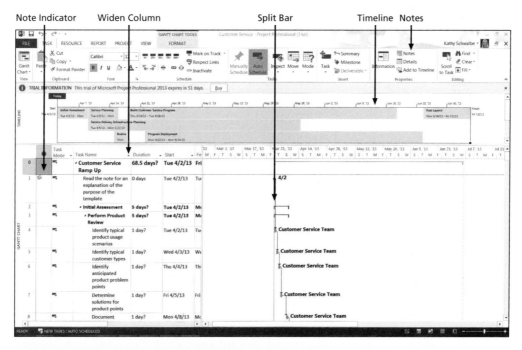

Created using Microsoft Project, used with permission from Microsoft.

FIGURE A-12   Customer Service template file

2. *Widen the Task Name column.* Move the **cursor** between the Task Name and Duration columns, and then **double-click** to widen the Task Name column so all of the text shows in one line.
3. *Move the Split Bar.* Move the **Split Bar** to the right so the entire Task Name column text is visible, but not the Duration column. The default table view is the Entry table.

4. *View the first Note.* Move your cursor over the yellow **Notes** symbol in the Indicators column for Task 1 to read it. You can insert notes by any task.

To show different WBS levels:

1. *Select Outline Level 1 to display WBS level 2 tasks.* Click the **View** tab and then the **Outline** button's list arrow, and then click **Outline Level 1**. Notice that only the level 2 WBS items display in the Entry table. The black bars on the Gantt chart represent the summary tasks. Recall that the entire project is normally referred to as WBS level 1, and the next highest level is called level 2.

2. *Adjust the timescale.* Click the **Zoom out** button (minus sign) on the left side of the Zoom slider on the lower right of the screen, as shown in Figure A-13. Notice the milestone task in row 143 indicating the project completion date. Recall that the black diamond symbol on a Gantt chart shows milestones.

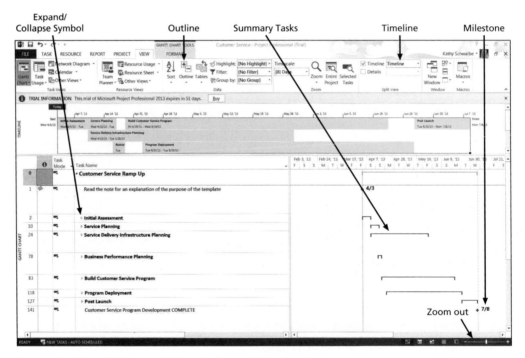

Created using Microsoft Project, used with permission from Microsoft.

FIGURE A-13 Showing part of the WBS on the Gantt chart

3. *Expand a task.* Click the **expand symbol** to the left of **Task 2**, Initial Assessment, to see its subtasks. Click the **collapse symbol** to hide its subtasks. Experiment with expanding and collapsing other tasks and resizing other columns.

4. *View all tasks*. Click the **Outline** button and select **All Subtasks** to see all of the items in the **Task Name** column again.

5. *Remove the Timeline*. Click the **Timeline** checkbox on the Ribbon to unselect it. Click it again to display it.

6. *Close the file without saving*. Click the **Close** icon in the upper right of the window, and select **No** when prompted to save the file.

Project 2013 Views

Project 2013 provides many ways to display or view project information. In addition to the default Gantt chart, you can view the network diagram, calendar, and task usage views, to name a few. These views allow you to analyze project information in different ways. The View tab also provides access to different tables that display information in various ways. In addition to the default Entry table view, you can access tables that focus on data related to areas such as the Schedule, Cost, Tracking, and Earned Value.

To access and explore different views:

1. *Explore the Network Diagram for the Customer Service file. Open the* **Customer Service** *file again. Click the* **Network Diagram** *button under the View tab, and then move the* **Zoom slider** *on the lower right of the screen all the way to the left. Your screen should resemble Figure A-14. Critical tasks display in red.*

Network Diagram

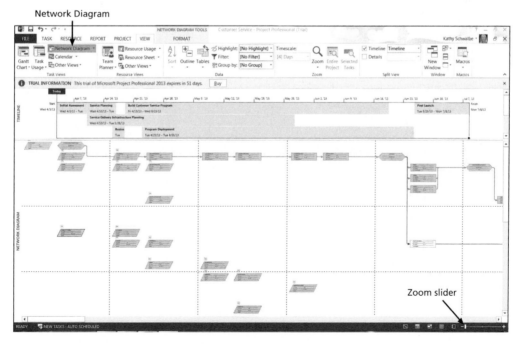

Created using Microsoft Project, used with permission from Microsoft.

FIGURE A-14 Network diagram view of Customer Service file

2. *Explore the Calendar view*. Click the **Calendar** button (under the Network Diagram button). Notice that the screen lists tasks each day in a calendar format.

3. *Change the table view*. Click the **Gantt Chart** button on the ribbon, click the **Tables** button under the View tab, and then click **Schedule**. Figure A-15 shows the table view options.

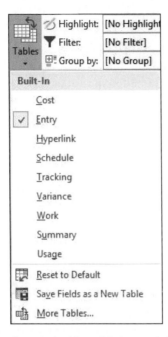

Created using Microsoft Project, used with permission from Microsoft.

FIGURE A-15   Table view options

4. *Examine the Schedule table and other views*. Select the **Schedule** table view and move the **Split bar** to the right to review the Total Slack column. Notice that the columns in the table to the left of the Gantt chart, as shown in Figure A-16, now display more detailed schedule information, such as Late Start, Late Finish, Free Slack, and Total Slack. Remember that you can widen columns by double-clicking the resize pointer to the right of that column. You can also move the split bar to reveal more or fewer columns. Experiment with other table views, then return to the **Entry** table view.

Created using Microsoft Project, used with permission from Microsoft.

FIGURE A-16   Schedule table view

Project 2013 Reports

Project 2013 provides many ways to report project information as well. In addition to traditional reports, you can also prepare visual reports, with both available under the Report tab. Note that the visual reports often require that you have other Microsoft application software, such as Excel and Visio. Project 2013 automatically formats reports for ease of printing.

To access and explore different reports:

1. *Explore the Reports feature.* Click the **Report** tab to see the variety of reports available in Project 2013.
2. *View the Project Overview report.* Click **Dashboards**, and then click **Project Overview**. Review the report and new options on the ribbon, as shown in Figure A-17.

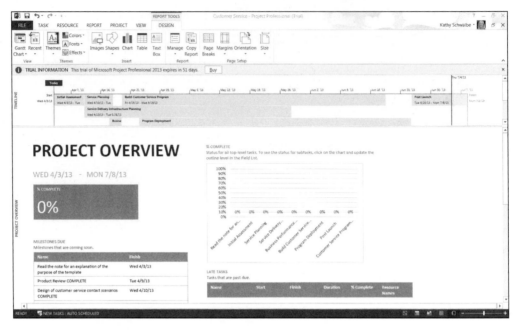

Created using Microsoft Project, used with permission from Microsoft.

FIGURE A-17 Project Overview report

> 3. *Open the Resource Overview report.* Click the **Report tab again**, click **Resources**, and then click **Resource Overview**. Review the report, as shown in Figure A-18.

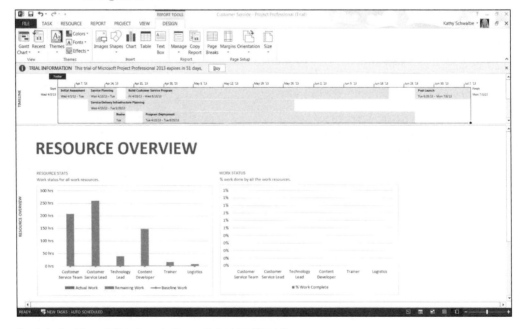

Created using Microsoft Project, used with permission from Microsoft.

FIGURE A-18 Resource Overview report

4. *Examine the report and experiment with others.* Click the **Report** tab, click **In Progress**, and then click **Critical Tasks** to display the Critical Tasks report, as shown in Figure A-19. Examine other reports.

5. *Return to the Gantt chart.* Click the **View tab, and then click Gantt Chart** to return to the Gantt chart view. You can close the file without saving it if you wish to take a break.

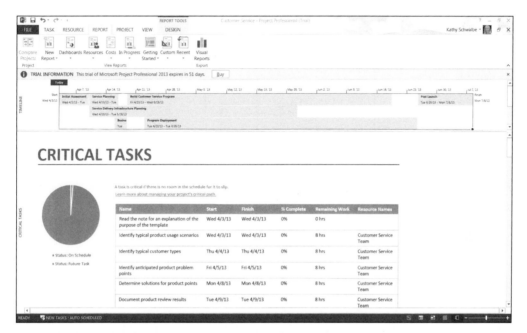

Created using Microsoft Project, used with permission from Microsoft.

FIGURE A-19   Critical tasks report

Project 2013 Filters

Project 2013 uses a relational database to filter, sort, store, and display information. Filtering project information is very useful. For example, if a project includes thousands of tasks, you might want to view only summary or milestone tasks to get a high-level view of the project by using the Milestones or Summary Tasks filter from the Filter list. You can select a filter that shows only tasks on the critical path if that is what you want to see. Other filters include Completed Tasks, Late/Overbudget Tasks, and Date Range, which displays tasks based on dates you provide. As shown earlier, you can also click the Show button on the toolbar to display different levels in the WBS quickly.

To explore Project 2013 filters:

1. *Access filters.* Click the **View** tab, if necessary, and make sure the Customer Service file is in the Gantt Chart: Table Entry view. Click the **Filter list arrow** (under the Data group), as shown in Figure A-20. The default filter is No Filter, which shows all tasks.

Filter list arrow

Created using Microsoft Project, used with permission from Microsoft.

FIGURE A-20 Using a filter

2. *Filter to show milestones.* Click **Milestones** in the list of filters. Notice that the Gantt chart only shows the summary tasks and milestones for the project. Your screen should resemble Figure A-21. Recall that milestones are significant events.
3. *Show critical tasks.* Select **No Filter** from the Filter list box to reveal all the tasks in the WBS again. Click the **Filter** list arrow, and then click **Critical**. Now only the critical tasks appear in the WBS. Experiment with other filters.
4. *Close the file.* When you are finished reviewing the Customer Service file, click **Close** from the File tab or click the **Close** button. Click **No** when asked if you want to save changes.
5. *Exit Project 2013.* Click the **Close** button for Project 2013.

Now that you are familiar with the main screen elements, views, reports, and filters, you will learn how to use Project 2013 to create a new file.

Created using Microsoft Project, used with permission from Microsoft.

FIGURE A-21   Milestones filter applied

CREATING A NEW FILE AND ENTERING TASKS IN A WORK BREAKDOWN STRUCTURE

To create a new Project 2013 file, you must first name the project, enter the start date, and then enter the tasks. The list of tasks and their hierarchy is the work breakdown structure (WBS). The file you create could be used for a class project which lasts approximately three months. It uses the project management process groups to reinforce use of several project management deliverables described in this text. You could modify this file to meet your specific needs.

> ### NOTE
>
> In this section, you will go through several steps to create a new Project 2013 file named mywbs.mpp. If you want to download the completed file to check your work or continue to the next section, a copy of mywbs.mpp is available on the companion website at *www.intropm.com*. Try to complete an entire section of this appendix (entering tasks in a work breakdown structure, developing the schedule, and so on) in one sitting to create the complete file.

Creating a New Project File

To create a new project file:

1. *Create a blank project.* Open Project 2013 and click **Blank Project**. A blank project file opens with a default filename of Project1, Project2, and so on.

(If Project 2013 is already open and you want to open a new file, click the **File tab**, select **New**, and then **Blank Project**.)

2. *Open the Project Information dialog box.* Click the **Project** tab, and then click **Project Information** to display the Project Information dialog box, as shown in Figure A-22. This dialog box enables you to set dates for the project, select the calendar to use, and view project statistics. The project start date will default to the current date. Note that in Figure A-22 the file was created on 4/3/13 and a Start date of 9/9/13 was entered.

Start date
text box   Current date

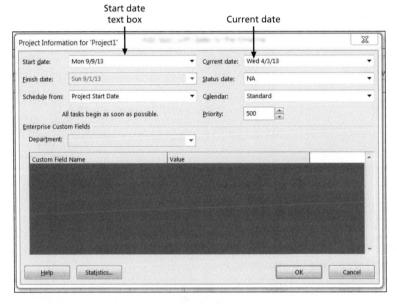

Created using Microsoft Project, used with permission from Microsoft.

FIGURE A-22   Project information dialog box

N O T E

All dates are entered in month/day/year or American format. You can change the date format by selecting Options from the File tab. Click the date format you want to use in the Date Format box under the General settings. You can also customize the Ribbon, change default currencies in the display, and so on under Project Options.

3. *Enter the project start date.* In the Start date text box, enter **9/9/13**. Setting your project start date to 9/9/13 will ensure that your work matches the results that appear in this appendix. Leave the Current date and other information at the default settings. Click **OK or press Enter**.

4. *Enter advanced project properties.* Click the **File** tab, and then click **Info**. Click **Project Information** on the right side of the screen, and then click **Advanced Properties**. Enter **Project A+** for the title, if you want to change the title. You can also enter a subject, author, and other information as desired. Click the **left arrow** at the top left of the screen to go back to the previous screen.

Creating a Work Breakdown Structure Hierarchy

As mentioned earlier, a work breakdown structure (WBS) is a fundamental part of project management. Developing a good WBS takes time, and it will make entering tasks into the Entry table easier if you develop the WBS first. For this example, you will use the project management process groups as the level 2 items and add some key deliverables and milestones under each one. You will use the information in Figure A-23 to enter tasks. Note that Microsoft Project uses the term tasks instead of deliverables or activities or milestones, so it is also used in this appendix.

Order	Task Name	Order	Task Name
1. Initiating	16. Deliverable 2
2. Stakeholder identification	17. Deliverable 3
3. Stakeholder register completed	18. Deliverable 1 completed
4. Stakeholder management strategy completed	19. Deliverable 2 completed
5. Project charter	20. Deliverable 3 completed
6. Project charter completed	21. Monitoring and Controlling
7. Kickoff meeting	22. Actual hours tracking
8. Kickoff meeting completed	23. Project documents updates
9. Planning	24. Progress report 1
10. Schedule	25. Progress report 2
11. Gantt chart completed	26. Team review meetings
12. Scope statement	27. Closing
13. Initial scope statement completed	28. Final project report
14. Executing	29. Final project presentation
15. Deliverable 1	30. Project completed

Schwalbe Publishing 2013.

FIGURE A-23 Task list for Project A+

To develop a WBS for the project:

1. *Enter task names.* Enter the 30 items in Figure A-23 into the Task Name column in the order shown. To not have the text wrap, click the **Format** Tab, click **Column Settings**, and then click **Wrap Text** to turn it off. Do not worry about durations or any other information at this time. Type the name of each item into the Task Name column of the Entry table, beginning with the first row. Press **Enter** or the **down arrow** key on your keyboard to move to the next row.

HELP

If you accidentally skip a row, highlight the task row, right-click, and select Insert Task. To edit a task entry, click the text for that task, and either type over the old text or edit the existing text. Entering tasks in Project 2013 and editing the information is similar to entering and editing data in an Excel spreadsheet. You can also easily copy and paste text from Excel or Word into Project, such as the list of tasks.

2. *Adjust the Task Name column width as needed.* To make all the text display in the Task Name column, move the cursor over the right-column gridline in the **Task Name** column heading until you see the resize pointer, and then click the **left mouse** button and drag the line to the right to make the column wider, or double-click to adjust the column width automatically.

This WBS separates tasks according to the project management process groups of initiating, planning, executing, controlling, and closing. These categories will be the level 2 items in the WBS for this project. (Remember the whole project is level 1.) It is a good idea to include all of these process groups because there are important deliverables that must be done under each of them. Recall that the WBS should include *all* of the work required for the project. In the Project A+ WBS, the WBS will be purposefully left at a high level (level 3). You will create these levels, or the WBS hierarchy, next when you create summary tasks. For a real project, you would usually break the WBS into even more levels and then enter activities to provide more details to describe all the work involved in the project. For example, each deliverable would probably have several levels, activities, and milestones under it. You can review other Project 2013 template files or other sources for more information.

Creating Summary Tasks

After entering the items listed in Figure A-23 into the Entry table, the next step is to show the WBS levels by creating summary tasks. The summary tasks in this example are Tasks 1 (initiating), 9 (planning), 14 (executing), 21 (monitoring and controlling), and 27 (closing). You create summary tasks by highlighting and indenting their respective subtasks.

To create the summary tasks:

1. *Select lower level or subtasks.* Highlight **Tasks 2** through **8** by clicking the cell for Task 2 and dragging the mouse through the cells to Task 8.
2. *Indent subtasks.* Click the **Indent Task** button on the Ribbon under the Schedule group of the Task tab (or press Alt + Shift + right arrow) so your screen resembles Figure A-24. After the subtasks (Tasks 2 through 8) are indented, notice that Task 1 automatically becomes boldface, which indicates that it is a summary task. A collapse symbol appears to the left of the new summary task name. Clicking the collapse symbol (filled triangle sign) will collapse the summary task and hide the subtasks beneath it. When subtasks are hidden, an expand symbol (unfilled triangle sign) appears to the left of the summary task name. Clicking the expand symbol will expand the summary task. Also, notice that the symbol for the summary task on the Gantt chart has changed from a blue to a black line with arrows indicating the start and

end dates. The Task Mode has also changed to make this task Automatically scheduled. You'll learn more about this feature later. For now, focus on entering and indenting the tasks to create the WBS.

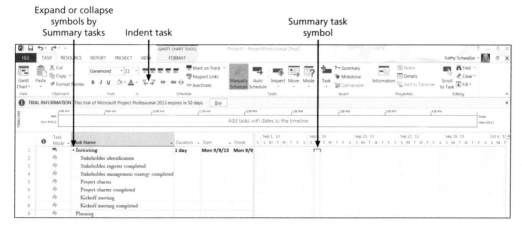

Created using Microsoft Project, used with permission from Microsoft.

FIGURE A-24 Indenting tasks to create the WBS hierarchy

3. *Create other summary tasks and subtasks*. Create subtasks and summary tasks for the other process groups by following the same steps. Indent **Tasks 10** through **13** to make Task 9 a summary task. Indent **Tasks 15** through **20** to make Task 14 a summary task. Indent **Tasks 22** through **26** to make Task 21 a summary task. Indent **Tasks 28** through **30** to make Task 27 a summary task. Widen the Task Name column to see all of your text, as needed.

TIP

To change a task from a subtask to a summary task or to change its level in the WBS, you can "outdent" the task. To outdent the task, click the cell of the task or tasks you want to change, and then click the Outdent Task button (the button just to the left of the Indent Task button). You can also press Alt + Shift + Right Arrow to indent tasks and Alt + Shift + Left Arrow to outdent tasks.

Numbering Tasks

To display automatic numbering of tasks using the standard tabular numbering system for a WBS:

1. *Show outline numbers*. Click **the Format tab**, and then click the **Outline Number checkbox** under the Show/Hide group. Project 2013 adds the appropriate WBS numbering to the task names.
2. *Show project summary task*. Click the Project Summary Task checkbox just below the Outline Number checkbox. Scroll to the top of the file to see that a new task, Project A+, the title of the project, has been added under row 0. Your file should resemble Figure A-25.

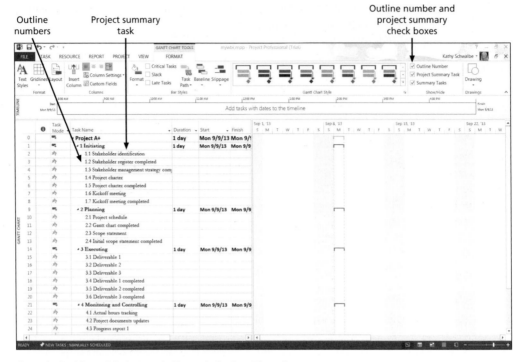

Created using Microsoft Project, used with permission from Microsoft.

FIGURE A-25   Adding automatic outline numbers and a project summary task

Saving Project Files Without a Baseline

An important part of project management is tracking performance against a baseline, or approved plan. It is important to wait until you are ready to save your file with a baseline because Project 2013 will show changes against a baseline. Since you are still developing your project file for the Project A+ project, you want to save the file without a baseline, which is the default way to save a file. Later in this appendix, you will save the file with a baseline. You will then enter actual information to compare planned and actual performance data.

To save a file without a baseline:

1. *Save your file.* Click the **File** tab and then click **Save**, or click the **Save** button on the Quick Access toolbar.
2. *Enter a filename.* In the Save dialog box, type **mywbs** in the File name text box. Browse to the location in which you want to save the file, and then click **Save**. Remember that you can move the Split bar to show more or fewer columns.
3. *Close Project 2013.* Click the Close icon to exit Project 2013.

HELP

If you want to download the Project 2013 file mywbs.mpp to check your work or continue to the next section, a copy is available on the companion website at *www.intropm.com*.

DEVELOPING THE SCHEDULE

Many people use Project 2013 for its scheduling features. The first step in using these features, after inputting the WBS for the project, is to change calendars, if needed, and then enter durations for tasks or specific dates when tasks will occur. You must also enter task dependencies in order for schedules to adjust automatically and to do critical path analysis. After entering durations and task dependencies, you can view the network diagram, critical path, and slack information.

Calendars

The standard Project 2013 calendar assumes that working hours are Monday through Friday, from 8:00 a.m. to 5:00 p.m., with an hour for lunch from noon until 1:00 p.m. In addition to the standard calendar, Project 2013 also includes a 24 Hours calendar and Night Shift calendar. The 24 Hours calendar assumes resources can work any hour and any day of the week. The Night Shift calendar assumes working hours are Monday through Saturday, from 12:00 a.m. to 3:00 a.m., 4:00 a.m. 8 a.m., and 11 p.m. to 12 a.m. You can create a different base calendar to meet your unique project requirements.

To create a new base calendar:

1. *Open a new file and access the Change Working Time dialog box.* With Project 2013 open, click the **Project** tab, and then click the **Change Working Time** button under the Properties group. The Change Working Time dialog box opens, as shown in Figure A-26.
2. *Name the new base calendar.* In the Change Working Time dialog box, click **Create New Calendar**. The Create New Base Calendar dialog box opens. Click the **Create new base calendar** radio button, type **Fiscal** as the name of the new calendar in the **Name** text box, and then click **OK**.
3. *Change the fiscal year start.* In the Change Working Time dialog box, click **Options** at the bottom of the screen. Change the **fiscal year** to start in October instead of January. Review other options in this screen, and then click **OK twice**.

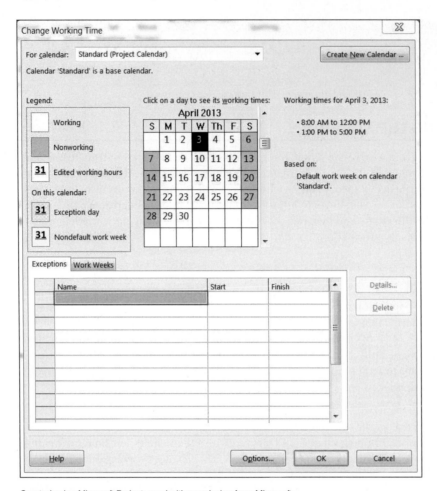

Created using Microsoft Project, used with permission from Microsoft.

FIGURE A-26 Change Working Time dialog box

You can use this new calendar for the whole project, or you can assign it to specific resources on the project.

To assign the new calendar to the whole project:

1. *Open the Project Information dialog box.* Click the **Project** tab, and then click the **Change Working Time** button.
2. *Select a new calendar.* Click the **For calendar** list arrow to display a list of available calendars. Select your new calendar named **Fiscal** from this list, and then click **OK**.

To assign a specific calendar to a specific resource:

1. *Assign a new calendar.* Click the **View** tab, and then click the **Resource Sheet** button under the Resource Views group. Type **Adam** in the Resource Name column, press **Enter**, and then select the word **Adam**.

2. *Select the calendar.* Click the cell under the **Base** column that says **Standard** on the right part of the screen for Adam. Click the list arrow to display the options, and then select **Fiscal** as shown in Figure A-27.

Resource Name	Type	Material	Initials	Group	Max.	Std. Rate	Ovt. Rate	Cost/Use	Accrue	Base
Adam	Work		A		100%	$0.00/hr	$0.00/hr	$0.00	Prorated	Fiscal

Created using Microsoft Project, used with permission from Microsoft.

FIGURE A-27   Changing calendars for specific resources

3. *Block off vacation time.* Double-click the resource name **Adam** to display the Resource Information dialog box, and then click the **Change Working Time** button, located on the General tab in the Resource Information dialog box. You can block off vacation time for people by selecting the appropriate days on the calendar and marking them as nonworking days. Click **OK** to accept your changes, and then click **OK** to close the Resource Information dialog box.
4. *Close the file without saving it.* Click the **Close** box, and then click **No** when you are prompted to save the file.

Task Durations

Recall that duration includes the actual amount of time spent working on an activity plus elapsed time. Duration does not equal effort. For example, you might have an activity that you estimate will take one person 40 hours of effort to complete, but you allow two weeks on a calendar for its duration. You can simply enter 2w (for two weeks) in the Duration column for that activity (called a task in Project 2013).

Manual and Automatic Scheduling

If you have used earlier versions of Project, you probably noticed that when you entered an item in the Task Name column, it was automatically assigned a duration of one day, and Start and Finish dates were also automatically entered. This is still the case in Project 2013 if you use automatic scheduling for a task. If you use manual scheduling, no durations or dates are automatically entered. The other big change with manual scheduling is that summary task durations are not automatically calculated based on their subtasks when they are set up as manually scheduled tasks. Figure A-28 illustrates these differences. Notice that the Manual subtask 1 had no information entered for its duration, start, or finish dates. Also note that the duration for Manual summary task 1's duration is not dependent on the durations of its subtasks. For the automatic summary task, its duration is dependent on its summary tasks, and information is entered for all of the durations, start, and end dates. You can switch between automatic and manual scheduling for tasks in the same file, as desired, by changing the Task Mode.

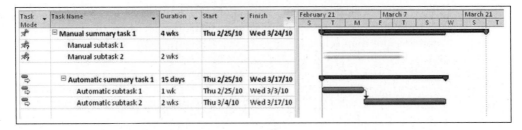

Task Mode	Task Name	Duration	Start	Finish	February 21			March 7			March 21	
					S	T	M	F	T	S	W	S	T
	⊟ Manual summary task 1	4 wks	Thu 2/25/10	Wed 3/24/10									
	Manual subtask 1												
	Manual subtask 2	2 wks											
	⊟ Automatic summary task 1	15 days	Thu 2/25/10	Wed 3/17/10									
	Automatic subtask 1	1 wk	Thu 2/25/10	Wed 3/3/10									
	Automatic subtask 2	2 wks	Thu 3/4/10	Wed 3/17/10									

Created using Microsoft Project, used with permission from Microsoft.

FIGURE A-28   Manual versus automatic scheduling

When you move your cursor over the Task Mode column (shown in the far left in Figure A-28) Project 2013 displays the following information:

- A task can be either Manually Scheduled or Automatically Scheduled.
- Manually Scheduled tasks have user-defined Start, Finish, and Duration values. Project will never change their dates, but may warn you if there are potential issues with the entered values.
- Automatically Scheduled tasks have Start, Finish, and Duration values calculated by Project based on dependencies, constraints, calendars, and other factors.

Project Help provides the following example of using both manual and automatic scheduling. You set up a preliminary project plan that's still in the proposal stage. You have a vague idea of major milestone dates but not much detail on other dates in various phases of the project. You build tasks and milestones using the Manually Scheduled task mode. The proposal is accepted and the tasks and deliverable dates become more defined. You continue to manually schedule those tasks and dates for a while, but as certain phases become well-defined, you decide to switch the tasks in those phases to the Automatically Scheduled task mode. By letting Project 2013 handle the complexities of scheduling, you can focus your attention on those phases that are still under development.

Duration Units and Guidelines for Entering Durations

To indicate the length of a task's duration, you normally type both a number and an appropriate duration symbol. If you type only a number, Project 2013 automatically enters days as the duration unit. Duration unit symbols include:

- d = days (default)
- w = weeks
- m = minutes
- h = hours
- mo or mon = months
- ed = elapsed days
- ew = elapsed weeks

For example, to enter two weeks for a task's duration, type 2w in the Duration column. (You can also type wk, wks, week, or weeks, instead of just w.) To enter four days for a task's duration, type 4 or 4d in the Duration column. You can also enter elapsed times in the Duration column. For example, 3ed means three elapsed days, and 2ew means two elapsed weeks.

You would use an elapsed duration for a task like "Allow cement to dry." The cement will dry in exactly the same amount of time regardless of whether it is a workday, a weekend, or a holiday. Project's default calendar does not assume that work is done on weekends. You will learn to change the calendar later in this appendix.

It is important to follow a few important rules when entering durations:

- To mark a task as a milestone, enter 0 for the duration. You can also mark tasks that have a non-zero duration as milestones by checking the "Mark task as milestone" option in the Task Information dialog box on the Advanced tab. You simply double-click a task to access this dialog box. The milestone symbol for those tasks will appear at their start date.
- You can enter the exact start and finish dates for activities instead of entering durations in the automatic scheduling mode. To enter start and finish dates, move the split bar to the right to reveal the Start and Finish columns. You normally only enter start and finish dates in this mode when those dates are certain.
- If you want task dates to adjust according to any other task dates, do not enter exact start and finish dates. Instead, enter durations and then establish dependencies to related tasks.
- To enter recurring tasks, such as weekly meetings, select Recurring Task from the Task button under the Task tab, Insert group. Enter the task name, the duration, and when the task occurs. Project 2013 will automatically insert appropriate subtasks based on the length of the project and the number of tasks required for the recurring task.
- Project 2013 uses a default calendar with standard workdays and hours. Remember to change the default calendar if needed, as shown earlier.

Next, you will set task durations in the file that you created and saved in the previous section. If you did not create the file named mywbs.mpp, you can download it from the companion website.

Use the information in Figure A-29 to enter durations. The Project 2013 row number is shown to the left of each task name in the table.

Task Row	Task Name	Duration
2	Stakeholder identification	1w
3	Stakeholder register completed	0
4	Stakeholder management strategy completed	0
5	Project charter	1w
6	Project charter completed	0
7	Kickoff meeting	3d
8	Kickoff meeting completed	0
10	Project schedule	5d
11	Gantt chart completed	0
12	Scope statement	8d
13	Initial scope statement completed	0
15	Deliverable 1	3w
16	Deliverable 2	5w
17	Deliverable 3	6w
18	Deliverable 1 completed	0
19	Deliverable 2 completed	0
20	Deliverable 3 completed	0
24	Progress report 1	0
25	Progress report 2	0
28	Final project report	4d
29	Final presentation	4d
30	Project completed	0

Schwalbe Publishing 2013.

FIGURE A-29   Task durations

Entering Task Durations

To enter task durations:

1. *Enter the duration for Task 2*. Open the mywbs file, and move the split bar to the right, if needed, to reveal the Duration, Start, and Finish columns. Click the **Duration** column for row 2, Stakeholder identification, type **1w**, and then press **Enter**. Notice that the duration for the first task, Initiating, also changed since it is a summary task and is an Automatically scheduled task,

as shown in the Task Mode column. When you created summary tasks earlier, Project changed their scheduling mode to Automatic. Also notice that the Start and Finish date for Task 2 remain blank, since that task is a Manually scheduled task.

2. *Enter the duration for Task 3.* In the **Duration** column for row 3, Stakeholder register completed, type **0**, and then press **Enter**. Remember that a task with zero duration is a milestone. Notice the milestone or diamond symbol next to the date 9/9 that appears on the Gantt chart, as shown in Figure A-30. Adjust the Task Name column width to see all of the text, and use the Zoom slider on the bottom right of the screen to change the length of the Gantt chart bars.

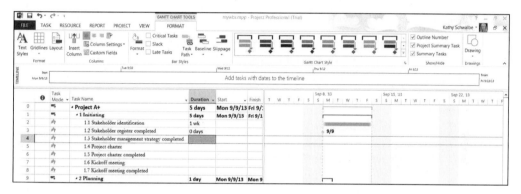

Created using Microsoft Project, used with permission from Microsoft.

FIGURE A-30   Entering task durations

3. *Make all tasks Automatically scheduled tasks.* To save time because you do want most of the tasks to be automatically scheduled, select all of the tasks by clicking the **Task Name** column heading, and then click the **Auto Schedule** button under the **Task** tab, Tasks group. Most of the durations change to 1.

4. *Enter remaining task durations.* Continue to enter the durations using the information in Figure A-29 or Figure A-31. Do not enter durations for tasks not listed in the figure. Notice that the Planning Wizard dialog box displays when you make the same entry several times in a row, such as after task 20. Click OK to close the dialog box. You can adjust the column widths and Zoom, if desired.

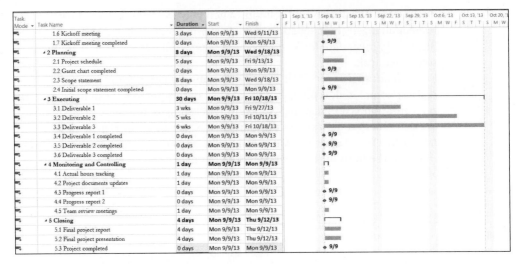

Created using Microsoft Project, used with permission from Microsoft.

FIGURE A-31   Entering more durations

5. *Insert a recurring task above Task 26, Team meetings.* Click **Team review meetings** (Task 26) in the Task Name column to select that task. Click **the Task tab, and click the Task button** drop-down box under the Insert group, and then click **Recurring Task**. The Recurring Task Information dialog box opens.

6. *Enter task and duration information for the recurring task.* Type **Team review meetings** as the task title in the Task Name text box. Type **15min** in the Duration text box. Select the **Weekly** radio button under Recurrence pattern. Make sure that **1** is entered in the **Recur every** list box. Select the **Thursday** check box. In the Range of recurrence section, type **9/12/13** in the Start text box (or select it with the drop-down calendar), click the **End by** radio button, and then type **12/5/13** in the End by text box (or select it in the calendar), as shown in Figure A-32. The new recurring task will appear above Task 26, Team review meetings, when you are finished. **Delete task 40**, Team review meetings, by right clicking anywhere in row 40 and selecting Delete Task.

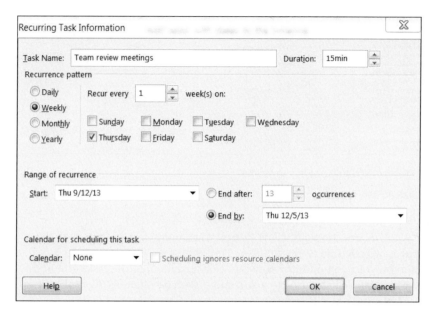

Created using Microsoft Project, used with permission from Microsoft.

FIGURE A-32 Recurring task information dialog box

TIP

You can also enter a number of occurrences instead of an End by date for a recurring task. You might need to adjust the End by date after you enter all of your task durations and dependencies. Remember, the date on your computer determines the date listed as Today in the calendar.

---

7. *View the new summary task and its subtasks.* Click **OK**. Project 2013 inserts a new Team review meetings subtask in the Task Name column. To collapse the recurring task, click the **collapse symbol.** Move your cursor over the Recurring Task symbol in the Indicator column for row 26 to read the note about it occurring 13 times. Notice that the recurring task appears on the appropriate dates on the Gantt chart.

8. *Adjust the columns displayed and the timescale.* Move the **split bar** so that only the Task Name and Duration columns are visible. If needed, increase the Duration column's width so all of the text is visible. Click the **Zoom Out** button on the Zoom slider in the lower right of the screen to display all of the symbols in the Gantt chart. Your screen should resemble Figure A-33.

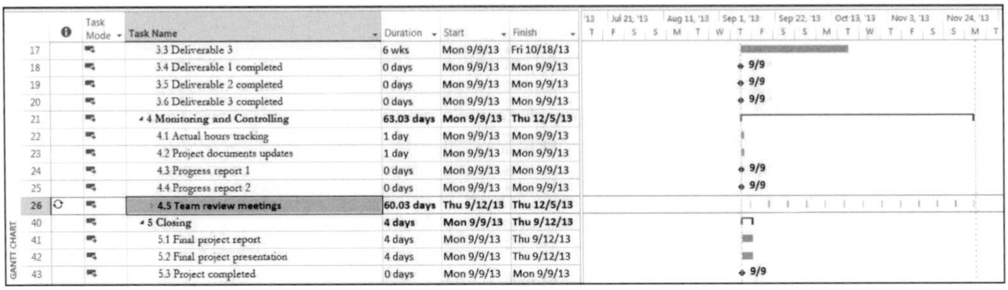

	ⓘ	Task Mode	Task Name	Duration	Start	Finish	Gantt Chart
17		🖩	3.3 Deliverable 3	6 wks	Mon 9/9/13	Fri 10/18/13	
18		🖩	3.4 Deliverable 1 completed	0 days	Mon 9/9/13	Mon 9/9/13	◆ 9/9
19		🖩	3.5 Deliverable 2 completed	0 days	Mon 9/9/13	Mon 9/9/13	◆ 9/9
20		🖩	3.6 Deliverable 3 completed	0 days	Mon 9/9/13	Mon 9/9/13	◆ 9/9
21		🖩	⁴ 4 Monitoring and Controlling	63.03 days	Mon 9/9/13	Thu 12/5/13	
22		🖩	4.1 Actual hours tracking	1 day	Mon 9/9/13	Mon 9/9/13	
23		🖩	4.2 Project documents updates	1 day	Mon 9/9/13	Mon 9/9/13	
24		🖩	4.3 Progress report 1	0 days	Mon 9/9/13	Mon 9/9/13	◆ 9/9
25		🖩	4.4 Progress report 2	0 days	Mon 9/9/13	Mon 9/9/13	◆ 9/9
26	↻	🖩	4.5 Team review meetings	60.03 days	Thu 9/12/13	Thu 12/5/13	
40		🖩	⁴ 5 Closing	4 days	Mon 9/9/13	Thu 9/12/13	
41		🖩	5.1 Final project report	4 days	Mon 9/9/13	Thu 9/12/13	
42		🖩	5.2 Final project presentation	4 days	Mon 9/9/13	Thu 9/12/13	
43		🖩	5.3 Project completed	0 days	Mon 9/9/13	Mon 9/9/13	◆ 9/9

Created using Microsoft Project, used with permission from Microsoft.

FIGURE A-33 All task durations and recurring task entered

9. *Save your file and name it.* Click **File** on the Menu bar, and then click **Save As**. Enter **myschedule** as the filename, and then save the file to the desired location on your computer or network. Notice that all of the tasks still begin on 9/9/13. This will change when you add task dependencies. Keep this file open for the next set of steps.

Establishing Task Dependencies

To use Project 2013 to adjust schedules automatically and perform critical path analysis, you *must* determine the dependencies or relationships among tasks. There are several different methods for creating task dependencies: using the Link Tasks button, using the Predecessors column of the Entry table or the Predecessors tab in the Task Information dialog box, or clicking and dragging the Gantt chart symbols for tasks with dependencies. You will use the first two methods in the following steps.

To create dependencies using the Link Tasks button, highlight tasks that are related and then click the Link Tasks button under the Task tab, Schedule group. For example, to create a finish-to-start (FS) dependency between Task 1 and Task 2, click any cell in row 1, drag down to row 2, and then click the Link Tasks button. The default type of link is finish-to-start. In the Project A+ file, you will also set up some other types of dependencies and use the lag option to set up overlaps between dependent tasks.

> **TIP**
>
> To select adjacent tasks, click and drag the mouse to highlight them. You can also click the first task, hold down the Shift key, and then click the last task. To select nonadjacent tasks, hold down the Control (Ctrl) key as you click tasks in order of their dependencies.

When you use the Predecessors column of the Entry table to create dependencies, you must manually enter the information. To create dependencies manually, type the task row number of the preceding task in the Predecessors column of the Entry table. For example, Task 3 has Task 2 as a predecessor, which can be entered in the Predecessors column, meaning that Task 3 cannot start until Task 2 is finished. To see the Predecessors column of the Entry table, move the split bar to the right. You can also double-click on the task, click the Predecessors tab in the Task Information dialog box, and enter the predecessors there.

Next, you will enter the predecessors for tasks as indicated. You will create some dependencies by manually typing the predecessors in the Predecessors column, some by using the Link Tasks button, and the remaining dependencies by using whichever method you prefer.

To link tasks or establish dependencies for Project A+:

1. *Display the Predecessors column in the Entry table*. Move the split bar to the right to reveal the full Predecessors column in the myschedule.mpp file you saved in the previous section. Widen the Task Name or other columns, if needed.

2. *Highlight the cell where you want to enter a predecessor, and then type the task number for its predecessor task*. Click the **Predecessors cell for Task 3**, Stakeholder register completed, type **2**, and press **Enter**. Notice that as you enter task dependencies, the Gantt chart changes to reflect the new schedule. Also notice that several cells become highlighted, showing *the Visual Change Highlights feature of Project 2013*.

3. *Enter predecessors for Task 4 and view the Task Path*. Click the **Predecessors cell for Task 4**, type **2**, and press **Enter**. Click the **Format** tab, and then click the **Task Path** button under the Bar Styles group. Experiment with the options to highlight Predecessor, Driving Predecessors, Successors, and Driven Successors, and then click Remove Highlighting.

4. *Establish dependencies using the Link Tasks button*. To link Tasks 5 and 6, click the **task name for Task 5** in the Task Name column and drag down through **Task 6**. Then, in the **Task tab**, click the **Link Tasks** button **(looks like a chain link)** under the Schedule group. Notice that the result is the same as typing 5 in the Predecessors column for Task 6, as shown in Figure A-34.

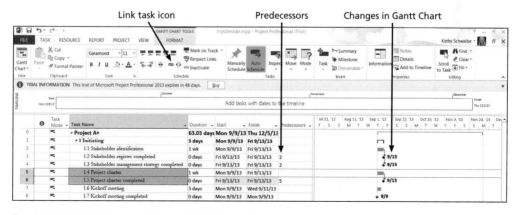

Created using Microsoft Project, used with permission from Microsoft.

FIGURE A-34 Entering predecessor

5. *Enter dependencies and lag time using the Task Information dialog box.*
Double-click the **Task Name** for task **5**, *Project charter, and then click the*
Predecessors tab in the Task Information dialog box. Click the cell under
Task Name, and then click the **Task Name** down arrow and select **Stake-**
holder identification. Click the **Type** drop-down arrow to see the various
types of dependencies. For this task, you will keep the default type of finish-
to-start. Click the **Lag drop-down arrow**, then **type -50%** and press **Enter**.
(Lag means there is a gap between tasks, and lead or negative lag means
there is an overlap). Your screen should resemble Figure A-35. Click **OK** to
close the dialog box. Notice that the Predecessor column for task 5 displays
2FS-50%, meaning there is a finish-to-start relationship with task 2 and a
lag of -50%, meaning the task can start when task 2 is 50% completed.*

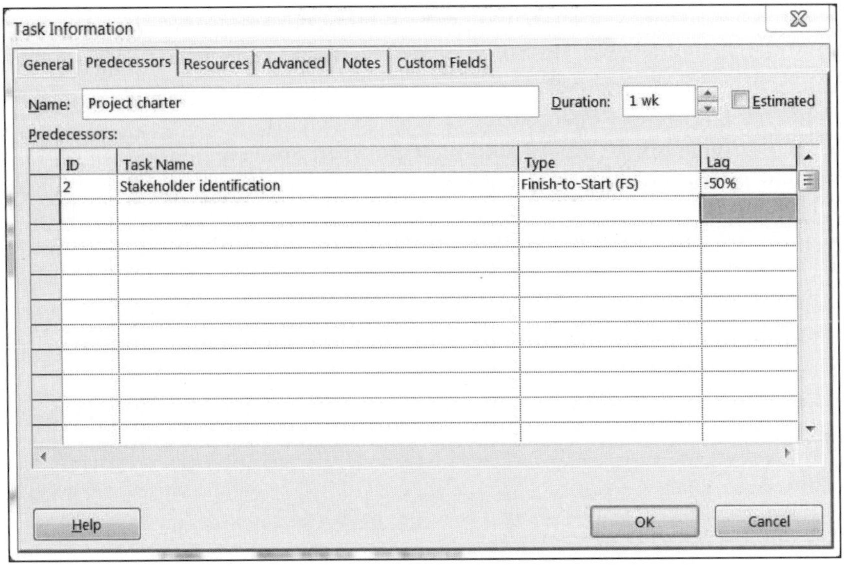

Created using Microsoft Project, used with permission from Microsoft.

FIGURE A-35   Entering predecessor information using the task information dialog box

6. *Enter remaining dependencies.* **Link the other tasks** by either manually
entering the predecessors into the Predecessors column, by using the Link
Tasks button, or using the Task Information dialog box. Use the information
in Figure A-36 to make your entries, being careful to leave some of the predecessors blank, as shown. If you have entered all data correctly, the project
should end on 12/6, or December 6, 2013.

Task Row	Task Name	Predecessors
3	Stakeholder register completed	2
4	Stakeholder management strategy completed	2
5	Project charter	2FS-50%
6	Project charter completed	5
7	Kickoff meeting	2,6
8	Kickoff meeting completed	6,7
9	Planning	
10	Schedule	5,12FS-50%
11	Gantt chart completed	10
12	Scope statement	5
13	Initial scope statement completed	12
14	Executing	
15	Deliverable 1	12
16	Deliverable 2	18
17	Deliverable 3	18
18	Deliverable 1 completed	15
19	Deliverable 2 completed	16
20	Deliverable 3 completed	17
21	Monitoring and Controlling	
22	Actual hours tracking	2
23	Project documents updates	3
24-40	Progress Report 1 through Closing	
41	Final project report	18,19,20
42	Final presentation	18,19,20
43	Project completed	41,42

Schwalbe Publishing 2013.

FIGURE A-36   Predecessor information for Project A

7. *Adjust several dates.* You know that you have to deliver the two progress reports on specific dates. Click the **Start dates for Tasks 24 and 25** and change those dates to October 10 and November 7. Also change the **Finish dates for tasks 22 and 23 to December 4** to make those dates more realistic. Project

2013 will display a yellow warning symbol to remind you that you are changing default dates, which is fine in these examples.

8. *Review the file.* If needed, click the **Zoom Out** button on the Zoom slider to adjust the timescale so all of the information shows on your screen. When you finish, your screen should resemble Figure A-37. Double-check your screen to make sure you entered the dependencies correctly.

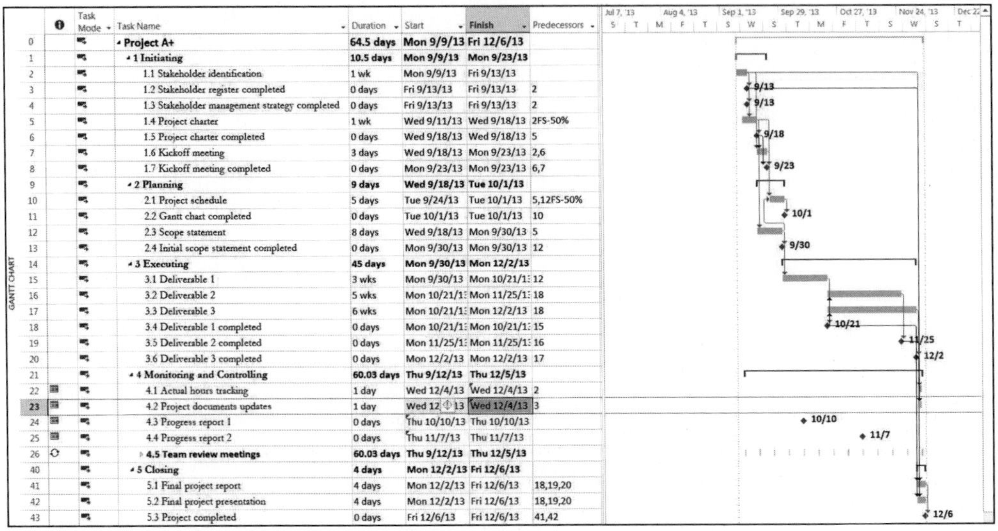

ID	ⓘ	Task Mode	Task Name	Duration	Start	Finish	Predecessors
0			⁴ Project A+	64.5 days	Mon 9/9/13	Fri 12/6/13	
1			⁴ 1 Initiating	10.5 days	Mon 9/9/13	Mon 9/23/13	
2			1.1 Stakeholder identification	1 wk	Mon 9/9/13	Fri 9/13/13	
3			1.2 Stakeholder register completed	0 days	Fri 9/13/13	Fri 9/13/13	2
4			1.3 Stakeholder management strategy completed	0 days	Fri 9/13/13	Fri 9/13/13	2
5			1.4 Project charter	1 wk	Wed 9/11/13	Wed 9/18/13	2FS-50%
6			1.5 Project charter completed	0 days	Wed 9/18/13	Wed 9/18/13	5
7			1.6 Kickoff meeting	3 days	Wed 9/18/13	Mon 9/23/13	2,6
8			1.7 Kickoff meeting completed	0 days	Mon 9/23/13	Mon 9/23/13	6,7
9			⁴ 2 Planning	9 days	Wed 9/18/13	Tue 10/1/13	
10			2.1 Project schedule	5 days	Tue 9/24/13	Tue 10/1/13	5,12FS-50%
11			2.2 Gantt chart completed	0 days	Tue 10/1/13	Tue 10/1/13	10
12			2.3 Scope statement	8 days	Wed 9/18/13	Mon 9/30/13	5
13			2.4 Initial scope statement completed	0 days	Mon 9/30/13	Mon 9/30/13	12
14			⁴ 3 Executing	45 days	Mon 9/30/13	Mon 12/2/13	
15			3.1 Deliverable 1	3 wks	Mon 9/30/13	Mon 10/21/1:	12
16			3.2 Deliverable 2	5 wks	Mon 10/21/1:	Mon 11/25/1:	18
17			3.3 Deliverable 3	6 wks	Mon 10/21/1:	Mon 12/2/13	18
18			3.4 Deliverable 1 completed	0 days	Mon 10/21/1:	Mon 10/21/1:	15
19			3.5 Deliverable 2 completed	0 days	Mon 11/25/1:	Mon 11/25/1:	16
20			3.6 Deliverable 3 completed	0 days	Mon 12/2/13	Mon 12/2/13	17
21			⁴ 4 Monitoring and Controlling	60.03 days	Thu 9/12/13	Thu 12/5/13	
22			4.1 Actual hours tracking	1 day	Wed 12/4/13	Wed 12/4/13	2
23			4.2 Project documents updates	1 day	Wed 12/ ◊ 13	Wed 12/4/13	3
24			4.3 Progress report 1	0 days	Thu 10/10/13	Thu 10/10/13	
25			4.4 Progress report 2	0 days	Thu 11/7/13	Thu 11/7/13	
26			⁴ 4.5 Team review meetings	60.03 days	Thu 9/12/13	Thu 12/5/13	
40			⁴ 5 Closing	4 days	Mon 12/2/13	Fri 12/6/13	
41			5.1 Final project report	4 days	Mon 12/2/13	Fri 12/6/13	18,19,20
42			5.2 Final project presentation	4 days	Mon 12/2/13	Fri 12/6/13	18,19,20
43			5.3 Project completed	0 days	Fri 12/6/13	Fri 12/6/13	41,42

Created using Microsoft Project, used with permission from Microsoft.

FIGURE A-37   Project A+ file with durations and dependencies entered

9. *Preview and save your file.* Click the **File** tab, and then select **Print to preview and print your file. Click Page Setup, and then click the option to Fit to 1 so it will print on one page, as shown in** Figure A-38. Be careful before printing any Project 2013 files so you do not waste a lot of paper. When you are finished, click Save to save your file again. Keep the file open for the next set of steps.

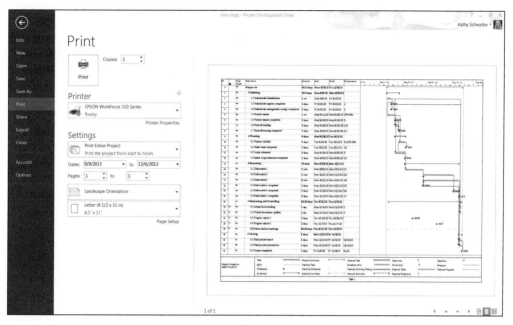

Created using Microsoft Project, used with permission from Microsoft.

FIGURE A-38   Project A+ set up to print on one page

Gantt Charts, Network Diagrams, and Critical Path Analysis

Project 2013 shows a Gantt chart as the default view to the right of the Entry table. As described earlier in this text, network diagrams are often used to show task dependencies. This section explains important information about Gantt charts and network diagrams and describes how to make critical path information more visible in the Gantt Chart view.

Because you have already created task dependencies, you can now find the critical path for Project A+. You can view the critical tasks by changing the color of those items in the Gantt Chart view. Tasks on the critical path will automatically be red in the Network Diagram view. You can also view critical path information in the Schedule table or by using the Critical Tasks report.

To make the text for the critical path tasks appear in red on the Gantt chart:

1. *Change the critical tasks format.* Using the myschedule.mpp file you previously saved, click the **Format** tab, and then click the **Critical Tasks check box** in the Bar Styles group, as shown in Figure A-39. Notice that the critical tasks display in red in the Gantt chart. You can also quickly change the Gantt Chart Style by clicking one of those options.

Critical tasks check box

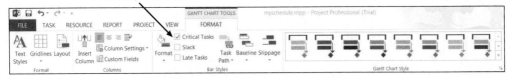

Created using Microsoft Project, used with permission from Microsoft.

FIGURE A-39   Formatting critical tasks

2. *View the network diagram.* Click the View tab, and then click the **Network Diagram** button under the Task Views group. Click the **Zoom Out** button on the Zoom slider several times and watch the view change. Figure A-40 shows all of the tasks in the Project A+ network diagram. Note that milestone tasks, such as Stakeholder management strategy completed, the fourth box on the top, appear as pointed rectangular boxes, while other tasks appear as rectangles. Move your cursor over that box to see it in a larger view. Notice that tasks on the critical path automatically appear in red. A dashed line on a network diagram represents a page break. You often need to change some of the default settings for the Network Diagram view before printing it. As you can see, network diagrams can be messy, so you might prefer to highlight critical tasks on the Gantt chart as you did earlier for easier viewing.

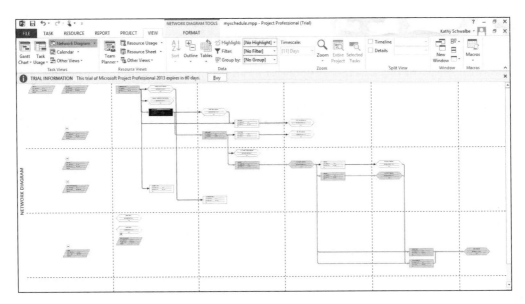

Created using Microsoft Project, used with permission from Microsoft.

FIGURE A-40   Network diagram view

3. *View the schedule table.* Click the **Gantt Chart** button under the **View** tab to return to Gantt Chart view. Right-click the **Select All** button to the left of

the Task Mode column heading and select **Schedule**. Alternatively, you can click the **View** tab and click the **Tables** button under the Data group and then select **Schedule**. The Schedule table replaces the Entry table to the left of the Gantt Chart. Your screen should resemble Figure A-41. This view shows the start and finish (meaning the early start and early finish) and late start and late finish dates for each task, as well as free and total slack. Right-click the **Select All** button and select **Entry** to return to the Entry table view.

Select All
button   Schedule table

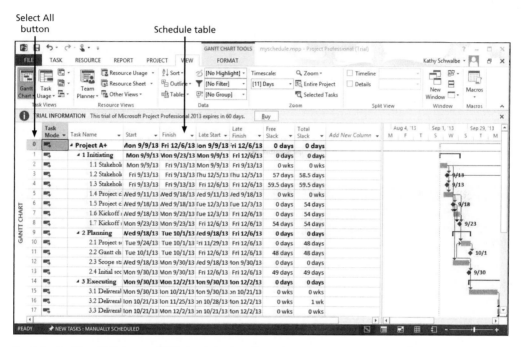

Created using Microsoft Project, used with permission from Microsoft.

FIGURE A-41   Schedule table view

4. *Open the Project Overview report*. Click the **Report** tab, and click the **Dashboards button under the View Reports group, and then click Project Overview** to open the Overview Reports, as shown in Figure A-42. Note that the report shows the milestones due and % complete. Examine other reports, as desired.

5. *Close the report and save your file*. When you are finished examining the reports, click the **Save** button on the Quick Access toolbar to save your final myschedule.mpp file, showing the Entry table and Gantt chart view. Close Project 2013 if you are not continuing to the next section.

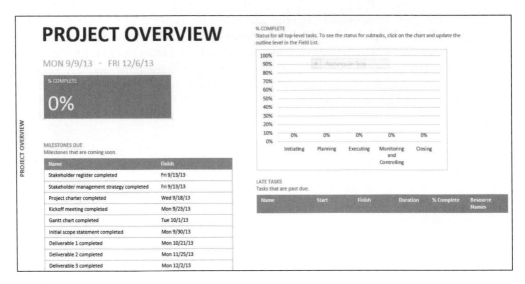

Created using Microsoft Project, used with permission from Microsoft.

FIGURE A-42 Project Overview report

Next you will explore some of the cost and resource management features of Project 2013.

PROJECT COST AND RESOURCE MANAGEMENT

Many people do not use Project 2013 for cost or resource management. Some organizations have more established cost management software products and procedures in place, and many people simply do not know how to use the cost or resource management features of Project 2013. However, these features make it possible to integrate total project information more easily. This section offers brief instructions for entering fixed and variable cost estimates, assigning resources to tasks, viewing resource histograms, and entering actual cost and schedule information after establishing a baseline plan. It also explains how to use Project 2013 for earned value management. More details on these features are available in Project Help, online tutorials, or other texts. See other chapters of this text for information on some of these concepts.

Entering Fixed and Variable Cost Estimates

You can enter costs as fixed or variable. Fixed costs include costs like a specific quantity of materials or costs for consultants hired at a fixed cost. Variable costs vary based on the amount of materials or hours people work. On many projects, human resource costs are the largest percentage of total project costs.

Entering Fixed Costs in the Cost Table

The Cost table allows you to easily enter fixed costs related to each task. You will enter a fixed cost of $200 related to Task 15, Deliverable 1.

To enter a fixed cost:

1. *Display the Cost Table view.* Open your Project 2013 file myschedule.mpp, if necessary. Right-click the **Select All** button to the left of the Task Mode column heading and select **Cost**. The Cost table replaces the Entry table to the left of the Gantt chart. **Widen** the Task Name column and then move the **Split bar** to the right, as needed, until you see the entire Cost table.
2. *Enter a fixed cost.* In the **Fixed Cost column for Task 15**, Deliverable 1, type **200** and press **Enter**. Notice that the Total Cost and Remaining Cost columns reflect this entry, and changes are made to the summary task, Executing, as well. Your screen should resemble Figure A-43.

Select all button   Fixed Cost column of cost table

	Task Name	Fixed Cost	Fixed Cost Accrual	Total Cost	Baseline	Variance	Actual	Remaini
0	◢ Project A+	$0.00	Prorated	$200.00	$0.00	$200.00	$0.00	$200.00
1	◢ 1 Initiating	$0.00	Prorated	$0.00	$0.00	$0.00	$0.00	$0.00
2	1.1 Stakeholder identification	$0.00	Prorated	$0.00	$0.00	$0.00	$0.00	$0.00
3	1.2 Stakeholder register completed	$0.00	Prorated	$0.00	$0.00	$0.00	$0.00	$0.00
4	1.3 Stakeholder management strategy completed	$0.00	Prorated	$0.00	$0.00	$0.00	$0.00	$0.00
5	1.4 Project charter	$0.00	Prorated	$0.00	$0.00	$0.00	$0.00	$0.00
6	1.5 Project charter completed	$0.00	Prorated	$0.00	$0.00	$0.00	$0.00	$0.00
7	1.6 Kickoff meeting	$0.00	Prorated	$0.00	$0.00	$0.00	$0.00	$0.00
8	1.7 Kickoff meeting completed	$0.00	Prorated	$0.00	$0.00	$0.00	$0.00	$0.00
9	◢ 2 Planning	$0.00	Prorated	$0.00	$0.00	$0.00	$0.00	$0.00
10	2.1 Project schedule	$0.00	Prorated	$0.00	$0.00	$0.00	$0.00	$0.00
11	2.2 Gantt chart completed	$0.00	Prorated	$0.00	$0.00	$0.00	$0.00	$0.00
12	2.3 Scope statement	$0.00	Prorated	$0.00	$0.00	$0.00	$0.00	$0.00
13	2.4 Initial scope statement completed	$0.00	Prorated	$0.00	$0.00	$0.00	$0.00	$0.00
14	◢ 3 Executing	$0.00	Prorated	$200.00	$0.00	$200.00	$0.00	$200.00
15	3.1 Deliverable 1	$200.00	Prorated	$200.00	$0.00	$200.00	$0.00	$200.00
16	3.2 Deliverable 2	$0.00	Prorated	$0.00	$0.00	$0.00	$0.00	$0.00
17	3.3 Deliverable 3	$0.00	Prorated	$0.00	$0.00	$0.00	$0.00	$0.00

Created using Microsoft Project, used with permission from Microsoft.

FIGURE A-43 Entering a fixed cost

Entering Resource Information and Cost Estimates

Several methods are available for entering resource information in Project 2013. The Resource Sheet allows you to enter the resource name, initials, resource group, maximum units, standard rate, overtime rate, cost/use, accrual method, base calendar, and code. Once you have established resources in the Resource Sheet, you can assign those resources to tasks in the Entry table with the list arrow that appears when you click a cell in the Resource Names column. The Resource Names column is the last column of the Entry table. You can also use other methods for assigning resources, such as using the Assign Resources button or using the split window, which is the recommended approach to have the most control over how resources are assigned because Project 2013 makes several assumptions about resources assignments that might mess up your schedule or costs. Next, you will enter information for three people working on Project A+ and assign them to a few tasks using various methods.

To enter basic information about each person into the Resource Sheet and assign them to tasks using the Entry table and toolbar:

1. *Display the Resource Sheet view.* Click the **View** tab, and then click the **Resource Sheet** button under the Resource Views group.
2. *Enter resource information.* Enter the information from Figure A-44 into the Resource Sheet. The three resources names are **Kathy, Dan, and Scott**. The Std. Rate and Ovt. Rate for Kathy is **40**, and the Std. and Ovt. Rates for Dan and Scott are **30**. Type the information as shown and press the **Tab** key to move to the next field. When you type the standard and overtime rates, you can just type the number, such as 40, and Project 2013 will automatically enter $40.00/hr. The standard and overtime rates entered are based on hourly rates. You can also enter annual salaries by typing the annual salary number followed by /y for "per year." Your screen should resemble Figure A-44 when you are finished entering the resource data.

Resource Name	Type	Material	Initials	Group	Max.	Std. Rate	Ovt.	Cost/Use	Accrue	Base
Kathy	Work		K		100%	$40.00/hr	$40.00/hr	$0.00	Prorated	Standard
Dan	Work		D		100%	$30.00/hr	$30.00/hr	$0.00	Prorated	Standard
Scott	Work		S		100%	$30.00/hr	$30.00/hr	$0.00	Prorated	Standard

Created using Microsoft Project, used with permission from Microsoft.

FIGURE A-44   Resource sheet view with resource data entered

> ## TIP
>
> If you know that some people will be available for a project only part time, enter their percentage of availability in the Max Units column of the Resource Sheet. Project 2013 will then automatically assign those people based on their maximum units. For example, if someone can work only 50% of his or her time on a project throughout most of the project, enter 50% in the Max Units column for that person. When you enter that person as a resource for a task, his or her default number of hours will be 50% of a standard eight-hour workday, or four hours per day. You can also enter the number of hours each person is scheduled to work, as shown later.

3. *Assign resources to tasks.* From the **View** tab, select the **Gantt Chart** button under the Task Views group, and then click the **Select All** button and switch back to the **Entry** table. Move the Split bar to reveal the Resource Names column, if needed.
4. *Assign Kathy to task 2, Stakeholder identification.* Click in the **Resource Names** cell for **row 2**. Click the list arrow, click the **checkbox** next to **Kathy**, and then press **Enter** or click on another cell. Notice that the resource choices are the names you just entered in the Resource Sheet. Also notice that after you select a resource by checking the appropriate checkbox, his or her name appears on the Gantt chart, as shown in Figure A-45. To assign

more than one resource to a task using the list arrow, simply select another checkbox. Note that Project 2013 will assume that each resource is assigned full-time to tasks using this method since the task is in automatically schedule mode. Also note that you can use filter by Resource Names to only show tasks assigned to specific resources after you enter the resources.

Filter Resource Names

	❶	Task Mode	Task Name	Duration	Start	Finish	Predecessor	Resource Names
0		➟	◢ Project A+	64.5 days	Mon 9/9/1:	Fri 12/6/13		
1		➟	◢ 1 Initiating	10.5 days	Mon 9/9/13	Mon 9/23/1:		
2		➟	1.1 Stakeholder identification	1 wk	Mon 9/9/13	Fri 9/13/13		Kathy
3		➟	1.2 Stakeholder register completed	0 days	Fri 9/13/13	Fri 9/13/13	2	☐ Dan
4		➟	1.3 Stakeholder management strategy compl	0 days	Fri 9/13/13	Fri 9/13/13	2	☑ Kathy
5		➟	1.4 Project charter	1 wk	Wed 9/11/1:	Wed 9/18/1:	2FS-50%	☐ Scott

Created using Microsoft Project, used with permission from Microsoft.

FIGURE A-45 Resource assigned using the entry table

5. *Assign two resources to a task.* Click in the **Resource Names** cell for **row 5 (Project charter).** Click the **list arrow**, then click the **checkbox next to Dan and Kathy**, and then press **Enter.** Notice that both resource names appear in the Resource Names column and on the Gantt chart for this task, and the task duration remains at 1 week.

6. *Change the resource assignments.* Click in the **Resource Names** cell for **Task 2**, Stakeholder identification, click the **list arrow**, and add **Dan** as another resource. Notice that when you change an original resource assignment, Project prompts you for how you want to handle the change, as shown in Figure A-46. Click the **Exclamation point** symbol to read your options. In past versions of Project, resource additions would change schedules automatically unless the user entered them a certain way. Now you have much more control of what happens to your schedule and costs. In this case, we do want to accept the default of keeping the duration constant.

keholder identification		1 wk	Mon 9/9/13	Fri 9/13/13		❗ ▾	Kathy,Dan	▾
keh	You added resources to this task. Do you want to:							
keh								
pjec	○ Reduce duration but keep the same amount of work.						Dan,Kathy	
pjec	◉ Increase the amount of work but keep the same duration.							
ːko	○ Reduce the hours resources work per day (units), but keep the same duration and work.							

Created using Microsoft Project, used with permission from Microsoft.

FIGURE A-46 Options when additional resources are added to tasks

7. *Review the cost table.* Right-click the **Select All** button to the left of the Task Mode column heading and select Cost. Notice that costs have been added to the tasks where you added resources. Project assumes that people are assigned full-time to tasks. It is showing a cost of $2,800 each for Task 2 and

Task 5. In the next section, you will see how to control resources entries even more. First, right-click the **Select All** button to the left of the Task Mode column heading and select Entry to return to the **Entry** table.

To control resource and work assignments using the Resource details window:

1. *Open the Resource Form.* Notice the **red symbols in the Indicator columns** for rows/tasks 2 and 5. Move your cursor over the symbol to read the message about resources being overallocated. Click the Task Name for row 2, Stakeholder identification, click the **Resource tab, and then click the Details button under the Properties group**. A Resource Form is displayed at the bottom of the screen, as shown in Figure A-47. Project 2013 assumes every task is assigned full-time, so since Kathy is scheduled on two tasks on the same day, it says she is overallocated.

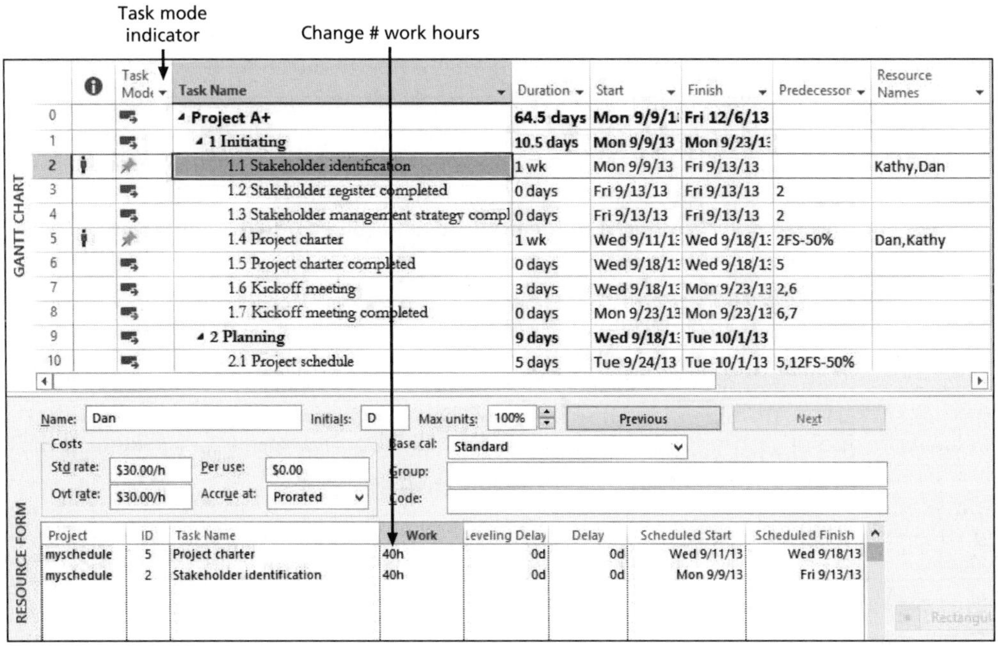

Task mode indicator

Change # work hours

		Task Mode	Task Name	Duration	Start	Finish	Predecessor	Resource Names
0			⊿ **Project A+**	**64.5 days**	**Mon 9/9/1**	**Fri 12/6/13**		
1			⊿ **1 Initiating**	**10.5 days**	**Mon 9/9/13**	**Mon 9/23/1**		
2			1.1 Stakeholder identification	1 wk	Mon 9/9/13	Fri 9/13/13		Kathy,Dan
3			1.2 Stakeholder register completed	0 days	Fri 9/13/13	Fri 9/13/13	2	
4			1.3 Stakeholder management strategy compl	0 days	Fri 9/13/13	Fri 9/13/13	2	
5			1.4 Project charter	1 wk	Wed 9/11/1	Wed 9/18/1	2FS-50%	Dan,Kathy
6			1.5 Project charter completed	0 days	Wed 9/18/1	Wed 9/18/1	5	
7			1.6 Kickoff meeting	3 days	Wed 9/18/1	Mon 9/23/1	2,6	
8			1.7 Kickoff meeting completed	0 days	Mon 9/23/1	Mon 9/23/1	6,7	
9			⊿ **2 Planning**	**9 days**	**Wed 9/18/1**	**Tue 10/1/13**		
10			2.1 Project schedule	5 days	Tue 9/24/13	Tue 10/1/13	5,12FS-50%	

Name: Dan   Initials: D   Max units: 100%   Previous   Next

Costs   Base cal: Standard
Std rate: $30.00/h   Per use: $0.00   Group:
Ovt rate: $30.00/h   Accrue at: Prorated   Code:

Project	ID	Task Name	Work	Leveling Delay	Delay	Scheduled Start	Scheduled Finish
myschedule	5	Project charter	40h	0d	0d	Wed 9/11/13	Wed 9/18/13
myschedule	2	Stakeholder identification	40h	0d	0d	Mon 9/9/13	Fri 9/13/13

Created using Microsoft Project, used with permission from Microsoft.

FIGURE A-47   Changing Work hours for tasks

TIP

You can right-click on the lower screen to review see additional forms/views. You can click the Select All button at the top right of the screen to view different tables at the top of the screen. You want to make sure that resource and work hour assignments do not adjust your schedules in ways you did not intend.

2. *Make tasks 2 and 5 manually scheduled.* Right-click the **Select All** button and switch to the **Entry table**. Click the drop-down in the **Task Mode** column for Tasks 2 and 5 to make them **manually scheduled**. When you assigned resources, Project 2013 assumed they were working full-time or 40 hours per week on each task. Because these two tasks have days that overlap, there is an overallocation. You do not expect each resource to work that many hours, so you can change them by using the Resource Form.

3. *Change the number of Work hours.* Select Task 2, **Stakeholder identification** in the top window, and then click the **Work** column in the Resource Form window for **Kathy** in the lower part of your screen. Type **10h**, press **Enter**, and again type **10h** and press **Enter** for the next task, Task 5, Project charter, and then click the **OK** button. Click Next to see Dan's Resource Form, as shown in Figure A-47.

4. *Enter additional work hours and review the Gantt chart.* Change Dan's work hours to **10h for Tasks 2 and 5** as well. Notice in the Gantt chart that the duration for Tasks 2 and 5 are still one week. The overallocation indicator should now disappear because the number of hours has been reduced from the default of 8 hours per day, or 40 hours for a 5-day task. To remove the Resource Form, click **Details** on the Ribbon under the Resource tab.

5. *Examine the new cost information.* Right-click the Select All button, and then click **Cost** to view the Cost table. Tasks 2 and 5 each show only $700 for Total Cost.

6. *Close the file without saving it.* Close the file, but do not save the changes you made.

Using the Team Planner Feature

Another way to assign resources and reduce overallocations is by using the Team Planner feature. Assume you have two people assigned to work on a project, Brian and Cindy, as shown in Figure A-48. Notice that Brian is assigned to work on both Task 1 and Task 2 full-time the first week. Therefore, Brian is overallocated. Cindy is scheduled to work on Task 3 full-time the second week, and Task 4, also scheduled for the second week, is not assigned yet.

Overallocation
indicator

Created using Microsoft Project, used with permission from Microsoft.

FIGURE A-48 Overallocated resource

You can click the Team Planner view under the View tab to see a screen similar to the top section of Figure A-49. Notice that Brian has both Tasks 1 and 2 assigned to him at the same time. These tasks and Brian's name display in red to show the overallocation. Cindy is assigned Task 3 the following week, and Task 4 is unassigned. By simply clicking and dragging Task 4 straight up so it is under Brian in Week 2 and Task 2 straight down so it is under Cindy in Week 1, you can reassign those tasks and remove Brian's overallocation, as shown in the bottom section of Figure A-49. Many people will appreciate the simplicity of this feature, first introduced in Project 2010!

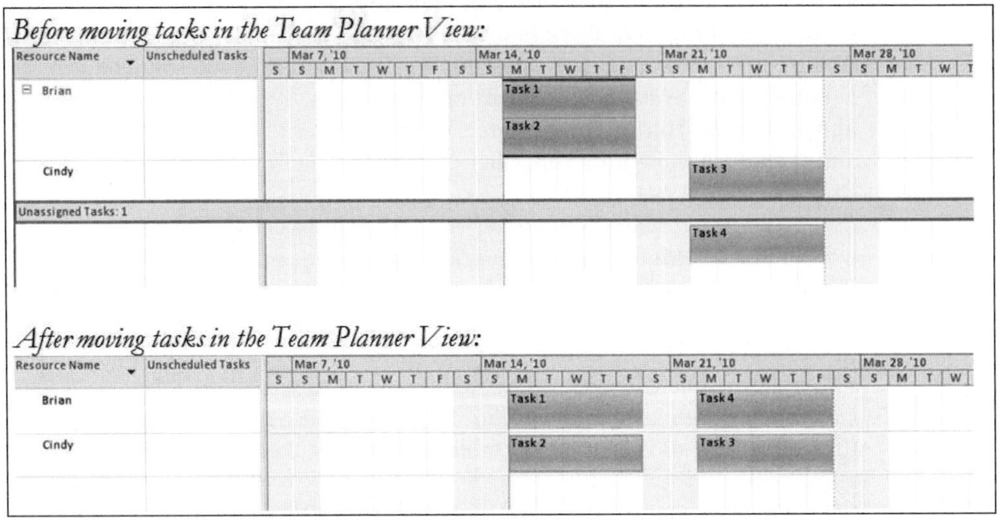

Created using Microsoft Project, used with permission from Microsoft.

FIGURE A-49   Adjusting resource assignments using the Team Planner feature

Entering Baseline Plans, Actual Costs, and Actual Times

After entering information in the Task Name column, establishing task durations and dependencies, and assigning costs and resources, you are ready to establish a baseline plan. By comparing the information in your baseline plan to actual progress during the course of the project, you can identify and solve problems. After the project ends, you can use the baseline and actual information to plan similar, future projects more accurately. To use Project 2013 to help control projects and view earned value information, you must establish a baseline plan, enter actual costs, and enter actual durations. In the next series of steps you will use a new file called tracking.mpp that you downloaded from the companion website (*www.intropm.com*).

To save a file as a baseline and enter actual information:

1. *Open the file called tracking.mpp.* The file should be showing the Cost table view. Notice that this short project was planned to start on January 7, 2013 and end on February 13 of the same year, have three resources assigned to it, and cost $11,200. Click the **Project** tab, click the **Set Baseline** button under the Schedule group, and click **Set Baseline**, as shown in Figure A-50.

Select All button   Set baseline

Created using Microsoft Project, used with permission from Microsoft.

FIGURE A-50   Saving a baseline

2. *Save the file as a baseline.* Examine the **Set Baseline** dialog box. Click the drop-down arrow to see that you can set up to ten baselines. Accept the default to save the entire project. Click **OK**. Notice that the Baseline column changes to blue.

3. *Display the Tracking table.* Click the **Task** tab, right-click the **Select All button** and then click **Tracking to view the tracking table**. Move the split bar to the right to reveal all of the columns in the table, if needed. Move your cursor over each tracking button on the Ribbon in the top line of the Schedule group to see what it does. Your screen should resemble Figure A-51.

4. *Mark Tasks 2 through 4 as 100% complete.* Click the Task Name for Task 2, **Subtask 1 under Main task 1**, and drag down through Task 4 to highlight those tasks. Click the **100% Complete** button on the Ribbon. The columns with dates, durations, and cost information should now contain data instead of the default values, such as NA or 0. The % Comp. column should display 100%. Adjust column widths if needed. Your screen should resemble Figure A-52. Notice that the Gantt chart bars for those three tasks now have a black line through them.

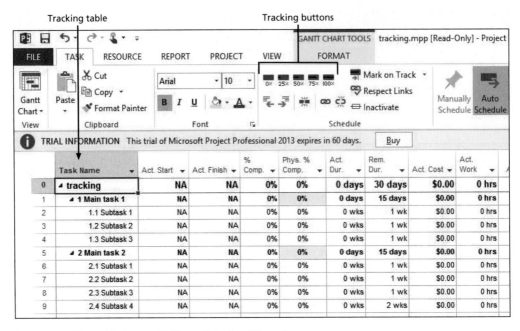

Created using Microsoft Project, used with permission from Microsoft.

FIGURE A-51   Using the tracking table and tracking buttons

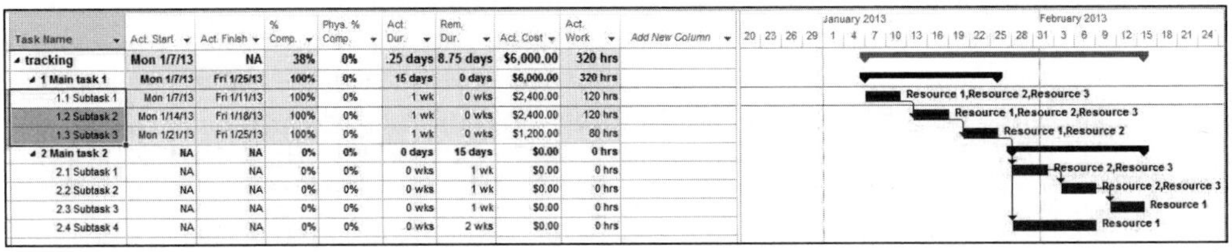

Created using Microsoft Project, used with permission from Microsoft.

FIGURE A-52   Tracking table information

5. *Enter actual completion dates for Task 6.* Click the Task Name for Task 6, **Subtask 1 under Main Task 2,** click the **Mark on Track drop-down,** and then click **Update Tasks.** The Update Tasks dialog box opens. For Task 6, enter the Actual Start date as **1/28/13 (the same as the Current Start date)** and the Actual Finish date as **2/11/13 (ten days later than the Current Finish date),** as shown in Figure A-53. Click **OK.** Notice how the information in the tracking sheet has changed.

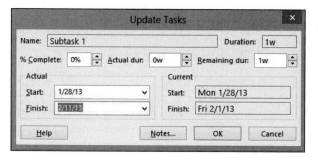

Created using Microsoft Project, used with permission from Microsoft.

FIGURE A-53   Update Tasks dialog box

6. *View the Tracking Gantt chart.* Click the drop-down arrow on the far left of the screen next to the Gantt chart, and then click **Tracking Gantt** to quickly switch to that view. Move the **split bar** and adjust column widths as needed. Use the **horizontal scroll bar** in the Gantt chart window to the right (move the slider to the left) to see symbols on the Tracking Gantt chart. Use the **Zoom slider** on the lower right of the screen to adjust the timescale so you can see all of the symbols. Your screen should resemble Figure A-54. The blue bar for Task 6 shows the actual time you just entered. Notice that the delay in this one task on the critical path has caused the planned completion date for the entire project to slip (now Feb 25 versus Feb 13). Also notice the Indicator column to the far left. The check marks show that tasks are completed.

Completion indicator

Tracking Gantt chart

	ⓘ	Task Name	Duration	Start	Finish	Predecessor	Resource Names		Dec 23, '12	Jan 13, '13	Feb 3, '13	Feb 24, '13
0		⊿ tracking	36 days	Mon 1/7/13	Mon 2/25/13							57%
1	✓	⊿ Main task 1	15 days	Mon 1/7/13	Fri 1/25/13				100%			
2	✓	Subtask 1	1 wk	Mon 1/7/13	Fri 1/11/13		Resource 1,Resource 2,Resource 3		100%			
3	✓	Subtask 2	1 wk	Mon 1/14/13	Fri 1/18/13	2	Resource 1,Resource 2,Resource 3		100%			
4	✓	Subtask 3	1 wk	Mon 1/21/13	Fri 1/25/13	3	Resource 1,Resource 2		100%			
5		⊿ Main task 2	21 days	Mon 1/28/13	Mon 2/25/13					35%		
6	✓	Subtask 1	2.2 wks	Mon 1/28/13	Mon 2/11/13	4	Resource 2,Resource 3			100%		
7		Subtask 2	1 wk	Tue 2/12/13	Mon 2/18/13	6	Resource 2,Resource 3			0%		
8		Subtask 3	1 wk	Tue 2/19/13	Mon 2/25/13	7	Resource 1			0%		
9		Subtask 4	2 wks	Mon 1/28/13	Fri 2/8/13	4	Resource 1			0%		

Created using Microsoft Project, used with permission from Microsoft.

FIGURE A-54   Tracking Gantt chart view

7. *Save your file as a new file named myactuals.mpp.* Click **File** on the Menu bar, and then click **Save As**. Name the file **myactuals**, and then click **Save**.

Notice the additional information available on the Tracking Gantt chart. Completed tasks have 100% next to their symbols on the Tracking Gantt chart. Tasks that have not started yet display 0%. Tasks in progress, such as Task 5, show the percentage of the work completed (35% in this example). The project summary task bar indicates that the entire project is 57% complete. Viewing the Tracking Gantt chart allows you to easily see your schedule progress against the baseline plan. After you have entered some actuals, you can review earned value information for the initiating tasks of this project.

VIEWING EARNED VALUE MANAGEMENT DATA

Earned value management is an important project management technique for measuring project performance. Because you have entered actual information, you can now view earned value information in Project 2013. You can also view an earned value report using the visual reports feature.

To view earned value information:

1. *View the Earned Value table.* Using the myactuals file you just saved (or downloaded from the companion website), right-click the **Select All** button, select **More Tables, and double-click Earned Value**. Move the split bar to the right to reveal all of the columns, as shown in Figure A-55. Note that the Earned Value table includes columns for each earned value acronym, such as PV, EV, AC, SV, CV, etc. Also note that the EAC (Estimate at Completion) is higher than the BAC (Budget at Completion) for Task 6 (and its summary task, Task 5), where the task took longer than planned to complete. Task 0 shows a VAC (Variance at Completion) of ($3,360.00), meaning the project is projected to cost $3,360 more than planned at completion. Remember that not all of the actual information has been entered yet. Also note that the date on your computer must be set later than the date of a completed task for the data to calculate properly.

	Task Name	Planned Value - PV (BCWS)	Earned Value - EV (BCWP)	AC (ACWP)	SV	CV	EAC	BAC	VAC
0	◢ myactuals	$11,200.00	$8,000.00	$10,400.00	($3,200.00)	($2,400.00)	14,560.00	11,200.00	($3,360.00)
1	◢ Main task 1	$6,000.00	$6,000.00	$6,000.00	$0.00	$0.00	$6,000.00	$6,000.00	$0.00
2	Subtask 1	$2,400.00	$2,400.00	$2,400.00	$0.00	$0.00	$2,400.00	$2,400.00	$0.00
3	Subtask 2	$2,400.00	$2,400.00	$2,400.00	$0.00	$0.00	$2,400.00	$2,400.00	$0.00
4	Subtask 3	$1,200.00	$1,200.00	$1,200.00	$0.00	$0.00	$1,200.00	$1,200.00	$0.00
5	◢ Main task 2	$5,200.00	$2,000.00	$4,400.00	($3,200.00)	($2,400.00)	$11,440.08	$5,200.00	($6,240.08)
6	Subtask 1	$2,000.00	$2,000.00	$4,400.00	$0.00	($2,400.00)	$4,400.00	$2,000.00	($2,400.00)
7	Subtask 2	$2,000.00	$0.00	$0.00	($2,000.00)	$0.00	$2,000.00	$2,000.00	$0.00
8	Subtask 3	$400.00	$0.00	$0.00	($400.00)	$0.00	$400.00	$400.00	$0.00
9	Subtask 4	$800.00	$0.00	$0.00	($800.00)	$0.00	$800.00	$800.00	$0.00

Created using Microsoft Project, used with permission from Microsoft.

FIGURE A-55 Earned value table

2. *View the earned value chart.* Click the **Report** tab, and then click **Costs** under the View Reports group, and then click **Earned Value Report**, as shown in Figure A-56. You can experiment with different report options or click the link to learn more about earned value, as desired.

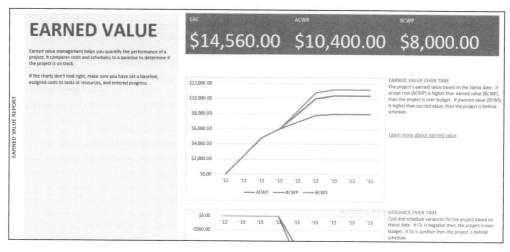

Created using Microsoft Project, used with permission from Microsoft.

FIGURE A-56   Earned value report

3. *Close Project 2013 without saving the file.* Click the **File tab**, click **Close**, and select **No** when prompted to save the file. You can also exit Project 2013 and take a break, if desired.

Next you will use a few more features of Project 2013 to help tie your Project to other applications.

INTEGRATING PROJECT 2013 WITH OTHER APPLICATIONS AND APPS FOR OFFICE

Project 2013 provides several features to make it easy to integrate with other applications. For example, you can copy data between Project 2013 and other applications (including the timeline), or you might want to create hyperlinks to project documents created in Word, Excel, PowerPoint, or other applications from within your project files. You can also purchase and add new apps to Project 2013 from Microsoft's Office Store.

Copying Information Between Applications

Most people are familiar with copying information between Office applications. For example, you can highlight a column of data in Excel, select Copy, and then select Paste in Project 2013 or other applications. You can also create a new Project 2013 file from an existing Excel file by select New from Excel Workbook. It is also easy to copy a timeline from Project 2013 into another application.

To copy a timeline from Project 2013:

1. *Open another Project 2013 template file.* Start Project 2013, and open a template file, such as **Residential Construction**, as shown in Figure A-57. Notice the timeline near the top of the screen.

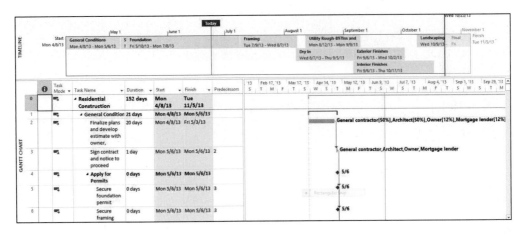

Created using Microsoft Project, used with permission from Microsoft.

FIGURE A-57   Residential construction template

2. *Make changes to the Timeline.* Move your cursor over the second item on the Timeline called Site Work. **Right-click Site Work**, and select **Remove from Timeline**.

3. *Open the Insert Hyperlink dialog box.* Click Task 4, **right-click Apply for Permits**, and then click **Add to Timeline**. (Note that this milestone could be worded better to indicate that it has no duration, such as Permit Applications Submitted). Make other adjustments to the Timeline, as desired.

4. *Copy the Timeline into PowerPoint.* Click anywhere on the Timeline, and then click the **Copy Timeline button** in the Copy group on the Ribbon, as shown in Figure A-58, and select **For Presentation**.

Copy Timeline

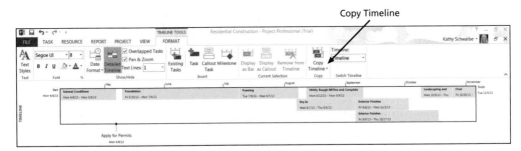

Created using Microsoft Project, used with permission from Microsoft.

FIGURE A-58   Copy Timeline

5. *Copy the Timeline into PowerPoint.* Open **PowerPoint**, change the slide layout, add a title to the slide, and change the theme, as desired, and then **right-click** and select **Paste picture**. Your screen should resemble Figure A-59, showing the Project 2013 Timeline in your presentation.

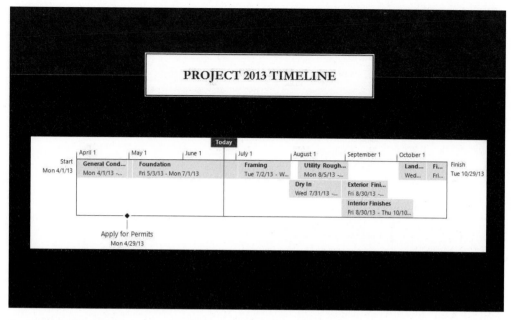

Created using Microsoft Project, used with permission from Microsoft.

FIGURE A-59 Timeline copied into PowerPoint

Creating Hyperlinks to Other Files

Some people like to use their Project 2013 file as a main source of information for many different project documents. To do this, you can simply insert a hyperlink to other document files. For example, you can create a hyperlink to the file with the stakeholder register you listed as a milestone in your Task Name column earlier.

To insert a hyperlink within a Project 2013 file:

1. Open the **myschedule.mpp** file. Use the file you saved earlier or download it from the companion website. The Entry table and Gantt Chart view should display.
2. *Select the task in which you want to insert a hyperlink.* Click the Task Name for Task 3, **Stakeholder register completed**.
3. *Open the Insert Hyperlink dialog box.* Right-click in that cell, then click **Hyperlink**. The Insert Hyperlink dialog box opens, as shown in Figure A-60. You will have different folders visible based on your computer's directory structure.

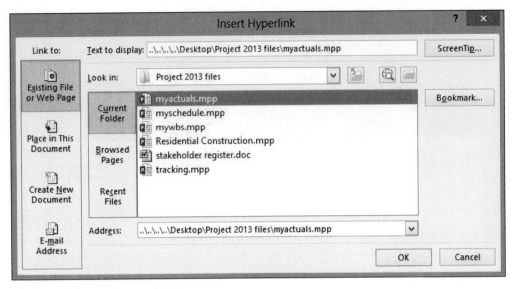

Created using Microsoft Project, used with permission from Microsoft.

FIGURE A-60   Insert hyperlink dialog box

4. *Double-click the filename of the hyperlink file.* Change the **Look in:** information until you find where you have saved the files you downloaded for this appendix. Double-click the Word file named **stakeholder register**, and then click **OK**. A Hyperlink button appears in the Indicators column to the left of the Task Name for Task 3. Move your cursor over the hyperlink button until the mouse pointer changes to the Hand symbol to reveal the name of the hyperlinked file. If you click on it, the file will open.

Using Project 2013 Apps

Microsoft has an Office Store where you can download special apps for Project 2013. New apps are added often.

To explore Project 2013 apps:

1. *Access the Office Store.* With Project 2013 open, click the **Project** tab, then click the **Apps for Office button** on the left of the Ribbon under the Apps group. The Apps for Office dialog box opens, as shown in Figure A-61.

Created using Microsoft Project, used with permission from Microsoft.

FIGURE A-61   Apps for Office dialog box

2. *Explore the Office Store.* Click the **Office Store button**. Your screen should resemble Figure A-62, which shows the apps available on April 6, 2013. Read information about various apps, and add them as desired.

Created using Microsoft Project, used with permission from Microsoft.

FIGURE A-62 New Apps for Project on the Office Store (April, 2013)

You have really just touched the surface of Project 2013's powerful features, but you probably know more than most people who have this software! There are several books with more detailed information on using Project 2013 that you can use to learn even more, or you can experiment with the software and Help feature to understand it more.

Discussion Questions

1. What are some unique features of project management software?
2. What are the new features of Project 2013?
3. How do you create a WBS in Project 2013?
4. How do you enter task durations and establish dependencies between tasks?
5. How can you make sure that resource assignments do not mess up your schedule?
6. How can you use the Team Planner to assign resources and reduce overallocations?
7. How do you establish a baseline in Project 2013 and enter actual information?
8. What type of information do you see in the Earned Value table?
9. How can you copy a Timeline from Project into other applications and access other application files from within Project 2013?
10. Where can you access apps created for Project 2013?

Exercises

1. To make sure you understand the information in this appendix, perform the steps yourself. Print out the following screens or send them to your instructor, as directed:
   a. The adjusted Customer Service file as shown in Figure A-13.
   b. The Schedule table view for the Customer Service file, similar to Figure A-16.
   c. The Customer Service file filtered to show only milestones, similar to Figure A-21.
   d. The mywbs file with automatic outline numbers and a project summary task, similar to Figure A-25.
   e. Create a new Project file called generic-wbs that shows the WBS for a generic project. Make the main categories phase 1, phase 2, phase 3, and phase 4. Include at least four tasks and one milestone under each of these main categories, using meaningful, fictitious names for them. Enter 0 for the duration of the milestones, but do not enter any durations for the other tasks. Be sure to indent tasks and show the outline numbers before printing or submitting the file. Note: If you are doing a project for your class, you can use data for that project instead.

2. Continue performing the steps in this appendix, starting with the section called Developing the Schedule. Print out the following screens or send them to your instructor, as directed:
   a. The myschedule file with durations and dependencies entered, similar to Figure A-38.
   b. The earned value table, similar to Figure A-55.
   c. Continue performing the steps, even if you do not have to print out more screens. Write a one-to-two page paper describing the capabilities of Project 2013 and your opinion of this software. What do you like and dislike about it?

3. Use some of the information in the body of the text (or find a sample WBS and Gantt chart on your own). Enter the WBS into Project 2013 to practice your Project 2013 skills.
   a. Review one of the sample WBSs. Indent tasks and use the automatic numbering feature. Print out or submit your file.

b. Use the information in Chapter 6 under the section called Developing the Project Schedule to create the Gantt chart for Project X. Also create the network diagram for Project X. Make sure both will print out on one page each, then print or submit them to your instructor. Assume the start date was 6/9/09, or June 9, 2009, to make your results match the screen shots in Chapter 6. (Or use a similar project you find elsewhere).

c. Make up actual information for Project X (or a similar project). Assume some tasks are completed as planned, some take more time, and some take less time. View and then print out or submit the tracking Gantt chart.

4. If you are doing a team project as part of your class or for a project at work, use Project 2013 to create a detailed file describing the work you plan to do for the project.

a. Create a detailed WBS, including several milestones, estimate task durations, link tasks, add tasks to the timeline, and enter resources and costs, assign resources, and so on. Save your file as a baseline and print it out send it to your instructor, as desired.

b. Track your progress on your team project by entering actual cost and schedule information. Create a new baseline file if there have been a lot of changes. View earned value information when you are halfway through the project or course. Continue tracking your progress until the project or course is finished. Print or submit your Gantt chart, Project Summary report, Earned Value table, and relevant information to your instructor.

c. Write a two- to three-page report describing your experience. What did you learn about Project 2013 from this exercise? How do you think Project 2013 helps in managing a project? You may also want to interview people who use Project 2013 for their experiences and suggestions.

Endnotes

[1] TopTenREVIEWS™, "Project Management Software," (*project-management-software-review.toptenreviews.com*) (accessed June 17, 2009).

[2] TopTenREVIEWS™, "Best Online Project Management Comparisons," (*online-project-management-review.toptenreviews.com/*) (accessed April 7, 2013).

5 whys A technique in which you repeatedly ask the question "Why?" to help peel away the layers of symptoms that can lead to the root cause of a problem

acceptance decisions Decisions that determine if the products or services produced as part of the project will be accepted or rejected

activity An element of work normally found on the WBS that has an expected duration, cost, and resource requirements; also called a task

activity attributes Information about each activity, such as predecessors, successors, logical relationships, leads and lags, resource requirements, constraints, imposed dates, and assumptions related to the activity

activity list A tabulation of activities to be included on a project schedule

activity-on-arrow (AOA) A network diagramming technique in which activities are represented by arrows and connected at points called nodes to illustrate the sequence of activities; also called arrow diagramming method (ADM)

actual cost (AC) The total of direct and indirect costs incurred in accomplishing work on an activity during a given period

adaptive software development (ASD) A software development approach used when requirements cannot be clearly expressed early in the life cycle

agile Quick and coordinated in movement; a method based on iterative and incremental development, in which requirements and solutions evolve through collaboration

agile methods An approach to managing projects that includes a workflow comprised of short iterations and incremental delivery of software

agile software development A method for software development that uses new approaches, focusing on close collaboration between programming teams and business experts

analogous estimates A cost-estimating technique that uses the actual cost of a previous, similar project as the basis for estimating the cost of the current project; also calledtop-down estimates

analogy approach Creating a WBS by using a similar project's WBS as a starting point

appraisal cost The cost of evaluating processes and their outputs to ensure that a project is error-free or within an acceptable error range

arrow diagramming method (ADM) A network diagramming technique in which activities are represented by arrows and connected at points called nodes to illustrate the sequence of activities; also called activity-on-arrow (AOA)

artifact A useful object created by people

backward pass A project network diagramming technique that determines the late start and late finish dates for each activity

balanced scorecard A strategic planning and management system that helps organizations align business activities to strategy, improve communications, and monitor performance against strategic goals

baseline The approved project management plan plus approved changes

baseline dates The planned schedule dates for activities in a Tracking Gantt chart

benchmarking A technique used to generate ideas for quality improvements by comparing specific project practices or product characteristics to those of other projects or products within or outside the performing organization

benchmarking Generating ideas by comparing specific project practices or product characteristics to those of other projects or products inside or outside the performing organization

best practice An optimal way recognized by industry to achieve a stated goal or objective

bid A document prepared by sellers to provide pricing for standard items that the buyer has clearly defined; also called a tender or quote (short for quotation)

blogs Journals on the web that allow users to write entries, create links, and upload pictures, while readers can post comments to journal entries

bottom-up approach Creating a WBS by having team members identify as many specific tasks related to the project as possible and then grouping them into higher-level categories

bottom-up estimates A cost-estimating technique based on estimating individual work items and summing them to get a project total

brainstorming A technique by which a group attempts to generate ideas or find a solution for a specific problem by amassing ideas spontaneously and without judgment

budget at completion (BAC) The original total budget for a project

budgetary estimate A cost estimate used to allocate money into an organization's budget

buffer Additional time to complete a task; a buffer is added to an estimate to account for various factors

burndown chart A chart that shows the cumulative work remaining in a sprint on a day-by-day basis

burst A single node followed by two or more activities on a network diagram

Capability Maturity Model Integration (CMMI) A process improvement approach that provides organizations with the essential elements of effective processes

capitalization rate The rate used in discounting future cash flow; also called the discount rate or opportunity cost of capital

cash flow Benefits minus costs or income minus expenses

cash flow analysis A method for determining the estimated annual costs and benefits for a project

cause-and-effect diagram A diagram that traces complaints about quality problems back to the responsible production operations to help find the root cause; also known as a fishbone diagram or Ishikawa diagram

champion A senior manager who acts as a key proponent for a project

change control board (CCB) A formal group of people responsible for approving or rejecting changes on a project

change control system A formal, documented process that describes when and how official project documents may be changed

checksheet A technique used to collect and analyze data; sometimes called a tally sheet or checklist

closing processes Formalizing acceptance of the project or project phase and ending it efficiently

coercive power Using punishment, threats, or other negative approaches to get people to do things they do not want to do

collaborating mode A conflict-handling mode in which decision makers incorporate different viewpoints and insights to develop consensus and commitment

communications management plan A document that guides project communications

compromise mode Using a give-and-take approach to resolve conflicts; bargaining and searching for solutions that bring some degree of satisfaction to all the parties in a dispute

configuration management A process that ensures that the descriptions of a project's products are correct and complete

conformance Delivering products that meet requirements and fitness for use

conformance to requirements Project processes and products that meet written specifications

confrontation mode Facing a conflict directly using a problem-solving approach that allows affected parties to work through their disagreements

constructive change orders Oral or written acts or omissions by someone with actual or apparent authority that can be construed to have the same effect as a written change order

contingency allowances Provisions held by the project sponsor or organization to reduce the risk of cost or schedule overruns to an acceptable level; also called contingency reserves

contingency plans Predefined actions that the project team will take if an identified risk event occurs

contingency reserves Dollar amounts included in a cost estimate to allow for future situations that may be partially planned for (sometimes called known unknowns) and that are included in the project cost baseline

contingency reserves Provisions held by the project sponsor or organization to reduce the risk of cost or schedule overruns to an acceptable level; also called contingency allowances

contract A mutually binding agreement that obligates the seller to provide specified products or services and obligates the buyer to pay for them

control chart A graphic display of data that illustrates the results of a process over time

cost baseline A time-phased budget that project managers use to measure and monitor cost performance

cost of capital The return available by investing capital elsewhere

cost of nonconformance Taking responsibility for failures or not meeting quality expectations

cost of quality The cost of conformance plus the cost of nonconformance

cost performance index (CPI) The ratio of earned value to actual cost; can be used to estimate the projected cost to complete the project

cost plus award fee (CPAF) contract A contract in which the buyer pays the supplier for allowable costs (as defined in the contract) plus an award fee based on the satisfaction of subjective performance criteria

cost plus fixed fee (CPFF) contract A contract in which the buyer pays the supplier for allowable costs (as defined in the contract) plus a fixed fee payment that is usually based on a percentage of estimated costs

cost plus incentive fee (CPIF) contract A contract in which the buyer pays the supplier for allowable costs (as defined in the contract) along with a predetermined fee and an incentive bonus

cost plus percentage of costs (CPPC) contract A contract in which the buyer pays the supplier for allowable costs (as defined in the contract) along with a predetermined percentage based on total costs

cost variance (CV) The earned value minus the actual cost

cost-reimbursable contracts Contracts that involve payment to the supplier for direct and indirect actual costs

crashing A technique for making cost and schedule trade-offs to obtain the greatest amount of schedule compression for the least incremental cost

critical chain scheduling A method of scheduling that takes limited resources into account when creating a project schedule and includes buffers to protect the project completion date

critical path method (CPM) or critical path analysis A project network diagramming technique used to predict total project duration

critical path The series of activities in a network diagram that determines the earliest completion of the project; it is the longest path through the network diagram and has the least amount of slack or float

daily Scrum A short meeting in which the team shares progress and challenges

decision tree A diagramming analysis technique used to help select the best course of action when future outcomes are uncertain

decomposition Subdividing project deliverables into smaller pieces

defect Any instance in which the product or service fails to meet customer requirements

definitive estimate A cost estimate that provides an accurate estimate of project costs

deliverable A product or service, such as a technical report, a training session, a piece of hardware, or a segment of software code, produced or provided as part of a project

Delphi technique An approach used to derive a consensus among a panel of experts to make predictions about future developments

dependency The sequencing of project activities or tasks; also called a relationship

deputy project managers People who fill in for project managers in their absence and assist them as needed

design of experiments A quality technique that helps identify which variables have the most influence on the overall outcome of a process

direct costs Costs that can be directly related to creating the products and services of the project

directives New requirements imposed by management, government, or some external influence

discount factor A multiplier for each year based on the discount rate and year

discount rate The rate used in discounting future cash flow; also called the capitalization rate or opportunity cost of capital

discretionary dependencies The sequencing of project activities or tasks defined by the project team and used with care because they may limit later scheduling options

DMAIC (Define, Measure, Analyze, Improve, Control) A systematic, closed-loop process for continued improvement that is scientific and fact based

dummy activities Activities with no duration and no resources used to show a logical relationship between two activities in the arrow diagramming method of project network diagrams

duration The actual amount of time worked on an activity plus elapsed time

early finish date The earliest possible time an activity can finish based on the project network logic

early start date The earliest possible time an activity can start based on the project network logic

earned value (EV) An estimate of the value of the physical work actually completed

earned value management (EVM) A project performance measurement technique that integrates scope, time, and cost data

effort The number of workdays or work hours required to complete a task

emotional intelligence Knowing and managing one's own emotions and understanding the emotions of others for improved performance

empathic listening Listening with the intent to understand

enterprise project management software Software that integrates information from multiple projects to show the status of active, approved, and future projects across an entire organization; also called *portfolio project management software*

estimate at completion (EAC) An estimate of what it will cost to complete the project based on performance to date

ethics A set of principles that guides decision making based on personal values of what is considered right and wrong

executing processes Coordinating people and other resources to carry out the project plans and create the products, services, or results of the project or project phase

executive steering committee A group of senior executives from various parts of the organization who regularly review important corporate projects and issues

expectations management matrix A tool that helps clarify expectations and lists project measures of success as well as priorities, expectations, and guidelines related to each measure

expected monetary value (EMV) The product of a risk event probability and the risk event's monetary value

expert power Using one's personal knowledge and expertise to get people to change their behavior

external dependencies The sequencing of project activities or tasks that involve relationships between project and non-project activities

external failure cost A cost related to all errors that are not detected and corrected before delivery to the customer

extrinsic motivation An approach that causes people to do something for a reward or to avoid a penalty

fallback plans Plans developed for risks that have a high impact on meeting project objectives and implemented if attempts to reduce the risk are not effective

fast tracking A schedule compression technique in which you do activities in parallel that you would normally do in sequence

features The special characteristics that appeal to users

feeding buffers Time added before tasks on the critical chain if they are preceded by other tasks that are not on the critical path

finish-to-finish dependency A relationship on a project network diagram in which the "from" activity must be finished before the "to" activity can be finished

finish-to-start dependency A relationship on a project network diagram in which the "from" activity must be finished before the "to" activity can be started

fishbone diagram A diagram that traces complaints about quality problems back to the responsible production operations to help find the root cause; also known as a cause-and-effect diagram or Ishikawa diagram

fitness for use A product that can be used as it was intended

fixed-price contract A contract with a fixed total price for a well-defined product or service; also called a lump-sum contract

float The amount of time a project activity may be delayed without delaying a succeeding activity or the project finish date; also called slack

flowchart A graphic display of the logic and flow of processes that helps you analyze how problems occur and how processes can be improved

flowcharts Diagrams that show how various elements of a system relate to each other

forcing mode Using a win/lose approach to conflict resolution to get one's way

forecasts Predictions of future project status and progress based on past information and trends

forward pass A network diagramming technique that determines the early start and early finish dates for each activity

free slack (free float) The amount of time an activity can be delayed without delaying the early start of any immediately following activities

function points A means of measuring software size in terms that are meaningful to end users

functional organizational structure An organizational structure that groups people by functional areas such as IT, manufacturing, engineering, and human resources

functionality The degree to which a system performs its intended function

Gantt chart A standard format for displaying project schedule information by listing project activities and their corresponding start and finish dates in a calendar format; sometimes referred to as bar charts

Google Docs Online applications offered by Google that allow users to create, share, and edit documents, spreadsheets, and presentations online

groupthink Conformance to the values or ethical standards of a group

hierarchy of needs A pyramid structure illustrating Maslow's theory that people's behaviors are guided or motivated by a sequence of needs

histogram A bar graph of a distribution of variables

human resources (HR) frame A frame that focuses on producing harmony between the needs of the organization and the needs of people

indirect costs Costs that are not directly related to the products or services of the project, but are indirectly related to performing the project

influence diagram A diagram that represents decision problems by displaying essential elements, including decisions, uncertainties, and objectives, and how they influence each other

initiating processes Defining and authorizing a project or project phase

intangible costs or benefits Costs or benefits that are difficult to measure in monetary terms

integrated change control Identifying, evaluating, and managing changes throughout the project life cycle

integration testing Testing that occurs between unit and system testing to test functionally grouped components and ensure that a subset or subsets of the entire system work together

interface management Identifying and managing the points of interaction between various elements of a project

internal failure cost A cost incurred to correct an identified defect before the customer receives the product

internal rate of return (IRR) The discount rate that results in an NPV of zero for a project

interviewing A fact-finding technique that is normally done face to face, but can also occur through phone calls, e-mail, or instant messaging

intrinsic motivation An approach that causes people to participate in an activity for their own enjoyment

Ishikawa diagram A diagram that traces complaints about quality problems back to the responsible production operations to help find the root cause; also known as a cause-and-effect diagram or fishbone diagram

ISO 9000 A quality system standard developed by the International Organization for Standardization (ISO) that includes a three-part, continuous cycle of planning, controlling, and documenting quality in an organization

issue log A tool used to document, monitor, and track issues that need resolution

IT governance The authority and control for key IT activities in organizations, including IT infrastructure, IT use, and project management

Joint Application Design (JAD) Using highly organized and intensive workshops to bring together project stakeholders—the sponsor, users, business analysts, programmers, and so on—to jointly define and design information systems

kaizen The Japanese word for improvement or change for the better; an approach used for continuously improving quality in organizations

kanban a just-in-time method of inventory control that can be modified used in conjunction with Scrum

kick-off meeting A meeting held at the beginning of a project so that stakeholders can meet each other, review the goals of the project, and discuss future plans

kill point A management review that should occur after each project phase to determine if projects should be continued, redirected, or terminated; also called a phase exit

known risks Risks that the project team has identified and analyzed and that can be managed proactively

known unknowns Dollar amounts included in a cost estimate to allow for future situations that may be partially planned for (sometimes called contingency reserves) and that are included in the project cost baseline

late finish date The latest possible time an activity can be completed without delaying the project finish date

late start date The latest possible time an activity may begin without delaying the project finish date

leader A person who focuses on long-term goals and big-picture objectives while inspiring people to reach those goals

lean An approach for improving quality that involves evaluating processes to maximize customer value while minimizing waste

learning curve theory A theory that when many items are produced repetitively, the unit cost of those items normally decreases in a regular pattern as more units are produced

legitimate power Getting people to do things based on a position of authority

lessons-learned report Reflective statements written by project managers and their team members to document important information they have learned from working on a project

life cycle costing The total cost of ownership, or development plus support costs, for a project

lump-sum contract A contract with a fixed total price for a well-defined product or service; also called a fixed-price contract

maintainability The ease of performing maintenance on a product

make-or-buy decision An organization's decision to make certain products and perform certain services inside the organization or to buy them from an outside organization

Malcolm Baldrige National Quality Award An award started in 1987 to recognize companies that have achieved a level of world-class competition through quality management

management reserves Dollar amounts included in a cost estimate to allow for future situations that are unpredictable (sometimes called unknown unknowns)

manager A person who deals with the day-to-day details of meeting specific goals

mandatory dependencies The sequencing of project activities or tasks that are inherent in the nature of the work being done on the project

matrix organizational structure An organizational structure in which employees are assigned both to functional and project managers

maturity model A framework for helping organizations improve their processes and systems

mean The average value of a population

measurement and test equipment costs The capital cost of equipment used to perform prevention and appraisal activities

merge Two or more nodes that precede a single node on a network diagram

methodology A description of how things should be done

metric A standard of measurement

milestone A significant event that normally has no duration on a project; serves as a marker to help in identifying necessary activities, setting schedule goals, and monitoring progress

mind mapping A technique that uses branches radiating from a core idea to structure thoughts and ideas

mirroring Matching certain behaviors of another person

monitoring and controlling processes Regularly measuring and monitoring progress to ensure that the project team meets the project objectives

Monte Carlo analysis A risk quantification technique that simulates a model's outcome many times to provide a statistical distribution of the calculated results

multitasking Working on more than one task at a time

Murphy's Law The principle that if something can go wrong, it will

Myers-Briggs Type Indicator (MBTI) A popular tool for determining personality preferences

net present value (NPV) analysis A method of calculating the expected net monetary gain or loss from a project by discounting all expected future cash inflows and outflows to the present point in time

network diagram A schematic display of the logical relationships or sequencing of project activities

node The starting and ending point of an activity on an activity-on-arrow diagram

normal distribution A bell-shaped curve that is symmetrical about the mean of the population

offshoring Outsourcing from another country

opportunities Chances to improve an organization

opportunity cost of capital The rate used in discounting future cash flow; also called the capitalization rate or discount rate

organizational breakdown structure (OBS) A specific type of organizational chart that shows which organizational units are responsible for particular work items

organizational culture A set of shared assumptions, values, and behaviors that characterize the functioning of an organization

organizational process assets Formal and informal plans, policies, procedures, guidelines, information systems, financial systems, management systems, lessons learned, and historical information that can influence a project's success

outsourcing An organization's acquisition of goods and services from an outside source

overallocation A state in which not enough resources are available to perform the assigned work during a given time period

overrun The additional percentage or dollar amount by which actual costs exceed estimates

parametric estimating A cost-estimating technique that uses project characteristics (parameters) in a mathematical model to estimate project costs

Pareto analysis Identifying the vital few contributors that account for most quality problems in a system

Pareto chart A histogram that helps identify and prioritize problem areas

Parkinson's Law The principle that work expands to fill the time allowed

payback period The amount of time needed to recoup the total dollars invested in a project, in terms of net cash inflows

performance How well a product or service performs the customer's intended use

PERT weighted average (Optimistic time + 4 * most likely time + pessimistic time)/6

phase exit A management review that should occur after each project phase to determine if projects should be continued, redirected, or terminated; also called a kill point

planned value (PV) The portion of the approved total cost estimate planned to be spent on an activity during a given period

planning processes Devising and maintaining a workable scheme to ensure that the project addresses the organization's needs

Point of Total Assumption (PTA) The cost at which the contractor assumes total responsibility for each additional dollar of contract cost in a fixed-price incentive fee contract

political frame A frame that addresses organizational and personal politics

politics Competition between groups or individuals for power and leadership

power The ability to influence behavior to get people to do things they would not otherwise do

power/interest grid A tool used to group stakeholders based on their level of authority (power) and their level of concern (interest) for project outcomes

precedence diagramming method (PDM) A network diagramming technique in which boxes represent activities

predictive life cycle A software development approach used when the scope of the project can be articulated clearly and the schedule and cost can be predicted accurately

prevention cost The cost of planning and executing a project so that it is error-free or within an acceptable error range

probabilistic time estimates Duration estimates based on using optimistic, most likely, and pessimistic estimates of activity durations instead of using one specific or discrete estimate

probability/impact matrix or chart A matrix or chart that shows the relative probability of a risk occurring and the relative impact of the risk

problems Undesirable situations that prevent an organization from achieving its goals

process A series of actions directed toward a particular result

process adjustments Adjustments made to correct or prevent further quality problems based on quality control measurements

procurement Acquiring goods and services from an outside source

product backlog A single list of features prioritized by business value

product owner The person responsible for the business value of the project and for deciding what work to do and in what order when using a Scrum method

profit margin The ratio of profits to revenues

profits Revenues minus expenses

program A group of related projects, subprograms, and program activities managed in a coordinated way to obtain benefits and control not available from managing them individually

Program Evaluation and Review Technique (PERT) A project network analysis technique used to estimate project duration when there is a high degree of uncertainty about the individual activity duration estimates

program manager A person who provides leadership and direction for the project managers heading the projects within a program

progress reports Reports that describe what the project team has accomplished during a certain period of time

project A temporary endeavor undertaken to create a unique product, service, or result

project acquisition The last two phases in a project (implementation and close-out) that focus on delivering the actual work

project and portfolio management software Software that integrates information from multiple projects to show the status of active, approved, and future projects across an entire organization; also called *enterprise project management software*

project archives A complete set of organized project records that provide an accurate history of the project

project buffer Time added before the project's due date

project charter A document that formally recognizes the existence of a project and provides direction on the project's objectives and management

project cost management The processes required to ensure that the project is completed within the approved budget

project feasibility The first two phases in a project (concept and development) that focus on planning

project integration management Processes that coordinate all project management knowledge areas throughout a project's life, including developing the project charter, developing the preliminary project scope statement, developing the project management plan, directing and managing the project, monitoring and controlling the project, providing integrated change control, and closing the project

project life cycle A collection of project phases, such as concept, development, implementation, and close-out

project management The application of knowledge, skills, tools, and techniques to project activities to meet project requirements

Project Management Institute (PMI) An international professional society for project managers

project management knowledge areas Project integration management, scope, time, cost, quality, human resource, communications, risk, procurement, and stakeholder management

Project Management Office (PMO) An organizational group responsible for coordinating the project management functions throughout an organization

project management plan A document used to coordinate all project planning documents and guide project execution and control

project management process groups The progression of project activities from initiation to planning, executing, monitoring and controlling, and closing

Project Management Professional (PMP) Certification provided by PMI that requires documenting project experience and education, agreeing to follow the PMI code of ethics, and passing a comprehensive exam

project management tools and techniques Methods available to assist project managers and their teams; some popular time-management tools include Gantt charts, network diagrams, and critical path analysis

project manager The person responsible for working with the project sponsor, the project team, and the other people involved to meet project goals

project organizational structure An organizational structure that groups people by major projects

project portfolio management or portfolio management When organizations group and manage projects as a portfolio of investments that contribute to the entire enterprise's success

project procurement management The processes required to acquire goods and services for a project from outside the performing organization

project quality management Ensuring that a project will satisfy the needs for which it was undertaken

project scope management The processes involved in defining and controlling what work is or is not included in a project

project scope statement A document that includes at least a description of the project, including its overall objectives and justification, detailed descriptions of all project deliverables, and the characteristics and requirements of products and services produced as part of the project

project sponsor The person who provides the direction and funding for a project

project time management The processes required to ensure timely completion of a project

PRojects IN Controlled Environments (PRINCE2) A project management methodology developed in the United Kingdom that defines 45 separate subprocesses and organizes these into eight process groups

proposal A document prepared by sellers when there are different approaches for meeting buyer needs

prototyping Developing a working replica of the system or some aspect of it to help define user requirements

quality The totality of characteristics of an entity that bear on its ability to satisfy stated or implied needs or the degree to which a set of inherent characteristics fulfill requirements

quality assurance Periodic evaluation of overall project performance to ensure that the project will satisfy the relevant quality standards

quality audit A structured review of specific quality management activities that helps identify lessons learned and that can improve performance on current or future projects

quality circles Groups of nonsupervisors and work leaders in a single company department who volunteer to conduct group studies on how to improve the effectiveness of work in their department

quality control Monitoring specific project results to ensure that they comply with the relevant quality standards and identifying ways to improve overall quality

RACI charts Charts that show Responsibility, Accountability, Consultation, and Informed roles for project stakeholders

rapport A relation of harmony, conformity, accord, or affinity

rate of performance (RP) The ratio of actual work completed to the percentage of work planned to have been completed at any given time during the life of the project or activity

Rational Unified Process (RUP) framework An iterative software development process that focuses on team productivity and delivers software best practices to all team members

referent power Getting others to do things based on a person's own charisma

relationship The sequencing of project activities or tasks; also called a dependency

reliability The ability of a product or service to perform as expected under normal conditions

Request for Proposal (RFP) A document used to solicit proposals from prospective suppliers

Request for Quote (RFQ) A document used to solicit quotes or bids from prospective suppliers

required rate of return The minimum acceptable rate of return on an investment

requirement A condition or capability that must be met by the project or that must be present in the product, service, or result to satisfy an agreement or other formally imposed specification

requirements management plan A plan that describes how project requirements will be analyzed, documented, and managed

requirements traceability matrix (RTM) A table that lists requirements, their various attributes, and the status of the requirements to ensure that all are addressed

reserves Dollar amounts included in a cost estimate to mitigate cost risk by allowing for future situations that are difficult to predict

residual risks Risks that remain after all of the response strategies have been implemented

resource breakdown structure A hierarchical structure that identifies the project's resources by category and type

resource histogram A column chart that shows the number of resources assigned to a project over time

resource leveling A technique for resolving resource conflicts by delaying tasks

resource loading The amount of individual resources an existing schedule requires during specific time periods

resources People, equipment, and materials

responsibility assignment matrix (RAM) A matrix that maps the work of a project, as described in the WBS, to the people responsible for performing the work, as described in the organizational breakdown structure (OBS)

return on investment (ROI) A method for determining the financial value of a project; the ROI is the result of subtracting the project costs from the benefits and then dividing by the costs

reward power Using incentives to induce people to do things

rework Action taken to bring rejected items into compliance with product requirements, specifications, or other stakeholder expectations

risk An uncertainty that can have a negative or positive effect on meeting project objectives

risk acceptance Accepting the consequences if a risk occurs

risk appetite The degree of uncertainty an entity is willing to take on in anticipation of a reward

risk avoidance Eliminating a specific threat or risk, usually by eliminating its causes

risk breakdown structure A hierarchy of potential risk categories for a project

risk enhancement Changing the size of an opportunity by identifying and maximizing key drivers of the positive risk

risk events Specific uncertain events that may occur to the detriment or enhancement of the project

risk exploitation Doing whatever you can to make sure a positive risk happens

risk factors Numbers that represent the overall risk of specific events, given their probability of occurring and the consequence to the project if they do occur

risk management plan A plan that documents the procedures for managing risk throughout a project

risk mitigation Reducing the impact of a risk event by reducing the probability of its occurrence

risk owner The person who will take responsibility for a risk and its associated response strategies and tasks

risk register A document that contains results of various risk management processes, often displayed in a table or spreadsheet format

risk sharing Allocating ownership of a risk to another party

risk tolerance The maximum acceptable deviation an entity is willing to accept on a project or business objectives as the potential impact

risk transference Shifting the consequence of a risk and responsibility for its management to a third party

risk utility The amount of satisfaction or pleasure received from a potential payoff

risk-averse Having a low tolerance for risk

risk-neutral A balance between risk and payoff

risk-seeking Having a high tolerance for risk

Robust Design methods Methods that focus on eliminating defects by substituting scientific inquiry for trial-and-error methods

rough order of magnitude (ROM) estimate A cost estimate prepared very early in the life of a project to provide a rough idea of what a project will cost

run chart A chart that displays the history and pattern of variation of a process over time

scatter diagram A diagram that helps to show if there is a relationship between two variables; sometimes called XY charts

schedule baseline The approved planned schedule for the project

schedule performance index (SPI) The ratio of earned value to planned value; can be used to estimate the projected time to complete a project

schedule variance (SV) The earned value minus the planned value

scope All the work involved in creating the products of the project and the processes used to create them

scope baseline The approved project scope statement and its associated WBS and WBS dictionary

scope creep The tendency for project scope to keep getting bigger

scope validation Formal acceptance of the completed project deliverables

Scrum team or development team A cross-functional team of five to nine people who organize themselves and the work to produce the desired results for each sprint

Scrum The leading agile development methodology for completing projects with a complex, innovative scope of work

ScrumMaster A person who ensures that the team is productive, facilitates the daily Scrum, enables close cooperation across all roles and functions, and removes barriers that prevent the team from being effective

secondary risks Risks that are a direct result of implementing a risk response

sellers Contractors, suppliers, or providers who provide goods and services to other organizations

sensitivity analysis A technique used to show the effects of changing one or more variables on an outcome

seven run rule If seven data points in a row on a quality control chart are all below the mean, above the mean, or are all increasing or decreasing, then the process needs to be examined for nonrandom problems

SharePoint portal A tool that allows users to create custom websites to access documents and applications stored on shared devices

six 9s of quality A measure of quality control equal to 1 fault in 1 million opportunities

Six Sigma A comprehensive and flexible system for achieving, sustaining, and maximizing business success that is uniquely driven by close understanding of customer needs, disciplined use of facts, data, and statistical analysis, and diligent attention to managing, improving, and reinventing business processes

Six Sigma methodologies Define, Measure, Analyze, Improve, and Control (DMAIC) is used to improve an existing business process, and Define, Measure, Analyze, Design, and Verify (DMADV) is used to create new product or process designs

slack The amount of time a project activity may be delayed without delaying a succeeding activity or the project finish date; also called float

slipped milestone A milestone activity that is completed later than planned

SMART criteria Guidelines to help define milestones that are specific, measurable, assignable, realistic, and time-framed

smoothing mode Deemphasizing or avoiding areas of differences and emphasizing areas of agreement

software defect Anything that must be changed before delivery of the program

Software Quality Function Deployment (SQFD) model A maturity model that focuses on defining user requirements and planning software projects

sprint A set period of time, normally two to four weeks, during which specific work must be completed and made ready for review when using Scrum methods

sprint backlog The highest-priority items from the product backlog to be completed in a sprint

staffing management plan A document that describes when and how people will be added to a project team and taken off it

stakeholder analysis A technique for analyzing information to determine which stakeholders' interests to focus on and how to increase stakeholder support throughout the project

stakeholder register A document that includes details about identified project stakeholders

stakeholder register A document that includes details related to the identified project stakeholders

stakeholders People involved in or affected by project activities

standard Best practices for what should be done

standard deviation A measure of how much variation exists in a distribution of data

start-to-finish dependency A relationship on a project network diagram in which the "from" activity cannot start before the "to" activity is finished

start-to-start dependency A relationship on a project network diagram in which the "from" activity cannot start until the "to" activity starts

statement of work (SOW) A description of the work required for procurement

statistical sampling Choosing part of a population of interest for inspection

status reports Reports that describe where a project stands at a specific point in time

strategic planning Determining long-term objectives by analyzing the strengths and weaknesses of an organization, studying opportunities and threats in the business environment, predicting future trends, and projecting the need for new products and services

structural frame A frame that deals with how the organization is structured (usually depicted in an organizational chart) and focuses on different groups' roles and responsibilities to meet the goals and policies set by top management

subproject managers People responsible for managing the subprojects of a larger project

sunk cost Money that has been spent in the past

SWOT analysis Analyzing Strengths, Weaknesses, Opportunities, and Threats; used to aid in strategic planning

symbolic frame A frame that focuses on the symbols, meanings, and culture of an organization

synergy An approach in which the whole is greater than the sum of the parts

system outputs The screens and reports the system generates

system testing Testing the entire system as one entity to ensure that it is working properly

systems Sets of interacting components working within an environment to fulfill some purpose

systems analysis A problem-solving approach that requires defining the scope of the system to be studied, and then dividing it into component parts for identifying and evaluating its problems, opportunities, constraints, and needs

systems approach A holistic and analytical approach to solving complex problems that includes using a systems philosophy, systems analysis, and systems management

systems development life cycle (SDLC) A framework for describing the phases involved in developing and maintaining information systems

systems management Addressing the business, technological, and organizational issues associated with creating, maintaining, and modifying a system

systems philosophy An overall model for thinking about things as systems

systems thinking A holistic view of an organization to effectively handle complex situations

tangible costs or benefits Costs or benefits that can be easily measured in dollars

task An element of work normally found on the WBS that has an expected duration, cost, and resource requirements; also called an activity

team development Building individual and group skills to enhance project performance

termination clause A contract clause that allows the buyer or supplier to end the contract

Theory of Constraints (TOC) A management philosophy that any complex system at any point in time often has only one aspect or constraint that limits the ability to achieve more of the system's goal

three-point estimate An estimate that includes an optimistic, most likely, and pessimistic estimate

time and material (T&M) contracts A hybrid of fixed-price and cost-reimbursable contracts

Top Ten Risk Item Tracking A qualitative risk analysis tool for identifying risks and maintaining an awareness of risks throughout the life of a project

top-down approach Creating a WBS by starting with the largest items of the project and breaking them into subordinate items

top-down estimates A cost-estimating technique that uses the actual cost of a previous, similar project as the basis for estimating the cost of the current project; also called analogous estimates

total slack (total float) The amount of time an activity may be delayed from its early start without delaying the planned project finish date

Tracking Gantt chart A Gantt chart that compares planned and actual project schedule information

triggers Indications for actual risk events

triple constraint Balancing scope, time, and cost goals

Tuckman model A model that describes five stages of team development: forming, storming, norming, performing, and adjourning

unit pricing An approach in which the buyer pays the supplier a predetermined amount per unit of service, and the total value of the contract is a function of the quantities needed to complete the work

unit test A test of each individual component (often a program) to ensure that it is as defect-free as possible

unknown risks Risks that cannot be managed proactively because they have not been identified and analyzed

unknown unknowns Dollar amounts included in a cost estimate to allow for future situations that are unpredictable (sometimes called management reserves)

use case modeling A process for identifying and modeling business events, who initiated them, and how the system should respond to them

user acceptance testing An independent test performed by end users prior to accepting the delivered system

user stories Short descriptions written by customers of what they need a system to do for them

variance The difference between planned and actual performance

virtual team A group of people who work together despite time and space boundaries using communication technologies

watch list A list of risks that have low priority but are still identified as potential risks

WBS dictionary A document that includes detailed information about each WBS item

weighted scoring model A technique that provides a systematic process for selecting projects based on numerous criteria

wiki A website that enables anyone who accesses it to contribute or modify content

withdrawal mode Retreating or withdrawing from an actual or potential disagreement

work breakdown structure (WBS) A deliverable-oriented grouping of the work involved in a project that defines its total scope

work package A task at the lowest level of the WBS

workarounds Unplanned responses to risk events when no contingency plans are in place

yield The number of units handled correctly through the development process

Q

Y

Z